SELECTIONS FROM THE SMUTS PAPERS

VOLUME V

SELECTIONS FROM THE
SMUTS PAPERS

VOLUME V

SEPTEMBER 1919–NOVEMBER 1934

EDITED BY

JEAN VAN DER POEL

CAMBRIDGE

AT THE UNIVERSITY PRESS

1973

Published by the Syndics of the Cambridge University Press
Bentley House, 200 Euston Road, London NW1 2DB
American Branch: 32 East 57th Street, New York, N.Y. 10022

Original Smuts Papers © The Smuts Archive Trust 1973
Editorial material © Cambridge University Press 1973

Library of Congress Catalogue Card Number: 64-21586

ISBN: 0 521 08602 7

Printed in Great Britain
at the University Printing House, Cambridge
(Brooke Crutchley, University Printer)

CONTENTS OF VOLUME V

page

Preface   vii

PART XIII: PRIME MINISTER
3 SEPTEMBER 1919–25 JUNE 1924
Documents 1–151   1

PART XIV: IN OPPOSITION
9 JULY 1924–28 JUNE 1929
Documents 152–262   231

PART XV: ALLIANCE WITH HERTZOG
9 AUGUST 1929–12 NOVEMBER 1934
Documents 263–370   415

PREFACE

The second series of *Selections from the Smuts Papers* (volumes v to vii) is the final instalment of a four-fold publication plan based upon the Smuts Collection and comprising a two-volume biography and seven volumes of documents. The second series covers the same period as that of *Smuts—The Fields of Force, 1919–1970*, the concluding volume of the biography by Sir Keith Hancock which appeared in 1968.

The entire Collection, including both public and private papers, has now been assembled and will be kept as a unit in its permanent repository—the state archives in Pretoria. Detailed lists and indexes of all but the minor papers have been made. Microfilm copies of the private letters and of the most important newspaper cuttings have been presented to the libraries of the University of Cambridge and the University of Cape Town. A brief descriptive catalogue of the Collection has been compiled.

In order to complete the publication programme and to finish the arrangement of the Collection, the Trust set up to have temporary charge of it had, in 1967, to find additional funds. An appeal to Mr Harry Oppenheimer was answered with a generous grant of R13,000 from the Ernest Oppenheimer Memorial Trust and this has provided enough to meet all remaining expenses and to make a substantial contribution to the cost of producing these volumes.

In selecting the documents for the second series the editor has applied the criteria which the co-editors of the first series explained in their preface; but, because of the far greater wealth of material for the later period, her choice has had to be even more severely limited. The number of in-letters has been drastically reduced; extracts from Smuts's academic writings have been omitted, since most of these have been published elsewhere; only key speeches and memoranda have been selected. Again, although almost all the selections are from the private papers, a few official documents of primary importance, both historically and in Smuts's political life, have been included: e.g. the memorandum circulated to the imperial conference of June 1921 and the papers on the Irish negotiations of July 1921. These last, from the Royal Archives at Windsor, appear by the gracious permission of Her Majesty the Queen.

Transcription of the selected documents has again been made according to the rules set out in the preface to the first series. It has, however, been necessary to make some additional excisions. These have been limited to a few passages which might invade the privacy of living persons and to the detailed descriptions of everyday family activities and events which Smuts usually included in his letters to close friends.

The editor wishes to record her deep gratitude to the Trustees of the Smuts Collection for invariable support and encouragement and to the secretary of the Trust for indispensable services. In preparing the biographical and other notes she has been capably assisted by Mrs Eleanor Katzschner and Miss Deborah Bates and she holds in grateful remembrance the late Miss Winifred Greenshields, who devoted many years of her life to the ordering of the Smuts Collection and the making of the books based upon it.

March 1972

JEAN VAN DER POEL

PART XIII

PRIME MINISTER

3 SEPTEMBER 1919–25 JUNE 1924

PRIME MINISTER

Smuts entered upon his first prime ministership with some apprehension and reluctance but soon recovered his characteristic self-confidence as well as the physical energy depleted by the strains of the war. Both were fully tested during the next five years which produced major crises both in South Africa and in Europe. The Smuts Collection contains important documents on all these events, for Smuts was not only a forceful prime minister but remained closely concerned with the problems of European and Commonwealth politics upon which his help was often sought.

The South African documents here selected deal mainly with (*a*) a renewed, and again unsuccessful, attempt to reunite the South African and National parties; (*b*) the alternative, and temporarily successful, manoeuvre of merging the South African and Unionist parties (**21, 23, 30, 31, 33, 34, 36, 42**); (*c*) eruptions of race and colour violence in the clashes at Bulhoek and with the Bondelswarts (**45, 98, 103, 104**); (*d*) the crucial strike on the Witwatersrand which led to Smuts's defeat by a Nationalist–Labour combination (**68–75, 87**). But other continuing themes of South African history also appear, such as the South West Africa mandate (**77, 140**) and relations with Rhodesia (**83, 85, 86, 88, 93**).

Smuts's European preoccupations at this time were the welfare of his 'own child', the League of Nations, and the rehabilitation of Germany. This led him to criticize the foreign policy of Great Britain as too tolerant of the punitive measures of France and later, on a visit to Europe in 1923, to make a personal intervention in the reparations impasse, culminating in a telling speech (**108–33**). These matters are well documented in his private papers.

An earlier visit to England in 1921 found Smuts drawn deeply, at the request of both sides, into the complications of the Irish nationalist movement. The part he played in this appears fully in nos. **48–62**. He also made at this time a notable contribution to Commonwealth history by circulating at the imperial conference a memorandum on Dominion status which anticipated the Balfour declaration and the statute of Westminster (**46, 47**. See separate note on pp. 65–7).

Records of his personal life during this period show him pursuing his botanical interests, climbing the mountains of the western Cape whenever he can, reading new books on science and philosophy. L. S. Amery becomes a regular correspondent; important letters are exchanged with W. S. Churchill, J. M. Keynes, E. H. Walton; and Smuts makes the first approaches to J. H. Hofmeyr (**35, 38, 136, 139**).

3

1 To S. M. Smuts

Vol. 22, no. 170

Civil Service Club
Cape Town
3 September 1919

Liefste Mamma, Wij zijn hier gister (Dinsdag) veilig aangekomen, en ik had tijd na aankomst om de meeste mijner ander collegas te zien over aan blijven in het nieuwe Cabinet. Ik moet Burton en Kowie Graaff nog zien. De anderen hebben allen in dankbaarheid aangenomen. Malan was 'quite nice about it'—dacht dat ik de eenige oplossing was. Het is jammer dat de *Friend* van gister een vergelijking tusschen hem en mij maakte die niet zeer vleiend voor hem was en die hij aan Nyssie R. zal wijten en mij voor blameeren als vriend van Nyssie. Buxton arriveert hedenochtend en het nieuwe ministerie (het oude onveranderd) zal vanmiddag ingezworen worden. Voor mij begint dan een kolossale verantwoordelijkheid en de oplossing van kwesties waarvoor zelfs ou Louis reeds jaren had teruggedeinst. Moge ik kracht en moed hebben het werk te doen. Jou hulp en geloof in mijn ster zullen mij veel helpen en hebben mij reeds veel geholpen op het lange afgelegde pad. Wanneer ik over de toekomst denk en alles wat zal moeten gedaan worden dan voel ik bijna beangst. Maar deze bergen van moeilijkheden, wanneer naderbij en 'closer seen, are but gigantic flights of stairs'. Wij zullen zien. Jij moet mij schrijven hoe alles op de plaats gaat en met jou en de kinderen. En houd maar duim vast voor mij in de nieuwe taak. Ik had zoo gedacht dat na al dat zware werk ik een tijdje van rust en recuperatie zou hebben. En nu? Ja het leven is zwaar; voor ons is het een zwaar en drukkend last geweest voor nu 21 jaren. Hoe lang nog? Maar ik ben niet ongeduldig, en moet maar voortgaan, op het werk ziende niet als een last maar een gelegenheid om werk te doen voor Z.A. en de menschheid. Tatta mijn liefste.

Jan

TRANSLATION

Civil Service Club
Cape Town
3 September 1919

Dearest Mamma, We arrived here safely yesterday (Tuesday) and I had time, after arriving, to see most of my other colleagues about staying on in the new cabinet. I have still to see Burton [H.] and Kowie [Sir J. A. C.] Graaff. The others have all gratefully accepted. Malan [F. S.] was quite nice about it—thought I was the only solution. It is a pity that yesterday's *Friend* made a comparison between him and me which was not very flattering to him, which he will attribute to Nyssie R.[1] and for which he will blame me as a friend of Nyssie. Buxton arrives this morning and the new ministry (the old one unchanged) will be sworn in this afternoon. A colossal responsibility then begins for me and the solution of questions from which even old Louis[2] had shrunk for years. May I have strength and courage to do the work. Your help and belief in my star will help me greatly and have already helped me greatly on the long, travelled road. When I think of the future and all that will have to be done I feel almost frightened. But these mountains of troubles when they are nearer and 'closer seen, are but gigantic flights of stairs'. We shall see. You must write me how everything goes on the farm and with you and the children. And hold thumbs for me in the new task. I had really thought that, after all that hard work, I would have a little time of rest and recuperation. And now? Yes, life is hard; for us it has been a heavy, oppressive burden for twenty-one years. How much longer? But I am not impatient and must go on, looking upon the work not as a burden but as an opportunity to work for South Africa and mankind. Good-bye, my dearest.

Jan

2   To M. C. Gillett   Vol. 22, no. 273

Civil Service Club
Cape Town
6 September 1919

I have just seen in the paper that a boat leaves in an hour's time for England and so I drop you a hurried line. I am down here for a short special session to ratify the peace treaty and have left Isie at Doornkloof. I am now prime minister but my heart is not in the thing and only an overwhelming disaster brought me there. Botha's loss to this country is quite irreparable. His was just the role which I temperamentally could not play, and you know how necessary that role is in the world. I shall do my best without being sanguine about success.

I still think a great deal of the world I left behind me, but lots of work and troubles peculiar to our young growing country keep me from any morbid dwelling on the past. Europe is a sad broken world—a world which touched me even more to the quick than did the Transvaal after the Boer War. Nobody seems able to bring

---

[1] Deneys Reitz.   [2] General Louis Botha.

healing to the disease from which she is suffering. If I had thought I could do any good, I might have felt tempted to stay on. But talking is not my line, and writing statements[1] which every newspaper throws into the wastepaper basket is not good business either. And there is a good deal of work to be done in South Africa. In the meantime, you must keep me in touch with the great world by letting me know what is doing and what currents are flowing. In a difficult time of world transition such as we are now passing through strange undercurrents and cross currents will develop which it would be interesting and useful to watch. I am sure you will keep your eyes open and tell me what you see or feel.

Apart from the great sorrow so suddenly come upon us, I have still been revelling in the joy of our young life and the fresh beauty of our country and climate. It is really a lovely country with a strange fascination. And yet the downs and the firs and the knolls keep crowding in on me in spite of all that South Africa has to show. Life to me has been very great and sweet and true. And I thank God for all I have gone through—the great fires of life which purge the soul and feed it with the food immortal.

I had a letter from May[2] last night from which I infer she is not well or happy—though of course she does not say so—and that she is going to America after all and contemplates a tour to Asia and where not next year. I have told her South Africa is a good little country to see—better than America or Asia.

Now love to you dear child; and love and blessings to all my little family. Arthur I assume is now quite well. Ever yours,

Jan

3   From A. F. B. Botha

Vol. 21, no. 16

8 September 1919

My dear Jannie, I have not wired to you to congratulate you or tell you how glad I am that you have been chosen to form the cabinet and carry on in Louis's place. Perhaps it was that there was no one else who could do so but you, and perhaps it was because I knew that you would know and understand exactly how I felt in the matter. It was always Louis's wish and ambition to see you prime minister, and now I say with him: God bless you Jannie; and may He give you strength and great wisdom, patience and His guidance in the difficult task before you. I know you are equal to it and we are all going to give you every possible support and assistance and

---

[1] See vol. IV, **1043**, **1057**.   [2] See vol. IV, p. 80, note 1.

if there is anything I can do, please just tell me. I am willing and glad to carry on if you think Louis would wish it. Your tribute to him at the opening of parliament was beautiful. Isie [Smuts] I have seen twice since your departure and she is just a dear, sweet, understanding friend.

We have not finished with our cup of sorrow. Helen's[1] youngest boy, Danie, is dangerously ill—the doctors have not decided what he has—and we are just in a state of anxiety and fear.

I just want to say once more many, many thanks for all your loving utterances in honour of the man who loved you so greatly during his lifetime. You never had a truer or more faithful friend and brother; and he thought the world of you and always said you were the greatest man in our country, the coming man of the age. I thought I would tell you this although I know you must often have realized what his thoughts and opinions were of you.

I cannot tell you all I wish for you, and I shall just end by saying again: God bless Jannie, Louis's faithful friend in storm and calm. Ever your loving

Aunt Annie

4　To M. C. Gillett　　　　　　　　　　　　Vol. 22, no. 274

Civil Service Club
Cape Town
14 September 1919

This is Sunday night and I have spent a most beautiful and enjoyable Sabbath day. In the morning after breakfast I went up Table mountain and after a good climb and a glorious three hours I returned for lunch—all by myself. A sort of Quaker Meeting at which I pondered over many things. I thought of all my dear ones and all my holy places in two continents. I thought of the difficulties behind and the great work ahead. And I thought of all you have been saying in your last dear letters. Oh, 102[2] is very dear to me and I can scarcely think of you all without moist eyes. And your letters are very precious. I was amused to see in your last letter the wish that I should not plunge right into work but have some time with my poor dear family. Well, I have been back forty days, of which I have only spent two or three at home—the rest have been spent all over South Africa. And it will be weeks before I am home again. Public life has to me been one long sacrifice of family life. Isie must surely

---

[1] *See* vol. III, p. 459, note 1.　　　　[2] *See* vol. II, p. 574, note 1.

feel all this very much, and looks very thin and worn out with labours which she has undertaken largely as a narcotic to dull this never-ending pain of living. But what can be done? Now I am prime minister and things will be worse than ever. My beginnings as prime minister have been quite successful and both my colleagues and party are very pleased with the way I have handled the peace treaty in parliament. Everybody of course knows that I abhor the document—all except the League of Nations. The Hertzogites and their republican propaganda I have handled quite vigorously—at which there is also rejoicing in the party. But all this cannot interest you. We are such a small world. And yet great issues have arisen here, and may again arise. I am very anxious that the name of South Africa shall not be tarnished with this peace. I am going to give our Germans good decent treatment in spite of the awful terms about their private property.[1] I had a wonderful letter from a German at München, written 1 July, in which he thanked me most profusely for the protest[2] and said it had brought hope and comfort to millions in Germany. So that was good work anyhow.

I am so glad that Arthur is getting all right. I hope Tona Wallis[3] will soon be well too. My dear love to you and all the children. You are all ever in my thoughts and in my heart.

Jan

5   To S. M. Smuts   Vol. 22, no. 181

Civil Service Club
Cape Town
18 September 1919

Liefste Mamma, Onze eerste (of laatste!) sessie is voorbij, en alles is zeer voorspoedig afgeloopen, en van alle kanten hoor ik lofbetuiging voor de wijze waarop het werk gedaan is. Mrs Botha krijgt een pensioen van £1,200 per jaar. Ik hoop zij zal daarmee tevreden zijn. Ik geloof niet dat jij ooit een pensioen zal krijgen want men houdt niet van mij zooals van ou Louis. Hij was waarlijk een man van vrede; terwijl ik steeds een vechter ben geweest.

[1] The terms of the treaty of Versailles relating to the property of German nationals in the territories of the allied and associated powers are contained in section IV, article 297. The powers are given the right 'to retain and liquidate all property rights and interests...belonging to...German nationals' and the German owner may not dispose of such rights and interests without the consent of the state concerned.

[2] Vol. IV, **1043**.

[3] *See* vol. IV, p. 192, note 1.

Denn ich bin ein Mensch gewesen
Und das heisst ein Kämpfer sein.

Jij onthoudt die regels uit de *West-östlicher Divan.*

Ik ben verbazend vol werk en zal heel mogelijk niet eens na Riebeek kunnen gaan. Een groot programma voor aanstaande week is voor mij uitgewerkt. Ik hoop avond van 4 of 5 Oct. hier te vertrekken en dus omtrent 7 Oct. thuis te zijn. Daar zal ik een 14 dagen vertoeven voor noodzakelijk werk voor ik verder ga. Ik zal zeer bezig zijn, Mamma, en gedurig van thuis wezen met mijn rondreizen door het land. Maar ik weet jij is geduldig en zal alles voor de goede zaak opofferen.

Nu, mijn liefste, een zoentje aan jou en de kleinen.

Pappa

TRANSLATION

Civil Service Club
Cape Town
18 September 1919

Dearest Mamma, Our first (or last!) session is over, and everything has gone off very well, and from all sides I hear praise for the way in which the work has been done. Mrs Botha gets a pension of £1,200 a year. I hope she will be satisfied with this. I do not think that you will ever get a pension because people do not like me as they did old Louis. He was truly a man of peace; whereas I have always been a fighter.

Denn ich bin ein Mensch gewesen
Und das heisst ein Kämpfer sein.

You remember these lines from the *West-östlicher Divan.*[1]

I have an astonishing amount of work and shall very probably not even be able to go to Riebeek.[2] A big programme has been worked out for me for next week. I hope to leave here on the evening of 4 or 5 October and so to be home about 7 October. I shall stay there for a fortnight for essential work before I go further. I shall be very busy, Mamma, and continually away from home on my journeys throughout the country. But I know you are patient and will sacrifice everything for the good cause.

Now, my dearest, a kiss for you and the little ones.

Pappa

[1] For I have been a man and that means being a fighter. Goethe, *West-östlicher Divan, Chuld Nameh, Buch des Paradieses,* 'Einlass'.
[2] *See* vol. i, p. 4, note i.

6 To S. M. Smuts
Vol. 22, no. 185

Civil Service Club
Cape Town
21 September 1919
Zondagochtend

Liefste Mamma, Ik ben niet naar de kerk gegaan daar ik verscheiden dingen heb in orde te brengen. Gister avond was ik op een diner mij door de Civil Service gegeven en moest daar een lange speech maken. Heden namiddag spreek ik de Y.M.C.A. toe in de City Hall. Ik denk het is goed tot de jonge lui te spreken. Zij worden allen Nat of rebelsch. En de waarheid is veel breeder dan het nationalisme, met zijn engheid en (soms) zelfzuchtigheid. Van avond vertrek ik dan op mijn toer door de noordwestelijke deelen. Laatst was ik daar 18 jaren geleden, vechtende voor de republiek. Nu ga ik daarheen om hen te vragen de republiek maar te laten staan. Dat is de ironie der geschiedenis, oogenschijnlijk tegenstrijdig; en toch zijn beide op het pad van zuiver plicht. Maar menschen verstaan zulke kiesingen niet maklijk. Ik hoop echter dat alles wel zal gaan en dat er goed uit mijn reis zal geboren worden. Het wordt mij steeds meer duidelijk dat het onmogelijk is met Hertzog en Co. samen te werken. Zij zijn bepaald onmogelijke menschen; ik meen de voormannen, niet het volk dat het eerlijk meent.

Mijn warm jas is aangekomen. Hartelijk dank. Jou brief was ook zeer welkom. Ik ben zeer blij dat de kleinen weer wel zijn. Ik hoop maar net dat wij regen zullen krijgen. Het moet waarlijk zeer droog zijn. Hier blijft het maar steeds koud en regenachtig...Zoentjes aan Mamma en de kleinen.

Pappa

TRANSLATION

Civil Service Club
Cape Town
21 September 1919
Sunday morning

Dearest Mamma, I have not gone to church as I have various things to put in order. Yesterday evening I was at a dinner given me by the civil service and had to make a long speech. This afternoon I am addressing the Y.M.C.A. in the city hall. I think it is a good thing to speak to the young people. They are all becoming Nats[1] or rebels. And the truth is much broader than nationalism with its narrowness

---

[1] *See* vol. III, p. 542, note 1.

and (at times) selfishness. This evening I leave on my tour through
the north-western region. I was last there eighteen years ago,
fighting for the republic. Now I go there to ask them to let the
republic go. That is the irony of history, apparently contradictory;
and yet both are in the way of pure duty. But people do not easily
understand such choices. However, I hope that everything will go
well and that good will come of my journey. It becomes more and
more clear to me that it is impossible to work with Hertzog and Co.
They are definitely impossible people; I mean the leaders, not the
common people who honestly mean it.

My warm coat has arrived. Thank you very much. Your letter
was also very welcome. I am very glad that the little ones are well
again. I only hope we shall have rain. It must really be very dry.
Here it continues to be cold and rainy...Kisses to Mamma and the
little ones.

Pappa

7   To M. C. Gillett   Vol. 22, no. 277

Civil Service Club
Cape Town
4 October 1919

I returned last night from a fortnight's tour through the north-
western districts of the Cape Province, having travelled about
700 miles by motor over bad roads mostly (and generally doing my
own driving) and visiting thirteen or fourteen towns and making
innumerable speeches and attending endless functions. I am glad
it is over; it has been a most trying time. But not without the
greatest interest and keen enjoyment. I was there last eighteen
years ago in command of the republican forces, calling upon the
population to join me. And now I was calling upon them to drop
all agitation for the republic and abide in the British connection.
Such is my fate. And yet I do not feel inconsistent. But it is somewhat mystifying to the plain man on the veld.

The Hertzog party is and has been working up a strong agitation
in favour of a republic movement, in which I see the seeds of fresh
troubles for the future. I have waged a great fight against them
since my return to South Africa, and the effects of my efforts are
beginning to be felt by them. My endeavour is to get the co-operation of all moderate sensible elements in the population for the
support of a stable government to see this young country through
the period of grave unrest which is before the world.

You have been passing through the great railway strike.[1] It must be a most exciting but also a most grave time. It is difficult to get the hang of the thing from the cables, and I suppose [Lloyd] George is exaggerating when he speaks of an anarchist conspiracy. I hope the trouble will soon be over and not leave a worse temper behind it. The world is truly in a bad way. Perhaps thus only could the new birth of society come about.

I have thought much of you and Arthur and the little ones on these travels. You have been very close to me in the great spaces. The day before yesterday when I was coming through my own native parts, now in full flower, a flood of emotions surged over my soul, and I had again that great experience in which Downs mixed with Veld and I felt uplifted beyond the limits of time and space.

Tonight or tomorrow I leave for Pretoria. It is just two months since I landed from England, and I have only been a couple of days at home. Jannie[2] will have nothing to do with me anymore. He has probably suffered too much through my long absence. Louis[3] is very dear. All are very well. But Isie in her last letter wrote to me that she hoped to see more of me in the life to come! What if we go to different destinations?

Good-bye, dear child. I have had no letter from you recently as they are waiting for me at Irene. Love and blessings on you and Arthur and my little family. Ever yours,

Jan

8   From P. J. G. de Vos   Vol. 21, no. 88

There is no reply to this letter in the Smuts Collection.   Stellenbosch
4 October 1919

Waarde Heer en Vriend! Laat my toe dat ik iets in alle bescheiden-heid onder uwe aandacht brenge. Geloof my dat ik 't alleen doe omdat de verdeeldheid onder ons volk voor my eene allerfataalste zaak is, en omdat er naar myne overtuiging geen genoegzame grond voor bestaat.

Ziet er wordt van de zijde der Z.A.P. gezegd dat er voor het *tegenwoordige* althans geen *propaganda* behoort te worden gemaakt voor eene republiek, dat men natuurlijk niet vooruit weten kan

[1] This began on 26 September because the government had announced a reduction in wages when the railwaymen were asking for an increase. An almost complete paralysis of railway transport followed. The strike ended on 5 October when it was agreed to maintain existing wages.

[2] *See* vol. III, p. 103, note 1.   [3] *See* vol. III, p. 265, note 1.

wat de Voorzienigheid in de toekomst mocht doen gebeuren, en men daarop wachten moet. Het is ook bekend dat op enkele uitzonderingen na al de leden den Z.A.P. ernstig hopen (evenals Onze Jan het als iets natuurlijks verwacht heeft) dat de tijd zal komen, dat wij geheel losgemaakt zullen zijn van het Engelsche rijk.

Die Nat partij weder houdt vol dat zij er niet aan denkt haar doel op eene andere dan constitutioneele wijze te bereiken, en door het publiek daartoe op te voeden, hoe lang 't mocht duren. Het verschil tusschen de twee partijen op dit punt waar zoo te zeggen alles om draait, is dus alleen een kwestie van tijd en wijse. Voor een 'outsider' derhalve, die evenals ik zich niet eigenlijk op politiek terrein beweegt, maar alleen met zijn gezond verstand vraagt, als voor Gods aangezicht, wat onder zulke buitengewoon ernstige omstandigheden, de plicht is van een volk met zulk eene geschiedenis en zulk eene roeping als de onze, is dit toch waarlijk geen genoegsame reden waarom het langer zoo verdeeld zal blijven en zich aan zulke ontzettende gevaren zal gaan blootstellen. Er is toch zoo oneindig veel dat ons zoo hecht aan elkander bindt als 't met eenig ander volk het geval is, en dat ons wel in staat moet stellen, op zulk een punt van tijd en wijse alleen, elkander te verdragen en de oplossing ervan aan de toekomst over te laten, en derhalve iedereen vrij te laten zijn gang te gaan. Hoe dikwijls worden niet ministers van het zelfde cabinet toegelaten in de eene of andere zaak, die niet zoo dadelijk tot eene cabinetskwestie behoeft gemaakt te worden van elkander te verschillen en te stemmen zooals zij willen!

De vraag is dus of 't niet noodzakelijk is, dat U en een of ander leidsman van de Nat. party de zaak privaat en openhartig met elkander zullen bespreken, en eerlijk en ernstig trachten zullen tot eene verstandhouding te komen. Als een derde persoon noodig is om den weg voor U daartoe te openen, zal zoo iemand wel te vinden zijn. Ik wil my geensins aan U opdringen, maar zou indien gewenscht gaarne al wat in mijn vermogen is daartoe willen doen. Geen mensch weet van dit mijn schrijven aan U; maar als U gereed is tot 't een of ander in boven aangeduide richting, en my wil zeggen aan wien ik in denzelfden geest schrijven moet en *waar* en *wanneer* U hem zou willen ontmoeten, zal ik zulke gaarne doen. Na minzame groete Uw Dw. Dienaar en Vriend

P. J. G. de Vos

TRANSLATION

Stellenbosch
4 October 1919

Dear Sir and Friend, Allow me, with all respect, to bring something to your attention. Believe me, I do so only because the division among our people is to me a most fatal matter, and because I am convinced that there are no sufficient grounds for it.

On the South African party side it is said that there should, for the *present* at any rate, be no *propaganda* for a republic; that one cannot know in advance what Providence might cause to happen in the future, and one must wait for it. It is also known that, with a few exceptions, all the members of the South African party earnestly hope (just as Onze Jan expected it as something natural) that the time will come when we shall be completely disconnected from the English empire.

The National party again maintain that they do not contemplate reaching their aim in any other than a constitutional way, and by educating the public to it, however long it may take. The difference between the two parties on this point, upon which so to speak everything turns, is therefore solely a question of time and manner. For an outsider who, like me, does not really move in political regions, but only asks, with his sound commonsense, as before God, what in such exceptionally grave circumstances is the duty of a people with such a history and calling as ours, this is really no sufficient reason why it should any longer remain so divided and expose itself to such terrible dangers. There is so infinitely much that binds us together, as closely as in the case of any other nation, and that should enable us, if only at this time and in this way, to bear with one another and leave the solution to the future, and so leave everyone free to go his own way. How often are not ministers in the same cabinet allowed to differ from one another and to vote as they please on some matter which need not immediately be made a cabinet matter!

The question is therefore whether it is not necessary that you and some leader of the National party should discuss the matter privately and frankly, and honestly and seriously try to come to an understanding.[1] If a third person is necessary to open the way to this for you, such a person will no doubt be found. I do not wish in

---

[1] During 1919–20 there were unsuccessful attempts at *hereniging* (reunion) between the South African and the National parties. Representatives of both parties met in congress on three occasions in 1919 to discuss it. At the October meeting agreement was reached on such matters as a distinctive Union flag and the right of neutrality but the South African party denied the right of secession from the Empire and refused to accept the National party's demand for freedom to advocate a republic.

any way to force myself on you, but I should, if that is desired, like to do all that is in my power. No one knows about this letter of mine to you; but if you are ready to do something in the direction indicated above, and would tell me to *whom* I should write in the same spirit and *where* and *when* you would wish to meet him, I would gladly do so. With friendly greetings, Your sincere friend,

P. J. G. de Vos

9   To J. X. Merriman   Vol. 22, no. 186

Prime Minister's Office
Pretoria
14 October 1919

Dear Mr Merriman, Thank you very much for your letter of 4 October and enclosures. It is clear that nothing that I said at Loxton could justify [A.] Le Fleur's remarks.[1]

I am very sorry that my undertaking Botha's life is quite out of the question. It should be done well by somebody who has the leisure for it, and you know how my time is taken up with other unavoidable duties. It seems to me that Professor Fouché, who wrote that celebrated Rebellion Blue Book,[2] could perhaps do justice to the task, as he had a fair personal knowledge of Botha, and is otherwise very able.[3]

I am amused at your reply that I don't appear 'to encourage outside opinion'. On the contrary your expression of opinion is always most welcome to me, even where I don't always agree with you. And I would do anything to encourage you sometimes to give me the benefit of your experience and judgment. Times are very difficult and mistakes may under present circumstances have far-reaching results. Please therefore do not pass me by, where I could be helped by friendly advice. Ever yours most sincerely,

J. C. Smuts

[1] A. Le Fleur was a supporter of Smuts and of J. X. Merriman among the Coloured people of the southern Cape Province. He seems to have been of Griqua descent and to have had some influence among the Reheboth Bastards. (*See* vol. III, p. 454, note 3.)
[2] *Report on the Outbreak of the Rebellion* (U.G. 10 of 1915).
[3] There are four biographies of Botha: E. H. Spender, *General Botha: the Career and the Man* (1916); Earl Buxton, *General Botha* (1924); F. V. Engelenburg, *General Louis Botha* (1929); J. Meintjes, *General Louis Botha—a Biography* (1970).

10   To A. Clark   Vol. 98, no. 102

Pretoria
21 October 1919

Last mail brought another welcome letter from you. I trust you are not over-meticulous on the point of replies, as it is not always possible to reply owing to my being so often absent. But it does me good to hear from you. You wear the laurels of the Ideal still fresh round your head, whereas with me they are faded and all awry! It is nice to hear you talk of Love and Truth and Life and the other great Capitals. Here I am immersed in the small things and console myself with David Harum's philosophy that 'fleas are good for a dog'.[1] But the auroral hues of the Ideal are so much pleasanter to the eye and to the temper!

I hear from Hilda [Clark] fairly frequently. I do not see clearly what could be done. We have coal and maize but absolutely no transport. Meanwhile Hilda paints the prospect in the darkest colour.[2] I sometimes fear that this war is simply the vanguard of calamity and that the Great Horror is still to come. What will become of the world? Is it still possible to believe in your great Ideals? My heart often feels cold and numbed when I think of the world situation today.

Thanks for the sprig of heather from the Quantocks. It made me think far back to that day when we three wandered over the dear hills. Will they ever come again, the long, long dances?[3] Arthur [Gillett] is, I suppose, in Vienna[4] and I hear a rumour that you too are going.

Give my love to the dear Parents and tell them I always think of them and the beautiful visits to Millfield. Ever yours,

Jan

11   From W. S. Churchill   Vol. 21, no. 35

War Office
Whitehall
London S.W.1
30 October 1919

My dear Smuts, I have been keeping your letter by me in my boxes for an opportunity to tell you how deeply I value it. All the many

[1] 'A reasonable amount o' fleas is good for a dog—keeps him from broodin' over bein' a dog.' Edward Noyes Westcott, *David Harum*, p. 284.

[2] Hilda Clark was leader of the Society of Friends relief mission in Vienna.

[3] *See* vol. IV, p. 40, note 1.

[4] Arthur Gillett was in Vienna to advise the relief mission on finance.

kindnesses and services you rendered to me in the stormy ups and downs of the great struggle have made a lasting impression on my mind. I can never forget your sympathy and comradeship. We shall always look back upon those fierce crowded days and in them I shall always see your friendship and courage and wise counsel.

Botha came to see me here before he sailed, and I did what I have so far done for no other visitor—escorted him downstairs and put him into his carriage myself. Almost immediately after (as it seemed) while the impression of his presence was strong with me I learned that he has gone. I know what a loss this will be to you, and believe me I felt a keen personal pang as if someone I had known all my life had passed away. He was one of the truly great men of the world, and, thank God, of the British Empire.

Now you stand in his place with all those difficulties and troubles to face. I am sure you will succeed. That wise and tolerant liberalism which is the peculiar product of our island is one of the keys; and your own gifts and courage make the other.

I am not yet through with my Russian troubles[1] but I think I shall get through to a good result for all—though not by the path you would have followed.

I send you my warmest wishes for good fortune. South Africa is dear to me and if at any time there is any service you think I can render her, or you, please do not delay to impart it to your sincere friend,

Winston S. Churchill

12 Speech   Box H, no. 29

This address was delivered on 3 November 1919 in Johannesburg at a reception given in Smuts's honour by the South African Zionist Federation and the South African Jewish Board of Deputies.

I need not tell you, you know better than I do, that the Jews have been one of the most national little peoples that have ever lived, national even to the extent of bigotry, and they have paid the penalty of being bigoted, of being national and of being small. They have been ground down between the upper and the nether millstone in history. The great empires which have marched hither and thither

---

[1] In March 1919 on the initiative of Churchill, then secretary for war, the Supreme War Council in Paris decided on large-scale intervention in the civil war in Russia to help the monarchists. British arms and volunteers were sent to the main centres of resistance to the Bolshevists. Churchill's policy was unpopular with Labour and, by this time, unacceptable to Lloyd George and the cabinet.

over the face of Asia have also come into repeated conflict with the
Jewish people, with the result, as you know, that 2,000 years ago,
they were, after previous transportations from their country, finally
ejected and scattered over the face of the earth. And since then their
history has been one of martyrdom. I do not think there is any record
in the whole history of the human race which compares to that of
the Jewish people. Yet through it all you have kept the faith, you
have kept up your self-respect, you have kept up your national ideals,
and you are surviving today, among the nations of the world. (Cheers.)
You have not been absorbed, you have not been merged, and you
have not lost your identity, but through all tribulations and persecu-
tions, through all the vicissitudes of human history you have survived.
You have survived, and the day will come when the words of the
prophets will become true, and Israel will return to its own land.
(Loud cheers.) I am very happy that in my own day I have had the
privilege to contribute however humble a share towards the great
result which has already been achieved in that direction. (Cheers.)

I remember very well the incident referred to by Mr [M.]
Alexander; how after I came back from East Africa and was lying
ill in my house, Mr Nathan Levi came to me with the resolutions
passed by the Zionist Federation.[1] I gave him my assurance that
whenever I had the chance, without knowing that I ever would
have the chance, I would help Zionism. It was like one of those
blank cheques that politicians sometimes sign. I said, 'Certainly,
I shall do my best, if I have the opportunity, to further these
resolutions of the Zionist Federation.' I did not know that I would
have to honour that cheque, and that the day would really come
when I would be in a position to help to carry out the aspirations of
the Zionist community all over the world. (Cheers.) But somehow
after I arrived in Europe fate in a curious way linked my fortune
with those of your people and your country. After I had been there
for a short while, I think it was in May 1917, Mr Lloyd George,
the prime minister, asked me to take command of the British forces
in Palestine.[2] I didn't want to accept that, as I had had enough of
fighting. After so many years of commanding in all sorts of campaigns I thought that I could probably be of more service and do
more useful work at the centre of things. And so I declined to seek
military glory in Palestine. But you can readily understand, ladies
and gentlemen, how an offer like that, pressed upon me repeatedly
before I finally declined it, brought home to me more than ever
before the consideration of Palestine and of the Jewish question

[1] The South African Zionist Federation was founded on 11 December 1898.
[2] The offer was made in April 1917. *See* vol. III, **743**.

generally. After I had refused to go to Palestine I became a member of the war cabinet and was really at the centre of things. And then began this movement in favour of a declaration on behalf of Palestine as the future home of the Jewish race. (Cheers.) The idea of course originated with Dr [C.] Weizmann and the other leaders of the Zionist movement. They approached certain members of the government. Dr Weizmann, who was a friend of mine, approached me and pressed me very strongly, and I told him of the promise I had made on my sick bed at Irene, and that I had to carry out that promise, and, ladies and gentlemen, I did my best to carry it out. (Cheers.) The matter was one of extreme difficulty and intricacy and delicacy, too. Palestine, as you know, is a country largely inhabited still by the Arab people; very few Turks, but mostly Arabs. And besides, at the time that this movement started in favour of declaring Palestine as the home of the Jewish people, it was still very strongly held by the Turkish armies. It seemed somewhat premature, to say the least, to make a declaration such as we were pressed to make. But all great things in the world are done in faith, and we acted in that spirit. We believed in the victory of our cause, we believed that the day would come, and was not far distant, when Palestine would be set free from the oppression of the Turk, and when a promise to the Jewish race could be fulfilled by us. That was one difficulty. The other difficulty was to discover a formula to which the various great powers would agree. That was a matter of extreme difficulty and delicacy and involved a great deal of negotiation before it was found possible to make a public declaration which would pledge and bind the British government and British policy. Finally, after a great deal of cogitation we hit on that formula which has become historic, and which was published in the declaration of Mr Balfour on behalf of the British government.[1] (Cheers.) That formula declared that the British government would do its best in future to make Palestine, the old historic Palestine of the Bible, the national home of the Jewish people.[2] (Cheers.)

I believe we must have tried a score of other formulas which we found would not suit the facts of the case, or the possibilities of the future political situation in the world. But finally that formula was evolved, and was settled upon as likely to do adequate justice to the Jewish cause, and at the same time as likely to carry the assent of the great powers. After we had published that statement it was

---

[1] The declaration was contained in a letter from Balfour, then foreign secretary, to Lord Rothschild dated 2 November 1917.

[2] The declaration included a proviso that the rights of the non-Jewish peoples in Palestine would be safeguarded.

almost immediately assented to by President Wilson and the American government—(cheers)—and shortly afterwards it also secured the approval of the government of the French Republic. And ever since then, since the November of 1917, I have looked upon the fate of Palestine as settled, and settled for ever. (Loud applause.) The events of the war have proved that our faith was not wrongly placed. The Turkish armies were driven away from Palestine, and in fact from the whole of Syria, and it then became possible for the British government to make good the promise which they have made. Ladies and gentlemen, that promise has not been executed yet because it has not yet been possible to have final peace with the Turkish Empire. You know that the negotiations with regard to the peace treaty with Turkey are still going on. But I think I am giving away no secrets when I say that it is looked upon as a settled policy that the mandate for Palestine, the old historic Palestine, is going to be given to the British Empire. (Loud and prolonged applause.) I think there can be no doubt about that, although it is one of the matters which have not yet been finally settled, as that particular treaty has not yet been signed. But I have no doubt in my mind that it won't be many months before you will see that is the result, and that Palestine will become linked in a very intimate way with the fortunes of the great British Empire.[1]

The idea of the British government is, as soon as practicable, to set up local autonomous institutions in Palestine. The problem there is one of great delicacy, because a large Arab population is still living in Palestine. You have a minority of Jews there, and the policy that will have to be promoted and fostered in future will be the introduction of larger and ever larger numbers of Jews into Palestine. (Cheers.) It is easy to see that there are possibilities of conflict, of misunderstanding, in a situation like that, between the old Arab population and the new Jewish population. The whole situation will have to be handled with great delicacy, with great tact; and I know of no people in the world, and of no government in the world better equipped by its large experience with all races and all parts of the world, to deal with a problem like that than the British Empire, and the British government. (Cheers.)

The problem will have to be dealt with in stages, and you will have seen recently a warning issued by Professor Weizmann to the Jewish people to have no extravagant expectations of what can be done immediately. Palestine was indeed a land flowing with milk and honey in Bible times. But since then it has been blasted by the

[1] The British mandate for Palestine was granted in April 1920 and Sir Herbert (later Lord) Samuel became the first high commissioner.

tyranny of the Turk, and it will take a good deal of time and capital to restore that country to its old fertile condition. And therefore we will have to proceed with the great task ahead of us with patience and with wisdom, but also with the fixed determination that we are going to carry it out. (Cheers.)

I have no doubt in my mind, ladies and gentlemen, that although we may not live to see the day when the whole of Israel will have returned to Palestine, yet more and more it will again become the national home of the Jewish people. (Hear, hear.) From those parts of the world where the Jews are oppressed and unhappy, where they are not welcomed by the rest of the Christian population, from those parts of the world you will yet see an ever increasing stream of emigration towards Palestine; and in generations to come you will see a great Jewish state rising there once more. And I hope that its glories will be greater than even those of the state of which we read in the Bible. (Cheers.)

Ladies and gentlemen, during the war I had the privilege to go to Palestine for some months.[1] The British government sent me to Palestine in order to consult with General Allenby and to work out plans for the final advance which was made when the whole country was occupied by us. I then had the privilege, which to me was an inestimable one, of seeing that country, of travelling over it and learning to know its physical conditions, and of seeing with my own eyes what I had read and heard of since I saw the light of day. And I assure you I speak no words of exaggeration when I say that when I arrived in Palestine in February 1918, it seemed to me almost as if I was once more in South Africa. It was the only part of the world away from our own continent which appealed to me as having something African about it. There, once more you had that wonderful air—clear, keen, distinct; you could see without difficulty, in those February days, almost a hundred miles away. Whereas in Europe your vision is mostly limited to five or six miles of distance, in Palestine and on the mountains of Judea you could see almost any distance just as in South Africa. I breathed that keen air, I saw that distant vision, I thought of my own country, and I could understand how it was that Jews love South Africa so much. (Cheers.) It was a wonderful country. I must say, ladies and gentlemen, as you may not know it, that I am really a barbarian by every instinct. I love the desert parts of the world, and you must bear in mind that Palestine has a very forbidding aspect to the ordinary European, accustomed to his gardens and his trees and his limited range of vision. Palestine is a forbidding country, just as

---

[1] *See* vol. III, **814**, **816**.

the Karroo is a forbidding country, but with my African heart that wild country appealed to every fibre of my being, the air and the spirit of Palestine penetrated me. I saw practically the whole of Palestine in that clear light from two points. One point was about fifteen miles north of Jaffa, a little eminence where we surveyed the lines of the enemy armies. And standing there one afternoon I could see before me practically the whole of the land of the Jews in days gone by. Looking to the left I saw the mountain of Carmel spread out before me. I saw the breakers of the Mediterranean foaming at the foot of Carmel. I saw those wonderful hills before me so full of Bible history. And then there was a dip, and then another line of mountains began which were the mountains of Judea. Looking through that dip I saw in the distance the land of Galilee, the highlands and the hills of Galilee spread out before me. And looking to the right of the dip the whole country of Judea, right on to Beersheba, lay spread out before me. I do not think in any part of Europe it would have been possible to see so much country from one point of vantage. And on another occasion I was standing on the Mount of Olives, and I was looking over the whole country once more. I saw the whole Jordan valley stretching out before me in one of the most wonderful panoramas it is possible to see. Nothing is more grand and majestic than the valley of the Jordan and the Dead sea as seen from the Mount of Olives with that wonderful mountain of Moab towering above the valley on the other side, with the peaks of Pisgah and Nebo and Bethpeor. Further to the north I saw in the far distance one mountain after another rising in the Hauran. Hermon[1] itself was not visible. But I saw the Hauran country rising in tiers of mountains in the distance. Well, ladies and gentlemen, I thought I was once more in South Africa, I thought I was standing again on some point of vantage in South Africa and was looking over my native land. I could feel, looking over Palestine there that day, that there was a great spirit in that land. I could feel how that apparently deserted country, so forbidding and grand, gave birth to the greatest religion on earth, the loftiest religious spirit in history, and to one of the most wonderful peoples, perhaps the most wonderful people that the world has ever seen. You do not get really great things from prosperity. In the fertile parts of the world there could not possibly have been born that great spirit which you see in the Bible, that great religious literature which you find in the Bible, or that indomitable spirit of the Jewish people. It required something rugged, something terrible to have bred and to have created that literature and that spirit, which

---

[1] Mount Hermon.

has been perhaps the most powerful influence in the history of the human race. (Cheers.) Well, ladies and gentlemen, why should the Jews not go back to that wonderful land? Why should they wander over the face of the world? And why should they not in future have as great a mission as they have had in the past? Your people, your little people has had a mission, a civilizing mission in the world, second perhaps to none among the nations of the earth. You have played a role in history such as no other nation has played, and that was in no small measure due to the physical conditions of your country. And I do not see, ladies and gentlemen, why it should not be possible under better circumstances—when this little people is once more gathered to their own country and once more subjected to the influences of that country, why they should not once more play a great part in the history of the world.

When I was in Palestine it struck me also how it was that the Jews have solved one of the greatest problems in the life of nations. As you know, you have remained an intensely individual, national people. Intensely national and individual, and yet perhaps more than any other people you are a great international people with a real international spirit. You have learnt how to reconcile the national with the international. (Cheers.) And when I was in Palestine thinking over the problems connected with the Jewish people it struck me how you had arrived at that reconciliation between the individual and the general, between the national and the international. You can see it there before your eyes. There was the Jewish people living on the mountains of Judea; and by them went the great highway of history, the great highway between Asia and Africa and Europe. That plain, that wonderful plain, between the Mediterranean and the mountains of Judea, the coastal plain of Palestine was the highway on which the most powerful nations and the greatest empires of the world passed to and fro in their marches of conquest and civilization in previous centuries. And the Jews sitting on their hills were the spectators of all this; they saw all this whilst they were living their own national life on their hills; they saw before them this whole panorama of the great empires, the marching and counter-marching of the great conquerors, and great armies, and great civilizations, from Assyria to Egypt and from Egypt to Assyria. And this went on generation after generation and century after century. There you learnt one of the valuable lessons in your history, namely how to reconcile the life of the nation with the life of the world, how to reconcile the national with the international. And it seems to me that that is one of the great lessons that you have to teach humanity.

Ladies and gentlemen, both these things are very valuable. It is a great thing to be patriotic, to have your people and to say, 'My people first and foremost'; that is the national point of view. But that has to be counter-balanced by the other, the larger point of view, which it is so very difficult for us to learn. It is difficult to learn in this country and in Europe it is just as difficult. They all see only themselves alone; they all tend only to see their own people and to love their own people, while the great world and other nations and the whole of civilization do not seem to affect them very much. You, after the very hard experiences of living the life that you lived thousands of years ago in your own country and in other countries, got it into your blood, and learnt how these two factors are to be reconciled in the forward march of the race. And you are therefore in a peculiar position to teach mankind in future the task, how to reconcile these two factors, which is going to be the great task before the world in the years to come. There is no doubt that the day of the purely national is past. There is no doubt that we will have to superimpose the international order on the purely national basis, and no people in the world understands better how to do that and can teach the world greater lessons of wisdom and experience in that respect than your little Jewish people. (Cheers.)

The League of Nations seems to be entirely in the line of development of the whole Jewish idea, and I hope therefore that in the years to come the Jewish people will play an important part in this international order, that they will infuse a great spirit into the League of Nations, that they will stand for this wider outlook which is now dawning before history, and that they will contribute on this new level and on this new line as much to human welfare and human progress as they did before when they were a little people producing a great religious literature.

As I have said before on the occasion referred to by Mr Alexander, I look forward to the Spinozas[1] and the Maimonideses[2] of the future. I do not see why not, because the race is there, the character is there, the spiritual flame is still burning strong in you. I must admit that in recent centuries it has been deflected a great deal into other channels, that the spiritual force and vitality of the Jewish people has very often been turned into other channels, and nowadays you have the reputation of thinking more of the material than of the spiritual, more of money making than of the great spiritual values of life. But I am sure that that is only a temporary phase and a phase which can be explained and entirely explained by

[1] The Dutch philosopher Baruch Spinoza (1632–77) was of Jewish birth.
[2] Maimonides (1135–1204), rabbi and philosopher, was born in Córdoba, Spain.

the historic circumstances under which you have lived for many centuries amongst the nations of Europe. There is no reason why Israel should not come back to her great historic mission, why Israel should not hold aloft once more the banner of the spirit among the other peoples of the earth. That was your mission in the past; I hope that will be your mission in the future. (Continued applause.)

Here in this country too you have had an important role to play. South Africa has done well by you. I was looking at these cadets tonight lined up there as a guard of honour to me. I could not help thinking of the many faces of Jewish boys that I had seen in Europe in recent months in those parts where there is oppression and poverty and distress. I could not help comparing those bright and brave faces with what I had seen in Europe. South Africa has done well by the Jews, and I am sure you are all determined to give of your best to South Africa. You have much to give to South Africa. I have always thought that the Jews will become one of the most powerful and one of the most beneficent factors in the national life of South Africa. You bring qualities into the common pool that the others don't have. And there is so much in common between us; your whole attitude, your historic religious standpoint is so very close to that of the rest of the white population in South Africa that really I do not see why there should not be a 'pooling' of all our energies for the common good such as we have never seen before in the past.

I need not remind you that the white people of South Africa and especially the older Dutch population have been brought up almost entirely on Jewish tradition. The Old Testament, the most won-derful literature ever thought out by the brain of man, the Old Testament has been the very marrow of Dutch culture here in South Africa. I am sure that there are thousands, tens of thousands of Dutch people in this country who know the Old Testament better than many Jews themselves. In my own case I may say that whenever I see anything great or anything really moving, my mind always passes into the language of the Old Testament, which is the greatest language ever spoken by the tongue of man. I do not mean the Hebrew language as spoken by Dr [J. L.] Landau, although it sounded very magnificent, just now. But I mean the universal language of the human heart, the language of the human mind and soul expressing pure human feelings and human emotions with a universality which appeals to all races and all ages. That is the language of the Psalms and the prophets.

That is the basis of our culture in South Africa, that is the basis of our white culture, and it is the basis of your Jewish culture; and therefore we are standing together on a common platform, the greatest spiritual platform the world has ever seen. On that platform I want us to build the future South Africa. I do not want to see merely a country full of wealthy men, I do not want to see many multi-millionaires in South Africa. It is our ambition to see in South Africa a country of men and women, where the poor man is as great as the rich man, where the great ideals which you find expressed in the prophets of the Old Testament will find their realization, where it will be recognized that the greatest thing on earth is the human soul, not the human pocket, but the human soul. (Loud applause.)

Well, ladies and gentlemen, that is the great ideal for which you stand, that is the fundamental point of view of the Jewish religion, of the Old Testament, of all that we have imbibed from that great culture of the past; that is what you stand for and what we stand for. And I hope that in the years to come you will continue to show, as your prophets have told us, that the great things in life are the spiritual values, that the greatest thing is the human soul, that the great things are love and purity and strength and truth—the great ideals of the spiritual life. If you do that then I am sure the Jews will do to South Africa the greatest service that they could possibly render to our young country. (Cheers.)

13   From A. Clark   Vol. 21, no. 52

London
6 November 1919

My dearest Jannie, I have had a dear note from Cato[1] this morning, and Margaret let me see your letter telling of your tour in the north-west. That must have been a great work. It matters little what name we bear—whether we are a republic, or a kingdom, or a member of a commonwealth—it is our character that counts; our essential being which can and will transform the organism of the state into harmony with itself.

It has made me very happy to think of you preaching the truth to your people and showing them the way of life, which you have also shown them by your acts. That is a great creative work. If the hearts of the people are right no outward calamity need be feared. As I thought of this my mind turned to Drinkwater's great drama, *Abraham Lincoln*, and I compared your life and his as I have often done before. There is a place in the play when Mrs Lincoln tells how she had known the greatness of his character and had saved

---

[1] *See* vol. II, p. 186, note 3.

him from losing himself in matters of secondary importance and so he was ready for the great occasion. Then suddenly many things became clear in my mind and I suppose they will always remain so, though you will think them but foolishness; and though they are true, I expect it is foolishness to tell them to you.

I have a photograph of you taken fourteen years ago. Two strongly developed characters are mingled there, striving for mastery—the creative and the instrumental. Seldom are the two so evenly balanced in one nature. I am very fond of that photograph; it is so like you. Nevertheless the strife should have an end and out of the strong must come forth sweetness.[1] It is the very excellence of your instrument which sometimes clouds your faith in creative power, for you never meet your equal in intellectual force; but you understand too much ever to be content apart from the creative life.

Looking back on the past years a strange sense has come to me of the relations of things and I wonder whether it is true or whether it is mere fancy; but why should one fancy such a thing.

I remember that Sunday at Oxford when you were in a state of such indecision as to whether you should take command in Palestine or not. I remember so well the arguments for and against by different people. Finally you decided against. It was your creative soul that made the decision, realizing your mission was to make the peace, rather than to win the war. It was the right decision; but afterwards the instrumental side of your character asserted itself, and though the creative force asserted itself again and again, you became greatly involved in winning the war—and were not ready for making the peace. Out of my ignorance and foolishness I am inclined to think that from the point of view of winning the war, it would have been better if you had taken the Palestine command. Six months of the war might have been saved and peace have been made before the Germans were completely exhausted. Might have beens are always uncertain, and I think you eschew reviewing the past; perhaps that is the wisest course. But remember that creative power has its scope in the hearts of men and women, not in the machinery of government, and that you have power to move those hearts. Don't tie yourself up with offices so that you have not time for sympathetic meeting with the common people.

It is late and I have not time to write of events which are happening here. If I had I doubt your getting through this letter as far as this. I send you much love as always. Affectionately yours,

Alice Clark

[1] 'Out of the eater came forth meat, and out of the strong came forth sweetness.' *Judges* xiv. 14.

14   From J. X. Merriman   Vol. 22, no. 91

Schoongezicht
Stellenbosch
23 November 1919

Dear General, You may perhaps remember my writing to you about
Botha's portrait. I have since heard from Lady Phillips, who is
much interested in such matters, that Gyngell [A. E.] whose name
was mentioned is a quite unsuitable man. I send her opinion on to
you, *quantum valeat*.[1] She also told me that Sir W[illiam] Orpen
whose name you mentioned, is quite in the top rank, and that we
should be lucky if we secured a portrait by him at anything like
£500. A local portrait *done from photographs* would be rather
a fiasco. I think you will agree with me that a full length picture of
our friend would in no sense do him justice. The modern trouser
in no sense lends itself to portraiture (pity we do not wear togas) and
Botha's figure of late years had developed. It is a misfortune that
he was not painted just after the Boer War. He was indeed a fine
figure of a man at that date! It will be a real misfortune if we do not
succeed in getting a fine portrait for those who come after. But after
all he is in no worse case than Washington whose portraits are very
poor.

What of his life? Do take some pains to collect *first hand* information of his early days, when he was a frontier fighter before his name
was known. Do not in any case let him share President Kruger's
fate, to be thrown to the book makers; or Rhodes's for that matter.
I only hope that Basil Williams who has *him* in hand will do as well
by him as he did by Chatham.[2]

But I expect your mind is full of graver matters. Events do not
seem to be shaping well anywhere in the world. We are submerged
by the influence of the golden calf. You have your own special
trouble with the 'pronouncing' Generals—at Johannesburg.[3] It is
a pity that your hand was stayed when you began dealing with
those military traitors! How two cultivated men like Hertzog and

---

[1] For what it may be worth.

[2] B. Williams, *Cecil Rhodes* (1921). *Life of William Pitt, Earl of Chatham* (1913).

[3] On 20 November 1919 General Hertzog arrived in Johannesburg to hold political
meetings. He rode into the city at the head of about a thousand mounted supporters,
who had elected Councillor Pretorius as their 'General', and was accompanied by
General J. C. G. Kemp, General C. H. Muller, Dr D. F. Malan, F. W. Beyers and
other National party leaders. There were minor clashes between bystanders and
members of the 'commando' outside the town-hall where Hertzog received an
address and later made a speech, the main theme of which was the 'ideal of ultimate
and absolute independence' and separation from the British Empire. (*See* the *Star*,
20–21 November 1919.)

Creswell can make such asses of themselves is beyond my com-
prehension. I often think of poor Rhodes in his happier days when
he used to say that the salvation of South Africa lay in 'the old
Boer and the Native'. Certainly times have changed, when we have
to deal with the young Boer of the Nat type and 'the worker' of
the [W. H.] Andrews variety; they might have graduated in South
America. Read Shuckburgh's *Life* of Augustus;[1] it will cheer you
up. I suppose your philosophy does not get much time to deal with
radioactivity and relativity and those other deep fathomless subjects
that go to the very roots of existence. How petty all our troubles
seem in the scheme of the universe! However, as Candide observed,
Il faut cultiver notre jardin and your own special row seems a pretty
hard one to hoe just now! With kind regards and best wishes,
Yours very truly,

John X. Merriman

15   To A. Clark   Vol. 98, no. 104

Irene
Pretoria
26 November 1919

I enclose a letter for Hilda which I wish you to read and forward to
her, as I am not quite certain of her address. You will see I have
written to her in one of my black moods. Not even your cheery
optimism and buoyant faith can keep me from sometimes feeling
very depressed. Sometimes it is physical; more often it is psychical
—this deep feeling of weariness and melancholy at the way this
universe is run. But it is very good to read your letters and to feel
the pulse of life and faith in your dear letters. So do not give me
up but continue to labour at the good of my soul.

   I think my state of mind is also partly due to the great amount
of political work in the party sense I have to do now, and you know
how much against my grain that sort of work is. I don't think I ever
was meant for a politician. In the world of action I always feel
surer and happier and more myself. And again in the world of
thought and study I am also happier. I could track an idea or watch
a vague filmy mood with far more interest than a question of party
politics.

   Now, dear child, this will reach you about Christmas time. And

[1] E. S. Shuckburgh, *Augustus: The Life and Times of the Founder of the Roman
Empire* (1903).

it is a friendly shake of the hand from the South. How gladly I would walk up with you to the Hood monument. But please not through that mud to that little hill in the valley! I still remember with lively feeling that Sunday walk through the mud. Remember South Africans emerged from the mud age long ago, unlike the Europeans who still revel in it.

I am so glad that Mrs Clark is well again. She really improved during the two-and-a-half years I was in England, and if her daughters take decent Christian care of her, she will be quite well when next time I come round to an imperial conference. That may be towards the end of next year, if my political opponents don't throw me out at the general election next March. That seems more than likely. I have been thirteen years in the government most of whose sins are visited on my undeserving head. Besides these is the aftermath of discontent which has followed the war. And lastly there is the general impression of me that I am not really interested in South Africa, that this dear country is too small or too dull for me, and that I hanker after a more spacious theatre! This impression is quite wrong, but then wrong is just as potent a force in life as right. So I *may* come to you before you come to me; but it may also be otherwise.

Now, a Merry Christmas and a Happy New Year to you, dear Alice. Ever yours,

Jan

16 To M. C. Gillett   Vol. 22, no. 284

Pretoria
30 December 1919

Your dear letters continue to arrive punctually with every mail. How refreshing they are, and cooling to the soul over-heated in the stress and struggle of life. To me your and Arthur's letters are a never-ending source of pure delight. Your visits to Street and Penrith, your walks to Ewelme and other sacred places, the innocent babblings of the children—all give no end of pleasure to read of. I owe you a letter for several weeks, and indeed I have three times begun letters but never got far enough to make it worth while to send them. I am deeply sorry to hear that Arthur is again suffering from indigestion. It may still be overwork. I am most grieved, as I had hoped the operation would effect a complete cure. But really you must come out soon, if his health remains indifferent. Here he will get the perfect rest and comradeship and change of physical conditions which may just do the trick. And it would be such a joy to have you all here! Oh, the very thought of it brings new life into my blood. So whether it is February or August, come and be welcome. Only do not hurry back as there is so much to see and to enjoy. How I would love to motor you round to the farms or to ride over the veld or to ox-wagon with you through the bush! I always see you coming but am prepared to wait patiently until the great joy is fulfilled.

This is the end of the year. A bad, unhappy year—the year of the Great Failure. For make no mistake about it, Margaret, I have failed, at the most critical point in human history. 1919 will remain the year of the greatest and deepest disappointments of my life. Even that little League of Nations is being done to death in America. My appeal has passed unheeded. God has retired into the background, and the prospect before the world is dark indeed. Have we reached a point at which the conditions of human life will begin slowly to deteriorate and life will henceforth be on a lower level? People are so apathetic about all the evils which surround us that I conclude the great reaction is as much inner as outward; our very souls have deteriorated. Will 1920 see a change for the better? Anyhow I wish you and 102 a Happy New Year. Kiss the dear ones all for me. I am always thinking of them. Yes, life cannot be quite bad so long as it holds such ties and treasures for us. I am making inquiries about Belger's[1] business. My love also for the Murrays and the Henry Gilletts.[2] The mimosas are in bloom outside and sometimes I feel almost drunk with the scent of them. Sundown and the smell of mimosa flowers and Kaffir children singing their melancholy native tunes have an effect on me which I cannot express. Good-bye dear,

Jan

17   To M. Murray   Vol. 23, no. 192

Prime Minister's Office
Pretoria
[1] January 1920

My dear Lady Mary, May I send you a line to wish you the compliments of the season? It seems like a mockery to speak of peace or good will at this time. And yet beyond that terrible tragedy in human fate which we witness in our day we are and remain simple human beings, with cravings for sympathy and elementary human fellow-

---

[1] Belger was a German friend of the Gilletts.   [2] *See* vol. IV, p. 37, note 1.

ship. And I feel that from that base—and perhaps from it alone— it will be possible to reconstruct the world. When the great Roman world broke down it was in the homes and the lives of the poor and the simple that Christianity found the real centres and beginnings of the new life. And so it may be again. And the process may be in operation even now in the midst of all this outward turmoil and anarchy which dominate our views. The complex is breaking down and the simple and elementary are once more coming to the front as the abiding factors in life. And if we could see into the hearts of men and women we would perhaps be strangely reassured as to the future. So let us be cheerful and trustful of the deeper things which move within the outward visible life of the world. Dark as is the riddle of our day, I do not believe there is any occasion to wring hands or to sit down in despair. Not even the United States senate —bad as it is—makes me despair. The League has come and it will stay. Obstruction cannot kill the new life but only limit or postpone its functioning. I see a way out of the American reservations[1] which I have cabled to Lloyd George; but I sometimes fear the British official world are not in earnest over the League.

Please give my kindest regards to Professor Murray, to dear Agnes,[2] and to the Toynbees.[3] I often think of you all, of the ideas and sympathies we share in common, of the strange history which brought us together twenty years ago; of all the trials and heart-breaking disappointments we have gone through in common. But God is very great, as the Mohammedan says, and in that great Whole alone can our partial and sectional selves find rest and peace. The world is the Valley of Soul-Making, as Keats has said,[4] and I believe in this furnace of history through which our generation is passing, the human soul is being purged as never before. I regret we saw so little of each other in all those harassing days. But perhaps better luck next time. Ever yours affectionately,

J. C. Smuts

[1] After long debates the United States senate adopted fifteen reservations to the League covenant. President Wilson refused to accept any amendments and in November 1919 the senate rejected the entire treaty.

[2] *See* vol. III, **798**.

[3] *See* vol. IV, p. 47, note 2.

[4] 'Call the world if you please "The vale of Soul-making".' Keats, *Letters*, To Fanny Brawne, 8 July 1819.

18   To A. Clark   Vol. 98, no. 106

Pretoria
10 January 1920

This mail you did not write to me—I suppose as a punishment to me for not punctually answering your letters. But remember, dear, that I am very busy, and that your letters are always very welcome.

You must tell me more about the reviews and the sale of your book,[1] in which I feel a deep personal interest. Did I not keep your nose to the grindstone and constantly encourage you to go on and complete it, in spite of ill-health and depression?

I have decided to make an appeal to South Africa for a great relief fund for Central Europe, and this evening I have spent in writing the appeal.[2] My mind and heart are simply torn with pity over all that measureless human misery. I have certain ideas as to what we as a government could do to provide credits; but the public should join in this great human work. After all we cannot forget our own case in 1902. I hope the appeal will have great effect. I hope Lloyd George will also issue one.[3] It sometimes looks to me as if there is going to be a permanent set-back to European civilization, as if the conditions of human life are slowly but steadily, and perhaps permanently, deteriorating. It is an awful thought— that the great storm has not merely blown off the rotten and weak branches of the human tree, but affected the tree itself, and that in future it will for generations have only a stunted growth. I believe in God and I believe in Good. But, dear Alice, I am often very low and despondent over it all. Only a few years ago we still saw the vision of the New Earth. In Paris that vision vanished. And now arises that other vision of human decay—where God rings down the curtain and darkness settles down once more on human destiny.

Give my love to the dear Parents. Perhaps they will be interested in the above pessimism. The eye of my faith is very dim just now. Ever yours lovingly,

Jan

[1] *See* vol. III, p. 335, note 1.

[2] An appeal by the Archbishop of Canterbury for the collection of relief funds had reached the Union government.

[3] Smuts urged Lloyd George to start a great British Empire collection. *See* Smuts Collection, vol. 23, no. 191.

19   From A. Clark   Vol. 23, no. 28

Millfield
Street
Somerset
11 January 1920

My dearest Jannie, Your last letter has been often in my thoughts during the three weeks since it came. It was a sad letter, telling of your weariness and discouragement. Since then I have been reading Maynard Keynes's book,[1] and that would almost make one despair. But I was glad to find in it a note of hope; not based on any of the obvious factors of the situation, but on the incalculable power of Good.

Thou art fond of speculations on the meaning of Good. Thou keeps them as a refuge from the clamouring demands of the political existence. Like Marcus Aurelius thou retires to that little farm of thy own mind where a solitude so profound may be enjoyed. But that is no place from which to draw creative force.

Speculations about the meaning of Good don't recreate us; they are rather idle; for we all know more about Good than we care to admit. Every one of us knows just as much about the meaning of Good as we are willing to put in practice in our lives. What we want to understand is the power of Good. Philosophy will never help us to understand that. No intellectual subtlety can trace it out. The only means is simple honesty, making our life perfectly harmonious with our thought, bringing our instincts and our emotions into this same harmony.

It is only when that is arrived at that our work and activity go forward without fatigue.

There are people whose instincts and emotions are better than their conscious thoughts but I don't think you are one of those. Yours is a character that develops and progresses. Your thoughts are therefore in advance, or on a higher plane as it were, than your subconscious emotions. To you the conscious thought seems to be what you are. But to the others the actions of the subconscious self are what you are judged by, that is to say by your past. Though you are right in believing that your thought is your real self, they are right also because you have not unified your personality. The people like simplicity in character and they are right because goodness is simple.

But progress is not incompatible with simplicity—only, if simplicity is to be preserved where you have developing ideas, the truth

---

[1] *See* vol. IV, p. 222, note 2.

as it is understood must be carried into the innermost recesses of your nature, so that old errors have no lurking places left. Nothing in your nature is concealed from God or man. Your own self is the only person who can be deceived.

Don't you think for example that, if the people think you feel South Africa too small a field, you have had feelings which give rise to such a suspicion? Consciously you know South Africa is a great country, but consciously you know too that it is part of a whole; subconsciously you feel sometimes a sense that what occupies so much attention there is of little real consequence. However much people's minds are engrossed with trivialities the fault is not because they are South African instead of European. Triviality only becomes more trivial the more it is multiplied. The great issues are to be striven for in South Africa just as much as in Europe. Wherever there is a group of human families there are the vital issues. The measure of your success is the enlightenment of the minds of those about you and yourself; the purification of life; the intensification of activity. This goes on while you think, while you speak, while you act, and may perhaps go on more while you are out of office than while you are in it.

My love to you, dear Friend, and I pray that you may find the source of life. Yours as always,

Alice

20   To M. C. Gillett   Vol. 23, no. 206

Doornkloof
[Irene, Transvaal]
19 January 1920

This is Sunday afternoon, hot and quiet, and I sit in the capacious study writing letters of which there is a great bundle to dispose of. I have just been pitching into some Americans over the doings of the senate.[1] I should not have conceived it possible for a great people to take so petty a line over issues of vast importance. The League must be wrecked because Wilson is disapproved of. The Dominions must be deprived of their new international status of equality, because England misbehaves towards Ireland. And yet the Dominions are going to be a great benefactor in the world and a strong reinforcement to the cause of peaceful progress. And the League is the creative seed of reform but for which Europe will continue to writhe in her convulsions into the blackness of final

---

[1] See vol. V, p. 32, note 1.

anarchy. With all his faults, Wilson is still the best and truest friend of progress.

Yesterday some delightful snaps of family scenes arrived from 102. Helen[1] and I. Helen and Nico.[2] Thank you, dear. My heart is always in that little garden, even when I walk over the wide prospect of Doornkloof.[3]

I have written an appeal to our public for funds for Central Europe. But I doubt whether South Africa is really interested in that world. All these reports of wars and campaigns make people here think that world is hopelessly mad.

I am still campaigning. This week in the western Transvaal, next week in the Free State; the following two weeks in the Cape. And so this futile game of politics goes on.

My love to you and Arthur and all the dear little family. Ever yours,
Jan

21   To A. Clark   Vol. 98, no. 110

Pretoria
8 March 1920

Two days before the poll! So you can imagine that my correspondence does not get a fair chance. This is just a line and a friendly handshake in return for your last letter. I am fighting very hard against the Nationalist republican movement, which is in essence a racial anti-British movement. But during the war it attained to a surprising strength, and since the war the dissatisfaction over the peace treaty has tended to help it; and not even my attitude at Paris has been able to turn the tide. I hope to be able to hold my own, but forbear to say more as, weeks before this reaches you, the papers will have acquainted you with the actual results. May Hobbs has written to say that she declines to wish me luck as she feels certain my heart is no longer in this sort of politics! This is rather rough on me. As a fact I have been engaged all my life in enterprises which I did not care for in a fundamental sense. We are not consulted in these matters. I am afraid in any case there is before me the ugly prospect of going or forming a coalition government with the Unionist party[4] (the old Jingo party now much sobered down). So you can realize my difficulties. Good-bye, dear. Ever yours,
Jan

[1] *See* vol. III, p. 471, note 1.
[2] Arthur Nicholas, youngest son of A. B. and M. C. Gillett.
[3] *See* vol. II, p. 537, note 2.   [4] *See* vol. II, p. 638, note 1.

22   **To A. Clark**   Vol. 98, no. 111

Cape Town
18 March 1920

First the good news and then the bad. Arthur and Margaret will
arrive about the middle of next week and it will be a great joy having
them here. Jan and Tona[1] will amuse themselves with a thousand
novelties at Groote Schuur;[2] Arthur will rest and Margaret will go
about the country visiting her numerous friends while I struggle
with a hopeless parliament. So much for the good news. Now for
the bad.

The elections have gone against me and I have no parliamentary
majority. Parties are as follows:

South African party (mine) 43;   Nationalists 43;
Unionists (British) 25;   Labour 21.[3]

I do not yet know what I shall do beyond meeting parliament and
making necessary financial provision. Some of my colleagues are
for resigning as our position is untenable in a parliamentary sense.
I am for holding on till parliament dismisses me; and it is possible
that it may hesitate to do so. But the position will be unbearably
uncomfortable and I fear some of my colleagues may leave me in
disgust. So you see, while you talk nicely and comfortably of Life
and Truth, my troubles are rapidly thickening on life's path; and
truth is in sad obscurity. And to add to my misfortunes Isie became
very ill the day I left Pretoria; she broke down from sheer overwork
at my election. My immense victory at Pretoria[4] was due to her
brilliant and hard work; but it proved beyond her powers, already
much enfeebled from heavy war work. Poor, dear thing. She is
a great woman, and not least great in her absolute devotion to me—
an ascetic of a radical type, who finds consolation only in her family
and her work. I hope she will be well enough to come to me in
a month's time.

I read the criticisms of the Book[5] you sent me with great interest;
the merits of the book are beyond their feeble praise or commenda-
tions. But so it ever is. It is only when the whole work is complete
that people will acclaim you as the Historian of Women. I am really
glad to hear your health is good and your appetite for work as usual.

---

[1] *See* vol. III, p. 27, note 1; p. 101, note 1.

[2] *See* vol. III, p. 65, note 2.

[3] The actual results were: South African party 41, National party 44, Unionist
party 25, Labour party 21, Independents 3.

[4] At Pretoria West Smuts's majority was 1247; his National party and Labour
party opponents polled 473 and 303 votes respectively.

[5] See vol. III, p. 335, note 1.

For months now I read, almost every night before I go to bed or sleep, a few pages in one or other of your African books.[1] What a consolation they are. Somebody said: 'The more I see of men the more I love dogs.'[2] I say 'The more I see of the present the more I delight in that barbarous virgin past of Africa.' Ever yours,

Jan

23   To C. P. Crewe   Vol. 102, no. 201

Prime Minister's Office
Cape Town
25 March 1920

My dear Crewe, Many thanks for your note. I agree with you that the Unionists ought now to disappear but the big wigs of that party do not agree; so we shall mark time for the present. My difficulties are very great. I have been talking to some of the party leaders but they do not appear very anxious to help me in the present difficulties. I am afraid to throw up the sponge because it means either another election (which would be very bad) or a short period of Nat rule with infinite resulting mischief. Meantime I am temporarily holding on in order to get more light on the situation. The trouble is increased by my having to introduce legislation (profiteering etc.) of a most difficult and contentious character.

Well, my friend, life is hard, and we must take it as it is. We have passed through graver troubles in our day than we are ever likely to meet again—let that be our consolation in present difficulties.

I hope to see you when you come to Cape Town and in the meantime I send you and Lady Crewe[3] my sincere regards. Ever yours,

J. C. Smuts

24   To A. Clark   Vol. 98, no. 112

Cape Town
9 April 1920

I had a very beautiful letter from you a couple of days ago—so full of your great, cheerful, invigorating spirit—the healing spirit of the Whole. I infer you are well and active and congenially

---

[1] Alice Clark had given Smuts a number of books on African exploration.
[2] 'The more I see of men, the more I admire dogs.' Madame Roland.
[3] Born Helen Orpen; married Sir Charles Crewe in 1887.

occupied. I need your encouragement now for I have a very difficult job, running this dear country with forty members of parliament out of a total 134! It is difficult enough nowadays to govern with a great parliamentary majority, as Lloyd George has found to his cost. But to govern with a small minority in such times is quite a new sort of undertaking. But I am making the effort. If I fail I fear there will be a great set-back politically, as the bulk of my own Dutch people are republicans and wish to secede from the British Empire while, of course, the English out here are more loyal than the English in England! If I fail, racialism would become very dangerous and anything might happen. And now, on top of all my troubles, comes a silly speech by Bonar Law in the commons that a Dominion may secede, and the British government will not use force to maintain the British connection.[1] This is fuel to the republican fire. Bonar Law and his friends used a great deal of force to get us *into* the British Empire, and I doubt whether a Nationalist secession will be such a peaceful affair as he suggests. It is curious how this nationalist wave in the world is reaching its climax just as we are entering on the great international order of the world. Perhaps this is the last great flickering up of a flame which will soon be quenched.

The Gilletts are very happy here, especially the little ones. Arthur is making grand progress, Margaret remains ever the same dear pal. I was sorry to hear that Hilda is unwell. Of course that Vienna work is quite beyond her physical powers. She needs Holism and rest. My health is very good, but my head has a feeling of tiredness sometimes. Ever yours lovingly,

Jan

25 To R. Bridges   Vol. 23, no. 199

Prime Minister's Office
Cape Town
21 May 1920

Dear Mr Bridges, Many causes have prevented me so far from replying to your letter and thanking you for the copy of your last volume of poetry.[2] I cannot tell you how much I value the honour

---

[1] Speaking in a debate on the Government of Ireland Bill on 30 March 1920, Bonar Law said *inter alia*: 'If the self-governing Dominions...chose tomorrow to say "we will no longer make a part of the British Empire", we should not try to force them. Dominion Home Rule means the right to decide their own destinies.' *House of Commons Debates*, vol. 127, col. 1125.

[2] *October and Other Poems*, London, 1920.

you have done me. The volume with its dedication[1] and inscription will remain as a precious possession in my family. I only regret that I saw so little of you in those strenuous years when I was in London—years which will ever remain among the most eventful in human history. But, as you know, I was very often away at the front or in the allied countries on some mission or other; and when in London I was generally overwhelmed with my immediate duties. Still, I count it a privilege to have met and known you. And I pray for blessings on you in your old age and that you may be spared to see some good arise out of the ruins in which poor mankind is struggling today. Perhaps I shall have the privilege next year to see you and Mrs Bridges[2] again in London. Then we could talk over things which it is difficult now to write about. Unless this war leads to some spiritual regeneration (in the widest sense) in the Old World, the fate of our white race is dark indeed. With best wishes, Ever yours most sincerely,

J. C. Smuts

26   To M. C. Gillett   Vol. 23, no. 214

Groote Schuur
[Cape Town]
26 July 1920

This is Monday morning before breakfast. Saturday and Sunday I went to spend with my youngest brother[3] on the farm Klipfontein[4] where I grew up, and on my return last night I found a letter from you written on the train to Irene; also a note from Arthur written at the same time. Thank you both very much. I was glad that you enjoyed yourself so much this second visit also at Onze Rust.[5] I trust you will find Doornkloof no less interesting. You certainly have there the additional variety of the children who to me, at any rate, are a great source of amusement. And Arthur can study his beloved birds there, though I am not quite certain that winter is a good time for birds in that valley. I enjoyed myself very much yesterday. I took a walk by myself over the farm humming my monotonous tune to myself to the accompaniment of a gentle rain most of the time, and I felt uplifted once more. Those hills of my

[1] The dedication is as follows: To General the Right Honourable Jan Christiaan Smuts, Prime Minister of the Union of South Africa, soldier, statesman and seer, with the author's homage.

[2] Born Monica Waterhouse; married Robert Bridges in 1884.

[3] Boudewyn de V. Smuts.   [4] *See* vol. I, p. 4, note I.

[5] President Steyn's farm near Bloemfontein.

beginnings always have a great effect on me. 'The land of sacrament' you once called the hills at Street. My native country too is very close to me and fills me with indescribable feelings. The places where I looked after sheep or cattle, or picked up tortoises, or dug out edible roots in the Bushman fashion, the hills where dim, unformed aspirations began to surge up, where I used to sit for half a day under a 'skerm'[1] in the rain while a roaring fire burnt in front—how close they are to me even at this great age of fifty! And the hopes and the dreams of that birth time!

> *Wie gross war diese Welt gestaltet,*
> *so lang' die Knospe sie noch barg,*
> *Wie wenig, ach, hat sich entfaltet:*
> *dies' Wenige wie klein und karg!*[2]

I came thus far when your second letter was brought in—written at Doornkloof and descriptive of that beloved family circle. I am really glad you like them all and the farm also. And yet I see very little of them or it. You can count the months I have been there the last sixteen years. Life certainly is hard on me. Sometimes I doubt whether it is really worth while, this prolonged effort of (so-called) human service which cuts you off all the dear things in life and turns you into a mechanism in the world's great machine, and a mechanism so absolutely insignificant that you sometimes can't help laughing at yourself! Levi (biographer)[3] writes to me that people in England and Holland ask him 'Who is really dead, Botha or Hertzog? And what is now exactly the position occupied by Smuts?' I am surprised that it is not asked whether I too am dead! Such is fame.

I love my willows dearly, but they change the river course.[4] Some big ones will remain I hope. There is a great variety of all sorts of forest trees belonging to the African bush. But Arthur is more interested in the birds.

Our work goes forward very slowly, heart-breakingly slowly. I still say to myself that 7 August will see the end, but all my colleagues think differently and say I shall have to stay here for Buxton's farewell, as there will be no time to go north! The [N. J.] de Wets are here, Ella trying hard to entertain me. But you know

[1] A shelter made of branches (Afrikaans).
[2] How vast this world was formed while the bud still hid itself;
How little, alas, has unfolded itself; how small and meagre this little.
                                        Schiller, *Die Ideale*.
[3] *See* vol. III, p. 367, note 1.
[4] Margaret Gillett had written asking that the Doornkloof willows should not be cut down.

I am not a great listener. And my mind is far away. Give my love to Arthur and the domestic circle. My heart leaps even to think of them. Ever yours,

Jan

27   To A. W. Gillett   Vol. 23, no. 216

2 August 1920

Dear Tona,[1] You have been away long enough and you must now come back, and tell Joan[2] you are sick of the Free State and the Transvaal, and the Cape is the only place for you, and Table mountain is the only mountain for you, and Groote Schuur is the only house for you. Why live in a tin house in these cold nights? Here it is warm, sunny, lovely, heavenly. Come soon.

Oom Jannie

28   To A. Clark   Vol. 98, no. 117

Cape Town
12 August 1920

We are now in the last days of the session and early next week the shutters will be up in the National Talking Shop. On the whole I have succeeded in putting through a great deal of excellent work.[3] It is really curious to see what one can do with a parliamentary minority. We have done more and better work than the strongest government relying on a powerful majority has attempted. But my position remains precarious and insecure, and some reform of the government will be necessary before parliament meets next January. The difficulties of this change are very great and may mean my downfall. To tell the truth I shall not break my heart if I am out of the government, after having been in it continuously for nearly fourteen years. My health and spirits are quite good, but I daresay one really gets tired of the work. And I am interested in other things besides politics as you know. Arthur and Margaret will be back from the Transvaal next week, and we shall be together for the week before they sail and I go on to South West Africa. I have not seen

[1] Second son, then aged eight, of A. B. and M. C. Gillett.
[2] Joan H. Boardman, born Rowntree 23 April 1895, daughter of the headmaster of the Society of Friends' Boys' School at York and a cousin of Arthur Gillett. She went to South Africa with the Gilletts in 1920 and later settled there.
[3] Some thirty Acts were passed during this session, including the Native Affairs Act (No. 23 of 1920) and the Currency and Banking Act (No. 31 of 1920).

so much of them here, they have been away so much and I have been so preoccupied with my parliamentary work. I am sure they have enjoyed themselves in the Transvaal and Free State. Isie has enjoyed their company very much indeed at Doornkloof. And they have been to the Bushveld[1]—that mysterious fascinating part of Africa.

The latest news in the papers show that the storm in Poland[2] may blow over. The Poles are hopeless—just like the Irish, and I fear this is only the foretaste of what is coming. The Poles will keep the pot on the boil for this generation and more. And in the end their misgovernment may again mean partition.[3]

Thanks for your last dear letter. I am not so downhearted. But this is a trying world. Ever yours,

Jan

29   To J. M. Keynes   Vol. 98, no. 297

Groote Schuur
[Cape Town]
27 September 1920

My dear Keynes, You may perhaps know that we have just passed that measure for the establishment of a Central Reserve Bank[4] in connection with which I asked for your advice. Strakosch [H.] was most helpful to me and the bill was framed largely on the lines of his advice. Now we are very anxious to secure the right man for governor of the bank. Both Strakosch and Gillett know the type of man we want as well as all other details. Will you attend a conference with them and F. C. Goodenough of Barclay's Bank in order to consult with them about the selection of the man? Our high commissioner will call the meeting and I shall be deeply obliged if you could manage to attend and give us the benefit of your advice on this matter also. Gillett and his wife have been staying with me in South Africa for some time, and he now returns with the ship which carries this letter.

[1] Sub-tropical region in the eastern Transvaal.

[2] The peace conference of 1919 had created the new state of Poland but not defined the boundaries. In July 1920, Teschen had been divided between Czechoslovakia and Poland but neither state was satisfied. At the same time Poland was at war with Soviet Russia over Lithuania and the Ukraine. By early August Russian troops were threatening Warsaw and the Poles, with French help, were preparing a counteroffensive.

[3] In the course of the eighteenth century Poland had been partitioned between Prussia, Austria and Russia.

[4] The Central Reserve Bank was established under Act 31 of 1920.

I do not refer to other general matters as we are badly informed in South Africa and the general world situation is to me most obscure and perplexing. More and more it is passing beyond the control of the statesmen, and these too are falling out among each other. In South Africa we are getting along all right. The country is very prosperous and on the whole conditions are quite sound.

I have seen your work on Probability[1] mentioned in the press, but I suppose it has not yet appeared, as I have not noticed any review. I hope you are getting on very well. With best wishes,

Yours very sincerely,

J. C. Smuts

30 To T. W. Smartt   Vol. 23, no. 200

30 September 1920

My dear Smartt, I was very sorry not to be able to visit your Irrigation Works,[2] but my presence at Pretoria was urgently demanded and I had to hurry through. Once more many thanks for your kind invitation to Burton and me.

Hereniging has miscarried,[3] as I expected. As regards the future I have issued a statement advocating a transformation of the South African party and starting a new party on a wider basis. I believe (unless I misread the signs) that the psychological moment has come for a great move forward, and for definitely breaking with the racial politics and parties of the past. If the South African party congress authorizes me to proceed, I intend to issue an appeal immediately after in favour of the new party. I hope sincerely you will be in a position on behalf of the Unionist party to accept my appeal and join hands with us definitely and unreservedly. The details in regard to the new party could then be worked out later, and probably a great conference will have to be called at a suitable time. But your acceptance of my appeal will be urgent because of the necessity to fill up various important vacancies without further delay. I am most anxious that the Unionist party should join unconditionally and not make the mistake of bargaining about portfolios etc. My task is already frightfully difficult; as it is, I shall scarcely have a parliamentary majority; and the hostility of the

[1] *Treatise on Probability*, published in 1921.

[2] Smartt had established a large farming syndicate near Britstown, Cape Colony, and built a great dam at Houwater.

[3] The last *hereniging* congress met at Bloemfontein in September 1920 with Professor P. J. G. de Vos (*see* **8**) as chairman. All the provinces and parties were represented. It failed, as before, to agree on the republic issue. (*See* p. 14, note 1 *supra*.)

Labour party will after this junction become undisguised. Personally I doubt whether I shall be able to get through next session without having to fight another general election. For these and other reasons I am very anxious that you should avoid trying to impose conditions on me; which might have the effect of making an already very difficult task impossible. At the same time I wish to tell you fully and frankly what I intend to do. Colonel [D.] Reitz I shall have to take into the cabinet in order to give representation to the Free State; that leaves two other vacancies in the cabinet. There will be a third vacancy if (as is likely) Kowie Graaff[1] goes out at this stage. These two (or three) vacancies I intend to fill up with Unionists. I am anxious to get Jagger and Macintosh [W.] into the cabinet where the business side is at present very weak. A third vacancy I wish to fill up with Duncan as soon as we can provide him with a seat in parliament. In regard to yourself I am still very keen that you should go to London as our high commissioner and principal representative (in the absence of the prime minister) on the League of Nations. If for the full period of five years so much the better; if you will not go for so long then for a shorter period. In any case you will pay us an annual visit here to keep in touch with the Union. Sending a man of your calibre to the highest post at the disposal of the Union will give general satisfaction and remove many anxieties at present felt. And it is of the utmost importance that at this juncture we shall be worthily represented in London and Geneva, and by appointing you we are putting our best foot forward, if I may say so. It is the post I would covet if I were not prime minister. Incidentally I admit quite frankly that your going to London rather than into the cabinet will ease some of my difficulties here. I therefore hope you will agree, even though it will be a great sacrifice for you to go to London. But I feel the situation in South Africa is today such that I am entitled to appeal to you to make sacrifices if necessary for the attainment of our great object. I am not very sanguine about immediate success, but I know we are moving on right lines and in the end (perhaps after a temporary reverse) the people will rally to the banner which we shall hold aloft.

Please keep the names I have mentioned with all possible secrecy in any talks with your friends, and let me know as soon as possible whether you generally agree with my ideas. Ever yours sincerely,

[J. C. Smuts]

[1] Sir Jacobus Graaff.

31   From T. W. Smartt   Vol. 23, no. 187

Glenban
Stellenbosch
10 October 1920

My dear Smuts, I may say at once that I very much appreciate your letter of 30 September in which you so freely and frankly refer to the situation which has arisen owing to the failure of *hereniging*, and the subsequent issue of your manifesto.

My delay in replying was due to the fact, which I mentioned in my note to you from Naauwpoort, that I only received your letter, which was re-directed to me from Stellenbosch, as I was on my way to Bloemfontein, and I therefore was desirous of having the opportunity of meeting the members of the Unionist executive, which met at Bloemfontein on 8 October—and at which there was a full attendance from the four provinces—before replying fully.

After a very full discussion the executive agreed to recommend to the party congress to be held at Bloemfontein immediately after the South African party meeting,—of course assuming that that gathering adopts your proposals—that we should accept your invitation to join in the formation of a new party. I believe our congress will adopt the recommendation, though I must point out that there may be considerable difficulty in preventing what may be termed the advanced democratic wing from breaking away, and although we may have some defection, I hope and believe that when the real and supreme issue is fairly put to them, we may be able to prevent such assuming serious proportions.

In regard to the latter portion of your letter, let me say that in the extremely grave crisis that the country is faced with, you may rest assured that I and others associated with me appreciate the difficulties that you are faced with, and that no spirit of bargaining will find any place in our relationships with you as the leader of the new party, either in connection with representation on the cabinet, or in any other respect. I personally think, without going into the details of personnel, which is a matter that at a later stage we should personally discuss, your proposals, under the circumstances, are fair and reasonable. With regard to your renewed offer of the high commissionership I very much appreciate the terms in which you have made it, and entirely agree with your view in regard to the importance and responsibilities of the post. Under the circumstances I thought it best to *confidentially* consult with the executive on this matter, and find that it is thought that my acceptance of the position is likely to be so strongly and widely opposed, that my doing so might seriously jeopardize the whole-hearted co-operation of our supporters, which is so essential to the success of a fresh start. Apart therefore from health and other considerations, I think I will find myself compelled to abandon the consideration of the proposal, anxious as I am to render you every assistance in my power.

There is another point which I think should receive your earnest consideration, and that is the tactical importance of a general election at the earliest possible moment. It would be taking a great risk to meet parliament as at present constituted, the majority being so small that the possible defection of one or two members might bring about a defeat. The best prospects of your obtaining a working majority would be by going to the country on the formation of the new party and government, as soon as the necessary machinery could be got into working order, and thus take advantage of the wave of enthusiasm which the fresh start, with a new constitutional party, is likely to engender throughout the Union. With kind regards, Yours very sincerely,

T. W. Smartt

32   From J. M. Keynes

Vol. 23, no. 153

King's College
Cambridge
22 October 1920

Dear General Smuts, I have been very glad to serve on the committee to recommend a governor for your new state bank. It is a very difficult post to fill, and well-qualified candidates are scarce; but we met yesterday, and there are good prospects, I think, of a strong appointment.[1]

I see from your letter that the Old World is beginning to seem a very long way away from you; all the happier for you. Things move slowly and sensational anticipations are not fulfilled. But below the surface the European situation (except, perhaps, in France and Belgium) steadily deteriorates. From the *budgetary* standpoint Germany, Austria and Poland (and probably Italy) are now bankrupt: it is *impossible* that their budgets should be made to balance. So far as opinion goes, France is, if anything, more opposed to revision[2] than six months ago. The less the French believe in

[1] The first governor of the Reserve Bank was William Henry Clegg who had been chief accountant of the Bank of England.

[2] The Supreme Allied Council had met at San Remo in April 1920 and decided to invite the German government to a conference in order to fix the total reparation liability. But when that conference took place in July the German proposals were not accepted.

the possibility of getting more money out of Germany, the more disposed they become to use the reparation commission[1] as an instrument for the purposes of the political, military and commercial hegemony of Europe, which is becoming every day the more and more conscious objective of many Frenchmen. Meanwhile Germany, from lack of nourishment I suppose, continues half-witted, and most of what emanates from them is impracticable and crazy.

Writings about the treaty now multiply amidst recriminations and partial disclosures from secret documents. The British Institute of Foreign Affairs (a new body under very strong auspices)[2] has produced a voluminous history[3] of the conference, which you have probably not seen. I enclose a copy of a letter which I wrote to the editor some weeks ago on a point touching you. This, however, has since been put in the shade by Baruch [B. M.] having printed in full (see the review of his book in *The Times* of October 21) your memorandum about war pensions.[4] I have not yet got Baruch's book, but I will send you a copy as soon as it is obtainable. It looks as though they were going to saddle *you* with responsibility for the Big indemnity, which is absurdly unfair, to anyone who knows the facts—though I am not sure it won't serve you right for writing that memorandum! Ever sincerely yours,

J. M. Keynes

ENCLOSURE

J. M. Keynes to H. W. V. Temperley
Private

Charleston
Firle
Sussex
29 September 1920

My dear Temperley, I have been reading with great interest the first two volumes of your *History of the Peace Conference*. Like all

---

[1] The reparation commission had been set up under articles 233 and 234 of the treaty of Versailles to determine the amount of damage for which compensation was to be made by Germany. It was to report by 1 May 1921 and thereafter to consider conditions and possibilities of payment. It was constituted with five members to ensure a majority vote. After the withdrawal of the United States the chairman, the French representative, could exercise a casting vote. The commission was abolished in 1930.

[2] Founded in 1920 'to encourage and facilitate the scientific study of international questions', this body became known later as the Royal Institute of International Affairs.

[3] *A History of the Peace Conference of Paris*, 6 vols. (1920), edited by H. W. V. Temperley.   [4] *See* vol. IV, **926.**

composite works, it strikes me as very unequal, some parts being a great deal better than others. But I cannot help regretting, what was perhaps the impossible, namely that much more space has not been given to the history of the conference proper. Most of the first volume deals with matters prior to the conference, while most of the second volume consists of an analysis of the treaty provisions. This was well worth doing. But the result is that the actual amount of space devoted to the history of the conference itself is extremely small; and this part, so far as I can check it, is very incomplete.

My reason for writing this letter, however, is concerned with an inaccuracy, which is perhaps important. In dealing with the arguments in favour of the inclusion of pensions and allowances under the reparation claim, it is stated on page 45 of the second volume that 'an argument in its favour was brought forward by General Smuts'. This is in a sense accurate, though I think rather misleading. But on page 14 this is amplified into the statement that 'the provision making Germany responsible for pensions and allowances was proposed by General Smuts'. This latter statement is very far indeed from being the fact. General Smuts's connection with the reparation chapter was of the slightest. He was never a member of any of the commissions or committees which dealt with it, and was not brought into the question at all until a very late stage, after we had been wrangling about pensions and separation allowances for many weeks. Week after week went by and President Wilson refused to succumb to any of the arguments that were addressed to him as to the inclusion of these charges being consistent with the Fourteen Points.[1] Finally General Smuts, as having been an outsider to the whole discussion up to date, was invited by the prime minister[2] to give his opinion. He gave this in a secret document which was seen by very few eyes, but which had importance because it was generally believed to have had some influence on the President. While, therefore, it is quite false to say that he *proposed* the inclusion of these charges, it is the case that an argument in favour was brought forward by him.

A great deal turns, however, on the nature of the argument. So many arguments were being concocted at that time that I myself do not clearly remember what the argument was. In any case, it is not fair, I think, that General Smuts should be saddled with the responsibility for the inclusion of pensions and allowances, when practically no one except the prime minister and the president really knows what he did say or what part he played in the matter.

[1] *See* vol. IV, p. 85, note 1.
[2] D. Lloyd George.

The document in which he expressed his opinion was an exceptionally secret one, and if it is to be alluded to in public there is a great deal of matter, certainly not more secret, which, if it were divulged, would be much more damaging to other parties.

I appreciate that the origin of the whole matter was the reference in [J. F.] Dulles's letter to *The Times*.[1] But your page 14 goes a good deal further than Dulles, and I am rather sorry that almost the only exception to the perfect discretion of the book should have had reference in this way to General Smuts. He was one of the strongest opponents of the reparation proposals in Paris; and whatever exactly took place, it is a substantial injustice to saddle *him* with a primary responsibility for them in their final form. Sincerely yours,

s. J. M. Keynes

33   To M. C. Gillett   Vol. 23, no. 221

Pretoria
25 October 1920

...I write you a line before leaving for Bloemfontein to attend our party congress where my appeal for an expansion of our party will be considered. My people are full of fears if the Unionists join us in a body as I think they will do. But I do not see any other exit out of the present political troubles. I cannot go on with forty members in a house of 134. If I fail now it means that I am going to be scrapped politically. If I succeed, South African politics will have made a great step forward on the path of racial unity and nationhood. My friends are all somewhat scared by my pressure forward. But I feel necessity is laid on me, as a great man once said.[2]

Isie has had another pitiable attack of malaria; in one day her temperature went up to 105 and then in a few hours down to 97. This, of course, is very bad. She is, however, up again and quite cheerful, dear thing. She has a great spirit.

From Lloyd George I have had a telegram fixing a meeting of prime ministers for next June. I have said that I could attend at the end of June, if I am still there. This, of course, is highly doubtful. You and Arthur had better keep this news to yourselves until

---

[1] J. Foster Dulles, in a letter published in *The Times* on 16 February 1920, wrote that opinion was divided at the peace conference as to the inclusion of pensions and separation allowances in the reparation calculations and that 'an argument in its favour was brought forward by General Smuts...who did not hesitate to express his disapproval of certain other features of the treaty'.

[2] '...for necessity is laid upon me; yea, woe is unto me, if I preach not the gospel.' 1 *Corinthians* ix. 16.

you see it in the papers. The constitutional conference will meet in
1922.[1]

Your affairs in the Old World are in an awful mess. Ireland in
a state of chaos;[2] England in a great coal strike;[3] the Poles in Vilna;[4]
Europe starving; millions in China dying from starvation, etc. etc.
When will the day dawn again over this scene of darkness? I suppose
some vast financial crisis is looming over the world which will pull
the prosperous countries down with Central Europe and make us
realize that mankind is one. It is far worse than the downfall of
the Roman world.

Good-bye, dear Friend. Kiss all the children and beat Arthur
for me! Ever yours,

Jan

34   To M. C. Gillett   Vol. 23, no. 222

Pretoria
1 November 1920

I enclose list of marked books[5] for purchase. It is really very good
of you to do all this hard work.[6] But I know you love to do it and
keep my mind in touch with the world which lies beyond politics.
One of these days I shall be out of politics and hope to retain the
faculty of rising into the world of thought. I have seen pretty well
enough action. Wallas [G.] I have. Alexander [S.] discussed his

[1] In 1917 the imperial war cabinet decided that a special conference should be held
after the war to consider the constitutional relations of Great Britain and the
Dominions. This had become necessary because of the enhanced status of the
Dominions and the emerging concept of a Commonwealth of equal states.

[2] At this time a guerilla war was being fought between the Irish Republican Army
and British government forces consisting of self-disciplined auxiliaries (the Black and
Tans and the Auxies). The war, brutally conducted on both sides, had begun early in
1919. In defiance of British rule an independent Irish parliament, the dail, had been
set up with De Valera as president.

[3] The coal-miners in England were at this time still under government control.
The price of coal was high for the German mines had not yet recovered. The miners
struck in October 1920 for a wage increase and got it.

[4] The Poles had launched a counter-offensive against the Russian army and forced
it into headlong retreat from the outskirts of Warsaw. The Poles took Vilna, ancient
capital of Lithuania, and the Bolshevik government agreed to the treaty of Riga
(1920) which gave Poland an eastern boundary far beyond the 'Curzon line' laid down
by the Allied powers, and some six million Russian subjects.

[5] S. Alexander, *Space Time and Deity* (1920); James Ward, *Psychological Principles*
(1918); A. N. Whitehead, *An Enquiry concerning the Principles of Natural Knowledge*
(1919) and *The Concept of Nature* (1920).

[6] After the death of H. J. Wolstenholme, Margaret Gillett became Smuts's book
buyer in England.

theories with me in London. He proves Time and Space = Deity! Ward [J.] will be most welcome. Whitehead [A. N.] is the mathematics man who collaborates with Bertrand Russell.[1]

I have a very heavy week behind me, having held a most successful congress at Bloemfontein. My party unanimously endorsed my appeal for a new party with the name of the South African party. I send you a copy of my speech, from which you will see that my attitude is not purely for 'law and order', but a constructive one aiming at the laying of the national foundations of the new South Africa. This week the Unionists are holding their return congress and I expect that they will virtually decide to join us in the new South African party. It will come as a great shock to many good Saps[2] when they find themselves under the same umbrella with the former Unionists, the party whose past has meant so much mischief for South Africa. But things have changed, the Unionists are much changed, and the talk of co-operation has at last to be translated into action. But I fear many of our old stalwarts will not be able to swallow the pill. I shall also have to take Duncan, Macintosh and Jagger into the cabinet and send Smartt to London as high commissioner. If there were a good man in South Africa I would like to come to London myself and devote my time mainly to the League. But now I cannot leave here, and I fear I am not destined to be resident again in London. I am pleased to see the Liberal papers applaud my appointment of Robert Cecil to the meeting of the League. The League is in a very bad way. The governments of the great powers leave it unsupported and it seems unable to do anything. I hope Cecil might awake some interest by his speeches. I have instructed our delegate to press for the admission of Germany and other ex-enemy powers. I fear the great governments do not see how sick Europe is. To me the writhings and contortions seem more and more the signs of decay than of new life. And it may be that we shall have to get down to a much lower level in order to rise again in the future of the world. I am glad that the coal strike was settled. It might have had the most dangerous developments.

Olive Schreiner is here, poor thing, and thoroughly unhappy because she finds nobody in sympathy with her at the Cape where she now is in a boarding-house. I feel deeply sorry for her. She is really quite out of things and simply keeps teasing her own nerves and eating her own heart.

[1] Russell and Whitehead had collaborated in writing *Principia Mathematica*, 3 vols. (1910–13).

[2] *See* vol. III, p. 542, note 1.

It is so delightful to read all your home news. You know how
I love to hear about the children and all the familiar things. And the
Downs! To me they stand out as among the great things in life.
And some day we three shall revisit those holy places and feel
reconciled again to this good God's world. I hope Arthur is not
again overworking. Please, Arthur, do be careful and go slow.
Enough money has been made. And we have lots of tramping still
to do. Give my love to all the dear children. I often think of you all.
Ever yours,

Jan

35 To J. H. Hofmeyr   Vol. 23, no. 201

The first recorded meeting of Smuts and J. H. Hofmeyr took place when
Hofmeyr and his mother were invited to Doornkloof in October 1920.
Hofmeyr was then twenty-six and had been for a year principal of University
College, Johannesburg. See A. Paton, Hofmeyr, pp. 89–91.

Confidentieel

Pretoria

5 November 1920

Vriend Hofmeyr, Hartelijk dank voor dat artikel dat ek met grote
belangstelling gelezen heb. Ik stem samen dat een bloot negatieve
houding niemand helpt. Vrijheid als objectief—maar bereikbaar
op het pad, niet van isolement en misschien geweld, maar van
ontwikkeling—als een gelijk en vrij lid der Britsche en Wereld
Liga; Zuid-Afrika als een deel der menschheid, het hare doende tot
bevordering der grote menschelijke idealen. Het idee van souvereine
onafhankelijkheid is formeel, juridisch en, voor de groote menschelijke toekomst van samewerking en organisatie onder de volkeren,
onvruchtbaar.

Tot sover is alles goed afgelopen, maar het einde is nog niet.
Doch een groot slag is geslagen en een historische stap vooruit-
genemen. De ontbinding van de party van Rhodes en Jameson is
een van de grootste overwinningen nog behaald op de weg van het
Zuid-Afrikanderisme of laat my liever zeggen van de Zuid-Afrikaansche geest. Ik hoop maar dat onze Hollandsche bevolking de
werkelijke betekenis ervan sal inzien en zicht niet zoo zeer bekom-
meren over de pure traditioneele beskouing van de rassen ver-
houding in Zuid-Afrika. De drie Congressen—Hereeniging,
Z. A. P., en Unionist—vormen een grootsche trilogie in onze geschiedenis, waarvan ik vertrouw dat groote gevolgen voor een edeler

Zuid-Afrika zullen volgen. Maar dat *dénouement* is nog ver af, en zware jaren en tijden zijn nog voor ons.

Met hartelijke groeten, ook aan 'Poor Relations' *t.t.*

J. C. Smuts

TRANSLATION

Confidential

Pretoria
5 November 1920

Friend Hofmeyr, Many thanks for that article[1] which I have read with great interest. I agree that a merely negative attitude helps no one. Freedom as the objective, but to be reached, not along the road of isolation and perhaps of violence, but of development—as an equal and free member of the British and World League; South Africa as a part of mankind, doing her share towards the advancement of the great human ideals. The idea of sovereign independence is formal, juridical, and unfruitful for the great human future of co-operation and organization among the nations.

So far everything has gone off well, but the end is not yet. But a great blow has been struck, and a historic step forward has been taken. The dissolution of the party of Rhodes and Jameson is one of the greatest victories yet achieved on the road of South Africanism, or let me rather say of the South African spirit. I only hope our Dutch population will see the true meaning of it, and not worry so much about the purely traditional view of race relations in South Africa. The three congresses—*hereniging*, South African party and Unionist—form a great trilogy in our history, from which I trust that great results for a nobler South Africa will follow. But that *dénouement* is still far off, and difficult years and times are still before us.

With best wishes, to 'Poor Relations'[2] as well, *totus tuus*,

J. C. Smuts

---

[1] 'The Republican movement and the problem of the British Empire', published in the *South African Quarterly* for December 1919 and signed N. K. R.—the final letters of Hofmeyr's names. Smuts and Hofmeyr had discussed *hereniging* at their Doornkloof meeting. *See* A. Paton, *Hofmeyr*, pp. 86–9 for Hofmeyr's attitude to republicanism.

[2] Hofmeyr's mother, who could be caustic, used to say, in claiming distant kinship with Smuts, that she and her son were 'the poor relations'.

36   From H. E. Fremantle

Cottesloe
Summerville
via Addo
[Cape Province]
7 November 1920

My dear Smuts, I was very glad to get your letter of 18 October, which evoked my cordial sympathy. I also very much liked your speech at Bloemfontein. And I am eager to co-operate. But I am not clear as to procedure. What do you want me to do? It is useless for me to join the South African party as an individual under circumstances which would make it impossible for any other Nationalist to follow. I take it that we are agreed in regarding this as a new start owing to the new situation created by the Nationalists in making secession the one question before the country. There is no very great difficulty in the Unionists joining the South African party and linking up with you because you have been co-operating for years in general, they supporting you. But it is a very different matter for us who thought you wrong in some ways in 1912 and onwards, but are in complete agreement with secession. Moreover, the jingo speeches of Fitzpatrick [J. P.] and others at the Unionist congress do yeoman work in the cause of Tielman.[1] Also Prince Arthur's[2] 'English mind'. I take it that you do not ask us to repent about 1913[3] any more than I ask you to, and that we can agree in believing that each meant right. But I think there should be a clear understanding about this. Supposing this settled, as I do suppose, then you must really deal a little tenderly with us. I personally rather welcome the chance of co-operating with the late Unionists, as I spy a chance of the whole of the English being weaned from jingoism that way. But I confess that I am frightened. You cannot keep the Dutch with jingoism, nor ought this to be done, and some of these devils are infernal jingoes. And if this is my feeling how much more that of other Nationalists. But even Smartt, as I understand, has not joined the South African party yet, but is negotiating with you. Do you ask the Nationalists who agree with you about secession—and you see that Hertzog agrees with me in thinking that there are thousands—to come over to you with none of the safeguards that Smartt gets for what is essential to his lot? I can hardly think this.

[1] Tielman Roos.

[2] Prince Arthur of Connaught, second governor-general of the Union of South Africa.

[3] In 1913 Fremantle had joined the newly formed National party.

I therefore ask you to discuss matters, so as to make it possible for Nationalists to co-operate. If you will agree to this, I will come up any time you like and see you and any of your people or Smartt's you think right. I very strongly press this on you. Otherwise it will not be possible to get the confidence of any section of the Nationalists.

As far as I myself am concerned I do not say that I will not join your party anyhow. I intend to do so if possible. But I want to draw as many as possible with me, and I really think you might help at least as much as Fitz and his crowd hinder. If not, I come alone. I shall then do my utmost to get the party to take the line which will win the confidence of Nationalist non-secessionists. But that will take years. I cannot think that you intend to turn a deaf ear to me and my lot.

Will you please let me know your decision, and will you also please tell the secretary of your party, whoever that is, to write to me and send me all necessary literature? All best wishes. Yours ever,

H. E. S. Fremantle

37 To A. B. Gillett

Vol. 23, no. 226

Doornkloof
[Irene, Transvaal]
20 November 1920

Your £2,500 arrived all right, although I did not know it was your money until the arrival of your note last week. I have placed it on fixed deposit for $5\frac{1}{2}\%$ for twelve months, and enclose a memo in respect of it which you should keep.[1]

We are very busy now with the coming election. The Unionists have dissolved and joined the South African party. There is no enthusiasm about this among our stalwarts, and I shall not be greatly surprised if I suffer defeat next February. In that case I hope to have the little holiday to which I have been looking forward in vain for some years. I hope it will be so arranged by a kind providence that we shall spend it together somewhere in Far Away and Quite Forget.[2]

---

[1] The Gilletts wished to buy a farm in South Africa; Smuts was to advise and help them in acquiring it.

[2] Fade far away, dissolve, and quite forget
What thou among the leaves hast never known,
The weariness, the fever, and the fret...'

Keats, Ode to a Nightingale.

Thank you very much for all your trouble about our Governor (Bank).[1] With love, Ever yours,

Jan

38   To J. H. Hofmeyr   Vol. 23, no. 202

Pretoria
25 November 1920

Waarde Hofmeyr, Ik verstaan natuurlijk heel goed uw bezwaren en neem u uw ontkennend antwoord niet kwalijk. Alleen zal het publiek eronder lijden dat het niet een duidelijke uiteenzetting van een moeilijke constitutioneele positie voor zich heeft. Ik vind overal grooter bereidwilligheid om de 'Verhoogde Status' kwestie op haar merieten te bespreken. Men begint in te zien dat er iets groots is gebeurd, dat zelfs in Engeland niet besefd werd voordat er met nadruk in Zuid-Afrika op gewezen werd.

Verder gaat de wereld naar verwachting. De Unionisten hebben zich stilweg uitgewisschen. Zij hebben zich uitstekend gedragen en al onze voorstellen aangenomen. En zoo is de partij van Rhodes de weg van alle vleesch gegaan. Waarlijk, een van de betekenisvolste overwinningen ooit door de Zuid-Afrikaansche geest behaald.

De huidige positie is niet houdbaar, en ik heb maar besloten weer naar een electie te gaan. Het volk *moet* besluiten en niet steeds blijven hinken op twee gedachten. Ik wil hebben dat wij komen op een [one illegible word] positie wat beginsels betreft. De rassenkwestie is geen blijvende basis, daar menschen van dezelfde ras niet noodzakelijk dezelfde opinies deelen. Met zeer hartelijke groeten, *t.t.*

J. C. Smuts

TRANSLATION

Pretoria
25 November 1920

Dear Hofmeyr, Of course I understand your objections very well and do not take your negative answer amiss.[2] But the public will suffer from not having before it a clear exposition of a difficult

[1] *See* **29, 32**.
[2] Smuts had asked Hofmeyr to write a pamphlet on the constitutional meaning of Dominion status. Hofmeyr declined pleading pressure of work and his duty as principal of a university college to have no party political connections. *See* an incomplete draft of Hofmeyr's letter to Smuts dated 13 November 1920 in the Smuts Collection (vol. 23, no. 149A).

constitutional position.[1] I find everywhere a greater readiness to discuss the 'increased status' question[2] on its merits. People are beginning to see that something great has happened, which was not realized even in England until it was pointed out with emphasis in South Africa.

For the rest things are going as expected. The Unionists have quietly wiped themselves out. They have behaved excellently and accepted all our proposals. And so the party of Rhodes has gone the way of all flesh. Truly one of the most significant victories ever achieved by the South African spirit.

The present position is not tenable, and I have decided to hold an election. The people *must* decide and not always remain halting upon two opinions. I wish us to arrive at a [one illegible word] position as regards principles. The racial question is not a permanent basis, as people of the same race do not necessarily share the same opinions. With very good wishes, *totus tuus*,

J. C. Smuts

39   To A. B. Gillett   Vol. 23, no. 228

Pretoria
6 December 1920

Your last letter was full of depression over the financial situation and I notice that since you wrote a great meeting of manufacturers have protested against the present heavy taxation.[3] There is no doubt that the public is awakening, but whether there will be a great response from the present government I don't know. Things may have to get much worse before they get better, as you say. I notice a great deal of activity in Quaker circles. I shall be glad if you will let me get their really important leaflets. The Quakers have the root of the business in them. Only they are so infernally rich and comfortable. But you will see a movement among the bones in Ezekiel's valley[4] as things get worse. And finally the spiritual values will

[1] The main point at issue was the right of secession from the Empire which the National party claimed and the South African party denied.

[2] South African party spokesmen countered republican propaganda by emphasizing the enhanced status of the Dominions as expounded in Smuts's speech of 15 May 1917 (*see* vol. III, **750**), and as implied in their recognition as signatories of the treaty of Versailles and members of the League of Nations.

[3] The post-war boom in Great Britain was coming to an end in the winter of 1920. Taxation rose to £1,426 million in 1920-1.

[4] The prophet's vision of the valley of dry bones symbolizes the restoration of Israel after the fall of Jerusalem. '...and as I prophesied, there was a noise, and behold a shaking, and the bones came together...' *Ezekiel* xxxvii. 7.

assert themselves and a new creative movement will begin which may reach far before the end.

You are right about us. This is a very material little community. The young look at the outward aspects of things. It is only with adversity that reflection and inwardness come. And we have also been so prosperous. And yet I detect everywhere an inner hunger after the great things. The world is not ripe, but it is ripening for a great spiritual revival. Not in the sense of the old evangelistic revivals. But in the sense of a reshaping of values and ideals, which must in the end reform and recast society too. I see no light at present. It is all a vague aspiration through very dark surroundings. I do not *see* the New World, but *feel* it is somehow darkly emerging in the pain and strife of things. It will be more spiritual than the old world. 'The Poet hath said: Dear City of Cecrops; and shall we not say: Dear City of God?' That was Marcus Aurelius. Ever yours lovingly,

Jan

40   To M. C. Gillett   Vol. 23, no. 231

Pretoria
26 December 1920

This is Sunday night after Christmas. I came home the night before Christmas and have spent a blessed time here—the first Christmas home for many many years. And I am leaving again just now for a tour through the eastern Transvaal from which I shall return some time in January, I hope the first week. I feel very tired. There is that dull pain in the head that warns me I am going beyond the limits even of my strength. And you can see my hand is shaky. And this will go on till February, and then there is parliament. I hope you and Arthur will just give me rest when I come to England. Far, Far away and Quite Forget—where there is healing and growth and holism beyond the factions and divisions and separations which constitute my working life.

I spent last night in writing an appreciation of Woodrow Wilson[1] to be published in America on his retiring 4 March next. I shall send you a copy next week when it has been typed. Wilson erred grievously, but he wrought a great work for the world, and the future will justify him. I want to tell the Americans something about it and at the same time break a lance for the League. In my heart of hearts, however, I feel that the League is my own child,

---

[1] Not in the Smuts Collection.

but it is wiser not to father this Moses of the future on a despised Israelite. He must be born in the purple, so to say.

Thanks for your dear presents, which have cheered us greatly. The snaps pulled heavily at my heartstrings. Life has been very hard on me, and yet when I glance at those snaps and think of all they mean, I admit that there has been a soul of goodness at the core.[1]

I have written a letter to the suffrage people to say that I and my party support them, but make no party question of the suffrage. With wisdom and tact it will come right, and I alone can make it right. So be quiet, dear soul.[2]

My love to you all. My thoughts are always with you. I have a fear that both you and Arthur are physically in a bad way. I hope I am wrong. Ever yours,

Jan

41   To M. C. Gillett   Vol. 24, no. 276

Irene
Transvaal
3 January 1921

I came home last night from my trip in the eastern Transvaal, having held meetings from Lydenburg in the north to Vryheid in the south. All good splendid meetings characterized by much enthusiasm. I am sure good work was done. In your previous letter you had written that you were sending me some books which you were sure I could not understand. Well, I took what appeared the most difficult of the three with me and read it through on the journey, and I believe thoroughly mastered it. That was Einstein's book on Relativity. I enjoyed it immensely, my knowledge of dynamics making it comparatively easy to follow it. So don't you belittle my intelligence too much!...

When I came back last night from my trip I found a most welcome letter from you and this morning another from Arthur from Cambridge. Cambridge is not very willing to give you the vote, and for once she is lagging behind your own Oxford of lost causes.[3]

---

[1] There is some soul of goodness in things evil,
   Would men observingly distil it out.

Shakespeare, *Henry V*, IV, i. 4.

[2] At this time women in the Union of South Africa were not enfranchised. Margaret Gillett was an ardent advocate of women's rights.

[3] At Oxford women were, in February 1920, admitted to membership of the university and to degrees and might vote in the congregation. At Cambridge a proposal

I note what you say about Keynes's article on Baruch's book. Arthur referred to the same subject from Cambridge. I cannot say that the matter troubles me. My opinion to the Big Four[1] was written at their express request, went on legal grounds which I think were quite correct, and were approved by the greatest jurists at the conference. It had little to do with the amount of the German indemnity as I was a known and consistent advocate of a reasonable fixed amount of indemnity. If, however, pensions had been excluded from civilian damage, France would have got practically the whole indemnity, whatever it was, as she had suffered by far the most devastation. That would have been quite unfair. Keynes's article not only misreports the opinion, but lays undue stress on the *secrecy* of the matter. There was no special secrecy about it. The Big Four had the confidence in me to consult me in preference to the other lawyers and in accepting my reasoning. I know the matter is painful to you. But I accept no blame for it, as it was done in good faith and expressed my view of a legal matter. Of course my enemies will say I was responsible for the heavy reparation demands! But that is nonsense. Even if we could legally demand a huge amount, I was always, on grounds of policy, an avowed advocate of a reasonable amount. So there, my child! Do not be angry with me, and remember how I suffered to do the right thing throughout. Now, good-bye, and wish me well in these elections which are being fought with great violence...

42   From H. Mentz   Vol. 24, no. 191

Departement van Verdediging
Pretoria
4 Maart 1921

Lieve Generaal, Ik het banje gedenk over wat u my gister gese het en het toen daar over geslaap maar kon dit niet eers doen en nou voel ik dat ik u moet seg hoe die ding van die 2ᵉ man in die kabinet my hinder. Hoe meer ik daarover denk hoe meer onmogelik kom dit my voor.

Ik wil u dus weer seg dat ik denk dit sal een fatale fout wees. Dit sal alreeds verschrikkelik swaar gaan om ons mense te krij om

to give women students of the university full membership was rejected in December 1920 by 904 to 714 votes. In October 1921 Cambridge admitted women to 'titular' degrees, but they did not become members of the university until 1947–8. The first women to receive honorary degrees at Cambridge were admitted by Smuts, who became chancellor in 1948.

[1] *See* vol. IV, p. 210, note 1.

die pil te sluk van Minister van Landbouw maar terwijl hij daarop staat kan ik sien dat u daarin sal moet toestem. Maar ons kan die ander ding niet voorby kom voor die volgende redenen

(1) Daar is maar een Holl. sprekende Minister in die lot van die Kaap en hij word achteruit gestoot om plek te maak voor —.

(2) Dit is die prijs wat betaald moet worde voor die overkom van hulle.

(3) Dus daar was altyd een amalgamatie op sekere condities en nooit een vrywillige aansluiting. Dis een van die condities.

Daar sal natuurlik nog honderde andere draaien aan die ding gegewe wordt wat ik niet eerst wil probeer om op te noem.

Ons gaat een moeielike tijd in van alle opsichte beschouwd en ik vraag u in alle ernst moet dit niet onmogelik maak ver jou ou seksie om u handelwyse te verdedig, moet hulle a.u.b. niet die schole geef. Dis te groot. Uw beste vriend,

H. Mentz

TRANSLATION

Department of Defence
Pretoria
4 March 1921

Dear General, I thought much about what you told me yesterday and then slept on it, but could not even do that, and now I feel that I must tell you how this matter of the second man in the cabinet troubles me.[1] The more I think about it, the more impossible it appears to me.

So I want to tell you again that I think it will be a fatal mistake. It will already be terribly hard to get our people to swallow the pill of minister of agriculture, but, since he insists on it, I can see that you will have to agree to it.[2] But we cannot get past the other thing, for the following reasons:

(1) There is only one Dutch-speaking minister from the Cape[3] among the lot, and he is to be pushed back to make room for —.[4]

(2) It is the price that must be paid for their coming over.

(3) Thus, it was always an amalgamation on conditions and never a voluntary linking up. This is one of the conditions.

[1] That is, the proposed appointment of a second Unionist in the new cabinet. In the end three Unionists became ministers—Sir Thomas Smartt, J. W. Jagger and P. Duncan.

[2] Smartt became minister of agriculture.

[3] F. S. Malan, who had previously been minister of education and minister of mines and industries and now retained only the second office.

[4] Blank in the original letter.

Of course, a hundred other twists will be given to the thing which I don't even want to try to enumerate.

We are entering on a difficult period, whichever way it is regarded, and I ask you in all seriousness: do not make it impossible for your old group to defend your action; please don't give them the schools.[1] That is too big. Your best friend,

H. Mentz

43 To L. S. Amery   Vol. 24, no. 243

Prime Minister's Office
Cape Town
8 March 1921

My dear Amery, Thank you very much for your kind congratulations on the elections. Though so many were nervous about the result, my action has been amply justified.[2] A very dangerous situation has been turned to first-class use; not only have the Nats been beaten and the elections won over this republican issue, but the two white races have at last been brought together to a degree that would have been scouted as impossible before. I had looked upon great imperial results as likely to follow on our victory. And now both you and Milner have gone! It is too bad. At a most eventful time, when really important work could have been done, you both have sought other consolations—the one in matrimony,[3] the other in the admiralty[4] of all places!

You have not gone to a bed of roses. Naval policy in the next few years will be one of the most difficult and most —[5] subjects possible. The naval lessons of the Great War are really most difficult to read, and the directions in which to move would require great foresight. However you have jumped into the breach. And I can only wish my stout-hearted and hard-working old colleague all the luck in the world in this new adventure.

I don't like all this trouble about German indemnities. Take care that the policy of the British Empire does not become subordinated to French aims. We are great enough in the world to stand

[1] P. Duncan became minister of education, the interior and public health.

[2] The results of the election were: South African party 79; National party 45; Labour party 9; Independent 1.

[3] Milner had retired from public life and married Violet Maxse, then Lady Edward Cecil, in February 1921.

[4] Amery, who had been under-secretary of state for the colonies with Milner, became financial secretary to the admiralty in February 1921.

[5] Blank in the typed copy in the Smuts Collection.

on the broad lines of our own imperial policy. We were too subservient in the war, we are now too subservient in the peace.

With kindest regards both to you and Mrs Amery, Ever yours sincerely,

s. J. C. Smuts

44   To A. Clark   Vol. 98, no. 128

Cape Town
21 April 1921

Your cheerful letters are always most welcome. I sometimes wonder whether you are as cheerful as you appear from your letters. The Good is much more impotent than you seem to appreciate—not only as an inner force in our personal lives, but also as an objective factor in the world's affairs. This industrial madness which is bringing about the economic and ultimately the political downfall of England[1] does not tend to make me feel cheerful. And as soon as the industrial situation clears a bit, France with her policy of keeping Europe's nerves on edge will start in. And the British government will of course back her. [Lloyd] George's Bristol speech of 1918[2] has put him apparently entirely in the hands of the French reactionaries. And so the marshals rule instead of the statesmen. And you continue very cheerful! To my mind the world is sinking to a lower economic and social level. We are going to be much poorer than we ever dreamt of being; we shall have to work much harder if these vast populations are to have a livelihood. Disease will grip us much more closely. Social conditions are going to be worse, much worse. And the danger is that under great economic stress and suffering, militarism will revive (as always in the world's past) and nations will eat up each other with the sword. And we all appear perfectly helpless against the inevitable fate which is in store for us. Suffering to me is very real, and the world is in for suffering, have no doubt of that.

[1] On 1 April a coal strike began in England when, following a slump in the export price of coal, the mine owners announced a drastic reduction in miners' wages. The miners were at first supported by the railwaymen and transport workers. A general strike of the 'Triple Alliance' was threatened and the government declared a state of emergency. But the Railway and Transport Unions reversed their decision to strike and the miners had to end their strike on 1 July and accept reduced wages.

[2] Lloyd George's speech at Bristol on 11 December 1918 included the following statements: 'I have always said we will exact the last penny we can out of Germany up to the limit of her capacity...' 'There is no doubt at all as to the demand which will be put forward...to make the Kaiser and his accomplices responsible for this terrible crime.'

I shall probably arrive in London on June 11[1] and I have asked the Gilletts to meet me, and hope soon to see you thereafter unless you could be in London on that Saturday evening when we shall have a joint spree in the Savoy Hotel in the old style. We must drown our public sorrows in private cheerfulness!

Now good-bye, dear. Ever yours affectionately,

J. C. Smuts

45 To C. P. Crewe   Vol. 102, no. 206

Prime Minister's Office
Cape Town
6 May 1921

My dear Crewe, Thank you for your note re Israelites.[2] I agree with you that there should be a limit to patience, even with these religious fanatics. A breach of the law where the actual administration of justice is concerned cannot be overlooked. The police are now going to act.

My main difficulty is the faulty old law which does not permit of the summary procedure you sketch. If I did what you suggest and our action is challenged in the courts, we shall be beaten. The Israelites have a white lawyer to look after their interests. However we must act and keep to the law as closely as possible.

Kind regards to you and Lady Crewe. Ever yours,

J. C. Smuts

46 Memorandum (1921)   Box G, no. 5c

The question of the constitutional relations of Great Britain and the Dominions came to the fore when, at the imperial conference of 1911, Sir Joseph Ward, prime minister of New Zealand, presented a plan, inspired by Lionel Curtis, for federating the self-governing units of the Empire. Sir Wilfred Laurier and General Botha successfully opposed it (*see* vol. III, pp. 29–30, 36) as did all the other prime ministers, but the federalists continued to propagate their views. At the imperial war conference of 1917 the constitution of the Empire was again on the agenda. Smuts helped to frame a resolution which was moved by Sir Robert Borden, seconded by W. F. Massey, and adopted by the conference on 16 April. The resolution declared that the readjustment

---

[1] To attend the imperial conference.

[2] Members of an African separatist church who were in illegal occupation of common land in the Bulhoek location near Queenstown. A police force sent to move them was defied and attacked on 24 May and some 300 Israelites were killed or wounded. *See* W. K. Hancock, *Smuts—The Fields of Force*, pp. 89–100.

of the constitutional relations of the Empire should be the subject of a special conference to be summoned after the war, but added that 'any such adjustment, while thoroughly preserving all existing powers of self-government and complete control of domestic affairs, should be based upon a full recognition of the Dominions as autonomous nations of an imperial Commonwealth...' Speaking to the resolution Smuts pointed out that, although the Dominions enjoyed great freedom, yet 'in the actual theory of the constitution' their status was still that of 'subject provinces of Great Britain' and their standing as equal nations of the Empire would have to be specifically recognized. He went on to draw attention to that part of the resolution which affirmed that all the existing powers of self-government of the Dominions should be preserved. This, said Smuts, meant that the 'federal solution' of their future constitutional relations was, by implication, negatived. (*See* Cd. 8566 of 1917, pp. 5, 42, 46–8).

Recognition of the principle of equal status having been secured and imperial federation excluded, Smuts could go on to expound his view of the British Commonwealth as a community of nations linked by common allegiance to the crown in a speech to members of parliament on 15 May 1917 (*see* vol. IV, pp. 506–17). The status of the Dominions was further enhanced by their recognition as autonomous states at the peace conference and their admission as member states of the League of Nations. But legal recognition of their independence and the removal of discrepancies between equal status and British law and administrative practice had still to be secured.

In 1920 Smuts was informed that a conference of prime ministers and representatives of Great Britain, the Dominions and India would meet in London in June 1921 and that the constitutional conference decided upon in 1917 would meet in 1922 (*see* **33**). As the agenda of the constitutional conference was to be decided at the 1921 conference, Smuts prepared, for circulation at that conference, the memorandum printed below. He sent a copy in advance to L. S. Amery who commented upon it in a letter of 20 June 1921 (*see* **47**).

It was clear from the opening speeches at the 1921 conference that the other Dominion prime ministers were not interested in clarifying and defining constitutional relations and regarded this as unnecessary and even dangerous. W. F. Massey of New Zealand and W. M. Hughes of Australia added that elections at home would prevent their attendance at the projected conference in 1922. Smuts did not circulate his memorandum but, in a speech on 11 July, he referred to its 'preliminary observations' and suggested that a sub-committee should frame a short list of 'principles or declarations' setting forth the status of equality in the Empire and the relations of its members. This received no support but informal conversations, initiated by Smuts, took place between the prime ministers. Several draft constitutional declarations were circulated, among them a set of resolutions for a future constitutional conference framed by Smuts. These embodied the leading ideas of his memorandum. By the time the drafts were discussed on 22 July Smuts knew that all the prime ministers were opposed to a constitutional conference. He therefore made an attempt to get his resolutions accepted as recommendations

for the consideration of their governments, but in vain. In the end a resolution
was adopted that there was no advantage to be gained by holding a constitutional conference and the whole matter was shelved. (*See* Cmd. 1474 of 1921,
pp. 9–10, 14–28.)[1]

THE CONSTITUTION OF THE BRITISH COMMONWEALTH

One of the most important matters for discussion at this meeting
of the imperial cabinet[2] is the agenda or programme to be laid
before the constitutional conference which will be held at an early
date. That programme will include such important matters as:
  1. The status of the Dominions.
  2. The relations of the king, as the common bond of unity, to
     the component parts of the Commonwealth.
  3. The methods of conference and consultation between those
     parts in all matters of common imperial concern, and
  4. Several other subsidiary but still important matters.
Before dealing with these points I wish to make two preliminary
observations:

In the first place, I would emphasize the urgency of the subject
and the necessity of as early a settlement as possible. Delay in the
settlement of Dominion status is fraught with grave dangers. The
British Commonwealth cannot escape the atmosphere of political
unsettlement and change which is affecting most other countries.
The national temperature of all young countries has been raised
by the event of the great war. The national sense, the consciousness
of nationhood of the Dominions has received a great impetus from
their share in the great war and from the experiences of hundreds
of thousands of Dominion troops in the campaigns of the great war.
While these experiences have strengthened the common bonds,
they have undoubtedly also deepened the Dominion sense of
national separateness, of the Dominions as distinct nations in the
Commonwealth and the world. And with this sense goes a feeling
of legitimate pride and self-respect which affects the rank and file
of these young nations just as much as their political leaders.
Unless Dominion status is settled soon in a way which will satisfy
the legitimate aspirations of these young nations, we must look for
separatist movements in the Commonwealth. Such movements

---

[1] The editor is indebted to Mr H. Duncan Hall for assistance in preparing this
introductory note.

[2] Smuts used this term, on the analogy of the imperial war cabinet of 1917, to
designate the gathering of the prime ministers of the United Kingdom and the
Dominions. But the 1921 conference was attended, in addition, by other representatives of the Dominions and also of India.

already exist, notably in South Africa, but potentially in several of the other Dominions also. And the only way to deal with such movements is not to wait until they have become fully developed, and perhaps irresistible in their impetus, but to forestall them and make them unnecessary by the most generous satisfaction of the Dominion sense of nationhood and statehood. The warning against always being too late in coming to a proper settlement, which the example of Ireland gives to the whole Commonwealth, is one which we can only neglect at our peril.

My second observation is this: that it is not sufficient merely to lay down a formal agenda of points or topics for the consideration of the coming conference. This imperial cabinet should give a definite lead to public opinion and to the conference by drafting and provisionally approving a number of definite resolutions for the consideration of the conference. If this is not done, there is every risk that the conference may resolve itself into a series of academic discussions on some of the most difficult and intricate questions in the whole range of constitutional law. In that way the conference might prove abortive and futile, and public opinion in the Dominions might become exasperated. From bitter experience in South Africa extending over about two years of public discussion, I feel that public opinion requires education—it requires a lead— it requires practical suggestions for its guidance through a maze of questions which even technical lawyers find it difficult to follow. If a series of resolutions were passed at this cabinet, not as a definite and final settlement but as a programme for discussion at the conference, and if these draft resolutions were published as soon as possible in order to guide the formation of public opinion all over the Commonwealth, we should go far in ensuring the success of the conference and in making it the greatest landmark in the history of the Commonwealth. Nay, more: with such draft resolutions before it from the imperial cabinet, the conference could be made a larger and more representative body and embrace representatives from other parties as well as from the government. The issues to be settled are so important that it would be most desirable not to confine the conference merely to the governing parties represented in the cabinets of the Commonwealth. For every Dominion the settlement should not be a party one but a national settlement accepted if possible by all important sections of public opinion. I fear, however, that such a large conference would prove abortive, unless it had before it the detailed proposals of the imperial cabinet. The conference should be a sort of legislative assembly convened to consider definite motions placed before it. This enlarged conference, if successful, could then become a precedent for the future and take the place of the present imperial conference which is not a very satisfactory body.

DOMINION STATUS

I now proceed to discuss the matters which will be embraced by the draft resolutions, and, firstly, the definition of the future constitutional status of the Dominions in the Commonwealth group and in the world. After the evolution in the status of the Dominions, culminating in their signature of the Versailles treaty and their membership in the League of Nations, what is their present position? What is clear in their present status, and what is still obscure or anomalous and requires further action? In general, the equal statehood of the Dominions with the United Kingdom and with other sovereign states has been affirmed both by Dominion and British statesmen, as following in principle from what has happened. Apart from general principle, however, it is most important to see what the position in actual practice is, for only in that way will it be possible to know what steps have still to be taken in order that the actualities of the situation may be brought to harmonize with theory or principle. The actual position may, I submit, be formulated as follows:

1. As regards legislative sovereignty.

As a matter of strict law, the parliament of the United Kingdom has sovereign power of legislation not only in respect of the United Kingdom but of the Empire as a whole, including the Dominions. Constitutionally, however, the parliaments of the Dominions have exclusive legislative sovereignty in respect of their several Dominions, and any attempt of the parliament of the United Kingdom to legislate for a Dominion would be unconstitutional and revolutionary.

Here two questions arise. Firstly, as the legislative sovereignty of the parliament of the United Kingdom over the Dominions is constitutionally obsolete, is it worth while formally abolishing it; or had it better be left alone as a sort of symbolic reminder of the historic unity of the Commonwealth? I submit that it is an archaic form devoid of all substance in our unwritten constitution and may therefore be left alone.

Secondly, the legislative sovereignty of the Dominions is territorially restricted in their present constitutions. These give them power to legislate 'for the peace, order and good government' of their respective Dominions. Extra-territorial legislation may be held to be *ultra vires*. I have contended successfully that the Dominions have power of legislation in respect of their mandated territories also. But beyond that their power is questionable. They could, for instance, not legislate for the annexation of new territories. This limitation on the legislative sovereignty of the Dominions should be removed by legislation of the imperial parliament which granted the Dominion constitutions. Several of the Dominion constitutions also reserve the power of their amendment to the imperial parliament. It would be desirable to amend these constitutions and, as in the case of the South Africa Act, give the power of amendment to the Dominion concerned. The application of the Colonial Laws Validity Act[1] to future Dominion legislation should also be abolished, as it places the Dominion parliaments in a position of inferiority and has clearly become an anachronism.

With these alterations in the *law*, the *constitutional* equality of the Dominion parliaments with that of the United Kingdom would be established.

2. As regards executive sovereignty.

Here the present position may be summarized as follows:

The Dominion executive, or the king in his Dominion government, has constitutionally unrestricted power of executive action within the Dominion, and the British government has not even a legal fiction of authority left. Outside the Dominions, however, that is to say in foreign affairs and international relations, the Dominions had no defined status until the Versailles treaty. Their membership of the peace conference and of the League of Nations and their signature of the Versailles treaty meant for them international recognition and an international status. But this is so recent an innovation that little has been done hitherto to carry this position to its logical applications. In practice the imperial government has continued to control the foreign relations of the Commonwealth *vis-à-vis* foreign powers. And in doing so the British government has done little more, even in the way of consulting the Dominions, than to send occasional summaries of the international situation to the Dominion governments. It is agreed that the Dominions are not constitutionally bound by treaties to which they are not parties by their own signature. It is agreed also that they can authorize the king to appoint Dominion representatives to foreign

---

[1] By this act of 1865 colonial laws that are repugnant to any act of the British parliament are invalid.

governments, and some of them contemplate doing so.[1] There has, however, not yet been time for any settled practice to grow up in regard to the foreign representation of the Dominions, and in consequence there is a good deal of obscurity about the whole position, not only in the United Kingdom and the Dominions, but also in foreign countries. Foreigners find it difficult to understand the unwritten British constitution, in which precedents mould and expand the constitution, and the legal aspect is nothing and the constitutional aspect everything. Even in America the senate debates over the reservations in regard to the voting power of the British Empire in the assembly of the League of Nations are a warning to us. Other people find it difficult to grasp the difference between legal theory and constitutional practice in the Empire and to see how the law of the constitution is moulded and finally abrogated by the practice of the constitution, and how, without a change of the law, a British colony becomes in constitutional fact an independent state. These abstruse matters might be cleared up in some formal way which would show the true nature of the Dominion status as distinct from legal archaisms. It has been suggested by Mr Duncan Hall in his interesting book on the British Commonwealth of Nations,[2] that a declaration of constitutional rights should be made which would explain the new developments in Dominion status, remove obscurities, set at rest doubts and abrogate what is obsolete—a declaration, in fact, which would become a precedent and a most important amendment of the unwritten law of the constitution. Such a declaration would set out that, as a matter of constitutional right, the British parliament has no legislative power in respect of the Dominions; that the king has no more constitutional right of vetoing Dominion bills than he has in respect of British bills; and that the king in his Dominion government has in respect of foreign affairs affecting the Dominions the same constitutional right that he has as king in his British government in respect of the United Kingdom. Other points might also be covered by such a declaration, which would definitely settle the new constitutional basis on which the Commonwealth rests and explain that basis to all the world. I heartily endorse Hall's suggestion which seems to me the easiest constitutional means of settling the international status of the Dominions, without

---

[1] On 10 May 1920 it was announced in the house of commons, Canada, that the king, on the advice of his Canadian ministers, would appoint a minister plenipotentiary at Washington to have charge of Canadian affairs.

[2] H. Duncan Hall, *The Problem of Dominion Status—the reconciliation of absolute equality of nationhood with the formal unity of the Empire* (1920).

changing the unwritten flexible character of the constitution of the British Commonwealth. If the suggestion is adopted, the declaration could be drafted by the imperial cabinet, considered and passed by the constitutional conference and by them presented to the king in a formal address for his acceptance.

3. As regards judicial sovereignty.

The only limitation at present existing to the judicial sovereignty of the Dominions is the right of appeal to the judicial committee of the privy council safeguarded in all the Dominion constitutions. This right of appeal, which is most extensive in the earlier constitutions granted to Canada and Australia, is so seriously curtailed in the later South Africa Act that appeals to the privy council from the supreme court of South Africa are most rare and, owing to a recent ruling of the privy council,[1] are likely to be still rarer in the future. The force of opinion in favour of this right of appeal to the privy council has greatly diminished in recent years, and there is now no strong reason why, if a Dominion so chooses, it should not have the power to abolish this right altogether. With the two larger Dominions it is now largely a question of internal arrangement as between the Dominions and their component states or provinces. If the power to amend their constitutions is granted to the Dominions by imperial act, as already suggested, this will necessarily also give them the power to deal with the right of appeal to the privy council as they please.

THE KING AND THE DOMINIONS

The relations of the king to the Dominions raise some very difficult questions in regard to the status of the Dominions and it is best to discuss this aspect of Dominion status separately. Equality of statehood with the United Kingdom requires that the king should have exactly the same relation to a Dominion that he has to the United Kingdom; and the Prince of Wales, in a recent celebrated speech, which read almost like a constitutional declaration, said that this was so. But as things stand in practice today, this is not so. The statement would be correct if the king were also the sovereign of a Dominion in his personal capacity. But this is not so. The king in his relation to a Dominion is not the king in his personal capacity, but the king in his official capacity as the constitutional sovereign

---

[1] By a ruling of 1920 the judicial committee of the privy council would only entertain appeals from the supreme court of the Union of South Africa if a broad principle of jurisprudence were involved.

of the United Kingdom. If, therefore, the king is to execute any act in relation to a Dominion he does so through the forms and channels prescribed by the constitution of the United Kingdom. His appointment of a governor-general to represent him in a Dominion is made technically on the advice of his British cabinet and bears the counter-signature of a secretary of state. The most significant illustration of this position is afforded by the recent appointment by the king of his Dominion ministers as plenipotentiaries to sign the peace treaty on behalf of their Dominions; this appointment was countersigned by a British secretary of state, although made on the advice of his majesty's Dominion executives. As long as this is so, it is impossible to contend that the Dominion governments stand on the same footing as the British government, their position being one of distinct inferiority.

There is another very serious instance of this inferiority. The Dominion executive has not direct access to their sovereign; they can only approach him officially through his British government. The relations of the king to his Dominion government have been placed under a British secretary of state through whom all communications pass. The governor-general, who represents the king in the Dominions, does not correspond direct with the king but communicates officially with the secretary of state. The placing of the Dominions under the secretary of state for the colonies or indeed under any other British department or ministry is therefore in itself a sign of the inferiority in status of the Dominion government to the British government. In practice this inferiority is carried even further: the governor-general is not merely a viceroy, representative of the king; he is also the agent in the Dominions of the British government and more particularly of the colonial office. This is of course a relic of the past—quite out of harmony with the new order of things.

This state of affairs positively cannot be tolerated much longer. It is imperatively necessary that equality of statehood should in practice be carried out to the full extent of bringing about an equality of status between the British and Dominion governments as co-ordinate governments of the king. This would involve:

  (a) that the Dominions should cease to be placed under the colonial office or any other British department;
  (b) that the Dominion governments should have direct access to the king who will act on their advice without the interposition of the British government or a secretary of state;
  (c) that the governor-general should become a viceroy simply

and solely and only represent the sovereign in his Dominion executive and not also the British government.[1]

The important principle is contained in paragraph (b). If that is carried, the changes involved in (a) and (c) will necessarily have to be made by administrative action. Now, one way of carrying (b) is the declaration of constitutional rights referred to. In such a declaration the king in the exercise of his royal prerogative could lay down that in future the Dominions will have direct access to him and that in his conduct as Dominion sovereign he will only act on the advice of his Dominion government. As the king resides in England, this would involve the residence there of a Dominion minister of the crown to remain in touch with him. Direct access of each Dominion executive to the king should, however, not have the effect of weakening the intimate relations which keep the British and Dominion governments in close touch with one another. Some machinery which will prevent their drifting apart under the new system will have to be devised. Perhaps the following suggestion might be considered:

A Dominions committee should be constituted consisting of the prime ministers of the United Kingdom and of the Dominions as *ex officio* members, with the right, however, of nominating representatives to take their places on the committee. This would not be a committee of the present privy council, which is merely an organ of the British government, but a real Commonwealth committee. The Dominion affairs [are] to be taken away from the colonial office and put in the charge of this Dominions committee through whom formal correspondence between the governments of the Commonwealth would pass. (The committee should, however, not be a post office, such as the colonial office has largely become, and all merely business or departmental matters should be sent direct as between the British and Dominion departments concerned without troubling the committee.) Business which concerns any Dominion particularly would be dealt with by that Dominion's representative and the United Kingdom's representative. If the two fail to agree, the matter [is] to be remitted to their principals, the two prime ministers concerned, for decision. It is assumed that in a purely Dominion matter the view of the Dominion representative shall prevail. In matters of common concern for the Commonwealth, the whole committee should meet and dispose of the matter on the

[1] Smuts had, in January 1919, after informal discussion between the Dominion ministers assembled in Paris, written a short memorandum on the position of the governor-general. Copies were circulated to the various prime ministers but the matter was not brought up before the British Empire delegation. The memorandum is in the Smuts Collection (vol. LXXVIII, no. 59).

principles which guide the deliberations of the imperial conference and the council of the League of Nations, viz., unanimity of resolutions and no attempted coercion of a dissentient Dominion. Members of the committee [are] to have direct access to the king who will be advised in regard to general Commonwealth matters by the committee as a whole, and in regard to matters affecting a particular Dominion by the two representatives referred to. Thus, in regard to the appointment of a governor-general or viceroy, the king would be advised by the United Kingdom and Dominion representatives who no doubt will be guided by the instructions of their principals. I sketch the general idea of this committee in outline and purposely avoid details.

It will be seen that the constitution of this Dominions committee will not only satisfy the requirements of the three points above stated, but that it will serve the further purpose of providing an imperial organ of 'continuous consultation', such as was contemplated in the resolution of the 1917 conference.

METHODS OF CONFERENCE AND CONSULTATION

After what has already been said in reference to the imperial conference and the Dominions committee, it is unnecessary to discuss this subject in detail, and I shall proceed to summarize my suggestions. There will be three organs of conference and consultation in regard to the common policies and concerns of the Commonwealth: the imperial conference, the prime ministers' conference (in place of the imperial cabinet) and the Dominions committee.

1. The imperial conference or Commonwealth congress will meet every four years and discuss general questions of common concern, such as will from time to time come up for legislation in the Commonwealth parliaments. It will no longer be confined to cabinet ministers but will be broadened in its membership so as to include representatives of the parliamentary oppositions also. Its sessions will go in rotation round the Commonwealth, and its president will be the prime minister for the time being of the country in which the session is held. It will generally sit in public.

2. The Dominions committee which will be a continuous organization and form the link between the throne and the Commonwealth cabinets. It will be continuously available for the discussion of questions of foreign policy and other common matters as they turn up. It will also discuss important matters coming from the League of Nations, on which group action by the Commonwealth may be desirable. It will have a Commonwealth secretariat.

75

3. The prime ministers' conference which I suggest should replace the present so-called imperial cabinet. This name is a misnomer, as it is no cabinet and takes no executive action, nor is there joint responsibility to any parliament. In the Dominions the name of imperial cabinet is already leading to serious misunderstanding and criticism. The imperial cabinet is really and substantially a prime ministers' conference, to which other British or Dominion ministers are also invited when the affairs dealt with by their departments are under discussion. It will be the Dominions committee in an expanded form and clothed with greater authority. It will meet at least once every two years to review the foreign or defence or other common policies of the Commonwealth as a whole. It will lay down, subject to the approval of the several countries, the general principles of the common policies to be followed from time to time, and the Dominions committee will take those principles as their general instructions in the intervals between the meetings of the prime ministers' conference. The Dominions committee and the prime ministers' conference may on occasion for purposes of consultation hold joint sittings with the committee of imperial defence.

There are only two other miscellaneous matters to which I wish to refer because of their great symbolic or sentimental significance. There is no doubt that the formal settlement of the above matters will complete the fundamental alteration in the basis of the British Empire which has taken place recently. It will no longer be an empire but a society of free and equal sister states. A new name should mark that epoch-making departure. For this there is all the more reason because the name of the British Empire is for various reasons not universally popular throughout our group of associated nations. I would therefore suggest that the time has come for the consideration of a new name for our group, such as the British Commonwealth of Nations.

Secondly, some great symbol should mark the equal statehood of the Dominions and their entry among the nations of the world. This could best be done by their adoption of a distinctive national flag for each, in addition to the Union Jack or other common symbol of imperial unity and allegiance.

To summarize the above suggestions:

1. The imperial cabinet should draft a general scheme of future constitutional relations for the British Commonwealth, and this scheme should take the form of a series of concrete resolutions to be submitted for the consideration of the constitutional conference

next year, and to be published for general information and public discussion in the meantime.

2. The scope of the resolutions should be the practical recognition of the equality of statehood of the Dominions with the United Kingdom and the methods of conference and consultation to be adopted in future in respect of common policies and concerns of the Commonwealth.

3. The resolutions should provide that legislation of the British parliament be passed (*a*) giving power of amendment in respect of their constitutions to the Dominions, (*b*) extending their legislative jurisdiction beyond their territorial limits, and (*c*) abrogating the Colonial Laws Validity Act in its application to future Dominion legislation.

4. The resolutions should further provide that a declaration of rights be presented by the constitutional conference for the acceptance of the king, providing (*a*) that the British parliament has no constitutional right of legislation in respect of the Dominions, (*b*) that the royal veto is in the same constitutional position in the Dominions as in the United Kingdom, (*c*) that the Dominions have direct access to the sovereign without the intervention of any British secretary of state, and (*d*) that the international status and rights of diplomatic representation of the Dominions is unquestioned.

5. The resolutions should further provide (*a*) that Dominion affairs be removed from the secretary of state for the colonies and placed under a Dominions committee, consisting of the Commonwealth prime ministers or their nominees and having direct access to the king; and (*b*) that in future the governor-general in the Dominion shall be simply and solely a viceroy, representative of the sovereign.

6. With regard to the methods of conference and consultation the resolutions should provide that there be (*a*) a quadrennial Commonwealth congress, (*b*) a biennial prime ministers' conference (in lieu of the imperial cabinet), and (*c*) a continuous Dominions committee; all with scope as above explained.

7. To mark the fundamental change in the character of the British Empire, the resolutions should provide that its name be altered to that of the British Commonwealth of Nations. (*b*) To mark the fundamental change in the status of the Dominions, the resolutions should provide that besides a common imperial flag (which may be the Union Jack) each Dominion should have its own distinctive national flag.

47   From L. S. Amery   Vol. 24, no. 3A

20 June 1921

My dear Smuts, I have read your draft memorandum with the greatest interest and with complete agreement on the main points. Working separately it seems that we have both arrived at more or less identical conclusions, not only on questions of principle but also of actual machinery, and that is at any rate not unhopeful as to the feasibility of what we advocate.

I entirely agree with you that it is desirable not only to secure at the forthcoming constitutional conference certain general declarations of constitutional right, as Duncan Hall suggests, but also to frame the draft of those declarations now at the present prime ministers' conference and have it in circulation during the next twelve months, in order to focus public opinion in the Empire. While we do not want anything in the nature of a fixed or written constitution for the British Commonwealth, we do want a general agreement and public understanding on fundamentals, and not always to be questioning these afresh or pulling our institutions up by the roots. The suggested declarations would have that desired effect and the process of constitutional evolution would then go on both as between the different parts of the Empire, and in each part of the Empire severally, without further questioning of the underlying fabric.

These declarations would of course include an affirmation not only of the complete independence and equality of the several partners but also of the indissoluble unity of all of them under king and crown. That is the issue which you have recently fought so successfully in South Africa.[1] But in your anxiety to lay stress on the other aspect—the one which requires action and a measure of re-organization—you have omitted to mention it in the draft memorandum. I think it would make it rather more complete in itself, and more acceptable to the members of the conference if you put in a few sentences making that clear.

The peculiar characteristic it seems to me of the British Empire is the combination of the complete independence of its parts (at any rate of the self-governing parts) as political entities and the underlying unity based on the fact that these independent political units are composed equally of British subjects and have thus a common and interchangeable citizenship, and that the same crown

---

[1] The attempts at reunion of the South African and National parties had foundered on the question of secession from the Empire and the elections of 1920 and 1921 had been fought mainly on this issue.

is an integral part in the constitutional framework of each. The unity created by the crown is an inherent constitutional unity and not a mere accidental and personal connection. The relation is quite different to that between say England and Hanover a century ago, or even Austria and Hungary up to the other day. In those cases the crowns are separate even though they happen to be worn by the same monarch, and the identity of monarch did not make a Hanoverian a British subject or a Hungarian an Austrian subject. With us not only the king but the crown and the status of British subject are one. That status may be limited from the point of view of citizenship in various parts of the Empire by restrictions as to franchise, immigration etc. etc., but fundamentally it remains one everywhere, and this is of course one of the greatest assets of belonging to the British Commonwealth. It means that each member of it can aspire to not only the ordinary rights of citizenship in other parts of the Empire but to its very highest posts. Nothing could be more typical of this community of citizenship than the fact that you, while a South African minister, were actually for a time also a member of the British war cabinet or the converse fact, that you picked a member of the British house of commons as one of South Africa's representatives at the assembly of the League of Nations.[1]

From this point of view I should be inclined to word somewhat differently the passage on page 9 (with the substance of which I entirely agree) as to the relationship of the king with the Dominion in his 'personal and official' capacity. It seems to me that it is not so much a contrast between 'personal and official' capacities as a survival in the highest political realm of all, viz., the dealing of the king with his ministers of the old supremacy of the United Kingdom. That supremacy went long ago in respect of ordinary internal administration. It has gone more recently in respect of foreign policy, and I entirely agree with you that it ought to go even as regards counter-signatures and personal access, and that ministers of the Dominions should have direct access to the king. Indeed, if I may say so, your coupling of this right seems to me one of the happiest features of your scheme.

As regards the machinery for co-operation my conclusions are the same as yours. We require an enlarged imperial conference which ought to be a conference of parliamentary delegations and no longer a conference of governments only, to discuss with the fullest publicity broad fundamental matters of common interest, not only questions of constitutional right but of defence, trade, shipping etc. in so far as they can be discussed in the general aspects

[1] Lord Robert Cecil.

and embodied in broad resolutions. Under present conditions of communication, I do not think you can summon this body conveniently more than once in four years. In the interval you would carry on firstly with the prime ministers' conference or imperial cabinet, meeting not less often than once in two years, and the imperial committee or commission sitting more or less continuously, though with no doubt a frequently changing personnel.

So much for the general points. I add a few notes on points of detail which have struck me in reading through the draft.

Page 5. I agree that the principle of equality of status demands the removal of the territorial limitation on the legislative sovereignty of the Dominions. But this point will want very careful investigation in order to avoid overlapping jurisdictions or a danger of the breaking up of the unity of the status of British subject. On a British steamer sailing from South Africa to England British subjects are South Africans till they leave the three miles limit and are then under the United Kingdom jurisdiction for the rest of the voyage. I do not know whether the proposition should be that if the steamer is registered in South Africa they should remain under South African jurisdiction until they enter Southampton Water. Another conceivable solution would be that we divide up the oceans among ourselves for inter-imperial jurisdiction purposes.

Again, at present a South African in Italy has exactly the same claim to the protection and support of the British representatives there as an Englishman, and it seems to me very undesirable it should be otherwise. Even if South Africa appointed a minister in Rome to deal specifically with South African interests, that would not, to my mind, make it any the less desirable, or from the point of view of individual South Africans less advantageous, that every representative of the British Empire abroad should regard it his duty to help and protect every British subject regardless of his domicile.

I raise this point very much as a layman but it does seem to me the resolutions and legislations in respect of this matter will have to be very carefully framed.

Page 8. I am not quite sure whether the question of appeals to the privy council is one which should be included among the declarations of constitutional right. For one thing the feeling in some parts of the Empire at any rate, more particularly in Canada, is still strongly in favour of maintaining the appeal, and it seems to me that this is a matter best left to the discretion of each Dominion.

There is also a further question which has not, I think, arisen in the past, namely of a conflict between two Dominions. If the nations at large are prepared to agree among themselves on an international court, then *a fortiori* we ought to preserve something in the nature of an imperial court for possible issues as between ourselves.

Page 9. I agree that the present double status of the governor-general as representative of the king on the one side and the agent of a British government department on the other, is an anomaly. Despatches should no longer be transmitted, to my mind, through the governor-general, but of course the governor-general, just as the king at home, should receive simultaneously a copy of every document of importance. I consequently agree entirely with A., B., and C. at the bottom of the page.

Page 11. I entirely agree with your idea of a minister resident or 'in-waiting' in England and it brings the whole thing into a much better and truer constitutional light to have him there as in attendance on the king and not in attendance on the British cabinet. For many reasons it would be desirable, I think, that this duty should be exercised by various members of a Dominion cabinet in rotation in order to give each of them, as far as possible, experience of the problems discussed at this end and to bring the whole of the Dominion cabinet in personal relations with the sovereign.

I am not quite sure there is not a slight overlapping between your definition of the Dominions committee on this page and your summary of the organization on page 13. In the latter place you distinguish between the prime ministers' conference as the expanded Dominions committee with greater authority and the committee itself as the intermediate link between the prime ministers' conference. On this page you use the words 'Dominions committee' to cover both. On the whole I think the nomenclature on page 13 is preferable. By the way, I am not exactly sure where and how you propose India should come in to this committee and if so, I am not sure whether imperial committee would not be a better name than Dominions committee.

You describe the privy council as merely an organ of the British government. I should have thought the privy council, i.e. the whole body of privy councillors, is like the whole body of British subjects, an imperial unit. In actual operation it functions in separate panels, though a meeting of privy councillors from all parts of the Empire, e.g. at an imperial cabinet, does constitute a real Commonwealth body.

Bottom of page 11. I am all with you in the desirability of letting corresponding departments in this country and the Dominions deal directly with each other and avoid the unnecessary amount of 'office work' which goes on nowadays. And of course I am with you in thinking that the Dominions work ought to be taken away from the colonial office. I fancy, however, that there will still be a residue of inter-imperial business and business between this country and particularly Dominions affecting several departments, or affecting matters as to which it is not always clear which department here corresponds to the department at the other end, in respect of which a Dominions department of some sort, though on a smaller scale, would be required. My own notion is that this should be attached to the president of the council, whose functions are largely honorific but who already deals with certain inter-imperial organizations, such as the imperial mineral resources bureau etc.

Page 13. I confess I do not quite agree with your description of the title 'imperial cabinet' as a misnomer. The essence of a cabinet is not that it is executive—the executive lies in that several ministers [*sic*]—nor that it is responsible to a single parliament. It lies in the sense of intimacy and collegiality, and though the name is at this moment criticized in one or two quarters, I should be inclined to let it run on concurrently with the phrase 'prime ministers' conference' in the belief that it will, before long, be generally accepted. There is a disadvantage from the point of view of ordinary phraseology in having two conferences, one the imperial conference and the other the prime ministers' conference. It would be simpler if the word 'conference' were used habitually of the imperial conference and the other came to be known as imperial cabinet, or if you like, imperial council.

I feel the same difficulty about your suggestions for altering the nomenclature of the British Empire itself. I am all with you in introducing as an alternative title some such phrase as 'United Nations of the British Commonwealth' or 'British Commonwealth' by itself, but there are to my mind considerable disadvantages in a formal rechristening of ourselves. For one thing the word 'empire' is convenient when it is applied not only to the partnership of free nations but to the whole, including dependencies and protectorates of all sorts and kinds. For another it is enshrined in history, literature and tradition and many good people would be desperately against a formal change. Last but not least the word 'empire' has a natural adjective belonging to it—'imperial', and none of the substitutes lend themselves with any ease to adjectival use. One of the difficulties which the word 'Dominion' has had in replacing 'colony' is just that the latter has a natural adjective which the former lacks. After all the connotation of a name depends mainly on its actual meaning in fact, and if we get the constitution of the Empire on the desired basis, the word 'empire' and 'imperial' will finally and definitely acquire the signification we desire, viz., the conception of a broader unity covering many nations dropping any idea of a domination or subordination.

As regards the flag, I am not quite sure whether this is a matter so much for the constitutional conference as for action by each Dominion; in any case I hope that the basis of the different flags will be the Union Jack as in the case of the present Canadian, Australian and New Zealand flags, each of which consists of a distinctive national device on some form of Union Jack. In strict logic there ought to be either a single common flag for the Empire, or, if the Union Jack is retained for that purpose, the United Kingdom ought to invent its own variant (it has its local variants for the original component parts).

Anyhow I think the immediate practical thing to do is to get the present imperial cabinet to appoint a committee to draft an agenda for the forthcoming constitutional conference and among other items on the agenda to include a definite set of draft resolutions. I may try my hand during the next few days at drafting some resolutions and if so will send them along to you. Yours ever,

L. S. Amery

48   From T. Casement   Vol. 24, no. 41

At the suggestion of Art O'Brien, President de Valera agreed that Tom Casement, who was a brother of Sir Roger Casement and had fought under Smuts in East Africa, should see him in London and try to get his support for the Irish nationalist cause at the imperial conference. Tom Casement had unofficial talks with Smuts in the latter half of June. (*See* D. Macardle, *The Irish Republic*, pp. 481–2.)

Castle FFrench
County Galway
[Ireland]
30 May 1921

Dear General Smuts, I am sending you some stuff to meet you at Madeira. It tells its own tale.

The Southern elections did not come off.[1] There were 124 Sinn

[1] Under the Government of Ireland Act of 1920 two parliaments were to be elected, one for southern Ireland and one for northern Ireland. In the twenty-six southern counties no elections took place because in all the ordinary constituencies the Republican candidates were unopposed. The four members for Trinity College were also unopposed. The Unionists were against self-government for Ireland.

Fein nominations and 4 Unionists (Trinity College Dublin). They all went without a contest on the thirteenth. In the Six Counties (Carsonia) the elections came off on the 24th.[1] I regret to say that the anti-Partitionists did not get a show. Intimidation, personation, etc. carried the day. It was not creditable to the winning side. In Belfast, the anti-Partitionists are roughly a quarter of the population. There are sixteen seats. The Partitionists got fifteen and the Anti's one.[2] A clear case of unfairness. There are about 3,000 men interned untried at Ballykinbar Camp. They were not allowed to vote. Arthur Griffith, also untried, is an inmate of Mountjoy Jail since November last. He was not allowed out. Still, he got in for Tyrone by an overwhelming majority.

I hope to see you in London, but I won't worry you until I feel that you have a few minutes to give to an old friend and comrade and one who has stuck to you through all kinds of weather. That is my excuse for bombarding you with Irish stuff the last few months, I know you are a busy man. You have many big things on hand in England and your time will be fully taken up. You understand me. My language is crude, I know, but when a man has stood through thick and thin and fought for another man he feels he has some slight excuse to bring his own affairs before him.

I want you to try and come for a few days to Ireland. I want you to meet the kindliest people in the world and I want you to see the country. You will then grasp what it means to us to have our country to ourselves.

Try and wade through some of the stuff I am sending to you. The *Terror in Action* is written by a good Englishman, who has been over here and seen with his own eyes.

I had a jolly nice letter from Mrs Smuts the other day. I hope you left her and the children well. She asks me not to be unhappy. It is a difficult thing at present.

We are living in great times. We have just come out of a war that was fought for peace. Look at the world today. England and the U.S.A. should naturally be friends. They are now drifting apart. Why? Ireland! If they were friends, the peace of the world would be assured, but the Irish question is causing untold bitterness in America and until it is settled there can be no real lasting friendship.

Privately, I have always felt that you would some day be a big

---

[1] In the six counties of Ulster a parliament of Northern Ireland was duly elected. 'Carsonia' refers to Sir Edward Carson, leader of the Unionists until 1921.

[2] The anti-Partitionists were nationalists, opposed to the division of Ireland into two separately governed parts.

factor in settling our question. I may be wrong, but I have pinned a lot of faith on you. You went through the mill years ago and see things quite differently from the narrow political point.

Sir Edmund Talbot (Lord Fitzalan), the new viceroy of Ireland, appears to be in a quandary. He accepted the post on an understanding. The promises have not been carried out. He only stayed two days in Ireland and then returned to London. Being a Howard and the most powerful family in England, he won't be let down without a fight.

You can't imagine how every one longs for peace in Ireland, but we cannot and won't submit to the Terror that is in force at present.[1] No one is safe. Any soldier, Auxiliary, Black and Tan, can pick one up and put him in a lorry. Later on one is found shot. 'Shot trying to escape'. The poor women are the worst sufferers. They never can tell from hour to hour when a lorry may roll up, take her husband or son away and it is a million to one he is never seen alive again. A fine band of men at Westminster daily try and get answers from the government without result. Amongst them are friends of mine, Commander Kenworthy, Wedgewood Benn and several others. Kenworthy is fine, and, being the heavy-weight champion of the navy, does not care a d— for the crowd. No doubt you will meet him in London. He is a fine man.

Don't throw my parcel overboard. You have a few days quietness on board. That is my idea for sending it to you. Lots of good wishes to you and best of luck. Your friend,

Tom Casement

49   From H. Plunkett   Vol. 24, no. 211A

Kilteragh
Foxrock
Co. Dublin
8 June 1921

Dear General Smuts, Twice during the war you were kind enough to listen to my appeal for help in getting the Irish problem settled. Few pronouncements upon that old sore in recent times have had a more profound effect than your warning to the Empire, when you last left Europe, that an unsettled Ireland would prove its ruin.[2] Many are looking to you for a further effort at the imperial conference.

Ever since the armistice the Irish Dominion League has been

---

[1] See supra, p. 51, note 2.   [2] See vol. IV, pp. 273-4.

striving to educate public opinion upon what, an increasing number of people are coming to see, is now the only way out of the disastrous impasse into which the government has drifted. When the elections were coming on we sent the enclosed memorial[1] to the prime minister. Lord Robert Cecil, Sir Courtenay Ilbert, Professor Adams (whom you will remember in the prime minister's war secretariat) and many other men of sound judgment on constitutional questions joined in a letter asking Mr Lloyd George to give favourable consideration to this proposal. It was, however, simply ignored, neither the memorialists nor their British backers getting so much as a printed acknowledgement from a private secretary that the letter had been received.

Probably the reason for this treatment of the moderate Irishmen, who worked out this plan, is that they gave answer to the oft repeated assertion of the government that no one had proposed, or could propose, any alternative to the Government of Ireland Act 1920. The memorial gives a direct denial to that statement. I need not tell you we should not have sent it in to the government unless we had very good reason to believe that it would have been accepted over here had the initial step—'a firm offer of full Dominion status' been made by the prime minister as proposed in the memorial. I sent the memorial to Dr Kelly, the Roman Catholic Bishop of Ross, who I think is universally regarded as politically the wisest in that hierarchy. In the course of his letter he thus comments on the proposal:

In my opinion your plan of settlement and procedure justifies your claim that you substantially give to all parties, both in Ireland and in England, what they have asked or offered; and that your proposal can be adopted without any climb down on the part of the government, the military, Sinn Fein, Ulster, or the moderates, both Nationalist and Unionist. I also agree in the belief of the memorial that a discussion in a constituent assembly would now lead to a united Ireland.

The holding of the elections on 24 May for the whole of Ireland, without any concession in regard to the constituent assembly, of course prevents the plan of the memorialists being carried out as originally proposed. Ulster has set up a parliament in which only the members of the Carson party will be present, both the Nationalists and the Sinn Feiners having given pledges at their election that they would not recognize the institution. In the rest of Ireland, out of the 128 seats 124 were conceded to Sinn Fein without any opposition. Dublin University returned (also unopposed) four

[1] Omitted by the editor.

members; and these alone will take their seats.[1] The chief secretary[2] goes on proclaiming that he hopes the Southern parliament will function; but he knows it will not, and all preparations are being made for a continuance of the military government.

I still believe that in 'full Dominion status' is to be found the only possible solution of the Irish problem. If the government would make the firm offer the memorial suggests, the plan could be worked. There would have to be a new election in Southern Ireland, because Sinn Fein has not put forward its best men and the Dominionists (as I think all the moderate people in Ireland who have given any thought at all to the problem may now be called) are wholly unrepresented. But the Northern elections would of course stand, and the Northern government could go on functioning while the constituent assembly was sitting.

I recognize, however, that the situation has become much more difficult owing to the government's persistence in military repression. They have staked their all on the success of partition. The king, I see in today's papers, is to open the parliament of the favoured six counties this month.

In this situation it occurs to me that you may see your way, on account of the imperial interests involved, to use your personal influence to promote an Irish settlement. From a pretty full knowledge of my countrymen at home and abroad I can truthfully say that no living statesman would be more acceptable to the majority of the Irish people as a political adviser than yourself. You would of course need to be satisfied that there were some definite issues which the imperial conference could be reasonably asked to decide and these are suggested in the very able memorandum[3] I enclose.

The author is Mr A. D. Lindsay, of Balliol College, Oxford, who paid me a visit a few weeks ago, with two other Oxford friends, in order to discuss the Irish situation with some of us who are in close personal touch with it. He tells me that you may be going to Oxford in which case you would have an opportunity of talking it over with him.

I find myself wholly in agreement with the memorandum, so far as its general principles—and ultimately these are, of course, what matter—are concerned. The only factor to which he may not have attached sufficient importance is the British party politics

---

[1] These four and two senators were the only members present at the opening of the parliament of southern Ireland which did not meet again until 14 January 1922 when it ratified the treaty with Great Britain.

[2] The chief secretary for Ireland in the British cabinet was Sir Hamar Greenwood.

[3] Omitted by the editor. It is entitled: 'The Application of Dominion Home Rule to Ireland'.

factor. For the last ten years—more particularly during the convention[1] and since the armistice—I have held that the saving of the face of the party in power at Westminster was the golden key to the Irish, and indeed to many another problem of world importance.

I have only to add that if at any time you wish to come to Ireland incog. and meet a few of the people who count over here but do not appear in public or go to London, I should most gladly do myself the honour of placing my house at your disposal. Believe me, with great respect, sincerely yours,

Horace Plunkett

50   From C. Courtney[2]   Vol. 24, no. 69

15 Cheyne Walk
Chelsea S.W.3
9 June 1921

Dear General Smuts, A few lines I must have written in any case to welcome you to England and to say how much I am looking forward to seeing you in this little house and soon: but I have also something definite to note.

You will soon find that people of many points of view are looking to you to help us about Ireland—in fact you are almost in as dangerous a position as Wilson was when he landed in France. I know you will not, like him, make glorious speeches first and realize or not realize their application afterwards. You will be hearing the government side of the Irish question and of course you will see some of that noble band of moderates of the Plunkett type; but I should like you to see a friend of mine who is an out and out Republican and deep in the counsels of the Sinn Fein organization —Sir Erskine Childers. You probably know him and certainly all about him. He is a man of very fine character and intellect but I think overwrought since his fine work in the war. He and his wife are great friends of mine and I believe a word would bring him over from Dublin to see me and if, as I hope, it would be quite natural for you to come here to dine or lunch one day—giving me four or five to arrange it—there might be a little quiet talk, the quicker the better, over that side of the problem.

I feel you could influence him and his colleagues on the side of moderation and what is practical. They sometimes seem to prefer

---

[1] An Irish convention sat from June 1917 to April 1918 to make proposals for the government of Ireland. *See also* vol. III, p. 521, note 2; p. 635, note 2.

[2] *See* vol. II, p. 230, note 1.

heroic martyrdom to getting what they want by consent. But both sides have got into a state of hysteria which makes them hardly responsible; and yet I feel as if a touch, or word, if it is the right one, might transform the whole scene.

You are probably already arranged for Sunday afternoon but, if not, I am always in to tea and this next Sunday the chief justice of New Zealand is coming to call—Sir Robert Stout, I believe an able man. At any rate he was an admirer of my husband which recommends him to me.

I have already written too long a letter and yet not said half I could in a fruitful visit! Your very friendly

Kate Courtney

51   From Lord Fitzalan   Vol. 24, no. 90

1 Buckingham Palace Gardens
S.W.1
13 June 1921

My dear General Smuts, Lord Stamfordham[1] has just rung me up saying he was most anxious I should see you.

I very much want to do so, only I am tied to my bed for a day or two with slight vein trouble and therefore cannot get to you.

Is it possible for you to find time to come to me here? Any hour you name I will keep free for you.

I am sending my private secretary, Mr [S. G.] Tallents, with this in case you are in and can give verbal answer.

If not, my telephone number is Vic: 1612.

Welcome back to England. Yours very sincerely,

Fitzalan

52   To Lord Stamfordham   Vol. 24, no. 261

Nos. 52–7, 59, 62 are copies of documents in the royal archives at Windsor Castle in the series numbered Geo. V. K. 1702. They have been added to the Smuts Collection with the gracious permission of Her Majesty Queen Elizabeth II.

Savoy Hotel
London
14 June 1921

Dear Lord Stamfordham, For your confidential information I enclose a copy of a letter to the prime minister with a draft declaration

---

[1] Then private secretary to King George V.

which will reach him tomorrow. I had a very satisfactory interview with Lord Fitzalan but thought it better not to show him the draft declaration before it has reached the prime minister. Ever yours sincerely,

J. C. Smuts

FIRST ENCLOSURE

To D. Lloyd George

14 June 1921

My dear Prime Minister, I am very sorry to hear that indisposition is keeping you away from London at this moment. The great urgency and importance of the following matter must be my excuse for writing you this note.

I need not enlarge to you on the importance of the Irish question for the Empire as a whole. The present situation is an unmeasured calamity; it is a negation of all the principles of government which we have professed as the basis of Empire, and it must more and more tend to poison both our Empire relations and our foreign relations. Besides, the present methods are frightfully expensive in a financial no less than a moral sense;[1] and what is worse they have failed. What is to be the next move, for the present situation may not last. I believe there are certain hopeful elements in the present position, of which full use should immediately be made— with perhaps far-reaching results. In the first place the establishment of the Ulster parliament definitely eliminates the coercion of Ulster, and the road is clear now to deal on the most statesmanlike lines with the rest of Ireland.

In the second place, the King (as he tells me)[2] is going to Belfast next week to open the Ulster parliament. Now it is questionable whether the King should go at all. But his going would be fully justified if the occasion were made use of by him to make a really important declaration on the whole question. I believe that in the present universal mistrust and estrangement the King could be made use of to give a most important lead, which would help you out of a situation that is well-nigh desperate. The Irish must accept it as coming from the King, and in that way the opening might be given you for a final settlement. I would suggest that in his speech to the Ulster parliament the King should foreshadow the grant of

[1] In reply to a question in the house of commons on 18 December 1919 Churchill said that the monthly cost of the 43,000 regular British troops then in Ireland was £860,000.

[2] Smuts had lunched with the King at Windsor on 13 June. For an account of their conversation about the Irish situation and what ensued *see* H. Nicolson, *King George V*, pp. 349–54.

Dominion status to Ireland, and point out that the removal of all possibility of coercing Ulster now renders such a solution possible. The promise of Dominion status *by the King* would create a new and definite situation which would crystallize opinion favourably both in Ireland and elsewhere. Informal negotiations could then be set going with responsible Irish leaders and the details—financial and strategic—might be discussed with the Dominion prime ministers, if you like to do so.

I enclose a suggested declaration to be inserted in the King's speech. Such a declaration would not be a mere kite, but would have to be adopted by you as your policy, and the King could of course only make it on your advice. I am not acquainted with the details of the Irish situation, but I should consider the attempt well worth the making and think you would in doing so be supported by all the Dominion prime ministers.

SECOND ENCLOSURE

Declaration

I have come here today not only to open this parliament but also and especially to testify to my love for and sympathy with Ireland and the Irish people as a whole. As the sovereign and executive head of the British Empire, I bring to Ireland today a message of good will and sympathy in all the trials and sorrows through which she is passing. My world-wide Empire is a system of human government which rests on certain principles and ideals of freedom and co-operation, which must find their application in Ireland no less than in the other parts. And it is my desire that the full and fair application of these principles to Ireland may lead her out of the miseries of the present to the happiness and contentment which characterizes all my other self-governing Dominions. I trust that the establishment of this parliament for North-east Ireland will be found to have removed what has in the past proved an insurmountable obstacle to the realization of this high destiny for Ireland as a whole, and that the path is now clear for a lasting settlement of the age-long misunderstanding and estrangement. God grant that there may be found here too that spirit of wisdom and moderation which under somewhat similar circumstances brought lasting appeasement and reconciliation to another great portion of my Empire.

53   From E. W. M. Grigg to Lord Stamfordham
Vol. 24, no. 151A

10 Downing Street
14 June 1921

My dear Lord Stamfordham, General Smuts came in to see me just after our conversation on the telephone this morning. He had just left Lord Fitzalan, whom I have also seen this afternoon. General Smuts's suggestions are going down to the prime minister by bag this evening.

I am much impressed by General Smuts's view, because he has great insight into political situations; but there is a very difficult balance to be struck between conflicting considerations. I know the prime minister has had the position much at heart, and I am sure he will give his whole mind immediately to General Smuts's suggestions. I am, Yours sincerely,

E. W. M. Grigg[1]

54   Memorandum   Box G, no. 5A

EXTRACT FROM A MEMORANDUM[2] SUBMITTED TO THE
KING BY LORD STAMFORDHAM, 29 JUNE 1921

I went to Downing Street this morning and saw Sir Edward Grigg for a moment. I reminded him how keen the prime minister had been on Friday morning on sending General Smuts to talk to de Valera,[3] and I ventured to express the hope, which I felt sure was Your Majesty's wish, that General Smuts might now go to Dublin. Sir Edward's reply was—that the prime minister had really placed the whole matter in General Smuts's hands, and that the latter was carefully considering whether affairs had arrived at a point when any conversations with de Valera would be helpful. Apparently that situation has not yet been reached, as General Smuts was at the moment at the imperial conference, listening to what Sir Edward Grigg said was a very important speech by Mr [A.] Meighen on the Japanese treaty.[4]

---

[1] Sir Edward Grigg, then one of Lloyd George's private secretaries, wrote the new draft of the King's speech incorporating Smuts's suggestions.

[2] The memorandum is annotated, in the handwriting of George V, as follows: 'If de V. won't come over I hope Smuts will go to him and make him come. G.R.I.'

[3] On 24 June the British government invited De Valera and Sir James Craig to a conference in London. Craig accepted. De Valera hesitated but did not refuse outright. In these circumstances it was suggested that Smuts should see him in Dublin.

[4] The question before the imperial conference was the renewal of the Anglo-Japanese alliance of 1902. At the imperial conference of 1911 all the Dominions

55   From E. W. M. Grigg to Lord Stamfordham
Vol. 24, no. 151B

Private   10 Downing Street
29 June 1921

My dear Lord Stamfordham, The prime minister wishes me to send you the enclosed message[1] which gives our latest information from Dublin Castle. Sir James Craig has replied to de Valera's request for a separate preliminary conference that he thinks they will do better by both attending the conference to which they have been invited in London. General Smuts is keeping touch with the Sinn Feiners, and is ready to give them his advice and assistance the moment he thinks he can usefully do so.[2] Yours very sincerely,

E. W. M. Grigg

56   To Lord Stamfordham   Vol. 24, no. 265A

Savoy Hotel
London
1 July 1921

My dear Lord Stamfordham, Will you please inform His Majesty that, after consultation with Mr Lloyd George, I have decided, at the invitation of Mr de Valera, to visit the latter in Dublin on Tuesday, 5th inst. I want to ascertain his views on the Irish question and to try and see whether it is not possible for him, when he comes to London to see the prime minister, to arrive at some satisfactory basis of agreement, so as to minimize the possibilities of a conference of this nature coming to naught. Under these circumstances I shall not be able to accept the command of Their Majesties to be present at the state banquet on 4 July, and I shall be very glad if you would ask Their Majesties to excuse me in view of the peculiar circumstances.

I may say that not more than half a dozen people are aware of my projected visit and I intend to keep matters as secret as possible.

On my return I shall ask you to arrange a time when I may have the opportunity of reporting to His Majesty what has transpired. With kind regards, Believe me, Yours sincerely,

J. C. Smuts

had approved its continuance but Canada now opposed renewal. In February 1922 the alliance was superseded by a four-power treaty between Britain, the United States, Japan and France. *See infra*, p. 110, note 2.

[1] Here is inserted in an unidentified handwriting: 'from, I think, H. Greenwood'.

[2] The document is annotated as follows: 'This seems all right. G.R.I.'; 'Just come 7 p.m. S.'

57   From Lord Stamfordham   Vol. 24, no. 237A

Buckingham Palace
1 July 1921

My dear General Smuts, The King desires me to say how delighted
he is that you have accepted Mr de Valera's invitation to visit him
in Dublin on Tuesday next. For His Majesty is impressed with the
belief that *you* of all men will be able to induce Mr de Valera to be
reasonable and agree to a settlement.

Their Majesties are only sorry that this important mission will
prevent your being present at Monday's state banquet.

The King will be here till the 9th when he leaves for the Channel
Islands and will be delighted to see you if you are back in London
before that date. Yours very truly,

Stamfordham

58   Notes   Box N, no. 89

These notes, in Smuts's handwriting, are headed: 'De Valera's position—
Dublin meeting'.

[5 July 1921]

Not willing to accept invitation to *joint* conference because

1. Ulster having been satisfied, dispute now is (as it has really
always been) between British government and majority in Ireland,
and conference should be confined to two. Ulster may be dealt
with separately where her interests are concerned.

2. Three-cornered negotiation will lead to no result, as British
government will only exploit differences between two Irish
sections.

(Real reason is de Valera does not wish to be put on same level as
Craig who has only minority behind him)

With regard to solution de Valera thinks Irish people should have
choice between republic plus treaty of limitations and Dominion
status without limitations. No offer to which force is only alternative will satisfy Irish.

Full Dominion status if offered will receive most careful consideration and republican administration will legalize Irish voting
on it, as they did last election.

If Dominion status is accepted Ireland wishes to be friend and considered as friend, and no limitations in respect of defence should be imposed.

59   Memorandum   Box G, no. 5B

MEMORANDUM OF A CONVERSATION BETWEEN THE
KING AND GENERAL SMUTS AT BUCKINGHAM PALACE,
THURSDAY, 7 JULY 1921

General Smuts explained that he was determined not to go to see de Valera until asked to do so by the latter, and after Sir James Craig's refusal to meet de Valera the latter wrote to General Smuts and asked if he would come and confer. He arrived in Dublin on the morning of the 5th and met at the Mansion House in Dublin, de Valera, accompanied by Griffith, Barton [R. C.] and Duggan [E. J.].

General Smuts explained that he did not come as an emissary of the British government, nor did he bring any offer from them. In fact he had nothing to do with the British government. He came as a friend who had passed through very similar circumstances, and he could assure them that in England there was an intense desire for peace; that the King himself was most anxious for a settlement; and General Smuts could assure them that the words uttered in the King's speech at Belfast were a true interpretation of His Majesty's feelings.

De Valera expressed distrust of the British government or of a conference at the invitation of the prime minister. The prime minister had asked de Valera to meet Craig at a round table, where they would be like two school boys—the two would be sure to disagree and the prime minister would profit by their disagreement and in this way place them both at a disadvantage. General Smuts pointed out to de Valera in the strongest possible terms that in refusing the invitation de Valera would be making the greatest mistake of his life. The invitation from the prime minister was unconditional, and a refusal on his (de Valera's) part would have the worst possible effect and would turn public opinion against him in America, indeed all over the world, and even in Ireland. General Smuts strongly urged him to offer to go to the conference with the prime minister without Craig,[1] but to avoid doing or saying anything

---

[1] De Valera and his colleagues did confer with Lloyd George (14–21 July) but the proposals of the British government, which offered southern Ireland Dominion status but insisted on recognition of the parliament of northern Ireland, that is, partition, were rejected by the republican government.

which would hurt public feeling in Ulster; accept the settlement of Ulster—it has got its own government; but tell the prime minister that he came as the representative of south Ireland. General Smuts thought both the prime minister and Sir James Craig would agree to such a proposal.

The next question which de Valera lay stress upon was the partition of Ireland, consequent upon the Home Rule Bill. General Smuts replied that it was not a partition, but merely that Ulster, which has always proved the obstacle, is now out of the way. Surely de Valera would recognize this. Both in Mr Gladstone's bill[1] and in Mr Asquith's[2] the one stumbling block had always been Ulster, with the result that Ulster, which did not want home rule, has got home rule, and the rest of Ireland is quit of Ulster but is left without the home rule she wants; therefore, obviously, the right thing for de Valera to do is to cease talking or troubling about the Ulster partition, accept what has been done, and talk to the British government about south Ireland.

During the argument about the conference in London, Griffith was evidently impressed with what Smuts said and supported his advice. The others were silent, but by their manner Smuts was inclined to think that they also agreed with him. Mr Erskine Childers came into the room for a short time, and struck General Smuts as being in a highly wrought and somewhat neurotic condition.

In the afternoon the conversations were resumed.

General Smuts asked de Valera the point blank question, 'What do you propose as a solution of the Irish question?' The reply to this was: 'A republic'. General Smuts: 'Do you really think that the British people are ever likely to agree to such a republic?' De Valera replied that he would be prepared to be bound by a treaty with England, as of course Ireland would always be dependent chiefly upon England for her markets. He then talked a great deal about self-determination, idealism, blood of martyrs etc. etc. General Smuts let him talk himself out in this direction.

General Smuts said: 'I can talk from experience as to republics bound by treaty,[3] for I served as a minister, attorney-general, in the

[1] Gladstone's bill, the first to give Ireland a measure of home rule, was introduced in 1886. It was defeated in the house of commons when a section of the Liberal party known as the Unionists joined the Conservatives to oppose it. The chief reason for opposition was the belief that home rule would subject Ulster to the rule of the south.

[2] Asquith's Home Rule Bill was passed by the house of commons in 1912 and rejected by the house of lords. Before it could be enacted in 1914 under the terms of the Parliament Act, a powerful Unionist agitation designed to prevent its implementation, by force if necessary, was set on foot in Ulster. The operation of the Act was suspended during the war and it became a dead letter.

[3] Smuts was referring to the convention of London of 1884. See vol. I, p. 21, note I.

Transvaal Republic, under such conditions. The result was, quarrelling day and night over breaches on our part of the treaty, in which we very likely were to blame;[1] but whoever were to blame, the end was a three years' war, at the end of which our country was devastated.' So he begged de Valera, even if the British people would give Ireland a republic under those conditions, not to take it. He told de Valera: 'We in the Transvaal have worked both systems, and look at the result. We have had a general election on the very question whether or not South Africa should again be a republic, and a large majority declared that they did not want a republic but free membership of the British Empire.' So General Smuts said to de Valera: 'As a friend I cannot advise you too strongly against a republic. Ask what you want, but not a republic.'

De Valera said that the question must be decided by the Irish people. They had elected him the president of the republic,[2] and he must do whatever they decided. 'If the status of Dominion rule is offered, I will use all our machinery to get the Irish people to accept it.' He talked seriously about the republic which had been set up some time ago[3] and had functioned regularly and was doing excellent work, but was upset and knocked out by the British army. The future form of the government must now be settled by the Irish people themselves.

The conversation then turned upon the question of Ireland having its own army and navy. De Valera said: 'We do not want to have a separate army and navy, but if such restriction is put into the act it would be regarded by us as an insult. We must be trusted not to set up an army or navy, and any condition suggestive of doubting our word would be looked upon as a stigma. Already there is a fear that if an agreement is come to, England will ask us to raise regiments and build battleships.'

De Valera thought that what Ireland wanted was a lasting settlement. Smuts asked what was the alternative to such a settlement, and de Valera replied: 'To go on as we are now; we are winning and the British army is beaten.'

Smuts spoke seriously about the murders. De Valera replied: 'They are not murders or crimes. We are at war and such methods

[1] As state attorney of the South African Republic Smuts had contested every charge of violation of the convention made by the British government against his government. *See* vol. I, **64** and p. 203, note 1.

[2] Having escaped out of Lincoln Gaol in February 1919, De Valera was elected president of the Irish Republic by the dail on 1 April.

[3] The Irish Republic was first proclaimed on 24 April 1916, but the republicans were unable to set up a government until 1919 when the first dail Eireann met on 21 January, ratified the Republic and issued a declaration of independence.

are our only means of warfare against a regular army such as that which is opposing us. We are winning; and if we continue, in two years' time we should have a republic. An ideal form of government would be to leave the British government out altogether and the north and south of Ireland to unite.'

Smuts thinks the invitation to the conference will be accepted, but they are small people and very suspicious both of the British government and of the prime minister, and are afraid that he will get the better of them in a conference.

General Smuts thought that de Valera was impressed with his arguments urging him not to refuse to come to the conference, his (Smuts's) views on the partition question, and also with regard to a republic bound by treaty; and on these three points General Smuts hoped that he had done good.

60   From A. S. Green   Vol. 24, no. 151

59 Cadogan Gardens
[London]
[July 1921]

My dear General Smuts, I think the first moves today are very promising. Negotiations once begun cannot stop short of a settlement.

I had a letter yesterday expressing the utmost general suspicion and distrust, and urging on me the view that without *your* support there would be no possibility of consenting to a parley. I now have the highest hopes, and I am confident that when you meet these men you will find they are not without reason, intelligence, and character.

More than a truce[1] will be needed if they are to come to London. After the identifications possible on such a journey (and photographs) they would return to a far greater danger than they left, that is, if peace were not made.

I am always at your disposal, and this note of hopefulness needs no answer. Yours most sincerely,

A. S. Green

[1] The assistant under-secretary for Ireland, A. W. Cope, had been exploring the possibility of a truce between the British and the Irish Republican forces. This was concluded on 9 July.

61 To S. M. Smuts

Vol. 24, no. 269

Savoy Hotel
London
14 Juli 1921

Liefste Mamma, Ik hoop 29 Juli van hier te vertrekken—over 14 dagen. Mijn hart is in Afrika. Maar ik heb goed werk hier gedaan, en over de geheele wereld politiek zal gevoeld worden de invloed die ik hier heb kunnen uitoefenen—Asië, Amerika, Ierland. Maar mijn hart is en blijft in Afrika—en te Doornkloof. Ik ben vol heimwee. Dankie voor jou laatste brief. Ik doe onderzoek omtrent Kate Opperman.

Ik slaap nog altijd snachts by de Gilletts, en ben gelukkig daar. Beide hij en zij zijn van de beste. Er is een sterk gevoel in Engeland om naar Z. Afrika te verhuizen. Ik hoop zij zullen ook komen. Laatste Saterdag en Sondag was ik te Street by de oude Clarks. Zout en goud der aarde. Geef mijn zoentjes en liefde aan de kleine Doornkloof familie. 1000 zoentjes voor jou.

Pappa

TRANSLATION

Savoy Hotel
London
14 July 1921

Dearest Mamma, I hope to leave here on 29 July, within fourteen days. My heart is in Africa. But I have done good work here, and the influence I have been able to exercise here will be felt throughout world politics—in Asia, America, Ireland. But my heart is and remains in Africa—and at Doornkloof. I am very homesick. Thank you for your last letter. I am making enquiries about Kate Opperman.[1]

I still sleep at the Gilletts at night and am happy there. Both he and she are of the best. There is a strong desire in England to emigrate to South Africa. I hope they will come too. Last Saturday and Sunday I was at Street with the senior Clarks. Salt and gold of the earth. Give my kisses and love to the little Doornkloof family. A thousand kisses for you.

Pappa

[1] Madame Kate Opperman was a South African professional singer who was consulted about singing lessons for one of Smuts's daughters.

62   To George V   Vol. 24, no. 273A

Savoy Hotel
London
4 August 1921

Your Majesty, It was my intention to ask Lord Stamfordham to arrange an interview when I might have the opportunity of saying good-bye, but I regret that I have to leave London before Your Majesty returns. I embark from Southampton at 4 p.m. on Friday, 5 August.

Knowing the great personal interest that Your Majesty has taken in the projected Irish settlement, I think that I cannot do better than enclose for Your Majesty's information a copy of a letter I have written to Mr de Valera on the negotiations to date.

There is at the present time an apparent impasse but I cannot believe that public opinion will allow this golden opportunity to pass when the alternative is so grave. It is my earnest hope that Your Majesty will be able to keep in close touch with the progress of events and will use your great influence towards a settlement, which means so much to us all.

I take this opportunity of offering my respectful congratulations to Your Majesty on the success that is attending the Royal Yacht at Cowes, and I hope that both Your Majesties, the Queen and yourself, will enjoy a needed respite from your labours.

It was my intention to discuss with Your Majesty the possibility of His Royal Highness the Prince of Wales visiting South Africa on the conclusion of his tour in India. Perhaps if the contemplated visit to Japan falls through, His Royal Highness may be able to consider the possibility of a visit to the Union where the most cordial welcome awaits him, and where he will probably be able to find some rest and quiet from his all too strenuous labours. I am, Sir, Your obedient and humble servant,

J. C. Smuts

ENCLOSURE

To E. de Valera

Savoy Hotel
London
4 August 1921

My dear de Valera, Lane [E. F. C.] duly reported to me the substance of his conversations with you and handed me your letter of 31 July. He told me of your anxiety to meet and discuss the situation with Ulster representatives. Since then I have, as I wired you yesterday, done my best to bring about such a meeting, but Sir James Craig, while willing to meet you in a conference with Mr Lloyd George, still remains unwilling to meet you in his absence, and nothing that I have been able to do or say has moved him from that attitude. If you were to request a meeting with him, he will reply setting forth his position and saying that Ulster will not be moved from the constitutional position which she occupies under the existing legislation; she is satisfied with her present status and will on no account agree to any change.

On the other hand, both in your conversation with Lane and in your letter, you insist on Ulster coming into a United Ireland constitution, and unless that is done you say that no further progress can be made. There is therefore an impasse which I do not at present know how to get over. Both you and Craig are equally immovable. Force as a solution of the problem is out of the question both on your and his premises. The process of arriving at an agreement will therefore take time.

The result is that at this stage I can be of no further use in this matter, and I have therefore decided to adhere to my plan of sailing for South Africa tomorrow. This I regret most deeply, as my desire to help in pushing the Irish settlement one stage further has been very great. But I must bow to the inevitable.

I should like to add a word in reference to the situation as I have come to view it. I have discussed it very fully with you and your colleagues. I have also probed as deeply as I could into the Ulster position. My conviction is that for the present no solution based on Ulster coming into the Irish state will succeed. Ulster will not agree, she cannot be forced, and any solution on those lines is at present foredoomed to failure.

I believe that it is in the interest of Ulster to come in, and that the force of community of interests will over a period of years prove so great and compelling that Ulster will herself decide to join the Irish state. But at present an Irish settlement is only possible if the hard facts are calmly faced and Ulster is left alone. Not only will she not consent to come in, but even if she does, the Irish state will, I fear, start under such a handicap of internal friction and discordance that the result may well be failure once more.

My strong advice to you is to leave Ulster alone for the present, as the only line along which a solution is practicable; to concentrate on a free constitution for the remaining twenty-six counties, and, through a successful running of the Irish state and the pull of economic and other peaceful forces, eventually to bring Ulster into that state. I know how repugnant such a solution must be to all Irish patriots, who look upon Irish unity as a *sine qua non* of any Irish settlement. But the wise man, while fighting for his ideal to the uttermost, learns also to bow to the inevitable. And a humble acceptance of the facts is often the only way of finally overcoming them. It proved so in South Africa, where ultimate unity was only realized through several stages and a process of years; and where the republican ideal for which we had made unheard of sacrifices had ultimately to give way to another form of freedom.

My belief is that Ireland is travelling the same painful road as South Africa, and that, with wisdom and moderation in her leadership, she is destined to achieve no less success. As I said to you before, I do not consider one single, clean-cut solution of the Irish question possible at present. You will have to pass through several stages, of which a free constitution for southern Ireland is the first, and the inclusion of Ulster and the full recognition of Irish unity will be the last. Only the first stage will render the last possible, as cause generates effect. To reverse the process and begin with Irish unity as the first step is to imperil the whole settlement. Irish unity should be the ideal to which the whole process should be directed.

I do not ask you to give up your ideal, but only to realize it in the only way which seems to me at present practicable. Freedom will lead inevitably to unity; therefore begin with freedom—with a free constitution for the twenty-six counties—as the first and most important step in the whole settlement.

As to the form of that freedom, here too you are called upon to choose between two alternatives. To you, as you say, the republic is the true expression of national self-determination. But it is not the only expression; and it is an expression which means your final and irrevocable severance from the British league. And to this, as you know, the parliament and people of this country will not agree.

The British prime minister has made you an offer of the other form of freedom—of Dominion status—which is working with complete success in all parts of the British league. Important British ministers have described Dominion status in terms which must satisfy all you could legitimately wish for. Mr Lloyd George in his historic reply to General Hertzog at Paris,[1] Mr Bonar Law

---

[1] On 5 June 1919 a National party deputation from South Africa met D. Lloyd George, then prime minister of Great Britain, in Paris. It consisted of General J. B. M. Hertzog and N. C. Havenga from the Orange Free State, A. D. W. Wolmarans and Dr H. Reitz from the Transvaal, Dr D. F. Malan and F. W. Beyers from the Cape Province, Dr E. G. Jansen and A. T. Spies from Natal and Dr J. H. Gey van Pittius as secretary. On 28 April 1919 the deputation had, while in London, sent the prime minister a statement of its case in which it declared that its chief object was to lay before the British government 'the claim of the former republics to the restitution of

in a celebrated declaration in the house of commons;[1] Lord Milner, as secretary of state for the colonies, have stated their views, and they coincide with the highest claims which Dominion statesmen have ever put forward on behalf of their free nations.

What is good enough for these nations ought surely to be good enough for Ireland too. For Irishmen to say to the world that they will not be satisfied with the status of the great British Dominions would be to alienate all that sympathy which has so far been the main support of the Irish cause.

The British prime minister offers complete Dominion status to the twenty-six counties, subject to certain strategic safeguards which you are asked to agree to voluntarily as a free Dominion, and which we South Africans agreed to as a free nation in the Union of South Africa. To my mind, such an offer by a British prime minister, who—unlike his predecessors—is in a position to deliver the goods is an event of unique importance.

You are no longer offered a home rule scheme of the Gladstone

their national status obtaining before the war of 1899–1902'. On 8 May 1919, apparently at the request of Lloyd George, Smuts sent him a carefully drafted 'suggested reply' to this statement. At the Paris meeting Hertzog was the only spokesman for the deputation. Lloyd George asked a few questions and promised to send his answer within forty-eight hours (Smuts Collection, vol. LXXVIII, no. 60 (a), (b), (c)). Lloyd George's letter to the deputation, dated 7 June 1919, is given in some detail, but in Afrikaans translation, in C. M. van den Heever, *Generaal J. B. M. Hertzog*, pp. 419–21 and in J. J. van Rooyen, *Die Nasionale Party*, p. 90 and briefly quoted in English in D. F. Malan, *Afrikaner Volkseenheid*, pp. 62–3. It is substantially Smuts's 'suggested reply', several passages of which are incorporated verbatim. The passage on Dominion status in Smuts's draft is as follows: '[South Africa's] status in the world is surely no mean one. As one of the Dominions of the British Commonwealth they control their own national destiny in the fullest sense, and in regard to common imperial concerns they have the fullest right to conference and consultation before action is taken.' The equivalent passage in Lloyd George's letter reads: 'Finally I would point to the status which South Africa now occupies in the world. It is surely no mean one. As one of the Dominions of the British Commonwealth, they control their own national destiny in the fullest sense. In regard to the common imperial concerns, they participate in the deliberations which determine imperial policy on a basis of complete equality.' Some members of the deputation, including Hertzog, suspected the mind and hand of Smuts in Lloyd George's answer (*see* van den Heever, *Generaal J. B. M. Hertzog*, pp. 418, 421–2). But D. F. Malan saw in the quoted passage an 'authoritative declaration' by the British prime minister himself of South Africa's 'right of self-determination' even to the point of republican independence and contrasted this with the 'Smuts standpoint' of 'subordination' to an imperial 'super state'! (*See* Malan, *Afrikaner Volkseenheid*, pp. 62–7.) Smuts's description of what was really his own letter (no doubt deftly edited by Philip Kerr who, as the prime minister's private secretary, was present at his meeting with the deputation) as 'Mr Lloyd George's historic reply to General Hertzog at Paris' adds a further touch of ambiguity to a richly ironical situation. For it raises the question whether Smuts, when he wrote his 'suggested reply' for Lloyd George, did not have it in mind to commit a prime minister of Great Britain in writing to an advanced interpretation of Dominion status.

[1] *See* **24**.

or Asquith type, with its limited powers, and reservations of a fundamental character. Full Dominion status with all it is and implies is yours—if you will but take it. It is far more than was offered the Transvaal and Free State, who fought for freedom one of the greatest wars in the history of Great Britain, and one which reduced their own countries to ashes and their little people to ruins.

They accepted the far less generous offer that was made to them; from that foothold they then proceeded to improve their position, until today South Africa is a happy, contented, united and completely free country. What they have finally achieved after years of warfare and political evolution is now offered you—not in doles or instalments, but at once and completely. If, as I hope, you accept, you will become a sister Dominion in a great circle of equal states, who will stand beside you and shield you and protect your new rights as if these were their own rights; who will view an invasion of your rights or a violation of your status, as if it was an invasion and a violation of their own, and who will thus give you the most effective guarantee possible against any possible arbitrary interference by the British government with your rights and position. In fact the British government will have no further basis of interference with your affairs, as your relations with Great Britain will be a concern not of the British government but of the imperial conference, of which Great Britain will be only one of the seven members. Any questions in issue between you and the British government will be for the imperial conference to decide. You will be a free member of a great league, of which most of the other members will be in the same position as yourself; and the conference will be the forum for thrashing out any questions which may arise between members. This is the nature and the constitutional practice of Dominion freedom.

The difficulty in Ireland is no longer a constitutional difficulty. I am satisfied that from the constitutional point of view a fair settlement of the Irish question is now possible and practicable. It is the human difficulty which remains. The Irish question is no longer a constitutional but mostly a human problem.

A history such as yours must breed a temper, an outlook, passions, suspicions, which it is most difficult to deal with. On both sides sympathy is called for, generosity, and a real largeness of soul. I am sure that both the English and Irish peoples are ripe for a fresh start. The tragic horror of recent events, followed so suddenly by a truce and fraternizing all along the line, has set flowing deep fountains of emotion in both peoples and created a new political situation.

It would be the gravest reflection on our statesmanship if this auspicious moment is allowed to pass. You and your friends have now a unique opportunity—such as Parnell and his predecessors and successors never had—to secure an honourable and lasting peace for your people.

I pray to God that you may be wisely guided, and that peace may now be concluded, before tempers again change, and perhaps another generation of strife ensues. Ever yours sincerely,

s. J. C. Smuts

63   To A. B. and M. C. Gillett   Vol. 24, no. 302

R.M.S. Saxon
Sierra Leone
20 August 1921

This is Saturday; we have been here since Tuesday, and tomorrow we transfer to the *Kenilworth Castle* and sail for Cape Town, where we hope to arrive on 30 August. All the fires in the coal bunkers have not yet been put out, and this ship will be here at least another ten days, and will then either leave for the Cape or return to England according to the extent of the damage. I have had a most excellent time; have spent every day ashore in explorations by motor, train, and on foot. I have just returned from climbing the highest mountain in the neighbourhood. It is only 2,000 feet high, but you must know that it is now the heavy rainy season and that all the conditions for the climb make it quite arduous. I and the rest of the party enjoyed it most thoroughly. The local people are amazed at our energy, as they are languidly meandering along between their homes and offices, and never dream of such a thing as mountain climbing. But I have preached and set them an example of physical fitness under all circumstances, and I trust some good seed has been sown, quite apart from the pleasure and enjoyment I have had. I found here a South African in the garrison artillery who has made a collection of the most gorgeous butterflies; I have bought the collection, and have in mind to transfer it to the little family at 102, after Doornkloof has had their enjoyment of it. One very funny thing which struck me here was the language of the Natives of this town. I took it to be some Native dialect and only this morning a doctor passenger on my questioning him told me it sounded like Zulu. Well, their language is none other than English! English as brought from America by the freed slaves, of whom the original population consisted, and now corrupted still further by generations of corrupt usage. It is truly a horrible language as spoken by them!

This has been a truly blessed time of quiet reflection and reading for me. It has been a first-class rest, such as you can only get on a voyage. We hear by wireless only the faintest echoes of what is passing in the great world. Thus the curious fact that the Supreme Council[1] is finally abdicating in favour of the League of Nations by making the Silesian problem over to them![2] Thus, too, the publication of the De Valera correspondence, including my letter to him just before leaving. I gave authority for its publication only in the very last resort; I only trust that the government have made no improper use of it.[3] I remain not without hope that the Irish question is now on the way to settlement. I only regret that I am not there to help, as I could really help. But 'South Africa first' as the Hertzogites say! I cannot afford to give the impression in South Africa that I remain away from my post in order to lend a hand in foreign questions. I am sure I have sown good seed in England this time, and I must leave the germination and growth to other forces...

64   To A. B. Gillett   Vol. 24, no. 309

Pretoria
18 October 1921

I have just found a letter which I wrote to you on 9 September but forgot to post! Now I have destroyed it as being out of date.

We are just going on as usual. I am much occupied with all the sorts of questions with which governments have to deal nowadays —unemployment, absence of credit, and the general malaise which has followed the superficial and shortlived post-war prosperity.

Last year you will remember I appointed a financial conference to go into the banking and currency question; this conference paved the way for the Central Reserve Bank. A similar conference is again sitting here to go into the question of our return to the gold standard, and our possible dissociation from British sterling in the years to come. You will remember that our act suspended the gold basis till 1923; and now the question of policy arises what to do after that date. A sudden return to the gold standard will mean the ruin of

[1] The Supreme Council of the Allies, the successor of the Supreme War Council. It had control over matters arising out of the peace settlement. The United States was not represented on it.

[2] Under the treaty of Versailles plebiscites were to be held in Upper Silesia to determine German and Polish claims to it.

[3] Lloyd George gave Smuts's letter to the press on 14 August without De Valera's consent and before publication of the terms to which it referred. His action elicited immediate protest by the dail. (*See* D. Macardle, *The Irish Republic*, p. 505.)

the banks and the export of vast capital out of the country. At the same time we must keep the gold standard as our ideal to work to. I think the Central Reserve Bank is going to be a success. Our system of banking is very faulty and really obsolete. Every year we are in the greatest straits to finance our annual crop of all sorts. In fact, the two existing banks[1] do not seem to respond to the rapidly expanding requirements of the country. I have repeatedly discussed the question with Clegg [W. H.], and hope for some useful results. With us the process of deflation is perhaps proceeding too drastically. At any rate we have said a final farewell to all that inflation which is still running riot in Europe.

I see that Lloyd George is after all going to Washington. Briand [A.] is going simply to flee from the wrath to come in the coming session of the French chamber. I hope there is not a similar motive operating on George. I am rather unhopeful about this Washington conference.[2] I believe a jingo lot are now in command in America just as a militaristic crowd are in command in France; and I fear no real disarmament will result. In that case bankruptcy will do what the statesmen have failed to do. I see the other Dominions will be there. Well. I have much else to do. What a poor, uninteresting letter—like a page from a financial journal! Love to you and Margaret and the little family.

Jan

65   Press statement (1921)   Box G, no. 7A

In a speech at Pretoria on 21 October 1921 Smuts said that if the Pacific Dominions were to attend the Washington conference without a direct invitation from the United States sent to them through British diplomatic channels, then Dominion statehood would receive 'a serious setback'. The United States was, he declared, the only Allied power which had not recognized that status. If the Pacific Dominions did not attend the conference 'in their own right' a bad precedent would be set and 'the American challenge to Dominion status' will not have been properly met. He continued: '...if South Africa is to appear at an international conference it will be in her own right, and not by cover of the international rights of the British government'. Accordingly the Union was not represented at the Washington conference. (*The Times*, 24 October 1921.)

[1] The Standard Bank of South Africa, founded in 1862, and the National Bank of South Africa, founded in 1901.

[2] In view of the rapidly rising expenditure on naval construction by the United States, Great Britain and Japan, President Harding called a conference on naval limitation. It met at Washington on 12 November 1921 and nine powers were represented.

General Smuts has issued the following to the press:

My statement made some weeks ago about Dominion status in connection with the Washington conference has attracted widespread attention. It is evident from much that has been said both in South Africa and outside of it that there is some misunderstanding both of my attitude and of the constitutional point which has been raised. It may be generally useful if I attempt to remove some misconceptions and state the constitutional position as briefly and clearly as possible. Dominion status is a matter which is not only fundamental for the present critical Irish negotiations but also for the future peace and welfare of the whole British Empire. It was with that larger point of view, and that only, that I was concerned in making my original statement.

To make the position of Dominion status clear it is necessary to compare what happened at the peace conference with what is now happening in connection with the disarmament conference.

The peace conference was organized by the Supreme Council and on their invitation the governments of the Dominions as well as that of the United Kingdom were represented at the peace conference as equal governments of His Majesty the King. The plenipotentiaries were appointed by the king who was moved thereto by resolutions of the respective executives of the United Kingdom and the Dominions. The Dominions were not only invited but directly represented by their own delegates who ultimately signed the treaty on behalf of their countries. While the United Kingdom and the Dominions were thus individually represented on a footing of equality they were all recognized as forming a special group in the conference, and their delegates acted together on what was called the British Empire delegation in close consultation and co-operation. At Paris the Dominions had all the advantages of a recognized individual status and of consultation and mutual support in the British Empire delegation. Our individual standing was unquestioned, while our team work made us a really effective force in the conference. This is the great precedent which settled our international status and which I feel should be followed in future.

But what has now happened at the first great international conference called after Paris? Only the government of the United Kingdom has been invited by the government of the United States to attend the Washington conference. The Dominions, in spite of the Pacific position of three of them, have been simply ignored. Owing to the courtesy of the British government some Dominion statesmen will figure in the United Kingdom delegation; but they will formally appear as British representatives who came on an invitation extended to Great Britain alone. As Canada has not been invited Sir Robert Borden will appear as a member of the British delegation and not as a representative of Canada and will sign the disarmament treaty (if any) as a British, not as a Canadian plenipotentiary. Whereas at Paris the Dominions were represented as such on a joint Empire delegation, at Washington there will be only a British delegation in which the Dominions *as such* will not be found. As the states of the Empire are not directly represented at Washington, the Empire will not be represented there in its full authority as a group of states, and the full weight of the British Empire will not be exerted or felt.

I have been told that I am for playing a lone hand, that I am against team work, that I do not wish to go to Washington as a member of the British Empire but favour separate action. These remarks show how completely the real position is misunderstood. I want the Paris precedent followed at Washington and every subsequent international conference. I want the British Empire represented through its constituent equal states; there is no other way of giving it representation. The United Kingdom is not the British Empire, and a United Kingdom delegation does not become an Empire delegation by kindly slipping in some Dominion statesmen through a back door. Unity of diplomatic and international action does not mean that the Dominions are swallowed up and lose their identity as free agents; that is the obsolete imperialism which has disappeared for ever. Unity of action in the Empire means that a group of equal states, recognized and represented as equals, freely consult together and co-operate in their external relations. At Washington team work has been rendered impossible because the team has disappeared, and there is only a one-horse show. I have spoken because I do not want Washington to become a precedent for the future; because so far as is possible I wish to see the position put right and the Dominion representatives at that conference formally empowered to speak and sign for their Dominions; and because I wish the American government to understand the Dominion standpoint and recognize the Dominion status as the other powers have recognized it at Paris with the whole-hearted advocacy and support of the British government.

In saying what I have said I did not intend to strike a jarring note, but merely to stand up for that Dominion status which to me, and I feel sure to the nations of the Dominions, is a reality and the basic constitutional reality of our free imperial Commonwealth. This constitutional question apart, I feel the gravest concern and the most fervent wish for the success of the Washington conference. The eyes which once were turned to Paris, are today fixed on Washington. At Paris we ended the war but failed to make the peace. Will the peace be made at Washington, and the great darkness be lifted from the souls of the peoples? Away from the blood-stained soil of Europe and amid the more hopeful surroundings of the New World, a greater spirit may visit the hearts of the statesmen. The simple human ideals of faith, forgiveness and generosity may open a new chapter in our human story. The great pledge may be signed, the great prohibition passed against war and all its growing horrors. Our vast international debts may cease to breed bitterness between the nations and hold peaceful commerce down. And East and West, frightened by the spectre of the greater Armageddon looming in the future, may agree on a better way for the future. On that way the League of Nations may yet realize the great hopes and prayers which surrounded its birth at Paris.

Such are some of our hopes for Washington. May they not also be turned to bitter disappointment and despair.

66 To A. B. and M. C. Gillett   Vol. 24, no. 315

Pretoria
6 December 1921

I am on the point of leaving for the Free State where I shall be on a short political tour, and I drop you a line to wish the little family at 102 my best Christmas wishes. I send you all my dear love and you may be sure I am ever very close to you all.

News has just arrived that the Irish question has been settled on the lines on which I advised last August.[1] I do most sincerely wish that it is all right and that a new beginning will now be made in that land of sorrows. Washington also seems to be going well and at any rate a naval disarmament treaty and a Pacific arrangement will result from the present conference.[2] These are all good things and may well be the beginning of still better things. The economic

[1] On 6 December 1921 Irish and British negotiators signed 'Articles of Agreement for a Treaty between Great Britain and Ireland'. It was approved by the dail on 7 January 1922 but by only 64 votes to 57.

[2] In February 1922 a five-power treaty was signed by representatives of the United States, Great Britain, Japan, France and Italy to restrict naval construction of large ships to an agreed ratio, but France and Italy did not ratify the treaty. In addition, the nine powers reaffirmed the policy of the 'open door' in China, that is, equal access for all foreign trade and, by the four-power treaty, the United States, Great Britain, Japan and France agreed to respect one another's territorial rights in the Pacific ocean.

mess in the world will then claim undivided attention, and who knows whether there too solutions may not be found for problems which now appear insoluble. Let us have faith.

'The Lord advances and ever advances', as Walt Whitman says.[1] Why should we assume that just now He is in retreat? Good-bye, dear children. I send you kisses and embracings. Ever,

Jan

67   Press statement (1921)   Press cuttings, Vol. 36, no. 56

The following message was sent to the *New York World* by Smuts and reported in the *Star* (Johannesburg) on 10 December 1921.

I congratulate Irishmen in America and over the whole world on the successful solution at last of the Irish question. The settlement follows clearly on the lines on which I advised the Irish leaders to proceed last summer. To my mind it is a generous, workable settlement, and even if Ulster stands out today, her early entry into the Free State must become inevitable on economic grounds and be much accelerated by the successful functioning of the Free State conception of Dominion status which has been evolved in constitutional evolution. The old British Empire has once more proved its wonderful power of combining, as it does, the complete freedom and independence of each state with close association in a world wide group of free states. It satisfies both the sentiment of nationality and the tendency towards international co-operation which are the two most powerful forces of our time.

The Irish Free State, while remaining a member of a great group, becomes mistress of her own fate and can now proceed to realize the ideals of Irish genius to the spiritual enrichment, not only of Ireland, but also of mankind. Our prayers and best wishes accompany her.

68   To A. B. and M. C. Gillett   Vol. 25, no. 298

Pretoria
18 January 1922

Last week I missed the mail; I had begun a letter but at the last moment I was called away to Johannesburg in connection with the strike[2] and could not continue the letter. The strike has now been

---

[1] *See* vol. IV, p. 48, note 2.

[2] The great Witwatersrand strike began on New Year's Day when the Transvaal coal-miners came out. They were followed on 10 January by the gold-miners and the

on for ten days or more and the end is not yet in sight. Happily it has so far been free from violence, but this may soon be expected. The men have withdrawn all their union men from the pumps and other essential services. Several mines are flooding and will never restart. The outlook is black—blackest of all for white labour. It will all be over when you get this so I shall drop the subject...

Lloyd George's plans are meeting with great difficulty. Poincaré will prove most difficult.[1] In fact the French are returning to the eighteenth [*sic*] century, and a European coalition may have to be formed against them as was done by William III.[2] Good-bye dears; love from

Jan

69   To M. C. Gillett   Vol. 25, no. 299

Pretoria
1 February 1922

I could not write last week as I was away in connection with the strike. You can imagine in what a turmoil we are here. So far the strike has been orderly but big commandos of strikers are now drilling daily on the Rand and untoward developments may take place any moment. The government did its level best to prevent the strike and bring the parties together in a conference. But the conference has failed, the Natives are going back to their homes and many mines are flooding. The prospect is black indeed. The movement has now assumed a political character as the Labour and Nationalist parties have persuaded the deluded miners that they will help them out. The end will have come before you receive this. I am very sad over it all. Against stupidity the Gods fight in vain. It is very bad luck...

Your letters are a great solace in these days. With love to all,

Jan

workers in the power stations and engineering industries. The strikers opposed wage reductions. But the gold-miners were chiefly concerned to stop an attempt by the Chamber of Mines, which had to cut costs, to increase the ratio of black to white miners in semi-skilled work.

[1] After the collapse of the Anglo-American treaty of guarantee in 1919, France sought security against Germany by, among other measures, the conclusion of an Anglo-French pact. At the Cannes conference in 1921 Lloyd George and Briand reached agreement on the linked problems of security and French reparation demands but the French chamber repudiated Briand. He made way for Poincaré who was expected to enforce to the limit French claims under the treaty of Versailles.

[2] In 1689 William III, as king of England, directed a Grand Alliance of European powers for war against France. It included Austria, Spain, Sweden, the Netherlands, Savoy, Saxony, Bavaria and the Palatinate.

70   To M. C. Gillett   Vol. 25, no. 302

Rondebosch
[Cape Town]
23 February 1922

I mourn with you the loss of Braithwaite [W. C.]. He was a good man, and I don't blame him if he did not feel much interested in Gillett's bank and left the drudgery to such a glutton for banking details as Arthur. Only a few weeks ago I saw that Marburg had made him an honorary doctor for his History of Quakerism.[1] Now he is no more, except in that unknown greater life of the whole whither we are all bound. Peace to his ashes. I am sorry I never knew Janet, though I have often heard you and Arthur speak of her...

The strike still continues and is taking more and more to ways of violence. It is a very bad business. The men have chosen to be unbending just at a time when all over the world labour has either to bend or to break before the wild economic storm which is raging. I am very sorry, but I feel that if the men win, half the gold industry is dead, and if the Chamber of Mines win, they will return to their old dictatorial attitude towards labour. On the whole I imagine public opinion is behind the attitude of the government but you know what an unreliable thing public opinion is.

Ireland is again in a frightful mess. De Valera is determined to fight Griffith and Collins [M.] and the battle is not only between the living, but the spooks of the dead past join in the fray, and God only knows what is going to happen.[2] A big man in Ireland will pull them through, but I did not see him in my negotiations with the Irish leader. I did not meet Collins, and from Ireland I get favourable accounts of him.

Lloyd George is in a great mess. His European policy[3] is opposed by France, and at home the coalition is going. The coalition Liberals would be nowhere without the genius and personality of Lloyd George. I am afraid my strong telegram about the French pact[4] must also have been a blow to him, and probably he knows that

---

[1] W. C. Braithwaite, *The Beginnings of Quakerism* (1912).

[2] Following the narrow vote in the dail in favour of the treaty, Griffith headed a provisional government with Collins as minister of finance. It was bitterly opposed by the anti-treaty party, led by De Valera, who had resigned the presidency and soon formed a new Republican party.

[3] Lloyd George hoped to establish a consortium of European powers, including Russia, to cure the economic ills of Europe. To this end he arranged an international conference which was to meet at Genoa.

[4] Smuts had warned Lloyd George that South Africa would not be a party to such a pact.

I don't stand alone among the Dominions in this attitude. We are sick of French chauvinism and black troops and guarantees and cryings for the moon. Poincaré is a really dangerous man, and I fear Grey[1] is too much of his way of thinking to be a safe guide in these troubles.

Good-bye, dear. Love to you and Arthur and the children.

Jan

71   From W. S. Churchill   Vol. 25, no. 22

Telegram

From: secretary to governor-general

To: Lane, secretary to prime minister

Undated. [13 March 1922]

Following message for prime minister begins—
Deeply concerned to hear you have been again under fire.[2] Warmest congratulations your escape. Urge you to take greatest care of yourself. Your life is invaluable South Africa and the British Empire. Winston Churchill.

72   To A. Clark   Vol. 98, no. 131

Cape Town
24 March 1922

My letters to you are as rare as angels' visits,[3] but I am glad that you don't mind and continue to send me your most cheerful, cheering and welcome notes. Not only am I a bad correspondent but circumstances have recently been very hard on me. You will have seen in the papers about the disturbances on the Rand which in the end

---

[1] There was a movement among the divided Liberals to close ranks once more under the leadership of Lord Edward Grey.

[2] After mobilizing the Active Citizen Force and declaring martial law on 10 March, Smuts left Cape Town for Johannesburg to command the government troops against the armed strikers. While travelling by car from Randfontein to his headquarters in Johannesburg, he, Louis Esselen, secretary of the South African party, and his chauffeur Hodgson, repeatedly came under rifle fire. (*See* J. C. Smuts, *Jan Christian Smuts*, p. 256.)

[3] (*a*) 'Like angels' visits, short and bright...' Rev. John Norris (1657–1711), *Collection of Miscellanies, The Parting*.

(*b*) The good he scorn's
Stalk'd off reluctant, like an ill-us'd ghost,
Not to return; or if it did, its visits
Like those of angels, short, and far between.
Robert Blair (1699–1747), *The Grave*, l. 586.

have led to heavy bloodshed and had to be forcibly quelled. I went up country for the purpose and have added further claims to the title of butcher and hangman![1] But I could not help it. Throughout I have been influenced by considerations of humanity and by kindly feelings towards the workers. But there was madness in their blood, and in the end blood-letting became necessary. It is all awfully bad luck on this country, and on me personally, but it could not be avoided. The doctors ordered me away for a month's rest at the beginning of December, and instead of a holiday I have been occupied with this sort of situation. Do you really think that under those circumstances I could practise your gospel of blind cheerfulness? I believe in the great ideals of life as you know, but I also believe that, as the flowers grow on a granite soil, so life with all its beautiful flowerings rests at last on a granitic foundation. Unless society is to go to pieces there must be the solid guarantee of force in the background, and this will remain so until human nature has undergone a thorough change. As in Russia, so elsewhere, the danger is that in a very short time the slow results of ages of progress may be undone. However, I believe your orderly mind will agree with me that no undue risks must be run.

Things continue very bad in the world, and yet I believe there is a slow improvement. Society has stood far greater strains than anybody ever thought it could bear. But the ups and downs are most harrowing. Take Ireland, for instance, today filling us with hope and tomorrow with despair. Genoa with its fair promise is also drifting on the rocks. George has surrendered to Poincaré and, I fear, all for nothing. It never pays to buy the devil.

Well, dear, your life continues deeply occupied with good works. God bless you. And if I don't write often, you will know that the great attachment continues and you are ever in my thoughts. Love to the Millfield[2] circle. Ever yours,

Jan

---

[1] After the declaration of the general strike on 7 March the strike commandos committed many acts of violence including the killing of Native miners. On 10 March there was fighting along the whole Reef. Government troops suppressed the rising in three days. For the casualties on both sides and among non-whites *see infra,* p. 131. A number of strikers were brought to trial. Of eighteen sentenced to death for murder, four were hanged.

[2] *See* vol. III, p. 582, note 2.

73 To M. C. Gillett Vol. 25, no. 304

Cape Town
24 March 1922

The last two weeks I have been away quelling disturbance in the north and therefore had no opportunity to write to you. But your letters have been most welcoming; one reached me at Doornkloof just when I was coming back, the other found me here. We have passed through a bad time, and the more I have of it the more I pity the lot of rulers in these days. The commandos, which had been drilling and marching on the Rand, suddenly and mysteriously became armed with rifles and attacked the police inflicting heavy casualties. So martial law and all the rest of it. And I have earned an additional claim to the titles of butcher and hangman. I am afraid the rest of the session we shall talk nothing but strike, revolution and martial law, and the shortcomings of the government. I have abandoned all idea of doing any real work. It is all very galling, and I would pray to the Lord to be well out of it. But how does one get out of it with decency and self-respect? That is the question I cannot answer. Perhaps other methods of government may go better with the nerves of this country, but I do not see how I am to be got out of the way, except by the way of the hospital, and so far my health is not bad. The rest which the doctors prescribed at the beginning of December has not come yet, but I manage to get along without appearing to be a physical wreck. However, enough about this.

I do hope the country will really settle down now after this disastrous flare-up. We cannot for ever continue to stand such shocks as we have had in 1913, 1914, 1915 and now in 1922. Recent experience in the world, however, proves that mankind can stand much more than was considered possible; look at the way Europe is slowly and painfully groping through all her agonies. But it is very slow and painful. Genoa, I suppose, will be a great failure. [Lloyd] George, having allied himself to his arch-enemy, Poincaré, must know that he is marching to disaster. In Ireland Griffith again has compromised with de Valera,[1] and I imagine all the good work there is in the gravest danger. There are occasions beyond all compromise, when men and nations have to be put to the test, whatever the issue. It would have been far better for both George and Griffith to have fought it out. I suppose a great political change is coming about in England. But the Liberals look paralysed. I cer-

---

[1] Griffith and De Valera had agreed that the elections to the new dail would be postponed so that the provisions of the new constitution and of the treaty could be put before the electorate before they voted. This was a concession to the Republicans.

tainly don't think much of any of the Liberal leaders. They are devoid of real courage and audacity, they lack conviction and some lack first-class intelligence. Labour is hopeless with its class selfishness. So what is to come out of the melting pot? Well, Isie is now down here; I brought her with me. We are happy and the little children frolic about the house all day.

My dearest love to you and Arthur and the little group at 102. Ever yours,

Jan

74   To C. P. Crewe   Vol. 102, no. 209

Prime Minister's Office
Cape Town
27 March 1922

My dear Crewe, Your letter of 17 March was very welcome, all the more so as I know you have not always seen eye to eye with the government in reference to the situation up north. Personally I ran no particular risk, nothing at least which old fire-eaters like you and me would call a risk. But on the Rand people were profoundly depressed and nervy, and I counted on the psychological effect of my presence with them in their day of trouble.

Parliament is even more depressing than was the revolution up north. I have never seen such a spirit of faction, of envenomed party, and more especially personal, animosity. Sometimes I doubt whether it is right for such a stone of stumbling (as me) to be the cornerstone of a government.[1] People are blinded politically at sight of me. Isn't it dreadful? And I would so much rather take a holiday and give this country a respite! No doubt we are working through a very difficult phase of our history. And we are not even a generation removed from the most painful things and happenings in South Africa.

My kindest regards to both you and Lady Crewe. I have my wife with me at Groote Schuur now. It is a great joy. Ever yours sincerely,

J. C. Smuts

[1] 'the stone which the builders disallowed, the same is made the head of the corner, and a stone of stumbling, and a rock of offence'. 1 *Peter* ii. 7–8.

75   Speech (1922)   Box H, no. 33

This speech was delivered by Smuts on 31 March 1922 when he moved the second reading of the Indemnity Bill in the Union house of assembly following the imposition of martial law on the Witwatersrand on 10 March. The document in the Smuts Collection is a typescript from the office of Blenkin and Ribbink of Johannesburg, 'official verbatim reporters and shorthand writers'. There was at this time no Union parliament Hansard.

The right honourable the prime minister (General J. C. Smuts), speaking before a full house and crowded galleries on Friday, 31 March 1922, on the occasion of the introduction of the second reading of the Indemnity Bill said:

Mr Speaker, the house, I am sure, does not expect me to go through everything, through all the trouble through which we have passed of recent months, the house does not expect me to cover the whole of that field. The strike follows on difficulties and disputes which had been going on in the gold-mining industry and in other industries from last November, and the strike took place early in January of this year. The matters in dispute have been raised from time to time and have been very fully discussed in this house for weeks. We have spent a good deal of our time, indeed practically all our time, in discussing these issues, and I think it would be unfair to the house and everyone if I were to attempt to go over all that again. I must limit myself and I am going to limit myself to the matters before us, that is the declaration of martial law, the circumstances which immediately led to that declaration, what happened during the time of martial law, and what course the government proposes with regard to the result of martial law, that is the various acts of misbehaviour which took place and the appointment of the various tribunals to deal with these cases. I am going to confine myself to that, and it is not necessary for me to go back further in the history of this matter than the declaration of the general strike on 7 March. The declaration of the general strike on Tuesday, 7 March, was a great and new development in this dispute. It marked to my mind the beginning of the revolution, from the declaration of the general strike the whole matter assumed a new light and a new character. (*Mr [J.] Christie*: From the 12th of February.)[1] And under those circumstances I am going to limit myself to what happened then. (*Mr [T.] Boydell*: What about the

---

[1] On 12 February 1922, after his attempts at mediation had failed, Smuts called upon the mines to re-open and on the miners to go back to work and promised those who did so government protection.

Chamber of Mines letter?)[1] Well, the honourable member is at liberty to argue the case from his point of view as fully as he likes, but I am trying not to roam over the whole field, but to limit myself in order to present an intelligible picture to the house of the circumstances under which martial law was declared, and of the circumstances which led up to martial law.

A week before the declaration of martial law there was every indication of the strike coming to a conclusion and practically fizzling out. I remember at the end of the previous week the whole trouble seemed to be subsiding, workers were returning in large numbers to the mines, the spirit became much wider all over the Rand, and the Augmented Executive,[2] who were in charge of the whole business on behalf of the workers, practically decided to hold a general ballot of the workers, and find whether they were prepared to return to work. That was the trend of things, the trend of events at the end of the previous week, in spite of the letter of the Chamber of Mines, on which I have already expressed my opinion very strongly.[3] In spite of every circumstance, the position was developing most favourably, the strike was subsiding and men going back to work, and the body in charge of these miners were themselves trying to hold a ballot of the workers. And what happened? Sir, a most sudden and unexpected and dramatic change took place. (*Mr Boydell*: Why?)

(*Mr Speaker*: Order, I must ask the honourable member kindly to desist from interruption.)

The prime minister: A most sudden and dramatic change in the situation took place, and instead of a ballot being author-

[1] After the breakdown on 27 January 1922 of the Curlewis conference between representatives of the South African Industrial Federation and the Chamber of Mines, the latter offered a ratio of 1 to 10·5 in the employment of black and white miners with a two-year guarantee. This was refused but later the Federation proposed a further meeting with the Chamber to discuss terms. The Chamber's reply, in a letter of 4 March, was a harsh rebuff—in the words of the Graham commission, 'a frank and brutal expression of their views' (U. G. 35 of 1922, para. 107). It was later suggested that this letter was the chief cause of the general strike and the revolution but the Graham commission regarded it as a lesser cause (para. 160). For the text of the letter *see* the *Cape Times*, 6 March 1922, pp. 9–10.

[2] This body came into existence shortly before the strike began when the president of the South African Industrial Federation, Joseph Thompson, invited all trade unions, whether affiliated to the Federation or not, to appoint representatives to augment the executive of the Federation.

[3] On 7 March 1922 Smuts said in the house of assembly that the reply of the Chamber of Mines 'not only negatived any further parleying and refused to recognize the Industrial Federation, but was couched in such a deplorable tone that it must be clear...that tempers were rising. Unfortunately...any bad move in the game was followed by a worse blunder on the other side and the miners' ballot had been dropped and a general strike declared.' (*Cape Times*, 8 March 1922.)

ized by the Augmented Executive, the general strike was declared.

Well sir, it has been said that this act from the Augmented Executive was an act of despair. It was said that they had been driven to despair, it was the last despairing movement they were making to save themselves. It is said that the attitude of the Chamber of Mines in that letter which has been referred to, that the attitude of this house in the resolution which had been taken,[1] and the various other circumstances had practically turned the minds, unhinged the minds of the workers, and the workers had plunged into this fatal step as a last resort.

That is the view urged of this sudden change. I think that that view will not stand a moment's examination. It was not the workers who changed. The Augmented Executive did not change its mind. It was doing its best to achieve a ballot and to have the men declare their opinions. No sir, the real significance of what happened was this, that the Augmented Executive and the workers, the genuine workers, the trade unionists of the country were practically superseded in this business and their place was taken by an entirely different body of men and leaders. There is no doubt about it. I have read a description of what took place that Tuesday afternoon when the Augmented Executive were sitting there in the Trades Hall, with a wild, howling mob outside, practically forcing them at the point of the bayonet to declare a general strike.[2] The workers did not change; what did happen was this, and I say it because the truth must be said, and though I am not the advocate for the Augmented Executive or the Labour party, or any other similar body, the truth must be said, and it is this, that at that stage the forces of violence, the militant forces, the forces of anarchy trying to come to the fore ousted the constitutional labour movement, and the labour organizations, and took their places. The Augmented Executive that afternoon abrogated [sic] and their place was taken by a military, revolutionary junta, called the Council of Action,[3] and they ran the business. In fact the strike had become

[1] On 28 February 1922 the house of assembly rejected Hertzog's motion to set up a select committee of inquiry into the strike. Smuts had declared that it must be settled by arbitration and that the government would consider the appointment of an impartial tribunal to investigate all issues in the dispute only after the miners had gone back to work.

[2] For a description of these events (6–7 March) by a principal actor in them see W. H. Andrews, *Class Struggles in South Africa*, a pamphlet published in January 1941 (pp. 34–5). Andrews's account bears out Smuts's impression. See also U. G. 35 of 1922, para. 110.

[3] The Council of Action was first formed in July 1921 in Johannesburg by labour leaders, some of them members of the South African Communist party, against whom

a revolution. The workers quietly dropped out of this business and in their place came this other, this sinister force which had been kept in abeyance in the meantime.

Now sir, what was the situation, how had this come about? I am not to-day going into any lengthy explanations of what the situation is on the Rand, and honourable members in this house are aware of the situation there and the character of the population on the Rand. We have on the Rand, in addition to some of the best people in South Africa, a fairly large percentage of people there who are of a very dangerous class. They are generally referred to as the hooligan element, but I think that would be a wrong term to use, to some extent anyhow.

But we have on the Rand a portion of the population who are very ignorant. Some of them are the poor whites of our own people who have in recent years, owing to various disasters in this country, owing to social conditions, owing to land conditions, gravitated into the town. People without calling or education, people who easily fall a prey to any mischievous movement which may be afloat are found on the Rand.

In addition to that, a portion of the population on the Rand is also recruited from less developed countries in the world, and people come from abroad with ideas, with social ideas of government, which are opposed to all the traditions of South Africa, and in that way you have a minority on the Rand, a minority of people who are very ignorant, who are very prone to any mischievous movement, and you have another small number of people who are advanced Communists, international Communists, who preach the most dangerous doctrines for a class of that kind. There is no doubt that it was the coming together of these two elements that set the revolution going.

I am not accusing the ordinary working class, the skilled working class of this. I am not making any charge against them, but there is no doubt that the situation on the Rand was such, so inflammable owing to the circumstances which I have described, that under favourable circumstances it was possible, and it may in future be again possible, to produce a conflagration. That conflagration did take place.

Let me say that most people who took part, the rank and file of this revolution were not members of the Labour party at all. (*Mr Boydell*: Hear, hear.) There is no doubt about it, sir. The vast

disciplinary action had been taken by the Mine Workers' Union for organizing unofficial strikes in 1919 and 1921. The chairman was F. W. Pate, the secretary, A. McDermid. The Council's published manifesto was Marxist. Its leading figure was Percy Fisher, a Communist. Other members were W. H. Andrews, George Mason, Ernest Shaw, Harry Spendiff, J. Wordingham. (*See* U. G. 35 of 1922, paras. 128–31.)

body of people who formed the rank and file in this sad and terrible business were Nationalists. I do not say this as a general charge against the Nationalist party. (*General Hertzog*: You need not apologize.) The truth would not be consistent with any apology. (Government cheers.) That is the absolute fact, sir. The Nationalist party have stood for a programme which must react necessarily most dangerously on ignorant people. It is quite easy for educated people to say, 'We are going to act in a constitutional manner. We are working consistently and deliberately for a subversion of the government, but we will do it constitutionally.' That reservation the educated section are always making. No one talks more of constitutional methods than they do. They are full of it. But you cannot expect the people whom I am referring to, the poor whites, the flotsam and jetsam of our urban population, to understand the fine distinction between constitutional methods and the objects they have been taught to aim at and are aiming at.

The result is this, that a spirit of lawlessness and anarchy which the international Communists teach these people from day to day is reinforced most dangerously by the doctrines which they pick up from their own party. The Nationalist leaders say 'no violence'. But the international Communists do not say that. They say, 'We want violent subversion from the ordinary state', and the combination of these two elements, the pernicious doctrines which have been preached by the Nationalist party, and which have affected the minds of the uneducated classes, together with the theoretical preachings of the international Communists, have set the match to this business.

And beyond that, sir, they read in their press day after day the most vile invectives against the government of this country. (*General Hertzog*: They deserve it.) The honourable member says they deserve it. I daresay that governments in general, and this government in particular, does deserve a good deal of invective, such as they get their full share of, but what is going on in the Nationalist press in this country is much more dangerous. These poor ignorant people are told day by day that the government of this country is a pack of scoundrels, murderers, people who are unfit to govern the lowest forms of society. They have not been taught to discriminate. They do not bring any trained political judgment to bear on these statements; they swallow these things. They hear this from all the men and leaders they look up to. Their minds have become inflamed and they have become the easiest prey possible to the Andrewses[1]

---

[1] W. H. Andrews was at this time secretary of the South African Communist party and editor of its organ, *The International* (*see* vol. IV, p. 295).

and the other Communists, socialists, Bolshevist leaders etc., who have preached to them. Well, that was the atmosphere.

And in this case, unlike other similar cases we have been through, there was unfortunately the special machinery through which they could operate, this commando system.[1] I do not know whose invention it was. (*Mr C. van Niekerk*, sarcastically: The Nationalists of course.) Well, it so happened that every commandant was a Nationalist. (*An honourable member*: What about Waterston?) No, the honourable member for Brakpan, although he holds a very great distinction, at a very early stage he simply stepped into an organization which was provided by the Nationalists. He found the work prepared. There is no doubt that this dangerous movement found an instrument ready at hand, and hence we saw for weeks and almost months these daily parades through the streets of the Rand, men training men, going through military evolutions, dismounted men trying to unmount horsemen, bomb throwing, special methods of dealing with police etc., all this went on. (*Mr [R. B.] Waterston*: No, it did not go on.) No, the honourable member did not go on, he came to this house. He left his bomb throwers behind, and he came here to throw other bombs.[2]

Well sir, this machinery of the revolution was developed there. It was very difficult; the government watched the movement very closely, but it was very difficult, not only for the government but for the country, and for every man, to make up his mind as to the ultimate tendencies of this movement. The people who were concerned said that it was for physical exercise, to keep themselves fit, and from vegetating at home. Others, again, said that it kept the workers together, and that it was not a military movement, nor a revolutionary movement, but that the object of the commandos was to keep the strikers together so that they might act as bodies and not surrender to the enemy individually and indiscriminately.

[1] The strikers formed 'commandos' in almost all the Rand townships. They stood under elected officers and some had cyclist and ambulance corps. Intelligence and signalling systems were organized. The commandos were openly and competently drilled and became more effectively armed as the strike developed. A 'general staff' was established to co-ordinate their action.

[2] R. B. Waterston was, apparently from its establishment on 14 January, officer commanding the Brakpan commando and was styled 'General'. He led this and other forces in various attempts to 'pull out scabs' at some of the mines. On 5 February he proposed a resolution at a large strikers' meeting in the Johannesburg town hall to proclaim a republic and form a provisional government in association with Labour and National party members of parliament who would assemble in Pretoria on the 6th. The resolution was passed with acclamation but rejected at the Pretoria meeting, whereupon Waterston disavowed it, deprecated violent measures, retreated to Cape Town to attend parliament (12 February) and was superseded as general of the Brakpan commando. (*See* U. G. 35 of 1922, paras. 116–17.)

That was one construction, so it was very difficult with all these considerations to say from the very start that these were illegal organizations, and that they served only one purpose and therefore had to be forcibly put down. I do not think the government was justified to do so, and it did not do so until it became clear that there was no other construction possible, but that these commandos were to be used for violence.

There was this state of feeling on the Rand, there was this military organization, and I must add this, that there was no doubt that these people expected support from the country.[1] (*Mr [J. H.] Munnik*: They were unarmed.) I will come to the arms just now. (*General Hertzog*: Perhaps they expected support from the government.) Well, I do not know whether they expected support from the honourable member for Smithfield, where they expected support from was their secret. (*Mr [J. H. H.] de Waal*: That is a very mean insinuation.) Well, I do not want to pursue that subject now. I did not know what happened at the secret strike meeting at Witbank, but I always give General Hertzog credit for being so intelligent as not to let himself in for a thing like this. No doubt stories were about but I have personally never believed them. (*General Hertzog*: Have not you?) No, I have not. (*General Hertzog*: You are a fool not to.) Yes, perhaps I am a fool. No sir, there is no doubt about it that assistance was expected from the country, and it was one of the disappointments which led rapidly to the end when these revolutionaries, these revolutionary commandos, found out that the only commandos which were coming to the Rand were the government commandos, and that the others from the Free State and the western Transvaal did not materialize. (Nationalist laughter.) Yes, sir, we know that they were called for. We know that. We know that emissaries were sent, and we kept trace of them.[2] In one case, for instance, which I may mention here, emissaries have been sent to the Lichtenburg district to all the principal officers who took part in the rebellion, and they were seen by these emissaries from the Rand and were called upon to come to the assistance of their friends. (*Mr [C. G.] Fichardt*: Who were the emissaries?) Oh, the government happens to be in full possession of all the information, and they sent the magistrate of Lichtenburg to these former rebel leaders to explain to them what the position was, and warned them that if they took part in this movement they would not receive

[1] Evidence was given before the Graham commission that the strikers expected large numbers of armed farmers to ride in to their assistance and also to be supplied with food from the farms (*see* U. G. 35 of 1922, para. 48).

[2] *See* U. G. 35 of 1922, paras. 34, 37, 39.

the same merciful treatment which they had received formerly. And they thanked the government.

Well sir, that was the position of affairs on the Tuesday afternoon when the general strike was declared.[1] The Labour organization was swept off the scene and anarchists took possession. That was the turning-point. The following day the commandos proceeded to put into force what seems to have been, from such information as the government has, the plan of campaign. Attacks would be made all over the Rand against the Natives, and the Natives would be goaded into revolt, and, once the Natives had been set going, the story would be spread that there was a general Native outbreak, and these commandos—the supporting commandos—were to come forward and assist. (*Mr* [*N. C.*] *Havenga*: You do not believe that surely.) I think it is true because it is supported by what actually took place.

On Wednesday morning the attacks started. There were indiscriminate massacres of Natives at Fordsburg and elsewhere on Wednesday morning. On Wednesday afternoon, the attacks were launched at Germiston, and massacres took place on the Primrose Mine. This policy was continued on Thursday, when large numbers of additional Natives were killed and wounded. My colleagues who were on the Rand issued a statement to the Natives calling upon them to be quiet. A similar statement was also issued to the public, and it was quite clear that in spite of all provocation which was given, the Natives were not rising to the occasion. On Friday the campaign entered upon a new phase. On that day, 10 March, martial law was declared.

On the Friday morning the commandos launched their attacks against the government forces from one end of the Reef to the other. They started by that most dastardly massacre of the mine officials at Brakpan,[2] an incident which is blacker than any incident we have of Native warfare or massacres anywhere. (*Mr. Havenga*: Except the incident of the Hanekoms).[3] These people at Brakpan

---

[1] On 7 March.

[2] On 31 January Waterston and his commando went to the state mines at Brakpan and threatened the officials when they would not come out on strike. On 10 March the same commando, under another commandant, attacked the mine at Brakpan and killed five mine officials, a lieutenant and two constables of the Special Police and one Native.

[3] The three Hanekom brothers, Pieter Albertus, Johannes Petrus and Barend Daniel and Marthinus Wessels Smith, commando members, were arrested on 16 March for committing illegal acts by soldiers of the Citizen Force. They were shot by an escort patrol. It was said in parliament and widely believed that they had been executed in cold blood and in revenge by order of the officer commanding the escort, Captain Kirby. The military authorities declared that they had been shot while trying to escape. After an exhaustive investigation the Graham commission upheld the second contention. (U. G. 35 of 1922, pp. 45–65.)

were shot down and killed and battered to pieces after they had put up their hands to surrender. My friends, the two ministers in Pretoria,[1] after hearing of these attacks on the Brakpan mine and the indiscriminate massacre of mine officials there, sent aeroplanes to reconnoitre. What happened? The aeroplane that went to Brakpan was attacked, and the observer, Lieutenant Carey Thomas, was shot dead. No bullet was fired from that machine, and Colonel van Ryneveld[2] followed with further machines. He himself was fired on at Benoni and brought down. While these matters were going on an attack was made on the police at Fordsburg.

The member for Langlaagte has given the house, not from personal observation but hearsay, his own account of what happened. According to his account eighty-five brave, well-armed, well-drilled policemen gave in to a small commando, to a small body of men with four rifles between them—eighty-five brave, well-armed, well-drilled men surrendered to a small coterie of men with four rifles between them. (Laughter from government benches.) Yes sir, that is the story, but the fact is that they were attacked and forced to surrender, those eighty fellows. (*Mr Christie*: I never said that, I said it commenced with four rifles.) No, I said it. At the same time that this attack was made on the government forces at Fordsburg, another attack was made on another body of police at Brixton. That was by the Vrededorp commando. We were told by the honourable member for Vrededorp (*Dr [T. C.] Visser*) that in the Vrededorp commando there were only fifteen rifles. (*Dr Visser*: No.) Well, the honourable member will no doubt inform the house of his facts in that eloquent manner which the house so much likes to hear.

Well sir, it is clear from the instances which I have mentioned to the house what the position was. Those brave police held out from Friday morning until Saturday night when a counter-attack was launched from another part. It is clear from the instances which I have mentioned to the house that on Friday morning the idea of provoking the Natives had been given up, and it was thought that the time had come to go for the government forces.

No doubt there was an expectation that there would be support from the commandos in the country. Now, that was the position in the parts which I have described. In the other parts the position was this. At Kurgersdorp,[3] although there was no actual fighting, the police and the authorities, the magistrates, etc. had to keep very much in the background, and I am sorry to say it, but Krugersdorp

---

[1] H. Mentz, minister of defence and F. S. Malan, minister of mines.
[2] Afterwards Sir Pierre van Ryneveld.   [3] Twenty miles west of Johannesburg.

was dominated very much also by a local commando, and the same happened at a number of other points on the Rand.

The same happened at Roodepoort.[1] You may see that on this Friday morning, while up to that day the government had, through the police force at its disposal, done its best to maintain a hold on the Rand, on this Friday morning the command passed from the government, and passed over to the revolutionary forces. Where fighting took place the government were generally defeated, and in other parts the government dared not show its face. It was then, when that climax had been reached, when matters had reached that pass, that martial law was declared. Now, sir, various questions arise here, and the first is this: why did not the government act sooner and declare martial law sooner? That is the question which is raised by two sets of people. There are people who clamoured for a declaration of martial law from the earliest appearance of trouble. There are people who only believed in martial law. (*Mr Munnik*: That is the government.) I am here defending myself and the government for not putting it into force sooner than we did. The facts are there, and if honourable members will not interrupt me, but listen to me they [will] have those facts. One set of people blamed the government, and they blamed the government very severely for waiting so long in declaring martial law, and they say that if we had acted more expeditiously, we might have avoided a great deal of trouble.

There are other people who blame us—they are the people who are dead against martial law. And the subtle charge they make against us, I believe it is honourable members on the Nationalist benches and their supporters, and they say that this snake-like government was sitting still. They wanted revolution first to take place in order that they might crush it with violence and lawlessness. (*Mr Fichardt*: You wanted revolution.) No, the government wanted the situation to develop; the government took this attitude that they could not agree with either the one or the other of these two extreme criticisms, that before they declared martial law they were bound in the interests of the country to let the situation develop, naturally, because it was possible that the situation might develop peacefully.

They knew what was going on, those members who now so strongly criticize us, and now they cannot understand why martial law was not declared, because they knew what took place. Well, I did not. I went on the assumption of keeping my eyes open all the time and being carefully on the watch. There was this possi-

[1] Twelve miles west of Johannesburg.

bility that the strike, which had lasted a long time in a peaceful manner, might end peacefully. A similar strike in England[1] had lasted three months and had ended peacefully, and I thought, and my colleagues thought, that if the government of this country could get through this great industrial crisis without the declaration of martial law it would be a great point scored in the interests of the country. We let the matter develop before we declared martial law, and when we got to this stage when the government authority was usurped and ousted, and the revolutionary forces were in possession practically of the Rand from one end to the other, there was no doubt that we had to act and we did act.

Let me add this for the information of the house. The government had to face this situation as it ultimately arose when they were delaying the declaration of martial law—we were bound to delay to the last possible moment the taking of such an extreme step as the declaration of martial law, and I think we acted wisely.

I asked the police authorities before I left the Transvaal for parliament whether they thought it was possible for them to get through the trouble without calling up the commandos,[2] and without declaring martial law, and Colonel [R. S.] Godley, who is in charge of the police, said that unless something very much larger took place than was happening on the Rand, unless practically a revolution took place, unless the disturbances spread to other parts of the country beyond the Rand, he thought that the police force which the government had placed at his disposal could maintain law and order.

I had that assurance when I came here to parliament, and I thought there was a great deal behind it to make my belief that that judgment was correct, that the police, having maintained control of the situation so long, would continue to maintain it to the end. But at the same time, behind this judgment of the police and of myself, I did have the fear that events might take a more fatal turn, and I told my colleagues, and they will bear me out, that the possibility might arise that for a couple of days, if we delayed the declaration of martial law and the calling out of the burghers, that we might lose control of the Rand, and that matters might get out of hand, and that a good deal of outrage and destruction might take place—the very contingency which ultimately did take place, but even with that risk, the government said, 'Let us run it. If there are revolutionary forces brewing in this country, if

[1] *See supra*, p. 64, note 1.
[2] That is, the burgher commandos or members of the Citizen Force Reserve who might be called up by the government.

we are continuously walking on the edge of a volcano, let the country see it, let us even at the risk, the very serious risk of a couple of days of revolution, delay the declaration of martial law and let the situation develop.'

That was the government's attitude and judging now from what has happened, now that it is all over, I think it is the judgment of the majority of people in this country that in so doing the government has acted rightly in not prematurely declaring martial law, in not prematurely marshalling the government forces when they might not be necessary, in not trying to coerce labour, and driving it back at the point of the bayonet. 'Let us wait and let the situation develop'. Well, it did. For a couple of days we did lose control, and during these days we saw a state of affairs on the Rand which I hope will be an object-lesson to the people of this country for ever.

On Friday these things which I have described happened. On the Saturday the position went much further. On Saturday the position was as black as possible, and sir, when I arrived in Johannesburg that Saturday night, early on Sunday morning,[1] it seemed to me that even that small portion of the Rand which we were holding might go too. In Johannesburg, as I explained before, we were just holding the mere centre of the town, and that centre was menaced from various places. Commandos from the east were holding Jeppestown and that area, and in Ellis Park we were trying to stem the tide. Vrededorp, Fordsburg, and all that area within a couple of hundred yards of the police headquarters was in the hands of the revolutionaries. That was the position on Saturday night, and it was in my opinion, that Saturday night, touch and go.

If there had been any real, daring spirit among the revolutionaries, the worst might have happened on the Sunday. But on the Sunday the tide turned. Our weary, tired forces, the police who had been on duty for weeks, our small citizen forces who for days had been fighting and suffered severe casualties, they were marshalled, and they took the field, and the situation was altered by that Sunday night as far as the centre of Johannesburg was concerned, and on the Monday the commandos began to appear. Sir, I do not think at any other time in the history of South Africa has there been such a magnificent and speedy mobilization as on this occasion. (Cheers from the government benches.) Neither on the occasion of the Jameson Raid or of the Rebellion has there been such a rush of the burghers, rushing to the help of their country. (*Mr Fichardt*: How

---

[1] The night of 11–12 March. Smuts now personally took command of the government forces.

many were commandeered?) Commandeering orders went out after the declaration of martial law—commandeering started on the Friday afternoon, and about 7,000 were commandeered.

The earliest commandos were assembling in their villages by Saturday morning, and I myself saw, when I arrived at Potchefstroom on Saturday night, I saw between 1,200 and 1,500 men there. This mobilization had started on Friday afternoon, and by Saturday night we had large forces already in the field. It redounds to the eternal honour and credit of the burghers of this country that in the hour of danger, when they realized what was going on, when they realized that it was more than an industrial dispute, and that the very foundations of public life were in danger and of public order, they did not ask for reason, they did not urge politics, but a vast bulk of them took to the field, got their horses and rode to the rescue. (Enthusiastic cheers from the government benches.) (*Mr [J. S.] Smit*: Yes, but when did they realize it?) They appeared on Monday and a good deal of the Witwatersrand was taken back, and by Tuesday[1] the whole of the Rand was again held by the government forces, and thereafter for the rest of the week the neighbouring villages were gone through in order to collect arms and restore law and order and public authority.

Now, sir, I will not detain the house longer with a description of these details. I submit that on the facts I have put before the house that the government acted under the most ample provocation when they declared martial law, that the government was right in declaring martial law at that date and not earlier or later, and what the government is asking here in this Bill should be granted, because there was no other course open for the government.

I just want to mention to the house before I go over the details of the Bill, certain figures which have been supplied to me by the defence department.

The question was asked here by an honourable member just now as to whether these commandos, these revolutionary commandos were armed. Now the defence department says that the following arms and ammunition were captured during military operations, and these figures do not include arms and ammunition handed in under the martial law notice:

Rifles	1,150
Shot-guns	231
Revolvers	745
Captured in action: one machine-gun	

[1] 14 March.

(*Mr Fichardt*: And one bicycle chain.) (Nationalist laughter.) Besides that, there were some unserviceable machine-guns which originally were taken from one of the stores. (Nationalist laughter.) Yes, this seems to amuse honourable members opposite very much —1,150 rifles and 231 shot-guns. (Nationalist laughter.) It is a matter of amusement to the honourable member for Smithfield[1] in the responsible position which he occupies here. (Nationalist jeers.) Then sir, the following ammunition was captured:

Rifle ammunition	43,519 rounds
Shot-gun ammunition	3,699 rounds
Revolver ammunition	13,298 rounds

And that, sir, is after days of fighting. (*Mr Fichardt*: You might call it ammunition recaptured.) The above is by no means all the rifles and ammunition of the revolutionaries, as all the commanding officers report that, immediately firing ceased, rifles were thrown away, buried and hidden in houses, fields, mealie patches and plantations, where they are still to be collected.

I proceed to mention another figure which is a sad figure, and that is the figure of the losses, so far as we have been able to ascertain them. That figure is as follows: On the government side, the military forces of the government engaged in operations: killed, about 50; it may be a little more, that includes the police, the Citizen Force[2] and the burghers—all the military forces who took part; wounded, 237.

On the other side, and when I mention the other side, the figure I am going to give does not all mean revolutionaries. The figure I am giving you is the figure of Europeans killed and wounded, and it includes revolutionaries and peaceful citizens who were shot in the course of these operations. There are simply the two classifications; those who did not belong to the government forces have not been sufficiently classified yet to enable us to say how many were revolutionaries and how many not. Killed and died in hospital, 138; wounded, 287; Indians and Natives and Coloured people killed and died of wounds, 31; wounded, 67. (*Mr Havenga*: Where does the machine-gun come from?) I have not the information, but you can take it from me that this was a machine-gun captured in action, and those others which I have referred to were found in a well in Vrededorp, but the latter can be traced in the Johannesburg municipality, which had kept them for a museum. And they were not used; at any rate the state in which they were found showed

---

[1] General Hertzog.
[2] That is, members of the Active Citizen Force under training.

that they had not been used. They were all German guns, and they, too, have been kept as trophies. The 130 killed on the other side would include a case such as that of Mrs Truter, who was perfectly innocent, and a number of others who have lost their lives in these disturbances.[1] Of course, these people are all dead, that is the point.

Now sir, let me say before I sit down, a few words about the clauses and provisions of this bill. The bill follows in its provisions, its main provisions, which are very few and simple, the usual form of an indemnity act.

In clause 2, as honourable members will see, the government asks for an indemnity for itself and its servants, officers and officials, who took part in the suppression of these disturbances and who acted in good faith. That is the usual formula always found in these Acts, and it is simply taken over from previous legislation. People who under cover of the military operations, and the suppression of disturbances, acted from private motives, and did not act in good faith, are not protected by this. The people protected and indemnified here are only people who in the ordinary way, and in the execution of their duty in good faith, did things and took part in the suppression of these hostilities.

That is the main provision of the bill. Clause 1 deals with the ratification of proceedings which have happened under martial law, and I wish to say a word about that. When martial law was declared, and the regulations were published, they were enforced by the government, not through courts martial. No court martial has been appointed, nor is there, as I have explained, any intention to appoint courts martial under martial law. We are entirely relying on the ordinary courts of the land to do justice where offences have taken place under martial law and against martial law regulations; there the magistrates are going into these cases. A man is for instance found in possession of loot or fire-arms or dynamite or any such thing. (*Mr Fichardt*: Or a red tie.) In all these cases the prosecution has taken place before the magistrate under the martial law regulations, and for breach of the martial law regulations, and what is asked for is the ratification of these sentences.

There is another clause to which I would refer, and that is the prosecution before the magistrates, and under martial law, of people who were commandeered and did not come out, did not respond. (Government cheers.) There is a very small percentage of these

[1] Mrs J. C. Truter was killed in her house in Benoni on 11 March by a bomb dropped from an aeroplane. Benoni was then held by the strike commandos and Mrs Truter's house was near their headquarters, the Trades Hall. Six other persons, including two youths and a child, were accidentally killed.

cases, but that makes it all the more necessary to make an example of these people. (Hear, hear.) Of the 7,000 or more people who were commandeered a couple of hundred did not respond, and they are getting an opportunity of explaining their conduct before the magistrate, and where they cannot give a valid excuse for their disloyal behaviour they are punished. The magistrates are sitting in various parts of the country, and are passing these sentences for breaches of the martial law regulations, and the house is asked to ratify these actions.

There remains one more regulation, provision 4, which deals, not with the offences under martial law, but with the really serious offences that took place during the disturbances.

In regard to them I have already explained what the course is which the government proposes to take. We are not going to appoint military tribunals or courts martial to deal with these cases. This bill provides the ordinary machinery. These cases can go before the ordinary courts of the land. If minor cases, the magistrates will dispose of them. If the case is serious it will go before the attorney-general, who will either send it to a judge and jury or to a special court of judges under the law. That special court was constituted under the legislation of 1917, and that legislation provided that in certain classes of offences, that is high treason, sedition, and public violence, for these three classes of offences the attorney-general can ask for the appointment of a special court of two or three judges, and in these cases the trial will take place, not before a judge and jury, but before a special court. That procedure stands, and stands in the present case too. But we go a step further and this bill asks that before this special court, already existing under the law, should be triable also other serious cases—cases of murder, attempted murder, or arson, and of malicious damage of property —these four classes of cases. The blowing up of railways, the setting on fire of houses, murder, or where attempted murder can be a proper charge—in these four very serious classes of crimes the attorney-general will have the option either of sending a case to a jury, or where he thinks that a fair trial before a jury is not likely, then he can ask a special court to try such a case, and I think the government and the house will have the strongest reason to amplify the jurisdiction of the special court in this case.

I think it goes without saying that every honourable member will recognize that to send these serious cases to a Rand jury might conceivably lead to a very grave miscarriage of justice. An accused may be tried before a jury of the people who are opposed to him, strongly opposed to him, people who have fought against him, and it would be most unfair to have him tried by such a biased jury. On the other hand the other case may also occur, that juries on the Rand may be so much in favour of the disturbances that it may be possible to get a jury which will not convict.

The attorney-general, who knows more about the facts, will look into them all and he must have a greater option than he has at present if justice substantial is to be done, and therefore the government asks that the jurisdiction of the special court should be amplified, and the discretion vested in the attorney-general should also be amplified, so that he might say in what cases, in what serious cases, he will send a case to a jury and in what cases he will send to a special court.

I think, sir, that that absorbs all the important provisions of this bill, and in conclusion I wish to say only this, that it has been argued here that martial law can be kept as a formality. I do not believe that it can be, and in no circumstances do I think would it redound to the credit of this country if martial law for any length of period continues where it is not necessary.

The case has been put before us, in this house, of South West Africa, which, for a long time, was administered under martial law as a so-called formality. Well, sir, it was not. In the case of South West Africa martial law was the very foundation of government there until we passed an act through the house. The military commander was absolutely the law there, because there was no other law under which the country could be administered. The low courts and even the high courts there were all constituted under martial law, and it was the basic reality in that country until an act was passed through here under which it was possible to administer that territory on a peaceful basis; and until that was passed it was not possible to repeal it.

With regard to the present case, you may whittle it down as much as possible, and withdraw as many of the regulations as possible, but you will continue to be told, and I shall continue to be told by my officers and officials that it would be dangerous to repeal this or to do that, and if martial law is to remain in force on the Rand I cannot undertake that it will not be administered and that acts will not be done under it. If the house wishes to do its duty to the country, and to take away the possibility of dangers, such as I have referred to, then there is only one course open, and that is to assert its authority, nullify the military will, and pass this bill into act as soon as possible.

Before this act is passed I shall not withdraw martial law, because as soon as that is done we are exposing ourselves to all sorts of trouble in the law courts and otherwise. Heaps of things have been done, I do not say against the law, but certainly not under the law, and it is inevitable and absolutely necessary that before martial law is withdrawn, there shall be this indemnity to the government and its officers; and in the circumstances I have the strongest reason and the best case for asking this house not to delay this matter unduly but to enable me to withdraw martial law.

I now move the second reading of the bill. (Government cheers.)

76 To A. B. Gillett

Vol. 25, no. 306

House of Assembly
Cape Town
27 April 1922

I write to you but without having any recent letter from you before me, and therefore for a talk and not for correspondence. I was deeply interested to see from Margaret's last letter that Henry and Lucy had had a great luck.[1] Please give them my most hearty congratulations. I would have written to them if I had a free moment. But just now I am rushed almost beyond endurance. The usual parliamentary grind is going on, and you have seen what that is. Besides I have just finished with the Rhodesian delegation who came to see me on the question of incorporation into the Union.[2] I am now busy with the Chartered Company[3] in order to see whether we can arrive at an agreement on the expropriation of their assets. The work really means a financial review of the history of Rhodesia. And over and above all this the Portuguese delegation have arrived from Lisbon to negotiate a new Mozambique treaty.[4] I am now like an Oriental despot giving audience to suitors from the ends of two continents. All very interesting, but very exacting.

[1] Dr H. T. Gillett and his wife. Their youngest child, Roger, had been born.

[2] Because the charter under which the British South Africa Company governed Rhodesia would expire in October 1924, the question of whether Southern Rhodesia should become a self-governing colony or whether it should seek incorporation in the Union of South Africa had, since 1919, been the subject of much debate and negotiation. Following the report of the Buxton committee in 1921, the British government had indicated that it would grant responsible government after a favourable memorandum. In July 1922 the Union government made known the terms upon which it would admit Southern Rhodesia as a fifth province. (*See* E. A. Walker, *A History of Southern Africa*, p. 598.)

[3] In August 1922 the Union government offered the company £6,836,000 for their assets in crown lands, railways and public works. The company would retain its mineral rights.

[4] *See* vol. II, p. 564, note 1. The treaty of 1 April 1909, concluded for a term of ten years, had been inherited by the Union of South Africa from the Transvaal in 1910.

It does not look like achieving success either—the Rhodesian or Mozambique business. But I am going to try very hard. It would be a great thing to round off the South African state with borders far-flung into the heart of this continent. But I fear I am moving too fast, and patience will be necessary.

It is a far cry to Genoa. But Genoa has been almost as much in my thoughts as South Africa. Genoa is going to be a failure, and not a splendid failure either. What with Chicherin [G. V.] on the one side and Poincaré on the other, poor Lloyd George seems almost bound to fail. Whether his attempt was a really great-hearted or unselfish one, or whether it was dictated by electioneering motives, I don't know. One never knows with George. But I fear Genoa will simply burst the band of Anglo-French relations on the one hand and cement Russo-German relations on the other, and thus produce just the opposite of what George intended.[1] Anglo-French agreement has been the pivot of George's policy, and in my humble opinion the aims of France cannot be reconciled with the rehabilitation of Europe. But what dismal prose I am writing.

I hope you are all very well now, with mumps permanently gone. The cold is gone too, and May is i-cumen[2] in all her glory. I see the Downs before me, I smell the May. I feel the touch of the dear hand of friendship. But I am under a sentence of hard labour, not a free man like you.

Good-bye, dear Arthur. My love to you all and ever,

Jan

77   To W. E. Rappard   Vol. 25, no. 241

W. E. Rappard was at this time director of the mandates section of the League of Nations. His letter, to which this is a reply, is not in the Smuts Collection.

Cape Town
4 July 1922

Dear M. Rappard, It was a pleasure to receive your letter of 23 May and I readily respond to the queries which you put to me. I enclose a newspaper report of what I said in September 1920 at Windhuk,[3] from which you will see that the newspaper paragraph you refer

---

[1] The Genoa conference failed when the Russian and German representatives signed a separate agreement, the treaty of Rapallo, on 16 April 1922. It restored diplomatic and commercial relations between the two powers.

[2] Summer is icumen in,
   Lhude sing cuccu!   *Cuckoo Song*, c. 1250.

[3] *See* the *Cape Times*, 18 September 1920.

to is substantially correct. It will help you to understand what I said if you bear in mind that we have quite a peculiar and unexpected problem on our hands with the German population in South West Africa. In other mandated African territories the German population was simply expelled or repatriated during the war or the armistice and the mandatory power is therefore rid of that source of trouble. The Union, however, adopted a much more merciful attitude and, with some exceptions, allowed the German population to remain in South West Africa in the hope that they would respond to the benevolence of our action and co-operate with us in every reasonable way.

This unfortunately they have not done. They remain aloof from us in their outlook and sympathies and cling to the German fatherland as if they were still a German colony, and they long for the day when they will again be a German colony. This unexpected attitude has made our task in South West Africa much more difficult than it should have been. And I have had to explain to the Germans that the mandate of the 'C' type largely ignores them as Germans and affords guarantees only in respect of the indigenous Native population. I have explained to them the futility of looking to the fatherland and the necessity of throwing their lot in with the people of the Union, where a large and prosperous population of German extraction lives. I have explained to them that the Union has full power of legislation and administration over South West Africa as an integral portion of the Union and that the effect is very much the same as if they were incorporated with the Union, subject of course to the four safeguards in the interests of the Native population.[1] In all this I have confined myself to the strict letter of section 22. The Germans, however, claim that they should have their own legislative institutions and apparently attach no meaning to the provision that the Union can administer the mandated territory under its laws as an integral portion of the Union.

I have no doubt that with a policy of patience and forbearance the Germans in South West Africa will in the end recognize that it is in their own interest to identify themselves with the Union and cease to look to Germany. The question is coming up in an acute form in the matter of nationality. Are they German subjects under the mandate? Will they and their children for ever remain German subjects, although born in a country which has nothing to do with Germany and although they themselves are not under German pro-

[1] Article 22 (5) of the covenant of the League of Nations laid down that the mandatory must guarantee freedom of religion, prohibit traffic in slaves, arms and liquor, prevent the setting up of military or naval bases and the military training of the Natives.

tection but under the protection of the mandatory? You see how anomalous the position is and how much more absurd it will become with the years. I believe the only solution is that they be made Union subjects by act of parliament with the right of objecting individuals to register themselves as German subjects. But it is to be feared that as long as they expect one day to be handed back to Germany they will resist such a step.

I see that the committee of the League has found that they are, and continue as, German subjects. This is probably correct. But in that case what is the nationality of the indigenous population which had become German by conquest and annexation in years gone by? Do the Natives also remain German subjects in perpetuity? This would be most absurd and yet it is difficult to draw any distinction in principle between born white German subjects and conquered black German subjects. I think in the end the Union will simply pass a law to settle the nationality question, but leave it to individual white Germans to register themselves as continuing German subjects.

Do not for a moment think that in my ideas or proposals I depart from the system of mandates which I consider one of the most beneficent advances in international law. We must only recognize the fact that 'C' mandates are in effect not far removed from annexation. The case is, of course, quite different with the other two far more important types of mandates.

I wish you all success in your very responsible work. And from me you will always have full support. I believe in the League as a new instrument of human progress. If it fails it will be because of its internal weakness. The idea is sound enough and vital enough to carry it to final success. But there is a long and very difficult road before the League. Europe is very sick and it may be that the curve will sink much lower before the upward movement begins again in the years to come.

I trust the administration of the League will become as economical and efficient as possible. I have my doubts whether it is either at present. The League is not a new diplomatic organization, but a missionary cause, and should be proud of simplicity and poverty and set the governments of the world a great example in that respect. Believe me, Ever yours sincerely,

s. J. C. Smuts

Prime Minister's Office
Cape Town
5 July 1922

My dear Cecil, I have asked [Sir E. H.] Walton to approach you
with a view to your representing South Africa once more at the
League of Nations assembly and I trust you will honour us once
again by acting as one of the Union's representatives. [Sir H.]
Strakosch and Murray [G. G. A.] will be asked to act again as
technical advisers. I do not think that my action in your renomina-
tion will be popular with the imperial government, especially in
view of your great and growing hostility to the government policy
and in particular to the methods of the prime minister. This hostility is no doubt a drawback. But, on the other hand, I am more
concerned for the League than for the government and I feel that
your continued presence at the assembly is of inestimable value to
that body. I trust, therefore, that you will accept my offer, even if
there is no cordiality on the part of the British government.

I am far away from the scene of operations where the battle of
Europe's future is being fought out and it is difficult to understand
the situation and appraise the factors. I have supported the Genoa
move, even if it was apart from the League, in the same way that
I have supported Washington. And Washington has produced
great results. Genoa has been somewhat barren, and yet its economic
and financial reports are a great advance on what was done at
Brussels. Besides, the moral isolation of France which it produced,
and which was to be foreseen, is certain to have a sobering effect
on France and thus to pave the way to better things in future. In
any case, Genoa helps to train and habituate the nations to
co-operative methods, which is the very idea the League stands for.
And the comparative failure of Genoa may produce a reaction in
favour of the League and its methods. You and the prime minister
have clashed your swords violently over Genoa, but I have a good
deal of sympathy with the prime minister. His fundamental instincts
are sound, even where his methods are faulty. And I have no doubt
that he has the laudable ambition of saving Europe from going on
the rocks. His European prestige is a great asset and ought not to
go unused. In spite of all I continue to have great faith. However,
that is the personal aspect.

On the European situation itself one sometimes feels tempted
to despair whether in our day the long lane will be turned and
whether the process to chaos will not go even further than it has

already gone. Sometimes I feel as if the only true policy for us is to concentrate on the British Empire and its utmost development as the only solid nucleus in all this moving chaos of European politics. But then again I feel that European civilization is one and that no solution will work which does not recognize that fundamental unity. The great, the real mistake which was made at the peace conference was to recognize the division of Europe into two camps and to exclude our enemies from the League. It was perhaps unavoidable but it was most far-reaching. The watchword of the Great Peace should have been European reconciliation and unity and all should have been included in the League from the start. With a divided Europe America had an excuse for standing out, and hence our woes.

If Europe is to be one once more, we have to deal with Germany and Russia who are now outside and whose continued exclusion will in itself produce a new menace in the separate joint action. At Genoa the prime minister wished to avoid French antagonism and therefore left the problem of Germany alone, and proposed to deal with Russia as a more promising beginning.

He may have been right, but frankly I expect very little from the efforts now made to restore Russia. Russia is politically and economically an almost insoluble problem today, and I fear at Genoa we have been, and at the Hague[1] we are still, ploughing the sands of the sea. Besides, Germany means infinitely more to European unity and restoration than Russia and, if French opposition could be overcome, is quite a soluble problem. I fear with Russia we begin at the wrong end. We must deal with Germany first. The immediate future of Europe depends on Germany and not on Russia. The first move should be to get Germany into the League, and I would go the whole length of getting her right into the council of the League. This undoubtedly would induce her to join and even perhaps to make the first move. But I think the British Empire should concentrate on this policy and, with the approval of the Dominions, the imperial government should at once begin the necessary spade work among the other powers, so that the change could be brought about at the next session of the assembly. France will not willingly agree, but neither would she willingly face isolation on this issue. The entry of Germany into the League may have very far-reaching effects on the future of

[1] After the failure of the Genoa conference another attempt was made by Lloyd George to pursue its aims, and particularly to draw Russia into economic co-operation with the West, by calling another conference at the Hague on 15 June 1922. The United States did not attend, Germany was not invited and the conference came to nothing.

both and it appears to me to be the obvious immediate step to be taken. It ought to be expressly understood that her entry does not affect the Versailles treaty, save in so far as the reparations chapter is concerned, and that a revision of that chapter will be the first task of the enlarged council to which the United States of America should be invited to send a representative for the purpose of joining in that revision.

I do not know whether this programme is possible, but if it is in any way possible I would postpone Russia for the present, if the Hague conference is not successful, and concentrate on Germany on these lines. If this is not done, there may be two dangers; either Germany sinks into the abyss and emerges later as a militant monarchy, or she pulls through now and snaps her fingers at the West and proceeds to consolidate Russia as a German annex. There is the third alternative—that she may continue to be a festering sore as at present and prevent the early recovery of Europe. The reparation arrangements have to be revised, but I would make her entry into the League and into the partnership of western Europe a condition of such revision. Russia will then become the next chapter.

I do not know in how far you are in agreement with these views, but I trust you will consult with your friends and let me know if you think I am wrong. Meantime I am also writing to the prime minister who, I fear, is inclined to be somewhat lukewarm on the League and rather scared by French opposition. Ever yours sincerely,

s. J. C. Smuts

79   To M. C. Gillett   Vol. 25, no. 316

Pretoria
31 July 1922

Last week I did not write to you as I had just got back from Cape Town and was recuperating at Rooikop. I took some of the children with me...

In two day's time Isie and I leave for a long trip to Rhodesia where I have been invited to open a show and will make use of the opportunity to get about and make friends with the Rhodesians. I hope they will vote to come into the Union, but I am told that the great current of opinion is still the other way. They are afraid of our bilingualism, our nationalism, my views of the British Empire. In fact they are little Jingoes and the sooner they are assimilated by the Union the better for them and for us. Isie will go on to the Falls;

what a chance you are missing! I go instead to the south and will see the Zimbabwe ruins which, some people say, are just as well worth seeing. I shall be back in three weeks' time. Don't expect many letters in the meantime. I shall be moving or speaking or eating most of the time and shall not have much opportunity for correspondence.

The weather is now most beautiful—cold nights but the most glorious sunny days. There are five or six good riding horses on the farm and I go out riding as often as I can for exercise. At the Cape it is mountain climbing; here it is riding.

I hope Exmoor has done you and Arthur much good. But I do long to see you all again. Ever with love,

Jan

80   To M. C. Gillett   Vol. 25, no. 318

Doornkloof
[Irene, Transvaal]
30 August 1922

Last week I was writing to Arthur when I was interrupted and had to go away to the western Transvaal. I have just returned after a most successful week of political touring. Feelings are subsiding and my backveld[1] friends are learning to understand my policy better. At a place called Ottosdal[2] the prophet van Rensburg,[3] who played such a part in the rebellion of 1914, sat next me and at the end of the meeting prayed 'for that great statesman'! Financial conditions are very bad in the rural districts; prices of produce are very low and farming implements and requirements are still expensive. In adversity the people who are really quite good and sound are learning the lessons of tolerance and self-help and co-operation. Political conditions are most difficult. I have never worked harder or amid more friction and trouble than at present. This is indeed a most difficult country to rule, and one is sometimes almost in despair. However, I always console myself with the reflection that rulers of other countries are infinitely worse off. Who for instance would like to govern Ireland today? With Griffith dead and Collins assassinated, I look upon Irish prospects as dark indeed. But the Irish people are no doubt learning their lesson at last. Or who would like to stand in the shoes of Ebert[4] or Wirth [J.]?[5]

[1] Literal translation of *agterveld* (Afrikaans), meaning the remote parts of South Africa.   [2] In the south-western Transvaal.
[3] *See* vol. II, p. 279, note 1.   [4] Then president of the German Republic.
[5] Then chancellor of the German Republic.

Germany seems rapidly going under. I fear that in their agony and despair the German magnates will turn to France and a combination will result which may have far-reaching consequences for the rest of Europe in another generation. I doubt whether the imperial government are sufficiently alive to the danger of a Franco-German combination; but if England does nothing, what else is left the Germans but to go into an unequal partnership with their enemies. God have mercy on this poor soiled world! With love,

Jan

81 To P. van der Byl   Vol. 25, no. 250

Pretoria

31 August 1922

My dear Piet, Many thanks for your letter and for sending for my information a copy of the *World's Work*. I was glad to see it and am much obliged to Mr Baruch for his friendly references.[1] He did an absolutely unpardonable thing by writing a book on the peace conference and publishing documents which were secret and which under no circumstances should have been published without authority. One of the documents which he published was a memorandum which I furnished;[2] I suppose he is now making an *amende honourable* in this manner.

We have had splendid rains here and the farming community are all looking forward to a good season.

I am just off to Natal and Zululand for a short visit and hope to inspect the famous Kosi bay.[3]

With very kind regards to all at Fairfield,[4] Believe me, Yours sincerely,

s. J. C. Smuts

[1] *The World's Work*, vol. 40, no. 237 (August 1922) contains an article by B. M. Baruch entitled 'Popular Fallacies about Reparations' in which (p. 162) he praises Smuts's 'integrity and ability' and continues: 'We do not think him "a master sophist", but believe that his remarks on pensions and separation allowances were honest and sincere.'

[2] *See* vol. IV, 926.

[3] The development of Kosi bay on the coast of Zululand as a harbour to serve the Witwatersrand and make it less dependent on Lourenço Marques had been considered from time to time every since 1890.

[4] Major van der Byl's farm near Caledon, Cape Province.

82   To M. C. Gillett   Vol. 25, no. 322

Pretoria
25 October 1922

What an excitement your cable brought us this week! I had given up all hope of your coming out in the near future. I saw nothing special to bring Arthur and without him you were not likely to come...

This week too we heard of the fall of the Lloyd George government. It is a Tory reaction which has knocked him over, and there is little to rejoice over. I can't blame George too much. He gambled too much on the ability of the Greeks to hold their own.[1] But the behaviour of the French and Italians was disgraceful.[2] And I fear the new government[3] will adopt a francophile policy which will be even more fatal than George's vagaries. We mean to keep out of it all.[4] But we want to see others keep out too. But enough.

Our dearest love to you all. Bon voyage.

Jan

83   From D. Chaplin   Vol. 25, no. 21

Personal

Administrator's Office
Salisbury
Rhodesia
30 October 1922

My dear Smuts, You will have received my telegram giving my impression as to the result of the referendum. Since that was sent off I have heard the Unionist estimate of the result of the voting at Bulawayo and also the responsible government estimate of the results for all Matabeleland. The former gives 64% to responsible government, the latter rather more, which would seem to point to a fairly large responsible government majority. These forecasts

[1] War between Great Britain and Turkey seemed imminent when Lloyd George took a personal decision to aid the Greeks in their struggle with Turkey for possession of the Aegean coastal region of Asia Minor. The crisis passed but it seriously weakened the position of Lloyd George.

[2] A neutral zone controlling the Straits was held, under the treaty of Sèvres (10 August 1920), by Allied forces. On 21 September 1922 France and Italy withdrew their forces.

[3] On 23 October a Conservative government took office with A. Bonar Law as prime minister.

[4] On 15 September 1922 the British government had asked the Dominions for military help in the event of war with Turkey. Only New Zealand promised support.

may, of course, prove to be quite wrong, but I fear there is little chance of this.[1] I still think that if more time had been allowed between the publication of the Union terms and the date of voting the result might have been different. The farmers, at any rate, after another six months of the present depression would have been practically solid for Union. However, there were very practical difficulties in the way of delay. The real mistake, I think, was made by Churchill when he appointed the Buxton committee and altered Milner's plan of leaving the question of responsible government to be voted upon at the general election for the legislative council, which would have taken place in the ordinary course next year.[2]

The main reasons for the support given to the responsible government cause seem to me to be:

(1) anti-Dutch feeling, especially among the women;
(2) the belief of the trade union element, including the commercial clerks and a proportion of civil servants, that under responsible government they will be in a position to dictate to the government;
(3) the feeling on the part of the trade union and kindred elements that, as most of the better-class people, merchants, representatives of large companies and employers generally —were for Union, their proper course was to vote the other way; loyalty to employers in these matters is a thing of the past;
(4) the satisfactory condition of administrative finances, of which the responsible government speakers have made the most and which has blinded people to difficulties of the future.

As regards the campaign itself, the Unionists had the most money, but in Salisbury at any rate their organization was none too good, and as a party—though some of their people worked hard—they lacked enthusiasm. They were much handicapped by want of effective speakers, and as a result were for the most part on the defensive. They put their case soberly and truthfully, but they did not do enough to counteract the aggressive and frequently unscrupulous tactics of the other side, and in my opinion if they had hit harder they would have had more success. Their method of putting the case seemed to be based on the assumption that the electors generally were reasonable and reasoning people. The support of such people they did as a rule secure, but unfortunately these are only a minority of the electorate.

[1] The result of the referendum was 8,774 for responsible government and 5,989 for incorporation in the Union of South Africa.

[2] Churchill had succeeded Milner as colonial secretary in January 1921.

Of the various sections of the community I should say that the majority of the farmers voted for Union. Most of the Labour people must, I think, for reasons already given, have voted for responsible government. Mrs [Mary] FitzGerald's interview in the *Star* on her return to Johannesburg indicates that she was of the opinion they would vote in this way.[1] The senior civil servants were nearly all for Union. The Public Services' Association, however, and the Post and Telegraph Association were captured by responsible government extremists, with the result that any number of demands were pressed first on [Sir Charles] Coghlan and then on you, with the result, which was of course foreseen, that Coghlan was ready to promise anything, whereas you rightly declined to go beyond what was reasonable. The police kept out of the fray, and I have no idea how they voted. The teachers under [K.] Bradley's lead appear to have carried on a very active responsible government propaganda. The Indians as a class voted anti-Union, which perhaps was to be expected. The Coloured people, having got a promise from Coghlan that he would give them facilities not allowed by the existing law for obtaining drink, probably did the same. The clergy and missionaries, except those of the Dutch Reformed Church, were I think, for responsible government, believing in the efficacy of the powers reserved by the draft letters patent to the high commissioner.[2] The Natives attached to the English Church asked the bishop and his clergy to support Union.

I fear a great many of these people, if responsible government is established, will in a comparatively short time be sadly disillusioned.

I thought your final message was excellent. Coghlan, as you will see from the papers, has repudiated your suggestion that the reservations in the draft letters patent are likely to cause friction between the responsible government and the Company. He will not want to begin by quarrelling with the Company, but I must say I cannot see how friction can long be avoided.

Coghlan, as time goes on, must begin to realize the difficulties he has to face. When his election comes on he will have opposition from pro-Union candidates; he will find the Labour people to whom he has deeply committed himself extremely embarrassing; and he will be lucky if he is not given concrete cause for regretting the grossly offensive things which he and his supporters have said about you and your government and the Union people generally.

[1] *See* the *Star*, 23 October 1922.

[2] The draft letters patent left the high commissioner in control of Native affairs, that is, the personnel of the department and the Native reserves. He would be independent of ministerial advice and recommendations affecting the Native affairs department would be submitted to him by the governor. *See* Cmd. 1573 of 1922.

For myself I greatly resent the reflections cast on yourself and on the South African party, of which the old Unionist party to which I belonged for so many years has now become a part. It is a disappointing result, but I have not the smallest doubt that the policy of working for Union was the right one. Rhodesia must eventually go into the Union, and at any rate a portion of the education which was necessary before the people would see this has now been imparted.

I am leaving for the Cape on 13 November, and shall probably go on to England for a short visit on 8 December. I am anxious to get down to the Cape as soon as possible to see about the starting of my house at Noordhoek, and unless we are wrong as to the result of the referendum, which I fear is not likely, I do not think that there will be any necessity for me to go to Pretoria on the way down. Probably I shall be back in Cape Town when you go down there for the session. Kind regards. Believe me, Yours sincerely,

Drummond Chaplin

84   To A. Bonar Law   Vol. 25, no. 274

Pretoria
20 November 1922

My dear Prime Minister, Hearty congratulations on your great victory![1] The last I wrote to you it was to condole with the breakdown in your health and your sudden retirement from office. Now you are sufficiently restored to take up the great burden at a time of unexampled difficulty. Good luck to you, and may you lead the nation in quiet paths, paths of peace[2] and recovery from the effects of the post-war conditions.

Foreign policy is going to be the acid test of your rule. And there I frankly fear that your government may lean too much towards France. French policy was for centuries the curse of Europe and it was only the rise of Germany to first place that changed her attitude. Now Germany is down and out, and France is once more the leader of the Continent with all the old bad instincts fully alive in her. Let the Germans be made to pay what and when and how they can. But let the reparation question not be a cloak for the dismemberment of Germany and the sowing of the dragon's teeth afresh for the world.

[1] At the general election on 15 November the Conservatives won 347 seats which gave them a majority of 88 over the other parties.

[2] 'Her ways are ways of pleasantness, and all her paths are peace.' *Proverbs* iii. 17.

The French are out for world power; they have played the most dangerous anti-ally game with Kemal [Ataturk];[1] and inevitably in the course of their ambitions they must come to realize that the British Empire is the only remaining enemy. We had better keep a sharp look-out in that direction.

Some of your friends may think that it is not French ambitions which have to be watched but French fears which have to be soothed. Hence they may revive the idea of an Anglo-French pact which luckily fell through at an earlier stage.[2] I fear such a pact very much. It would tie us up to France and to French policy in a way which is not safe for the British Empire. It would alienate American feeling which is becoming alive (after Washington) to the true trend of French policy. It would not change French policy but simply cover the British Empire with the world-wide odium which that policy is sure to provoke. It would kill the League of Nations, for the present French spirit is alien to all true ideals of international peace and co-operation. Last and not least, it holds grave perils for the unity of the British Empire. South Africa would not join in an exclusive Anglo-French pact beyond the general pact in section 10 of the covenant of the League.[3] I doubt whether Canada would, or whether she could afford to do so in view of internal tendencies in that Dominion. Australia and New Zealand would join heartily. But you will already have driven that wedge into the Empire which time will drive deeper. And I believe in these dangerous years of transition it is to the good of the world that the Empire should hold together. And I would oppose any foreign policy of the Empire which introduces elements of division into the Empire itself. I write thus freely and strongly to you, as I have always written and spoken to [Lloyd] George, because I am most acutely conscious of the danger which a policy of exclusive alliances must hold for so heterogeneous and huge a concern as the British Empire.

I would not conciliate France at the cost of the Empire. If Poincaré pursues his policy of guarantees[4] which is nothing but disintegration of Germany, let him do so on the sole responsibility

---

[1] France had, after September 1921, failed to co-operate in Allied efforts to enforce the treaty of Sèvres against the Turkish nationalists and had, in return for trade concessions, made separate agreements with the Turks. *See also supra*, p. 144, note 2.

[2] *See supra*, p. 112, note 1.

[3] Article 10 bound members of the League to protect the independence and territory of all members against external aggression.

[4] The sympathetic attitude of the British government to the German request for a moratorium on reparation payments was countered by a French proposal that, as conditions of a moratorium, a series of 'productive guarantees' should be required, including expropriation of the Ruhr mines (August 1922).

of France and let our hands be clean in the matter. Any other course I fear would produce a frightful entanglement for us.

[Lloyd] George's policy was to keep in with France in order to keep her back—to act as a restraining influence on critical occasions. The result was a suspicion and wrath on the part of France, continual charges of bad faith and perfidy. You could not escape similar charges, and the best is to keep out of the policy. I have never believed in marrying the reprobate with a view to his reformation!

When you think of foreign policy, think at the same time of the Empire. Foreign policy is a truly imperial function, and before any far-reaching departure, the Dominions should be consulted, either at a conference or through correspondence.

Perhaps my fears are groundless. But our old friendship enables me to write to you with perfect freedom. Ever yours sincerely,

s. J. C. Smuts

85   To A. Bonar Law   Vol. 25, no. 273

Prime Minister's Office
Pretoria
20 November 1922

My dear Prime Minister, As the new secretary of state for the colonies[1] does not know me, and the question of Rhodesia is one of very great importance, I write you this brief note in the way it strikes me.

A very bad mistake was made last year when Buxton's committee was appointed by Churchill to report on a scheme of responsible government for Rhodesia. The result was in effect to commit the British government to the grant of a constitution after a referendum. It was a sharp reversal of Milner's previous policy which had laid down that Rhodesia must wait till the charter expires in 1924. I tried to save the situation by interpolating an alternative in the referendum which would thus be either for responsible government or for joining the Union of South Africa on definite terms. But I have not been able to repair the initial mistake. And thus Rhodesia will now become a self-governing colony with a responsible government. The Chartered Company remains intact with all the assets, while the new régime will have nothing at all, except the power to tax its handful of small farmers and other small fry. The country will remain stagnant for want of funds and of the means of development.

[1] The Duke of Devonshire.

And after a few years of toying with responsible government it will accept the inevitable and apply to come into the Union—at a time when it will be much more awkward to receive her than now.

Two alternatives are now open to your government. You may either revert to the Milner policy and postpone the constitutional settlement till 1924, or you may act at once on the referendum and start Rhodesia with responsible government about the middle of next year, when I suppose all the preliminary arrangements can have been completed.

In favour of postponement is the consideration that it is necessary first to ascertain the liability of the crown to the Chartered Company and that can only be after the petition of right instituted by the Company has been disposed of. It would be extremely awkward to grant letters patent to Rhodesia and then to find (if the Company wins) that you have unwittingly obliged the British taxpayer to pay up £5 million to the Chartered Company, especially when you further find that even land sales in Rhodesia will never recoup you for that outlay and interest thereon.[1] No doubt postponement will be a very great disappointment to the majority in Rhodesia and you will be charged with a breach of faith. But as against that you will have to weigh up the financial risk in case the petition of right is decided against the crown.

The other alternative is to run the financial risk and to give Rhodesia her constitution as soon as the preliminary arrangements are completed. The choice between these two alternatives lies before the British government. I am satisfied that, whichever you choose, it will only be a few years before Rhodesia is in the Union. The next two years are going to be most difficult financially, and I should not be surprised to see Rhodesia in the Union as a result of the financial storm.

It is however important that Rhodesia shall not come under the impression that she is being dragooned to enter the Union. Should you, therefore, decide to postpone the letters patent till 1924, I would advise that Sir Charles Coghlan, the leader of the Responsible Government party, be invited to come to London and that the position be fully explained to him. It may be that after such

---

[1] Milner had, in 1918, appointed the Cave commission which fixed at £4,435,000 the amount which the crown should pay to the Chartered Company on taking over the government of Rhodesia. The British government delayed payment and the Company started legal proceedings by means of a petition of right against the crown, whereupon the government claimed a war debt of two millions from the Company. In the end the 'British taxpayer' paid the Company £3,750,000, and the crown waived its claim to war expenditure while the new Rhodesian government was to pay the crown £2,300,000 in respect of lands and public works. (*See* E. A. Walker, *A History of Southern Africa*, pp. 596–9.)

an explanation he may decide to avoid two further years of Chartered rule, and to come into the Union at once.

If you decide to give her a responsible constitution immediately, that would be taking the path of least resistance so far as Rhodesia is concerned, and the Union will have no fault to find, knowing that in a few years' time she will be knocking at the door of the Union. But I would add that it would not be good public policy to extend any financial favours to Rhodesia, as she ought to seek relief from her financial troubles in the Union. Indeed, finance would be one of the principal causes to bring her into the Union, and the British government should not in any way lessen the force of that cause. For the entry of Rhodesia into the Union is not only in her own interest and in that of the Union but also in the interest of the British Empire. Rhodesia as a separate state struggling vainly with her impossible task is certain to become an embarrassment to the British government in the end.

It may be useful for you to have a talk with Sir Drummond Chaplin, the administrator of Rhodesia who is now on his way to London. Ever yours sincerely,

s. J. C. Smuts

86   To W. G. A. Ormsby-Gore   Vol. 25, no. 277

Prime Minister's Office

Pretoria

21 November 1922

My dear Ormsby-Gore, Hearty congratulations on your well-deserved promotion. Your position as colonial under-secretary will give you the most ample opportunity for the exercise of your gifts and the furtherance of the causes you have at heart.

I enclose for your private information a copy of a letter I have written the prime minister on Rhodesia. To me it is a matter of indifference which course the colonial office follows—whether they revert to the Milner policy or whether they give responsible government forthwith to Rhodesia. I know Rhodesia will be in the Union in a few years, and all I am really anxious about is that (in case responsible government is granted) no financial inducements are offered Rhodesia. If they get no assistance from the government they must inevitably come into Union soon and repair the mistake which they have just made in a fit of local patriotism. Rhodesia is going to be a heavy incubus to the colonial office, unless it joins the Union soon. Chaplin is really better informed than anybody on the details of the Rhodesian situation, and I trust you will discuss the whole position carefully with him. He is a man of very great ability—quite out of the common among colonial governors.

I trust you will also keep your interest in Palestine. In the new government will be strong forces trying to pull the government out of what they consider an expensive and dangerous entanglement. But I would advise holding on strongly to Palestine. For the sake of the world-wide Jewish question, for the sake of our position in Egypt, for the sake of the ideals we fought for, I think we should stand by the 'national home' policy and the mandate. With kind regards, Ever yours sincerely,

s. J. C. Smuts

87   From Earl Buxton

Vol. 25, no. 16

Newtimber Place
Hassocks
Sussex
21 November 1922

My dear Smuts, I feel sure that you must have been terribly worried over the question of these executions.[1] I should like therefore, if I may, to send you one line of sympathy (which is *not to be answered*).

As far as I can judge over here, the advice you gave to the governor-general appears to me to have been entirely right. I feel confident that if I had still been there, I should have fully agreed with it, and acted on it.

I have read carefully the Graham commission [report],[2] an able document, and a full justification of the strong action taken by the government.

As regards the incidents, the only doubtful one seems to be the Hanekom case,[3] but I was much struck by the argument and

[1] Eighteen participators in the Rand strike of 1922, after trial by the ordinary courts, were sentenced to death for murder. Of these four were hanged. They were: Herbert Hull and David Lewis, who both had criminal records; Carl Christian Stassen, who had shot two Natives in Sophiatown; and Samuel Alfred (Taffy) Long, a popular strike leader whom many miners regarded as unjustly executed.

[2] *Report of the Martial Law Inquiry Judicial Commission* (U. G. 35 of 1922). The two commissioners were both supreme court judges, T. Lynedoch Graham and John H. Lange.

[3] For the Hanekom case *see supra*, p. 125, note 3. The other two incidents investigated by the Commission were those of Jacobus Johannes Christoffel van Wyk and William Edward Dowse. They were shot, after arrest for concealing arms and ammunition, on 16 March by members of the government forces. The commission found that both were shot while attempting to escape. (U. G. 35 of 1922, pp. 35–45.)

inference contained in the latter part of paragraph 273 as a strong point in favour of Captain [W. H.] Kirby's bona fides.[1]

I have seen [Sir T.] Watt once or twice. He is certainly the better for his rest.

Our best remembrances to Mrs Smuts. Yours very sincerely,

Buxton

88   To W. S. Churchill   Vol. 25, no. 278

Pretoria

22 November 1922

My dear Churchill, First the news of your serious illness and then the news of your defeat at Dundee have come as great shocks to your friends in South Africa. I am really awfully sorry, whatever view you may take of the defeat. But perhaps it is as well that you get a short spell of rest after the very heavy labours you have had to bear recently. I trust you will soon be all right and all the better to do the great work which is still before you.

[Lloyd] George must have misjudged the situation very seriously. Either he should have pushed through the formation of a centre party while it still had a chance, or he should have precipitated an election at his own time. Instead he has waited for Sir George Younger and the Die-Hards, and they have successfully ambushed him.[2] In politics it is as in war, as soon as you start drifting you are lost. For the present anyhow the British people are in a quiet mood, and I think it would be a mistake to harass Bonar Law too much. His act of courage[3] has already had its reward, and people would like him to get a fair chance. Even with his overburden of dukes and marquises etc.[4]

Rhodesia has also gone wrong. It is a great blow to me. It is a worse blow to Rhodesia. But it will be temporary. Hard times are the best school for wisdom, and hard times are only just coming

---

[1] Captain W. H. Kirby was in command of B Company of the Transvaal Scottish Regiment of the Active Citizen Force and led the escort which fired upon and killed the Hanekom brothers and M. W. Smith. He had joined the army in 1914 and served in South West Africa and France. He was second in command of his regiment from 1923 to 1929 but resigned as colonel when he was passed over for the command. He rejoined the army in 1939 and was killed in action in 1941. See also supra, p. 125, note 3.

[2] For the circumstances of the fall of Lloyd George's coalition government see C. L. Mowat, *Britain between the Wars 1918–1940*, pp. 137–42.

[3] Bonar Law had, in spite of ill-health, reluctantly come out of retirement to lead the Conservative party against the coalition.

[4] Bonar Law's cabinet included seven peers, one a duke.

there. If the colonial office avoids the mistake of giving them financial assistance, they will be knocking at the door of the Union in a few years.

Give my very kindest regards to Mrs Churchill. Ever yours sincerely,

s. J. C. Smuts

89   To N. Talbot   Vol. 25, no. 284

Pretoria
5 December 1922

Dear Bishop Talbot, I was glad to hear from you the other day and hope, if you have at any time any views to offer, that you will feel that you can freely communicate with me. I am sure there are many things in which we can help each other and I shall always be glad to hear from you.

I hope that you found your mother and father in England well. I expect that you got a tremendous welcome when you arrived there.

You write to me about the Native affairs department and Native affairs generally.[1] I have been dealing with this matter myself recently and the public service commissioners are, from their point of view, making certain recommendations in regard to the better administration of the department. These recommendations we shall have to consider and we must see, in their recommendations for economical working, that the real welfare of the Natives is not prejudiced.

All of us have been feeling during the last few years the growing importance of Native affairs but, at the same time, I have felt that it is far better to proceed slowly and not to rush in with hasty legislation, which will only have the effect of adding confusion to the difficulties which will eventually have to be overcome. Besides, during the last few years, I think everybody will admit, that governments have had their attention very fully occupied by matters arising out of the post-war situation and that the atmosphere has not been entirely favourable to placid consideration.

The Native Urban Areas Bill,[2] I hope, will give us machinery to deal with Natives in towns and after that we shall have to tighten up

[1] Bishop Talbot had written (Smuts Collection, vol. 25, no. 327) urging improvement in the administration of Native affairs and in the personnel of the department. Smuts was at this time minister of native affairs.

[2] The Native (Urban Areas) Bill was enacted in 1923. It contained provisions to control the influx of Natives into the towns and to improve their housing in locations.

our district administration and see that the existing state of affairs is improved.

In regard to the personnel, I note your views. I do not want to commit myself in regard to details but I agree that the Native affairs department requires really first-class men and that those appointed must realize their grave responsibilities and be capable of carrying out the very important duties entrusted to that department.

I hope that you may be successful in your mission in England and be fortunate enough to secure men of high character and ability to come and assist with the beneficent work on which you are engaged. I know that in this matter finance, alas! plays an important part and although I feel confident that we are slowly getting out of our difficulties, I know that church accounts are the last that feel any improvement. With good wishes, Yours very sincerely,

s. J. C. Smuts

90   From E. H. Walton   Vol. 25, no. 349

Trafalgar Square
London
12 December 1922

My dear Smuts, I enclose you an extract from the *Daily Telegraph* containing an article by Lloyd George. This is the first of a series, and I will see that you get them. The little man will probably be successful in the bid he is making for the leadership of a united Liberal party, and it will not be surprising to find him leading a very strong contingent by the time the next general election comes round.

I note that you are making agreements with the Marconi Company, and if you are brought into contact with the late postmaster-general, Kellaway [F. G.], you should know that he is not too highly thought of on this side.

The colonial secretary has sent me a copy of your telegram dealing with the proposed economic conference. I should have thought that the time mentioned by you would have been more convenient to ministers on this side, except for the fact that the date might interfere with the shooting, etc. We must remember that people of the Devonshire type have never been broken in to work as we were.

I saw a report the other day that several of our Kaffirs had been sent to Moscow to pass through the Bolshevist training college there to qualify them as Bolshevist missionaries among their own people. The existence of such a college has been known for some time. I don't know whether you would think it worth while to ascertain the names of the South Africans who may be there, but if you do, I will make the attempt through our local police here. This propaganda work seems to be the one thing for which the Russians can find money.[1]

If the delivery of lectures will do us any good, we ought to be prospering. Last week I took the chair for a lecture written, I understand, by Zechariah and delivered by Boshoff [S. P. E.] at the Royal Colonial Institute, and last night I took the chair at a lecture on South African history by [Sir George] Cory, and in another hall last night, Professor [I. J.] Rousseau was also delivering a lecture on South Africa. We are getting many enquiries but we do not gush, nor go beyond saying there is a good living for honest work.

I note that you have agreed to accept liability for the League of Nations contribution on the Postal-Union basis for 1921, the liability involved to be liquidated by annual instalments. I am sure this decision will much gratify both [Sir Herbert] Ames and [Sir Eric] Drummond. I will write to both and put to the latter your point about South Africans on the League staff. I may say that I had some conversation on this subject, and was told when in Geneva last that the British representation on the staff was already in excess of their proportion, and that no more British were likely to be appointed for some time. You will be amused, knowing the absolutely sincere enthusiasm of our friend, Robert Cecil, for the League, but there is no doubt that this very fact has given him the idea that he has a claim to appoint his friends to jobs, and that this has been done fairly extensively. My wife was much amused at a remark made by Lady Mary Murray when she heard that the British list was full: 'Well, we shall not be able to get any more of our friends on the League of Nations.' However, we have a claim, and I will put it to Drummond.

Rhodesia. I don't suppose that Devonshire has thought more about this question than that it is one of those bothering things somebody or other will have to deal with some time. There is, however, quite an able permanent under-secretary at the colonial office in [Sir James] Masterton-Smith, who will be able to put a clear statement of the case before the prime minister. [Sir Dougal Orme] Malcolm came to dinner the other night and said that they are pressing their claim and have no doubt of succeeding.[2] Milner

---

[1] A marginal note inserted here in Smuts's handwriting reads: 'Ask for report. J.C.S.'.

[2] Sir Dougal Malcolm was at this time a director of the British South Africa Company.

was also there, but he did not say anything. Of course Masterton-Smith holds Milner responsible for the policy laid down by the colonial office and adopted by Winston when he appointed the Buxton commission. However, all that is fading into ancient history. He would, naturally, very much prefer that Rhodesia should come in, and would work for any practicable scheme in that direction. I note your suggestion to Bonar Law that Coghlan should be sent for to discuss the situation. You know Coghlan as well as I do, and I should say that it would require a very substantial inducement to persuade him to drop the prize for which he has been working harder than he ever worked for anything before. Even if Coghlan himself could be persuaded in the matter, failure on the part of the imperial government to accept the results of the referendum would create a very bad impression in Rhodesia, and give us some very discontented fellow citizens.

I heard of the discussion in the United States on the Bondelswarts rising, and have been asked to be interviewed, etc. I have repeated what I said at the League congress when I appealed for suspension of judgment pending publication of the official report.[1] I felt inclined, however, to tell the Americans to go and read their own history and their attitude towards Natives as evidenced in their daily press by their lynchings and murders, and I might have added that I hoped the day would never come when South Africa would take the United States as a model for its treatment of the Coloured races.

With regard to the forthcoming exhibition,[2] the high commissioners had a meeting on Friday, with reference to the restriction of exhibits, restaurants etc. to British products. I know your views on the subject, and the Australians have taken a similar line, and they wish to make it a condition that no exceptions should be made to the rule, unless with the consent of the high commissioners. Canada has not yet agreed to come in, but their high commissioner assured us that they would come in if the condition we proposed was accepted.

13 December. I cabled you last night on the subject of the cattle

[1] The Bondelswarts were a South West African people who had come into armed conflict with a Union government force in May 1922. In July Smuts appointed a commission of three members of the permanent Native affairs commission to inquire into the circumstances of the clash. It reported in March 1923 and the matter subsequently came before the permanent mandates commission of the League of Nations. Both commissions made adverse criticisms of the government's handling of the disputes which led to Bondelswart defiance.

[2] The British Empire exhibition at Wembley in north-west London. It was opened on 23 April 1924.

embargo fiasco. On Monday night, in a very thin house, while many of the members were at dinner, [Sir Robert] Sanders, the minister in charge of this bill, accepted an amendment for the deletion of clause 4, which provided that all Dominions etc. should share in the advantages given to Canada. As soon as I could get hold of the under colonial secretary yesterday, I tackled him about this and went down to the house of commons. I could not see the Duke of Devonshire himself, but he instructed his secretary to show me a copy of a cablegram he had sent to you on the subject. I spoke to several members at the house of commons, and the subject was renewed last evening at the third reading. I was hoping to get some answer from you this morning but have not done so, and at three o'clock I went down to the colonial office again and saw the Duke. The government had not heard from you either, but I said I was sure you would be very much disturbed at the incident, and pointed out its gravity. It was not as if discrimination between the Dominions had been legislated for by accident or oversight. Here was a case in which provision for equal treatment was deliberately withdrawn from an act of parliament, and the principle of discrimination and unequal treatment was therefore deliberately laid down. It was difficult to conceive anything more dangerous, and I asked the Duke to imagine what your position would be if, as a result of this act, someone moved in the Union parliament the abolition of the customs preference on British goods. However, the government is only going to take the second reading in the house of lords today; they are thinking hard as to what can be done, and there is no doubt that they are sincerely anxious to remedy the blunder. I shall add any later news before I close this letter tomorrow, and trust it may be more satisfactory.

Please accept my best wishes for the New Year, and I sincerely hope that it may be free from the anxiety that brought upon you so terrible a strain at the beginning of this year, and thank you very much for your kind message. It is a real pleasure to work with you, and a great satisfaction to know that I have been able to be of real help. Kindest regards to you and yours, Yours very sincerely,

E. H. Walton

91   To E. H. Walton   Vol. 25, no 289

Pretoria
13 December 1922

My dear Walton, In your letter of 27 September you made the suggestion that it would be a good thing if we were to invite Ranjitsinhji[1] to visit South Africa in order to make himself acquainted with the Indian problem on the spot.

I am forwarding for your information a copy of our despatch to the Indian government in reply to one of theirs in which they put forward certain representations on behalf of the Indians. From it you will see the line we have taken.

We fully appreciate the attitude of Ranjitsinhji as disclosed both in his speech and in his letter. He has expressed himself very moderately in both.[2] At the same time it does not appear advisable to invite him here because we have only recently declined to invite Mr [S.] Sastri here when pressed to do so by the British Indian Association. Under these circumstances an invitation to Ranjitsinhji would be misunderstood and any chance he might have of doing good here would thereby be destroyed.

The question of inviting a prominent Indian here is one on which there is much to be said on both sides and while I don't want to make any promise on the matter now, I think we might well discuss the matter if there is a prime ministers' conference in the near future. With kind regards, Yours sincerely,

s. J. C. Smuts

92   To M. C. Gillett   Vol. 25, no. 325

Pretoria
20 December 1922

I have missed two mails—partly due to ill health and partly to pressure of work. I am at present the only minister in Pretoria and my soul is eaten up with all the daily worries of all the offices, at least all such as cannot wait. Life is really a burden, sometimes almost insupportable. And it is never the great things, which one would rejoice to do, but the small things which create friction and bad temper and ill will...

I am really in a despondent mood, due I suppose to exhaustion after all the awful work of this year. But there is also exhaustion of

---

[1] Kumar Shri Ranjitsinhji, the famous cricketer and Maharaja of Nawanagar.

[2] Walton had enclosed, in his letter of 27 September, both Ranjitsinhji,s speech and his letter (to Walton), but neither is in the Smuts Collection.

soul. In this country there is the dreadful wash up of all the revolutionary business. To me one of the hardest things is to take life. And yet the matter is not so simple as it appears to your good Quaker soul. And in the great world I see nothing but black ruin staring us in the face. I have cabled very strongly to Bonar Law about the latest threats of Poincaré[1] and he has replied that he is generally in agreement with me. But I still fear the madness of France. What a world we have come to! The peace completely lost in the East, and Turk triumphant over Christian and booting him out of Asia Minor. And in the West a fratricidal strife continuing among the Christian nations which can only lead to the decay of our Christian civilization.

You were right. Figs do not grow on thistles.[2] And the Great War could not be expected to lead to the spiritual salvation of mankind. I had hoped that the great lesson had gone home. But evidently the Great War has taught us nothing but evil so far. And yet some unseen Power may be guiding us through this dark night. If I did not have this last vestige of a faith, I would really not be able to go on. Who knows whether light may not be dawning on human souls long before it becomes visible in human society? Christianity began in the slaves' quarters of the decadent Roman Empire. And so some seed of good may be germinating even now in the hearts of men.

... It is a great pity that your original plans could not be carried out. It would have done us all good to have gone about the country at this time of the year. Beautiful rains have made this part of South Africa more gorgeous than I have seen it for years. Now we shall just go slow.

Good-bye, dears. God bless you all. And be assured that you are remembered ever and always lovingly.

Jan

93   To W. Ormsby-Gore   Vol. 27, no. 173

Private and personal

19 January 1923

My dear Ormsby-Gore, In your letter of 13 December you ask for a private expression of my views in regard to Northern Rhodesia. I was sorry that we were so much hurried over the Southern

---

[1] Poincaré had, on 9 December, added to his list of 'productive guarantees'. *See supra*, p. 148, note 4.

[2] 'Do men gather grapes of thorns, or figs of thistles?' *St Matthew* vii. 16.

Rhodesia negotiations at Cape Town that there was no time to deal also with Northern Rhodesia. The lines along which I would have sought a solution were more or less as follows:

The Chartered Company conduct the administration of Northern Rhodesia at a loss of about £100,000 per annum. They are naturally anxious to pass this costly burden on to somebody else. But they claim much of the land and the mineral rights, as well as compensation for expenditure on public buildings and other improvements. If the colonial office or the Union would relieve them of the burden of administration and leave them to nurse their assets and wait for the unearned increment they would be on velvet. This, however, is not a policy that could for a moment be agreed to. And I would suggest that if they are relieved of the administration, they should also renounce all their other claims, to land and minerals etc. I understood from confidential information from Churchill that the treasury were willing to reduce the war claim against the Chartered Company in connection with Northern Rhodesia to £250,000. This amount the British government were willing to forego in case of a favourable referendum and the petition of right not being proceeded with. As neither of these conditions have been fulfilled the claim for war expenditure revives. This is a debt of the Chartered Company and should only be wiped out if they renounce all their rights to Northern Rhodesia. The administration of the territory could on these conditions be taken over by the crown and later on (when Southern Rhodesia comes into the Union) by the Union.[1]

I believe the Chartered Company would have accepted this solution if the referendum had gone right. It is now for the colonial office to put it through if they agree with my suggestion. I would not pay the Chartered Company any compensation for their assets and I would not advise taking over the territory unless all other rights are also taken over. Ever yours sincerely,

s. J. C. Smuts

[1] The rule of the British South Africa Company in Northern Rhodesia ended on 1 April 1924. The Company's claim for excess of administrative expenditure over revenue and the crown's counterclaim for war debt were abandoned. The Company was to receive half the net proceeds of all alienation of land until 1965 and it retained in freehold two-and-a-half million acres. It would receive mineral royalties in perpetuity. The mineral rights, worth some £13,000 a year in 1924, had risen to over £300,000 by 1939. (See A. J. Hanna, *The Story of the Rhodesias and Nyasaland* (1960), pp. 167–8.)

94   Press statement (1923)   Box G, no. 8

The charge that Smuts had been responsible for greatly increasing the
amount of reparation which Germany was required to pay by the treaty of
Versailles had its origin in the publication of his memorandum on pensions
and allowances by B. M. Baruch in 1920 (**926, 32**) and comment upon
the memorandum in a review of Baruch's book by J. M. Keynes (**41**).
H. G. Wells, returning from the Washington conference early in 1922, declared that it was Smuts who had added the last straw to the intolerable load
put upon Germany. When, a year later, Hertzog repeated and enlarged the
charge in the Union house of assembly, Smuts at last defended himself against
it in this statement to the press on 6–7 February 1923. *Die Burger* printed it
in Afrikaans but, in a long editorial note, preferred to believe H. G. Wells,
whose comment it quoted, and added: 'Generaal Smuts mis die moed om
eerlik sy fout te erken en die sedelike krag om te probeer dit te herstel.'
(General Smuts lacks the courage honestly to admit his fault and the
moral strength to try to put it right.) *See Die Burger*, 7 February 1923,
p. 5.

General Hertzog in his reply last week on the 'no-confidence'
motion accused me of having been responsible for the huge reparation amount which Germany has to pay under the peace treaty.
He indicated that but for me the reparation figure would have been
2,000 million sterling instead of 6,000 million. As I had no opportunity at the end of that debate to reply or to make a statement in
reference to this charge I tried to do so the following day. Owing,
however, to objections raised by the opposition I did not avail
myself of the Speaker's permission to make the statement and said
I would seek for another opportunity to do so. As the charge does
not arise from anything before parliament and is more of an historical and personal character, the proper course under the circumstances would be not to encroach on the time of parliament but to
give my statement to the press.

The charge is on the face of it ridiculous as it assumes a personal
influence on my part at Paris so overwhelming as to be incredible.
Imagine a representative of one of the smallest and least of the
states at the conference so influential and powerful that his voice
could settle the biggest and most difficult of all the issues which
confronted the peace conference. The thing is on the face of it
absurd.

It is advisable, however, to state the facts and I shall do so as
briefly and simply as possible.

The reparation question was entrusted by the conference to the
reparation commission of which I was not a member. The commission discussed the question for months but failed to come to

any conclusions and in the end referred the matter to the so called Big Four who represented the great powers.

One of the most important issues raised had to do with pensions and separation allowances, and the question was whether they could be included in the reparation amount. In the correspondence between President Wilson and the German government, which preceded the armistice, it was stipulated that Germany should pay reparation for all damage done to Allied civilians by land or sea or air. It was contended in the reparation commission that the subsequent armistice terms had superseded this stipulation. The Big Four, without expressing an opinion on this contention, raised the purely legal question whether, assuming the stipulation still to hold, the claim for pensions and allowances could be included in the reparation amount. In other words whether the interpretation of the phrase 'civilian damage' would cover and include pensions and allowances. I was one of the lawyers at the conference whom the Big Four consulted on this point. On the legal question, and apart from questions of policy, I had no doubt whatever, and I wrote an opinion, which I fully argued out, that civilian damage did cover pensions and allowances. This opinion along with the rest was considered by the Big Four, and in the result they included pensions and allowances in the reparation account. It was subsequently stated that it had been my argument that had convinced President Wilson and carried the day against the opinion of his own lawyers.

These are the simple and incontrovertible facts, and I ask how responsibility could be attached to me for an opinion on a technical question of law? A lawyer who gives a legal opinion on a statement of facts does not thereby become responsible for the actions of the client who has consulted him. It may be said that my opinion was wrong. Mr Keynes, who is not a lawyer, has said so. I can only say that I had no doubt in the matter. And I know that many of the greatest lawyers at the conference shared my opinion. The late lord chancellor,[1] the present lord chief justice,[2] Lord Sumner, the distinguished lord of appeal in the house of lords, the present English attorney-general,[3] all held the same view. And I could mention many of the greatest continental lawyers who also agreed. The American lawyers differed, but it was not my fault that President Wilson, himself a distinguished jurist, adopted my argument and not theirs.

Even if my opinion had not prevailed, there would still have been left the point, already mentioned, that in the actual armistice agreement the terms of President Wilson's stipulations had been

[1] Lord Birkenhead.   [2] Lord Hewart.   [3] Sir Douglas Hogg.

superseded. This was the view of another set of jurists. And if this obstacle had been surmounted there were still more formidable issues raised in the reparation commission, which would then have had to be dealt with by the Big Four, and which would in all probability have led to the inclusion of pensions and allowances in the reparation amount in any case.

I cannot go into these matters here. But it is quite wrong to single out my opinion from a vast mass of relevant matter and make it the pivot round which the whole decision moved. That may be flattering to me but it is a complete distortion of the truth.

So much for the point of law. What was my attitude on the question of policy, whether an extortionate sum should be claimed from Germany? The majority of the reparation commission favoured the highest possible damages from Germany. There were some who held that Germany could and should pay the whole war damage of all the Allies, a sum in the neighbourhood of 25,000 million sterling, and that President Wilson's terms were no bar to such a claim. Others were somewhat less extreme in their claims, but even their ideas seemed to me to go far beyond what was either possible or expedient. Both in the British Empire delegation and out of it in other sections of the conference I used every scrap of such influence as I possessed to get the reparation figures down to a fair, moderate and fixed amount. It is perfectly well known to those who took part in the conference that I was probably the most active protagonist at the conference for fixing the reparation amount at a reasonably low figure. I incurred bitter odium and obloquy at the conference because of the energy with which I pushed my view on this dangerous subject. The view which I consistently advocated was that, whether pensions were or were not included—indeed whatever items or valuations of damage were accepted as between the Allies—as regards the Germans the total amount due should be definitely fixed in the peace treaty and that it should be such as Germany could reasonably pay without dislocation of her economic life. Unfortunately this view did not prevail. The peace treaty did not fix the amount due by Germany and left it to the determination of the reparation commission, no doubt in the hope that the commission would act in a fair and judicial spirit. This commission, however, became hopelessly lopsided owing to the failure of the United States to ratify the treaty and to be represented on the commission. The sum which this truncated commission ultimately fixed in May 1921 was 6,600 million sterling, a sum which was absolutely beyond the power of Germany to pay. And this impossible amount is now being used as a lever for the dismemberment of Germany and the reduction of the whole central Europe to a condition of industrial and economic chaos. All this has been brought about against my advice and in the teeth of my strongest opposition. And I disclaim all responsibility for the results.

Bad as the peace treaty was (and I protested against it even when I had no option but to sign it), it was not so bad as it has worked out in actual practice. America's entry was the keystone of the victory, and her collaboration was the keystone of the peace. When she decided to retire from the position, the peace was lost. I do not blame her but the facts speak for themselves. The reparation commission that resulted from her withdrawal was not a judicial body, nor was it in a position to exercize the power of moderation and mitigation which was expressly vested in it by the peace treaty. Finally matters have reached such a climax that the representative of the British Empire has ceased to function; and the reparation commission has lost all semblance of a non-partisan character and has virtually become an annexe of the French foreign office. The promise which was held out to the Germans in the covering letter to the peace treaty, and for which I claim some small credit, viz., that if the treaty proved unworkable the League of Nations would be the destined instrument for its eventual amendment,—that promise has not yet been carried out. The sands are running out and unless some strong hand can even now clutch Europe and rescue her from the slope down which she is slipping, the catastrophe of the peace may yet become far greater than that of the Great War.

95   To M. C. Gillett   Vol. 27, no. 349

Cape Town
1 March 1923

I failed to write last mail owing to parliamentary difficulties and encroachments on my time. But I know you don't expect a letter every week. Last Sunday we went up Table mountain to unveil a memorial[1] to members of the mountain club who fell in the Great War. It was a unique occasion, with the most delightful weather, and thousands were there. I made a little speech which found great favour and I send you a copy.[2] It is a bit of me and not merely a speech....

[1] At Maclear's Beacon on the summit.
[2] *See Greater South Africa, the Speeches of General J. C. Smuts* (Johannesburg, 1940), pp. 31–5 for the text of this speech which was made on 25 February 1923.

I have had a handsome letter from Keynes about my reparation memo.[1] As his books have been the principal ground of attack on me both here and in America, I was glad to hear him say that grave injustice had been done me and that nobody had worked harder for a sane and wise peace than I had done at Paris. This might interest Arthur.

Yesterday the Belgian representative here[2] came to speak to me about the Ruhr position.[3] His point was that without reparations Belgium was bankrupt. I told him that the only advice I could give the French and Belgian governments was to increase their armies very largely and to prepare for the next war which their action was making a certainty. He appeared much disconcerted. Poor devils, they know not what they do. With a friendly handshake to all,

Jan

96   To J. M. Keynes   Vol. 98, no. 301

Groote Schuur
Rondebosch
Cape Town
10 March 1923

My dear Keynes, Thank you very much for your last note. I appreciate very much what you say.

My statement on reparations was intended not so much to be an apologia as an attack on the reparation commission which has become a body quite different from what was originally intended, and become a mere subservient tool of French policy.

I fear British statesmen have seen too late that the French were intent not so much on reparations as on the Rhine frontier. [Lloyd] George took the French seriously and so did Bonar Law. But while Poincaré *talked* reparations he really meant the old Rhine policy. We now sit with the fruits of this misunderstanding. We seem even to have given France our blessing in trying to get more reparations *via* the Rhine and the Ruhr, whereas it is these two that are wanted. And if the French get them I fear Great Britain will sink to a secondary position on the continent of Europe. In fact that is already happening. Bonar Law says that he will not move for fear of displeasing France. And in spite of it all we talk as if the

[1] Smuts Collection, vol. 26, no. 198.
[2] G. Stadler.
[3] Having received a notification by the reparations commission of a trifling German default in coal deliveries to France, Poincaré ordered French troops to occupy the Ruhr basin on 11 January 1922.

Entente[1] is still in existence. The way out of this imbroglio will be difficult to find, unless France makes such a mess of it that she breaks down in her effort to dismember Germany.

America still remains the key if she will only act with Great Britain. That may perhaps happen two years hence,[2] but it may then be too late.

If I come to London next autumn I hope to see something of you, as we missed each other last time. And I am anxious to keep in touch with you. With best wishes, Ever yours sincerely,

J. C. Smuts

97   To M. C. Gillett   Vol. 27, no. 350

Groote Schuur
[Cape Town]
15 March 1923

Last week I found no opportunity to write but I received a most welcome letter from you, full of plans for the future. Now let me say at once that nothing yet is settled about the prime ministers' conference. Two dates have been proposed to both of which I have had to object as they make my attendance impossible. I know there are difficulties for some of the other prime ministers too, and personally I am doubtful whether the conference will take place this year. It is a time of great unsettlement in all the Dominions. Governments are everywhere unstable and in trouble. I have just lost another most awkward bye-election.[3] And you can understand that our difficulties are not lessened by three or four months' absence from our countries in these critical times. At the same time a conference this year (if it does not come too late) could assist to shape our Continental policy and do good in that way. I don't know whether the evils which afflict the European peoples are beyond cure. But I do believe mere passiveness on the part of the British Commonwealth will be fatal all round, and that another most earnest unselfish effort should be made to pull the world out of the abyss into which it is visibly slipping. If I could help in this respect,

[1] The Entente Cordiale between Great Britain and France which arose out of an agreement on colonial questions signed on 8 April 1904 and later led to joint naval and military plans which became operative when war broke out in 1914.

[2] When a presidential election would normally be due. But President Warren G. Harding died in August 1923.

[3] At a bye-election at Oudtshoorn (8 March 1923) caused by the death of Dr J. A. Raubenheimer, South African party, the National party candidate, S. P. le Roux, polled 1,781 votes against 1,254 for the South African party candidate, J. H. Schoeman.

I would not care a farthing about my position in South Africa. Europe is plunging to destruction, and the great crisis which is rapidly coming may either mean one thing or the other—either ruin all round, or a great effort to pull out of the danger and to make a fresh start, such as was missed at Paris in 1919. It is very late now but the mere desperateness of the situation may create the opportunity for salvation and the beginnings of a new Europe. I would therefore make great sacrifices to attend a conference if it can be at all arranged. The rest of our plans are all dependent on this major issue, and need not be discussed now.

Today a year ago I had just succeeded in stamping out the Red revolution on the Rand. What a time it has been! Sometimes even the memory of it all is like a nightmare. Such public and personal dangers have been gone through and overcome; such crowded events reaching down to the foundations of things have been breathlessly lived through. The world is undoubtedly acquiring a new temper which is very puzzling to me. Things which I should have thought impossible are happening as a matter of course, and are taken quite coolly all round. Perhaps we of the older generation are no longer in close touch with the hidden springs of life and don't appreciate or understand what is taking place.

We have Frank Hirst here lecturing on the orthodox political economy. It sounds all very wise, and yet like so many of the formulas of liberalism it sounds out of tune with the new economic and political environment. He is a good fellow and I like Mrs Hirst too. Mrs Rowntree goes next week. Isie and the small ones have arrived and Groote Schuur is most cheerful and merry. I have a bad cold but am otherwise physically well. Good-bye, dears. Love to you all,

from Jan

98   To E. H. Walton   Vol. 27, no. 198

Cape Town
16 March 1923

My dear Walton, I am much obliged for your letter of 21 February. I agree entirely with your views in regard to the position of Indians in South Africa[1] and you should maintain the position which you outline in your letter in any discussions which may take place.

[1] In a letter of 21 February 1923 Walton had written to Smuts as follows: 'The Indian question will stand on its own merits—we cannot hand Natal over to the Indian population and that, I suppose, would be practically the result of giving them equal political status. Nor, I think, are we prepared to see our retail businesses put into the hands of the Indian population and our own shopkeeping class dispossessed.'

I will have copies of our communications with the government of India sent to you by next mail, to show you the views which they have put forward and the answer we have sent to the viceroy.

With regard to the Bondelswarts, I am sorry to say that I am not in a position to send you the report. The commission has kept on promising it but so far it has failed to materialize.[1] It is not very creditable to the commission that they have taken this long time to come to a conclusion, but one of the real difficulties in the way of signing the report is—between ourselves—that the commissioners talked rather freely as soon as they had completed taking evidence and stated that they were going to report and condemn [G. R.] Hofmeyr's administration root and branch. However, when they came to examine the report more carefully and to weigh up the evidence which they had taken, they found that a great deal of the evidence could not bear out the interpretation which they had put on it in the first instance. The result is now that they have to sign a very modified report and their friends, to whom they spoke in the first instance, will be asking them how is it that they now come to change their tune. There is no doubt that we were on the right track when we appointed a Native affairs commission,[2] but whether we have got the right personnel on the present commission[3] I sometimes very much doubt. I will send you the report as soon as possible with some suggestions, which may be useful to you when discussing it in the League of Nations, but I fancy the report will not cause the sensation that Mr [J. H.] Harris and his friends expected it would.[4]

I shall see that Hofmeyr's administrative report[5] is sent to you in plenty of time for transmission to the permanent mandates commission. Hofmeyr and Herbst [J. F.] are down here at the present

[1] See supra, p. 157, note 1.

[2] The schedule to the South Africa Act had provided for the appointment of a commission to advise the prime minister on the administration of the British protectorates when they should be incorporated into the Union. The main function of the Native affairs commission, set up in 1920, was, however, to advise the government on Native administration in general. By the Native Affairs Act, No. 55 of 1959, a Bantu affairs commission, presided over by the minister of Bantu affairs and development, was constituted. Its functions also are advisory.

[3] The members at this time were General L. A. S. Lemmer, Dr C. T. Loram and Senator A. W. Roberts.

[4] J. H. Harris (q.v.), then secretary of the Aborigines Protection Society, had written a sensational article on the Bondelswarts affair in the New Statesman of 28 August 1922 headed 'A Punitive Expedition under the League of Nations' and reprinted by his society. In the New Statesman of 12 May 1923 he criticized adversely the report of the Native affairs commission.

[5] Report of the Administrator on the Bondelswarts Rising, 1922 (U. G. 30 of 1922). The report was tabled on 19 July 1923.

time and the report will be completed here before the former returns to South West Africa.

I mentioned to you last week that Romyn [A. C.] had been down here on behalf of the Pretoria Iron Works, and that he was grievously ill. He died the same evening and what is the terrible tragedy is that his wife, who was also very ill, died on the following Monday in Pretoria.

I think that the whole Pretoria Iron business will now come to a standstill pending the return of Delfos [C. R.], who will now come out I expect and discuss matters locally.

Sir Bouchier Wrey, Bart., who is the chairman of the Rhodesia Chamber of Mines and a great stalwart of the Unionist party in Rhodesia, went to England last mail. He lives half the year in Bulawayo and half the year in England. He is a very charming gentleman and quite reliable and if he calls on you, perhaps you would see him. I doubt very much whether we can do anything in regard to Rhodesia at the moment. However, if we ever want to make any use of Wrey's services they are at our disposal and we could rely on him in every way.

I had hoped by this time that the Beef Export Bounties Bill would have made some progress but unfortunately we had to refer it to a select committee and I very much doubt whether we shall get it through before the recess.[1] It is rumoured that the opposition wish to kill it by holding it up, but I shall certainly do my best to get it through as I feel convinced that farmers are quite unable to export unless they get some form of subsidy. Even then the exporting companies, with the price they can get on the Continent, will have a very small return.

I have been approached by individual members in Kenya to support them in their protest against the imperial government's policy regarding Indians in Kenya. I have told them that I am not prepared to discuss the matter unless officially asked to do so by their executive council in Kenya, but if any member of the delegation should call on you, while they are in London, perhaps you would give him such facilities for communication with me as you think will meet the case. The people up there are a very nice lot and one wants to do what one can for them, though of course at the present time the quarrel is between them and the colonial office.

You will be interested in the debates on Jagger's railway estimates. The question of the recognition of the Nurahs[2] has created

---

[1] The bill became Act No. 12 of 1923.
[2] The National Union of Railway and Harbour Servants, founded 7 June 1916.

quite the sensation of the session. The debate is being continued today and I will tell you more about it next week. With kind regards, Yours sincerely,

s. J. C. Smuts

99   To I. B. Pole-Evans   Vol. 27, no. 203

Groote Schuur
[Cape Town]
29 March 1923

My dear Doctor, I was so sorry to see from Mary's[1] wire that you were ill in bed. The wire arrived here in the form 'ill. Tyd in bed'.[2] As if father Time had taken to bed at long last. I hope it is nothing serious and that you will soon be fit again. I had dropped some of my engagements in order that we might grass down the Olifants river and on to the Karriesbergen.[3] But if you don't come I shall not go so far afield and content myself with the neighbouring mountains.

Oryza sativa has been a first-class excitement to me. Thank you very much for the beautiful specimen, also for those of Eulalia villosa and Erag. aspera. It is all very interesting, but Oryza does intrigue me deeply. Rice could not have come during the time of the whites. The natives cultivate and eat rice in the Rufigi valley as well as on the islands of the Victoria Nyanza. And it is possible that in bygone centuries rice was cultivated farther south. But it may be an African indigenous plant. Your discovery opens quite a vista of speculation.

I am going this morning to have a look at Mrs [H. M. L.] Bolus's herbarium, as my grass knowledge is growing rusty. It would be so much more interesting to have you here too at such a time when one has a few days off from the daily grind.

The water on Droogegrond[4] is a great find, and I am duly grateful. The boring will cost me about £800 but this find is well worth it. With kindest regards and love to you both, Ever yours,

J. C. Smuts

I read Mary's researches into rust with great interest. I hope those researches will be continued. I deeply regret that she has left our service.[5]

---

[1] Wife of Dr Pole-Evans.

[2] Dr Pole-Evans's first name is Illtyd; *tyd* is Afrikaans for *time*.

[3] The Kareebergen in the noth-western Cape Province.

[4] One of Smuts's farms near Rust der Winter in the north-eastern Transvaal. He bought it in 1916.

[5] She had been employed in the Union department of agriculture.

100   From W. S. Churchill   Vol. 26, no. 48

Villa Rêve D'Or
Cannes, A.M.
7 April 1923

My dear Smuts, I never answered your very kind letter to me when I left office.[1] But I have been looking forward ever since to sending you a copy of my new book about the opening phase of the war.[2] I dwell a good deal in those dazzling terrible times, and I like to think of how we were together in so many important things. As Botha said to my Mother[3] in Westminster Hall in 1907,[4] 'we have been out in all weathers'.

Your friendship is always very much cherished by me. Believe me, Yours very sincerely,

Winston S. Churchill

101   To M. C. Gillett   Vol. 27, no. 351

Rondebosch
[Cape Town]
Good Friday [30 March] 1923

This is a glorious day and we intend spending the day on Table mountain, but I wish to write you a line before we go. I wish you and Arthur were here today. You know it is one of those wonderful days that send a subdued thrill through you from the time you get out of bed. You feel like singing, and even the humble task of shaving seems somehow to share in the delight. It will be great on the mountain.

I find my little address on Table mountain a month ago has had a good effect and attracted very widespread attention. The consecration of life by the spirit of joy seems somehow to be considered only a topic for poetry and not a subject for a politician with a reputation for worldliness. Some have said to me that *that* was the last thing they would have expected from me. And I retort by saying that when the last book is opened, I shall surprise them much more. But this is egotistical.

[1] Churchill had been secretary for the colonies in Lloyd George's coalition government. He was defeated at Dundee in the election of October 1922 and was recuperating at Cannes after an operation for appendicitis.

[2] The first part of *The World Crisis, 1911–1914*. It was followed by two further parts on the periods 1915 and 1916–18 published in 1923 and 1927.

[3] Lady Randolph Spencer-Churchill, born Jennie Jerome in New York on 10 January 1854; married Lord Randolph Churchill on 15 April 1874; died 1921.

[4] Botha was in London to attend the colonial conference of April 1907.

So you are still thinking of that farm. That is good. It looks now as fairly certain that I shall be in London in October. But it will be a very brief and hurried visit as I am badly wanted out here. I shall be there only for the month and hurry back probably before the end of the conference. In fact I wish I need not go as I am much out of tune with the British government over their policy. I have written stiffly to Bonar Law. Good-bye dears. Blessings from

Jan

I spent yesterday morning with Mrs Bolus over her grass herbarium. In all my troubles I don't forget my grasses.

102   From C. F. L. Leipoldt   Vol. 27, no. 6

De Volkstem[1]
Pretoria
21 May 1923

Dear Oom Jannie, This is, in the first place, to wish you many happy returns on the 24th when you celebrate what the French call your name day. I sincerely hope that it may be a really enjoyable day for you so that you may look forward to its return with pleasurable anticipation. Here we are alone now. Dr Engelenburg has departed, after giving us somewhat of a scare with his fluttering heart. Digitalis, however, came up to our fondest expectations, and his natural virility contributed to the successful issue from what was undoubtedly a serious attack of influenza.[2] On 1 July, as soon as paper supplies are available, we hope to start on an eight page paper, and make the old rag a little more presentable. I am still hoping that Pretoria may get its decent English newspaper, but so far negotiations are at a standstill. The *News*[3] is not at all working for union; it has plenty of ignorant little paragraphs, largely inspired by the Sons of England,[4] that are irritating. The latest is [V. P.] Stent's screech for a test case to settle the question of the validity of Afrikaans as an official language. I have suggested to Preller that we might anticipate this, by getting the Akademie[5] to take counsel's opinion on whether the word Dutch in the Africa Act includes

[1] *See* vol. II, p. 167, note 1.
[2] Leipoldt had taken a degree in medicine in London but was at this time an assistant editor of *De Volkstem*. Dr F. V. Engelenburg was the editor until 1924.
[3] The *Pretoria News*, established in June 1898.
[4] A patriotic and benevolent society established in the Cape Colony in 1881. It now has lodges throughout South Africa and Rhodesia. The members are men of British descent.
[5] *See* vol. III, p. 103, note 2.

Afrikaans.[1] You may remember that Melius de Villiers expressed himself categorically on this subject.

I am looking forward to the debate on the Bondelswarts. I sent the *Manchester Guardian* a synopsis of the report, and also of Hofmeyr's memorandum, and laid stress on the desirability of reading both together. Last week I sent them translations of the opinions of the Native press; these are, on the whole, quite favourable; much less alarmingly anti-Lemmer[2] than the opinions of some of our English papers. If you think it worth while, I will summarize the reports, with some criticism, for the *Fortnightly* [*Review*] or *Contemporary* [*Review*]. If there is anything you wish me to do, I hope you won't scruple to let me know.

By the way have you read that extraordinary second volume of Spengler's book on the Decline of the Occidental Nations?[3] The chapter on Roman Dutch law is peculiarly interesting, and the amazing encyclopaedic knowledge of the man *slaan 'n mens dronk*.[4] It is equally extraordinary that such a book, in many ways similar in tenor and ideal to the *Sittenlehr* of Fichte,[5] should have been produced at a similar period of German decadence. If you have not got it, I can send you both volumes.

It may interest you to hear that [Lord] Morley, in reply to a letter of mine, asking him if the statement in Steyn's autobiography that he (Morley) told him (Steyn) that if the Republics had fought on until June 1902 they would have got their full independence back, states that 'he never had the pleasure of meeting Mr Steyn' to the best of his knowledge and belief.[6] My letter to [Sir George] Arthur, asking him for his authority re that alleged letter of yours found at Reitz,[7] has so far not had a reply.

With kind regards and best wishes for your birthday, I remain, Yours truly,

C. Louis Leipoldt

[1] The South Africa Act of 1909, which constitutes the Union of South Africa declares in section 137 that 'both the English and Dutch languages shall be official languages of the Union'.

[2] In the report of the commission on the Bondelswarts rising issued in March 1923, one of the members, General L. A. S. Lemmer, differed on almost every finding from the other two, Dr C. T. Loram and Senator A. W. Roberts, who were to some extent critical of the action of the government.

[3] The second volume of *Der Untergang des Abendlandes* (*The Decline of the West*) by Oswald Spengler was subtitled *Welthistorische Perspektiven* (*Perspectives of World History*) and published in 1922.

[4] Takes one's breath away (Afrikaans).

[5] Johann Gottlieb Fichte's *System der Sittenlehr* (*System of Moral Philosophy*) was published in 1798.

[6] See N. J. van der Merwe, *Marthinus Theunis Steyn*, vol. II, p. 88 footnote.

[7] See vol. I, p. 389 and p. 391, note 1,

103   To G. R. Hofmeyr   Vol. 27, no. 221

Cape Town
25 May 1923

My dear Hofmeyr, The Bondelswarts debate is over[1] and has proved to be of unprecedented bitterness. I declined to go into the origins and causes, and directed attention to the two salient facts, viz. that Morris's return synchronized with a sinister gathering of the tribe to Haib, and that his military plans were ripe and you were only in the nick of time able to forestall an attack on Warmbad.[2] The Nats kept out of the debate and left the fight to the Labourites. My statement about Herbst being available with the evidence at Geneva you will have seen.

I wish to write to you about several other points. In the first place the depression in South West Africa. As I said to you it will probably be impossible to prevent certain people from going under. But we shall have to watch carefully the general condition of the people as a whole. I hope you will keep in touch with the banks especially, in order that they may supply you with all necessary information. The rank and file of the population should be saved from ruin, and any great setback of the German population will affect the Union population also. I feel sure you will carefully watch developments and advise action should it become necessary. Your financial position will be much easier with the great improvement in the diamond situation, and you will be able to afford assistance which some months ago might have appeared out of the question.

Secondly, a great deal was made in parliament of the Rehoboth position. I shall be glad if you could come to some reasonable settlement with the Rehoboths,[3] especially with the recovery and restoration to them of the white farms inside their reserve. If this could be done before next session it will prove helpful, especially as the Coloured people at the Cape have the impression that the Rehoboths have a grievance, and are treated by us worse than by the Germans. Do not stick at small concessions in order to carry your main point and fix up an agreement without undue delay.

[1] It took place on 21–3 May 1923.

[2] Abraham Morris was the military leader of the Bondelswarts. He returned illegally to the tribal capital, Guruchas, in May 1922 and the tribesmen prevented his arrest. Meanwhile it was widely believed that Morris was preparing for war against the whites. Hofmeyr decided to send a punitive force against the tribe. Bombs were dropped on Guruchas and 250 retreating tribesmen pursued southwards. On 4 June Morris died of his wounds and next day the remnant of his force surrendered.

[3] *See* vol. III, p. 454, note 3, and for an account of the Reheboths, J. S. Marais, *The Cape Coloured People*, pp. 98–108.

Thirdly, our main contention on the naturalization question has been conceded by the council of the League,[1] and it will now be possible for us to introduce legislation next year. I shall be glad if you would prepare a draft bill, and if you could, induce the Germans to write a letter to me, asking me to take such action. They may not have the same objection to this course that they have against public resolutions. But a letter or petition will suit me just as well. You can point out to them how difficult it is for me to take action in the face of the Windhoek meeting and resolution.[2] If we can put through the naturalization law next year,[3] we could put through a constitutional bill the following year (1925), under which South West Africa gets a legislative council and some members in the Union assembly. This matter will raise quite knotty points to which I wish you to begin to give your serious consideration as soon as possible. I mention the following:

1. Should there be a minority of nominated members in the council, the majority being elective?
2. What should be the powers of the council—the same as or different from those of a provincial council?
3. Should the position of the administrator be the same as that in our provinces, or should he have wider powers (as you now have)?
4. Will Union services be run from the Union or will the administrator run them for the Union? e.g. Natives, mines, finance, justice?
5. How should the executive committee be constituted, and what powers should it have? Will it be like the provincial executive or different?
6. How many members in the Union assembly? Will there be any in the senate?[4]

[1] The Union government proposed to offer the 7,000 German settlers South African nationality and to allow those who did not wish to accept to remain as alien residents without suffering any penalty. This proposal was agreed to by the council of the League of Nations in April 1923.

[2] On 23 February 1923, at a public meeting at Windhoek, resolutions proposed by Colonel de Jager were passed asking the administrator to approach Smuts to introduce legislation forthwith to make the South Africans in South West Africa citizens of the Union and to enable those German inhabitants who wished to do so to obtain Union citizenship.

[3] A South West African Naturalization of Aliens Act was passed in 1924.

[4] Act 42 of 1925 provided for (a) a legislative assembly of twelve elected and six nominated members, (b) an executive committee consisting of the administrator and four members elected by the assembly, (c) a nominated advisory council. The assembly had the right to make ordinances, subject to the approval of the Union government on matters not reserved to the Union parliament. The reserved subjects included Native affairs, mines, justice, railways and harbours, defence, customs, currency, banking.

The form of this legislation will have to avoid the appearance of making the territory a province or incorporating it into the Union. The mandate will have to be safeguarded, and the bill will have to say that its object is the better carrying out of the terms of the mandate. In effect South West Africa will become part of the Union, but it must not be called a province, and its constitution will be somewhat different. It will really be *sui generis*.[1] Indeed, it may become a precedent for the future when other territories, situated far from the Union but still on the African continent, come to be under our mandate or administration.

You will see how necessary it is to give attention in time to these great problems. And your knowledge of administration and constitution-making,[2] as well as your present position point you out as the man best qualified to advise the government on these matters. Please therefore begin to think them over as soon as you have some vacant moments. With kind regards, Ever yours sincerely,

s. J. C. Smuts

104   From E. F. C. Lane to S. M. Smuts   Vol. 27, no. 2

Prime Minister's Office
Cape Town
28 May 1923

My dear Mrs Smuts, I annex hereto, for purposes of more convenient record, the *Cape Times* reports of the recent debate on the Bondelswarts rising. The debate was carried on with unprecedented bitterness on the part of the Labour people, and what was rather surprising was that there was no defence of the government's action by the Nationalists, who were ostentatiously absent from the house and took no part in the debate whatsoever.

The real object of this letter is to put on record with you, for the purpose of the prime minister's biography in years to come, a telegram which has tremendous bearing on the debate. You will see that the Labour people were beside themselves and in extravagant language referred to General Smuts as 'the murderer of Bulhoek' and various other epithets indicating that he was 'steeped in blood'. It was perfectly wicked to hear it when one knew what the other

The intention to give South West Africa representation in the Union parliament was not carried out until 1949. The first assembly election was held on 25 May 1926.

[1] In a class by itself, unique

[2] Hofmeyr had between 1907 and 1920 been clerk of the Transvaal house of assembly, Transvaal secretary to the National convention and clerk of the Union house of assembly.

side of the story was and if you will look at the enclosed, which was the draft of a telegram sent on 6 June 1922 to Mr [G. R.] Hofmeyr, you will see how the General strove to maintain peace and to prevent further bloodshed after Mr Hofmeyr had had his first collision with the Bondelswarts. One of the most severe taunts was that no attempt had been made to send an emissary to discuss the matter with the Bondels. This telegram shows you how keen the General was to do this. One of the most remarkable features of the matter is that it was never shown by Mr Hofmeyr to Major [J. F.] Herbst, who went down with him to the scene of action and was military secretary to the forces. Herbst told me that he saw the telegram for the first time months afterwards. If the General had published the telegram it would have had the effect of making the people who had abused him take back their words in a most abject manner. On the other hand, of course, the administrator would have had to resign because he certainly made no attempt to carry out the suggestions. Morris was killed four days before the wire was sent[1] but we didn't know that. The peaceful intentions of General Smuts are, however, quite clear.

I think that this certainly should be on record and all you have to do is to put this letter and its enclosure in your safe with your other biography papers. With kind regards, Yours sincerely,

E. F. C. Lane

ENCLOSURE

Telegram

From: General Smuts, Cape Town

To: Hofmeyr, administrator, Kalkfontein South and Colonel Mentz, Pretoria

Dated 6 June 1922

The situation as regards the Bondelswarts rebellion is giving me much concern. Unknown number of Hottentots are in the field armed and apparently well supplied with ammunition. They are operating in most difficult country and our force which is dealing with them is very small and will soon be tired out. Hottentots have had severe handling and aeroplanes have greatly frightened them but in rough mountainous country they will soon learn how to take effective shelter. To treat situation merely as military problem and fight it out with Hottentots may mean long and expensive business. After great losses and punishment inflicted on Hottentots

---

[1] Morris was wounded on 3 June and died at dawn on the 4th. *See* R. Freislich, *The Last Tribal War*, pp. 75–9.

I consider time has come to start conversations with them with a view to ending trouble amicably if possible. Morris seems to be chief leader and I wish you to consider sending to him an emissary who is well known to him and who might talk over matters with him and inform you of results. It is quite possible that if this emissary is well chosen results may be successful and spare us long and expensive campaign in impossible country. Have you any man available who knows Morris well and with whom he would be willing to talk. Morris was chief scout to Major Carel van Zyl of Carnarvon commando in South West campaign. Captain van der Hoff[1] who, I believe, is now shooting somewhere in the Territory also knows him well. But you may have suitable man ready at hand to use for purpose whom you can send to Morris with message to talk things over. Think matter over and let me know your views.

105   To M. C. Gillett   **Vol. 27, no. 356**

Cape Town
31 May 1923

It seems as if I have not written to you for weeks, and yet it cannot be so. But the dreary and exhausting work of parliament drags on and makes time seem longer than it really is. Your letters, however, continue to arrive punctually for which I am grateful, as it is always a delight to get a letter from you or Arthur. Arthur writes in his last letter that he finds the trouble of the world beyond him and falls back more and more on the philosophy of home life. The greatest and truest of all philosophies in my humble opinion. It only shows that Arthur is wiser than I and others who toil at problems beyond their powers. And yet what can one do? Is it possible for those who occupy positions of leadership to fold their hands and admit defeat? Even the wisest of us are in a fog and do not see what solution there is for the troubles of the world. We may feel that something far more fundamental is required than has yet appeared. It is a new spirit, a new heart, in fact a new religion that is wanted and that alone can bring healing to the wounds that the war and its aftermath have inflicted. And yet we cannot wait till the new religiona ppears, till the Great Word is spoken by some authority greater than any among us today. And so we have to labour on with our little palliatives and keep the show going with some appearance of human decency. And that is hard enough in all conscience. Several of the gravest problems will come up for

[1] Not identified.

consideration at our conference in October, and I am really terrified to think that we shall have to lay down an international policy for the coming year or two. The eye of faith is almost blind in all this international gloom. Indeed I could wish that I were, like Arthur, out of it. But we shall have to do our best. And the senior partner has now become a purely die-hard government[1] which I do not know or presume to understand. It may be that Robert Cecil has assurances which have induced him to enter it.[2] But I do not know. But enough.

It will be extremely nice to stay with you in London[3] during October and thereafter to bring you out with me. If you find that I am more than usually busy during October I hope you will understand. My stay will necessarily be so short, and there will be so much to do—heaps of difficult South African questions besides the work of the two conferences[4]...Thanks for your birthday greetings. Love to you both and all the dear little ones. Kisses for Nico and Helen. Ever yours lovingly,

Jan

106   To W. S. Churchill   Vol. 27, no. 249

Pretoria
13 August 1923

My dear Churchill, Thank you very much for your last letter and the most acceptable gift of your Book. I have read the Book with the deepest interest. It is indeed a very brilliant affair and its subject will remain one of the greatest of all time. I envy you the great gift of being a man of action and a great writer at the same time. Julius Caesar was that rare combination. And although you are not as Francophobe as he was, your book will stand comparison with the *Gallic War*!

This morning I read in the papers the substance of the last British note to France.[5] Quite good so far as it goes, but I fear too late. It is impossible to stem the great moving tide of affairs with this thin trickle of correspondence. And the Ruhr affair may yet turn

---

[1] Stanley Baldwin's first cabinet which held office from May 1923 to January 1924.

[2] Lord Robert Cecil was lord privy seal.

[3] The Gilletts took a house in London as a 'retreat' for Smuts who lived at and conducted business from the Savoy Hotel.

[4] The economic conference and the imperial or prime ministers' conference.

[5] This was sent on 11 August. It proposed that Germany's capacity to meet reparation demands should be examined by a group of experts and implied that French action in the Ruhr was illegal. Poincaré rejected both the proposal and the implication.

out to be one of the most far-reaching and fatal in the history of Europe.[1] With Germany crumbling, and Europe shooting Niagara, I see but a bleak prospect before the world. Even the British Empire will feel the effects for many a day. If the friends of Europe had been as determined and ruthless as Poincaré, how different the future would have been!

I hope to see you next October and to discuss some of these matters with you.

With very kind regards both to you and to Mrs Churchill, Ever yours sincerely,

s. J. C. Smuts

107 To M. C. Gillett   Vol. 27, no. 362

Doornkloof
[Irene, Transvaal]
14 August 1923

I have been confined to bed for two weeks and in consequence have not written to you. After my return from Cape Town I did a lot of riding for exercise and chafed the skin off the inside of one of my legs in the vicinity of the main artery. This did not appear to be of any importance at first sight, and I went through my Natal trip with the sore leg. As things got worse I consulted a doctor on my return and he at once put me to bed, saying the sore was in a very dangerous place, might spread and affect the artery, with very grave results. So put to bed I was in order that the nuisance might heal. I could do my main office work but correspondence proved too awkward. Now I am well again and back in office since yesterday. The enforced rest had its uses but it came at a most inconvenient time, as I had a big tour in the Cape, which [F. S.] Malan had—bad luck for him—to take off my hands. Tonight I leave for Bloemfontein where our party congress will be held tomorrow.

I am glad that Baldwin has at last spoken out frankly to France

[1] French occupation of the Ruhr had been answered by a policy of passive resistance by the Germans. They refused to work the mines and railways and to co-operate with the French authorities who consequently extended the area of occupation and took other reprisals, such as encouraging the separatist movements in the Rhineland. Violent clashes occurred. The financial crisis in Germany was accelerated and Great Britain and France were estranged. On the other hand, the drop in coal production in the Ruhr raised the volume and the price of British coal exports. Smuts had advised the British government to stop its 'futile negotiations' with the French and take the initiative in a new reparations policy apart from her war-time ally. (See Smuts Collection, vol. 27, no. 245.)

and Belgium.[1] The Entente is now dead. But the action has, I fear, come too late to save Germany. The collapse of her currency[2] may now lead to a dissolution of the Reich which is what Poincaré is after. The next move will be a most important one. I have advised a conference with France and Belgium left out if they will not come. The important thing is to mobilize and consolidate European opinion. If Europe has not the courage to speak out, why then it is lost and nothing could save it. I have, however, the feeling that if one of the great powers courageously takes the lead, it will find strong backing. And the British government should take the lead. The imperial conference may now become an occasion of first-class importance. I am only afraid it is already too late to save Germany and that matters have gone too far. What a stroke of luck it would be if Coolidge turns out to be a first-class man, as Roosevelt turned out under similar circumstances![3] But luck is not very plentiful nowadays. Good-bye, dear children. Ever yours lovingly,

Jan

108   To S. M. Smuts   Vol. 27, no. 265

R.M.S. Arundel Castle

19 September 1923

Liefste Mamma, Morgen arriveeren wij te Madeira en ik zend een paar regels om jou to zeggen dat alles zeer wel gegaan is tot dus ver. Ik ben niet zeeziek geweest, mijn been is gezond, en alles is wel. De eerste week ben ik geheel stil gebleven in mijn kajuit en heb gelezen en geschreven; en dit tezamen met het warm zeewater heeft het zeer plek op de been geheel genezen. De zee is tamelijk onstuimig geweest, en was het niet dat de *Arundel* zoo goed zeilt zou ik zeker zeeziek geworden ben. Maar tot dusver, alles wel. Ik heb veel gelezen, boeken, papieren voor de Conferentie ens.

Het was smartelijk te hooren van den dood van Lady Watts en Mrs Merriman. Ik meen dat deze slag ook voor Mr Merriman doodelijk zal zijn. Watt hoop ik zal niet zijn slag zoo voelen als om

[1] The British note of 11 August was sent on the initiative of the secretary for foreign affairs, Lord Curzon.

[2] By August the mark, normally standing at twenty to the pound, had depreciated to almost twenty million to the pound.

[3] When Warren G. Harding died in office in August 1923 the vice-president, Calvin Coolidge, became president of the United States. Theodore Roosevelt had, as vice-president, succeeded to the presidency after the assassination of William McKinley in 1901.

uit de regeering te gaan. Want waarlijk ik weet niet hoe zijn plek op te vullen vanuit Natal.

Ik ben natuurlijk geheel bezig met het werk dat voor my ligt. De wereld is in zoo een toestand dat een dienst vandaag meer zal beteekenen als ooit tevoren. Maar alles is donker als de nacht. Een *overeenkomst* tusschen Frankrijk en Duitschland is zoo goed als onmogelijk in hun tegenwoordige gemoedstoestand. En een oplossing kan niet op hen geimposseerd worden. Daarvoor is er geen machinerie, en in vroeger jaren moest een oorlog altijd de oplossing geven waar overeenkomst niet mogelijk was. En wij willen toch niet weer oorlog. En toch zijn wij bezig met het begin van een ander wereld oorlog in de toekomst. Voor mij is de toekomst zoo duister als de nacht. Ik zie nergens een oplossing, nergens licht. Ik meen dat ik niets zie waarin andere zullen toestemmen. En nog ben ik optimist. Ik voel er zal redding komen.

Joan, de doctor en Mary en de rest van de partij zijn allen zeer wel. Zeg Jannie en Louis dat van ochtend by Tenerife wij een verschrikkelijk groote haai in het water gezien hebben. Ik heb nooit zoo iets gezien. Het heeft bijna zooals een klein walvisch geleken. Nu baing zoentjes aan allen.

Pappa

TRANSLATION

R.M.S. Arundel Castle

19 September 1923

Dearest Mamma, Tomorrow we arrive at Madeira and I send a few lines to tell you that everything has gone very well so far. I have not been seasick, my leg is cured, and all is well. I stayed very quietly in my cabin for the first week and read and wrote; and that, together with the warm sea water, has completely healed the sore spot on the leg. The sea has been rather rough, and if the *Arundel* did not sail so well, I should certainly have been seasick. But so far, all well. I have read a lot—books, papers for the conference, etc.

It was painful to hear of the death of Lady Watt[1] and Mrs Merriman.[2] I think that this blow will be fatal for Mr Merriman too. I hope Watt will not feel his blow so much as to leave the government. For I really do not know how to fill his place from Natal.[3]

Of course, I am entirely busy with the work that lies before me. The world is in such a state that a service today will mean more

---

[1] Sir Thomas Watt married May Lindup in 1886.
[2] J. X. Merriman married Agnes Vintcent in 1874.
[3] Sir Thomas Watt was at this time minister of posts and telegraphs and of public works. He did not resign.

than ever before. But everything is as black as night. An *agreement* between France and Germany is as good as impossible in their present frame of mind. And a solution cannot be imposed on them. There is no machinery for that, and in earlier years a war always had to provide the solution. And we do not want war again. And yet we are busy with the beginning of another world war in the future. To me the future is as dark as night. Nowhere do I see a solution, nowhere light. I mean that I see nothing with which others will agree. And still I am an optimist. I feel there will be rescue.

Joan,[1] the Doctor and Mary[2] and the rest of the party are all very well. Tell Jannie and Louis that we saw a tremendously big shark in the water this morning at Tenerife. I have never seen anything like it. It looked almost like a small whale. Many kisses to all,

Pappa

109   To B. M. Baruch   Vol. 27, no. 322

Telegram

From: [J. C. Smuts]

To: Bernard Baruch, New York

Dated [1 October 1923]

Deeply appreciate your grave appeal.[3] Ground being explored to see what action advisable. Will let you know. Smuts.

110   To B. M. Baruch   Vol. 27, no. 271

Telegram

To: Baruch, New York

From: General Smuts

Dated 3 October 1923

Your message. It will be most helpful for me to know whether there is any prospect that United States will be willing to join in repara-

---

[1] Joan Boardman.   [2] Dr I. Pole-Evans and his wife.

[3] Baruch had, on 30 September 1923, sent Smuts, for publication if desired, a long telegram setting out his views on the reparation question, stressing the urgency of establishing 'peace and order' in Europe, emphasizing the necessity for an effective League of Nations and appealing to Smuts to 'state the world's case'. The telegram closes as follows: 'In earnestness and confidence the friends of peace and progress everywhere look to you to rescue and help render practical the ideals which the world has recently sacrificed so much to attain.' (*See* Smuts Collection, vol. 26, no. 15.)

tion and inter-Allied loan settlement which will bring permanent peace to France and Germany. I mean settlement agreed to by France and England and accepted by Germany. Or better still settlement in which United States will take a hand in bringing about. Without moral and financial support of United States it is doubtful whether there is sufficient strength left in Europe to save herself. Great gesture by United States now will have most far-reaching effect. Perhaps you explore ground unofficially or suggest to me other channel through which I could work and let me know result as soon as possible.

111   From R. H. Brand   Vol. 26, no. 23

Furneux Pelham Hall
Buntingford
3 October 1923

Dear General Smuts, May I congratulate you most heartily on your speech?[1] I think what we want now is courageous speaking. Making all allowances for the difficulties of the British government, I think the position of this country lamentable and humiliating at the present moment. Yours sincerely,

R. H. Brand

112   From E. F. C. Lane to R. H. Brand   Vol. 27, no. 93

Savoy Hotel
[London]
6 October 1923

My dear Brand, I am so glad that you sent that line to the General. It bucked him up tremendously.

He is now very busy on an important memorandum on reparations,[2] which I think, judging by the careful way he is preparing it, will be read very attentively by all concerned. As soon as it is written I will try and get a copy and send it to you, because I should like to know from you as an old friend, as well as one of the greatest

[1] On 1 October 1923, at the opening of the imperial conference in London, Smuts declared that the influence and authority of the British Empire must be used to the full to secure a settlement in Europe. Britain must again 'speak with a voice that will be listened to'. The League of Nations must be strengthened and supported. Britain's own financial stability depended upon the restoration of tranquility in Europe. (*Manchester Guardian*, 2 October 1923.)
[2] *See* **114**.

experts in England, whether it is a line that you can support. With very kind regards, Believe me, Yours sincerely,

s. E. F. C. Lane

113   From B. M. Baruch   Vol. 26, no. 16

Telegram

From: Baruch, New York

To: General Smuts, London

Dated 6 October 1923

I wish I could give you reliable information in answer to your inquiry as to the probable policy of the present American government in respect of joining in any reparations or inter-Allied loan settlement or both which may be agreed to by France and England and accepted by Germany but for obvious reasons I cannot prophesy what the American government will do. For equally obvious reasons I am perhaps the least qualified man to inquire as my motives would be suspected as political at Washington. The only source from which I think you could get reliable information would be through some direct representative of the United States government. So far as I personally am concerned I have favoured and still favour American participation in the reparations settlement. The inter-Allied debt settlement however I regard as a matter for the nations of Europe to adjust among themselves.

114   To J. M. Keynes   Vol. 98, no. 303

The Smuts Collection contains three draft memoranda by Keynes headed 'Prepared for General Smuts, 5 October 1923' (vol. 98, no. 302). They make suggestions for dealing with the political and economic situation arising out of the reparation question but Smuts's reparation plan as set out in his letter takes little, if any, account of Keynes's drafts.

Savoy Hotel
[London]
9 October 1923

My dear Keynes, Many thanks for your suggestions. I incline to the following reparation plan:

1. Call a conference now of the powers represented on the reparation commission to fix the amount. United States of America to be pressed most strongly to join. I suggest the following scheme:

2. Fix amount at £2,500 millions ('A' and 'B' bonds) with

a moratorium of so many years. Ten years after moratorium has begun, a similar conference shall decide on 'C' bonds, that is, either in favour of or against them or further postponement.

3. This conference (more than ten years hence) also to decide question of inter-Allied debts—that is, French and Italian debts to Great Britain and America.

Effect of proposal would be to lump 'C' bonds and inter-Allied debts for simultaneous decision in the future and in the meantime practically to give a very long moratorium for both.

This may pave the way to cancellation of both, if the circumstances justify such a course.

What do you think? Yours very sincerely,

J. C. Smuts

115   To S. M. Smuts   Vol. 27, no. 278

Savoy Hotel
London
11 October 1923

Liefste Mamma, Laatste Maandag is een zeer welkomme brief van jou van Zoutpansberg aangekomen. Ik was zeer geïnteresseerd in al jou werk en ook in jou beschrijving van de spelonken wereld waar ik nog niet geweest ben. Ik hoop er echter eendag heen te gaan en jou zamen te nemen als gids en adviseur.

Het moet droog by jullie zijn. Een telegram van Malan zegt dat laatste week er nog geen regen in de Transvaal gevallen was. Ik hoop er is genoeg gras en voer voor ons vee beide te Doornkloof en Rooikop.

Ons werk gaat fluks aan en ik ben zeker op 9 of 16 November te vertrekken—ik kan nog niet zeggen welke week van de twee.

De positie is zeer ernstig en ik doe mijn best een oplossing te vinden. Duitschland is op haar uiterste, en de vraag is wat gedaan kan worden om de Fransche regeering in toom te houden. Ik voel de situatie zeer ernstig. Van alle kanten in Europa, zelfs van Pres. Wilson in Amerika, wordt een beroep op mij gemaakt om een oplossing te vinden. Ik ben gewillig maar de moeilijkheden zijn zeer groot. Indien ik niet vastgebonden was aan Zuid-Afrika zou ik de bul bij de horens nemen. Maar daar ik in enige weken weer naar Zuid-Afrika moet vertrekken zou het verkeerd zijn dingen hier in de war te stooten. Ik kan maar advies geven, en ik twijfel of mijn drastisch advies altijd welkom is. De de Wets vertrekken op 26 Oct. en willen niet langer wachten. Zij zijn zeer gelukkig. Van avond gaan wij allen by de koning dineeren. Ik was alreeds bij hem en hij is nog zoo opgenomen over mijn Iersche optreding twee jaar geleden.

Mijn gezondheid is goed. De dokter kijkt weer naar mijn been en die is snel aan het verbeteren. Met zoentjes en groeten

Pappa

TRANSLATION

Savoy Hotel
London
11 October 1923

Dearest Mamma, A very welcome letter arrived from you last Monday from Zoutpansberg. I was very interested in all your work and also in your description of the cave region, where I have not yet been. But I hope to go there one day and to take you along as guide and adviser.

It must be dry with you. A telegram from Malan [F. S.] says that up to last week there had not yet been any rain in the Transvaal. I hope there is enough grass and fodder for our cattle both at Doornkloof and Rooikop.

Our work is going on fast and I am sure of leaving on 9 or 16 November—I cannot yet say which of the two weeks.

The position is very grave and I am doing my best to find a solution. Germany is at her last gasp, and the question is what can be done to keep the French government in check. I feel the position very gravely. From all sides in Europe, even from President Wilson in America, appeals are made to me to find a solution. I am willing, but the difficulties are very great. If I were not tied to South Africa, I would take the bull by the horns. But, as I shall have to leave for South Africa in a few weeks, it would be wrong to push things into confusion here. I can only give advice, and I doubt whether my drastic advice is always welcome.

The [N. J.] de Wets leave on 26 October and do not want to wait longer. They are very fortunate. This evening we are all going to dine with the King. I have been with him already and he is still pleased about my Irish intervention two years ago.

My health is good. The doctor is again attending to my leg and it is improving fast. With kisses and good wishes,

Pappa

116   From E. Hobhouse   Vol. 26, no. 170

164 Elm Park Mansions
Park Walk, Chelsea S.W.
16 October 1923

Dear Oom, Time passes, and your days here are few. If the Gilletts do not tell you, let me impress upon you how the world is looking to you on all sides (not merely my own intimates). I hear reiterated 'Smuts is the man'; 'there is no one to help if he does not'. It's an awful responsibility, people looking to you like that in their despair but you earned that reputation over Ireland and have to live up to it!

Do chuck that imperial conference which is itself powerless for good to the Dominions till Europe is settled.

Do—if Baldwin won't send you—go to Germany incognito and study in reality what you only know theoretically. It would give immense power to your pleading. Even if your political position in South Africa is temporarily endangered by a prolonged absence it would matter less than the ruin and misery which increases as Europe sinks lower. Do devolve all other work to devote your unequalled powers to this one all-important end. Find a way of getting at the mass of the French who are *not* behind Poincaré and might cause his fall next election.

See for yourself the abject misery of middle-class intellectual Germany and then you won't rest; suicides increase. I am told that the cruelties practised in the Palatinate[1] are far greater than in the Ruhr for the public attention has escaped that part.

Professor [V.] Goldschmidt (whom I told you of) says Heidelberg is the place to study this for it is on the borders. His main reason for coming here was the hope of appealing to you to help—by perhaps arranging a joint English–American action. His house is open to you if you care to go there privately to see things. Do see [H. G.] Kleinwort and [R. von] Schröder[2] and Max Warburg—all international bankers of London and Hamburg and make them beat out financial plans.

If Baldwin, having egregiously failed himself, is stubborn do act privately; have a diplomatic illness and let Burton be deputy-premier while you save the world.

Do not delay. Yours,

Tante

[1] The Bavarian Palatinate was the scene of serious disturbances caused by forces of the Rhineland separatist movement supported by the French authorities who, on 24 October 1924, recognized the Palatinate as an autonomous state.

[2] Baron Johann Rudolph von Schröder, born 28 September 1878, controlled the banking house of Schröder Bros. of Hamburg and was a director of the Hypotheken-bank and Vereinsbank of that city. Died *c.* 1956.

P.S. I am able to go about a good deal now besides seeing callers and so I can and do hear what people are saying. I know you are trying, but chuck everything else and try harder.

117 To S. M. Smuts Vol. 27, no. 282

Savoy Hotel
London
18 October 1923

Liefste Mamma, Ik had zoo 'n mooi brief van jou van Pietersburg laatste mail. Het was baing interessant dat alles te lezen omtrent jou reis in het Zoutpansbergsche. Mijn eenige objectie is dat jij te veel tijd gegeven hebt aan die eene kiesafdeeling. Twee weken is te veel en in vervolg moet jou programma anders geregeld worden. Jij moet naar een paar voorname centrale plekken gaan en mindere personen moeten de kleinere buitenplekken bezoeken. Van Santa had ik ook een zeer interessante brief met al het plaats nieuws.

Op 26 Oct. vertrekken Klaas en Ella per *Windsor Castle*; Dr. en Mary gaan met hetzelfde schip. Ik heb mijn terugkeer op 9 Nov. vastgesteld. Joan zal een paar weken langer hier vertoeven; ook de Lanes. De Gilletts met 2 kleinen en een compagnon (zooals Joan laatste keer) zullen my vergezellen. Met my gaat het verder zeer goed. Ik heb maar min in het publiek gespreken, maar heb ernstige studie aan de Duitsch–Fransche kwesties gegeven. Ik meen aanstaande [*sic*] op de South African dinner daarover te praten en ik zal niet verwonderd zijn indien wat ik zeg een groot bohaai gaat maken. Duitschland gaat vinnig naar de maan en de zaak moet in alle ernst aangepakt worden. Maar 'nobody will bell the cat'. Ik ga het doen—en 'damn the consequences'.

Ik hoor van de vreeslijke droogte in Zuid-Afrika en van sprinkhanen uitbroei zonder regen. Ik hoop dat de couranten de toestanden overdrijven. Anders zou het toch te treurig zijn. Lady en Lord Gladstone zenden groeten. Ook Miss Hobhouse die nu veel beter is. Groeten aan jullie allen, ook de Wilds. Zoentjes van

Pappa

TRANSLATION

Savoy Hotel
London
18 October 1923

Dearest Mamma, I had such a nice letter from you from Pietersburg last mail. It was very interesting to read all about your
journey in the Zoutpansberg area. My only objection is that you
have given too much time to a small constituency. Two weeks is
too much, and in future your programme must be differently
arranged. You must go to a few important central places and lesser
people must visit the smaller outer places. I also had a very interesting letter from Santa[1] with all the farm news.

Klaas and Ella [de Wet] leave on 26 October on the *Windsor
Castle*. Dr and Mary go on the same ship. I have fixed my return
for 9 November. Joan will stay here a few weeks longer—also the
Lanes. The Gilletts with two little ones and a companion (like Joan
last time) will accompany me. For the rest, I am very well. I have
spoken little in public, but have made a serious study of the
German–French questions. I intend speaking about it at the South
African dinner next [one word omitted] and I shall not be surprised
if what I say will cause a great fuss. Germany is fast going to pot
and the thing must be tackled with all seriousness. But nobody
will bell the cat. I am going to do it—and damn the consequences.

I hear of terrible drought in South Africa and of locusts hatching
without rain. I hope that the newspapers are exaggerating the
conditions. Otherwise it would be too sad. Lord and Lady
Gladstone[2] send good wishes. Also Miss Hobhouse, who is now
much better. Good wishes to you all—also the Wilds.[3] Kisses
from

Pappa

118   From J. M. Keynes   Vol. 26, no. 199

King's College
Cambridge
21 October 1923

Dear General Smuts, It is rumoured in the newspapers that you
are interesting yourself in the details of reparation schemes. I can-

---

[1] *See* vol. II, p. 141, note 1. Santa Weyers died in August 1966.
[2] *See* vol. II, p. 606 and note 2.
[3] Commander Frank Wild, the Antarctic explorer, and his wife. They had settled
in South Africa.

not help writing to say that I hope this is not so. Surely at this moment of time such things are utterly useless.

No action now has any value except something that frightens France or encourages Germany or both. If we are not prepared to take such action, either for lack of courage or for better reasons, then there is nothing to be done. But plans about fifty milliards (or whatever it is) are as remote from realities now as plans about four times that amount used to be. The more I reflect upon it, the more convinced I am that no advantage can accrue to this country from still continuing to base policy on the infliction of imaginary milliards. Europe is not going to be saved by devices based on the hope of collecting, even at this time of day, substantial reparations for this country. Ever yours sincerely,

J. M. Keynes

I shall be in London in the middle of this week.

119   To J. M. Keynes   Vol. 98, no. 304

Savoy Hotel
London
22 October 1923

My dear Keynes, Thanks for your note. I agree with you that the reparation question is being swallowed up in a much graver situation. Tomorrow night I shall speak on this situation at the South African dinner and hang my remarks on the peg of the reparation question. You cannot and should not avoid that question, but place it in its proper perspective to what is now happening on the Continent. I hope I shall be able to do so. Look me up when you come to London. Yours ever,

J. C. Smuts

120   Speech (1923)   Box H, no. 38

Smuts delivered this speech at a dinner of the South Africa Club in the Savoy Hotel on 23 October 1923.

I am deeply grateful for the words which have fallen from the chairman, for the great reception you have given me tonight, and for the honour you have done me in giving me this magnificent banquet. I am very happy indeed to meet so many of my old friends again tonight.

On a night like this South Africa is foremost in our thoughts, as she is always in our hearts. Her mysterious spell is upon us, we forget we are in London, the world around us dissolves away, and we find ourselves once more upon the warm veld, breathing the great air, sniffing the scents and seeing the sights so dear to us. I know you would like me to speak about South Africa tonight and I feel very much tempted to do so. But it may not be. I am going to ask your attention for a more difficult and less pleasing subject. But allow me, before I do so, to say just a few words about our country. I know you would like to have my opinion about present conditions and prospects in the Union. Let me say at once that I am entirely satisfied with the recovery which is being made from the devastating depression of 1921 and 1922—certainly the worst every seen in South Africa. The economic and industrial outlook is improving; mining prospects are better than they have been for many years. Agriculture is going forward by leaps and bounds and becoming not only much more productive, but also much more scientific. Our youthful manufacturing industries, under the stimulus of our recent tariff, are also progressing favourably. We are striking out into new lines which are very promising such as cotton. The cost of living has come down more than in almost any other country. In every way we have turned the corner, and now look forward to a great advance in the immediate future. My doubt is not about the productive capacity of South Africa, but about the power of absorption of the European markets in the present depressed conditions. Labour troubles have been satisfactorily overcome, the political atmosphere is on the whole improving and causes me no undue anxiety. Much remains still to be done, but our problems are all of such a character that with courage they can be solved, unlike the situations with which you have to deal in this country and in Europe, which are so vast and difficult as to be almost beyond human power to cope with.

Let me also say a word about the two conferences now sitting—the economic conference and the imperial or prime ministers' conference. I believe they are going to be landmarks in their economic and political importance for the Empire. The preferences on Dominion and colonial products which the British government have already announced are going to be of very great advantage in our development. They do not amount to what is called the policy of imperial preference.[1] They do not touch foodstuffs or raw

---

[1] The policy of imposing lower import duties on Empire products. It was propagated by Joseph Chamberlain at the turn of the century but made little headway because the Dominions framed their tariffs to protect their own developing industries and Great Britain adhered to free trade. But in the 'twenties British tariff policy veered towards protectionism and imperial preference became feasible.

materials of industry. But they are nevertheless most useful and important from our Dominion point of view. It would be most undesirable to raise the issue of imperial preference at such a time as the present, to throw this great apple of political discord among the people of this country at a time when not discord but unity is above all required, when the nation is passing through what I believe to be a very grave crisis, and requires the concentration of every ounce of its strength and attention on the gigantic task which confronts it in this country and in Europe.

These conferences meeting at the present time are really a wonderful spectacle. Behind and beyond the material trade and tariff and other questions which occupy our attention you have the deeper significance of what we are and stand for in the world. It is an inspiring, I have almost said awe-inspiring spectacle to see our great Commonwealth, or rather our League of Nations, gathering from the ends of the earth. Here in a tumbling, falling world, here in a world where all the foundations are quaking, you have something solid and enduring. The greatest thing on earth, the greatest political structure of all time, it has passed unscathed through the awful blizzard and has emerged stronger than before. Why has it stood the test where so many others have failed and gone under? It is because in this Empire we sincerely believe in and practise certain fundamental principles of human government, such as peace, freedom, self-development, self-government and the like. Other empires founded on force have passed away. Force is again being tried today as a principle by others in spite of the lessons of the war. The result is a foregone conclusion. We on the contrary believe in certain great ideals of government and are practising them as best we can in a difficult world. South Africa, Ireland, Egypt[1] and India[2] all bear testimony to the political faith which we hold and practise in the Empire. That is the faith which holds us together and will continue to hold us together while the kingdoms and empires founded on force and constraint pass away.

In the imperial conference we are wrestling with the problems presented by so vast a group of states as ours. But we are not thinking of ourselves alone. The weight of the great world lies heavy on us. I trust before we part we shall be agreed on some general lines

[1] On 28 February 1922 the British protectorate of Egypt ended and it became an independent state. On 19 April 1923 Egypt was proclaimed an hereditary constitutional monarchy under King Fuad I. Rights of Empire communication and defence were reserved by the British government.

[2] The Government of India Act (1919) had set up a form of representative government for India. The new constitution came into force on 1 January 1921 but was strongly opposed by the Nationalists led by Gandhi.

of policy which will not only be in the interests of our group but will also prove helpful to the suffering distracted world around us. It will be a great thing if we could issue a message of hope to Europe, a message of good will which will once more bind the nations together, and ease the pain and lighten the burdens resting on millions of our fellow beings today.

I am not going to say more about the work of the conference. But I do wish to speak to you tonight about the European situation, the dangerous position into which we are drifting, and the way out as I see it. What I shall say commits nobody and constitutes simply my personal observations and suggestions on a situation dark and dangerous enough to perplex the wisest. And I shall not go into particulars, but shall try to indicate in a general way in what spirit I think the difficulties should be approached. Things have gone very far; and it is only quick and resolute action that can now save a large part of Europe from disaster.

Speaking here tonight as a South African to a great gathering of South Africans I feel that the occasion is specially appropriate for a reference to the present troubled Europe. We South Africans have no special interests to serve, we stand outside the arena of disputants, we have no antagonisms and we cherish no bitterness. What is more, we are connected with them all and in a measure we sympathise with them all. Besides Holland, which is very dear to many of us, France and England are the principal mother countries of our people. Our attitude is one of all-round good will, friendliness and helpfulness.

We have not only the right to speak with frankness and candour, but I also feel that I have a very plain personal duty in the matter. Of the great number of public men whose names stand under the peace treaty there are only two or three who still survive in power today. For better for worse I am one of them, and the responsibility for what was done at Paris, for the settlement contained in the peace treaty, weighs heavily on my conscience, in spite of the fact that I signed it only under protest, and under a sense of foreboding of future calamities which have come only too true. And I have therefore all the more reason and inducement to express my views on the situation with complete frankness and sincerity.

But there is another and more important reason why South Africa should speak in the present crisis. We have very good evidence to give. South Africa is an expert witness. Small and comparatively unimportant as we are among the nations of the world, we have yet a rich and a unique experience of the sort of trouble through which Europe is now passing. We also had our age-long

contention between the white races in South Africa, which culminated in a great war, with all its horrors of loss and suffering.
We also had our devastated area, which covered not merely a small
strip of our own land, but practically the whole of the interior of
South Africa. Defeated, broken, utterly exhausted, my little people
also had to bow to the will of the conqueror. But it was not an
impossible peace. The war was not continued in another form
after the peace. The Boers were not treated as moral pariahs and
outcasts. Decent human relations were re-established and a spirit
of mutual understanding grew up. The human atmosphere improved
until in the end simple human fellow-feelings solved the problems
which had proved too difficult for statesmanship. Four or five years
after the conclusion of the war a new settlement was come to, based
on mutual trust and friendship between the races. And South Africa
today is perhaps the most outstanding witness in the realm of
politics to the value of a policy of give and take, of moderation and
generosity, of trust and friendship, applied to the affairs of men.
What wisdom and moderation could achieve in Africa they can
also achieve in Europe. Let us have faith in the great human
principles and values and our faith will not be brought to confusion.
Human nature is the same in all continents, and what could be done
for the descendants in Africa can surely also be done for the parent
peoples in Europe.

Tonight I am bringing a message from South Africa to the parent
peoples of Europe. We are now more than four years from the
peace of Versailles, but there has been no peace yet. The war among
the peoples has been merely transferred to the economic plane,
and is today being carried on in a more intensive and destructive
manner than during the great war. Four or five years ago we were
singing our songs of victory; today we are all marching to certain
and inevitable defeat—victor and vanquished alike. The international chaos is growing. The economic and industrial structure of
Europe is cracking in all directions. Weariness and despair are
sapping the morale of the peoples. Military hysteria is sapping their
depleted financial resources. Everywhere you see armed men, everywhere gigantic armies, even among the small new states which cannot possibly afford them. In spite of the disappearance of the German
army there are now almost a million-and-a-half more men under
arms than in August of 1914. The black hordes of Africa have
been called into redress the moral and political balance of this mother-
continent of civilization. The human principles are everywhere
derided and degraded. The standards of living for the peoples are
everywhere sinking to lower levels. Famine for large numbers is not

far off. Can we continue much longer on this march to destruction, this pilgrimage, this crusade of suicide on which Europe has started?

I wish to declare with all the seriousness possible that the situation which has arisen in Europe, partly under the peace treaty, partly apart from the peace treaty, and partly in defiance and breach of the peace treaty, is such as was never contemplated or intended by anybody at the peace conference. We are today confronted with a situation which not only makes the execution of important sections of the peace treaty impossible, but which is actually a menace to the general peace settlement come to at Paris. And there looms before us, not the distant possibility, but the near and immediate prospect, of the disasters to which I have just referred. What are we to do? Drift will be fatal; half measures, palliatives, expedients, such as politicians resort to when hard pressed, will no longer avail anything. Either a comprehensive settlement now with some measure of finality about it, or else let the situation drift and develop until it brings about its own horrible nemesis, and shocks and shames the conscience of the whole world into action. And who knows what may then happen? Who can conceive the suffering before that happens? I vote for a gallant attempt now to save Europe from the dangers which threaten. But whatever we do let us avoid the process of patching, of temporizing, of playing with the dreadful reality which has already made possible the slow, steady, fatal deterioration of conditions all round. Faith, courage and real statesmanship are wanted. A thorough overhauling of the position into which we have drifted is wanted. A radical reconsideration and, where necessary, revision of existing arrangements are wanted.

The time has come for the convocation of a great conference of the powers who are mainly interested in the reparation question, and at this conference the governments of the powers should be directly represented. The situation is much too difficult and threatening to be dealt with by any subordinate authorities. Neither the reparation commission nor even the council of the League of Nations should be called upon to deal with it. They have not the authority or the responsibility which rests on the governments of the powers. It is a business for principals, not for agents. The conference may decide to refer certain inquiries to subordinate bodies, but it must act and decide itself. Decisions of far-reaching importance will have to be taken. There may even be the parting of the ways, and the history of Europe may never be the same thereafter. If the task before it has to be done, it will be a conference unlike any that has been held in Europe since the peace conference. Its

importance therefore cannot be overestimated. I know that negotiations are afoot to bring about such a conference, and shall therefore refrain from saying any more about it except this: I have no
reason to think that any of the powers concerned would decline to
come to such a conference, but I am clear in my mind that the
absence of one or other power should not prevent the rest from
meeting and dealing with the situation to the best of their ability.
It is, however, in my judgment, vitally important that the U.S.A.
should be there as an active member and bear her full weight,
which under the circumstances may be more decisive than that of
any other power. In her distress Europe is today more than ever
turning her eyes and stretching out her hands to the great daughter
nation in the West. The appeal is not so much for material assistance
as for moral support in this dark hour. It is lack of moral justice
which is Europe's undoing. The peoples of Europe have faith in
America, they believe in her impartial justice, and they feel that
without the reinforcement of her moral idealism Europe has no
longer the strength to save herself. I share that faith and that
feeling, and I have complete confidence in America's readiness to
act at the right time. President Coolidge has already in his recent
statement[1] taken up the initiative; it is being followed up. And the
New World may once more come in to redress the balance of the
Old, as it did one hundred years ago,[2] and as it again did six or
seven years ago.

The main issue for settlement at the conference will be the
reparation question. And the stage which this question has now
reached renders a satisfactory solution possible, if only statesmen
will be reasonable and desire a solution at all. It is now universally
recognized that the amount fixed by the reparation commission in
May of 1921 (£6,600 million pounds sterling) was too high, could
not be paid, and even if it were paid, the consequences for industry
would be calamitous. It would mean that the standard of living
for German workers must be lowered to an extent which would
render industrial production in other countries in competition with
Germany almost impossible. The amount has to be reduced to
a reasonable figure, and from the recent correspondence between the

[1] On 11 October 1923 President Coolidge had made a speech approving the setting
up of a committee of experts to investigate Germany's capacity to pay reparation demands.

[2] In opposition to the aims of the Continental Holy Alliance which wished to preserve autocratic dynastic rule and dominate European politics, George Canning,
foreign minister of Great Britain, supported the struggle of the Spanish American
colonies for independence. Defending his policy in a speech in the house of commons
on 12 December 1826 he said: 'I called the New World into existence to redress the
balance of the Old.'

British, French and Belgian governments, it appears possible to arrive at such a reasonable figure. It would in addition be necessary to give Germany a moratorium of about two years before payments are begun in order that she may in the meantime reform her currency, re-establish her credit and balance her budget. I have consulted many of the most competent financial authorities, both in this country and on the Continent, and they are all agreed that if the total reparation amount is fixed at a reasonable figure (about which there is also a great measure of agreement) and if a reasonable moratorium is given in order to enable Germany to put her financial house in order, large and increasing annual payments of reparations could thereafter be made by her. In short, they are all agreed that, if only the political questions are out of the way, the technical financial questions are all capable of solution, and it may not even be necessary to go as far in the way of credit assistance to and financial control of Germany as was necessary in the case of Austria, in view of the greater financial and industrial resources of Germany and her inherently sounder position. Germany is therefore still in a position to pay reasonable reparations which will be a very large amount, and go far to ease the burdens resting on the tax-payers in Allied countries. The danger is that if the situation is not gripped and stabilized now, the disintegration, economic and political, of Germany, which has already begun, may soon be completed, and then all chance of recovering reparation payments will disappear, perhaps for ever. I am afraid it is not generally realized how serious a position that would be for this country. By the printing press and the disappearance of the mark, Germany has cancelled her internal debt. She has since the peace vastly improved her industrial plant and equipment and organization, which are now much in advance of what you have in this country. And if, for one reason or another, she is also freed of reparation payments, her industries could restart in the future to a large extent unhampered by the vast tax burdens which will continue to depress industry in this country. Here your money, your currency, is still quite close to the gold value and your war debts, both internal and external, will have to be paid in full. The people, and especially the industries of this country, will have to bear a colossal burden of taxation for two generations which their competitors abroad will largely escape.

Apart from all other considerations, this country has therefore every possible financial inducement to press for a settlement of the reparation question without further delay. There are other considerations also. The delay which has already taken place has opened up other and more difficult issues than the reparation question itself. And unless the reparation issue is speedily got out of the way, Europe may soon be faced with a situation in which the reparation issue will be swallowed up and disappear in far more grave issues.

I am going tonight to refer to some of these issues and I shall do so quite frankly. The position in Europe and in this country today demands sincerity and candour from all of us and especially from public men.

The Ruhr occupation is one of the grave issues I refer to. It is a grave matter from whatever point of view it is considered. From the purely reparation point of view all the experts whom I have consulted are unanimously of opinion that as long as the Ruhr occupation continues there can be no reparation payments by the German government. The occupation will not only yield no payments but will render the payment of reparations impossible. While the industrial heart is severed from the body of Germany, her government cannot restore their finances and cannot even prepare to pay reparations. From the purely reparation point of view the least that should be done is that the Ruhr occupation should without further delay become an invisible occupation, and that all barriers between the Ruhr and the Rhineland on the one hand, and the rest of Germany on the other should be removed, and that free and unhampered trade relations between the two should be restored. Unless at least that is done, all discussions and settlements of the reparation question will be in the air and have no relation to facts at all. This is grave enough, but there is more.

The Ruhr occupation can also be considered from the point of view of a productive pledge, to be worked by the occupying authorities in default of official reparation payments by the German government. This is the official French viewpoint. But see what it means. It is not merely a bare occupation to exercise pressure on the German government. It is a direct exploitation of German territory, entirely unprovided for in the Versailles treaty. It cannot be squared with the reparation provisions of the treaty. It means the substitution by France of her own scheme for that which is contained in the treaty. If the agreements, now being concluded between General [J. M. J.] Dégoutte and the Ruhr industrialists, were to come up before the reparation commission for confirmation, the legal issue would at once be raised, as the commission can only carry out the provisions of the treaty, and have no other authority or power. The French hate the word revision, and yet they have actually begun the revision of the Versailles treaty! They are enforcing a settlement outside and different from that provided for in the treaty. They have the congratulations of all those who hate the treaty. They have begun a process which will go very far. And it is as well for the world at once to recognize the far-reaching significance of the French initiative.

But there is a far graver aspect from which the Ruhr occupation can be considered and will more and more come to be considered in the future. In the recent correspondence, the British government have stated their view that the occupation is illegal. With all their authority and responsibility they have declared before the world that the Ruhr occupation is a breach of the Versailles treaty on the part of France and Belgium. They have asked that the question should be decided by the supreme court of appeal among the nations, by the high court of international justice. Their request has not been granted, and will not be granted, for the simple reason that there can be no doubt in the matter. If the action of France and Belgium is right and legal under the treaty, then any one signatory of the treaty can at any time allege a breach of the treaty by Germany, and thereupon proceed to invade her territory, and claim to do so under the treaty. Such an interpretation of the peace treaty is on the face of it unfair and wrong.

Let us realize the gravity of the declaration made by the British government; the issue raised by them is fundamental. The greatest issue in the international relations not only of Europe but of the whole world has once more come to the front. We are back in August 1914. It is again the scrap of paper.[1] Once more a great instrument of European settlement has been broken. We entered the Great War to avenge such a breach. It bodes ill for the future peace of Europe that four years after the war we should have to face the same sort of situation again.

The British people will no doubt be invited to share in the spoils of the Ruhr; our hard-pressed industrialists may feel tempted to accept the invitation. My advice is to have nothing to do with the Ruhr. The declaration of the British government has made it impossible for this country to join in any shape or form in the Ruhr business. The shame and humiliation would be more than any proud people could bear. If we are to go into the Ruhr, let it be by way of a general legal settlement, and not by the back door of an illegal occupation.

Besides, I do not believe there will be any great spoils in the Ruhr. The productive gauges will only produce confusion and the burden of keeping a starving population alive. It will produce misery and

[1] *See* vol. IV, p. 207, note I.

hatred without measure and in the end such an indelible impression on the public opinion of the world as will cost France more than the devastations of the Great War. Let us by all means keep out of this disastrous business.

For the present the Ruhr occupation bars the way to reparations. There is another danger on which I wish to say a word. I refer to the menace of German disintegration. There are many disquieting signs that Germany is going to pieces. This is due partly to the inherent weakness of the republican régime established after the war and to the absence of real leadership in Germany, partly to the mistaken financial and reparation policies of her successive governments, and partly to the dreadful policy of France, which on the Rhine and the Ruhr and elsewhere has applied a relentless pressure far, far beyond the feeble power of the new Germany. A very grave responsibility rests on France before history. France can perhaps afford to regard the prospect of Germany's dissolution with equanimity, though even from her angle that would be a short-sighted view. But this country and the small countries which surround Germany on the Continent cannot be indifferent to Germany's fate. To all of them the economic and political dissolution of Germany would be a first-class, an irreparable disaster. For them it would mean immediate economic chaos, and it would open up the possibility of future political dangers to which I need not here refer. Germany is both economically and politically necessary to central Europe, and her complete breakdown would shake and render insecure the whole European position to an extent far beyond what anybody can foresee today. It is therefore to the interest of this country as well as to that of the central European states in every legitimate way to prevent the breakdown of Germany. How can we do this? In my opinion we can at any rate follow the benevolent policy which this country adopted towards France after the Napoleonic wars. We can give Germany the moral support which will mean very much indeed, perhaps everything to her, in her hour of adversity. It is not enough merely to express pious opinions favourable to her. The position which this Empire occupies in the world entitles it to an authoritative voice in the affairs of Europe. And it is for us to assert that great position and to see that a state of affairs is not brought about in spite of us which will profoundly affect the industrial position and political relationships of this country and bring about chaos on the Continent. To all whom it may concern we should make it perfectly clear in friendly but unmistakable language that in certain eventualities this country will have regard to its own interests and take whatever steps are necessary to that end, irrespective of the effect that they may have on old friendships.

Today's news is so grave as almost to justify the conclusion that it is now too late to save Germany from disruption and from at least temporary disappearance.[1] I think that view would go too far. Even yet I do not despair. A resolute and determined diplomacy even now would work wonders. And if (as I hope she will do) Germany makes a last despairing appeal and throws herself on the compassion of her conquerors in the Great War I trust this great Empire will not hesitate for a moment to respond to that appeal and to use all its diplomatic power and influence to support her and to prevent a calamity which would be infinitely more dangerous to Europe and the world than was the downfall of Russia six or seven years ago. In any case, what we do should be done quickly, for the crisis in its most acute form has arrived.

I wish finally to say one word on the subject of inter-Allied indebtedness which is closely connected with that of reparations. This country has been very strongly pressed to cancel all her claims against the Allies; so has America.[2] Here too I see the general lines of a satisfactory solution both from our own and the American point of view and shall not go into further details. I would however urge a point which seems to be of fundamental importance. Do not let us from mistaken motives of generosity lend our aid to the further militarization of the European continent. People here are aready beginning to be seriously alarmed about French armaments —on land and in the air. In addition to these armaments, the French government have also lent large sums to the smaller European states around Germany, mainly with a view to feeding their ravenous military appetites. There is a danger lest a policy of excessive generosity on our part or on the part of America may simply have the effect of enabling France still more effectively to subsidize and foster militarism on the Continent. If there is to be generosity

---

[1] The struggle for power in Germany between Conservatives, Socialists and Communists was much exacerbated by the collapse of the currency. One of the chief centres of revolt against the Reich government was Bavaria. On 22 October 1923 the Bavarian government took over the Reichswehr in Bavaria and challenged the authority of Berlin.

[2] On 2 August 1922 Balfour had published his note to the French government calling for a cancellation of all inter-Allied war debts and adding that what Great Britain would ask her European debtors to pay would depend on what she would have to pay to the United States. In January 1923 congress offered Great Britain terms of settlement extending over 62 years at 3–3½% which congress, but not the British government, regarded as generous. In Curzon's note of 11 August 1923 he said that Britain would demand from Germany and the Allies only what she had to pay the United States.

on our part, let there also be a cessation of militarism on the Continent. If things continue on the present lines this country may soon have to restart rearming herself in sheer self-defence. It would be monstrous if her generosity only resulted in placing her rivals in a more favourable position for purposes of aggression. This people should not be called upon to pay for Continental militarism. The peace was based on the idea of disarmament, and the covenant of the League made provision for disarmament. We have shown our good faith by disarming, almost beyond the safety limit. Let there be good faith all round in carrying this policy out, and let both America and Great Britain use their position as creditors in order to promote this policy of disarmament which is so essential to the welfare of Europe and the peace of the world.

Before I end, I beg leave to say a word in all modesty to France. My message is for France too. Much of what I have said tonight may sound like an indictment of French policy. And in a sense that is true. But while I am in total disagreement with the policy of the French government, I do feel a profound sympathy with the people of France. The French people sincerely thought they were going to get reparations out of the Ruhr adventure, and in embarking on it had no deliberate intention of breaking up Germany. I recognize too that the French agreement to the treaty of Versailles was only obtained by the promise of the treaty of guarantee by Great Britain and America, and that the breach of that promise let the French down badly and made them feel alone in the world.[1] No wonder that they were in consequence led to adopt a policy of force as an alternative. But it is a barren policy. There is no real security to be obtained by the sword. And in the end the burden of dominating Europe by force must prove insupportable. France knows from her own history and past sufferings that there is a nobler way, and we desire with all our hearts that she should return to that way. Even now the real liberal France is very much alive, although it is no longer vocal or in power. And liberal France knows that pacts of guarantee are not as powerful as the comradeship of liberal ideals. In the dark period in which Europe is now entering there is far more security for France in the company of liberal England and America than in all the legions white and black which she is mustering, and in all the unstable combinations which her government is laboriously building up in Europe. I sympathize with France. But I am equally moved by profound pity for Europe and horror of the fate to which she seems to be moving. And that fate must

[1] The promised treaty collapsed when congress rejected Wilson and the treaty of Versailles.

in the end affect France too. You cannot be a patriotic Frenchman unless you are also a good European. France occupies today a proud and pre-eminent position in Europe. Let her in the day of her victory and greatness not forget her noble historic mission as the great bearer of the liberal tradition in Europe. To abdicate that proud position and to place herself at the head of the reaction in Europe would be a defeat and a disaster, greater than any she has known in all her history. It may involve the whole cause of liberalism all over Europe in irretrievable disaster. And I would implore her for her own sake as much as for that of Europe to return to the faith of her past and become once more the great liberal leader of the Continent.

I have finished. I have said things which are seldom if ever said by those in responsible positions but which must be said quite frankly, unless all hope of a better and more satisfactory European settlement has to be given up. My purpose all through has been not to be a respecter of persons or governments, but to stand up for the human causes for which we made unmeasured sacrifices in the Great War. And in the reparation and Ruhr questions most of these causes are involved. They involve the final question which goes to the root of the whole matter: shall we have peace based upon law and justice? Infinite sacrifices have been made to establish the ideal of a peace between the nations based on justice and the faithful observance of international law and treaty obligations. For that ideal the young men fought and died in their millions. And the root question for us who remain and on whom the responsibility rests today, is whether that sacrifice shall be a total loss, or whether with our earnest and courageous backing, it shall yet be saved for the future. The future of the world depends largely on the answer which we in this generation shall give to that great question.

121   From Lord Curzon   Vol. 26, no. 69

10 Downing Street
Whitehall
[October 1923]

Dear Smuts, May I congratulate you on your speech. Most important and most helpful. Yours,

C.

122   From M. P. A. Hankey   Vol. 26, no. 156

Offices of the Cabinet
2 Whitehall Gardens
24 October 1923

My dear General, Just a line to congratulate you on your wonderful speech last night. I feel sure it will do a lot of good.

After six years with Lloyd George I thought myself case-hardened against speeches, but I must confess I was moved by yours. On no account trouble to answer. Yours ever,

M. P. A. Hankey

123   From G. N. Barnes   Vol. 26, no. 13

76 Herne Hill
[London]
24 October 1923

My dear General, Thanks for your speech of last night. You will have noted also that of Mr [G.] Harvey.[1] You have, be assured, the people of this country behind you. Surely France cannot defy both the British Empire and the United States. Don't go away till that conference is fixed up. But don't acquit the Germans. Damn them. Good luck. Had hoped to see you tomorrow at 'Cecil' but confined to house by sickness. Yours sincerely,

Geo. N. Barnes

124   From B. M. Baruch   Vol. 26, no. 17

Telegram

To: General Jan Smuts, London

From: Baruch

Dated 24 October 1923

Congratulate you upon your speech yesterday it has made most profound impression here.

[1] *See The Times,* 24 October 1923. George Harvey, United States ambassador in Great Britain, had indicated that the United States was ready to help in the economic recovery of Europe and that she had a moral obligation to act in the reparations problem.

125   To B. M. Baruch   Vol. 27, no. 323

Telegram

From: J. C. Smuts

To: Bernard Baruch

Dated [24 October 1923]

Many thanks. Universal indications that speech will be helpful.
Much depends on America.

126   From E. Hobhouse   Vol. 26, no. 171

24 October 1923

Three Cheers! Bravo, dear old Oom. The world will breathe a bit
easier.

Just off; but fully expect to see you again—bossing a world
conference.

Tante

127   From J. M. Keynes   Vol. 98, no. 305

26 October 1923

Dear General Smuts, I am sorry that I was not able to get hold of
you during my weekly visit to London. I enjoyed your speech
enormously, and wanted to say how grateful I felt to you for it.
I expect that the general line you adopted is the one right for the
occasion, especially as I now gather from several sources that there
is a real chance of the United States accepting an invitation to
participate in a conference. (I do not know whether you see *The
Nation* regularly. I am now the chairman of the company owning
this paper, and besides contributing myself am generally in close
touch with what appears there.)

I cannot much complain of your references to the reparation
question. But all the same I do feel that there is here a difference of
opinion between us. If you have in mind some such figure as fifty
milliard gold marks you must not include me amongst the experts
who are alleged to be in unanimous agreement about this. To have
the nominal German debt fixed at this figure would represent real
progress. But I am perfectly convinced that there is not the faintest
chance of Germany's paying anything approaching this sum. Nor
do I agree that from the point of view of her industrial competition
with ourselves we should have less to fear if she was held down to

very burdensome reparation payments than we should have to fear otherwise. Indeed, I think we should have to fear more.

As regards the possibility of fifty milliards, I have briefly three things to say:

(1) This is a good deal higher than the total figure for reparations which I used to estimate in peace conference days when I was trying to put the figure as high as I possibly could, and when circumstances were far different from what they are now and far more favourable to German payments. My figure at that time never exceeded forty milliards. And the arguments which led me to make it as low as that at that time lead me to make it much lower now.

(2) My figure of forty milliards at that date included what Germany would discharge out of various surrenders and deliveries which she would make once and for all. These have now been made and cannot therefore be taken into account in calculations for the future. People generally forget what an enormous sum Germany has paid already. I enclose an article on this point which I am publishing in next Saturday's *Nation*. It is quite a mistake to fix Germany's future liability on the assumption that she has not paid anything already.

(3) Since 1919 an enormous lot has happened to diminish both the expedience and the practicability of large payments; besides which experience has opened our eyes, I think, to many obstacles which have existed all the time, but of which we were not as vividly aware then as we are now.

I had quite another subject on which I wanted to say a word to you. It now looks as though you might be staying in England until well into December. If this is the case is there any chance of persuading you to come to the Founders' Day Feast at King's on 6 December? I have been asked by the college to convey to you an invitation to come as one of their guests. It would be a great pleasure to see you in Cambridge, and a great advantage and satisfaction to the undergraduates of the college to have you amongst them. This banquet is not, like so many that you are attending, one primarily composed of old gentlemen. All the scholars and all the third year men of the college are present, and it would be to them that you would be showing yourself and (I hope) speaking. Ever yours sincerely,

J. M. K.

128   From E. D. Morel   Vol. 27, no. 29

Orchard House
2 and 4 Great Smith Street
Westminster, London
[October 1923]

Dear General Smuts, I met you once at lunch with Lord Courtney and Lord Morley.

I want to express my admiration of your magnificent pronouncement which may, at the eleventh hour, save Europe and save a future Anglo-French war which, unless our diplomacy acts and speaks now, I regard as absolutely inevitable.

I had meant to ask you whether you had time for a conversation in private. I have recently had conversations with [G.] Stresemann, [Ritter Gustav] Von Kahr and other personages—in fact I have only just returned from the Continent, and my view of the situation might interest you. But you are no doubt fully conversant with what the situation actually is. However if you were at liberty, I should be very glad to pass on to you my own reading of the position.

My address is Cherry Croft, King's Langley, Herts. (Telep. 34, King's Langley) and [I] shall be there all this week, preparing a number of speeches I have to deliver in the north. Yours very truly,

E. D. Morel

129   From G. Stresemann   Vol. 27, no. 161A

Berlin, den 29. Oktober 1923

Sehr geehrter Herr General! Die Rede, mit der Sie des an Deutschland durch die Ruhrbesetzung verübten Unrechts in so offener und eindrucksvoller Weise gedachten, hat mich ebenso mit Dank erfüllt, wie die mir von Herrn de Haas freundlichst überbrachte Mitteilung von Ihrer Bereitschaft, uns in unserer Lage beizustehen. Es ist für unser Land ein erhebendes Gefühl, bei einem Manne von Ihrer Weltbedeutung und Kenntnis der Verhältnisse der Völker und Geschichte so viel Verständnis für die wirklichen Zustande in Deutschland und für die Notwendigkeit der Änderung dieser Verhältnisse zu finden. Den von Ihnen angeregten Konferenzgedanken begrüssen wir mit Freude; nur muss diese Konferenz schnell zusammentreten, da unsere jetzige Lage nicht länger andauern kann, ohne dass eine verheerende Katastrophe über uns hereinbricht.

Wir sind, wie ich wiederholt ausgeführt habe, bereit, auch

äusserst schwere Belastungen auf uns zu nehmen, aber jede Last ist unmöglich, wenn dass Reich durch die Politik Frankreichs weiter zerstückelt wird, und wenn dem deutschen Volke nicht die Lebensmöglichkeit erhalten bleibt. Die durch Herrn de Haas mir gegebenen Anregungen habe ich mit den Massgebenden Herren besprochen und gern in Erwägung gezogen. Herr de Haas ist beauftragt, mit Ihnen, Herr General, unsere Absichten hinsichtlich eines solchen Aufrufs zu besprechen. Für Ihr Urteil über die Wirkung dieses Aufrufs würden wir Ihnen besonders dankbar sein.

In den wenigen Zeilen, die ich Ihnen hierdurch übersende, kann ich nur in ganz grossen Strichen unsere Situation kennzeichnen. Ich würde es sehr begrüssen, wenn ich Gelegenheit fände, mit Ihnen an einem noch zu bestimmenden Orte zusammenzutreffen, um die derzeitigen Weltprobleme und Deutschlands Stellung innerhalb der Geschehnisse der Gegenwart mit Ihnen zu besprechen. Ich würde mich freuen, wenn sich dies ermöglichen liesse und wenn dem mittelbaren Gedankenaustausch die persönliche Bekanntschaft mit Ihnen folgen und vielleicht der Entwicklung die Dinge nützen könnte. In aufrichtiger Hochschätzung bin ich Herr General Ihr Ihnen sehr ergebener

G. Stresemann

TRANSLATION

Berlin
29 October 1923

Dear General, The speech in which you in such an open and impressive manner referred to the wrong done to Germany through the occupation of the Ruhr, filled me with gratitude, as did the friendly message, delivered by Mr de Haas,[1] of your readiness to stand by us in our present situation. It is uplifting for our country to find so much understanding of the true situation in Germany and of the need to change that situation, in a man of your world stature and knowledge of the history and relations of the nations. We greet with pleasure the idea initiated by you for a conference; but this conference would have to meet soon, as our present condition cannot continue without a great catastrophe breaking upon us.

We are, as I have repeatedly explained, prepared to shoulder very heavy burdens, but every load is impossible, if the Reich is to be further dismembered by the policy of France and if satisfactory living conditions for the German people are not maintained. I have discussed with the authorities the suggestions made to me by Mr

[1] Not identified.

de Haas, and would gladly consider them. Mr de Haas has been empowered to discuss with you our intentions in connection with such an appeal. We should be particularly grateful for your opinion on the effect of this appeal.

In the few lines which I now send you I can describe our situation in broad outline only. I should be very glad if I could find an opportunity to meet you, at a place to be arranged, to discuss with you contemporary world problems and Germany's position in the existing circumstances. I should be delighted if this were possible, and if an exchange of ideas were followed by a personal acquaintance with you which might well assist the development of these matters. With sincere esteem I am, Sir, Yours faithfully,

G. Stresemann

130   To J. M. Keynes   Vol. 98, no. 306

Savoy Hotel
London
30 October 1923

My dear Keynes, Many thanks for your note and for what you say about my speech. The experts will now once more start the task of Sisyphus[1] and try to settle the figures. My feeling is that events are moving very fast and that they will cut the Gordian knot.[2] Meantime I hope we shall succeed in getting America into the business before the great crisis arrives. It will be something if we have not to face the storm alone.

I am sorry I cannot accept the invitation for Founders' Day. I shall be gone by that time. With best wishes, Ever yours,

J. C. Smuts

I am talking over matters quietly with [K.] Melchior.

[1] The task of Sisyphus, legendary king of Corinth, in the underworld was endlessly to roll uphill a great stone which rolled back just as it reached the top.

[2] Gordius, king of Phrygia, fastened his wagon to a beam with an untieable knot. Alexander the Great, having been told that whoever untied it would rule the entire East, severed the rope with one quick stroke of his sword.

131   To Lord Curzon   Vol. 27, no. 332

Savoy Hotel
London
15 November 1923

My dear Curzon, I send you a copy of a letter I have sent to *The Times* on the reparation conference which will probably be published tomorrow.[1]

It is written in a spirit meant to be helpful to your policy.

The French attitude is alarming me more and more. Either they have lost their heads or they are deliberately courting a break with this country.

I am glad that Mussolini also suggests a strong lead from Great Britain. I trust the world will get it from you. Ever yours sincerely,
s. J. C. Smuts

132   To the Editor of 'The Times'   Box G, no. 8A

Savoy Hotel
[London]
14 November 1923

Sir, The attempt to get an expert committee to inquire into the reparation question has failed. Great Britain, the United States, Italy, and Belgium were all in favour of such an inquiry, but France would only agree to it on conditions which neither Great Britain nor the United States could accept. What is the next step?

In my speech at the South African dinner a few weeks ago I advocated a conference of the powers interested in the reparation question, including the United States. The United States in its correspondence with the British government declared itself in favour, either of such a conference, or of a more limited expert inquiry, such as Mr [C. E.] Hughes had suggested at the end of last year.[2] There can, however, be no doubt that the conference is the more desirable of these two alternatives, and, as the limited inquiry is now apparently dead, the wider conference, acceptable to both Great Britain and the United States, should be reverted to.

The imperial conference, in considering the principles which should guide our foreign policy in the European situation, came to the double conclusion that it was essential for us to secure the

[1] *See* **132.**
[2] Charles Evans Hughes, then American secretary of state, first suggested such a joint enquiry in a speech to the American Historical Association in December 1922.

co-operation of the United States and that Great Britain should take
the initiative in calling a conference, if the proposal for an expert
inquiry were to break down. I quote the words of the report of the
imperial conference:

The conference, after careful consideration of the policy which has been
pursued, was of the opinion that the European situation would only be lifted
on to the plane of a possible settlement by the co-operation of the United
States of America, and that if the scheme of common inquiry to be followed
by common action were to break down, the results would be inimical both to
the peace and to the economic recovery of the world.

It felt that in such an event it would be desirable for the British government
to consider very carefully the alternative of summoning a conference itself
in order to examine the financial and the economic problem in its widest
aspect.

These last words are important. They indicate that in the opinion
of the imperial conference the scope of the reparation conference
to be called by Great Britain should not be confined to the narrow
issue of what amount Germany could pay, but should be extended
to an examination of the whole reparation question in its widest
aspects, both from a financial and economic point of view. Not only
should such a conference have to consider the total reparation
liability of Germany under all heads (such as reparations, costs of
occupation, deliveries in kind, and so forth), in order that finality
may be reached. It would also have to consider the measures and
devise the means of putting Germany's finances into order, reform-
ing her currency, balancing her budget, and securing her the
necessary foreign credit, very much as was done in the case of
Austria.[1] With a view to this rehabilitation, and in order that Germany
may be enabled to pay reparations, the conference would further
have to consider how real peace can be secured to Germany and
how she can be accorded a fair opportunity to work out her salvation without constant menace and interference from outside.
Germany cannot pay reparations unless her currency and credit are
restored; and this restoration is impossible unless the total reparation sum is fixed at a fair and reasonable figure, and Germany is
allowed in peace and without constant hampering to resume her
productive industry.

These are the matters for the conference to consider; and,

---

[1] The dismemberment of Austria–Hungary by the treaty of Versailles resulted in
so serious an economic dislocation in Austria that, to prevent her from veering either
to Soviet Russia or to Germany, the European powers organized financial relief,
suspended reparation claims, advanced loans and set up a committee of control to
supervise her economy.

unless it has this wide scope, the conference will not be of much, if any, use. The situation has become so grave and threatening that any procedure adopted now should be calculated to lead to real solutions, and not to a further marking of time. And a conference of such wide scope and of real authority seems to me the only chance still remaining of staving off disaster.

It may be said that France, having just declined to agree to the narrower inquiry, is not likely to take part in this wider conference. I sincerely hope that this is not so, but even in that unfortunate event I am clear that the conference should be called. That clearly is what the imperial conference contemplated. That probably is what the British government contemplated when they hinted at a separate action in the note of August 11.[1] It is a course which nobody would take lightly or willingly. Such a decision would be, indeed, a momentous one. But so is the situation facing us. For it is no longer merely a reparation matter with which we are concerned. The reparation question is rapidly becoming a vast moral question. It is no longer a question merely whether Germany can, and shall, pay reparations, but whether Germany shall live or whether she shall become a gaping wound in the body of western civilization.

Where we are faced with a situation so terrible we can but do our duty. And our duty is clearly to go forward, even if France does not march with us. France on January 11 went forward without us to seek reparations in the Ruhr;[2] and shall we shrink from going forward without her when something far deeper, far more fundamental is at stake?

It may be argued that France, apart from and outside of such a conference, could render much of its work futile by pursuing a policy the reverse of that which the conference may recommend. While there is some danger of this, it must not be lightly assumed that France will deliberately or for long set itself against the policy of European appeasement which commends itself to the approval of other nations. Rather is it to be anticipated that if the work of the conference is done in the right spirit and with due regard to the interests of our Allies also, French opinion, too, will eventually fall into line. I feel confident that if even now it were possible to effect a fair and just settlement of the whole complex of questions, of which the reparation question is the centre, and the obsession of this great trouble could be lifted from men's minds, we shall find that it will be welcomed in unexpected quarters. The downward movement of Europe is very rapid and the growing unsettlement may soon reach such a pass that those who, like the French, have

---

[1] *See supra*, p. 203, note 2.   [2] *See supra*, p. 166, note 3.

everything to gain from stability, will welcome any reasonable settlement instead of insisting on their own. Let the conference, therefore, proceed with its work without delay, in the faith that the results will commend themselves to the conscience of mankind.

Even if France does not come to the conference, I sincerely trust that that will not prevent the United States from attending. And I also trust that the British government in calling the conference will make certain in advance of the support of the United States. To the imperial conference it appeared all important that the British Empire and the United States should act together in the grave European situation. And to me the only hope of saving Europe to-day lies in joint action by these two great powers, whoever else may be, or may not be, with them. Never before in history has there been such an opportunity of moral leadership, of great human service, as has come to these two English-speaking powers. Never before has there been so grave a responsibility. They could have saved the peace if they had whole-heartedly co-operated at Paris. Alas, they did not. But many obstacles to their co-operation have disappeared since then. And as the great tragedy of Europe has deepened, the people of the United States have become ever more responsive to its poignant appeal. The way has thus been smoothed for most fruitful co-operation in this great crisis. To both of them the downfall and decay of central Europe is a matter of the gravest concern—not only in an economic but far more still in a human sense. For both great peoples the human aspect of Germany's downfall is rapidly coming to dwarf every other aspect. So deep is her ruin that this winter vast numbers of the most docile, the most hardworking, the most intelligent people in Europe must surely die—unless the charity of other nations can keep them alive. We cannot wash our hands of this situation. If we did so, our sin before history may well become as great as Germany's. And the greatest charity, the greatest service that we could render Germany in this crisis, is to keep her on her legs, to help her to set her house in order, and to enable her government to discharge their proper functions—in fact, to assist Germany to save herself. That would not only be a service to Germany but to ourselves, for it is only by keeping Germany going and promoting her financial restoration that we can ever hope to get substantial reparations from her. It is from both these points of view that I would press most strongly for the speedy calling of the conference. Yours etc.,

J. C. Smuts

133   To G. Stresemann   Vol. 27, no. 334

Savoy Hotel
[London]
15 November 1923

Dear Herr Stresemann, I thank you for your note of 29 October. My point of view you will have learnt from the messages which I gave to Dr Melchior and Mr de Haas. It seems to me that your task is to keep Germany going while a more favourable public opinion is being slowly formed externally especially in the British Empire and the United States. I know how hard this task must be, and I fear it is going to be harder still this coming winter. But if only you can keep Germany going, you will find that the increasing gravity of your internal situation will react favourably on public opinion outside and will in the end secure you strong support. My conviction is that there is a real and rapid improvement under the surface, which may at an early date find open expression. In the meantime I trust you will be able to hold your people together in patience and strength of soul. Especially do I hope that, as the responsible government for a united Germany, you will do everything possible to feed the starving not only in unoccupied but also in occupied Germany.

I have done something to improve the situation. I have now to go back to South Africa but my interest in this situation will remain unabated. Even from South Africa I shall continue to be helpful, and in case of necessity I am prepared to come back again. But I trust the improvement will continue in an ever increasing measure.

With best wishes for your success in your almost superhuman task, Yours very sincerely,

s. J. C. Smuts

134   To E. Wilson   Vol. 30, no. 59

Telegram

To: Mrs Woodrow Wilson[1]

From: J. C. Smuts

Dated 4 February 1924

My deepest sympathy with you in great loss which you share with the world. A prince among the sons of men has departed.

[1] The second wife of President Wilson, formerly Edith Galt, née Bolling; born 1873, married Woodrow Wilson 1915, died 28 December 1961.

135   To the Editor of the 'New York World'
Vol. 30, no. 58

Telegram

To: Nyworld
From: J. C. Smuts
Dated 4 February 1924

My view Wilson's work and historic position was fully expressed in statement on his retirement March 1921 published America. That statement still expresses my opinion. Wilson's untimely eclipse was due to temporary and accidental circumstances. As these pass away his heroic figure will stand out ever more clearly and his work will be recognized as among America's greatest contributions to the world.

136   From J. H. Hofmeyr   Vol. 29, no. 152

On the resignation of the administrator of the Transvaal early in 1924, Smuts offered the position to J. H. Hofmeyr who was then principal of the University of the Witwatersrand.

Telegram

To: J. C. Smuts
From: J. H. Hofmeyr
Dated 20 February 1924

Council would release me if desired by you but hopes it will be given reasonable time for making arrangements for my work here under present difficult circumstances.[1]

137   E. F. C. Lane to S. M. Smuts   Vol. 30, no. 71
Private and personal

Prime Minister's Office
Cape Town
21 February 1924

Dear Mrs Smuts, I annex a letter[2] which was sent off today. Do not let anybody know that you have a copy, please, but I feel that it

---

[1] Hofmeyr was required to assume office on 1 March. The 'difficult circumstances' had arisen out of disputes between the council and the senate of the university following Hofmeyr's attempt to dismiss one of the professors. *See* A. Paton, *Hofmeyr*, chapters 10, 11.   [2] **138.**

must come to you because it is the young man's Magna Charta and will make very interesting reading in the biography for which no doubt you are quietly amassing interesting papers. Yours sincerely,

E. F. C. Lane

138 To C. L. Leipoldt   Vol. 30, no. 71A

Prime Minister's Office
Cape Town
24 February 1924

My dear Leipoldt, Thank you for your and Preller's wires re appointment of Hofmeyr. I can understand your views, while not sharing them. The plain fact is that it is most difficult to get a fit and proper person for the post. Your wire mentioned the name of Curlewis,[1] but you could not have meant this seriously. Other names were considered—Neser [J. A.], Kleinenberg [T. J.], etc. Rooth [E.] is out of the question because of the dickiness of his seat. It would indeed be foolish to try and keep Wakkerstroom,[2] only to lose Pretoria Central. It is no use being merely critical. Who is your better man, abler, more experienced and with more energy?

Hofmeyr is admittedly one of the ablest men in South Africa and has impressed even those able men with whom he has been associated in his recent commission work.[3] He will go into politics soon in any case and will go very far in my opinion. His youth and ability are in his favour, especially as it is essential for the South African party to encourage and push on young men. He is of course wanting in administrative experience but I hope he will overcome that difficulty, and none of the men mentioned have had bigger administrative exprience than he has for the last four years in the running of a new concern[4] like the Rand University. The *Volkstem* already committed the great mistake of making a veiled attack on him when he was appointed on the provincial relations commission. I really do think you will make a greater and more mischievous one if you repeat the attack after his appointment. As in your own case on

[1] J. S. Curlewis was a judge of the Transvaal division and became president of that division in 1924.

[2] The previous administrator of the Transvaal, A. G. Robertson, had resigned his post in order to fight a crucial bye-election at Wakkerstroom, a rural constituency in the eastern Transvaal.

[3] Hofmeyr served on the provincial finances commission (U. G. 19 of 1923) and the education administration commission (U. G. 41 of 1923). Fellow members included J. R. Leisk, W. D. Baxter, Sir Ernest Chappel, Professor F. Clarke,

[4] The University College of Johannesburg, formerly the South African School of Mines, became the University of the Witwatersrand in 1922.

the *Volkstem*, I want new blood, new ideas, courage and the forward look, and you will get them from Hofmeyr much more than your old estimable gentlemen whose inertia will mean the disappearance of the South African party. When I was appointed state attorney in the Transvaal at the age of twenty-eight, a member of the volksraad said: 'My God, het Paul nou sy kop verloor!'[1] It would be unpardonable if now a young man like you[2] said the same thing. Kind regards,

s. J. C. Smuts

139   To J. H. Hofmeyr   Vol. 30, no. 75

Kantoor van de Eerste Minister
Kaapstad
28 Februari 1924

Lieve Jantjie, Zeer hartelijk dank voor jou briefie van 24 dezer. Niets heeft mij grooter pleizier gegeven dan de gelegenheid jou tot Administrateur te bevorderen en bij mij rust geen twijfel dat jij aan onze beste verwachtingen zal beantwoorden. Zoals ik jou laatste te Groote Schuur zei was het mij plan jou so spoedig mogelijk van het zuiwer academisch werk weg te nemen en in het politieke leven in te leiden. Met het oog op de toekomst zou het een fout zijn indien jij te academisch zou ontwikkelen. Gelukkig is de opening spoediger gekomen dan ik verwacht heb, en ik ben jou dankbaar dat jij niet geaarzeld heeft [om] van de gelegenheid gebruik te maken. De Transvaal Administratie is een moeilijk werk en sal jou een ruimer school van de grootste waarde zijn. Veels geluk en veel meer in dit jou nieuwe loopbaan. Waar ik jou kan helpen en daardoor de land helpen, zal ik niet voor een oogenblik aarzelen.

Hartelijke groeten aan Poor Relations. Steeds getrouw

J. C. Smuts

TRANSLATION

Prime Minister's Office
Cape Town
28 February 1924

Dear Jantjie,[3] Very many thanks for your note of 24 inst. Nothing has given me greater pleasure than the opportunity to appoint you administrator and I have no doubt that you will fulfil our best

---

[1] 'My God, has Paul [Kruger] taken leave of his senses'. (Afrikaans.)
[2] Leipoldt was then aged forty-three; Hofmeyr was thirty.
[3] Diminutive of Jan in Afrikaans.

expectations. As I told you at Groote Schuur the other day, it was my intention to take you away as soon as possible from purely academic work and to introduce you into political life. With a view to the future it would be a mistake if you were to develop too academically. Fortunately the opening has come sooner than I expected, and I am grateful to you that you have not hesitated to make use of the opportunity. The administration of the Transvaal is a difficult task and will be a wider school of the greatest value to you. Good luck and much more than that in your new career. Wherever I can help you and so help the country, I shall not hesitate for a moment.

Good wishes to Poor Relations. Ever sincerely,

J. C. Smuts

140   To E. H. Walton   Vol. 30, no. 78

Cape Town
7 March 1924

My dear Walton, Thanks for your letter of 13 February.

I received by last mail an agreement from Bruce [S. M.] which I had telegraphed to you about. The proposal is that there should be a reciprocal tariff agreement between South Africa and Australia, and we are now going into the matter to see what can be arrived at. Hitherto dumping has been imposed in both countries in respect of certain goods and this did not make for satisfactory relations.

I got your cable reporting that Godfrey Isaacs had been to call upon you about the report of the wireless committee.[1] We are not prepared to take any action in this matter until there has been an opportunity of discussing things with van der Byl [H. J.] who arrives next week. The situation is far from clear and I expect that van der Byl will want to await the receipt of [R.] Donald's report before making his recommendations. The local Marconi Company have already made representations to the minister of posts and telegraphs[2] as they consider the recommendations contained in the report affect adversely the interests of the South Africa Company and its shareholders.[3]

[1] This committee, under the chairmanship of Robert Donald, was one of several appointed from time to time by the British government to make recommendations on the offer of the Marconi Company to establish direct wireless communication throughout the Empire.

[2] Sir Thomas Watt.

[3] The Donald Committee had recommended that all wireless stations in the Empire should be owned by the post office, whereas some of the Dominions had already made agreements with local subsidiaries of the Marconi Company for their own stations.

Replies will be sent to you to enable you to deal with the Anti-Slavery and Aborigines Protection Society.[1] Hofmeyr [G. R.] has got their letters under consideration now and I expect to be able to furnish you with particulars next mail.

We have decided that Hofmeyr should attend in person the next meeting of the permanent mandates commission to explain matters generally. He is anxious to take a holiday and I have decided under the circumstances that he should visit Geneva when the commission are considering the various reports and assist them in coming to a proper understanding in regard to the state of affairs in South West Africa. I hope that it will be convenient for you to accompany Hofmeyr to the meeting and introduce him. I have not yet received his report but he informs me that it is now being drafted and that we shall be able to comply with the requirements of the commission in regard to date of its receipt.

There will be a considerable stir in England in regard to the question of Singapore. I have just had a confidential cable from the prime minister saying that he expects to make a statement on this matter on 17 March to the effect that his majesty's government have decided not to proceed with the creation of this naval base.[2] He has asked for an expression of my views as the matter was discussed at the imperial conference last year and Australia and New Zealand displayed very great interest in it. I have informed him that I concur in the policy of his majesty's government which is entirely in accordance with my views. I have always had misgivings about this scheme and welcome its abandonment. I do not suppose that Messrs Bruce and [V.] Massey will be of the same opinion and there will be considerable outcry amongst the Conservative newspapers to the effect that the Labour government are neglecting to take precautions for the safety of the Empire.

I have had two telegrams from the secretary of state[3] in regard to the ratifications of

(a) customs formalities convention,

(b) liquor treaty with the United States of America.

[1] The Anti-Slavery Society was one of a cluster of English humanitarian organizations which were active in Great Britain particularly in the nineteenth century. They grew out of the British and Foreign Bible Society founded in 1804. The Anti-Slavery Society was in existence by 1824. The Aborigines' Protection Society, founded in 1833, sought to advance the rights and welfare of the natives in British colonies. The headquarters of the societies was Exeter Hall.

[2] After the naval disarmament measures agreed upon in February 1922 (see p. 110, note 2, supra) the admiralty decided to make Singapore an up-to-date naval base but in 1924 the Labour government stopped work on it, partly to save expenditure and partly as a pacific gesture.

[3] The secretary of state for the colonies was J. H. Thomas.

With regard to (*a*) in my letter of 1 February I asked you to ratify on our behalf, and with regard to (*b*) I have told the secretary of state that the British ambassador should be asked to ratify on our behalf when he does so for his majesty's government.

There has been another death amongst members of parliament. This time a very decent quiet Nationalist who was the member for Pretoria North, Jan Joubert. He has been in indifferent health for two or three years. We have not yet heard who they will put up, but the South African party in any event will vigorously contest the seat.

Clegg leaves by today's boat and will tell you how things are here. Yours sincerely,

s. J. C. Smuts

141   From R. Marloth   Vol. 29, no. 188

Cape Town
17 March 1924

Dear General Smuts, Kindly excuse the delay in returning your specimens, but I had to wait for the Saturday afternoon to attend to them.

Some interesting plants among them, e.g. the *Gladiolus carmineus* which is not in the *Flora Capensis*.[1] Yours sincerely,

R. Marloth

142   To R. Marloth   Vol. 30, no. 45

Prime Minister's Office
Cape Town
[March 1924]

Dear Dr Marloth, Thank you very much for so kindly naming my Hermanus[2] specimens. I have also collected a fairly full parcel of the timber trees in the Table mountain gorges,[3] and will trouble you to name them a little later. As soon as there is a clear weekend I shall consult you with a view to our going to the mouth of Palmiet river[4] to explore its vegetation. Ever yours sincerely,

J. C. Smuts

[1] A systematic description of the plants of the Cape Colony by various authors.

[2] A small town on the coast of the Indian ocean about eighty miles from Cape Town. The surrounding veld and mountains are rich in flowers and grasses. Smuts often went there to walk, swim and collect plants and usually stayed at the house of his sister, Adriana Smuts.

[3] Smuts was deeply concerned about the afforestation of Table mountain.

[4] Some ten miles west of Hermanus. The river mouth is on a large lagoon.

143   To I. B. Pole-Evans   Vol. 30, no. 85

Cape Town
26 March 1924

My dear Doctor, Thank you very much for sending me the beauti-ful specimens of *Stiburus* and other grasses which interested me greatly.

Don't you think you should write a short account of Greig's farm after being unburnt for such a long period? The fact that on the unburnt veld *Themeda* has supplanted the dune grass of the surrounding farms is most useful and important and should be generally known.

I have spoken to Lionel Phillips about Marloth's book.[1] The result is that Phillips is going to fix up the whole matter with Marloth this week.

Hill [A. W.] has sent me the *Kew Bulletin No. 1* for this year with a note asking that we should appoint a South African assistant there as soon as possible. I hope you are keeping the point before you.

I have been doing some useful exploring of the mountain gorges for timber trees and have now a fair collection. But I have not yet had Marloth to name them. I see from the Kew report that Miss [H. J.] Davison[2] has been working up the Celastraceae. Has she published her research?

During the Easter vacation I shall spend a fortnight in the Transkei[3] and Eastern Province[4] on a political tour, and hope to find time for collecting some plants too. With love to you and Mary, Ever yours,

J. C. Smuts

[1] In May 1905, on the initiative of Florence, Lady Phillips, Marloth had agreed to prepare a book on the South African flora to be published at her expense. Volumes I and IV appeared in 1912, volume II in June 1924. This richly illustrated work entitled the *Flora of South Africa* is now a rare item of Africana. *See* T. Gutsche, *No Ordinary Woman.*

[2] Of the division of botany, department of agriculture.

[3] The Transkeian territories lie between the Great Kei river and the southern border of Natal.

[4] The eastern region of the Cape Province. It is not a separate province.

144   To E. H. Walton   Vol. 30, no. 89

Telegram

From: General Smuts, Cape Town
To: Sir Edgar Walton, London
Dated 8 April 1924

In view Wakkerstroom election result[1] government have decided advise dissolution of parliament[2] and intend holding general election approximately 19 June. Challenge of Pact parties[3] had to be accepted and we must now fight it out. I trust you will continue in your important position as our representation in London during this year requires someone in whom we have the utmost confidence.

145   To L. S. Amery   Vol. 30, no. 100

Prime Minister's Office
Pretoria
7 May 1924

My dear Amery, Many thanks for your note of 9 April and your good wishes in the fight.

The Labour government in Great Britain has done us much harm, as people here say: 'Labour can't be so bad after all, look at what has happened in England. There they already sit in the seats of the mighty!' Besides, the imperial preference business is a very bad one for Dominion governments.[4] I am afraid this item of the Labour policy will yet cost the Empire dear. To think of the Empire Exhibition and the veto on imperial preference synchronizing!

I have had these knocks and others, and I have come to the conclusion that it could only weaken, still further weaken, my position if I delayed an appeal to the country. What is going to happen is

---

[1] This was as follows: A. S. Naudé (National party) 1,420; A. G. Robertson (South African party) 1,207.

[2] The decision to advise dissolution and hold an election was announced by Smuts without consulting the cabinet or the caucus and within a few hours of the Wakkerstroom result being known.

[3] The National party led by Hertzog and the Labour party led by Creswell had, during and after the Rand strike of 1922, made an agreement, popularly known as 'the Pact', to join forces for the purpose of ousting the Smuts government. For the conditions of the agreement *see* J. J. van Rooyen, *Die Nasionale Party, sy opkoms en oorwinning—Kaapland se aandeel* (1956), pp. 102–4.

[4] The Labour government, with Snowden as chancellor of the exchequer, repudiated the tariff preferences promised by the previous government. *See supra*, p. 193, and 193, note 1.

quite uncertain, more so than usual. I hope to win; if not, I shall be strong enough to be a check on the wreckers, I hope.

You mention Singapore. It is too much of a challenge to Japan, but yesterday our ally. Besides, Washington has cut down our fleet to such an extent, that in an emergency we could not spare sufficient warships for the Pacific. Singapore means *another* British navy, strong enough to cope with Japan. Therefore, from discretion as much as on principle, I would try the other way.[1] I admit Singapore and imperial preference appear a bad let down for Australia.

Good-bye. Love to Mrs Amery. Success to you. Ever yours,

s. J. C. Smuts

146   To E. H. Walton   Vol. 30, no. 105

Pretoria
7 May 1924

My dear Walton, By next mail Sturman [E. A.], postmaster-general, will be coming to England and I have told him we want him to open up negotiations with your assistance with the Union-Castle Company concerning the extension of the existing mail contract.[2] We feel very strongly that considerable reductions should be made in rates of freight and hope that Kylsant[3] will be able to meet us in this matter. An extension from September is necessary and then the new government will be able to call for tenders. I am convinced that no one in South Africa will be satisfied until we have called for tenders and have ascertained whether anybody is prepared to compete with the Union-Castle.

I am much obliged to you for sending a copy of the reparations report.[4] I saw the report in *The Times* last week, but the copy you send me now is in a much handier form.

I have received a message from Ramsay MacDonald regarding the attitude of the French on this matter, and thought I should

---

[1] *See supra*, p. 221, note 1.

[2] The contract for carrying mail between Great Britain and South Africa was at first (1876) shared between the Union line, which, from 1857, provided the first regular steamship service between Cape Town and England, and the Castle line, founded in 1872. In 1900 the two lines amalgamated as the Union-Castle line.

[3] Lord Kylsant, formerly Sir Owen Cosby Philips, chairman of the Royal Mail Steam Packet Company which controlled the Union-Castle line from 1912–32.

[4] Following an appeal by the British government to the government of the United States to collaborate in an investigation into Germany's capacity to meet reparation demands, a committee was appointed at the end of 1923 under the chairmanship of an American general, Charles G. Dawes. The Dawes report, issued on 9 April 1924, presented a new plan for stabilizing Germany's finances by granting her loans and lightening reparation payments.

encourage him to press on towards settlement. The attitude of the French seems to be holding the matter up very much indeed, and now I fear it is again complicated by the result of the German elections.[1] The question is of supreme importance and I hope the foreign office will not allow the French to postpone settlement indefinitely. I enclose a copy of my telegram to Ramsay MacDonald, dated 1 May.

We have had a great deal of negotiation in regard to our candidates and our nominations are more or less in order except that at Port Elizabeth at the present moment we have a difficult situation arising in the Centre constituency where Reitz [D.] is being opposed by Kayser [C. F.] who, despite tremendous pressure, refuses to stand down. I have hopes that we may settle it before the official nomination day, 22 May, and I will let you know next week what has been done.

I am very glad to see that the Prince of Wales visited our exhibit at Wembley, and is reported to have been pleased.

In my last letter I mentioned that Hertzog was preparing a manifesto. It has now been fired off and you will see it in the *Cape Times* of 5 May. Unfortunately I have not got a copy I can send you. I do not think he has put a very attractive programme before his people and I shall answer him at a suitable opportunity in the near future. As soon as the nominations are settled I shall make a very quick tour and return here just in time for polling day. My wife in the meantime is looking after my constituency, where I am being opposed by Mr George Hay of Johannesburg.

I enclose a copy of our manifesto. With kind regards, Sincerely yours,

s. J. C. Smuts

P.S. Reitz has asked me to tell you how much he appreciates the support you yourself have given him, and also the assistance he is getting from your son[2] in the Port Elizabeth *Herald*.[3]

---

[1] The general election of May 1924 had not improved the position of the government which was an uneasy coalition of Social Democrats, Democrats, Centre and People's parties holding 237 out of 471 seats. Wilhelm Marx was chancellor and Stresemann foreign minister. On the other hand, the French elections of that month had been won by the Radicals and Socialists and the new government, under Herriot, was ready to seek accommodation with Germany.

[2] Edgar Brocas Walton, the editor.

[3] This was the *Eastern Province Herald*, established as a weekly in Port Elizabeth in May 1845. It became a daily newspaper in 1898.

147   To C. P. Crewe   Vol. 30, no. 108

Pretoria
14 May 1924

My dear Crewe, I am very glad to know you are back in East London, and now look forward with more confidence to the election there.[1] I shall be in East London the week after next or somewhere there in order to give a helping hand.

I trust you are very well after your long absence and special treatment. And I hope Lady Crewe is also very well.

Owing to your movements I did not answer your last letter. There you warned me that I was losing British support by my leaning too much towards the other side. I imagine I have held the scales pretty evenly. But unfortunately the arid parts of South Africa have suffered most during the last three years of unprecedented drought and a great deal of my time and attention has therefore been occupied with the problems of the Backveld.[2] It was inevitable. I fear you are right and British support for the government has somewhat weakened. Labour has gone towards nationalism, and loyal Britishers have tended somewhat towards political independence. This has been due more to depression and other inevitable factors than the shortcomings of the government. Bear in mind too that we are a mixed crowd and that free-traders and protectionists foregather in our camp. It has always been difficult to pursue rigid policies. However, whatever the diagnosis, the crisis has come, and we must fight our hardest to get through it with credit and with victory if possible. Kindest regards, Ever yours,

s. J. C. Smuts

148   From K. Spilhaus   Vol. 30, no. 25

Telegram

From: Commissioner of Commerce, 's Gravenhage

To: Prime Minister, Pretoria

Dated 16 May 1924

Personal. Secret. Upon invitation from Cuno [W.] have had conversation with him. He expressed earnest wish that you should be available in Europe as soon as negotiations open in respect to European settlement so that you can on account of your influence

---

[1] Crewe controlled the *East London Daily Dispatch*, established in September 1872.
[2] Literal translation of *agterveld* (Afrikaans), meaning the more remote parts of the country.

and experience insure quick arriving final settlement of all pending reparation questions in a just and fair manner on a basis of your London speech and experts' report.[1] He has stated you have full confidence of all desirous of fair settlement because your London speech opened the way to such settlement. He has asked me if I thought cable from him to you will be well received. As late chancellor and not being a party man[2] Cuno will have good will of immense majority in parliament and nation on this subject and act in close touch with leader majority party in reichstag. Final negotiations will not begin probably before about middle of June. He asked me to suggest in what form your influence might be secured to guide and advise in respect to final negotiations.

149   To M. C. Gillett   Vol. 30, no. 148

Pretoria
24 June 1924

As the cables will have told you your wish has been gratified[3] and I have been beaten. Yesterday I resigned and for the present it is all over. For two months now I have worked my hardest to fight this last battle. Well, you know the rest. It will take me some time to adjust myself to the new situation. But first and foremost, I want a bit of rest and hope I shall get it now.

I was away from Pretoria practically the whole of the last two months and could therefore not write to you. But it was a consolation to receive your letters. Now I hope to return to better ways. I have had very nice letters from the children for my birthday. Please thank them from me. I was very pleased to see Jan was again all right.

At Doornkloof all is well. They had much fun over the elections and are by no means heart-broken over my defeat—double defeat.[4] Soon I shall have to leave for Cape Town to attend the new session and see how the new horses run. I am sure there will be some fun. I wish the new team well. But I have my doubts and fears.

[1] The Dawes report.

[2] Cuno had formed a non-party cabinet responsible only to the president in November 1922. It fell in August 1923. He had also, as managing director of the Hamburg-Amerika line, restored German shipping to its pre-war position.

[3] Arthur and Margaret Gillett had both written saying they almost hoped for Smuts's defeat so that he could have leisure for non-political pursuits. The results of the election were: National party 63; South African party 53; Labour party 18; Independent 1.

[4] Smuts had lost his own seat, Pretoria West, to G. A. Hay (Labour party) by 385 votes.

It is a bitterly cold day; hence this terrible scrawl. With much love—aye, more than much!

Jan

150   To J. X. Merriman   Vol. 30, no. 117

Prime Minister's Office
Pretoria
24 June 1924

Dear Mr Merriman, Thank you very much for your most kind letter of two weeks ago. It was very good of you to think of me in my troubles and to wish me well in my work. Well, the fight is over and the battle is lost. The Pact will now have a chance to run this country. It is clear that the people had made up their minds to have a change and to give the others a chance. We shall now see what they can do to carry out all their promises.

Well, my dear friend, I am very pleased that your health still permits you to attend to your large correspondence. I hope and trust that in your old age[1] you may have strength to enjoy the quiet pleasures which still fall to your lot, and that the farm and your books may make up for the loss of the doubtful pleasures of parliament and public life. I hope as soon as I am back for the session to come over to Schoongezicht and pay my respects to my dear old friend. Ever yours sincerely,

J. C. Smuts

151   To C. P. Crewe   Vol. 102, no. 212

Prime Minister's Office
Pretoria
25 June 1924

My dear Crewe, Just a line to thank you for your letter of 22 June. There are many things to put right, and I shall be most grateful if you will lend a helping hand in our reorganization. We have done badly but after all the country is all right. Over 48% of the electorate has voted for us, and with practially half the country behind us, even a minority may feel heartened. I only hope the Pact will form their coalition government[2] because that will make our work easier in many ways. A purely Nationalist government will be an appeal to many unthinking Saps to go over and save them from

---

[1] Merriman was eighty-three.   [2] This did, in fact, happen.

Labour; and a Pact government will on the contrary send many good sensible Nats our way.

I intend going to Standerton within the next fortnight to thank my new constituents. And then I shall try to give some lead to our party. To my mind the maintenance intact of our non-racial party is absolutely necessary in the public interest. With us there (even though in a minority) things never will go too far wrong. Though we must prepare for curious developments, e.g. Kemp as commandant-general and Grobler [P. G. W.] as ambassador on the Continent![1]

Good-bye, my friend. My love to Lady Crewe. I had a really good time with you. Ever yours sincerely,

J. C. Smuts

[1] They both became cabinet ministers.

PART XIV

IN OPPOSITION

9 JULY 1924–28 JUNE 1929

IN OPPOSITION

As leader of the opposition Smuts had to engage the Nationalist–Labour (Pact) government under Hertzog mainly on two issues. These were: English–Afrikander conflicts and irritations aroused by the determination of the Nationalists to give the country a distinctive flag, and the optimistic attempt made by Hertzog to reduce the formidable complications of black–white–Coloured relations to an orderly 'policy'. Smuts's attitude to, and his tactics on, both issues come out well in his private papers.

The flag quarrel stretched over two years and in the end the government was forced into a reluctant compromise (**174–7, 197, 199, 201, 229, 231, 233**). The challenge of Hertzog's Native bills compelled Smuts to give thought to a matter which he had previously tended to avoid. He wrote a long critical memorandum on the bills (**204**), recorded talks with Hertzog in February–March 1928 (**240–3**), explained his position in frequent letters to party colleagues and his English friends. No accord could be reached between the two leaders and Hertzog was unable to get the required two-thirds majority of both houses of parliament to pass his bills.

Although he was not now in touch with other governments Smuts's concern about Europe and the Commonwealth remained acute. This appears most notably in his correspondence with L. S. Amery, now secretary for the colonies, and G. G. A. Murray, an official of the League of Nations Union. The Locarno agreements and the attitude of the Dominions to the obligations undertaken by Great Britain, and his doubts about the effectiveness of the League made Smuts increasingly uneasy (**156, 157, 162, 173, 191**). But hopefully he urged upon Amery an East African policy which would create 'a great white state or system of states' in that region (**155, 245**). Hertzog's claims, on returning from the 1926 imperial conference, aroused some ironical private comments from Smuts—the real begetter of Dominion status. Publicly he welcomed the conference report. Yet he was disturbed by Hertzog's emphasis on the right of secession and its implications and warned the country not to read too much into the report of the conference (**213, 218, 222, 224, 239**).

Exchanges on the Native bills, Dominion status and the flag were acrimonious and renewed attempt at uniting the two main parties had no chance of success (**212, 216, 221, 225, 235, 252**). The election of 1929 was bitter and the Pact won it by playing on racial fears and prejudices (**255, 256, 258, 262**).

This period of Smuts's life gave him more leisure than any other before or after. The product of that was the publication of *Holism and Evolution* in

July 1926; a presidential address before the South African Association for the Advancement of Science in 1925 (**163, 165, 166**); participation in a discussion on the nature of life at the meeting of the British Association in Cape Town in 1929 (**249–53**). He also became an authority on grasses and added to his botanical studies a new one—palaeontology. The papers dealing with these pursuits which are printed below have been sparingly selected from a great many. A few items of intrinsic interest have also been included such as **193**, Smuts's tribute to Emily Hobhouse (**207**), and delightful letters from Monsignor F. C. Kolbe.

152   To M. C. Gillett   Vol. 30, no. 150

Irene
[Transvaal]
9 July 1924

I have just read your dear and welcome letter on my defeat. Thank you very much for what you say. It did me good and I felt much better for your sympathy. The situation is more difficult and complex than one anticipated. I had longed to get out of it and to clear my own thoughts in a period of release from official duties. My own election result was one of the first to be announced, and when I heard it (in the quiet of the house at Doornkloof) my first impression was that my secret desire had indeed been gratified and that now I would be free. But then came the other results, showing that all the most important of my old South African party colleagues had also been sacrificed—Malan [F. S.], Burton and Mentz.[1] I felt at once that under these distressing circumstances I ought not to clear out, that the South African party might go to pieces in the rout, and that irreparable mischief might be done to South Africa. And so I have had to 'dash down that cup of Samian wine'[2] and to renounce the vision of freedom and leisure. I am now member for Standerton,[3] leader of the opposition in a house where we are outnumbered by a larger majority than that ever seen in South Africa, and with most of my important old colleagues gone. It will once more be a hard political grind. But what else can I honourably do? I dare not desert my friends, I dare not leave my own work alone in the hour of defeat. People would not understand, and might be driven to despair, and I might later on reproach myself. So the road to freedom is not yet clear. That is why I say the matter is

[1] F. S. Malan had been defeated at Malmesbury, H. Burton at Ladismith and H. Mentz at Soutpansberg.
[2] 'Dash down yon cup of Samian wine!' Byron, *Don Juan*, canto III. lxxxvi. 16.
[3] This seat was offered to Smuts by Gert Wessels.

difficult and complicated. My own philosophy makes me feel perfectly serene and free from all regrets. Still, it is an eye-opener, to find how a large portion of the people you have slaved to serve view your efforts. It is a very humbling experience. But then life is itself a very difficult business. I have made for the great things in our life as a people, and the small things have appealed more to those who feel the pinch and the difficulties of the times. But enough of all this. At present it is all rather dark and puzzling. But I hope I shall see the way to go a little more clearly later on. At present I can but hold on and await developments. You will be glad to hear that I have had beautiful days in the Bushveld, days of enjoyment of the life around me, and of quiet turning round of the thoughts within me. It was all very healing, holistic and calming.

Well, dear children, God bless you all. I send you my dearest love. Ever yours,

Jan

153   To M. C. Gillett   Vol. 30, no. 156

Irene
[Transvaal]
17 September 1924

I have had a succession of such nice and welcome letters from both of you from Porthcothan.[1] The place seems to have stimulated you both very strangely, and I have felt the glow of your beings as far as 7,000 miles away. How I would have loved to have gone with you on Sundays over that strange dreamy or sleeping country to meetings in the distant villages. And what a splendid name is Come to Good![2] We have so many places that might appropriately be called after the legend; Go to the Devil, but Come to Good sounds so comforting that even the sound makes you inclined to be happy. So you and Jan [Gillett] continue at botany. It is a good complement to birding, and together they are about the happiest ways of spending the time in these days that I know. I again sleep outside[3] and in the early dawn the birds come to look for seeds quite close to my bed invisible behind the netting. They are most charming. The hoopoos come now to feed at the kitchen in the morning. Many strange and beautiful birds put in an appearance. To them this place is Come to Good. So it is now to me. I enjoy every day.

[1] On the north coast of Cornwall near Newquay.
[2] An ancient meeting house of the Society of Friends near Falmouth.
[3] Smuts was in the habit of sleeping on the verandah outside his bedroom.

I attend to a minimum of political business, and read and read and read; and think and think and think. It is all so restful and satisfying. My soul had begun to dry up literally in these years of arid politics. But now I begin to feel at rest again. And God is very good. Of course I continue to attend to a heavy correspondence in which Joan [Boardman] is useful. Ten to twenty letters every day is a lot for me. But I have time now to read and to ride and not to feel on edge all the time. Is it not a good feeling to be dead to the world? The family is very happy, all doing very well at school. Louis [McIldowie] writes stories: 'The Story of an Apple Tree', 'The Lost Boys Part 1' etc. etc.; Sylma [Coaton][1] works for matriculation, Cato [Clark] for B.A. Japie [Smuts][2] is very good at mathematics which he is taking for his degree. I suppose he will go to Cambridge. Santa [Weyers] rears chickens and keeps Sally the lioness (eleven months old) company. The house down at the farm[3] is practically finished. Then another will begin at Rooikop. Love to you all, dears.

Jan

154   To M. C. Gillett   Vol. 30, no. 157

Irene
[Transvaal]
25 September 1924

Your final letter from Porthcothan has arrived. You have become almost lyrical about the place and its surroundings. I should like to sample it myself on some future occasion, not omitting Come to Good!

I have spent two most delightful weeks at home. Nothing but reading and riding and even a little writing all the day. The reading is mostly botanical and biological, though physical speculations have not escaped me. I have read all you have sent me in recent years in that line, including Einstein whom I begin to understand thoroughly. I only believe it ought to be possible to devise some simpler scheme to explain the unitary character of time, space, matter and all physical appearances and activities. I have never yet applied holism in this domain, which is so purely mathematical.

I enclose a list of books which I find referred to and which I should like you to send me.

---

[1] *See* vol. II, p. 451, note 1.   [2] *See* vol. IV, p. 383.
[3] Apparently Droogegrond, one of the two farms near Rust der Winter in the Bushveld some fifty miles north-east of Pretoria.

I am glad you and Jan continue at botany. You ought to be an authority worth appealing to on your next angel's visit.[1]

With love to all,

Jan

155   To L. S. Amery   Vol. 30, no. 136

Personal   Irene

Transvaal

25 November 1924

My dear Amery, It is unnecessary for me to tell you how pleased I am that you are at last at the colonial office. You should have been there before and no one has your qualifications for the great post. Good luck to you; I am sure you will get it too. The resounding victory of the Conservatives[2] will have a great effect all over the world, and will make people everywhere realize that the nation wants stability and strength, and not this neurotic pandering to Bolshevism. It is already having a very good effect here where Thomas's patting on the back of Hertzog[3] has not been a particularly happy gesture. You will find that the putting into force of the preference resolutions now will have a most salutary effect, as the scrapping of those resolutions by MacDonald gave deep offence in all directions, and all that we and the other Dominions could do was to keep quiet and not make the mischief worse.

I regret that we do not see eye to eye on the Singapore business. What I fear most is that we are gratuitously driving Japan into the arms of our potential enemies of the future. Leading Japanese statesmen have repeatedly expressed their views on the project and I fear we are simply making powerful enemies who will reinforce your European opponents and make your foreign policy very difficult all round. Already a great friendship is arising between France and Japan, and at the last Geneva assembly they seem to have played effectively into each other's hands.[4] On the whole I much prefer the

---

[1] *See supra*, p. 114, note 3.

[2] In the third general election in three years (29 October 1924) the Conservatives won 415 seats against 152 Labour and 42 Liberal seats. L. S. Amery became secretary of state for the colonies in Baldwin's second cabinet.

[3] J. H. Thomas as secretary for the colonies had visited South Afrca in September 1924. On 7 September he said in a speech in Pretoria that he was convinced that Hertzog loved South Africa as much as Smuts did.

[4] The framers of the Geneva Protocol (*see* p. 239 *infra*, note 2) had excepted from its provisions disputes arising out of matters solely within the domestic jurisdiction of the parties but the Japanese had secured modifications which would bring such

Japs as friends, rather than as an estranged and possibly hostile power. Of the naval utility of Singapore I think very little, as we could never in a real crisis afford to divide our reduced fleet (after the Washington limitations) between European waters and the far Pacific. However I am afraid Australian pressure for Singapore will combine with your own views as a government to carry this useless and dangerous project, which will put our foreign policy out of gear for this and the next generation.

Now a word about Africa. While I approve the energetic action taken in Egypt I trust we shall keep within limits and let the Egyptians stew in their own juice rather than saddle the Empire with an impossible task. The separation of the Sudan is really punishment enough.[1]

I sent Lane to Kenya to have a look round and bring me first-hand information. You will have to watch the whole East African situation very carefully if that great territory is not to become a purely Native state with an Indian trading aristocracy in charge. All the highlands of eastern Africa from the Union to Abyssinia are healthy for Europeans and can be made into a great European state or system of states during the next three or four generations. It is one of the richest parts of the world and only wants white brains and capital to become enormously productive. But the present tendencies seem all in favour of the Native and the Indian, and the danger is that one of the greatest chances in our history will be missed. The cry should be 'the highlands for the whites' and a resolute white policy should be pursued. The fruits of such a policy will be a white state in time more important than Australia. There is land enough for all the vast Native population on the flanks of the highlands. But the Natives by themselves will continue to stagnate as they have stagnated for the last ten thousand years. A great white Africa along the eastern backbone, with railway and road communications connecting north and south will be a real first-class addition to the Empire and will repay all the capital put

matters as the immigration policy of a member state within its arbitration terms. The United States and Great Britain had objected to these modifications but France had supported them.

[1] Although Egypt had been recognized as an independent state in 1922, there was strong opposition by the nationalist 'Wafd' party to the retention of certain powers by the British government, notably control over the Sudan, first established in 1898, and the maintenance of British military garrisons in and around the Suez canal zone. After the victory of the Wafd at the general election of 1923 there was considerable disorder culminating in the assassination of the governor of the Sudan. The high commissioner, Lord Allenby, now presented a stiff ultimatum which was accepted in full and the British government put pressure on King Fuad to dissolve parliament and hold another election.

into it. It is an expansion of the Rhodes policy. Why should it not become your policy? While France in the north-west and north is building up a black Africa, you will be pursuing the great historic policy of the Empire in the east and leave behind a chain of white states which will in the end become one from the Union to Kenya. It is a policy which will be intelligible and capture the imagination, and it will have far-reaching effects on the future of the Empire. Please consider this carefully and avoid the Scylla and Charybdis of the Native and Indian policies which have so far seemed to influence unduly the colonial and India offices. With kind regards, Ever yours sincerely,

s. J. C. Smuts

156   To G. G. A. Murray   Vol. 30, no. 137

Irene
Transvaal
25 November 1924

My dear Professor Murray, I read your letter to *The Nation*[1] on the Protocol[2] with great interest, but I regret to say that it has seemed to me quite unconvincing. As you can well imagine, this Protocol has interested me profoundly. I have not yet made any public statement[3] although I have been most strongly pressed to express my views on it. Frankly, people are puzzled and want a lead, and I am not presumptuous enough to think the lead should come from me.

The effect of the Protocol is to declare war illegal and punishable through the economic boycott at least. This is, of course, an enormous change from the original covenant, which made provision for arbitration and conciliation but in the last resort left it to the parties to fight it out if they were so minded.[4] We certainly did not imagine

[1] *The Nation and the Athenaeum*, 18 October 1924, p. 108. In his letter Murray criticizes the leading article of 11 October headed 'A False Step at Geneva'.

[2] The Protocol for the Pacific Settlement of International Disputes or the Geneva Protocol was put before the assembly of the League of Nations by Herriot and Ramsay MacDonald which on 2 October 1924 unanimously recommended the governments of the member states to accept it.

[3] Smuts prepared a statement soon after the Protocol had been adopted by the assembly but did not publish it (*see* Smuts Collection, Box G, memorandum 6).

[4] Behind the Geneva Protocol and the criticisms of it were two opposed opinions. One was that the machinery provided in the covenant of the League to prevent war (articles 12, 13, 15, 16) was not effective and that, until security could be ensured, attempts at disarmament would not succeed. The Geneva Protocol thus sought to improve the League machinery mainly by making arbitration compulsory in all international disputes and subjecting recalcitrant states to the punitive measures of the

in 1919 that the world was ripe for the outlawry of war. Is it ripe now? Will nations submit vital questions of national honour and existence to arbitration in one form or another and agree to be outlawed if the decision goes against them? That is the fundamental question, and I fear the assembly has gone too far and proposed something which in the existing world organization is wholly impracticable. I also fear that the two Japanese amendments on domestic questions will keep America permanently out of the League and possibly drive the British Empire out of it.[1] I would rather see France keep up her bloated armaments and pay the penalty than attempt an advance on the covenant which is going to prove fatal to the League. I fear the Protocol is such an advance. No folly could be greater for the League than that of attempting too much: the effort must inevitably ruin her in the present international situation and temper.

Such are my fears as at present advised. Ever yours sincerely,

s. J. C. Smuts

157   To H. Strakosch
Vol. 34, no. 1

Irene
Transvaal
25 January 1925

My dear Strakosch, Many thanks for your letter of 1 January. I have said nothing so far in public about the draft Protocol but I am naturally much concerned to see that nothing is done which will injure the League. And the Protocol places the League between the proverbial devil and the deep sea. If the Protocol is rejected the League will deeply suffer; if it is adopted, it will probably disrupt the League. A way out by way of reform and amendment is therefore imperative. In recent press notices the British government have adumbrated the possibility of returning to a policy of security for France. This Pact business which I had considered dead is even worse as an alternative for it means the disruption of the Empire in the first great European crisis, as the Dominions are not likely to be dragged again into a European war as they were in 1914. The Protocol raises the most serious issue in the whole history of politics and international law and it should not be rushed through.

covenant. The contrary opinion was that, while the League was valuable as an international forum, its provisions for restraining aggressors, mainly by the application of economic and other sanctions, were unworkable and dangerous to peace.

[1] *See* p. 237 *supra*, note 4.

Time should be given for ample consideration and discussion and the first draft of Geneva should be amply scrutinized and amended before its final adoption and ratification. And when finally adopted, all the great states should adhere to it, whether as members of the League or not. Naturally I prefer them to be in the League. But the United States of America might find it easier to adhere to a reformed Protocol than to join the League now that it has grown into so difficult a political issue in the States.

You ask why I make it a condition that Russia should join the League. My reason is this: the Protocol is merely preliminary to the disarmament protocol which is to come. Now I cannot conceive all the other European nations disarming while Russia can continue and develop as an armed camp. That is simply to invite disaster for Europe as well as the League. No protocols and mutual guarantees will help unarmed Europe *vis-à-vis* a mobilization of the vast war resources of a resuscitated Russian state with over 100,000,000 people. You know what the history of Czarist Russia has been, how it conquered all the Baltic countries, then turned south and beat Turkey, and then went on wars of conquest as far as Vladivostock. That which hath been will be again, unless Russia disarms like the rest. And if she does not disarm, it would be criminal to disarm the rest. The Baltic states and Roumania and Poland will be attacked in turn and a helpless Europe will find its Protocol a broken reed to lean on, and a new cycle of world wars will begin. No, a disarmament policy *must* include Russia. And it is for this reason that I consider it necessary that she should join the League and adopt the Protocol when she is still impotent and before she has in another generation recovered from the waste and exhaustion of the great war and her great folly. Statesmen seem to think that Russia can be treated with contempt and can for the present be ignored. No greater mistake is possible. Hence I say: let the League now rise to the full expansion which was the original ideal. Let *all* nations and states belong to her. Only then could protocols and disarmament have any chance whatever on the road to permanent peace. The U.S.A. if not a member should be an associate; all the other great powers should be members. The last few years have taught us the unwisdom and impracticability of resting the League on a fraction of mankind. Let us now repair the error. Don't you agree with me? With best wishes,

s. J. C. Smuts

158 To R. Dart Vol. 34, no. 5

Irene
[Transvaal]
4 February 1925

Dear Professor Dart, I wish both personally and as president of the South African Association for the Advancement of Science[1] to send you my warm congratulations on your important discovery of the Taungs fossil. Your great keenness and zealous interest in anthropology have led to what may well prove an epoch-making discovery, not only of far-reaching importance from an anthropological point of view, but also well calculated to concentrate attention on South Africa as the great field for scientific discovery which it undoubtedly is. The recognition of the unique importance of our Rhodesian Broken Hill skull in human evolution has now immediately been followed by your discovery which seems to open up a still further vista into our human past.

I congratulate you on this great reward of your labours which reflects lustre on all South African science, and I wish to express the hope that many further triumphs await you and those who have so willingly co-operated with you on the road on which you have begun so well. Yours very sincerely,

s. J. C. Smuts

159 To C. Niekerk Vol. 34, no. 57

19 Maart 1925

Waarde Niekerk, Mnr. Malan het my jou brief gewys, waarin jy over die Colour Bar skryf. Ek dink jy verkeer onder 'n misverstand, en daar ek weet dat jy 'n baie verstandig man is, wil ek het graag wegneem.

Wat Generaal Botha aan jou gesê het jare gelede stem ek volkome mee saam en dit is ook my standpunt. Volgens beslissing van die Hof bestaat daar nou glad nie 'n kleurlyn nie en is die bruinman en naturel altwee vry om te doen die werk waarvoor hy geskik is. Nou wil die Regering kom en 'n kleurlyn stel vir die Naturel en Asiaat op die wetboek van die land om hulle te belet om sekere klasse werk te doen. Ek dink dit is baie verkeerd en dat ons nie so 'n beletsel in ons wetboek moet opneem nie. Ons moet regverdig wees vir almal en ek dink jy sal met my saamstem dat so 'n wet nie

---

[1] This Association was founded in Cape Town in 1903. Smuts was its president in 1925.

regverdig is nie. Die posiesie van die bruinman is glad nie 'n kwessie nie. Jy moet dus nie dink dat ek teen die bruinman is nie. Ek waardeer baie die vooruitgang wat ons bruinmense gemaak het en ek hoop dat die vooruitgang nog verder sal gaan. Ek hoop jy verstaan nou wat my posiesie is.

Ek hoop dit gaat jou wel. Dienstwillig die uwe,

get. J. C. Smuts

TRANSLATION

19 March 1925

Dear Niekerk,[1] Mr Malan has shown me your letter in which you write about the colour bar. I think you are under a misapprehension and, as I know that you are a very sensible man, I should like to remove it.

I agree entirely with what General Botha said to you years ago; that is also my standpoint. According to the court decision, no colour bar at present exists and the Coloured man and the Native are both free to do the work for which they are fitted. Now the government wants to put a colour bar for Natives and Asiatics on the statute-book of the country in order to prohibit them from doing certain classes of work.[2] I think this is very wrong and that we should not include such a prohibition in our statute-book. We must be fair to all and I think you will agree with me that such a law is not fair. The position of the Coloured man is not in question at all. So you must not think that I am against the Coloured man. I value very much the progress that our Coloured people have made and I hope that this progress will go even further. I hope you now understand what my position is.

I hope all is well with you. Yours sincerely,

s. J. C. Smuts

[1] Not identified.

[2] Under the Mines and Works Act, No. 12 of 1911 the government could make regulations for issuing certificates of competency in skilled work in mining and engineering. When, in 1923, certificates were withheld from 'coloured persons' (in effect Natives and Asiatics) in the Transvaal and Orange Free State, the courts declared the regulations to be *ultra vires*. Thereupon the Nationalist–Labour government proposed to limit the granting of certificates of competency in a number of skilled occupations to Europeans and Cape Coloured people and this was enacted in the Mines and Works Amendment Act, No. 25 of 1926, known as the 'Colour Bar Act'.

160   To S. L. Polak[1]   Vol. 34, no. 52

18 March 1925

My dear Polak, Thank you for your note of 27 February.[2]

I hope that what I have said on the colour bar policy of the government[3] will prove helpful, and pave the way for a satisfactory solution of the whole very difficult question. Yours sincerely,

s. J. C. Smuts

161   To J. J. Kotzé[4]   Vol. 34, no. 73

26 Maart 1925

Waarde Colonel, Dank vir uw briefie van 20 Maart. Ek wil nie die vraag stel door U aan die hand gegee, maar ek sal gebruik maak van die argument. Comdt. L. P. Boshoff, wie ek bedank het vir sy trouwe dienste, vraag my wat raad ek gee aan lede van die Skietvereniginge wat nou dreig om te bedank. Sê hom s.v.p. en ook alle andere belanghebbende dat ek er sterk voor is dat onse vriende by die organisasies bly en nie help afbreek wat so swaar opgebouwd is.

Hertzog het nou die segregasie gister feitelik oorboord gewerp en gesê hy kan maar voortgaan op die lyne wat ek gewerk het in die laatste jare. Wat een erkenning! Secessie en segregasie is altwee daarheen, en net die Pact bly oor. U vriend,

get. J. C. Smuts

TRANSLATION

26 March 1925

Dear Colonel, Thank you for your letter of 20 March.[5] I do not want to put the question suggested by you, but I shall use the argument.[6]

[1] Honorary secretary and treasurer of the Indians Overseas Association.

[2] Smuts Collection, vol. 33, no. 26.

[3] In a debate in the house of assembly on 25 February 1925 Smuts said *inter alia* that the terms of the Colour Bar Bill would discriminate between white and Coloured persons on the one hand and Natives and Asiatics on the other. He regretted the inclusion of Asiatics in the bill; not many Asiatics would be affected by it but it would place a stigma on all Asiatics. He advised the government to separate the Asiatic from the Native question for they were very different problems.

[4] Not identified; lived at this time at Bultfontein, Orange Free State.

[5] The letter is dated 22 March 1925 (Smuts Collection, vol. 32, no. 169).

[6] Kotzé wished Smuts to question in the house of assembly the fitness for the position of head of the Bultfontein commando of the person nominated in his (Kotzé's) place. He alleged that the person concerned was physically unfit, a Cape rebel and a pensioner.

Commandant L. P. Boshoff,[1] whom I have thanked for his faithful service, asks me what advice I give to members of the Rifle Associations[2] who are now threatening to resign. Please tell him and also others who are interested that I am strongly in favour of our friends remaining in these organizations and not helping to break down what has been built up with such difficulty.

Yesterday Hertzog practically threw segregation overboard and said that he might as well proceed on the lines followed by me in recent years.[3] What an admission! Secession[4] and segregation have both gone and only the Pact remains. Your friend,

s. J. C. Smuts

162   To G. G. A. Murray   Vol. 34, no. 105

House of Assembly
Cape Town
23 April 1925

My dear Murray, Thank you very much for your letter of 20 March, with its most interesting information.

I am very grateful for Mrs Sidgwick's[5] report on your thought transference experiments. The subject interests me profoundly as it points to the limitations of our present science compared with the facts they are intended to explain. To my mind telepathy is a great new fact which calls for readjustment of old views and new categories of explanation. Subconscious hyper-aesthesia is only a Latin and Greek combination to express a fact without giving any explanation. Some day I hope I may have the privilege of discussing this matter further with you.

[1] Commandant Louis P. Boshoff had served under Smuts in the Anglo-Boer War. *See* vol. 1, **174** (a) and p. 501.

[2] Under the Defence Act, No. 13 of 1912, all citizens who are required to register but who do not undergo peace training must serve for four years in a Rifle Association. Members are provided with free rifles and ammunition by the department of defence.

[3] In a debate in the house of assembly on 25 March 1925 Hertzog largely endorsed the policy of preceding governments in respect of *territorial* segregation and added: 'I hope it will be the last time we shall hear the word "segregation" used as if we were going to drive the Natives into any particular area.'

[4] The right of the Union of South Africa to secede from the British Empire had been one of the main planks in the platform of the National party but the Pact agreement, summarized in a letter of 12 April 1923 from Creswell to Hertzog, included the following: 'Both parties wished to guard against the "secession" question and should make a clear statement that neither wanted to make a constitutional break from England to establish a republic.' (*See* D. W. Krüger, *South African Parties and Policies 1910–1960*, pp. 74–5.)

[5] *See* Smuts Collection, vol. 32, no. 236. Eleanor Mildred Sidgwick, born Balfour, married Henry Sidgwick. Principal of Newnham College, 1892–1910.

I am afraid the Protocol for the present is dead.[1] It was too ambitious. It attempted too much. And it has met the fate of all efforts that aim too high. The next phase will be the exploration of the German offer of security.[2] When I was in London two years ago, I pressed the representatives of the German government very strongly to look upon the appeasement of France as a matter of primary concern for German policy, and to make the offer to France which would lay the foundations of a new peace for Europe. They thought the mentality both of France and Germany such at that moment that an effort in that direction would be in vain. However I am glad to see that at long last Stresemann has come round to this point of view, and I think [Sir Austen] Chamberlain is right in working this new proposal for all it is worth.

If success is achieved a great step forward will have been taken towards the lasting pacification of Europe. Then Russia alone will remain, and the political kaleidoscope there may yet bring about a situation where a similar fruitful policy may become possible even in respect of Russia. Once the foundations are thus laid, the superstructure of universal arbitration will become a possibility, which today I do not think it is. I think we are in face of a situation where we must be guided by facts and practical developments, more than by general considerations of policy, which in their vagueness and generality only create suspicion and difficulties.

The German offer is such a new fact, and I hope that, with all openness of mind, we shall explore it to the uttermost.

I hope you will do your best to keep the League of Nations Union[3] on non-party lines. Our cause is great and must win, and will win. The lines of wisdom for us is to minimize friction and not to call forth any party opposition. In your Union there has been a wonderful co-operation between the British parties, and I hope that will continue.

I am interested to hear that you have just finished translating *The Eumenides*.[4] Like Fitzgerald's translation of *Omar Khayyam*, your renderings often exceed in force and beauty the original. Often phrases from your previous translations keep murmuring in my head. I am sure that the work is as great a consolation to you as

---

[1] After criticism in the British Conservative press and in the Dominions the British government's rejection of the Geneva Protocol was announced in a speech by Sir Austen Chamberlain in the council of the League on 12 March 1925 and this killed it.

[2] On 9 February 1925, encouraged by the British government, the German government proposed a non-aggression pact to the French government with respect to the German–French boundary.

[3] Founded in April–May 1917. *See* **737**, **753**.

[4] The third play of the trilogy, the *Oresteia*, by Aeschylus.

to the thousands of readers to whom you have interpreted perhaps the most human of the ancient poets.

With very kind regards to you and Lady Mary, Ever yours sincerely,

s. J. C. Smuts

163   To I. B. Pole-Evans

Vol. 34, no. 122

House of Assembly
Cape Town
8 May 1925

My dear Doctor, I send you by the same post a first rough draft of my address for the S_2A_3.[1] I shall be very pleased if you will look through it. I am far from satisfied with it, and suggestions from you may improve it both in form and substance. Wilkinson [J. A.][2] has still to give me any events or happenings of the year which I should mention at the beginning.

You will see that there is a good deal of geological and climatological stuff in the address. I have therefore sent a copy to Dr A. L. du Toit of the irrigation department and asked him also for suggestions. Perhaps you two could have a talk over the matter. I want to be certain about the facts, and I want also any other relevant material which may help the case I am trying to make. On climate I have followed partly Brooks on Climate[3] and Wegener.[4] But I have naturally attempted my own version of the material in them.

I don't know what you think of the length of the address. It seems to be a good deal shorter than your address and most of those I have seen. But it will take at least an hour to get through what I have written.

I am sorry to trouble you. But you can appreciate my anxiety not to make a fool of myself.

With kind regards and best wishes to you and Mary, Ever yours sincerely,

J. C. Smuts

[1] Abbreviation of S. A. A. A. S.
[2] President of the association in 1924–5.
[3] C. E. P. Brooks, *The Evolution of Climate* (1922).
[4] A. Wegener, *The Origins of Continents and Oceans* (English translation 1924).

164   To M. C. Gillett   **Vol. 34, no. 280**

Civil Service Club
[Cape Town]
11 May 1925

Monday morning. We had a glorious week-end, Nyssie [Denys] Reitz and I. On Saturday morning we left for Caledon[1] to open a party bazaar. We were both very sick about this new labour after a very arduous week in parliament. But the day was gorgeous, such a May day as you only get in this land of God. And we gradually cheered up as we motored along. I opened the bazaar; we lunched and Nyssie made a good speech. And then after lunch I looked at that great mountain behind Caledon,[2] and my heart took flight. I said to the good people I was going up the mountain. They stared at me in astonishment. 'It was too rough, I would lose my way. Nobody ever went up there.' So I went up by myself, accompanied by my own thoughts and memories, with the flowers and rare ericas[3] and proteas smiling at me. Up and up until I was on the top and viewed the glorious landscape in that perfect air, and heard the *grysbok*[4] whistle and 'was made one with Nature'.[5] Then I came a little way down, took off these clothes, which are alien to that sort of surrounding and had a glorious sunbath. I gathered many plants, and laden with inner and outward treasures I arrived back at Caledon in the evening. Then dinner and once more speeches—till midnight. But I was satisfied because I had been refreshed by contact with the Great Happiness. On Sunday morning we motored back in perfect weather once more, and in the afternoon you would have found me once more grappling with the problems of holism. And so back to the new week's task and the weary round of parliament.

Do you remember Norie, the Coloured cook on the farm? She is dead, but out of gratitude to her memory Isie is keeping her two daughters on, although they are not really satisfactory. Norie was a good soul, better than most.

Isie writes me that Jannie [Smuts], who has been reading up Dart's discovery[6] and Neanderthal man, is now writing a poem on the 'Men who died thousands of years ago and lie buried under

---

[1] A town in the south-western Cape Province about seventy miles east of Cape Town.

[2] The Klein Swartberg.

[3] A wild flower species of which there are over a hundred varieties in the Cape Province. The yellow *Erica jasminiflora* of Caledon is a rare local variety.

[4] Literally 'grey buck', a small antelope.

[5] 'He is made one with Nature...' Shelley, *Adonais* XLII.   [6] *See* **158**.

the sands'! Louis is writing a serial story, and was last at part 6. There are strong literary leanings in the family.

Thank you for Bragg's book[1] and Cytology,[2] both very useful. I only wish I had more time to read but parliament is most exacting and exhausting. And what is worse I somehow feel that the labour there is not really worth while, that the waste and the friction are out of all proportion to the real work done. Love to you all. Ever yours,

Jan

165   To I. B. Pole-Evans   Vol. 34, no. 136

House of Assembly
Cape Town
27 May 1925

My dear Doctor, Thank you very much for your letter and for the trouble you have taken in connection with my address. I am agreeably surprised at your good opinion of the address. To me it seemed crude and vague, and to miss the mark. I had intended recasting the whole thing. But I have so little free time for this sort of thing, and I am now so emboldened by your good opinion that I shall merely make essential changes and leave it in substance untouched. I shall send you a new draft early for any further suggestions you may wish to make.

I think there is too much geology in the address and I shall somewhat compress that and somewhat expand the botanical part. It is curious that I had arrived at the same conclusion as to the origin of our floras as yourself. But I was afraid to say a thing which ran counter to all the expert opinions I have seen. It is however impossible to study [H. G. A.] Engler's account of the main features of our African flora without coming to the conclusion that it is largely indigenous; yet Engler himself is a northern. It only tends to show the power of the northern or European fallacy as I shall call it—this deciding everything from Europe.

Yes, we must do that trip later, as soon as I can command some free time and you can accompany me. It is sheer waste to devote so much of your valuable powers to mere administrative routine. You will yet settle several of our great botanical questions, I am sure.

Give my love to Mary. Good-bye to yourself. Ever yours sincerely,

J. C. Smuts

[1] Sir William Bragg, *Concerning the Nature of Things.*
[2] E. V. Cowdry (ed.), *General Cytology.*

166   To E. F. C. Lane   Vol. 34, no. 181

[1] July 1925

My dear Lane, I hear off and on about your excellent work at Wembley from returning South Africans, and it is evident that you have done a great deal to make our exhibit for this year a real credit to South Africa. I'm glad to hear everybody speak well of your work.

Here things are going much as might be expected under the circumstances. In parliament the Pact is making a sad mess of things. We've passed through the assembly a colour bar bill which will set the Native and Asiatic population by the ears,[1] and a minimum wage bill which is as bad as anything they have in Australia.[2] The Labour wing is driving the Pact on to the rocks, and although it may take some years for the public to realize the inwardness of all that is happening, in the end their eyes will surely be opened and they will get rid of the Pact government. That may, however, take time.

We hear very little of Empire or foreign relations. Hertzog says never a word on these subjects, and the cable news is not very informative. I have a suspicion that Chamberlain has blundered over the security pact negotiations, but at the same time I have to admit that our information is very scrappy.

Next week I shall be at Oudtshoorn to address the S_2A_3 of which I am president this year. I send you a copy of the address which, I'm informed by Pole-Evans, contains a theory which is not only novel but also valuable, and may lead to the reconsideration of a number of scientific problems. I shall be glad if you will give the copy to our old friend Watt[3] and ask him to see that proper publicity is given to it in the press. I want no money, but only such publicity as may be useful to get my views discussed in the press. And the copyright must in any case be reserved, as it is certain to be published in full in the *Journal of South African Science*[4] which will appear next year, or at any rate some months hence. I'm also sending copies to Professor [A. C.] Seward, Downing College, Cambridge and to Dr [O.] Stapf at Kew Gardens for their information. I do not wish to give you any trouble over the matter but Watt may be glad to make use in some form or other of my address.

[1] *See supra*, p. 243, note 2.

[2] The Wage Act, No. 27 of 1925, provided machinery for fixing the wages of unskilled workers and distinguished for this purpose between employees with 'civilized' and 'uncivilized' habits of life.

[3] A. S. Watt, Smuts's literary agent in London.

[4] Smuts's paper, entitled 'Science from the South African point of view', was published in the *South African Journal of Science*, vol. 22, November 1925, pp. 1–19.

You will be glad to hear that I am rewriting my work on holism[1] and that about two-thirds is already finished. By the end of the year I hope to be finished with the whole volume. I shall be glad to be done with it as it has given me considerable trouble. The views put forward are largely original and may prove of some scientific and philosophical value. It may therefore be that I shall proceed to publication next year. You may just mention this matter to Watt also.

With very kind regards to both you and Mrs Lane, Ever yours,

s. J. C. Smuts

167   To L. S. Amery   Vol. 34, no. 192

17 July 1925

My dear Amery, Thank you very much for your letter of 28 May. I trust that [Sir Edward] Grigg, who is in all respects a very high class man, will also prove the right man for East Africa. I formed a very high opinion of him and hope he will supply the sort of guidance which East Africa's development requires. I believe the highlands of the Eastern Africa, South and Central, are the makings of one of the greatest future Dominions of the Empire. But white settlement will have to be pushed all the time.

I feel concerned over the new security pact negotiations, just as I felt nervous about the Protocol developments. The sub-committee of the imperial defence committee which sat over the Protocol did most useful work, and I hope you will insist that the same com-mittee should also examine the pact proposals. It seems to me inevitable that under the pact Great Britain will be drawn into a war in eastern Europe, say of Polish origin, in which France participates under her post-war engagements. If this is so, the position would be most lamentable indeed. The attitude of the Dominions over the Protocol kept Great Britain out of a first-class mistake, which Macdonald was prepared to make. Now your government propose to act on your own apart from the Dominions, and the attitude of the Dominions will therefore no longer act as a brake. All the more reason for extreme caution.

I must confess the idea of separate action by Great Britain and the Dominions strikes me as a great step backward, and I hope the implications of such a departure will be most carefully scrutinized before it is embarked upon.

[1] *Holism and Evolution,* published in 1926. For the earlier unpublished book *see* **519, 520.**

I am very sorry that I could not join the Milner memorial committee. Personally I would gladly have done so, but you know how our domestic politics is influenced by a certain type of consideration, and more harm than good would have been done by my joining the committee.

With my very best wishes and kind regards, also to Mrs Amery, Ever yours very sincerely,

s. J. C. Smuts

168   To Modjadji   Vol. 34, no. 205

Irene
Transvaal
27 August 1925

To the Chieftainess Modjadji[1]

My daughter[2] has told me that some months ago she had a motor accident in the neighbourhood of your *stad*,[3] and that you most kindly put her and her party up for the night and were kind to them in other ways. I wish to thank you for this kindness to my daughter and to tell you that I appreciate it very much.

My wife has made up a small parcel of gifts which she is sending you as a token of her gratitude also.

I wish you good health and other blessings.

General J. C. Smuts

169   From F. S. Malan   Vol. 32, no. 212

Mount Pleasant
Oranjezicht
Kaapstad
11 September 1925

Geagte Vrind, Ek moet jou gelukwens met die gunstige afloop van jou reis in die noordweste gedurende ons Sapweek. Oor die algemeen was die poging om belangstelling op te wek 'n volslae sukses. Dit het duidelik uitgekom op die vergadering van ons uitvoerende komitee van môre.

Op die vergadering het die naturelle-voorstelle van Generaal

---

[1] Mujaji III was at this time queen of the Lovedu tribe living in a reserve in the north-eastern Transvaal. *See* E. Jensen Krige and J. D. Krige, *The Realm of a Rain-Queen* (1943).

[2] Cato Clark. *See* W. K. Hancock, *Smuts—The Fields of Force*, pp. 474–5.

[3] Afrikaans for an African village.

Hertzog en sy raadpleging met die opposisie ook ter sprake gekom. In die loop van die bespreking word veral op drie punte nadruk gelê: 1. Dat ons versigtig moet wees om wit-op-swart van Hertzog sy voorstelle te verkry. Dit kan al te lig gebeur dat hy met ons kalf sal wil ploeg, of dat daar misverstand sal ontstaan omtrent wat werkelik plaas gevind het. 2. Dat daar verskil van gevoele is in ons eie party—veral wat betref die insigte van die Kaapse Provinsie en die van die Transvaal. As dit kan wil ons hierdie saak nie as 'n party-saak behandel nie; maar ons moet daarom oppas dat dit nie ons party sal opbreek nie. 3. Dat dit dus wenslik is om die deur oop te hou en nie ons hele party onvoorwaardelik deur 'n ooreenkoms met Hertzog te bind nie.

Die begeerte word uitgespreek dat ek die geleentheid moet neem om hierdie saak onder jou aandag te bring. Ek twyfel daar nie aan nie, dat jy die waarskuwing om versigtig te handel nie nodig het nie. Maar dit is 'n moeilike en ingewikkelde vraag, en ek meen dat dit sal goed wees as jy van ons voormanne sal raadpleeg, voordat jy 'n vaste verstandhouding met Hertzog aangaan.

Ek twyfel of die land ryp is vir 'n oplossing van die naturelle vraagstuk, soos deur Hertzog bedoel; en die houding van Tielman Roos bevestig my twyfel. En tog sal dit nodig wees om die saak grondig publiek te bespreek, en opening te gee vir verskil van mening, anders sal die volk nooit ryp genoeg word nie. In 'Ons Land' het ek vier artikels oor 'Die plek van die naturel in ons samelewing' gehad. Dit sal afsonderlik afgedruk word, en dan sal ek jou 'n kopie daarvan stuur. Die bedoeling van die artikels is hoofsaaklik om die publiek in te lig en tot nadenking te stem.

Die jaar vergadering van die S.A. Akademie sal op die 9 Oktober te Pretoria gehou word. Miskien kry ek dit reg om die vergadering by te woon en dan 'n kans te hê om een en ander met jou te bespreek. Sal jy teen die tyd op Pretoria wees? O ja—want jy moet deel neem aan die Kruger-feestelikhede op die 10 Oktober.

Die Preller-sensasietjie is gewees en verby. Op my vergaderinge in die kiesafdeling van Dordrecht het Vermooten geprobeer daar voordeel uit te trek, maar ek glo nie hy het veel indruk gemaak nie.

Sal Madeley ons elfde minister wees? 'What a come-done!'

Met hartelike groete van huis tot huis. Jou toegeneë vrind,

F. S. Malan

TRANSLATION

Mount Pleasant
Oranjezicht
Cape Town
11 September 1925

Dear Friend, I must congratulate you on the favourable outcome of your journey in the north-west during our S.A.P. week. On the whole the attempt to arouse interest was a complete success. This came out clearly at the meeting of our executive committee this morning.

At the meeting General Hertzog's Native proposals and his consultation of the opposition also came up.[1] In the course of the discussion three points in particular were emphasized: 1. That we must be careful to get his proposals from Hertzog in writing. It can happen all too easily that he will want to plough with our calf, or that misunderstanding will arise about what really took place. 2. That there are differences of opinion in our party—especially as regards Cape Province and Transvaal views. If possible, we do not want to treat this matter as a party question; but we must nevertheless take care that it does not break up our party. 3. That it is therefore desirable to keep the door open and not to bind our whole party unconditionally by an agreement with Hertzog.

The wish was expressed that I should take the opportunity of bringing this matter to your attention. I do not doubt that you do not need the warning to act carefully. But it is a difficult and complicated question and I think it would be well if you were to consult some of our leaders before you come to a firm understanding with Hertzog.

I doubt if the country is ripe for a solution of the Native question as Hertzog intends; and the attitude of Tielman Roos confirms my doubt. And yet it will be necessary to discuss the matter thoroughly in public and to allow openings for differences of opinion, otherwise the people will never become ripe enough. I had four articles in *Ons Land* on 'The place of the Native in our society'. They will be separately printed and I shall then send you a copy. The object of the articles is chiefly to inform the public and set them thinking.

The annual meeting of the Suid-Afrikaanse Akademie[2] will be held at Pretoria on 9 October. I may be able to attend the meeting and have a chance to discuss one or two matters with you. Will you

---

[1] Hertzog had, in 1923–4, made several speeches on Native policy but his first comprehensive public statement of his views and intentions in this matter was made at Smithfield on 13 November 1925.

[2] *See* vol. III, p. 103, note 2.

be in Pretoria at that time? Oh yes—because you must take part in the Kruger festival on 10 October.[1]

The little Preller sensation has come and gone.[2] At my meetings in the Dordrecht constituency Vermooten [O. S.] tried to turn it to his account, but I do not think he made much impression.

Will Madeley be our eleventh minister?[3] What a come-down!

With best wishes from my family to yours, Your sincere friend,

F. S. Malan

170   To F. S. Malan   Vol. 34, no. 216

Doornkloof
Irene
29 September 1925

Waarde Fransie, Hartelik dank vir jou brief wat ek ontvang het op my terugkoms uit Natal, waar ek 'n seer voorspoedige twaalf daagse toertjie gemaak het en op twee na al die afdelings besoek het. Ek het die gees daar gunstig gevind evenals in die noordelike distrikte van die Kaap. By my is dit duidlik dat ons toekoms goed en seker is, en dat ons net geduldig en arbeidsaam in tussen moet wees.

Ek is baie bly om te verneem dat jy met die eeufees hier sal wees. Kom direk naar Doornkloof en bly die slag by ons, sodat ons 'n goeie kans kan hê om dinge te bespreek. Indien enigsins mogelik bring jou vroutje ook saam.

Ek is nog nie door Hertzog genader oor sy naturelle voorstelle, maar ek weet dat die Naturelle Departement besig is 'n wet op te trek en ek verwag dus dat Hertzog my sal nader. Ek stem helemaal saam met die gevoelens van jou uitvoerende komitee en jou eie. Hartelike groete, Jou vrind,

get. J. C. Smuts

[1] To celebrate the centenary of the birth of President Kruger.

[2] G. S. Preller had been assistant editor of *De Volkstem*, which supported the South African party (*see* vol. II, p. 167, note 1), since 1903 and editor since October 1924. He resigned to become editor of *Ons Vaderland* (*see infra*, p. 394, note 1) which was the Pretoria organ of the National party. His reasons for resigning, one of which was that the editor of *De Volkstem* was no longer free but a party tool, were set out in his last leading article in that paper on 28 August 1925.

[3] W. B. Madeley became minister of posts and telegraphs and of public works in 1925.

TRANSLATION

Doornkloof
Irene
[Transvaal]
29 September 1925

Dear Fransie, Many thanks for your letter which I received on my return from Natal where I made a very successful twelve days tour and visited all the divisions except two. I found the spirit there favourable and also in the northern districts of the Cape. It is clear to me that our future is good and sure and that we have only to be patient and hard-working in the meantime.

I am very glad to hear that you will be here at the time of the centenary festival. Come straight to Doornkloof and stay with us this time so that we can have a good chance to discuss things. If at all possible bring your wife too.

I have not yet been approached by Hertzog about his Native proposals, but I know that the Native affairs department is busy drafting a bill and I therefore expect that Hertzog will approach me. I entirely agree with the views of your executive committee and with your own views. Best wishes, Your friend,

s. J. C. Smuts

171   From G. Elliot Smith   Vol. 33, no. 128

University College
Gower Street, London
1 October 1925

Dear General Smuts, It was very kind of you to write so generously of what after all was the little that I did to advise Captain Lane with reference to making your interesting address more widely known, for it needed no advocacy to get the press to take up the matter.

The southern point of view that you put so lucidly in your address is one which is exciting a good deal of interest in this country, and I do not think that there is any risk of it being neglected in future.

I am particularly grateful for the remarks you make about Dart, and the other young men who are developing the great scientific field in South Africa. We, of course, are always only too willing to do anything in our power to help them in their work and to back them up when they publish their results, so long as they will let us help them.

It has always been a great disappointment to me that I just missed

you twenty-nine years ago, when I went up into residence at
Cambridge. I think that you had left only a month before I arrived
there, and the men I got to know best were the men who had been
associated with you. With kind regards, Yours very truly,

G. Elliot Smith

172   To M. C. Gillett   Vol. 34, no. 299

Irene
[Transvaal]
2 October 1925

I was most pleased to see from your last letter that you were home
once more and that a perfect motor ride had ended a beautiful
holiday. But I was very sorry to hear of the relapse of your dear
father.[1]

I was wrong in writing you last week that I had had an attack of
muscular rheumatism. The cause of my intense agony was happily
quite different and I had quite forgotten an incident of my recent
Natal tour. My pain was due to an effort to save the life of a Native!
At Vryheid we came across a wagon loaded with cement which
had backed down a very steep mountain pass and had pinned
a Native against the bank adjoining the road. We extricated the
poor Native after desperate efforts. Hence the internal sprain and
pain! Still it was comforting to know that it was not rheumatism.

I am sending you a copy of the new MS on holism. It is quite
different from the last[2] and is in fact a new work on the same idea.
Please look it over and pass it on to Professor Gilbert Murray, whom
I also want to read it, and pass it on to Dr J. S. Haldane of New
College (unknown to me) who has written books round the fringe
of the subject without actually understanding it or coming to grips
with it. I have sent some copies to Lane and asked him to look for
a publisher. The holism which interests you is not yet in this book
which explores holism in nature and in its scientific aspects and
does not yet deal with its spiritual and philosophical aspects.[3] But
a preliminary canter over the ground is essential, and I don't know
what time I shall have in future. I have written to Gilbert Murray
and told him that Agnes [Murray] was an enthusiastic holist
according to the original version. The idea and the work itself are
so thoroughly original that I sometimes wonder how it will strike

[1] W. S. Clark.   [2] See 520.
[3] In the 'thirties Smuts wrote four chapters of a projected work on these aspects of
holism but never finished it.

other people. To me of course it is the key which unlocks the entrance to the innermost recesses of the spirit...Good-bye, dear, to you all. Love from,

Jan

173   To A. Chamberlain

Vol. 34, no. 230

Doornkloof
Irene
Transvaal
21 October 1925

My dear Chamberlain, Amery sent me your note to him[1] in reference to what I had said to the *Daily News* about the Pact, and I felt relieved to see your statement of the case and thank you very much for the trouble you have taken to enlighten me. Now the news has just come of the brilliant success of the Locarno conference,[2] and I congratulate you on that great event and on your principal share in the success achieved. Hitherto only very vague summaries of the Pact and other conventions[3] have been cabled out here and it is very difficult to form an opinion on such scanty material. But I gather that the international situation has been much improved in consequence and that the temper of the nations is now easier. One hopes that the corner has at last been definitely turned and that Europe will now set its face resolutely in the direction of peace and concord for the future.

I am especially glad that the Pact is not a disguised substitution for the covenant but a reinforcement of it and that under it the final decisions will rest with the council of the League. Knowing how subtly the League had been fought ever since its origin I rejoice to think that the Pact is only a further triumph for it and roots it still more deeply in the public life of civilization. To my mind nothing greater has been done in our day than the League and I am therefore perhaps unduly jealous of its success and its reputation.

In definitely guaranteeing the Rhine frontier Great Britain undertakes an obligation she has never yet known in her history, and one hopes that this great sacrifice on her part will be justified

---

[1] *See* Smuts Collection, vol. 31, no. 13.

[2] The Locarno agreements were initialled on 16 October 1925. They comprised a number of undertakings the chief of which (the Pact) was a treaty of mutual guarantee of the Franco-German and Belgo-German frontiers between Germany, France, Great Britain, Italy and Belgium.

[3] The Locarno agreements included arbitration treaties between Germany and the following powers: Belgium, France, Poland and Czechoslovakia.

by its good results for the permanent peace of Europe. My mind remains troubled by the Polish situation as it affects that peace.[1] Will trouble between the Continental nations not start on the eastern frontier and from there involve the Rhine frontier, which will thus inevitably involve Great Britain too? Does the guarantee of the Rhine frontier not in this way mean the guarantee ultimately of all frontiers? This seems to me the bigger question back of the guarantee of the western frontier. In Poland we have not only an unstable, but an inequitable, situation[2] and trouble arising there will and indeed must involve military movements and war in the West too.

I am afraid the Dominions will keep out of this Pact and will look upon this as a precedent to disinterest themselves in future more and more in the foreign policy of Great Britain.[3] Thus for the Empire too the Pact will become a new departure. This is a serious matter which no doubt you have carefully considered. It may be that the future peace of Europe outweighs such considerations as arise in this connection. But I look upon the British Empire as, with the United States of America, the main guarantee of any public life that is worth living in the world. And I should be most sorry to weaken the voice of the Empire as a united whole in the councils of the world. Perhaps the reinforcement you have brought the League through this Pact will prove so salutary and effective that the League will in time become an even more powerful guarantee of future peace and liberty than the Empire could ever be. One can only hope for the best and in the meantime watch developments with sleepless vigilance. It seems to me almost inevitable that Locarno should weaken the case for a united Empire foreign policy and this is a matter which requires most careful watching.

I write to you frankly what is on my mind as I admire the spirit in which you are working for world peace and I feel that in this grave matter of future world peace the voice of the Empire would be something greater than the voice merely of Great Britain.

Please do not trouble to answer this note, which is merely by way of an answer to yours to Amery. With kind regards, Ever yours sincerely,

s. J. C. Smuts

[1] Another aspect of the Locarno agreements was a Franco-Polish and a Franco-Czechoslovak treaty of mutual assistance in case of aggression by Germany.

[2] Smuts had always regarded the inclusion of the free city of Danzig in Polish territory as unfair to Germany (see 1011).

[3] Article 9 of the Pact exempted the Dominions and India from British obligations under the treaty.

174   J. B. M. Hertzog   Vol. 32, no. 114

Kantoor van die Eerste Minister
Pretoria
10 November 1925

Waarde Smuts, Ooreenkomstig ons afspraak tydens die laaste sessie word tans ontwerpe gevra vir 'n Unie-vlag en sal ons later 'n gesamenlike Kommissie benoem om 'n keuse te doen. Hierdie benoeming, sal, naar ek aanneem, moet geskied voor of onmiddellik na 1 Desember, wanneer die tye vir insending van ontwerpe sluit.

Dit kom my egter voor dat die Kommissie, wat vermoedelik uit politieke voormanne sal bestaan, onmoontlik hul taak sal kan vervul sonder die voorafgaande arbeid en advies van vakmanne. Om tot 'n behoorlike keuse te kom sal ons die hulp nodig hê van manne, wat kennis het van heraldiek en van die vlae van die nasies van die wêreld.

Ek wil aan die hand gee dat ons dadelik 'n Kommissie van drie sulke manne sal benoem, wat die plus minus 300 ontwerpe, wat reeds ingekom is, saam met ander wat nog mag inkom, vir ons sal sif, sal uitskakel wat uit heraldies of kuns oogpunt onmoontlik is of reeds die besit is van 'n ander volk, en sal rapporteer omtrent die oorblywende ontwerpe, wat in aanmerking sou kan kom. Hul sal natuurlik ook die reg hê om individueel of gesamenlik nog ander moontlike ontwerpe te suggesteer.

As u met hierdie gedagte instem wil ek aan die hand gee dat twee van die Kommissie van vakmanne sal wees Dr Blommaert, professor van geskiedenis aan die Stellenbosch Universiteit, verteenwoordigende die Hollands-sprekendes en Prof. Walker, professor van geskiedenis aan die Kaapse Universiteit, verteenwordigende die Engels-sprekendes. Albei is vakmanne en stel biesonder belang in die saak. As u met hulle benoeming instem sal ek bly wees as u 'n derde wil aan die hand gee, ek sou sê, liefs iemand uit die Noorde en in Suid-Africa gebore.

Ek sal bly wees as u so gou as moontlik is hierop kan antwoord, aangesien ons geen tyd te verlies het nie. Vriendelike groete, Die Uwe,

J. B. M. Hertzog

TRANSLATION

Prime Minister's Office
Pretoria
10 November 1925

Dear Smuts, In accordance with our arrangement during last session,[1] designs for a Union flag are now being invited and we shall appoint a joint commission later to make a choice. This appointment will, I should think, have to be made before or immediately after 1 December when the dates for sending in designs close.

It seems to me, however, that the commission, which will probably consist of political leaders, cannot possibly fulfil their task without the preparatory work and advice of experts. To arrive at a proper choice we shall need the help of men with knowledge of heraldry and of the flags of the nations of the world.

I wish to suggest that we at once appoint a commission of three such men who would sift for us the approximately 300 designs that have already come in together with others which may still come in, who will discard what is heraldically or artistically impossible or already the possession of another nation and will report on the remaining designs which might be considered. They will, of course, also have the right, individually or collectively, to suggest other possible designs.

If you agree with this idea, I would propose that two of the commission of experts should be Dr [W.] Blommaert, professor of history in the University of Stellenbosch to represent the Dutch-speaking citizens and Professor [E. A.] Walker, professor of history in the University of Cape Town to represent the English-speaking citizens. Both are experts and are particularly interested in the matter. If you agree to their appointment, I should be glad if you would suggest a third, preferably, I should say, someone from the north and born in South Africa.

I should be glad if you would reply to this as soon as possible as we have no time to lose. Friendly greetings, Yours sincerely,

J. B. M. Hertzog

[1] Dr D. F. Malan had, earlier in the year, introduced a Flag Bill but Smuts had asked that the bill be delayed for a year and that in the meatime designs for a national flag be invited and a joint committee appointed to sift them. Malan accordingly withdrew his bill and in August designs were invited. (*See* D. F. Malan, *Afrikaner Volkseenheid*, pp. 104–6 and Smuts Collection, vol. 32, no. 209.)

175   To J. B. M. Hertzog

Vol. 34, no. 235

Doornkloof
Irene
11 November 1925

Waarde Hertzog, Uw brief van 10 November, 1925.

Ek twyfel of dit gewenst sal wees om eers een voorlopige sifting van ideë en ontwerpe te maak deur middel van die tegniese komitee. Een klein tegniese komitee sal noodsakelik wees, maar die moet haar werk gelyktydig met die politieke komitee doen. Feitelik sal die twee komitees moet saamwerk, en miskien sal die politieke komitee geen een van die ingesonde ontwerpe aanneem nie, maar self een uitwerk waaroor sy dan die tegniese komitee sou wil raadpleeg. Myn wenk is dus dat beide komitees terselfder tyd aangestel word en dat die politieke komitee die ontwerpe deurgaan en wanneer een of ander ontwerp haar geval sy die dan vir tegniese advies aan die tegniese komitee submitteer. Ek het nog geen lede vir die beide komitees in die oog en stel voor my vrinde te raadpleeg, en dit sal moeilik wees tot een finale beslissing te kom voordat ons alle met die sessie te Kaapstad by mekaar kom. Ek twyfel of grooter haast meer spoed sal beteken. Met groete, Getrou die uwe,

J. C. Smuts

TRANSLATION

Doornkloof
Irene
[Transvaal]
11 November 1925

Dear Hertzog, Your letter of 10 November 1925.

I doubt if it will be desirable to make a provisional sifting of ideas and designs by means of the technical committee. A small technical committee will be necessary, but it must do its work simultaneously with the political committee. Actually the two committees must work together, and perhaps the political committee will not accept any of the submitted designs, but work one out itself about which it would then wish to consult the technical committee. My suggestion therefore is that both committees be appointed at the same time, that the political committee should go through the designs and that if it approves any design it should submit this to the technical committee. I have as yet no members for either committee in view and propose to consult my friends, and it will be difficult to come to a final decision before we all meet for the session in Cape Town. I doubt if greater haste will mean more speed. With good wishes, Yours sincerely,

J. C. Smuts

176   To T. W. Smartt   Vol. 34, no. 238

Doornkloof
Irene
[Transvaal]
12 November 1925

My dear Smartt, I spoke at Johannesburg on the *hereniging* question[1] a few nights ago as I don't want any misunderstanding to arise among our rank and file. The decent Nationalists are getting much perturbed, and their fears will grow when they see Madeley in the cabinet. We must therefore make it possible for them to view us in a more favourable light. But we must do nothing to weaken the bonds in the South African party. The definite refusal of my overtures by the Nationalist leaders has cleared the air and will help us considerably. Hertzog and Co. are furious with me and that makes me think that our tactics are quite right.

Hertzog has written me that he wants to appoint two committees to deal with the flag question—a technical committee to do the sifting of all the designs sent in from a heraldic point of view, and a political committee to select the winning design from the balance passed by the technical committee. He wants me to suggest names for our side on both these committees. On the technical committee he suggests Professor Blommaert at Stellenbosch, not known to me, and Professor Walker of Cape Town. He wants me to suggest a third (a South African from the interior). Do you know the views of Walker on this important matter? It might be advisable for you to have a talk casually with him and see whether he is sound as I don't want to move in the dark in so important a matter. You must also think over two or three names for appointment on the other (political) committee which is practically to decide the matter. Struben [R. H.] told me last session that he was anxious to serve on it. Please think of some more names. The Nationalists seem in a mood to hurry this matter on, which makes me think that they may contemplate a general election in 1927 (after passing the flag next session). The Native question may force them to an early general election and they want to do some flag-wagging of their

---

[1] *See supra*, p. 14, note 1.

own when that comes off. We shall have to deal very warily with this question which presents difficulties and troubles of a delicate nature. With kind regards, Ever yours sincerely,

s. J. C. Smuts

177 From J. B. M. Hertzog Vol. 32, no. 115

Kantoor van die Eerste Minister
Pretoria
23 November 1925

Waarde Smuts, Jou brief van 11 deser is my ter hand en in antwoord daarop geliewe die volgende:

Ek het die saak met Dr Malan bespreek en hoewel hy van oordeel is dat dit beter sou gewees het as jy kon meegegaan het met die suggestie van 'n tegniese Komitee wat die andere sou voorafgaan, het hy daar geen beswaar teen dat jou wenk gevolg word om beide Komitees min of meer terselfder tyd aan te stel en te doen funksioneer.

Myns insiens, sou dit beter gewees het as ons kon ontmoet het voordat die Parlement weer sit, dog daar jy geen kans sien om met jou vrinde die saak te bespreek voordat ons weer te Kaapstad bymekaar kom, sal dan die benoeming van lede maar moet oorstaan tot dan.

Ek hoop ewewel dat ons nie lang sal versuim na die opening van die Parlement om daarmee voortgang te maak nie, want jy weet self hoe met die loop van die Sitting dit steeds drukker word vir almal, sodat teen die eind haas niemand meer tyd ter beskikking het. Met agting, getrou die uwe,

J. B. M. Hertzog

TRANSLATION

Prime Minister's Office
Pretoria
23 November 1925

Dear Smuts, I have your letter of 11 inst. and reply to it as follows:

I have discussed the matter with Dr [D. F.] Malan and although he considers that it would have been better if you could have accepted the suggestion of a technical committee to precede the other, he has no objection to your suggestion that both committees should be appointed and set to work more or less simultaneously.

In my view it would have been better if we could have met

before parliament is again in session; however, as you see no chance of discussing the matter with your friends before we again gather in Cape Town, the appointment of the members will have to stand over until then.[1]

I hope nevertheless that we shall not long delay in going forward with it after the opening of parliament for you know yourself how in the course of the session everyone becomes more and more busy so that towards the end hardly anyone has time to spare. Yours faithfully,

J. B. M. Hertzog

178 From J. B. M. Hertzog   Vol. 32, no. 116

Kantoor van die Eerste Minister
Pretoria
1 Desember 1925

Waarde Smuts, Soas jy jou sal herinner, het ek kort voor die sluiting van die jongste Sitting van die Parlement, die vryheid geneem om jou as leier van die opposiesie te nader aangaande die voorgenome poging deur my om 'n oplossing van die naturelle vraagstuk te bewerkstellig.

My doel daarmee was, soas aan jou meegedeel, om deur jou die medewerking te verkry van die opposiesie tot 'n oplossing wat sou staan buite die arena van party politiek; en daar ek gevoel het dat ek nie geregtig sou wees tot enig toesegging van hulp van jou sy voor en alleer ekself 'n praktiese uitweg aan die hand kon gee, het ek jou voorgelê wat volgens my 'n aaneembare oplossing behoor te wees, en wat ek gereed sou wees om aan die volk te onderwerp.

Tereg het jy my toe meegedeel dat jy my geen onmiddellike antwoord kon gee nie op my versoek, maar dat jy die opposiesie sou raadpleeg om my dan later in kennis te stel.

Sedert die tyd het ek nog niks verder van jou verneem nie, en het ek op 13 November l.l. te Smithfield die oplossing by ons gesprek aan jou uiteengesit, voor die volk gelê, en veroorloof ek my tans om jou bygaande 'n kopie te doen toekom van my toespraak.

Dit sal jou in die geleentheid stel, naar ek hoop, om meer geredelik tot 'n beslissing te geraak omtrent die verlange deur my aan jou geuit om medewerking.

Jy sal my dit toestem, nie alleen dat ons by die naturelle vraagstuk

---

[1] The two flag committees were duly appointed in February 1926. The political committee consisted of, for the National party, Dr N. J. van der Merwe, W. Rood and Dr D. F. Malan; for the Labour party, H. W. Sampson and G. Reyburn; for the South African party, P. Duncan, Joël Krige and Sir Charles Smith. The technical committee consisted of Professors W. Blommaert and E. A. Walker.

te doen het met 'n saak van die aller grootste en dreigenste gewig vir ons toekoms, maar ook met een waar die volk daarna uitsien dat ons onsself sal vergeet als party-leiers om als volksmanne te kan optree en handel.

Daarom sal dit my dan ook verbly als jy so goed wil wees om die saak verder te oorweeg, en om my ter gelegenertyd te doen weet in hoeverre jy met die opposiesie gesind sou wees om my en die Regering behulpsaam te wees by die oplossing als deur my voor-gestel. Met agting die uwe,

J. B. M. Hertzog

TRANSLATION

Prime Minister's Office
Pretoria
1 December 1925

Dear Smuts, As you will remember, I took the liberty shortly before the close of the last session of parliament to approach you, as leader of the opposition, in connection with my proposed attempt to bring about a solution of the Native question.

My object was, as I told you, to obtain through you the co-opera-tion of the opposition in a solution which would be outside the area of party politics; and as I felt that I should not be entitled to receive any help from your side before and until I could myself suggest a practical way out, I put before you what, in my view, ought to be an acceptable solution which I should be ready to submit to the people.

You then rightly told me that you could not give me an immediate reply to my request, but that you would consult the opposition in order to inform me later.

Since then I have heard nothing further from you and have, on 13 November last at Smithfield, put before the people the solution explained to you at our discussion and I now beg to send you a copy of my speech.[1]

I hope this will give you an opportunity to come more readily to a decision about the wish for co-operation which I expressed to you.

You will agree that we are faced in the Native question not only with a matter of the very greatest and most ominous gravity for our future, but also with a matter in which the people expect us to forget ourselves as party leaders so as to be able to bear ourselves and act as national leaders.

I should therefore be glad if you would be so good as to consider the matter further and to let me know in due course to what extent

[1] See supra, p. 254, note 1.

you and the opposition would be prepared to assist me and the government in the solution I suggest. Yours sincerely,

J. B. M. Hertzog

179   To J. B. M. Hertzog   Vol. 34, no. 244

Doornkloof
Irene
14 Desember 1925

Waarde Hertzog, Dit spyt my dat ek weens gedurige afwesigheid van huis nie in staat is gewees om jou brief van 1 Desember eerder te beantwoord nie. Wat betref die inhoud daarvan het ek my vrinde geraadpleeg en kom ons tot die meening dat die ontwerpe behelsende als een geheel die naturelle voorstelle van die regering eers ter tafel van die huis moet geleg word alvorens een raadpleging met nut kan plaats vind in een of ander vorm; en jy sal seker gesien het dat ek te Bloemfontein een Nationale Conventie voor die doel aan die hand het gegee [*sic*]. In elk geval is dit moeilik so een omvattende saak behoorlik te oorweeg tensy al die uitgewerkte voorstelle in die vorm van concept wette voor ons is, en ek stel dus voor die introductie van daardie ontwerpe in die Volksraad af te wag. Dienstwillig de uwe,

get. J. C. Smuts

TRANSLATION

Doornkloof
Irene
[Transvaal]
14 December 1925

Dear Hertzog, I regret that I have not been able, because of continued absence from home, to answer your letter of 1 December sooner. As regards its contents, I have consulted my friends and we are of the opinion that drafts embracing the whole of the Native proposals of the government should first be laid on the table of the house before consultation, in some form or other, can usefully take place; and you will no doubt have seen that I suggested at Bloemfontein a national convention for this purpose. In any case it is difficult to consider such a wide matter properly unless all the worked-out proposals are before us in the form of draft bills and I therefore propose to await the introduction of these drafts in the house of assembly. Yours truly,

s. J. C. Smuts

180   From E. F. C. Lane   **Vol. 32, no. 188**

British Empire Exhibition
Wembley, Middlesex
17 December 1925

My dear General, My last letter to you was dated 10 December, about *Holism*. Since then I have made a little progress and hope to be able to cable to you in the near future and therefore my cable will be rather more up to date than this letter.

Macmillans have made an offer for the book; namely £100 down and 15% on the first thousand copies and 20% thereafter. I have told Watt to tell them that this is in my opinion a little on the low side and they must be prepared to pay 20% on the first thousand copies and 25% thereafter because it is necessary to get a move on in view of my early return to the Union. They went to a good deal of trouble to get the privilege of publishing your work and I do not think we are asking too much. I happened to meet A. G. Gardiner the other day and he told me that I was perfectly entitled to get 20% for a start and to ask for a little more if possible. He himself is just bringing out a book which he tells me will bring him 20% and he said 'Such a great gun as Smuts can easily demand more.'

Another reason why I know I can go ahead with Macmillan is that, curiously enough, the man who read the work for them was the Master of Balliol!!![1] So that the man who wrote to me and said the work wanted doing is the same man who has commended it to the publishers! They don't know, of course, that I have got the Master to give me a private opinion and they don't know that I know he read the work for them. So that when it comes down to the pure business side of the bargain they are trying to beat me down as far as possible. I, knowing that their reader has recommended it to them and also knowing that they are particularly anxious to get the privilege of publishing some of your work, am hoping to go ahead and persuade them to put up better terms.

I think that you probably will not have got the work on *Emergent Evolution*[2] and so I got Joan to cruise about the booksellers' shops in Charing Cross Road to try and get it. She was successful, I am glad to say, in obtaining a copy and I send it out with my warmest wishes for Christmas although I fear it will be somewhat late for this occasion.

I hope that you have not been alarmed in any way about the suggestion that we have got into bad hands in regard to publishers and agents. Gardiner told me yesterday that we could not

---

[1] Alexander Dunlop Lindsay.   [2] By C. Lloyd-Morgan, published in 1923.

have a better adviser than A. P. Watt and a testimonial about Macmillan is not necessary. I know that Joan and her late employers have other views but we are on the right lines and it only remains for us to screw the publishers up a bit more; then they can go ahead and send out proofs to you and publish in the early spring.

Feetham [R.] returns to South Africa on this mail and we leave England on 8 January to see you next in Cape Town. With warmest regards, Believe me, Yours very sincerely,

E. F. C. Lane

181   From J. B. M. Hertzog   Vol. 32, no. 117

Privaat en konfidensieel   Kantoor van die Erste Minister
                                                                 Pretoria
                                                          18 Desember 1925

Waarde Smuts, Jou brief van 14 deser in antwoord op die van my van 1 Desember is my ter hand.

Ek merk op dat jy sê, dat geen *raadpleging met nut kan plaas vind* alvorens ek alle voorstelle omtrent naturelle sake op die tafel van die Volksraad gelê het. Dit is miskien nodig dat ek onderwyl jou aandag daarop vestig, dat ek voor als nog geen versoek aan jou gerig het om raadpleging; maar enkel om my te sê, of jy bereid is om my behulpsaam te wees by die soek naar 'n oplossing van ons naturelle probleem, hetsy langs die weg reeds deur my aan jou in hoofsaak voorgelê, of langs 'n ander weg. Daar raadpleging bereidwilligheid tot medewerking veronderstel, is dit te begryp dat solang as jy geen terme vind om medewerking te verleen, daar ook geen raadpleging met nut kan plaas vind.

Volgens jou skrywe moet ek aanneem, dat tot tyd en wyl ek in alle besonderhede met my voorgestelde oplossing voor die Volksraad verskyn, jy weier om my die versekering te gee, sowel om die saak buite die party politiek te hou, as om my hulp toe te sê by die poging om 'n oplossing te verkry.

As dit werkelik jou bedoeling is, dan spyt dit my van harte. Soas jy weet, het ek reeds gedurende jou Eerste-Ministerskap jou meegedeel hoe noodsaaklik ek die oplossing van die naturelle probleem beskou, en hoeseer ek my oortuig gevoel van die noodsaaklikheid dat waar 'n oplossing beproef word, die saak sal behandel word as 'n volkssaak en nie as 'n party-kwessie nie; en het ek jou verder daarby, uit eie beweging, aangebied, dat as jy gereed sou wees om 'n oplossing te beproef, ek jou met my party, afgesien van party politiek, daartoe sou bystaan.

My voersoek aan jou bevat dus niks meer dan wat ek self teenoor
jou as Eerste Minister my gereed toe verklaar het. Jy kan dus my
teleurstelling verstaan wanneer ek van jou verneem, dat waar ek
gereed was om jou my hulp toe te sê sonder 'n enkel voorstel tot
oplossing van jou kant af te wag; jy dit sou nodig vind om as voor-
waarde van medewerking van my te eis, dat ek eers alles in alle
bijsonderhede op die tafel van die Huis sal lê.

Jou weiering tref my des te meer as iets vreemds, omdat jou
voorstel van 'n *Nasionale Konvensie* getuig, dat ook jy besef die
dringende noodsaaklikheid van 'n oplossing, sowel as die groot
erns van die saak; en ek dink jy sal my dit toegee, dat om met
dieselfde adem waarmee 'n weiering tot medewerking geskied,
'n Nasionale Konvensie voor te stel, 'n bietjie inkonsekwent is, en
nouliks berekend om *die* voorstel as ernstig gemeend te doen beskou.

Hoe dit ook sy, ek dink nie dat jy dit van my sal verwag om, hetsy
nou of later, weer my versoek aan jou te herhaal, en moet die reg
sowel as die verantwoordelikheid by jou gelaat word om dit te
aanvaar of te verwerp. Dienswillig die uwe,

J. B. M. Hertzog

TRANSLATION

Private and confidential   Prime Minister's Office

Pretoria

18 December 1925

Dear Smuts, I have received your letter of 14th inst. in answer to
mine of 1 December.

I note that you say that no *profitable consultation can take place*
until I have laid all proposals on Native affairs on the table of the
house of assembly. It is perhaps necessary that I should in the
meantime draw your attention to the fact that I have as yet made no
request to you for consultation, but only to tell me if you are prepared to assist me in searching for a solution to our Native problem,
whether on the lines which I have already broadly put before you,
or on other lines. Since consultation presupposes readiness to co-
operate, it is understandable that as long as you find no grounds
for co-operation, there can also be no profitable consultation.

According to what you write I must take it that, until such time
as I come before the house with all the details of my suggested solution, you refuse to give me an assurance to keep the matter outside
party politics and to proffer help in the attempt to get a solution.

If this is really your meaning then I deeply regret it. As you
know, I told you during your premiership how necessary I con-

sidered a solution of the Native problem to be and how strongly
I was convinced of the necessity, were a solution attempted, that
the matter be handled as a national and not as a party question;
and I also, of my own accord, offered, if you were prepared to
attempt a solution, that I and my party would, eschewing party
politics, assist you.

My request to you therefore contains nothing more than I declared myself ready to do for you as prime minister. So you will
understand my disappointment at hearing from you that, whereas
I was ready to help you without waiting for a single proposal for
solution from your side, you should find it necessary to demand
from me, as a condition of co-operation, that I should first lay
everything on the table of the house.

Your refusal strikes me as the more strange in that your suggestion of a *national convention* shows that you also realize the urgent
necessity of a solution and the great gravity of the matter; and I
think you will admit that to suggest a national convention in the
same breath with a refusal to co-operate, is a little inconsequent and
hardly calculated to cause that suggestion to be regarded as
seriously intended.

However that may be, I do not think that it will be expected of
me, whether now or later, to repeat my request to you, and the right
as well as the responsibility of accepting or rejecting it must be
left to you. Yours truly,

J. B. M. Hertzog

182   To C. P. Crewe   Vol. 102, no. 217

Irene
[Transvaal]
18 December 1925

My dear Crewe, I have been so much on the move ever since last
August that there has not been much time for private correspondence. You must not chide me for my silence, and especially you
must not curtail your letters which I always like very much to get.

Our Bloemfontein conference was a great success and the spirit
in our party is both solid and optimistic—in spite of bye-election
figures. But it will be to our interest not to precipitate a general
election prematurely. The country is still in the mood of giving
them a chance, and I am not in favour of fighting bye-elections
unnecessarily, even though I would much like to have Burton's
powerful assistance in the house.

The leaders at Bloemfontein carefully considered our line of action on Hertzog's Native proposals, and finally decided in favour of a national convention in order to avoid the grave danger of party strife in the house on so contentious a subject. The position seems to me briefly this: that the Transvaal will not have Hertzog's scheme and that it is therefore foredoomed to failure. But Hertzog wants to place the onus of this failure on the South African party and to say to the Coloured people at the Cape: 'I was for equal rights but your friends the S. A. P. made my plan impossible.' To the Natives he will use a similar argument. And the result might be very much to our disadvantage at the next general election. We shall have to deal with Hertzog's proposals in such a way that we do not alienate the Coloured or Native voters at the Cape. And a national convention seemed to us the better way of procedure with this end in view.

My best Christmas and New Year wishes to you and Lady Crewe. With best regards, Ever yours sincerely,

J. C. Smuts

183   To J. B. M. Hertzog   Vol. 34, no. 246

Irene
29 December 1925

Waarde Hertzog, Jou brief van 18 dezer is my ter hand. Die toon en inhoud daarvan het my pynlik aangedoen en is betreurenswaardig vir eenige vorm van medewerking.

Ek weet natuurlik dat ek nog nie door jou geraadpleeg is nie oor die Naturelle kwestie. Maar nou moet ek ook verstaan dat daar selfs geen bedoeling is my te raadpleeg nie alvorens ek eers my bereidwilligheid tot medewerking op die kwestie vooraf te kenne gegee het.

Daarop wil ek alleen sê dat die bereidwilligheid aan my kant altyd bestaan het, maar dat jou Smithfield voorstelle beginsels insluit waar ek bepaald nie mee kan saamgaan nie, en dat ek der- halve, om onnoodige verdeeldheid te vermy, aan die hand gegee het dat die hele naturelle kwestie naar een Naionale Conventie sal verwys word met opdrag naar een bevredigende oplossing te soek.

Als door medewerking van my kant verstaan word aanname van jou vorstelle als een geheel, dan moet ek my leedweze betuig dat ek nie sulks kan doen nie. En als medewerking beteeken een oplossing langs ander weg vind, dan kom dit my voor dat sulks best gedoen kan word by wyze van een Nationale Conventie. Ek het alleen gerefereer naar die voorlegging van jou wetsontwerpe omdat jy self publiek beloofd had sulks te doen, en omdat ek meende dat dit sou behulpsaam wees om jou voorstelle aan te vul en te verduidelik. Ek sou natuurlik nie die minste bezwaar hê nie dat die heele saak voor een oplossing naar een conventie verwys word selfs voordat jou wette ter tafel van die Parlement geleg word; dat wil sê als sulks overeen te breng is met jou belofte aan die publiek.

Jy refereer naar een gesprek tussen ons van eenige jare gelede. Daardie kasueele gesprek, meen ek, had te doen met die tersyde zetting van naturelle areas onder die wet van 1913 en geenszins met die oplossing van die naturelle probleem. Ek het nie op jou wenk gehandel omdat ek destyds al gevoel het, wat ek vandaag nog voel, dat beide van blanke en naturelle oogpunt daar sterke en gegronde bezware was teen die tersyde zetting van die biesondere areas deur die verskillende kommissies onder daardie wet aanbeveel. Dienswillig de uwe,

get. J. C. Smuts

TRANSLATION

Irene
[Transvaal]
29 December 1925

Dear Hertzog, I have received your letter of 18th inst. The tone and contents of it pained me and are lamentable for any sort of co-operation.

I know, of course, that I have not yet been consulted by you about the Native question. But now I am also to understand that there is no intention of consulting me before I indicate in advance my readiness to co-operate in the matter.

To that I wish only to say that on my side the readiness always existed, but that your Smithfield proposals include principles with which I can definitely not agree, and that I therefore, to avoid unnecessary division, suggested that the whole Native question should be referred to a national convention with a commission to search for a solution.

If co-operation on my side is interpreted as acceptance of your proposals as a whole, then I must express my regret that I cannot do this. And if co-operation means finding a solution on other lines, then it seems to me that this can best be done by means of a national convention. I only referred to the submission of your bills because you yourself publicly promised to do this, and because I thought that it would be helpful to supplement and explain your proposals. I should, of course, not have the least objection to referring the whole matter for solution to a convention even before your bills are laid on the table of parliament; that is to say, if this can be reconciled with your promise to the public.

You refer to a conversation between us of some years ago. That casual conversation had to do, I think, with the setting aside of Native areas under the act of 1913[1] and not in any way with the solution of the Native problem. I did not act upon your suggestion because I thought at the time, as I still do today that, from the point of view of both whites and Natives, there were strong and well-founded objections to the setting aside of special areas by the various commissions as recommended under that act. Yours truly,

s. J. C. Smuts

184   From J. B. M. Hertzog   Vol. 35, no. 159

Kantoor van die Eerste Minister
Kaapstad
16 Januarie 1926

Waarde Smuts, Jou skrywe van 29 Desember in antwoord op die van my van die 18de in verband met my versoek aan jou vir medewerking in sake die naturelle vraagstuk, is my ter hand.

Jy sal my verskoon as ek, met die doel om misverstand te voorkom, hier weer eens verwys na die inhoud van die versoek wat ek aan jou gerig het. Dit is die volgende, nl.:

dat die poging wat staan om deur my aangewen te word om 'n bevredigende oplossing te bewerkstellig insake die naturelle-vraagstuk, die medewerking sal geniet van jou en jou party afgesien van partye en partygeskille.

Die versoek bevat dus twee voorstelle:

1. Dat die saak sal beskou en behandel word as staande buite die arena van partye en party getwis;
2. Dat jy, en sodanige andere van jou party as jy mag goeddunk, met my sal te rade gaan en meewerk by die poging om 'n bevredigende oplossing in die lewe te roep.

Tot hiertoe is hierdie versoek deur jou van die hand gewys, en moet dus aangeneem word dat die saak deur jou beskou en behandel sal word op die gewone wyse, as staande binne die strydperk van

[1] The Natives Land Act, No. 27 of 1913, sought to ensure territorial segregation by designating areas where Natives could not own land and other areas where they alone could do so. These latter, besides the existing Reserves, were to include additional land to be purchased by the government. A commission was appointed to make recommendations as to additional Native areas.

die party politiek. Daardeur sal dit dan ook, soos jy sal besef, onmogelik wees om die strydmotiewe te vrywaar teen die invloed van party-belange en party-oogmerke.

Wanneer jy dus in jou brief tans voor my sê:

'Maar nou moet ek ook verstaan dat daar selfs geen bedoeling is my te raadpleeg nie al vorens ek eers my bereidwilligheid tot medewerking op die kwessie vooraf te kenne gegee het.'

dan moet ek jou antwoord deur die vraag: Hoe kan jy iets anders verwag? Solang dit jou keuse is om die gewone politieke spel te speel moet ek jou natuurlik volgens die reëls van *die* spel behandel.

Nou gaan jy voort in jou brief en sê verder:

'Daarop wil ek alleen sê dat die bereidwilligheid aan my kant altyd bestaan het, maar dat jou Smithfield voorstelle beginsels insluit wat ek bepaald nie mee kan saam gaan nie.'

Wat die beginsels is waar jy nie mee kan saam gaan nie het jy my nog nie meegedeel, en weet ek dus nie. Ook weet ek nie of jy enige ander beginsels of voorstelle het wat jy in die plaas sou wil sien gestel van die deur my aan die hand gegee.

Dog wat ook al *die* beginsels mag wees wat jy afkeur en of jy al iets om daarvoor in die plaas te stel of nie, in enig geval sien ek nie waarom dit jou rede sou gee om my versoek tot medewerking te verwerp—temeer daar, soos jy sê, by jou altyd die bereidwilligheid daartoe bestaan het.

Ek eis geensins van jou dat jy enig beginsel of voorstel van my sal onderskryf waar jy van my verskil. Inteendeel is die strekking van my versoek, dat waar jy van my verskil ons gesamentlik sal raadpleeg en soek om 'n betere oplossing te vind wat in plaas kan gestel word van wat deur my aan die hand gegee is.

Dit is natuurlik juis omdat ek sodanige verskil van mening verwag het, dat ek om jou medewerking gevra het, 'n versoek wat oorbodig sou gewees het as ek gemeen het dat jy dit met my eens sou wees oor al my voorstelle.

Jy sal my dus verskoon as ek sê, dat ek geen gegronde rede kan vind vir jou weiering. Die hoofrede waarom ek my tot jou gewend het om medewerking, was om die noodlottige gevolge te vermy van 'n partystryd oor hierdie gewigtige volksaak, en jy kan dus besef hoe seer ek dit betreur, dat dit jou nie moontlik is om my van die medewerking te verseker.

Ek mag ewewel nie oor die hoof sien, dat in jou brief jy verder sê dat: 'om onnodige verdeeldheid te vermy' jy 'aan die hand gegee het dat die hele naturelle kwessie na een Nasionale Konvensie sal verwys word met opdrag na een bevredigende oplossing te soek'. Daar hierdie voorstel van 'n Nasionale Konvensie tans weer deur jou herhaal word, moet ek aanneem dat jy dit ernstig daarmee bedoel nietteenstaande die ongerymdheid daarvan waar ek in my vorige brief op gewys het.

Die naam 'Nasionale Konvensie' gee my ewewel nog niks te kenne, en voor dat ek in staat kan wees om 'n oordeel te vel oor die doelmatigheid of aanneembaarheid daarvan, sal ek natuurlik moet weet wat ek daardeur moet verstaan.

Jy sê dat die doel waarmee jy die voorstel maak, is om 'onnodige verdeeldheid te vermy'. Ek sou van harte *alle* verdeeldheid wil vermy sien, maar, soos tans ingelig, kan ek nie insien hoe deur so iets as 'n konvensie—al is dit dan ook 'n Nasionale—selfs 'onnodige' verdeeldheid sal vermy word. Dit kom my voor dat verdeeldheid en die mate daarvan by hierdie vraagstuk, soos by alle grote politieke kwessies, alleen kan bepaal en beteugel word deur die gesonde leiding en vaderlandsliefde van die leiers van partye; en of dit plaas vind op 'n Konvensie, of in die Raadsaal, of om 'n tafel, kom my voor vrywel dieselfde te wees. Dog miskien is ek verkeerd en word my mening daardeur geïnfluenseer, dat tot nou toe ek nog nie in staat is gestel om te wete te kom wat eintlik moet verstaan word onder 'Nasionale Konvensie' met betrekking tot die naturelle-vraagstuk. Ek sien b.v. uit 'n besluit my toegesend deur 'n naturelle Kongress, dat ook die naturelle ten gunste daarvan is, mits dat ook hul daarop sal verteenwoordig wees.

Ten einde dus te kan beslis of jou voorstel een is wat kan aanvaar word, sou ek graag van jou wil verneem wat ek moet verstaan deur die term Nasionale Konvensie, en sal ek bly wees om van jou te verneem jou antwoord op die volgende vrae:

1. Deur wie en uit welke kringe sal die afgevaardigde na die Konvensie gekies of benoem word?
2. Sal die afgevaardigde by meerderheid van stemme beslis?
3. So nee, hoe sal die beslissing geskied en wat sal die verbindende krag daarvan wees?
4. So ja, sal die minderheid by 'n genome besluit daarna verplig wees om hul aan die beslissing te onderwerp en om aan die besluit hulle ondersteuning te verleen? Of sal dit hul vrystaan om daarna in hulle opposisie te volhard asof daar geen Konvensie plaas gevind het en geen besluit geneem is geword?
5. Wat gaan jou houding wees as die Konvensie deur sy besluit goedkeur die beginsels in my Smithfield voorstelle waarteen jy tans beswaar gevoel?

Deur die hier gestelde vrae sal dit jou duidelik wees hoe vaag en onprakties die voorstel van 'n Nasionale Konvensie my moet voorkom solang ek nie in besit is van die informasie wat ek deur *die* vrae van jou hoop te verkry; maar wat meer is, jy sal ook daaruit besef die gegrondheid van my vrees dat so 'n Konvensie uiters noodlottig kan wees vir enige poging om die saak buite party politiek te hou, of om verdeeldheid te vermy.

Voordat ek dus tot 'n beslissing kan kom aangaande die voorstel, sal dit noodsaaklik wees dat my die gevraagde informasie gegee word, en sou dit van groot nut wees as jy my sou kan meedeel wat, volgens jou mening, te behaal sou wees langs die weg van 'n Nasionale of ander Konvensie, wat nie verkrygbaar sou wees deur middel van onderlinge beraadslaging en besprekinge om 'n tafel deur die erkende leiers en voormanne van partye, bygestaan, waar nodig, deur andere geskikte persone.

Dit spyt my dat ek reeds soveel van jou tyd moes in beslag neem, maar jy sal my verskoon as ek verder nog die geleentheid neem om jou te reg te wys waar jy aan die slot van jou brief sê, dat jy van mening is dat my gesprek van enige jare gelede, waarna ek gerefereer het in my vorige brief, te doen had met die tersyde setting van naturelle areas. Jy het dit volkome mis. My gesprek was met betrekking tot die Naturellevraagstuk in die algemeen; en op meer dan een geleentheid daarna het ek, met verwysing na wat ek jou by *die* geleentheid aangebied het, my aanbod in die Volksraad herhaal, weer sonder enige beperking. Dienswillig die uwe,

J. B. M. Hertzog

TRANSLATION

Prime Minister's Office
Cape Town
16 January 1926

Dear Smuts, I have received your letter of 29 December in answer to mine of the 18th in connection with my request to you for co-operation in the matter of the Native question.

You will pardon me if, in order to prevent misunderstanding, I once more refer to the content of the request which I made to you. It is as follows:

> that the attempt which is to be made by me to bring about a satisfactory solution of the Native question shall enjoy your and your party's co-operation, free of parties and party differences.

The request therefore contains two proposals:

1. That the matter be regarded and treated as standing outside the arena of parties and party quarrels;
2. That you, and such others of your party as you may think fit, should consult with me and co-operate to bring a satisfactory solution into being.

So far this request has been rejected by you, and it must therefore be supposed that the matter will be regarded and treated by you in the usual way as being inside the ring of party politics. It will therefore, as you will realize, be impossible to keep the motives of the struggle free of the influence of party interests and party objects.

When, therefore, in the letter now before me, you say:

'But now I am also to understand that there is no intention of consulting me before I indicate in advance my readiness to co-operate in the matter.'

then I must answer you by asking: How can you expect anything else? As long as you choose to play the usual political game I must of course treat you according to the rules of this game.

Continuing your letter you say further:

'To that I wish only to say that on my side the readiness always existed, but that your Smithfield proposals include principles with which I can definitely not agree.'

You have not yet informed me what are the principles with which you cannot agree and so I do not know. I also do not know if you have any other principles or proposals which you would like to see put in the place of those suggested by me.

But, whatever may be these principles of which you disapprove, and whether or not you have something to put in their place, I cannot in any case see why this should give you cause to reject my request for co-operation—especially since as you say, readiness to do so has always existed on your side.

I do not in the least demand of you that you should subscribe to any principle or proposal of mine on which you differ from me. On the contrary, the tenor of my request is that where we differ we should consult together and try to find a better solution to put in the place of what I have suggested. It is of course precisely because I expected such differences of opinion that I asked for your co-operation, a request which would have been superfluous had I thought that you would agree with me on all my proposals.

You will pardon me then if I say that I can find no well-founded reason for your refusal. The chief reason why I approached you for co-operation was to avoid the fatal results of a party contest on this grave national question, and you will therefore realize how much I deplore it that it is not possible for you to assure me of co-operation.

I can, however, not overlook that you say further in your letter that 'to avoid unnecessary division' you 'have proposed that the whole Native question be referred to a national convention with a commission to seek a satisfactory solution'.

As you now repeat this proposal of a national convention, I must suppose that you mean it seriously in spite of the absurdity of it which I pointed out in my earlier letter.

The name 'national convention' still indicates nothing to me, and before I am able to decide on its effectiveness or acceptability, I shall, of course, have to know what I should understand by it.

You say that your object in making the proposal is to 'avoid unnecessary division'. I would fervently wish to see *all* division avoided, but, as at present informed, I cannot see how even 'unnecessary' division will be avoided by a convention—even if it is national. It seems to me that division and the degree of it can only be determined and curbed in this question, as in all great political questions, by the sound guidance and patriotism of the party leaders; and whether this occurs at a convention, or in the house, or round a table, seems to me pretty well the same. But perhaps I am wrong and perhaps my view has been influenced by my not as yet having been put in a position to get to know what exactly must be understood by a 'national convention' with reference to the Native problem. I see, for example, from a resolution sent to me by a Native congress that the Natives also are in favour of it on condition that they too will be represented on it.

In order, therefore, to decide whether your proposal is one which can be accepted, I should like to hear from you what I am to understand by the term 'national convention' and I should be glad to have your answer to the following questions:

1. By whom and in what quarters will the delegates to the convention be elected or appointed?
2. Will the delegates decide by majority vote?
3. If not, how will decisions be made and what will be their binding force?
4. If so, will the minority be obliged, after a resolution is taken, to accept the decision and give the resolution their support? Or will they be free to maintain their opposition afterwards as if no convention had taken place and no resolution been adopted?

279

5. What will be your attitude if the convention by its resolution approves the principles of my Smithfield proposals to which you at present object?

From the questions put above, it will be clear to you how vague and impractical the proposal of a national convention must seem to me as long as I do not possess the information which I hope to get from you by these questions; and, what is more, you will also realize from this how well-founded is my fear that such a convention could be utterly fatal to any attempt to keep the matter outside party politics or to avoid division.

It will therefore be necessary, before I can come to a decision about the proposal, that I am given the required information, and it would be very useful if you could tell me what, in your view, would be achieved by a national or other convention which would not be obtainable by means of mutual consultation and discussions round a table by the acknowledged leaders and leading men of the parties, assisted, where necessary, by other suitable persons.

I am sorry to have had to take up so much of your time, but you will pardon me if I take the further opportunity to correct you when you say, at the close of your letter, that you are of the opinion that my conversation some years ago, to which I referred in my earlier letter, had to do with the setting aside of Native areas. You are quite wrong. My conversation had reference to the Native question in general, and, on more than one occasion after that, in referring to what I offered you on that occasion, I repeated my offer in parliament, again without any limitation. Yours sincerely,

J. B. M. Hertzog

185   From J. B. M. Hertzog   Vol. 35, no. 160

Kantoor van die Eerste Minister
Kaapstad
23 Januarie 1926

Waarde Smuts, Jou brief van 21 Januarie in antwoord op die van my van 16 deser is my ter hand.

Die ernstige beskuldiging wat jy daarin maak teen my van 'verdraaing en valse voorstellings' sou my diep getref het as daar enige waarheid in was. Daar dit so volkome onwaar is, en daar jy self, deur na te laat om my die minste aanduiding te gee van waar ek my skuldig gemaak het aan 'verdraaing' of 'valse voorstellings', die bewys lewer van dit nie ernstig te bedoel nie, kan ek dit slegs aanneem as 'n voorwendsel deur jou aangewend om te dien as verontskuldiging vir jou onwilligheid om aan my versoek tot medewerking te voldoen.

Dit spyt my van harte dat jy nie jou weg skoon gesien het om 'n minder beledigende uitvlug te vind nie.

Dog hoe dit ook sy, ek het geen begeerte om tot weder beskuldiginge tans oor te gaan nie, en sal my dus beperk tot die versekering dat, wat my betref, jy verskoon sal 'bly van verdere private gesprekke en korrespondensies in verband met hierdie onderwerp' en, as jy verkies, ook van andere. Dienswillig die uwe,

J. B. M. Hertzog

TRANSLATION

Prime Minister's Office
Cape Town
23 January 1926

Dear Smuts, I have received your letter of 21 January[1] in answer to mine of 16th inst.

The grave accusation which you make in it against me of 'distortion and misrepresentation' would have hurt me deeply if there had been any truth in it. Since it is so completely untrue, and since you yourself, by neglecting to give me the slightest indication of where I have made myself guilty of 'distortion' or 'misrepresentation', give proof of not seriously meaning it, I can only regard it as a pretext adopted by you as an excuse for your unwillingness to accede to my request for co-operation.

I am deeply sorry that you have not seen your way clear to find a less insulting way out.

But, however that may be, I have no desire to resort to counter-accusations and I shall therefore confine myself to the assurance that, as far as I am concerned, you will be excused 'from further private conversations and correspondence in connection with this subject' and, if you prefer it, from others also. Yours sincerely,

J. B. M. Hertzog

[1] Not in the Smuts Collection.

186   To S. M. Smuts   Vol. 36, no. 125

House of Assembly
Cape Town
25 Februarie 1926

Lieve Mamma, Dit lyk of die weer nou glad gek geword het. Die laaste paar dae het dit hier hard gereent en het dit net soos winter gevoel. Dit kan wees dat die somer weer terug kom; maar daar is reeds een gevoel van herfst in die lug, en ek vrees dat die vrugte boere baie daaronder gaan ly. Wat in die droe dele van die binneland gaan gebeur weet ek nie, want dit lyk byna of ons sonder gras sal wees vir die winter. En ons het soo baie diere op ons hande dat 'n mens werkelik besorg word vir die toekoms.

Wanneer kom jy af? Bibas sal a.s. Maandag namiddag met twee meisies arriveer. Ons sal dus genoeg hulp in die huis hê.

Die werk in die Parlement vlot mooi aan en ek dink ons gaan klaar kom by einde van Mei of middel van Juni. Dit sal baie beter wees om dit maar een korte sitting te maak, viral daar 'n mens meer noodig sal wees thuis als hier.

Baie wil hê dat ek naar Amerika moet gaan. Ek kan egter nog nie besluit nie. Ek is bang ons kry een algemeene electie aanstaande jaar oor Hertzog's Naturelle politiek, en dit kan dus een beetje gevaarlik wees hierdie jaar lang afwezig te wees uit die land. Ma het ek Sondag gesien; sy was baie fluks en opgeruimd; baie bly dat jy afkom. Soentjes van

Pappa

TRANSLATION

House of Assembly
Cape Town
25 February 1926

Dear Mamma, It looks as if the weather has now gone quite mad. It rained hard here during the last two days and it felt just like winter. It may be that summer will return; but there is already a feeling of autumn in the air, and I am afraid the fruit farmers are going to suffer badly. What will happen in the dry parts of the interior I do not know, for it almost looks as if we shall be without grass for the winter. And we have so many animals on our hands that one is really worried about the future.

When are you coming down? Bibas[1] is arriving next Monday afternoon with two maids. So we shall have enough help in the house.

---

[1] *See* vol. I, p. 405, note 2.

The work in parliament is going ahead nicely and I think we shall be done by the end of May or the middle of June. It will be much better to make it a short session especially as one will be more useful at home than here.

Many people want me to go to America. But I cannot yet decide. I am afraid that we shall have a general election next year about Hertzog's Native policy, and so it could be a bit dangerous to be absent from the country this year. I saw mother[1] on Sunday; she was very active and cheerful; very glad that you are coming down. Kisses from

Pappa

187   From G. G. A. Murray   **Vol. 36, no. 30A**

Yatscombe
Boar's Hill
Oxford
1 March 1926

My dear Smuts, About *Holism*. I have at last had the typescript back from J. A. Smith, and enclose his note upon it.[2] I chose him as being not only about our best philosopher here but also the most entirely ruthless and critical. It is very interesting to see that *Holism* has made a real impression upon him. His main objection is one which is characteristic of his school: that no scientific conception can ever solve a philosophical difficulty – an objection which I never fully understand.

For my own part *Holism* seems to me the most striking and interesting book on philosophy that I have read for a great many years. It does combine and hold together a number of the new conceptions—results of scientific advance—which have seemed so destructive to the ordered world which we believed in thirty years ago. It seems to give one again an ordered and intelligible universe, or at least a glimpse of such a thing. I have been living with the idea of Holism for some months now, and find that it works—I mean, that in ordinary experience I find that it makes things intelligible.

I do not much like the word, but still it is properly formed and I do not see how to improve upon it. I am more worried over 'Personology'. I am not really sure that you want a new word; if you do, what about 'autology' from αυτος—*ipse*? When the parts become a Whole, that Whole is αυτος, Itself.

---

[1] Smuts's widowed step-mother (*see* **183**). His mother died in February 1901.
[2] Omitted by the editor.

One of the charms of the book is that there is so much thought to the page, and that the thought has been clarified before being written down. One feels that you have lived with the ideas and got them quite clear in your own mind, so that they come out alive—as a whole in fact, and not as a collection.

And meantime there is Poland! And, almost worse, Spain![1] We are by no means out of the wood, but your message,[2] and [Lord] Grey's letter and speech,[3] and the protest of the Conservative M.P.s have saved the situation for the time being. I have never before known the country to be so stirred over a League question, and so unanimously on the right side. I can hardly understand how Austen made such a sheer obvious blunder,[4] but I think he was intoxicated by the success of Locarno and bubbled over with promises of friendship and support to Briand, Skrzynski and Quinones[5] without realizing what he was doing. It will be difficult to trust him again. We have had rather a feverish time at the LNU,[6] trying to prevent the intrigue going through and at the same time avoiding unnecessary bad blood. The Poles have behaved rather well; the Spaniards not. Yours very sincerely,

Gilbert Murray

188   To F. C. Kolbe   Vol. 36, no. 133

The House of Assembly
Cape Town
17 March 1926

My dear Dr Kolbe, It is a pleasure to me to know that you think of me even in your dreams. Alas, we see so little of each other! But

[1] After the Locarno agreements, Germany was to be admitted to the League of Nations and to a permanent seat on its council, the other permanent seats being held by Britain, France, Italy and Japan. Now Spain and Poland made a bid for permanent seats, the latter being supported by her ally, France.

[2] Not traced.

[3] Speaking at Newcastle on 26 February 1926, Lord Grey said that discussion at Geneva on the admission of other nations as permanent members of the council should begin only after Germany had taken her seat.

[4] Speaking at Birmingham on 23 February 1926, Sir Austen Chamberlain had given the impression that he supported the French proposal to sponser Poland's claim to a permanent seat on the council.

[5] A. Briand (q.v.) was at this time foreign minister of France; Count Alexander Skrzynski (q.v.) was prime minister of Poland. José Maria Quiñones de Léon (born 1873) was Spanish ambassador in Paris in 1919, chief representative of Spain on the League of Nations until 1931 and president of the council of the League 1920, 1922, 1925.

[6] The League of Nations Union.

I hope that when *Holism and Evolution* has appeared, as it will next May, we shall be able to compare notes over it and that you will be able to put me right on the points where I have gone wrong. I have told my publishers to send you a copy and I hope you will accept it from me as a token of my admiration for what you have done and been to South Africa.

I have never had an opportunity to tell you how much I enjoyed reading your last autobiographical work;[1] it appealed profoundly to me as a great record of the spirit and of the interior development of a great soul. I have recommended it to many of my friends who had not heard of the book and they have since told me that reading it was a great eye-opener to them.

I am still confined to my bed with a minor operation for a carbuncle, but if all goes well I hope to be up and doing again in a week or two. With best wishes, Yours ever sincerely,

J. C. Smuts

189   To M. C. Gillett   Vol. 36, no. 225

Mount Pleasant[2]

25 March 1926

I am up again and have been for the last four or five days. The wound is healing nicely and I hope to be at my work in the house again in a couple of days. I am once more being innoculated with my own serum. I hope this time with more success. Isie is still here but has to leave early next week. The Boardmans[3] are leaving today on a visit of inspection to Port Elizabeth. . .

I have read a great deal since you left—geology, botany, philosophy, politics—what have I not read the last fortnight! It seems a pity to get back to politics in the house after such a spell of freedom from it. The more I see of politics the more I love my studies. And the work in parliament is doubly unpleasant just now. We are to hold a joint sitting of both houses over the Colour Bar Bill, the senate having once more rejected the bill.[4] After that the Asiatic Segregation Bill[5] will come on, as dangerous and unpleasant a

---

[1] *Up the Slopes of Mount Sion, or, A progress from Puritanism to Catholicism* (1924).

[2] F. S. Malan's house in Cape Town which Smuts had rented.

[3] Joan Rowntree had married H. Boardman.

[4] After a second rejection of a non-financial bill by the senate a joint sitting of both houses may, under clause 63 of the South Africa Act, be convened.

[5] In 1924 the Smuts government had introduced the Class Areas Bill to segregate Indians in urban areas but went out of office before it could be passed. The bill of 1926 contained provisions for segregation and repatriation of Indians. It was referred to a select committee and then dropped.

measure as has ever been before our parliament. Then Hertzog will bring forward his Native segregation bills. This will become a most unhappy country with policies such as these. And yet for the moment these policies are popular and the Nat–Labour Pact is no doubt scoring heavily and entrenching themselves in public opinion. I feel profoundly unhappy over it all, and I am not free of blame either. Worse luck. Well, good-bye, dear children. Good [*sic*] be with you ever.

Jan

190 To A. A. Roberts   Vol. 36, no. 138

[March 1926]

My dear Roberts, I have received your note of 20 March and have also heard from Dr Pole-Evans. I have much pleasure in agreeing to the proposal that the proceeds of the Louis Botha fund should be devoted to the payment of the salary of a professor of botany at the Transvaal University College.[1] I make no condition or reservation and leave full discretion to the council of the college in regard to the use of the money for the above purpose. But I would express the wish that the council lay it down as a rule that the professor paid out of this fund should once a year deliver a public lecture in which he deals with the general problems of botany and with any recent advances in botany, especially in South Africa. Yours sincerely,

J. C. Smuts

191 To G. G. A. Murray   Vol. 36, no. 142

Houses of Parliament
Cape Town
8 April 1926

My dear Murray, I received your note about *Holism* with the enclosure from Smith by the last mail. I am more than grateful for the trouble you have taken in this personal matter. I have written Smith a note to thank him for his trouble and interest. And I wish to thank you very much too. Your high praise is indeed welcome. When one ploughs a lonely furrow, as I have done in thought all these years, one never knows whether one has not perhaps lost the

---

[1] Founded in May 1910 in Pretoria; became the University of Pretoria in October 1930.

trail altogether. Holism has been my synthetic creed, and I do not know how I would have done without it.

I feel very sad over the last great failure of the League.[1] That it should be in the power of a minor state to upset the whole machinery of civilization is surely intolerable. I can imagine your anxieties in this connection. It is not only the human factor that has failed us this time, but evidently something wrong in the covenant itself. This great failure will either rouse public opinion to a sense of the dangers, or it will be acquiesced in, and thus fatally weaken the League. I am really very much perturbed and do not know what to think. Did we attempt too much in the League scheme? Lord Bryce, when he read my original memorandum which, as you know, was closely followed in the covenant, told me that such a scheme was quite impracticable and could never be adopted. Was he right? I mean, was he wise, and have we attempted too much? I have not taken previous failures of the League so much to heart as this one. I only trust that Germany will not change her mind,[2] and that the situation will not be worse next September at Geneva. If I can free myself from local entanglements I have a great mind to run over to England and Europe next July in order to get into closer touch with the situation. My fear is deep that the League has arrived at a critical point and that a fatal turn may be taken not only in her fortunes but in those of Europe and civilization too. In some way or other America *must* become associated with the League; but it is not clear to me how this is to be done, even if it is possible under the present conditions of American public opinion. The chance for another effort like the League will not come again until the world has been once more engulfed. And we must therefore move heaven and earth to keep the League going and to give it a chance for the future. I feel genuinely alarmed. Please let me know how you really view matters. Ever yours,

J. C. Smuts

192   To L. Esselen   Vol. 36, no. 143

12 April 1926

My dear Louis, I have been giving the subject of a change of chairmanship of our party on the Rand a good deal of consideration

---

[1] *See* **187**.

[2] Germany had been reluctant to join the League of Nations. Now the pretensions of Spain and Poland and the attitude of France (*see supra*, p. 285, note 1) revived her mistrust and caused her to veer towards Russia with whom she made a treaty of friendship and neutrality on 26 April 1926.

recently, and the more I think over the matter, the more it appears to me to be a mistake to make a change at this juncture. Julius[1] has served us very well, and I am afraid our dropping him now would make the impression that it is done simply because of [Sir A.] Bailey's difficulties with us. Julius has been so loyal to us and served our party so well on the Rand that I should not like it to appear to the world that we are punishing him for Bailey's sins. It seems to me very inopportune to drop him now.

I have also an uncomfortable feeling that with [C. F.] Stallard's peculiar views on the Native question, our party might be placed in a very awkward position if Stallard as chairman of our party on the Rand were within the next twelve months to come into conflict with the line which our party might generally take in reference to Hertzog's proposals. Stallard honestly takes a very much stronger line on the segregation ideas than the rest of us do, and I see the elements of a clash which might be most inopportune, and bad for the party. These and other reasons make me feel that we would be doing Julius an injustice and our party no service if we made a change at this juncture.

I want you to think over the matter carefully and, if you agree with me, discuss the position with Julius and, if necessary, show him this letter and try to induce him to remain on as chairman for the next twelve months. Much will clear up during that period, and at the end of twleve months it may be possible for us to arrange our difficult affairs much more satisfactorily. It may be a sacrifice for Julius to remain on, but I feel sure that if he is convinced that such a course is in the interests of the party, he will not hesitate for a moment. I have reason to think that Bailey would be quite pleased if he stayed on, as Bailey is by no means hostile to us, and has no reason whatever to do us any harm. As the general meeting will be held some time this month, I hope you will lose no time in dealing with this matter. Yours sincerely,

s. J. C. Smuts

193   To an editor   Vol. 36, no. 160

26 April 1926

Dear Sir, I enclose a contribution for the first issue of *Voorslag*[2] which I have promised Mr Lewis Reynolds.[3] It is called 'Beauty

[1] Sir Julius Jeppe.

[2] A South African journal in English edited by Roy Campbell and William Plomer. It appeared between June 1926 and May/June 1927. *Voorslag* is Afrikaans for whiplash.

[3] He had assumed financial responsibility for *Voorslag*.

in Nature',[1] and I hope you will find it suitable. Kindly note that I wish to retain the copyright of this article.

I also enclose cheque for 25s. for one year's subscription to *Voorslag*. Yours sincerely,

s. J. C. Smuts

194   From E. Hobhouse   Vol. 35, no. 179

c/o Barclay's Bank Ltd.
137 Brompton Road
London
2 May 1926

Dear Oom, When I look at the cover of the Scientific Presidential address you have so kindly sent me and see the list of letters after your name I realize that I have not kept myself *au courant* with all your honours. Please forgive that I have omitted them from your address in the past, and from very bad memory I may do so in the future. Meanwhile many thanks for sending me this reprint. I read it with interest as I do all that you write, but your main points were reproduced in the English press at the time of delivery—so, instructed by you, we have been turning our minds to look to South Africa or at least your continent as our most hoary ancestress.

I am still looking out for your philosophic book...

Now May has come I realize your birthday is near and I send you my warmest congratulations together with earnest wishes for many happy returns of the day. *How* young you still are! and *how* old I am! Soon to go hence and be no more seen. Probably you do not know that I have been through six months of most severe illness. The uprooting from my cosy little home in Tor Gardens was too much for me and nearly killed me. I cannot describe how terrible the heart attacks were—the struggle to draw a breath. Then they brought me to this place (Isle of Wight) for milder air but it has proved much colder and wet and foggy to boot. I have not left my room, hardly my bed. *So* weak. In June I am to be taken back to London in an ambulance car—so I am trying to find lodgings there.

Your session will be over when you read this and I hope you will have a restful time at Doornkloof. Please give my love to Santa and my kind regards to her husband, and with old love to Mrs Smuts, Believe me yours ever affectionately,

Emily Hobhouse

---

[1] This article was published in the first number of *Voorslag*. It may have suggested to Campbell the first line of his satiric quatrain on Smuts entitled 'Holism' and beginning: 'The love of Nature burning in his heart'. *See* R. Campbell, *Adamastor*, p. 103.

Have you read Colonel House's *Intimate Papers*?[1] Of deep interest. Also for vivid description Paléologue's *Memoirs*[2] are fascinating, and you should read Count Michael Karolyi's book *Fighting the World*.[3] He and his wife are exiles in England and we find them most charming people.

Lord Bertie's *Diaries*[4] are poor stuff and gossipy. Well, well, how inept they all show themselves to be and the minds run to dinners, lunches, wine parties and excursions while we poor creatures were half starved and the Tommies and Poilus in agony. They make one sick.

I think now the little Neutrals ought each to produce a book describing the great Drama from *their* points of view. I am writing to urge them to do so—particularly Holland and Switzerland.

Do you ever mean to bring the sunlight of your intelligence to shine on Europe again? Good-bye, Yours ever,

Emily Hobhouse

195   To E. Hobhouse   Vol. 36, no. 168

6th May 1926

My dear Tante, I have now several letters from you to reply to, and I hope you will not mind if I dictate it for typing so that you are spared the trouble of deciphering my hieroglyphics. Thank you very much for the 'Nature Cure' and 'Lemon Cure' which you have suggested. I feel quite well now and hope that it will not be necessary to try the lemon cure which does not sound very cheerful.[5]

I take plenty of out-door exercise and eat fresh uncooked vegetables as much as possible, and I doubt whether it is necessary for me to go in for any violent remedies. I cannot help thinking that that is a mistake that you are making. At our age we cannot try tricks on our poor bodies, and these forced measures exact a heavy toll from our poor frames.

I am indeed sorry to hear that you are at such a low ebb, and I cannot help feeling that your housing troubles have added very considerably to your state of mind and body. Perhaps it was a mistake

[1] Colonel E. M. House, *Intimate Papers* (1926–8).
[2] G. M. Paléologue, *An Ambassador's Memoirs* (1923).
[3] Count Michael Karolyi, *Fighting the World: the Struggle for Peace* (1924).
[4] *The Diary of Lord Bertie of Thame, 1914–18*, edited by Lady A. Gordon Lennox (1924).
[5] Emily Hobhouse, concerned about Smuts's carbuncles, thought his blood needed 'a thorough purification'. The climax of the 'lemon cure' was eleven lemons on the eleventh day! (*See* Smuts Collection, vol. 35, no. 178.)

for you to have sold that house, and I hope that next time you
settle down comfortably, you will not easily make a change. I wish
most fervently that you will soon be well again. It must be hard
indeed for a person of your active mind to be so reduced in bodily
health.

I am sorry that I cannot take a cheerful view of public affairs. In
Europe reaction is rampant, and the last fiasco at Geneva is indeed
a most pitiable affair. Now you have a general strike in England,
the consequences of which no man can foresee.[1] The industrial
position of England in the post-war period has been in continual
danger, and this disastrous affair may cause a set-back of the most
far-reaching character. One hopes against hope, and does one's best
to take a cheerful view of things, but there is no doubt that the outlook is black, and the outcome will be blacker than any of us can
foresee today. One's sympathy is with the workers in their efforts
to maintan a decent standard of living. But with competition
from other countries where longer hours are worked, less wages are
paid, and industrial efficiency is no less than in Great Britain, it may
be a physical impossibility to maintain the high standard for the
worker which has been achieved in Great Britain.

Things in South Africa are proceeding very much as usual.
Parliament is sitting, but we have no first-class measures of importance, and therefore the session is on the whole quiet and dull. The
only variation is the Colour Bar Bill which the opposition is
resolutely fighting. There was also a grave Asiatic trouble pending,
but this for the present has been postponed, owing to the decision of
the government to have a conference with the Indian government.[2]
We shall probably have finished with our work by the end of May.

I had at one time thought of going to America after the session,
but I have given up that idea, largely because I fear that the trip
would be much too strenuous for my present state of health. If I
could manage the time, I would like to run over to Europe rather,
and get into closer touch with the march of events there which it is
most difficult to understand and follow at this distance. But I doubt
if it will be possible to do even so much.

[1] In June 1925 the coal-miners struck against a decrease in wages announced by
the owners. When they were supported by the general council of the Trades Union
Congress a general strike became likely. Negotiations and the investigations of a commission failed to bring the parties to agreement. On 30 April 1926 the government
declared a state of emergency. On 1 May the trade unions' executives voted for
a general strike. Last minute talks with the cabinet failed and the strike began at
midnight on 3 May.

[2] *See supra*, p. 285, note 5. A deputation from India came to South Africa and a
deputation of the Union parliament went to India.

The family is very well. Cato is settled at Newnham and Japie, who is a very promising mathematician, will also probably go to Cambridge at the end of the year.

It has been very dry over large parts of South Africa, in fact in large parts of the Transvaal we have never had a worse time within memory. And this, coming after the very bountiful and beautiful season we had last year, is disheartening people very much.

This is a very doleful letter and I am afraid will do little to cheer you up. Perhaps it might make a difference if you knew that my book on *Holism* will soon be out, and that the publishers will send you a copy. I want you to read it, and I think there is something in it. I am anxious to know what your brother would think of it. I speak with the highest praise of his work in it. With my very best wishes, Ever yours affectionately,

s. J. C. Smuts

196 To S. M. Smuts

Vol. 36, no. 170

Volksraad
Kaapstad
12 Mei 1926

Liefste Mamma, Ek het met die laaste mail een mooi brief van Cato gehad. Sy lykt heel gelukkig te Newnham en is ook al besig met haar werk. Ek is bly dat alles so geloop het en dat daar geen moeilykheid daar gewees is nie. Ek sal haar briewe van introductie stuur aan die Masters van X's and Downing [*sic*], want die is altwee groot vrinde van my.

Die nuus is nou net aangekom dat die strike in Engeland beeindig is. Dit is waarlik een seen, want die voortduring daarvan sal die fataalste gevolge gehad het. Daar is een woeling en gisting onder die arbeidsklasse oor die hele wereld, en ek wonder soms wat die toekoms gaat baar. Dit is nie onmoontlik nie dat die beskawing nog ten gronde sal gaan, nie deur aanvalle van buite soals in die geval van vorige ryke, maar deur inwendige botsinge tussen klasse van die maatskappy. Hier in die land sien ons hoe ver, hoe uiterst ver, die een klas van die bevolking bereid is om te gaan teen die andere.

Ek is nou besig met die laaste korreksie van *Holism* en is by hoofd. 8 gekom—aanstaande week hoop ek klaar te kom, en dan behoort die boek in Juli uit te wees. Ek sal waarlik bly wees as hierdie zaak van my hande is, want dit het vir 2 jare nou baie van my tyd in beslag geneem. Ek meen die boek sal een kleine bydrage wees tot die nuwere filosofie en hoop vir een gunstige ontvangst.

Ons is nou besig met die Colour Bar debat. Hertzog het sig weer te buite gegaan in sy vernynige aanvalle op my en ook in een bittere aanval op die ou aartsbiskop en andere wat een doodonschuldige memorie oor die saak na hom gestuur het. Dit lyk my soms asof hy nie by sy volle sinne is nie. Nou hoor ek dat hulle tog die £700 per jaar gaat deursit, al is dit so onpopulair, en dat hulle ook die nuwe vlag gaat deursit. Ek meen eenige nuwe vlag moet deur overeenkomst vasgesteld word en nie maar van een kant of party van die bevolking kom nie. Maar die Pakt sal aandrywe tot hulle op die rotse is. Dit is net koud en nat hier en nou lyk dit of hierdie maatregels ons tot midde Juni hier sal hou. Nyssie kom na die sitting vir 4 of 6 weke alleen by ons bly. Sy vrou bly hier.

Pappa

TRANSLATION

House of Assembly
Cape Town
12 May 1926

Dearest Mamma, I had a nice letter from Cato [Clark] by last mail. She seems quite happy at Newnham and is already busy with her work. I am glad everything has turned out like this and that there has been no trouble. I shall send her letters of introduction to the Masters of Christ's[1] and Downing[2] for they are both great friends of mine.

News has just come that the strike in England has ended.[3] That is really a blessing, for its continuance would have had the most fatal consequences. There is activity and ferment among the working classes all over the world, and I sometimes wonder what the future will give birth to. It is not impossible that civilization will yet go to ruin, not through attacks from outside as in the case of previous empires, but through internal clashes between social classes. Here in this country we see how far, how extremely far one class of the population is prepared to go against the other.

I am now busy with the final correction of *Holism* and have reached chapter eight; next week I hope to finish and then the book should be out by July. I shall really be glad when this matter is off my hands for it has taken up much of my time for two years now.

[1] Sir A. E. Shipley.
[2] Professor A. C. Seward.
[3] The nine-day general strike ended on 12 May 1926 after suggestions for renewed negotiations made by Sir Herbert Samuel were accepted by the general council of the Trades Union Congress. But the coal-miners continued their strike for another six months before capitulating to the owners.

I think the book will be a small contribution to the newer philosophy and hope for a favourable reception.

We are now busy with the colour bar debate. Hertzog has again gone to excess in his venomous attacks on me and also in a bitter attack on the old archbishop[1] and others who sent him an entirely harmless petition on the subject. It sometimes seems to me that he is not in his right mind. Now I hear that they are nevertheless going to put the £700 a year[2] through, although it is so unpopular, and that they are also going to put the new flag through. I think that any new flag must be determined by agreement and not come only from one section or party of the population. But the Pact will drive on until they are on the rocks.

It is cold and wet here and now it looks as if these measures will keep us here until mid-June. Nyssie is coming to stay with us for four or six weeks after the session—alone. His wife[3] stays here.

Pappa

197   To C. P. Crewe   Vol. 36, no. 172

House of Assembly
Cape Town
14 May 1926

My dear Crewe, Thank you for your letter and for what you say about my speech. The harm done by the Colour Bar Act, especially in its effect on Native opinion will be very great. Yet I believe our resolute opposition to it during the last two years will now have this effect, that the government will be frightened to go beyond the old Transvaal regulations, and that it will hesitate, under the sanction of this act to proceed on a large scale with industrial segregation. Hertzog's attack on the English churches and missionaries was in shocking bad taste. One's only consolation is to know that it has done him far more harm than the churches concerned.

I note what you say about the segregation bills which are yet to come before us. My personal feeling is very much on the lines on which you write. Our party caucus will have to consider them after they have been laid on the table, and decide on some line of action which will be endorsed by our party generally over the Union. The subject is one of immense difficulty for the Nationalists, but it has also its difficulties for us, as the Native question is not looked upon

[1] The Right Reverend William Marlborough Carter.
[2] The proposed increase of the salary of members of parliament.
[3] Born Leila Wright; married Deneys Reitz in 1920; member of the house of assembly for Parktown, 1933–43; died in 1960.

from the same angle from the North and from the South. I have no doubt that Hertzog's main reason for taking the franchise away from the Cape Natives[1] is the fact already stated by him at Smithfield that in twelve seats at least the Native vote is decisive, and the seats therefore held by South African party men. We shall have to look at the question both from this angle very closely and also from the point of view of the country's future. As I say, the question bristles with difficulties for us, but I hope it will be possible for our party to adopt a policy which will be both in the party's interests and in the country's interests.

We have heard a great deal about the flag recently, and both Nationalists in the lobby and *Die Burger* declare that the bill will be proceeded with this session. If so it will lead to very prolonged debate. The decision of the Pact to eliminate all reference to the Union Jack in our flag is bound to be taken up as a racial challenge and to lead to great bitterness over the whole country. Indeed I am afraid that much of the good work of racial conciliation to which Botha devoted the best years of his life will soon be in rack and ruin, if the Pact proceed with their policy of setting one section against another and one colour against another. We can but do our best to uphold the cause and unity and co-operation for which our party stands. And I say no new flag without agreement between the two sections of our population.

I put the question this afternoon to Hertzog in the house whether it was the intention of the government to introduce any further legislation this session. His answer was: 'No, only small administrative bills may be brought forward beyond those already on the list.' From this I gather that it cannot be the intention to proceed with the Flag Bill. But of course one can never tell. With Hertzog it is the tail that wags the dog. And the poison of the Nationalist party is distinctly in its tail, where the racial animosity, although usually suppressed, is very bitter indeed.

I was very glad to get your letter and to see your firm handwriting. I hope you will excuse my dictating a letter which you might otherwise waste your time in trying to decipher.

With my kindest regard both to you and Lady Crewe, Every yours sincerely,

J. C. Smuts

[1] *See* vol. I, p. 94, note 1; vol. II, p. 239, note 1.

198   From D. J. Sioka   Vol. 36, no. 62

34 New Scotland
Pietermaritzburg
17 May 1926

Sir, I have the honour herewith to forward the enclosed resolutions for your information.

Could you kindly inform us how the Colour Bar Bill will affect us—what trades, especially, it will affect? I am informed that some Natives employed at Eddels Ltd. boot factory have already been dismissed. This is the biggest boot factory in Natal and a good number of Natives and Indians are employed.

The Natives here greatly admire your effort and we hope you will ever stand for what you consider is right for all sections and races of South Africa.

I am further requested to ascertain from you what the position of the exempted Natives[1] will be under this bill.[2] I have the honour to be Sir, Your obedient servant

D. J. Sioka
General Secretary Natal African Congress[3]

ENCLOSURE

NATAL AFRICAN CONGRESS AND THE
INDUSTRIAL AND COMMERCIAL WORKERS UNION

Resolutions

1. That this mass meeting of Natives, composed of all classes and all stages of civilization, assembled at the Market Square, Pietermaritzburg, on Sunday afternoon under the auspices of the Natal African Congress and the Industrial and Commercial Workers Union (I.C.U.)[4] herewith beg to proclaim its protest against the action of the government in forcing through the Colour Bar Bill to our very greatest regret and entire disappointment.

[1] Some Natives, such as clergymen and teachers, were exempted from carrying passes but carried an exemption certificate.

[2] The letter has an annotation in Smuts's handwriting as follows: 'Acknowledge. General Smuts wishes me to tell you in reply that it is impossible to answer your questions until the government has published the regulations which will be necessary to put the act into force.'

[3] The African National Congress, a political organization founded in January 1912, had provincial congresses in each of the provinces of the Union. It was banned on 8 April 1960.

[4] This general labour union for non-whites was founded in Cape Town in 1919. It became an important political organization but, after 1928, split into three opposed bodies.

2. That this meeting feels that the present government is not conducive to the welfare of this country so far as we have been following it up in their individual speeches and also in parliament, but be it as it may, the Natives have an equal claim for consideration.

3. That this meeting expresses its heartfelt thanks and congratulates the leader of the opposition, General Smuts, and the missionaries for the life and death fight they manifested which showed that they and they only are the true servants of God and the fathers of the Natives and guardians of South Africa.

4. That it is not true that the missionaries and others who fought for us in this particular bill are misleading us. We are quite aware of the consequences of the Colour Bar Bill and the intentions of the legislators of the same from their own lips.

5. That had the prime minister agreed to a deputation, composed of Natives only, being heard at the bar of the house, he and his supporters would have heard the views and the true views of the Natives themselves, and the idea that they have been misled by the missionaries and others, would have been cleared to the present government.

6. That this meeting humbly prays and earnestly appeals to our only true father, our beloved king through the governor-general of South Africa, and the supreme chief over the Native population not to give his assent to this fearful bill.

That copies of these resolutions be forwarded to the secretary to the governor-general, the prime minister, the chief native commissioner, Natal, General Smuts, and the Bishop of Cape Town and others who fought for us.

Dated at Pietermaritzburg, this 16th day of May in the year of our Lord 1926.

199   To S. M. Smuts   Vol. 36, no. 184

M[oun]t Pleasant
23 Mei 1926

Liefste Mamma, Volgens jou laaste briewe is jy nog op reis, maar wanneer Japie jou dit oorhandig sal jy al thuis wees. Ek is bly dat jy die lange toer geniet het. Ek is seker die besoek aan verafgeleë plekke het baie goed gedoen en genoeë gebreng aan baie gemoedere. Maar dit is baie vermoeiend; hoe ouer ek word hoe minder lyk ek die menslike gedoente en gewemel. En dit is maar seker met jou ook soo. Jy sal seker later met my weer moet rondreis en dit sal dus gewenst wees as jy nie verder aparte bestellinge maak nie.

Ons het hier een verbasende bakkly gehad oor die Vlag Wet, en ek denk die wet is nou ook seker dood. Ek het geen gevoel vir Eric Walker se vlag. Ek voel vir die liewe ou Vierkleur, en versta ook die gekleefdheid van Engelse aan die Union Jack. Beide vlae is groote historiese feite. Maar wat is Walker se vlag? Die Natte met hul malkop secessie propaganda wil met alles in ons verlede breek. Maar ek is nie daartoe bereid nie. As ons volk nie in syn beide dele kan saam stem nie oor een nuwe vlag is ek dus bereid om langer te wag totdat hul kan ooreenkom.

Gister, Saterdag, was ek by die Universiteits sports. Ongelukkig het dit baie van die tyd gestort reent en ons het almal maar nat thuis gekom. Japie het tot halfpad goed gehardloop in die 2 myl stryd, maar het toe maar uitgesak. Ek was bly want ek glo nie dat so iets goed kan wees vir syn hart. In die aand was ek op een Social in die Harbour Division, waar die vroue my een pragtige geskenk gegee het vir morre se dag. Een hoorlosie met inkpot en pencil vir my tafel—dit lyk alles in goud. Ek sal dit saambreng naar Irene. Alles is pragtig afgeloop. Die reen het vandag voortgeduur en dit on-moontlik gemaak om lang uit te gaan. Ons het Lion's Head opge-gaan, maar weens die reent moes ons weer omdraai. Japie het egter die kop in die tyd 2 *maal* uitgeklim—nie by die voetpad nie maar regop langs die kranse. Ons het werklik verys om dit te sien. Hy is darem fiesies (physisch) goed ontwikkel en ek is verbaasd om te sien wat hy kan doen. Hy vertrek vanaand. Ek het eerst gedag om hom hier te hou en dan met hom naar die Transvaal terug te motor aan die end van die sessie. Maar daar kom nog so baie wette voor dat ek bevrees is dat ons miskien langer als die eerste week van Juni sal sit. Dit wet teen die Senaat sal tyd neem. Die wet vir hoër parlementaire salarisse moet ook nog voorkom. Dit is almal spykers in die doodkist van die Pakt. Dit is waarlik wonderlik om te sien hoe baie kwaad die Pakt sigself hierdie sessie gedoen het. Die publiek is waarlik disgusted. En as dinge so aangaan is hul dae getel en hul einde gewis. Mooi so. Hul maak hulself dood. Die einde van Judas sal die einde wees van hierdie groot verraad van die ware en blyvende belange van Suid Afrika.

Nou Mamma, dit is genoeg. Ek stuur my soentjies en liefde totdat ek self in een week of 2, 3 terug kom.

Pappa

TRANSLATION

Mount Pleasant
[Cape Town]
23 May 1926

Dearest Mamma, According to your last letters you are still travelling, but when Japie gives you this you will already be home. I am
glad that you enjoyed the long tour. I am sure the visit to distant
places has done much good and given pleasure to many hearts.[1]
But it is very tiring; the older I get the less I like the human bustle
and crowd. And it is no doubt the same with you. You will probably
have to travel about with me again later and so it would be well if
you made no further separate engagements.

We have had an astonishing fight here over the Flag Bill, and I
think the bill is now probably dead.[2] I have no feeling for Eric
Walker's flag.[3] I do feel for the dear old Vierkleur[4] and also understand the attachment of the English to the Union Jack. Both flags
are great historical facts. But what is Walker's flag? The Nats.
with their crazy secession propaganda want to break with everything in our past. But I am not prepared to do that. If our people
cannot, in both its sections, agree on a new flag, I am ready to wait
until they can.

Yesterday—Saturday—I was at the university sports. Unfortunately it poured with rain much of the time and we all got home
rather wet. Japie ran well half the distance in the two-mile race, but
then fell out. I was glad because I do not think it can be good for
his heart. In the evening I was at a social in the Harbour Division[5]
where the women gave me a lovely present for tomorrow[6]—a clock
with inkpot and pencil for my table—it seems to be all in gold. I shall
bring it with me to Irene. Everything went off splendidly. The rain
continued today and made it impossible to go out for long. We went
up Lion's Head[7] but had to turn back because of the rain. However,
Japie climbed to the top of the Head *twice* in the time—not by the

---

[1] Isie Smuts at this time undertook speech-making tours in support of the South
African party.

[2] As a result of strong opposition and differences of opinion on the bill in the
cabinet it was withdrawn for that session (*see* D. F. Malan, *Afrikaner Volkseenheid*,
pp. 111–12).

[3] The government had in its bill put forward a design by Professor E. A. Walker
which consisted of a green vertical band against the flagstaff and horizontal bands of
red, yellow and blue (*see* Malan, *ibid*. pp. 108–11).

[4] The four-colour flag of the South African Republic which consisted of a vertical
green band against the flagstaff and horizontal bands of red, white and blue.

[5] A Cape Town constituency.

[6] Smuts's birthday.

[7] A peak, 2,175 feet in height, to the right of Table mountain.

footpath but straight up the ravines. It really turned us cold to see it. He is really well-developed physically and I am surprised to see what he can do. He leaves this evening. I thought first of keeping him here and then of motoring back to the Transvaal at the end of the session. But so many bills are still to be submitted that I am afraid we shall perhaps sit longer than the first week in June. The bill against the senate[1] will take time. The bill for higher parliamentary salaries must also be submitted. They are all nails in the coffin of the Pact. It is really remarkable to see how much harm the Pact has done itself this session. The public is really disgusted. And if things go on like this their days are numbered and their end sure. Good. They are killing themselves. The fate of Judas[2] will be the fate of this great betrayal of the true and lasting interests of South Africa.

Well, Mamma, enough of this. I send my kisses and love until I return myself in a week or two.

Pappa

200   To L. T. Hobhouse   Vol. 36, no. 197

Irene
Transvaal
15 June 1926

My dear Hobhouse, Last Friday when I reached home from the session of parliament I found a cable that Emily had passed away.[3] She had been moving up and down in her ailments for so long that one had come to believe that the end was really in the distant future. And now the sweet, brave soul is no more. I loved her very tenderly, and I reverenced her as one of the great women of my time. To her it was given to do a work such as few women of our time have done. And now she has her rest and peace at last.

We found a will of hers of 1908 of which I enclose a copy for

[1] Clashes between the government and the senate which, as in the case of the Colour Bar Bill of 1925, led to joint sittings of both houses caused the Pact government to introduce legislation to prevent such clashes. The Senate Bill, which became Act 54 of 1926, provided that the government might dissolve the senate within 120 days after a general election, upon which dissolution and whenever a change of government has occurred, the eight nominated senators vacate their seats instead of sitting, as before, for ten years.

[2] According to St Matthew (xxvii. 5) Judas Iscariot, the twelfth apostle, after betraying Jesus Christ committed suicide by hanging himself. But according to *The Acts* (i. 18) 'falling headlong, he burst asunder in the midst, and all his bowels gushed out'. The equivalent passage of *The Acts* in both Tyndale's New Testament and the Wycliffe Bible say that Judas was hanged and burst asunder in the middle.

[3] She died on 6 June.

your information. It speaks for itself. The question is whether it is her last will, and I hope you will be able to enlighten me after going through her papers. I shall be most glad to do whatever I can at this end. Mr Roos and I have looked after her investments here, and I believe everything is in good order. The Trust will have to be liquidated; that will take a little time in order to realize the mortgages which we hold. Please let me know whether any other will has been found.

To my surprise I received a letter some weeks ago from the British Institute of Philosophical Studies,[1] inviting me to become a member of the council of the Institute. This I must owe to your kind consideration as I notice that you are the chairman of the Institute. The honour can of course only be intended as an honour, as I have no real claim to this great distinction.

I wrote you about my *Holism*. The publication has, owing to various delays, been postponed till the autumn. I hope you will read the book, although it is quite possible that you will find nothing in it. Still in my own mind and experience the idea of holism has worked—I mean has proved of practical value in solving difficulties and rendering intelligible what otherwise was a hopeless puzzle.

I trust your health is now much better and that the revision of your works for a new edition, of which Emily told me, is going forward without undue delay. There is much in your thought that appeals to me. At any rate you have avoided all that irritating finesse which now passes current for philosophy. With very kind regards, Ever yours sincerely,

J. C. Smuts

201   To C. P. Crewe   Vol. 102, no. 219

Irene
Transvaal
29 June 1926

My dear Crewe, Thank you very much for sending me your articles on government policy. I have read the first two with deep interest and look forward to more. I doubt whether your idea of forming a constitutional league on non-party lines is feasible, but in any case your analysis of the situation is very valuable and informative. I expect that a grave blunder of the Pact in regard to the flag question will turn people's minds to their other first-class blunders also, and that in the end all moderate people will turn from them in disgust.

[1] Probably the Royal Institute of Philosophy founded in 1925.

You must bear in mind that it was the support of the non-political moderates which gave them victory two years ago. They are now doing everything in their power to alienate and disgust these people.

As soon as I have time I hope to write a short explanatory memorandum for the party of Hertzog's Native bills[1] which everybody finds so obscure and involved as to be almost unintelligible. I have no doubt that his proposals will miscarry. The crux seems to me to be the deletion of the existing Natives' names from the voters rolls which I trust our party will sternly oppose. If Hertzog fails to carry this point by a two-thirds majority at a joint session he is certain to drop his whole scheme. I must honestly confess that apart from all party considerations I personally feel no sympathy for Hertzog's proposals, which are to my mind no approach even to a solution of the Native question and must, on the contrary, create only greater confusion. However, it would be wise for us to avoid the party aspect as much as possible and discuss the question in an impartial spirit. The press has bestowed a great deal of praise on Hertzog's courage, and we must proceed warily.

The flag question has now to my mind become a screaming farce. The two stream policy has now become a two pole policy.[2] You may be sure the Nationalists will never vote for making the Union Jack one of the equal flags of South Africa. I await developments with amusement and utter contempt for the chief actors in this sorry melodrama. With kind regards, Yours sincerely,

J. C. Smuts

202   To M. C. Gillett

Vol. 36, no. 239

Irene
[Transvaal]
30 June 1926

Last week I did not write to 102 as I was far away on the Magalikwin,[3] as the Nyl river is called after it has left Potgietersrust.[4] Du Plessis[5] is there with the Rooikop cattle...We had a glorious time. Far away in the hushed bush with plenty of cattle and big game and silence...I also collected all the plants worth collecting in winter.

[1] See 204.

[2] For 'two stream policy' see vol. III, p. 286, note 4. 'Two pole policy' refers to a proposal by A. Barlow, M. Kentridge and others that the Union Jack should always be hoisted alongside the national flag.

[3] There are various versions of this name now called the Mogalakwena, a tributary of the Limpopo river.

[4] About 140 miles north of Pretoria.   [5] Manager of Rooikop.

The vegetation was however not very different from what we had seen at Rooikop and behind Magaliesberg.[1] It is mostly *acacia combretum* bush with a fair number of sub-tropical species which we did not see farther south. The place is *behind* Blaauwberg[2] and we looked at Blaauwberg from the west; and my mind again and again dwelt lovingly and longingly on the two days we tramped over that mountain of God. We had four riding horses which added to our comfort. I hope to go again next week and take the children who are now in their school holidays. Coming back I found your welcome letter and a long list of interesting books which you had secured after interviewing Huxley [J. S.].[3] There was also a nice letter from Huxley, mostly about a friend who has applied for a professorship at Cape Town.[4] I am reading a good deal during this holiday before the political campaigns start again next month. What a bore politics is! And one feels it is all so ineffective and not really touching the great issues of life. The more the state grows in power, the more complicated the machine becomes, and the less the individual citizen or even parliament apart from the executive government can do to affect the course of events. And in this country, with its long distances and the low tone of party politics, it is often really a painful business to venture on a political tour. However, one must do one's job, whether one likes it or not. The government through its recent extravagances like the flag and other issues is doing itself much harm, and its stock is falling. Hertzog has now issued his Native bills[5] and they are really farcical as a solution of the Native question. Instead of giving the Natives additional land to satisfy their urgent needs, he is setting aside areas for open competition between whites and blacks; and you know what chance the Native stands under those circumstances. The vote is to be taken away from the Cape Natives who have had it ever since parliamentary institutions have existed there, and instead lists of chiefs and headmen and selected Natives will be prepared *by the government* to vote for seven members of parliament all over the Union. You can understand what chance of getting his views before the country that sys-

[1] *See* vol. I, pp. 553–5, for Smuts's own description of this mountain range.

[2] Mountain in the north-western Transvaal rising to over 6,000 feet.

[3] R. Lydekker, *A Geographical History of Mammals* (1896); E. L. Thorndike, *The Measurement of Intelligence*; H. H. Dale and others, *Lectures on Biochemistry* (1926); J. B. Watson, *Psychology from the standpoint of a Behaviorist* (1919).

[4] This was Professor Lancelot Hogben who was appointed to the chair of zoology in the University of Cape Town in 1927.

[5] There were four bills: The Coloured Persons's Rights Bill; The Representation of Natives in Parliament Bill; The Union Native Council Bill; The Natives Land (1913) Amendment Bill. They were published in Government Gazette Extraordinary, no. 1570, 23 July 1926.

tem will give the Native. It is all very bad business and bound to embitter the Natives still more. On this great question I fear the Nationalist influence is thoroughly reactionary and bad for the future of the country. I hope we shall be able to defeat these plans next session.

It is very cold here at nights, as you can see from my handwriting. The days are however as beautiful and pleasant as only our days can be in winter. I don't think there are any questions to answer in your letter. Give my love to the children and thank them for their birthday letters. Ever yours,

Jan

P.S. Please get me (1) De Selincourt's edition of Wordsworth's *Prelude*[1] and (2) Doughty's new edition of *Arabia Deserta*.[2]

203 To F. S. Malan

Vol. 36, no. 203

Irene
Transvaal
6 August 1926

Liewe Fransie, Ek druk my innige sympathie met jou uit in die verlies van jou moeder. Die troos is dat haar werk gedaan was en haar kinders regvaardig haar in die wereld. Ek sluit in een briefie aan jou lieve ou vader wat ek graag wil hê jy moet aan hom deurstuur. Ek het nie sy adres nie.

Ook send ek jou vir oorweging en bespreking met Burton my memo. oor Hertzog's Naturellepolitiek. Dit is bedoeld vir circulatie onder ons parlementslede, maar die vraag is of ons nie een of ander houding oor die ontwerpe publiek moet opneem nie, en of dit nie wenslik is om wat ek sê oor my naam te publiceer nie. Is daar punte in die memo. wat ons sou kan kwaad doen? My kom dit voor asof die memo. min of meer die lyn is wat ons as party in die Parlement sal moet neem. En ek is bang dat dit ons kwaad sal doen indien daar nie namens ons party een leiddraad vir vorming van een gesonde publieke opinie gegee word. Bespreek dus die kwessie met Burton en gee my s.v.p. jou sienswyse.

Ek glo nie dat Gysie's betoog oor Hereeniging ons baie vrede sal breng nie. Soos voorgestel het die ding ongelukkig een rasse kleur. Dit maak die Engels sprekende suspicieus terwyl die Natte die spot drywe. Hartelike groete *t.t.*

get. J. C. Smuts

[1] E. de Selincourt, *Wordsworth's Prelude edited from the MSS.* (1926).
[2] C. M. Doughty, *Travels in Arabia Deserta*, new edition 1921.

Irene

Transvaal

6 August 1926

Dear Fransie, I express to you my deep sympathy in the loss of your mother. The comfort is that her work was done and her children justify her in the world. I enclose a letter to your dear old father which I should like you to send on to him. I have not his address.

I send you also, for consideration and discussion with Burton, my memorandum on Hertzog's Native policy.[1] It is intended for circulation among our members of parliament, but the question is whether we should not publicly take up an attitude on the bills and whether it is not desirable to publish what I say under my name. Are there points in the memorandum that could harm us? It seems to me that the memorandum is more or less the line that we, as a party, shall have to take in parliament. And I am afraid that it will do us harm if no guidance for the forming of a sound public opinion is given in the name of our party. So discuss the matter with Burton and please give me your view.

I do not think that Gysie's disquisition about reunion[2] will bring us much peace. As proposed the thing has, unfortunately, a racial colour. It makes the English-speaking people suspicious while the Nats mock. Best wishes, *totus tuus*,

J. C. Smuts

204   Memorandum (1926)   Box G, memorandum no. 7

Smuts wrote this memorandum on General Hertzog's Native bills early in August 1926. There is no manuscript draft or typescript of the memorandum in the Smuts Collection. The version here reprinted is that circulated in September 1926 by the South African party.

MEMORANDUM ON GOVERNMENT NATIVES AND COLOURED BILLS

I. *Introductory*

At the close of the last session of parliament, the prime minister laid on the table of the houses four government bills on Native policy.[3] Through this formal act these bills became the official

---

[1] *See* **204**.

[2] In July 1926 Gysbert R. Hofmeyr had issued a call for the reunion of the National and South African parties. *See* **212** and Smuts Collection, vol. 35, no. 188, enclosure.

[3] *See supra*, p. 303, note 5.

policy of the government as a whole, and the Native policy which General Hertzog had repeatedly foreshadowed to the country ceased to be merely his personal policy for which his colleagues and his party were not responsible.

Our parliamentary party met to consider the position thus created. It was felt however that there was no time at that last stage of the session for the study or discussion of these important measures, and for coming to any conclusions in respect of them. The party therefore expressed the wish that during the recess I should write and circulate a memorandum which would discuss the principles of the new bills and that, without attempting to come to final conclusions or to lay down a hard and fast policy for the party, I should express my own views and give a personal lead to the party. I have now had time to study these bills and to write the memorandum referred to. It deals only with general principles and does not go into criticism of details, nor does it give more than my own opinions and my advice to the party, which of course remains free to consider the whole policy embodied in these bills and to formulate its definite conclusions at the right time.

The bills deal with the subjects of Native land rights and of Native and Coloured franchise or political rights. It is advisable to deal with these subjects separately, and the proposed amendment of the Natives Land Act (1913) will be first referred to.

II. *The Natives Land Act (1913) Amendment Bill*

(a) The segregation policy.

To appreciate the character and scope of this bill it is necessary to go back to the provisions and intentions of the Natives Land Act of 1913. Previous to 1913 the great scarcity of land available for Natives had made itself felt and had led to Natives buying land among the whites wherever they could get it. In consequence, in areas which had up to then been held almost exclusively by whites there was a steady infiltration of Native buyers of land. This proved so alarming and led to such agitation, especially in the northern provinces, that it was felt necessary by the government and parliament to take action in 1913. It was felt that this evil of promiscuous buying of land by Natives among whites should be stopped, and at the same time, and as a *quid pro quo*, that reasonable additional land should be set aside by parliament for the exclusive occupation of Natives. A policy of territorial segregation was adopted, and steps taken to prevent whites and Natives from encroaching on each other's land. The act of 1913 therefore made the following main provisions:

(*a*) It declared all existing Native reserves to be scheduled areas reserved exclusively for Natives.

(*b*) It empowered the government to appoint a commission for the purpose of recommending, *inter alia*, additional areas to be reserved for exclusive acquisition by Natives, that is to say, in which Natives only could acquire land. Its recommendations were to be laid before parliament for its decision.

In the meantime, and to prevent promiscuous buying of land as between whites and Natives, it was laid down that no such buying of land by whites from Natives or by Natives from whites would be legal without the consent of the government.

The policy of the 1913 act was thus to prevent territorial mixture of white and Native and to secure their territorial segregation by providing additional areas for the exclusive occupation of the Natives, and as a *quid pro quo*, to free the whites from the fear of continual Native encroachment on the white areas by land buying.

To carry out the provisions of the act the Beaumont commission was appointed, and it recommended additional Native areas in the various provinces. These recommendations did not please the whites in all their details, and in consequence committees were appointed for the various provinces to revise the Beaumont areas. Even so however the whites continued to object to details of the committee areas, and no action was taken by parliament to declare these areas scheduled Native areas. However, even without waiting for the ultimate ratification of parliament, the government treated these committee areas more or less on the basis of the 1913 act. That is to say, they did not allow whites to buy from Natives and gave the Natives all possible facilities for buying land in those areas. Thus even without formal action by parliament the government were carrying out the policy of the 1913 act, and assisting the Natives to obtain land in the committee areas. Both the Botha and Smuts governments did so, and the Hertzog government followed in their footsteps.

What does the new bill propose to do? In the first place it makes certain small adjustments to the boundaries of the committee areas. In the second place it does not propose to make them additional Native areas in which Natives only can acquire land, as was intended in the 1913 act; it makes them *released* areas, that is to say, it releases them from the act of 1913, and sets them free (so far as they are at present held by whites) for open competition between whites and Natives, or rather specified Natives or Native tribes in respect of specific areas. The policy is thus the exact opposite of that of 1913. While the act of 1913 intended to constitute additional areas for Natives exclusively, the new bill sets these areas open to be bought by whites or Natives in competition with each other; in these areas whites may buy freely just as Natives may buy, without let or hindrance, and the policy of segregating whites and Natives is frankly abandoned. To this free buying and selling certain limits are however imposed. Thus inside these areas a Native may not, without government permission, buy land which would be entirely enclosed by white holdings; and similarly a white may not, without similar permission, buy land right in the midst of Native holdings. In other words, a Native can only buy land adjoining other Native holdings, and similarly a white can only buy adjoining to white holdings. In one respect the Native is favoured in this competition. Such crown land in these areas as adjoins Native reserves is reserved for Natives and cannot without parliamentary sanction be sold or let for more than a year to whites. The bill also contains certain fencing provisions. Thus the white or Native neighbour of a buyer in a released area may claim that the land bought be fenced, and in such a case the expense of fencing is shared between them. In other cases, where thieving or wilful trespass has taken place, the government can order the guilty party (white or Native) to fence at his own expense.

It is quite clear that under these conditions of practically free competition between whites and Natives for the available land in released areas the segregation policy goes by the board. But the bill goes further. It goes on to provide that Natives may, with the permission of parliament or the government, even overflow into adjoining white areas, so long as (1) they only buy land adjoining Native holdings, and do not buy ground which is remote from the boundaries of scheduled or released areas, and (2) so long as they do not buy land which in the aggregate amounts to more than the whole of the particular released areas in question. In other words, if a particular released area is 25,000 morgen[1] in extent, and after free competition with whites, the Natives cannot get more than 5,000 morgen in it, they are entitled, with parliamentary or government approval, to encroach for the balance of 20,000 morgen on other outside areas adjoining the released area, and to go on with this gradual encroachment until they have exhausted their right of buying up to a total of 25,000 morgen. It is clear that no whites in the neighbourhood of scheduled or released areas would be safe; their land would be subject to the fear of this creeping paralysis which will sooner or later overwhelm them. Only whites at a comparatively remote distance from scheduled or released areas

[1] Morgen is a measure of land used in South Africa. It equals about 2.1 acres.

would be able to breathe freely. In other words, both inside and outside released areas the policy of land segregation which was laid down in the act of 1913 is in substance reversed, and the door is once more set open to all the evils of mixed or piebald landholding against which the act of 1913 was intended to provide.

To assist Natives financially a Native fund is constituted into which certain revenues are paid and from which advances can be made to Natives for buying land or meeting the expenses of fencing and the like. Prospecting and mining on Native land in scheduled or released areas can only take place with the permission of the government and two-thirds of all mining revenue accruing to the state from such areas are to be paid into the Native fund. Power for expropriating land for Natives inside scheduled or released areas is given to the government. Power is also given the government to exchange crown land inside these areas for Native-owned land outside these areas.

Even with these powers it is doubtful whether the position of Natives in regard to the acquisition of land is substantially improved beyond what the existing practice has been under the Natives Land Act of 1913. While an opening is once more made for the introduction of the great evil of mixed holdings by whites and Natives both inside and adjoining these areas, no real attempt is made to solve the native land question which the act of 1913 set out to solve.

(b) The new licences.

In spite of this, however, provisions are included in this bill of which the only apparent object is to get the Natives moved off private white farms. Where are they to go to? In the released areas they are to compete with white purchasers and are not likely to get accommodated to a large extent; the same holds with respect to land which they may be permitted to buy outside these areas and where the same unequal competition will prevail. It is to be feared that under this bill they will continue to flock in ever increasing numbers to the towns, and the new legislation will therefore only add to the evils, already so great, of Native influx to the great urban centres. These provisions, intended to shift the Natives from white areas, are contained in the second chapter of this bill. They empower the government to declare that after a certain date a Native shall not live on land outside scheduled or released areas belonging to Natives except as an owner of the land on which he is living, or as a servant working on it, or as a licensed squatter or labour tenant on it, or with special government permission to live on it. Servants are persons who are continuously employed all the year

round on the land or in domestic service or on any farm work, and
they may live on farms without let or hindrance. Labour tenants
are half-time servants, serving at least six months per annum under
written contract of service, who do not give their masters anything
but service for their residence or occupation. Squatters are neither
full-time servants nor half-time labour tenants as above defined and
probably comprise the great bulk of the Native farm labour in at
least three provinces of the Union. In the first place, the bill provides that an owner may not keep more labour tenants or squatters
on his farm than his divisional council (at the Cape) or a special
district board appointed by the government in other provinces may
authorize. They are therefore at the mercy of this board. An ag-
grieved owner may appeal to the minister of Native affairs whose
decision is final, and the local magistrate will issue the owner
a licence for the number finally authorized. In the second place,
heavy licences are imposed for the number authorized. The annual
licence for each squatter is £3 where the owner resides on his farm,
and £5 where he does not so reside. The annual licence for each
labour tenant of a resident owner is nil for the first five tenants,
2s. 6d. each above five and up to nine, and 10s. each for any number
from ten to thirteen, while if the number is over fifteen the licence
is 10s. each for the first five and £2 each for any over that number.
If the owner is non-resident or absentee (as most owners of low
veld or bushveld farms are) the licence is 10s. each for up to three
labour tenants; if more than three and less than ten tenants 10s.
each for the first three and £1 each for the following six; and if ten
or more labour tenants 10s. each for the first three; £1 each for the
following six, and £2 each for every tenant after that. These licences
are so drastic and lay such an additional burden on the farmer that
the only possible inference is that the government wants to shift
the bulk of the rural Natives away from the farms. Even if the
farmer tries to evade the licence by making his present squatter
and labour tenants full-time servants, and pays them accordingly,
it is clear that he will not require the full labour of all of them and
a large process of weeding out will become inevitable.

Where are these rural Natives, said to be between 700,000 and
900,000 in number, on private farms, to go to when the owner
cannot meet these heavy licences? The scheduled areas are mostly
full; and in the released areas the Native newcomer will have to
submit to unequal competition with the whites for all except
certain crown land. The only alternative will be the already over-
crowded urban locations. The already excessive flooding of Natives
into the great white centres will be accentuated, and the Native

problem, instead of being 'solved', will become worse. In fact the main difficulty of the Native problem is already how to ease the increasing Native pressure on the towns. The influx under the new system will become worse. Surely this cannot be intended by the authors of the new policy; but in all probability it is going to be the direct and ever accelerating effect of this ill-considered policy of penal licences. From the farmers' point of view it may be pointed out that labour once driven from the land to the towns will probably be permanently lost to farming.

Very serious objections can therefore be taken to the new bill on the three grounds:

1. That it is no genuine attempt to solve the Native land question, and is a complete negation of the segregation policy which General Hertzog has always been understood to preach.
2. That it once more opens the door to mixed white and Native landholdings on a large scale, both inside and outside the released areas, against which the act of 1913 was passed; and
3. That it imposes a ferocious licensing system for farm squatters and labour tenants, which will force farmers to get rid of them, and which will drive them mostly to the towns where the Native influx is already reaching dangerous dimensions.

III. *Native representation in parliament*

The bill dealing with this matter provides that there shall be seven Native constituencies in the Union, in which the Natives will elect white representatives to sit in the house of assembly; one such constituency will be in the Free State and two in every other province. The clauses in the constitution dealing with the Native and Coloured franchise at the Cape are repealed and it is provided that no Native can in future be put on the parliamentary register, those already on it will be taken off by a special commission to be appointed by the government, and even if any Native names are left on the electoral rolls by mistake, they will not be able to vote at parliamentary elections with the white or Coloured electors. The existing Native franchise is however left intact so far as elections for the Cape provincial council are concerned. Under the new system the Natives will not individually have the vote for the election of their representatives, but the government will prepare lists of chiefs or headmen and other representative Natives who will be the voters, and the value of their votes will be based on the quota or number of persons in respect of whom they are selected as voters. Thus, presumably, the vote of a chief will depend on the number of his tribe. The members of parliament thus elected by the Native communal vote will be on a different footing from the other members of the house in two respects; they will not be competent to take part in any proceedings in the house which deal with increased Native representation or the Native franchise, nor can they take part in any vote in the house after the government have declared that they look upon such a vote as a matter of confidence or no-confidence in the government. There is, however, a qualification to this last point, as no such government declaration will deter a Native representative from voting on any matter involving Native taxation or education, Native local government or testaments, or administration of Native estates, Native contracts, or locations or reserves, townships or settlements, Native titles to property, the sale or supply of liquor to Natives, any race or colour differentiation against Natives, or any other matter which parliament may add to this list. Several points of very great importance arise on this scheme of Native representation.

(a) Removal of Native names already on registers.

In the first place the removal of the names of Native voters from the present electoral roll in the Cape Province is a direct violation of the spirit and intention of the constitution. This will be clear from section 35 of the South Africa Act, which provides that the existing Cape franchise for Natives shall not be taken away for race or colour reasons without a two-thirds majority vote of both houses of parliament at a joint session, and then proceeds to lay down that in no case will the names of voters already on the roll be taken off, no provision being made in this case for an alteration even by a two-thirds majority vote. It was thus the clear intention that no change of the Native franchise shall in any case affect Natives already on the roll. It is true that parliament has the power under section 152 to amend this section by a two-thirds majority at a joint session of parliament. But the absence of any provision for amendment from section 35 (2) is so striking, compared with its insertion in section 35 (1), that one can only come to one conclusion, that is, that the National convention and the British parliament intended that no change in the Native franchise should in any case affect Natives already on the Cape electoral registers.

Section 35 of the South Africa Act is here set out in order to make this clear:

35 (1) Parliament may by law prescribe the qualifications which shall be necessary to entitle persons to vote at the election of members of the house of assembly, but no such law shall disqualify any person in the Cape Province of the Cape of Good Hope who, under the laws existing in the colony of the

Cape of Good Hope at the establishment of the Union, is or may become capable of being registered as a voter from being so registered in the province of the Cape of Good Hope by reason of his race or colour only, unless the bill be passed by both houses of parliament sitting together, and at the third reading be agreed to by not less than two-thirds of the total number of members of both houses. A bill so passed at such joint sitting shall be taken to have been duly passed by both houses of parliament.

(2) No person who at the passing of any such law is registered as a voter in any province, shall be removed from the register by reason only of any disqualification based on race or colour.

Whatever therefore one may think of the policy or impolicy of taking away the Native franchise at the Cape, one point is perfectly clear and that is, that the names of Natives already on the rolls should remain there according to the intention of the South Africa Act. To delete these names would not only be a grave violation of existing rights but also a most serious violation of the spirit and intention of the South Africa Act. If the Cape franchise for the Natives is to be taken away, existing Native names should be left on the voters roll until within a generation they disappear through death and similar causes in the ordinary course of events. This will spread the change from the old system to the new over a transition period which would not only be fair in itself but carry out the provision of the constitution in this regard. There could be no doubt whatever that under all the circumstances, this transition period would be a wise and statesmanlike step, if a change is made at all.

(b) Government to choose Native voters.

It is proposed to extend political representation to the Natives in the three northern provinces, while at the same time it is admitted that they are not individually capable of exercising the franchise. In other words the vast bulk of the Natives are excluded from the franchise, which is entrusted only to chiefs and other representative Natives selected by the government. It is a very grave question whether political rights should be given to people who are thus admitted to be as yet incapable of properly exercising them. In other words, can it be claimed that the Natives in the northern provinces are ripe for these political rights when the government say that they clearly are not yet ripe to exercise the vote? Is this grave step, which the government are proposing, not premature and uncalled for in view of the backward political development of the vast bulk of the Natives in the northern provinces? We are asked to take a vast leap into the dark, at the same time that the government are themselves of opinion that the Natives are not ripe for the political franchise. And what makes the position worse is that for seven members of parliament the settlement of the electoral rolls will rest with the government or their officers. Knowing the Native mind and the way the chiefs look up to the government and its representatives one may feel grave misgivings about a step which will put in the hands of the government and its officers the selection of the chiefs and headmen who will be the Native electors under the new scheme. The seven members representing Native constituencies will be fully aware how much they are in the hands of the government, and it is to be feared that the influence of the government on parliament will not be less on that account. The proposed system is open to abuse by an unscrupulous government and may be applied in such a way that the government would practically, by an indirect method, influence the election of seven additional members to parliament.

(c) Native representatives may hold balance in parliament.

But the most serious objection to the new proposals goes deeper. What is the influence of the seven new members for the Natives going to be on the politics of South Africa? The Natives will see to it that they are not members of the white parties, but representatives solely and simply of Native interests. So far the Native voters at the Cape have been merged with the white voters in the same constituencies, and the members of parliament elected partly by their votes have been members of the big parties and have been in no sense different or distinguishable in their outlook or aims from the other members of parliament. But in future under the new system all this will be changed. The seven members will be a purely Native party, representing only the Native outlook, aims and points of view. With the other parties more or less balanced these seven men may hold the scale and exercise an influence out of all proportion to their numbers. The parliamentary influence of the Native vote will become far more important than it has been in the past. In fact, in many a parliament of the future this Native representation may be the balancing factor, with a power out of all proportion to its comparatively small numbers. Where the other parties are more or less equal in numbers, the real political power in the country will be wielded by the separate Native representation. The establishment of a Native block vote, the segregation of the Native vote *inside the white parliament*, with its consequent consolidation and independence, may thus become a matter of the most serious and far-reaching importance for South Africa as a whole. Can we face this, and can we afford to take this leap into the dark? The government are evidently impressed with the dangers of the situation and wish to limit the power of the Native representatives in the two respects mentioned above. But is that sufficient? Is this precaution not really futile? The government proposal to exclude the seven Native members from votes of confidence presupposes that future governments will be independent of them, and have proper and fair parliamentary majorities without them. But this may often not be the case. It may often happen that the government will be dependent on their vote, indeed so dependent that it could not do without them, and will only suffer defeat by their exclusion from the vote. And here their power will come in; they will be able to dictate their policies; they will be in a position to bargain and sell their support in order to keep a weak parliamentary government going, and the government they support will not dream of excluding them from any vote of confidence. No, the precaution taken in the bill is quite futile. To make it effective the bill should go on to make the provision (admittedly absurd) that in no case shall there be a government unless it has a fair parliamentary majority independent and exclusive of the members for Natives. In fact, this whole attempt to safeguard the position by creating two classes of members of parliament is futile and ineffective. If a member of parliament may vote on the budget or any other measure coming before parliament, you do not really curb his influence and power by excluding him from votes of confidence. And a government with a small parliamentary majority will come to terms with him, without inflicting on him the indignity of excluding him from a vote. Not even the attempt to keep down the Native representation to seven members will succeed in such a case. If Native opinion for an increase is strong enough, and the parliamentary majority weak enough, the seven Native representatives will, even without their vote in parliament, influence a government dependent on them to bend to Native wishes. Once make the Natives a real independent political force in parliament, as this bill does, and it becomes impossible to draw the line at any particular representation in future, and to say to the Natives: thus far and no farther. It is the first step now taken which counts; and no conditions or limitations will really prove effective in the long run and no precaution could undo the fatal initial blunder. The number seven has nothing sacrosanct or mystic about it; it is an arbitrary figure resting on no basis of principle. Just as it is fixed today at seven for political reasons, so any other higher figure may in future be similarly adopted for other political reasons. Let us act open-eyed and not deceive ourselves. Dividing members of parliament into two classes with different voting power will in the end fail to achieve its objects. The country must make up its mind whether it is or is not safe enough to make the Native an independent political power in the parliament of the country. If that is a dangerous step, as the government seem to think, the danger cannot be warded off by limiting the voting power of the Native representatives in certain respects. This position is final and there is no arguing round it. If it is necessary to limit the votes of the separate Native representatives in parliament, then it is too dangerous to have them there at all, and some other way out must be explored. It is a parliamentary monstrosity to have two sets of members in parliament with two sets of rights and powers. And the monstrosity will be futile and ineffective for the purpose for which it is intended. There can be no effective distinction in the powers and privileges of members of parliament, and if equality would be too dangerous in the interests of the country, then the proposals of the government for separate Native representatives in parliament are too dangerous and should be abandoned. That is the simple sense as well as the logic of the situation.

(d) Native danger in Cape Province.

What is the policy behind these far-reaching changes? The prime minister said at Smithfield[1] that the position is dangerous at the Cape, where the Native vote already holds the balance in twelve seats, and that if action is not taken in time, the situation for white South Africa may be lost within fifty years. The question is whether this danger at the Cape justifies the extension of another undefined danger throughout the Union. And another question is whether the position is really so bad at the Cape as it is painted. Certainly the type of representative whom the Native voter has sent to parliament in conjunction with the European voters has been no danger to the European position in South Africa. And if the representatives of the twelve constituencies to which General Hertzog referred are passed in review, it will be found that in political outlook or capacity they do not differ in any real sense from the rest of the parliamentary representatives of the Cape Province. So far the Cape system has failed to produce the dangers which have frightened the prime minister. Nor have the numbers of Native voters grown to any alarming extent. Although the Natives have had the parliamentary franchise since the original grant of representative institutions to the Cape, the number of Native voters at Union was only 6,633. Since Union the white voters at the Cape have increased by 35,185 (from 121,346 in 1910 to 156,331 in 1926) while the Native

---

[1] See supra, p. 254, note 1.

voters have only during the same period increased by 7,549 (from 6,633 in 1910 to 14,182 in 1926). Since 1923 only 334 additional Natives have acquired the vote. If in more than seventy years the Native vote has only grown to 14,182, we need not be unduly alarmed at the prospect for the next generation. It is clear from General Hertzog's repeated statements that he is above all anxious to get rid of the Native vote at the Cape, and in order to achieve this end he is even prepared to embark on a Native policy for the whole of the Union the results of which no man can foresee. If the Native voters have not increased unduly at the Cape during three-quarters of a century, and if they have in no real sense abused or been unworthy of their political rights one fails to understand what the policy is behind the prime minister's proposals. It cannot be statesmanship to take a step which not only violates the intention of the South Africa Act, but is also calculated to upset the Native mind more than any other step ever taken in our history.

IV. *Coloured representation in parliament*

(a) The exclusion of Indians.

The bill dealing with this subject provides that the political rights of Indians shall remain as at present, unaffected by the proposals embodied in the new bills. There are 2,034 Asiatics registered as voters in the Cape Province, and 26 in Natal, none in the other two provinces. There are 20,657 Coloured people registered as voters in the Cape Province, 326 in Natal and none in the two other provinces. The vast bulk of the Indian population of the Union is resident in Natal and the Transvaal where they are without political rights, and the question arises on what principle political representation is to be given to the Natives and the Coloured people in those provinces, but not to those Indians (about 60 to 70 per cent of the total Indian population) who have been born there and are permanently settled there. We have to consider the new policy with open eyes and from all points of view, and with a view not only to the actual present proposals, but also their implications for the future. If the Coloured people and the Natives obtain political rights in the northern provinces on what principle could we in the long run defend the exclusion of South African born Indians from such rights? Whatever we do now should be done with a full appreciation of the inevitable future consequences. It may be too late to try and retrace our steps hereafter. In this respect the present proposals raise very serious questions, especially for Natal.

(b) Coloured parliamentary representatives.

In the Cape Province the Coloured voters will continue to vote with the Europeans as heretofore in the various constituencies. But in the other three provinces the future Coloured voters will, for seven years and until parliament has otherwise resolved, vote for one white representative in parliament, the three provinces being taken as one constituency for the purpose of electing this Coloured representative. He will have the same rights and powers in parliament as the representatives of the European voters. After seven years parliament can by resolution decide that this separate constituency for Coloured people shall be abolished and that the Coloured voters in all the provinces shall vote with the European voters in their various electoral constituencies. It will be very difficult for parliament not to pass this resolution after seven years, if the policy of the government is now adopted. The adoption of the new policy by the country now would mean that the separate Coloured constituency for the three northern provinces is only a temporary expedient, and after seven years the Coloured voters in the northern provinces will join in every constituency with the European voters in electing members for parliament.

What the number of Coloured voters in the northern provinces will be no one knows. There will be no franchise qualifications in the Transvaal and the Free State, and any Coloured male of twenty-one and over who can read and write in a simple way will be registered as a voter. The number at present will not be large, and the policy must be judged, not so much from its present effects, as from its future implications and results.

(c) The Coloured list.

The new policy involves that there will be a new colour bar in South Africa. The bill called the Coloured Persons Rights Bill provides that a commission shall be appointed to erase all Native names from the existing voters rolls and to compile a new list of Coloured persons for the whole of the Union. This list will govern the political rights of the Coloured people in future. No Coloured person, whether at the Cape or in any other province of the Union, will in future be registered as a voter unless he passes the civilization test and his name is first put on this new Coloured list. If his name is on this list and in addition he passes the severer education test prescribed in this bill and also possesses the qualifications necessary for parliamentary voters under the law of his province, he will be put also on the register of voters. It is clear that interesting situations may arise in connection with the new Coloured list. Many a Coloured person with a preponderance of white blood who has hitherto by courtesy passed as a white will in future have to run the gauntlet of the Coloured list if he wishes to preserve his political rights. Perhaps also many a person who has hitherto been accepted as unquestionably white will, because of some disaster in the past, be caught in the colour definition of the new bill, and will have to undergo the mortification of figuring on the Coloured list. The Coloured list may become a terrible ordeal for many. The Coloured people at the Cape, who have been repeatedly told by the prime minister and other leaders that they will in future be completely taken up into the white community, will instead find themselves pilloried in a new Coloured list. The official memorandum issued by the prime minister with the publication of his bills, says on this point: 'For the first time in the history of the Union a statute lays down unequivocally the principle of political equality as between the European and the Coloured population.' The irony of this statement is seen in the separate Coloured constituency for the interior, in the inability under this statute of a Coloured person to sit in parliament, in the two differential education and civilization tests applied to Coloured voters, and last but not least, in the new Coloured list of the Union, on which every male Coloured person of twenty-one years and over will have to figure. The bill provides that the original Coloured list for the Union will be compiled by a commission of a judicial character with full power to enquire into anybody's present or past or pedigree; and in future the list will be kept up to date by district committees under the chairmanship of the local resident magistrate.

(d) The definition of Colour.

The most extraordinary provision of this bill is however its definition of Coloured persons. In the first place 'Coloured' person is a person born before the bill becomes law; there will be no more Coloured persons after the act, unless parliament by resolution declares a person a Coloured person. Miscegenation in future will have no effect in adding to the Coloured population so far as this bill is concerned. A Coloured person born before the act is a Coloured person; a Coloured person born after the act is a Native, unless parliament specially declares him a Coloured person!

This absurd and arbitrary distinction shows that the government are really doubtful of the Coloured policy they are recommending to the country, and that they wish to call a halt at a point where a halt is clearly impossible. The definition of a 'Coloured person' in this bill is made to depend on that of a Native, while that of

a Native is again hedged round with qualifications in such a way
that it requires a skilled metaphysician to make out what a
'Coloured person' is. Generally one may say that the term will
include, besides Cape Malays, any person born before the act of
parents, both Coloured, or one of whom is a Native or Coloured
person and the other is a European, as well as the offspring of such
unions born before the act. Besides, the person must wish to be
considered a Coloured person, and the government commission
must be satisfied that his language, associations, and habits of life
are more like those of the Cape Coloured people than those of the
Natives. Thus the practically black child of a Coloured mother and
a Native father born before the act and complying with the
civilization test will be a Coloured person with a practically white
status, while a practically white child of a white father and Coloured
mother born *after* the act will in any case be a Native with Native
status, unless parliament declares him a Coloured person. A boy
born before the act is Coloured; his brother born after the act is
a Native. Incredible as this may appear it is yet the outcome of the
definition in this bill. It is surely impossible to keep up this grotesque
distinction between the effects of miscegenation before and after
the act, and any political provision for Coloured people will have
to be the same for all alike. Otherwise (as miscegenation will continue in any case) there will in future be a class of people in all
respects alike and indistinguishable, some of whom will yet be
Coloured people with a more or less white status, and others will
be Natives with the status of Natives. And it will all depend on the
accident whether their forefathers were born before or after the
act! These childish distinctions are really quite impossible. Equally
childish is it to suppose that parliament will be bothered to give
serious attention to long lists of people who apply to be declared
Coloured people! The white people of the Union will have honestly
and frankly to make up their minds whether they confer the superior white status on all Coloured people without distinction now
and hereafter throughout the Union, or whether the risks of such
a policy are too grave and whether it is wise to wait and see whether
miscegenation is or is not on the wane in the Union. Whatever action
is taken let it be honest and defensible in principle and not based
on untenable subterfuges and evasions which could not be maintained in the long run. The Coloured people at the Cape will also
have to consider what guarantee there will remain for their rights in
future, once the entrenchments of section 35 of the South Africa
Act are abolished. The bill repeals this section, and in future a bare
parliamentary majority can do with the Coloured franchise what

it likes. It cannot be said that this bill offers them an honest square deal.

V. *The Union Native council*

This bill is an immense extension of the policy which has been followed in recent years and which is embodied in the Native act of 1920. In this act the Transkei precedent of Native local councils for purely local affairs was followed and a fairly liberal scheme of local Native government for Native areas was laid down. This act made provision also for the holding of annual conferences or pitsos, to which the government could invite Native chiefs and other representative Natives to deliberate over Native matters and advise the government as to the general trend of Native feeling. The present bill gives a much more formal character to this conference, and gives it a definite constitution and a very wide and vague scope of authority. The new council will consist of fifty Native members, thirty-five of whom will be elected for three years, while the remaining fifteen will be appointed by the government. The chairman will be the secretary for Native affairs or an officer of that department who will frame and enforce the rules of debate and procedure. Of the elected members ten will come from each of the provinces of the Cape, Natal and the Transvaal, while five will come from the Free State. The division of each Native parliamentary constituency into five areas will therefore give the necessary number of thirty-five Native constituencies. The electors will be the selected list of headmen, chiefs and other representative Natives who form the parliamentary electors for Native representation in parliament. Of the nominated members five will be nominated by the government for the Cape, four for Transvaal and Natal each, and two for the Free State.

The authority of the Native council will be to deliberate and pass resolutions on all matters affecting the social, economic or industrial condition of the Natives, to consider any proposed legislation specially affecting Natives which is to come before the Union parliament, and to consider any matter submitted to it by the government or the minister of Native affairs. Besides, parliament may delegate to the council any matter which solely affects the Natives of the Union or part of it, and in such a case the council may, on the initiative of the minister of Native affairs, pass valid ordinances on such matters binding Natives only. It is difficult to see what such matters could be affecting only the Natives. Does Native taxation affect only them? Do pass laws affect only them? Does Native education affect only them? Still, crude and ill-digested as this bill is, it will be well worth the while of parliament to endeavour to put it into shape and make of it as far as possible a workmanlike and workable measure. At any rate it is a measure to which the South African party could, with many reservations and amendments, give its discriminating support. I would have preferred the development of local Native councils under the act of 1920 before beginning another great change. But if the government are determined to make this change without further delay we should be prepared to make the best of it and amend it so as to become a safer and more practical measure than it is at present.

VI. *Conclusions*

The four government bills embodying their Native and Coloured policy have now been discussed and analysed, and the question arises what should be the attitude of the South African party to them. They deal with matters which are vital to the future of this country as a European civilization and embody principles which, if they turn out to be wrong, must work fatal and irremediable mischief in the future. In such circumstances an attitude of caution and reserve becomes imperative—an attitude all the more incumbent on us in view of the compromise come to in the South Africa Act after incredible difficulty. Although a waiting policy may have its dangers, they cannot be compared to the fatal consequences which may arise from undue haste and precipitation.

The misgivings and doubts of the government are revealed by their absurd definition of Coloured persons and their delaying any real settlement of the Coloured franchise for seven years at least. They are revealed also by the dangerous power given to the government to nominate the Native voters who are to elect the seven Native representatives, and by the attempt to give Native representatives in parliament an inferior status and thus to introduce another colour bar into parliament. In view of these doubts and fears and misgivings, and of the complexity and obscurity of the whole position, and the risk of grave and fatal blundering in matters of far-reaching national importance, it would be wise to abandon all idea of passing the two Native and Coloured rights bills at once, and instead to devote the next few years to a thorough exploration of the whole question in all its bearings.

The proper course would appear to be for the government at this stage either to call a small National convention as was suggested last year or preferably to appoint a strong commission of inquiry into the subject matter of these two bills on Native and Coloured representation in parliament, on which fair representation should be given, not only to the parliamentary parties, but also to those sections of the public who take a deep and intelligent interest in Native and Coloured affairs. A well-balanced representative commission, somewhat on the lines of the Native affairs commission of 1903–5, will be able to investigate and report on the difficult and important question: in what form and to what extent political rights can be wisely and usefully extended to the Native and Coloured peoples in the northern provinces. And parliament in eventually dealing with the matter will have before it ample information and argument to help it to come to a statesmanlike conclusion. If ever there was a subject on which the collection and sifting and reasoned weighing of information is necessary before action is taken it is the two bills under discussion.

There remain the Land Bill and the Council Bill, which are not similarly subject to fundamental objections in principle, and which are capable of amendment and improvement in important respects. These two bills might be proceeded with if the government so desire, and the South African party should be ready to render all possible assistance in amending them into fair measures of reform.

The Land Bill in its present form is an uncalled-for reversal of General Botha's segregation policy. At the same time it gives no substantial relief to the acute land position among the Natives. It is highly doubtful whether the committee areas of ten years ago are still practicable. It is also certain that no fair and proper use is made of the present Native areas under the very primitive agricultural methods in vogue. The bill should provide for a thorough reform in this respect, and the government should retain the power of expropriating private land taken in the bill or settling crown land with Natives in the vicinity of Native areas whenever such a course is necessary. The continuous and growing influx of Natives to the towns, which is the most unsatisfactory feature of present Native developments, should be dealt with, the powers of repatriation or exclusion under the Urban Areas Act[1] should, if necessary, be strengthened and enforced, and the repatriated Natives should, if land is not available in the scheduled areas, be settled in their neighbourhood on land acquired by the government for the purpose. The phenomenal migration of the Natives to the towns arises from a variety of causes and this evil should be met at the source by improving agricultural methods in the existing reserves and enlarging them in necessary cases under powers of expropriation

[1] The Natives (Urban Areas) Act of 1923, passed during the premiership of Smuts, contained measures to control the influx of Natives into the towns and provide for their housing in urban locations established by local authorities.

given to the government. The bill should also provide that in this expropriation the principle of segregation should be maintained to the fullest extent. On such expropriated or crown land the Natives would be able to pay an economic rent to the government for their holdings, while they would in most cases be unable to command the necessary capital for purchasing whole farms or blocks of farms in released areas. It would also be necessary to revise radically the far too onerous licensing provisions for squatters and the like, contained in the bill. If the private farms did not absorb a large portion of our Native population the Native land situation would soon become intolerable and possibly lead to trouble. The above improvements would help to make of the Land Bill a useful measure. Indeed, a land bill on these lines is a matter of great urgency.

It is not necessary here to go into the question of how the council can be improved. It is a very difficult matter, and a wrong council may easily be a hot-bed for agitation and Bolshevism among the Natives, who are at present orderly and law-abiding. But parliament in its wisdom may be able largely to redraft it and to make of it a political institution which would for many years to come satisfy the political aspirations of the Natives, and afford them genuine opportunities of administrative and legislative training. If the Native council is made a wise and practical institution for the ventilation of the Native point of view, it may go far to make them look to it rather than to parliament as an outlet for their political activities. This would in any case be far preferable to the proposal for a Native block vote in parliament which has above been criticized. While the general Native council would have its dangers at this early stage of Native political development it might prevent the still greater dangers which one may anticipate as the result of giving them separate parliamentary representation.

A good workable land bill and a fair council bill would be a very substantial measure of advance for the present; and the other two exceedingly contentious measures could stand over for careful inquiry and reflection. A few years of serious public thought and inquiry devoted to them would be well spent and by no means lost time.

205   From F. S. Malan   Vol. 36, no. 18

> Mount Pleasant
> Oranjezicht
> Kaapstad
> 21 August 1926

Geagte Vriend, Gister het ek die geleentheid gehad om jou memorandum met Burton te bespreek. Hy sal direk aan jou sy opinie meedeel. Ons kom oor die algemeen ooreen dat dit 'n goeie kritiek van Hertzog se skema is. Ek sou jou egter die volgende punte in oorweging wil gee:

1. Dit is nie wenslik om die hele dokument te publiseer nie—veral die deel wat betrekking het op die party-politiek sou ek liewer nie in 'n offisiele dokument wil sien nie.

2. Sal dit nie goed wees om *die hele* stemreg-kwessie na 'n Kommissie te verwys nie: blanke, vroue, gekleurde, naturelle, asiate? Dit lyk my die land het opvoeding op die hele kwessie nodig.

3. Sal dit nie nodig wees om 'n vergadering van die hoofbestuur te belê om die saak te bespreek nie? Ek dink dit sal goed wees om die basis van ons memo so breed te maak as moontlik.

Persoonlik is ek bereid om 'n meer positieve lyn te neem as wat in die memo. uitgedruk is. Soos jy weet is ek vir 'n algemene stemreg vir die hele Unie, met 'n besondere 'beskawingstoets' vir die non-Europeane.

Ek erken egter dat die land nog nie ryp is vir 'n algemene oplossing nie—ek glo ook nie dat 'n 'klein nasionale konvensie' nou al 'n oplossing wat aanneembaar is sal kan ontwerp nie—daarom is die idee van 'n kommissie vir my aannemelik. Dit is my meer te doen om die publieke opinie op te voed en te konsentreer, as om juis 'n rapport van die kommissie te kry.

Ek sien hul het jou vergadering op Joh[annes]burg laat misluk—altans dit was hul bedoeling. Die uitskel politiek is 'n teken van swakheid. Met groete *t.t.*

F. S. Malan

TRANSLATION

> Mount Pleasant
> Oranjezicht
> Cape Town
> 21 August 1926

Dear Friend, I had the opportunity yesterday of discussing your memorandum with Burton. He will give you his opinion directly. On the whole we agree that it is a good criticism of Hertzog's scheme. But I should like to put the following points to you for consideration:

1. It is not desirable to publish the whole document—especially the section which refers to party politics I would rather not see in an official document.

2. Would it not be well to refer the *whole* franchise question to a commission—whites, women, Coloureds, Natives, Asiatics? It seems to me the country needs educating on the whole question.

3. Will it not be necessary to call a meeting of the central executive to discuss the matter? I think it would be well to make the basis of our memorandum as broad as possible.

Personally I am prepared to take a more positive line than is expressed in the memorandum. As you know I am for a general franchise for the whole Union, with a special 'civilization test' for the non-Europeans.

But I admit that the country is not yet ripe for a general solution —I also do not think that a 'small National convention' will already be able to devise an acceptable solution—thus the idea of a commission is acceptable to me. I am more concerned to educate and concentrate public opinion than actually to get a report from the commission.

I see that they wrecked your meeting in Johannesburg—at least, that was their intention. The politics of abuse is a sign of weakness. With good wishes, *totus tuus*,

F. S. Malan

206 To S. G. Millin

Vol. 102, no. 2

Irene
[Transvaal]
1 October 1926

Dear Mrs Millin, I found *The South Africans*[1] more exciting and interesting than any of your novels, and that is saying a good deal. I read it through from cover to cover at one sitting, and wish to send you my congratulations on as fine a bit of work as I have read for many a day. I like the style, with its short and simple and almost colloquial sentences, inset with unforgettable vignettes of South African life and scenery. The historical introduction was like galloping over the veld; it made one realize the magic of your treatment.

---

[1] Published in 1926.

The *wacht-een-beetjie*[1] touch with which you start is wonderfully appropriate; I could wish you had returned to it at the very close after dealing with the Native problem. In many senses it is really the last word of wisdom on that subject.

I am very grateful for the references to General Botha. And I am also well satisfied with what you say about myself. I find all you say in this regard inspired by sincerity and kindness and there is also high praise, for which I am grateful. But I doubt whether you are right in attributing indecent haste to Botha and myself in the conciliation policy. We could not sit on the fence and await developments. We *had* to choose, and our choice has meant the apparent miracle of the new South Africa. We made it impossible then for Hertzog and his friends to carry out their ideas when their chance of power came.

On the Native question you have spoken with adequate information and much judgment and sympathy. Of course your role as an artist is to put the subject in its own great setting, without attempting to apply solutions. And in this you have admirably succeeded.

And you have brought out the wonder and the charm of this great country, as nobody has done since Olive Schreiner. And over Olive you have this advantage that you are calmer and saner, while she, with all her intense vehemence, often fails to give the right perspective. South Africa is and remains a mystery, and this you have well brought out. As the ambassador said of the young Catherine of Russia: 'What an awful future is written on that brow!' You have shown yourself willing to write on so great a subject. And greater praise I could not give you.

Once more my hearty congratulations. Ever yours sincerely,

J. C. Smuts

207   Speech (1926)   Box H, no. 45

Smuts delivered this address on 26 October 1926 when the ashes of Emily Hobhouse were buried at the foot of the Vrouemonument in Bloemfontein which commemorates the women and children who died in concentration camps during the Anglo-Boer War.

We are gathered here today from every part of South Africa to pay our last tribute of respect and love to the memory of Emily Hobhouse. It was her wish that her ashes should be buried in this land,

---

[1] Common name of a thorny bush or tree. S. G. Millin had found the name, meaning 'wait a bit', expressive of the South African attitude to 'the question of the black man' (p. 5).

should become part and parcel of the land where the best service of her life had been rendered. She now becomes one with us everlastingly. In life, in the greatest moments of our history we were together, and in death we shall not be divided,[1] but be united for ever.

It was the strong wish of Emily Hobhouse during the later years of her life to come back to us in South Africa, even if it were only for a visit. She often told me that personally, and in her last letters to me she again expressed the wish that the state of her health might yet permit her to undertake the difficult journey. It was not to be. But her heart was always with us; and now dear mother Africa will fold the remains of her adopted daughter to her bosom for ever in the last loving embrace.

In full health and strength she came to us in the dark days of 1901; she finally left us ten years after with shattered body and suffering from an illness from which she never recovered. During those ten eventful years she gave to us all she had; she gave her health and she poured out her soul. But her work and her sacrifice have not been in vain. Her work for us has produced enduring results, and her name and memory will remain inseparably connected with our history.

It is not necessary for us today to discuss the sad events which first brought Emily Hobhouse to our shores. After twenty-five years they are still vivid in the minds of this generation, most of whom in one form or another, took part in those events. War is at best a terrible business, and during the last twelve years we have seen war at its worst; we have seen hell let loose on earth among the Christian nations of the old motherlands of European civilization. By the side of the sufferings and tortures endured during the Great War our South African war of twenty-five years ago looks small and mild in comparison. We can today see the events of the Anglo-Boer War in a larger truer perspective. We have seen the influenza epidemic[2] carry off in a few weeks more lives than were lost in the whole course of the Boer War. We have been submerged and almost drowned in such world-wide calamities in recent years that our senses have been dulled; we have been stunned, and our sense of the sacredness of life is no longer what it was in the more peaceful time of the nineteenth century. To our small handful of whites in South Africa human life has always appeared specially precious, and the grievous and avoidable loss of child life in the concentra-

---

[1] 'Saul and Jonathan were lovely and pleasant in their lives, and in their death they were not divided...' 2 *Samuel* i. 23.

[2] The pandemic of 1918.

tion camps came as a terrible shock. A wrong policy had been
adopted by the military authorities, with results which were never
foreseen nor intended, but which threatened to decimate a whole
generation in the life of the people. It was at that dark hour that
Emily Hobhouse appeared. We stood alone in the world, friendless
among the peoples, the smallest nation ranged against the mightiest
Empire on earth. And then one small hand, the hand of a woman,
was stretched out to us. At that darkest hour when our race almost
appeared doomed to extinction she appeared as an angel, as a
heaven-sent messenger. Strangest of all, she was an Englishwoman.
It was providential, both for the immediate crisis and for the
after history of South Africa, that this great work should be done
by an Englishwoman. She could speak to her people, even in that
hour when the passions of war and of patriotism ran high. She
spoke the word, it was heeded by the British government, reforms
were instituted, and the young life, which was ebbing away in the
camps, was saved for the future. The precious little vessel which
was carrying the future of this subcontinent did not perish in the
storm. That great service—great beyond all power of words to
express it—was rendered by Emily Hobhouse, and for that service
the name of this Englishwoman will be for ever engraved in the
hearts and the memories of the Boer people.

She rendered other services to us. After the war she came to live
and work among us and taught home industries to our daughters.
In part this work still survives among us, and I only regret that the
conditions of life in this country have prevented her spinning and
weaving industry from becoming the general practice in the homes
on the veld. But here, too, important results of her work remain.
And the example of steadfast courage she set us was an inspiration
to many who did not join her spinning schools. Her service here
was great and her labour so hard that in the end it permanently
ruined her health. But to me her great signal service was rendered
not in that after-war period, but in connection with reform of the
concentration camps during the war.

I have not time to refer to her later activities before, during and
after the Great World War. The last remains of her health and
strength she spent in Germany, in succouring women and children
who were suffering and hungry, and living amid the terrible conditions at the end of the Great War. Her name is great and
reverenced not only in South Africa but in thousands of homes on
the continent of Europe.

Let me conclude with two brief remarks, which I feel sure will
also express the mind and ideals of Emily Hobhouse as I knew her

in life. Two great impressions remain with me from her life and work.

The first impression is that of the power and profound influence of women in the affairs of the world. The life of Emily Hobhouse is a striking instance of this power. Here was a great war in which hundreds of thousands of men were engaged, in which the greatest Empire on earth was exerting all its strength and force. And an unknown woman appears from nowhere, and presses the right button; and the course of our history in South Africa is permanently altered. For the future of South Africa the whole meaning and significance of the Anglo-Boer War was permanently affected by this Englishwoman. And she becomes the great symbol of reconciliation between two closely kin peoples who should never have been enemies.

How often in the great happenings of history, a woman appears at the decisive moment, and in her weakness turns the flowing tide of events! It is the inner spiritual force in the world which comes to the surface in pain and anguish and sorrow. And once it appears everything else shrinks into insignificance before it. In the end the spiritual values of life are supreme.

My second thought takes me back to the words of another Englishwoman spoken in the Great War. I refer to Edith Cavell's dying words before she was shot as a spy: 'Patriotism is not enough'. To me that statement has always seemed the truest utterance of the World War—in some respects greater than the speeches of President Wilson on which a bleeding world hung spellbound. It expresses the deepest meaning and message of that unparalleled tragedy for the future of the world: Patriotism is not enough. Great and noble and pure an emotion as it is, it is not enough. And if patriotism alone is going to be our rule and guide in the future, the world will surely perish just as it almost perished from patriotism in the Great War. It is a lesson which we Boer people should specially lay to heart. As a very small people that has suffered much at the hands of history, we are prone to exalt the virtue of patriotism above everything else. Let us not forget Emily Hobhouse. She was an Englishwoman to the marrow, proud of her people and its great mission and history. But for her patriotism was not enough. When she saw her country embark on a policy which was in conflict with the higher moral law, she did not say: 'My country right or wrong'.[1] She wholeheartedly took our side against that of her own people, and in doing so rendered an im-

---

[1] Said by Stephen Decatur (1779–1820). *See* his biography by A. S. Mackenzie, chapter 14.

perishable service, not only to us, but also to her own England and to the world at large.

For this loyalty to the higher and greater things of life she suffered deeply. Her action was not understood or appreciated by her own people. But to us her example makes a special appeal. Emily Hobhouse will stand out in our record as a trumpet call to the higher duty, to our duty and loyalty to the great things which do not merely concern us as a nation, but which bind together all nations as a great spiritual brotherhood. The Roman emperor[1] has put in unforgettable words the difference between this narrower patriotism and the wider loyalty which we owe to the great human ideals: 'The poet hath said: dear city of Cecrops, and shall we not say, dear City of God?' More than anything in our history the example of Emily Hobhouse reminds us that we are not merely citizens of South Africa, but that we belong also and above all to the greater City of God.

208   To F. C. Kolbe   Vol. 36, no. 213

Irene
[Transvaal]
28 October 1926

Dear Dr Kolbe, What a pleasure it was to get and read your letter! You evidently understand the idea I have been labouring at because you have been living in its atmosphere, so to say. That is a wonderful quotation which you give from St Thomas,[2] and if I had been aware of it, I would have used it as a motto for the book. Several of my passages seem to be literally translations of Thomas's great thought. I am very grateful for what you say, because you clearly *understand* it all. So many letters I get leave the impression that the fundamental notion has not yet been grasped.

No, I fear the *Kerkbode*[3] will not approve of *Holism*, and soon

---

[1] Marcus Aurelius.

[2] In a letter of 23 October 1926 (Smuts Collection, vol. 36, no. 3A) Kolbe had written: 'Doesn't this sentence appeal to you—from Thomas Aquinas—*Forma substantialis totius non superadditur partibus, sed est totum complectens materiam et formam cum praecisione aliorum*'.† Or again—*Anima est actus corporis organici* (i.e. the actuation of an organized body). Or again—*Anima rationalis est tota in toto, et tota in qualibet parte corporis sui.*'‡ († Nothing is added to the whole of the substantial form by the parts that constitute it, but it is the whole that embraces both the content and form while maintaining the precision of the different parts that constitute the whole. ‡ The rational soul is as a whole in the whole [body] and as a whole in every part of the body to which it belongs.)

[3] *De Kerkbode* became in 1894 the organ of the Nederduitse Gereformeerde Kerk, the largest of the three Dutch Reformed Churches in South Africa. *See* vol. I, p. 72.

some heresy hunt will be instituted. I don't mind. I *know* that the book has brought me close to the great spiritual values. Catholic mysticism is simply one particular version of holism in the spiritual sphere.

I wish you all possible luck on the flag commission.[1] But I fear you will have very little *dans cette galère*.[2] However, you are actuated by good will. And according to Kant there is nothing else good in the world.

Good-bye, my friend. With kind regards and best wishes, Ever yours sincerely,

J. C. Smuts

Thank you very much for your book,[3] which I shall read carefully.

209   To A. B. Gillett   Vol. 36, no. 257

Irene
[Transvaal]
10 November 1926

I owe you now a reply to two letters. But as a rule I touch on your points in the letters to Margaret which you also see. So that there is no harm or discourtesy. But I always love to get your letters. They bring us close together, they bring you very close to me.

I am glad you are interested in *Holism*. Nor apparently is it merely the interest of the wild guffaws of laughter with which you greeted some chapters in MS. You now realize that it is not all a huge joke. I sometimes myself wonder whether it is not really at bottom a huge unconscious joke. We know so little; our poor human thought and language are so totally inadequate to measure up the great mysteries of our existence, that our attempts at explanation may in the end prove nothing more than idle childish babblings. And yet I feel that *Holism* is a sincere groping towards the spiritual core of things. Proceeding along scientific and philosophic lines, I find no God of Theology at the end. But I say and recognize explicitly that the Divine Ideal rests on other grounds and other evidence. Science and philosophy will not unlock the great Door, but they may bring us right up to the threshold. Whether you can

---

[1] A new commission to advise the government in the selection of a design for a national flag had been appointed. The chairman was Sir William Campbell and the members included Professor W. Blommaert, Sir George Cory, Professor J. J. Smith, Mrs E. G. Jansen and Dr F. C. Kolbe. (*See* D. F. Malan, *Afrikaner Volkseenheid*, pp. 114–16.)

[2] In that company.   [3] *The Mysteries of the Christian Religion.*

enter into the Great Mystery depends on certain attitudes, certain inner affinities, which alone can draw you in spirit into the Great Kinship of Spirit, the inner mystic union of Holism. On that I say nothing in this book. Perhaps (if I am wise) I shall never say anything at all in writing. But I know this communion from inner experience. And I know that millions through the ages have seen and followed the unseen Inner Light. Some people will think that *Holism* is anti-theistic or godless. I don't think so, nor is that the spirit in which the book was written. That you know.

I am very hard busy[1] with politics and find it a most troublesome world—certainly not of my choosing.

Good-bye, dear Arthur. Is there no business which can bring you out here soon? Ever yours,

Jan

210   From C. Lloyd Morgan   Vol. 36, no. 28A

79 Pevensey Road
St Leonards on Sea
[England]
15 November 1926

Dear Sir, Thank you for the copy of *Holism*. I have read it with all the care it deserves as a remarkably fine bit of work. I'm not going to say anything more about it here and now; for I have been asked to review it in *The Journal of Philosophical Studies*.

Years ago I spent five years at the Cape in the then Diocesan College, Rondebosch[2] under Ogilvie,[3] returning to England in 1883.

I have heard much of you from my wife's nephew, Colonel [H. W.] Madoc, whom you may or may not remember. It does one good to hear the terms in which your junior speaks of his senior. One says: That's a bit of 'all right'!

But I write these few words around the central word of 'thanks'. Of course, there is much in your book with which I don't and can't agree. But I care little for a bit of work to which I am saying 'ditto' all the time. You have given us some real good stuff. Yours gratefully,

C. Lloyd Morgan

[1] Literal rendering of *hard besig* (Afrikaans).
[2] *See* vol. I, p. 30, note 3.
[3] The Reverend Canon George Ogilvie.

211   To M. C. Gillett   Vol. 36, no. 258

Irene
[Transvaal]
17 November 1926

This is Wednesday forenoon; I have just read your mail letter and others; and now I reply to as many as possible, the mail going from here this afternoon. Sir Arnold Theiler is bringing Professor [C.] Schroeter, the Zurich botanist, to spend the afternoon with me, so I shall try to get as far as possible this morning. Besides Schroeter we have also Lotsij [J. P.], the Dutch botanist, here at present. As you know, he is the author of a new theory of evolution (hybridization) which I incidentally criticize in *Holism*. I have asked the dear old man and his daughter to come and stay with us, and I shall be much interested in what he has to say about hybrids, at which he is working hard on the coast at present. I find botany entrancing, but our time is so frightfully limited. And this year it is so exceptionally dry that there is little of interest in the veld. No rains yet, though we have passed the middle of November. Cattle dying everywhere, little mielies sown. A farmer's life is a hard and hazardous one.

Have you seen anything of Hertzog at Oxford?[1] Do you ever see his son? I am interested in what you say about the Macmurrays,[2] I never met them here. I too have the highest opinion of White-head's *Science and the Modern World*. The curious thing is how we were working by different methods at the same problems and arrive at somewhat similar results.

(1) He gets away from the idea of *simple location* by a new analysis of space, I by the introduction of the concept of *fields* from electromagnetism.

(2) He substitutes for the idea of physical mechanism that of *organism* or organic mechanism, while I introduce the more powerful concept of holism. I think it is somewhat misleading and mystifying to speak of an atom or a table as an organism; it tends to confuse things with plants and animals. And again 'organism' scarcely applies to minds and souls and ideals. I therefore think the more generic concept of holism the better solution, and I hope in time it will be found that holism and not organism is the new way of thought. But his book is full of good things, and he speaks with an authority which I of course completely lack. You should

---

[1] General Hertzog was in England to attend the imperial conference of 1926. His son, Albert, was a student at Oxford.

[2] John Macmurray who had been professor of philosophy at the University of the Witwatersrand and his wife, born Elizabeth Hyde Campbell of Umsinga, Natal.

read it—though one reading is not enough, as the language at the critical points is most obscure.

I am glad the coal strike seems over.[1] But I fear it has crippled England for years. And the standards will be lowered. Stupidity does appear a powerful factor in the world. Ever yours,

Jan

212   From G. R. Hofmeyr   Vol. 35, no. 187

Confidential   Welgemeend
Cape Town
6 December 1926

My dear General Smuts, The time has arrived for bringing things to a head on the *hereniging* question and I will accordingly write letters in identical terms to yourself and General Hertzog at an early date.[2] I hope there will be a favourable response.

The Nationalist party leaders, having been swept into the maelstrom of imperialism by the inevitable course of events,[3] may try political expedients to justify their conduct to some bewildered sections of their followers and in an endeavour to score party advantage out of the new situation. [Tielman] Roos spoke perhaps too soon and too emphatically and on reflection will try to extricate himself by abusing the opposition for an imaginary attitude. I see he already predicts that the opposition will be responsible for any friction which may eventuate in consequence of what he regards to be an entirely new constitutional position and there is an echo of the same sentiment in today's issue of *Die Burger*. The declaration was perhaps intended to reconcile Labour on the flag question and thus save the Pact, but even on that score it may prove to have been a doubtful leap. Dr Malan is still more mischievous though amusing; he tells willing ears what must be some of his pet dreams as to the attitude of the opposition on the constitutional issue.

At the same time, it would seem a thousand pities that just at this juncture the flag issue is there to queer the pitch and it would be a great advantage if that weapon could be blunted or smashed by, say, a declaration to the effect that now that the secession issue

---

[1] *See* p. 293 *supra*, note 4.
[2] *See* p. 44 *supra*, note 3. For Hofmeyr's letter *see* Smuts Collection, vol. 35, no. 187. Nothing came of it.
[3] In November 1926 the report of the inter-imperial relations committee of the imperial conference incorporating the 'Balfour declaration' had been issued. The report defined the mutual relation of the members of the British Commonwealth. General Hertzog had played a significant part in securing it.

is dead and buried for good and all the flag question should be left in abeyance in order to give time for calmer and more rational consideration. There should on the merits be less ground for objection to the Union Jack as part of the flag now that South Africa is to remain permanently within the British Empire; at any rate, there would seem to be no ground now for wishing to force a flag, minus the Union Jack, on a section of the people. Naturally a forced flag will never become a national flag—it will remain a party flag and may in consequence prove most dangerous.

I wish you and yours the best of everything for this festive season. Yours very sincerely,

Gys

213   To M. C. Gillett   Vol. 36, no. 263

Irene
[Transvaal]
13 December 1926

The mail which carries this letter will also carry Japie to Cambridge. Unfortunately I shall not be able to see him off at Cape Town, but Isie is going with him. He will arrive the Monday after New Year and Cato, I hope, will meet him either at Southampton or in London and show him the way he should go. I shall advise him to spend a couple of days with you at Oxford before proceeding to Cambridge. I know you will mother him in that strange land and make him feel at home.

I am very glad that I am finished with political meetings till the beginning of January. On 16 December I have to be at Krugersdorp for the Paardekraal ceremony[1] but then I shall avoid politics and refresh my botany of which I have not been able to do much recently. Lotsij, the great Dutch botanist, will lecture at Pretoria at the end of this week and I shall get him and his daughter to stay with us so that I can pick up some hints and suggestions from him. You know he is the man who says that all evolution proceeds by crosses or hybrids. He finds hybrids in plenty in nature where nobody has found them before. I should like to know how he does it, for everything specifically different is for me a species.

We have had an amusing time recently over Hertzog's claim that he is bringing back our 'sovereign international status' from London. The Nats are delighted (or feign to be) and say Hertzog has done what Botha and I could not do. They are even prepared

---

[1] *See* vol. III, p. 426, note 1.

to bury the republic. This is of course all to the good; though I have quietly reminded them that the status is the same against which they have kicked so violently the last six years. Of course, psychologically it makes a great difference to them who has done it; the thing itself does not seem to matter so much. It is all a matter of personal rivalries—to such a pass our politics has come.

I hope you will have a good Christmas and a happy New Year. Give my love to all the little ones of whom I often think lovingly. Perhaps I shall see them next year, but who knows. With love,

Jan

P.S. A. N. Whitehead's *Religion in the Making* (Lowell Lecture 1926).[1]

214   To O. Hobhouse[2]   Vol. 36, no. 220

Irene
Transvaal
18 December 1926

My dear Oliver, Thank you for your kind note which I was very glad to get. It was a great occasion, and we buried her like a Princess.[3]

With kind regards and good wishes to you for the New Year. Ever yours sincerely,

J. C. Smuts

215   To F. S. Malan   Vol. 36, no. 221

Irene
21 December 1926

Waarde Fransie, Dit lyk vir my of ons Engelse vrinde hulle koppe heelmaal verloor oor Hertzog in hul blydskap dat hy nou die Empaaier geloof aangeneem het. Ons het alle rede om versigtig te wees. Hertzog het ons maar baie min indikasie gegee van wat hy werklik bedoel. Hy mag eerlik een nieuwe orientering bedoel. Maar hy mag ook maar net mooi phrases gebruik in sy ingenomenheid met sigself. Ek meen ons moet met alle kalmte en selfs welwillendheid die loop van sake afwag. Is Hertzog bereid om die Vlag te laat staan? Is hy gewillig om te breek met Arbeid? Ons weet niks wat sy werklike bedoeling is nie. Ek het aan Long geskrywe om versigtig te wees, daar dit moontlik is dat ons alleen met een slim

---

[1] Smuts means that M. C. Gillett is to send him this book.
[2] Nephew of Emily Hobhouse.   [3] *See* **207**.

manoever te doen het om die Provinciale Eleksies te wen. Ek hoop
jy sal ook jou invloed gebruik om ons vrinde privaat tot kalmte te
breng. Daar is geen die minste rede tot al die uitbundigheid.

Wel, ek wens jou een aangename Kerstmis en gelukkig Nieuwe
Jaar. Wat dit vir ons sal oplewer weet niemand, en ek voel dat ons
saak sterk genoeg is dat ons met moed en vertroue die toekoms kan
afwag. Hartelike groete, Jou vrind

get. J. C. Smuts

TRANSLATION

Irene
[Transvaal]
21 December 1926

Dear Fransie, It looks to me as if our English friends are completely
losing their heads over Hertzog in their joy at his now having
accepted the Empire faith. We have every reason to be careful.
Hertzog has given us very little indication of what he really means.
He may honestly mean a new orientation. But he may also, in his
self-satisfaction, only be using pretty phrases. I think we must,
quite calmly and even with good will await the course of events.
Is Hertzog prepared to let the flag go? Is he willing to break with
Labour? We know nothing about his real intentions. I wrote to
Long[1] to be careful, as it is possible that we have to do merely with
a clever manoeuvre to win the provincial elections. I hope you also
will use your influence to calm down our friends. There is not the
least reason for all this excessiveness.

Well, I wish you a pleasant Christmas and a happy New Year.
What it will bring for us no one knows, and I feel that our cause is
strong enough for us to await the future with courage and faith.
Best wishes, Your friend,

s. J. C. Smuts

216   To N. Levi   Vol. 36, no. 222

Irene
29 December 1926

Liewe Levi, Ek send terug eenige stukke wat u sal wil behou. Ons
moet die initiatief van Hertzog afwag. My is dit glad nie duidelik
nie wat sy plan is. Ek twyfel of dit Hereeniging is. Heel moontlik
bedoel hy maar weer die oorloopery van laaste jaar toen ek

---

[1] B. K. Long was at this time editor of the *Cape Times. See* vol. I, p. 92, note 2.

vroeg om Toenadering. H[ertzog] sit vas in die slagyser van die Pakt, en hy weet nie hoe daaruit te kom nie. Hartelike groete, *t.t.*

J. C. Smuts

TRANSLATION

Irene
[Transvaal]
29 December 1926

Dear Levi, I return some papers which you will wish to keep. We must wait for Hertzog to take the initiative. It is not at all clear to me what his plan is. I doubt if it is reunion. Very probably he again means merely the going over to the other side which happened last year when I asked for a rapprochement. Hertzog is caught in the snare of the Pact, and he does not know how to get out of it. Best wishes, *totus tuus*,

J. C. Smuts

217   From F. C. Kolbe   Vol. 36, no. 3B

St Mary's
Cape Town
31 December 1926

My dear General Smuts, Please excuse pencil: I dislocated my right arm on Christmas Day—N.B. *before* dinner—and shall not have free use of it for several days yet.

As for the point you refer to,[1] you must please give me time. I have not yet reached the positive exposition of *Holism*. My 'review' seems to be growing into a treatise.[2] The things you omit because you are writing for scientists are precisely the things whose absence would prejudice Catholic students against the book, and my purpose is to persuade Catholic men of intelligence to read the book. We shall not of course agree four-square, but I went one better than your typist. On first reading the book I said to a friend, 'This is a *deeply* religious book'.

I hope to give you reason to think that you might have strengthened your position by not over-emphasizing the isolation of the *cell* in organic wholes, as I think you have done. But you must give me time.

---

[1] The letter from Smuts here referred to is not in the Smuts Collection.

[2] Between 10 November 1926 and 9 March 1927 Kolbe wrote sixteen articles on *Holism and Evolution* for the *Southern Cross*, an organ of the Catholic church in South Africa.

In my article in *The Cape*,[1] which I hope you saw, I said there was one sentence in the book not clear to me. It is not clear yet. It is on page 113, and there seems to me to be an omission of a word or words:

'The field of an organism is its extension beyond its sensible limits, it is the more there is in the organism beyond these limits.'

With regard to one prophecy you make (p. 180), is the 'creative' process necessarily always forward? Do you not foresee the possibility of frigid degeneracy and stagnation for the earth, as perhaps, e.g. for the moon and other planets?

The question of terminology is here as elsewhere in philosophy a trouble. When *we* say 'substantial form', both *substance* and *form* have so many other uses that there is perpetual misunderstanding. The word 'whole' has a similar drawback. I shall wriggle out of that difficulty by occasionally using the word *totum*. A dead language is often the most alive.

I daresay we shall come to grips again in a few weeks' time when our divergences and convergences shall have been more clearly stated. Wishing you a very happy New Year, I am yours most sincerely,

F. C. Kolbe

P.S. It seems a shame to come down from cosmic speculations to political storms, but I cannot help alluding to the 'new' status. I hope I am not over-cynical, but this 'conversion' of Tielman Roos and 'inflation' of Hertzog has a sinister aspect for me. I look upon it as Tielman's latest joke—whose point will appear hereafter in the backveld. I cannot take that man seriously. Shakespeare's 'Triton among the minnows'[2] runs in my head as 'Kilimanjaro among the *kopjes*'. But I wish you had seen your way to accepting the compromise of the crown for the Union Jack.[3] I do not think you will ever bring the Boers to accept the latter. However, this is more your job than mine. Cosmic speculations are on even terms.

F. C. K.

---

[1] A weekly paper established in Cape Town in 1907; ceased publication in 1935. Kolbe's article entitled 'General Smuts's Great Book *Holism and Evolution*' appeared in the issue of 19 November 1926.

[2] 'Hear you this Triton of the minnows? mark you his absolute 'shall'?' *Coriolanus*, III.i.88.

[3] General Hertzog had suggested, as a concession to British sentiment, that a crown be included in the design for a South African national flag instead of the Union Jack (*see* D. F. Malan, *Afrikaner Volkseenheid*, p. 114).

218   To M. C. Gillett   Vol. 39, no. 266

Irene
[Transvaal]
5 January 1927

So the years mount up. What pathetic things we humans are! Like
the *langbeinige Cicada* in *Faust* we make our sudden spurt and then
sink back into the eternal grass to which we belong.[1] This seems
a poor way of welcoming the New Year. But I am bound to confess
that the coming of the New Year is no longer an agreeable prospect
to me. However, let us hope that this particular one will bring us
something good. Japie [Smuts] has just landed in England and has
I hope visited you at Oxford and given you all the local news.
Though he is not a very communicative spirit. I am under
the impression that Cato [Clark] is in Switzerland and will therefore not have met him on arrival. Still he is capable of taking
care of himself. I hope he will be happy at Cambridge and
get out of the place whatever good it can do for his type of
mind.

Your letter has just arrived, thank you. You chide me for not
sending you my memorandum on Hertzog's Native bills.[2] The fact
is that the bills are most difficult to follow for any person not conversant with the details of our Native problem; and my memorandum had reference merely to the bills and did not go into wider
aspects of policy. Both the bills and the memorandum have fallen
flat as few people, except a small number of enthusiasts, have studied
either. We shall come to the parliamentary session and these bills
without the public having any enlightened opinion on the subjects
with which they deal. It is all most disheartening, as on the due
understanding of the Native question the future of our European
civilization on this continent will depend.

Yes, things politically are in great uncertainty. Hertzog and Co.
have adhered to the Empire, have secured the 'independence' of
the country, and the poor efforts of Botha and myself are merely
things to sneer at. It is said that the greatest success is to let your

[1] *Er scheint mir, mit Verlaub von Ew. Gnaden,*
Wie eine der langbeinigen Cicaden,
Die immer fliegt und fliegend springt,
Und gleich im Gras ihr altes Liedchen singt.

He seems to me, with Your Grace's permission,
Like one of the long-legged cicadas
Which always flies and, flying, leaps
And falls back into the grass to sing its old tune.

Goethe, *Faust I, Prolog im Himmel.*

[2] **204.**

own work supersede you;[1] I may claim that sort of success! And perhaps I shall not be needed further. But on these great matters it is always wise to go slow and watch events. For things are not always what they seem, and least in South Africa. One thing is certain—that if I leave politics it will be without regret. I shall have done my bit and leave the rest to another generation. But I shall only go when it is possible to do so with a clear sense of duty. The Lotsij's have left and I go for a week's politics to my constituency. With love to all,

Jan

219   From L. S. Amery   Vol. 37, no. 7

Dominions Office
Downing Street, S.W.
24 January 1927

My dear Smuts, I should much like to have had a talk with you about all that happened at the imperial conference. To attempt to deal with it by letter is, I fear, more than I can do just now. All I would say to sum it up is that we worked very much on the lines which you and I have often discussed in the past and the outcome is, I think, one with which you wholly agree. The effect here on Hertzog was, I think, very great once he realized he was not being met with suspicion or opposition, but simply being invited to make clear what was in his own mind and see how far it really differed in essentials from what the rest of us had in our minds. As to the effect in South Africa, no doubt there is a certain amount of making of political capital connected with it all, but in the main his declarations and those of his colleagues must be to the good and provide a better basis for South Africa's public life in future. If I may say so I was very delighted that you met the matter in so broad and generous a spirit, treating it from the point of view of South African unity and of the future rather than of what was really in fairness due to your own party in the past.

I had many talks with Hertzog about his Native policy. It is the biggest thing before him and I do not see how you can get a reason-

---

[1] Hertzog had based his case in the inter-imperial relations committee at the imperial conference of 1926 on the memorandum prepared by Smuts in 1921 (46) which he had found among the prime minister's papers when he succeeded Smuts in that office. He let it be known in the committee that he was using Smuts's arguments. (*See* H. Duncan Hall, 'The genesis of the Balfour declaration of 1926' in the *Journal of Commonwealth Political Studies*, vol. 1, no. 3, November 1962, p. 173, and C. M. van den Heever, *General J. B. M. Hertzog*, p. 485.)

able policy on party lines when each leader is to some extent at the mercy of the extremer wing of his own party. This is a question which requires a national settlement and I cannot help feeling that Hertzog, at the bottom of his mind, realizes this and would be willing to get on to that basis if an opportunity were offered him. Incidentally I think that if public opinion could get concentrated on a real national settlement of the Native question, people would realize that it is foolish to raise controversy over the flag issue at this moment. However, these are your affairs and you will no doubt find the way out somehow.

I have had three weeks of good exercise and holiday in the Alps. I took *Holism and Evolution* with me but I confess I have not yet got very far though the line of thought interests me very much. Have you read Trevelyan's new *History of England*?[1] It is really a good piece of work. Yours ever,

L. S. Amery

220   From W. S. Churchill   Vol. 37, no. 50

Treasury Chambers
Whitehall, S.W.
21 February 1927

My dear Smuts, Some months ago you sent me a deeply interesting book on philosophy, into which I have peered with awe. I now venture to retaliate by sending you a couple of volumes in which I am sure you will find yourself much more at home.[2]

I follow always the course of your affairs with that enduring sympathy which springs from wartime comradeship. I hope it will not be long before you pay us a visit. You will find a warm welcome awaiting you from your many friends, and from none more than those who with you have faced the battle and the breeze[3] of the twentieth century of the Christian era. Your sincere friend,

Winston S. Churchill

[1] G. M. Trevelyan, *History of England* (1926).
[2] The third part of Churchill's book *The World Crisis* dealing with the period 1916–18 was published in two volumes in 1927.
[3] Thomas Campbell, *Ye Mariners of England*.

221   To N. Levi   Vol. 39, no. 19

Parlement
21 Februarie 1927

Waarde Levi, Dank vir u twee laaste briewe. Die resultate in die Transvaal is nie erg gunstig. Maar daar is die eleksie ook nie geveg nie. Dit lyk my dat van weerskante daar een flaauwe gees was en die Nattes met hul beter organisasie het daaruit die voordeel getrek. In die Kaap en Natal waar die geveg hard was, en die vlag viral die gemoedere gaande gemaakt het is die resultate meer gunstig. My leer dit dat die tyd vir ons nog nie ryp is nie, die platteland siet nog nie die gevaar van die Pakt nie, en dinge moet nog verder gaan om hul te affekteer. Trouens $2\frac{1}{2}$ jaar is nie lang nie.

Van Hereeniging denk ek nie dat iets sal kom nie. Ook is daar vir ons vandag geen nut in. Ons sal as aanhangers van die Nattes met 3 of 4 setels in die Cabinet moet kom en al hul gedane werk insluit. Ons party sal daarvoor bedank. In kaukus is die saak nie geopper nie. Roos het met Oppenheimer gepraat, maar as daar iets in die saak is kan Hertzog met my praat. Maar hy het dit nie gedoen en sal dit ook nie doen.

Dit spyt my dat jy en Louis nie in geduriger kontak bly nie. Jullie moet tweemaal per week minstens saam lunch by die Club of elders om sodoende kontak te hou.

Wat ons organisasie betref is dit sleg op die Rand, maar ek geloof dat op die platteland dinge beter is as hulle lyk. Neem geen pessimistiese beskouing van die situasie. Alleen is dit duidelik dat daar meer tyd nodig is op die platteland. In die stede is daar al een geheele omspring.

Ek sie maar min van die doctor die nou seker druk besig is met sy *magnum opus*.

Jy is altyd so welkom op Doornkloof dat ek vertrou dat jy daar meer dikwels jou Sondae sal deurbring. Hartelike groete *t.t.*

J. C. Smuts

TRANSLATION

Parliament
[Cape Town]
21 February 1927

Dear Levi, Thank you for your last two letters. The results in the Transvaal are not very favourable.[1] But the election was not fought

---

[1] The results of the provincial council elections in the Transvaal were as follows: South African party 19, National party 23, Labour party 8.

there. It seems to me there was a feeble spirit on both sides and the Nats, with their superior organization, benefited from that. In the Cape and Natal where the fight was hard and the flag stirred up strong feeling, the results were more favourable.[1] This teaches me that the time is not yet ripe for us; the rural districts do not yet realize the danger of the Pact and things must go further yet to affect them. Indeed, two-and-a-half years is not long.

I do not think anything will come of reunion. Besides, it is no use to us at present. We should have to go into the cabinet with three or four seats as dependents of the Nats and include all they have already done. Our party would not accept that. The matter has not been raised in caucus. Roos spoke to [Sir Ernest] Oppen-heimer, but, if there is something in the thing, then Hertzog can talk to me. But he has not done so and he will not do so either.

I am sorry that you and Louis [Esselen] are not in more regular contact.[2] You should lunch together at least twice a week at the club[3] or elsewhere in order to keep contact.

As regards our organization, this is bad on the Rand, but I think things are better in the rural districts than they look. Do not take a pessimistic view of the situation. It is merely clear that more time is needed in the rural districts. In the towns there is already a complete turn about.

I see very little of the Doctor who is probably hard at work on his *magnum opus*.[4]

You are always so welcome at Doornkloof that I hope you will spend your Sundays there more often. Best wishes, *totus tuus*,

J. C. Smuts

222   To L. S. Amery   Vol. 39, no. 20

[Cape Town]
22 February 1927

My dear Amery, Thank you very much for your long and interesting letter in reference to the work of the imperial conference. You should not be under the impression that I am other than pleased with the

---

[1] The results in the Cape Province were: South African party 26, National party 21, Independents 3, Labour party 1. In Natal the results were: South African party 20, National party 2, Labour party 1, Independents 2. In the Orange Free State the National party took all the seats (25).

[2] N. Levi was at this time assistant editor of the South African party newspaper *De Volkstem* and Louis Esselen was general secretary of the party.

[3] The Pretoria Club.

[4] Dr F. V. Engelenburg was writing *General Louis Botha* (1929).

results. The recommendations in reference to the constitutional position had indeed become inevitable, and the results, as far as South Africa is concerned, have been highly satisfactory. The ghost of the republic is—for the present at any rate—laid, and there is the reality or the appearance of a more cordial acceptance of the imperial position in quarters where before there was nothing but indifference or downright hostility. This is all to the good and I rejoice at this result. In any case the definition of Dominion status in some formal manner had become overdue, in view of the changes since the peace conference, and I have no fault to find with the expressions used for the purpose. It is, of course, true that here perhaps more than elsewhere attempts have been made to score a party triumph out of this achievement, and the change (if any) has in consequence been exaggerated far beyond its real scope. But this was only to be expected, and has to be dealt with by us locally on the usual party lines. All I wish to say in this connection is this: It would be most mischievous to let the impression take root either in South Africa or Canada that a radical transformation of the Empire has been brought about, and that the Empire in fact has ceased to exist except as a mere collective name. This mischievous impression may easily become the source of new separatist troubles in future. And I think it would be very necessary either for you or the prime minister or both in clear terms to state that the report made no change but simply formulated and declared the existing situation and practice as it had developed since the peace conference. Such an unequivocal declaration would ease the minds of many good and loyal friends of the Empire, and would nip in the bud certain separatist tendencies which I fear will develop to great mischief if we are not careful. I am for full Dominion nationhood and independent status; but I equally recognize the value of the Empire as a whole and the necessity of keeping it intact. Unless both points of view are maintained *pari passu*[1] there is certain to be a one-sided development in the direction of Dominion separatism. But I need not elaborate this point, as no one can more fully realize its importance than you.

The provincial elections in the Cape and Natal (less so in the Transvaal) have gone heavily against the Labour party which is practically extinguished in these provinces. This result is in no small measure due to the Flag Bill and the disappointment with the Labour leaders in this connection. Perhaps this rude reminder may give the government pause in their flag policy. If they proceed with their policy, I foresee a very grave recrudescence of racial feeling.

[1] Equally and together.

I see from the press that you are not likely to come out here this year. This I much regret. At the same time I recognize that it would be somewhat awkward for you to be here when a violent flag campaign or referendum[1] is on in the summer, and it may even lead to misunderstanding. But if the flag is dropped and your work will allow of it, it would be a very good thing from every point of view if you could visit us. With kind remembrances, Ever yours sincerely,

s. J. C. Smuts

I shall read Trevelyan's History. I liked his previous works on Italy[2] very much.

223   To L. S. Amery   Vol. 39, no. 37

Civil Service Club
Cape Town
11 March 1927

My dear Amery, You have sprung several real surprises on me by your last long and interesting letter.[3] I sent you *Holism* as a token of old friendship and thinking that you would look at the preface and stop there with the conclusion that I had got into my dotage. Now I find not only that you have read through the book, but you have even taken the trouble to dissect it critically, and you have even gone the length of developing an alternative view of a most interesting and plausible character. Well, although I will not hope that you may soon have sufficient leisure to write your book on philosophy, I *do* hope that you will write it before the years have sped too far, and that the writing will give you as much pleasure and consolation as the writing of *Holism* gave me. I believe that philosophy is not entirely a matter of studious seclusion but that we who have battled through the storm and stress of life have our own contribution to make. I look forward with deep interest and keen expectation to yours.

I suppose you had a talk with Philip Kerr[4] after his return from South Africa the other day. I have had a good deal of talk with him over the future of the southern half of this continent. I do believe that the eastern plateau from Kenya to the Karoo has the makings

[1] The suggestion that there should be a referendum on the flag question had come from the opposition (*see* D. F. Malan, *Afrikaner Volkseenheid*, p. 117).
[2] G. M. Trevelyan, *Garibaldi and the Defence of the Roman Republic* (1907), *Garibaldi and the Thousand* (1909), *Garibaldi and the Making of Italy* (1911).
[3] Smuts Collection, vol. 37, no. 7.
[4] Afterwards Lord Lothian.

of one of the finest things in the Empire, and has possibilities for white settlement and development which might provide the next great phase of Empire development.

Ormsby Gore's commission[1] was good but did not show sufficient vision. May the great African Empire to come not be looking to *you* to give it a start? Ever yours sincerely,

s. J. C. Smuts

224   To S. M. Smuts   Vol. 39, no. 43

Civil Service Club
Cape Town
18 Maart 1927

Liefste Mamma, Vrydag ogtend. Ons had eergister 'n interessante debat in die Huis omtrent die Imperiale Konferensie en die Status. Hertzog het soas gewoonlik heelmaal sy kop verloor en geskree en te keere gegaan voor een rasende. Ek was maar heel kalm en bedaard en die kontrast was dus al die grooter en sterker. Ek stuur een uit-knipsel uit die *Argus* deur sy gallery man geskrewe wat jou een indruk van die okkasie sal gee. Ek gaan net nou een kaukus hou van ons Kaapse Volksraadslede om hul te vra om vir Fransie Malan as die nuwe senator in plaas van Dr Watkins te stem. Ek sien geen ander kans om hom in die parlement te kry nie. Ons kry geen be-hoorlike vakature in die Volksraad en ek het hom gesê as hy nie na die Senaat gaan kan dit die volle 5 jare duur voor hy weer in die Parlement is. Hy het dus besluit na de Senaat te gaan en dan by die komende Algemeene Eleksie te beslis of hy weer vir die Volksraad sal staan. Na die vergadering gaan ek na Stellenbosch waar daar agtermiddag die vroue Sap. bazaar is en ek die sal open. Malan moet dit gedoen het maar hy het skielik uitgevind dat hy een of ander werk het te Wellington, en daar men baie begerig is dat ek my gesig te Stellenbosch sal wys, het ek aangeneem te gaan. Dan kan ek ook sien hoe dit met Ma gaan.

Ek sien uit die koerante dat dit nou ooral of byna ooral baie mooi reen. Ek hoop by jullie ook. Dit sal goed wees vir die winter, al is dit nou nie so noodig by ons nie.

Ek is weer by Dr Welman die tandaarts om na my tande te kyk daar ek een beetje bang is vir pyorrhoea (is dit die woord?) Hy het dan ook twee ou tande gevind, beide met swere daaronder, wat

---

[1] W. Ormsby-Gore was chairman of the East Africa commission appointed to report on the economic development of British East Africa. It reported in 1925 (*see* Cmd. 2387).

nou moet uit. Maar hulle is vergroot by die wortels en dit sal maar swaar gaan. Anders gaan dit met my gesondheid en wonde baie goed. Soentjies van

Pappa

TRANSLATION

Civil Service Club
Cape Town
18 March 1927

Dearest Mamma, Friday morning. We had an interesting debate in the house yesterday about the imperial conference and status. Hertzog, as usual, completely lost his head and shouted and went on like a madman. I was quite calm and composed and the contrast was therefore all the greater and stronger. I send a cutting from the *Argus*, written by their press gallery man, to give you an impression of the occasion.[1]

I am just about to hold a caucus of our Cape members of the house of assembly to ask them to vote for Fransie Malan as the new senator in the place of Dr [A. H.] Watkins. I see no other chance of getting him into parliament.[2] We shall not be getting a proper

[1] For this debate *see House of Assembly Debates*, vol. 8, cols. 1477–1519. In the course of it Hertzog said repeatedly that the imperial conference of 1926 had rejected Smuts's view of the Empire as a 'super-state' with the Dominions as 'subordinate appendages' and had recognized his own view. He went on: 'I find from the records in my office that [Smuts] himself in 1921 made an attempt to obtain a declaration from the imperial conference of that year...before he got so far he became afraid, for some reason or other.' Neither in this debate nor elsewhere did Hertzog ever publicly acknowledge any debt to Smuts's memorandum (46), but in a letter of 26 July 1925 to L. S. Amery he said that he had been struck by the similarity of Smuts's ideas, as expressed in the memorandum, and his own (*see* C. M. van den Heever, *General J. B. M. Hertzog*, p. 485). In the debate Hertzog rebuked Smuts for saying in a speech that he [Hertzog] had described the Empire as an orange to be sucked dry and thrown away. This, he said, was untrue and 'an act of inconceivable meanness'. In reply Smuts said that the imperial conference was 'an occasion of great importance' and its report 'a great document'. He praised the 'good work' done by Hertzog but found the tone of his speech 'deplorable' and 'unworthy of him as prime minister'. He apologized for the 'orange' reference. He denied that he had ever advocated a super-state in the Empire, pointed out that the doctrine of equality of status had not been questioned by thinking people since 1917, defended his action at the 1921 conference and claimed that it was largely due to his efforts that the idea of equal status had gained ground. He reminded the house that the work of the conference of 1926 must not be 'misrepresented or exaggerated'. The report had carefully avoided the word 'independence'. It was not a new departure. Its value consisted in its explicit recognition of existing practices. Smuts ended by appealing to Hertzog to 'work together', for the country now had 'a God-given opportunity to get out of the bog in which we have been wandering for years'.

[2] F. S. Malan had lost his seat in the house of assembly in the 1924 election. Dr Watkins died on 18 March 1927.

vacancy in the house of assembly and I have told him that if he does not go to the senate it might be a full five years before he is again in parliament. So he has decided to go to the senate and then to consider at the coming general election whether he will again stand for the house of assembly. After the meeting I go to Stellenbosch where the South African party women's bazaar takes place this afternoon and I shall open it. Malan should have done it but he has suddenly discovered that he has some work or other at Wellington, and as there is a strong desire that I should show my face at Stellenbosch, I have agreed to go. I shall then also see how Mother is getting on.

I see from the papers that it is now raining well everywhere, or nearly everywhere. That will be a good thing for the winter although we do not need it so much now.

I again visited Dr Welman, the dentist, to have my teeth examined as I am rather afraid of pyorrhoea (is that the word?). He duly found two teeth, with abscesses under them, which must now come out. But they are enlarged at the roots and it will be difficult. Otherwise all is well with my health and my wounds.[1] Kisses from

Pappa

225   To E. Rooth
Vol. 39, no. 69

[Cape Town]
29 March 1927

My dear Rooth, Thank you for your two letters in regard to *hereniging*. I note what you say, but do not wish to discuss the matter further as it is full of pitfalls in all directions and I do not think the time ripe for wise decisions. With kind regards, Yours sincerely,

s. J. C. Smuts

226   From D. J. Sioka
Vol. 38, no. 150

P.O. Box 167
Pietermaritzburg
29 March 1927

Dear Sir, Will you please excuse me and allow me to address you these few lines. I wonder if you know that all the Natives admire your action in defending them whenever there is a bill affecting

[1] Smuts had undergone an operation for carbuncles on 3 March.

them in parliament. I am writing to thank you not only on my own behalf but on behalf of all the Natives in Natal and in the Union generally. We follow with great interest the speeches you make in parliament and we therefore depend on you and the other members who are fighting for us. We take it that you and those members who are looking after our interest are far better than the seven members which the present bill intends to provide for us.[1] We followed all your speeches in the Colour Bar Bill and I believe that you will do the same when the prime minister's Native bills come up. Please let us just look into these bills and follow the speech of the prime minister at Smithfield and I think we will see the whole intention of the bill. To my mind the intention is take the Coloured persons and the Natives right of vote away so that those members of the South African party who are returned through them will be reduced in order to give the Pact members a chance of getting in and thereby putting the South African party in a position that it will be difficult for them to get into power again. Secondly, in order to segregate the Natives and keep them as down as they possibly can do or to take them back a thousand years if it be possible. I also read from the papers that you or your party are willing to help the government if the Cape franchise is not taken away at once but to allow those that have it to do so until their death. I must therefore point out that we are totally against that also. I must further thank you for the point you raised yesterday about the bills having to come before both houses jointly, but there is one more point which I believe none of the members touched upon and that is that after the bill has been passed it has to get the sanction of His Majesty the King. This point, together with that of the joint houses, is provided in the constitution of the Union. There is nothing that is good in these bills either for the Natives nor for the Coloureds. Allow me please to say this. There is absolutely no Native question if it is approached in a true and faithful spirit. Why does the government not simply say 'You Coloureds in the whole Union, because you follow the European custom, you live like them and speak their language and you have no chiefs, we give you full rights in everything, and you Natives who are civilized and fully educated, you must also get better rights.' Any legislation brought up in these lines would be favourably considered by all nations and the whole world. Why try to drive the educated Natives back where you took them out from and why divide the Coloureds into two camps. I am sorry to say the prime minister did not carry out a fraction in these bills of what he said at Smithfield.

[1] *See* **204**, section III.

I pray that these bills may not pass until the next election comes when we hope the South African party will come into power again because if they do pass I have a great fear that they will never come in again. We rejoiced greatly over the defeat of the Labour members at the last provincial elections and we hope the next parliamentary election will pull in the same line. You will greatly excuse me if I said some things which you do not approve of but I think in order that we understand each other we must speak the truth.

One more thing I nearly forgot to mention is that we were promised that the report of the government Native conference and resolutions will be printed and distributed to all the members of parliament so that they may refer to them when the bills are discussed in parliament. You will find that the whole of the bills were rejected on account of the taking away of the franchise. We said we wanted the franchise extended to all the other provinces.

Allow me to close with kindest regards. May the Almighty God bless you and keep you for many years. Yours sincerely,

D. J. Sioka

227 To S. M. Smuts

Vol. 39, no. 128

Volksraad
Kaapstad
4 Mei 1927

Liefste Mamma, Ek sluit in cheque vir deposit van £100, synde die legaat van Emily Hobhouse aan my. Dit is een welkomme windfall in hierdie slegte tye.

Hier word dit sterk aan winter en die dae is reeds taamlik koud —die nagte nog baie meer. Ons werk gaat maar langsaam vooruit. Ek hoor binne kort sal die vlag voorkom en dan sal die poppe begin te dans. Woensdag spreek ek Stellenbosch toe oor Holisme. Barlow het gesê dat die boek bewys my een atheist te wees. Ek wil nie daarop antwoord, maar laat deurskyn dat die boek nie oor die theologie is nie. Prof. C. G. S. de Villiers sê my daar is baie belangstelling.

Lou Geldenhuys is daar nie in geslaag om Barberspan te verkoop nie. Louis Esselen het nou aan Andrew Conroy geskrywe die meer grond vir skape wil hê. Ek is bereid om Kromdraai vir £10,000 te verkoop. Sê bietjie vir Andries indien hy van iemand hoor. Ek wil egter nie die plaas laat rond 'hawk' nie. Soentjes en groete,

Pappa

TRANSLATION

House of Assembly
Cape Town
4 May 1927

Dearest Mamma, I enclose for deposit a cheque for £100—Emily Hobhouse's legacy to me. It is a welcome windfall in these bad times.

Here it is fast becoming winter and the days are already fairly cold—the nights much more so. Our work goes on slowly. I hear the flag will come up soon—and then there will be the devil to pay. On Wednesday I speak to Stellenbosch about *Holism*. Barlow [A. G.] said that the book proved me an atheist. I don't want to answer that but do want to make it apparent that the book is not on theology. Professor C. G. S. de Villiers tells me there is much interest.

Lou Geldenhuys has not succeeded in selling Barberspan.[1] Louis Esselen has now written to Andrew Conroy who wants more land for sheep. I am prepared to sell Kromdraai[2] for £10,000. Please tell Andries,[3] in case he hears of someone. But I don't want to have the farm hawked around. Kisses and good wishes,

Pappa

228   To M. C. Gillett   Vol. 39, no. 287

Cape Town
5 May 1927

...I am addressing the Stellenbosch students on Wednesday next on holism, a subject on which they seem to be interested, but I almost despair of making it really intelligible to the average un-trained student, especially as I intend to speak in Afrikaans, a medium which is dear to me in the ordinary relations of life but in which I have never thought philosophy. I addressed the Cape Town students a few weeks ago on our status in the Empire, and hence the visit to Stellenbosch as a counterweight. We are very busy now in parliament, especially as most of our mornings are spent on a select committee on Hertzog's Native bills.[4] They are a frightful mess and

---

[1] *See* vol. III, p. 634, note 1. Smuts's financial position was at this time precarious. The salary of the leader of the opposition was then the same as that of an ordinary member—£700 a year—and farming hardly paid. Smuts told his wife that Doornkloof should be called 'Money Sunk'. To meet a large overdraft he proposed to sell his Lichtenburg farms. Barberspan was sold in 1928.

[2] One of the three farms in the Lichtenburg district, western Transvaal.

[3] *See* vol. III, p. 481, note 1.

[4] This was the second of three successive select committees of 1927–8 appointed to consider the four 'Native' bills which Hertzog had introduced on 4 April 1927.

one despairs of making anything coherent or beneficial of them. Still the attempt has to be made. There is grave danger that Hertzog's policy will mark a new departure in the alienation between white and black South Africa. A thousand pities and to be prevented at all costs. Now a flag bill has to be forced through to save the *amour propre* of the Nats. It will lead to 'a bitter wrangle and an ugly situation all over the country. The English section were prepared to forgive Hertzog all his past errors, but this expulsion of their flag will be unforgivable. Well, now, this is a doleful tale, written as you are basking in the sun at Porthcothan. However, we also have our compensations, and on the whole I find this land a good place to live in. But I would love to be at Porthcothan with you. Only it is a vision to be kept before the mind's eye for the future. Love from

Jan

229   To J. Martin   Vol. 39, no. 165

Civil Service Club
Cape Town
28 May 1927

My dear Martin, Many thanks for your note and the enclosure. I need not say that I thoroughly approve of your reply to Crewe, whose proposal would place our well-disposed press in an altogether false position.[1] It is that sort of unwisdom which accounts to some extent for the troubles in which we find ourselves. Thus we have the admission of Hertzog last night that he had thought of leaving the flag bill in abeyance for one or two years on his return from London, but the Empire group decided him the other way!

Hertzog's speech is a most disastrous event—especially coming after my olive branch two days before.[2] Long before this ugly and sad business is over we shall have forgotten the flag issue, and shall be straining all our nerve to maintain the Union of South Africa. Such is the evil spirit which will be let loose among our

[1] Crewe had proposed to secure concerted newspaper action against the flag bill. Martin replied that the Argus group would not take any step that would bind, or even appear to bind newspapers to a pre-arranged policy or in any way circumscribe their independence of action. (*See* Smuts Collection, vol. 38, no. 85.)

[2] Smuts's 'olive branch' was an amendment on the motion for a second reading of the flag bill to the effect that the national flag should 'embody the historic flags representative of the two races'. The proposed flag, at this stage, excluded both the Union Jack and the flags of the former Republics. Hertzog, in reply, refused to consider inclusion of the Union Jack. *See Cape Times*, 26 May 1927 and *Die Burger*, 28 May 1927.

people. Let the press be very firm, but calm and unprovocative. The passions are there among the people and will soon be boiling over in all directions. What a bankruptcy after the great era through which we have passed! 'Give them a chance', it was said; and this is how it is being used. The press should not spare political Labour who are the real traitors. With kind regards, Ever yours sincerely,

J. C. Smuts

230   To I. B. Pole-Evans   Vol. 39, no. 167

Civil Service Club
Cape Town
30 May 1927

My dear Doctor, My wife has written me that you have found *Wolffia arrhiza* in the Rietvlei above Doornkloof. I congratulate you. It only shows what one can find in our *vleis*.[1]

I have not done much botany recently, as there have been so many other calls on my time at week-ends. I made a good collection for Goddijn [W. A.], filling two petrol boxes; but they were all more or less well-known Table mountain plants. The great thing would be to spend a month in these and neighbouring parts in spring and early summer. We may this year have a special session over the flag question in October or thereabouts, and then I shall have a good look at the south-west grasses. This flag calamity threatens to engulf everything, and botany will help to keep me from getting too deeply involved in it.

Well, this was simply to congratulate you over *Wolffia*, and I must now stop. Every good wish to you and Mary. Ever yours,

J. C. Smuts

231   To S. M. Smuts   Vol. 39, no. 233

Civil Service Club
Cape Town
26 Juni 1927

Liefste Mamma, Zondag aand. Ek is vandag weer op die berg gewees. Die verrekte senuwe oor die hart pla nie meer dus kan ek weer goed klim. Die is een heerlike warm somerdag gewees—so warm dat ek een sonbad op die berg kon neem. Ek had eerst gedag om visites te maak vir die laaste Sondag—by Ella en Vaatje, by die

---

[1] A marsh or small temporary lake.

Graaffs, by Michaelis, by Sir Hugh Levick. Maar na ontbyt was die 'lure of the mountain' te veel vir my. Vir weke heb ek geen behoorlike oefening kon neem om bowegemelde rede, en so heb ek maar *cito cito* besluit om die visites te laat vaar. Nomineel was ek alleen, maar in werklikheid was ek die heele dag met mense daar so baie partye die berg op is. Met die afkom vond ek Stokoe wat so baie pragtige blomme in die Hottentots Holland berge gevind het, onder ander die *Orothamnus Zeyheri* wat miskien ons mooiste S. A. blom is—dit is goed geskilder vir die *Flowering Plants*. Platklip gorge op, by Disa gorge en die reservoir en die Hut, en toe by Kasteelpoort of—van 9.15 tot 5. Een allerheerlike dag. Ek het voorloopig gereel om Dinsdag 4 p.m. hier na die noorde te vertrek, en hoop dat daar nie oponthoud sal kom nie. Dit sal my dan Donderdag voormiddag thuis breng. Ek verlang al baie om julle almal en die plaas te sien. Wat ons nog een beetje ophou is die Diamant Wet en die Vlag Wet. Ons het besluit om een vlag as amendeert in die Senaat voor te stel—die combinasie vlag bestaande uit een witkruis en die ou vlae in die kwartiere, en een blou grond met 4 sterre in die vierde so:

U. J.	OVS
Transv.	* * * *

Die vlag is geteekend en maak een goeie vertooning, howeel Hertzog dit een gedrog noem. Sy vlag laat my koud. Maar omdat die skild met die ou vlae in die klein daarop is hoor ek dat baie nou aan wankel is en sy vlag wil ondersteun. Vir my is dit slegs een skyn om die mense te vang wat wil gevang word.

Sally is al laaste Dinsdag weg daar haar ma siekerig is. Ek het maar so aangesukkel met die baie correspondentie. My typewriter laat ek hier en sal een klein portable in die Transvaal kry. Soentjies,
Pappa

TRANSLATION

Civil Service Club
Cape Town
26 June 1927

Dearest Mamma, Sunday evening. I was on the mountain again today. The stretched nerve over the heart has stopped troubling me so I can climb well again. It has been a lovely, warm, summery day—so warm that I could have a sunbath on the mountain. I had thought of paying visits on the last Sunday—to Ella and Vaatje,[1] the Graaffs, [Sir Max] Michaelis, Sir Hugh Levick. But after breakfast the 'lure of the mountain' was too much for me. For the abovementioned reason I have not been able to take any proper exercise for weeks and so I decided *cito cito* to let the visits go. Nominally I was alone but actually I was among people all day as so many parties went up the mountain. Coming down I came across Stokoe [T. P.] who has found so many beautiful flowers in the Hottentots Holland mountains, among others the *Orothamnus Zeyheri*[2] which is perhaps our loveliest South African flower—it has been well painted for *Flowering Plants*.[3] [I went] up Platklip Gorge, past Disa Gorge and the reservoir and hut and then down by Kasteelpoort— from 9.15 to 5. A most lovely day.

I have arranged provisionally to leave here for the north on Tuesday at 4 p.m. and hope there will be no delay. That will see me home on Thursday morning. We are somewhat held up by the Diamond Bill and the Flag Bill.[4] We have decided to propose an amended flag in the senate—the combination flag consisting of a white cross with the old flags in the [three] quarters and four stars on a blue ground in the fourth thus:

Union Jack	Orange Free State
Transvaal	* * * *

The flag has been sketched and looks well although Hertzog calls it a monstrosity.[5] His flag leaves me cold. But because the shield with the old flags in miniature appears on it, I hear that many are

[1] *See* vol. I, p. 404, note 3; vol. III, p. 445, note 3.

[2] Its popular name is the Marsh Rose.

[3] *The Flowering Plants of South Africa*, an annual publication begun in 1921 and edited by the chief of the Botanical Research Institute of the department of agriculture.

[4] The bill, which laid down that the national flag should be the 'Van Riebeeck' flag with a shield enclosing the two republican flags and the Union Jack, and that the Union Jack should fly beside it at times and places to be determined by the government, was rejected by the senate in which the South African party had a majority.

[5] The 'Smuts' flag was passed by the senate but rejected by the house of assembly. To resolve the deadlock a joint sitting of both houses was to take place in November 1927. (*See* D. F. Malan, *Afrikaner Volkseenheid*, p. 128.)

now wavering and wish to support his flag. It seems to me merely a pretence to catch people who wish to be caught.

Sally[1] left last Tuesday as her mother is not well. I have been struggling along with all the correspondence. I shall leave my typewriter here and get a small portable in the Transvaal. Kisses,

Pappa

232   To M. C. Gillett   Vol. 39, no. 305

Irene
[Transvaal]
31 August 1927

I am not answering any letter in particular this time as the mail has not yet arrived, having been delayed by storms. They have had awful weather down at the Cape, much rain, snow and storms. We have felt the cold effects even up here. Luckily the bad drought has now been broken and there is rejoicing in the land. It is wonderful how the rainfall dominates everything in this country. They say that all Egyptian culture and religion centre ultimately in father Nile. Here it would be mother Rain. I have spent most of this last week reading and digesting B. Russell's *Analysis of Matter*,[2] a book very well worth careful study. Russell and I do not see eye to eye on philosophy—he is an atomist while I am a holist. He would call holism mysticism, while I am trying, from the rich resources of mysticism, to rescue this concept of holism for knowledge and science. But in spite of our ultimate differences, I can learn a lot from him. His attempt to connect quanta with qualities is interesting and gives me a clue for which I have long been looking. Science gives only quantities or extensive magnitudes. How do qualities or qualitative differences arise? The curious mystery of the quantum may hold the secret of this origin.

I see that Cecil has resigned from the cabinet.[3] The Geneva disarmament failure has been the last straw. Naval armaments are no doubt a great danger. But to me the continued occupation of the Rhineland, even after the ambassador's report of the final disarmament of Germany, is a far more serious matter and a far greater danger to the future peace. But to this his letter of resigna-

[1] Sally Richardson, who did secretarial work for Smuts.
[2] Published in 1927.
[3] Lord Cecil had been chancellor of the Duchy of Lancaster. He resigned after differences with W. C. Bridgeman, first lord of the admiralty, about the conduct of negotiations at the naval conference with the United States which had begun at Geneva on 20 June 1927 and broken down on 4 August.

tion does not even refer. The risk of war is not between the United States and Great Britain, but in central Europe where the old pre-war mentality is kept alive by short-sighted statesmen. One had thought that Poincaré had reformed after the Ruhr business of 1923. But he is just the same and poisoning the atmosphere of Europe with his narrow hatreds and fears. I feel profoundly sad over all this. And in England the Conservative government with the weak Chamberlain shortsightedly backs up France in this disastrous policy. Sometimes I feel a real bitterness over all this awful bungling which means a terrible legacy to the next generation. France learns nothing and forgets nothing. It is the old Bourbon mentality persisting. Love to you all, ever, from

Jan

233   To S. M. Smuts   Vol. 39, no. 249

Civil Service Club
Cape Town
27 October 1927

Liefste Mamma, Gister is die vlag settlement in die Volksraad aangeneem en daar heers vir die oomblik een baie mooi gevoel. Ek had een beetje moeilikheid in die caucus viral met Natal. Maar ek het hul daarop gewys hoe hul al die jare trou by Genl. Botha gestaan het en daarna by my, en dat ek diep gebonde voel aan my party in Natal en dat hul my moet vertrou en dinge in my hande laat. Die beroep het een verbasende effekt gehad en daarop is eenparig besluit om die compromise aan te neem.

Wat die toekoms gaan baar weet niemand. Wat ek gedoen het was alleen ter wille van land en volk, want onteenseglik was die vlag kwestie een kragtige wapen in ons hand om die regeering te breek. Oënskynlik is die regeering versterk deur wat gebeurd is. Maar ons sal een beetje moet wag om met klaarheid te sien. Indien ek my hart verhard had kon dit ons baie groot kwaad as een party gedoen het.

Dit is snaaks dat Frank Joubert gister by my was om te vra waar ek een huis wil hê wat my vriende my ter bewoning wil aanpresenteer. Ek dag dit was weer die Gillett idee en vroeg hom een beetje uit en vond toe dat dit niks met die Gilletts te doen had, maar een geheel nuwe idee [was] van een tal Kaapse vriende en admireerders. Ek het hom gesê om beetje in die rigting van Rondebosch Common te kyk, omdat ek baie van daardie lug hou en jy van Ella's nabyheid sal hou. Dit lyk my of een huis ons sal opgedring word en dat ons maar sal moet meegaan met die idee. Bibas kan huis hou. Sy doet dit goed en goedkoop.

Alles verder wel. Sally sal jou die *Cape Times* stuur met my speech van gister wat baie byval gevind het by die toehoorders. Soentjes,

Pappa

My neus gesond. Jeuk nie eens!

TRANSLATION

Civil Service Club
Cape Town
27 October 1927

Dearest Mamma, Yesterday the flag settlement was accepted in the house of assembly and very good feeling reigns for the moment.[1] I had a bit of trouble in the caucus, especially with Natal. But I pointed out how they had all these years stood faithfully by General Botha and, after him, by me, that I was deeply attached to my party in Natal, and that they must trust me and leave things in my hands. The appeal had a surprising effect and afterwards it was unanimously decided to accept the compromise.

What the future will bring no one knows. What I did was solely for the country and the people, for the flag issue was unquestionably a powerful weapon in our hands to smash the government. Apparently the government has been strengthened by what has happened. But we shall have to wait a bit to see clearly. If I had hardened my heart it might have done us great harm as a party.

It is odd that Frank Joubert saw me yesterday to ask where I should like to have a house which my friends want to present to me to live in. I thought it was the Gillett idea again and asked him some questions and then found that it had nothing to do with the Gilletts but was quite a new idea of a number of Cape friends and admirers. I told him to look about in the direction of Rondebosch Common because I like that air very much and you will like being near Ella [Louw]. It looks to me as if a house will be forced on us and that we shall have to go along with the idea. Bibas [Smuts] can keep house. She does it well and cheaply.

For the rest all is well. Sally [Richardson] will send you the *Cape Times* with my speech of yesterday which pleased those who heard it very much. Kisses,

Pappa

My nose is better. Does not even itch!

[1] At this stage the flag issue had been reduced to the relative prominence of the Union Jack and the Republican flags within the 'Van Riebeeck' tricolour. After personal talks between Hertzog and Smuts the compromise of the present flag was reached.

Volksraad
Kaapstad
29 Oktober 1927

Liewe Jantjie, Die Raad van die Science Association het my genader
om my te vra of ek jou nie kan ompraat om as President van die
Assoc[iation] op te tree in 1929 wanneer die Brit[ish] Ass[ociation]
hier sal sit nie. Hul gevoel baie sterk dat jy die beste man is vir die
doel en daarmee stem ek van harte saam. Ek weet nie wat jou planne
is, maar dit wil my lyk of jy noodsaaklik dan in die land sal wees,
daar een eleksie stryd dan op touw sal wees, òf net voor òf net na
die stryd. En ek neem aan dat na alle waarskynlikheid jy by die
geleentheid naar die Volksraad sal gaan.

Nou voel ek dat dit een uitstekende geleentheid sal wees om op
die voorgrond te kom en meer as ooit algemeene aandag te trek.
Met die oog op die toekoms wil ek graag hê dat jy van die geleentheid gebruik sal maak daar dit so uniek is. Die indruk wat jou
toespraak op die Commercial Congress gemaak het is uitstekend.
'Een van die beste wat hul ooit gehoor het'. Dit help Suid-Afrika
en dit help die goeie saak en dit help jou persoonlik. Denk dus baie
ernstig oor die saak na, want so'n kans kom nie gou weer nie.

Ek meen die vlag is goed beslis. Tielman's brief was as 'spoof'
bedoel maar dit het ernstige gevolge gehad. Ek hoor ons Nat.
vrinde hier is bitter teleurgesteld, maar by ons is algemeene
tevredenheid.

Met baie groete en beste wense aan jou en Borrie, Jou vriend,

J. C. Smuts

TRANSLATION

House of Assembly
Cape Town
29 October 1927

Dear Jantjie, The council of the Science Association has approached
me to ask if I can persuade you to act as president of the association
in 1929 when the British Association will meet here. They feel very
strongly that you are the best man for the purpose and I agree
wholeheartedly. I do not know what your plans are, but it looks to
me as if you will then necessarily be in the country as an election
fight will then be afoot, either before or just after the fight. And I expect that you will in all probability go into the house of assembly on
that occasion.

Now I feel that this will be an excellent opportunity of moving into the foreground and more than ever attracting general attention. With an eye to the future I should like you to use the opportunity for it is unique. The impression made by your address at the Commercial Congress is excellent—'one of the best they had ever heard'. It helps South Africa and it helps the good cause and it helps you personally. So think over the matter very seriously, for such a chance will not come again soon.

I think the flag has been well settled. Tielman's letter[1] was meant as a spoof but it had serious consequences. I hear our Nationalist friends here are bitterly disappointed, but with us there is general satisfaction.

With best wishes to you and Borrie,[2] Your friend,

J. C. Smuts

235 To M. C. Gillett

Vol. 39, no. 322

Irene
[Transvaal]
30 November 1927

I have just read your mail letter. I think it was good of Arthur to decide to send Nico to boarding house. The children are too tenderly brought up at home and require boarding house for hardening. Of course there is the danger of coarsening too. But with Nico the risk is small. All our children greatly improved by leaving home, Japie most of all. I think there is something in nature which requires severance from the too intimate home bonds in order to give proper scope to the young individuality. So don't make a song about it! But you and Helen will miss the dear thing.

You refer again to my delay about the Cape Town house. The fact is that I am most undecided about the future. You know how I long to get out of politics. All political ambition—if ever I had any—is quite dead in me. Sometimes my feeling goes deeper and I feel as if I would get out of everything and bury myself in meditation, botany and the like. However, my *political* future is most uncertain. If parties should come together, I would look upon that as a suitable time to clear out and be free. There is a great deal of *hereniging* talk about. Nobody knows how things will shape. I should

---

[1] In a statement to the *Pretoria News* on 11 October 1927 Roos, then deputy prime minister, had said that any reasonable suggestion made by the senate for settling the flag design controversy would be seriously considered.

[2] Shortened form of Deborah, the first name of Hofmeyr's mother.

welcome a good successor in the South African party so that I could retire. There has been no opening for me to do so during the last three or four years. But my chance may come sooner or later; hence I am averse to any sudden moves about the house.[1] Next year is time enough to see how politics and parties are shaping. I have a great longing to cut myself off people and things and retire to meditate. Whether this is a wholesome feeling or not, I cannot say, but it is deep and genuine. Next year it will be thirty years since I got into this hard grind, and one feels that there is a limit to the world and its claim on one.

I spent part of last week in getting my collections made in October in the Cape area in order. But it is really a devil of a job; and I can sympathize with you when you say that your occupations kept you away from botany last term. All these things take time and will not be hurried over.

The weather continues beautiful and I enjoy my daily rides and walks. With much love to you all,

Jan

236   To J. H. Hofmeyr   Vol. 39, no. 264

Irene
14 December 1927

Liewe Jantjie, Jou brief 30 ewe ontvang. Ek stuur die aanbod van die Science Ass. terug. My sterke wens is dat jy die aanbod sal aanneem. Jy weet wat my begeerte en plan vir jou is, en hierdie unieke eerbewys sal baie tot die uitvoering daarvan bydra.

Die mentaliteit van Hertzog is my nog altyd een raaisel, maar in hierdie geval wil dit amper lyk asof hy een eleksie omtrent daardie tyd (Augustus 1929) verwag en Julie wil vry hou. Jy sal dus dan ook hier moet wees, en sal jou vakansie soo moet inrig dat jy einde van Mei of in Junie 1929 terug sal wees van jou reis.

Die presidentskap by soo'n geleentheid is een van die grootste distinksies wat jou ooit kan te beurt val en *mag* nie geweier word nie. In Suid-Afrika moet jy jou kans waarneem solang jy jong is, en hier is die kans, nie alleen persoonlik nie, maar ook in belang van Suid-Afrika. Jou oud kollegas van die Rhodes Scholarship sal dit jou nooit vergewe, as jy dit deur die vingers laat gly. My is dit meer te doen vir die toekoms van die land en volk, en van daardie oogpunt mag jy nie aarsel nie. Oor een onderwerp behoor daar geen moeilik-

---

[1] A house was acquired in December. It was then called 'Tsalta' and is in Bowwood Road in Claremont—one of the southern suburbs of Cape Town.

heid te wees nie, daar die Association in die geheel nie beperk is tot die *natuur*wetenskap maar wetenskap in die breedste sin opvat. Ek wens jou baie geluk en voel as of dit een groot persoonlike overwinning is wat goeie vrugte gaan afwerp. *t.t.*

J. C. Smuts

TRANSLATION

Irene
[Transvaal]
14 December 1927

Dear Jantjie, Your letter of the 30th just received. I return the offer of the Science Association. It is my strong wish that you should accept the offer. You know what my desire and plan is for you, and this unique honour will contribute much to its realization.

The mentality of Hertzog remains a riddle to me, but in this case it would almost appear as if he expects an election about that time (August 1929) and wants to keep July free. So you would have to be here then and will have to arrange your holiday so as to be back from your journey at the end of May or in June 1929.

The presidency on such an occasion is one of the greatest distinctions that could ever come your way and *may* not be refused. In South Africa you must seize your chance while you are young, and here is the chance, not only personally, but also in the interests of South Africa. Your old Rhodes Scholarship colleagues will never forgive you if you let it slip through your fingers. I am more concerned about the future of the country and the people, and from that point of view you may not hesitate. There should be no difficulty about a subject, as the Association as a whole is not limited to natural science but interprets science in the broadest sense. I congratulate you heartily and feel as if it is a great personal victory which is going to bear good fruit. *Totus tuus,*

J. C. Smuts

237   To N. Levi   Vol. 40, no. 131

Irene
17 Januarie 1928

Waarde Levi, U notas so juis ter hand. Ek voel geheel seker van H. en wat Watson sê verdien geen notisie. Hy wil uitmaak dat daar meer verraaiers is soos hy. H's ma is ook geheel te vertroue. Roos vry erg in daardie rigting maar hul dryf die spot daarmee. Mentz lyk beetje teen H., waarom weet ek nie; dus moet U maar met een beetje sout eenige gedagte van daardie kant ook ontvang. Jooste is beter op hoogte.

Die Creswell affaire kan sake tot een breekspeul breng; anders hoor ek is dit nog Hertzogs plan die eleksie midden van 1929 te hou. Die rusie onder die arbeiders word onheelbaar en kan dinge verspoedig. Beste groete, *t.t.*

J. C. Smuts

Ek meen die posisie van Roos is baie sleg; niemand vertrou hom meer, nog Nat. nog Arbeid.

TRANSLATION

Irene
[Transvaal]
17 January 1928

Dear Levi, Your notes just received. I feel quite certain of H.[1] and and what Watson [H. G.] says deserves no notice. He wants to make it appear that there are more traitors like himself. H.'s mother is also entirely trustworthy. Roos is assiduously paying court in that direction but they laugh at it. Mentz seems to be somewhat against H., why I do not know; so you must also take any ideas from that side with a pinch of salt. Jooste [J. P.] is better informed.

The Creswell affair[2] may bring things to a smash-up; otherwise I hear it is still Hertzog's plan to hold an election in mid-1929. The quarrel in the Labour party is becoming incurable and may hasten matters. Best wishes, *totus tuus*,

J. C. Smuts

I think [T.] Roos's position is very bad; no one trusts him any more, neither Nationalists nor Labour.

238   To M. C. Gillett   Vol. 40, no. 214

Tsalta
[Claremont, near Cape Town]
18 February 1928

I am writing a line to you in my bedroom upstairs just before going to my work in town for the day. There is a good desk for the pur-

[1] J. H. Hofmeyr.
[2] At the Labour party conference in Bloemfontein on 1 January 1928 differences between Creswell, leader of the party, and his supporters and the national council of the party came to a head when Creswell insisted that the parliamentary caucus, and not the national council, must control the policy of the party in parliament.

pose. Downstairs there is a nice little working room in which my books are and in which I usually read and work when I am here. There, too, my plant specimens are kept in very useful shelves, put up for the purpose so to say. When you come out in August you will find a good assortment of our Cape plants classified and arranged, and both you and Jan will find them very serviceable for further comparison with new collections.

Last Saturday I went up Skeleton gorge alone as no companion was available. It is half an hour's walk from this house to Kirstenbosch;[1] from there to the first reservoir is somewhat under an hour for me. I explored to the south along the tops of the Twelve Apostles[2] but at 11.30 it began to mist heavily and later to rain, and as a result I was wet through and through and arrived drenched at home in the afternoon. But down below the sun was shining and no drop of rain had fallen, and people were all surprised to see me look like a ducked fowl. But it was really quite enjoyable and I even made a fair collection of plants, some new to me, which have dried well on the whole. I love these days on the mountain, best with a good companion, but even alone I delight in a ramble and fossicking among the wealth of plants. It will be glorious when you come in August or September when all the spring plants will be appearing.

The cables have just spread the news of Asquith's passing away. I was never greatly attracted by him, although he was a good man. He was so curiously formal and cold and even colourless. I was amused sitting once next him when he was making a little speech and finding that all his fine phrases had been carefully written down.

We are busy discussing Hertzog's Native bills in committee; I am doing my best to be helpful and to get him to make a fair and reasonable offer to the Natives. The fact is that it will be almost impossible to get the Natives to accept anything else in place of their existing Cape rights. But the Nats are determined to alter the present system, and with the growing colour prejudices I am afraid of a general election on this issue. I am prepared to face a change provided substantial justice is done to the Natives in the new proposals, which have, however, not yet materialized. I see Lord Olivier is once more on the rampage in the *Manchester Guardian*. Ever yours,

Jan

---

[1] The well-known national botanic garden founded in 1913. It is laid out on the southern slope of Table mountain and covers some 1,200 acres.

[2] Part of the Table mountain range overlooking the Atlantic coast south of Cape Town. Formerly called the Gewelberge (Gable mountains).

239   To N. Levi   **Vol. 40, no. 156**

Volksraad
Kaapstad
15 Maart 1928

Waarde Levi, Dank vir u briefie van 9 Maart. Reitz sal opkom vir
die aksie. U houding re Status is heel verstandig. Ek sal wat meer
te sê hê hedenamiddag. Ek is bang dat die Nattes een nuwe bakkly
punt oor neutraliteit gaan opwerk om die pot aan kook te hou, en
dus ag ek dit noodig om heel duidelik te praat. Hertzog is op baie
gevaarlik terrein, en die saak *moet* deur die Imp. Conferensie
behandel word, en nie deur die Dominies afsonderlik. U beheer en
beleid in die *Volkstem* is deurgaans uitstekend. En alles sal reg
kom. Ek is vol moed. *t.t.*

J. C. Smuts

TRANSLATION

House of Assembly
Cape Town
15 March 1928

Dear Levi, Thanks for your note of 9 March. Reitz[1] will come up for
the action. Your attitude on status is very sensible. I shall have
something more to say this afternoon. I am afraid that the Nats are
going to work up a new row about neutrality to keep the pot on the
boil and so I consider it necessary to talk quite plainly.[2] Hertzog
is on very dangerous ground and the matter *must* be dealt with by
the imperial conference and not by the Dominions separately. Your
control and policy in *Die Volkstem* is excellent throughout. And all
will be well. I am full of heart. *Totus tuus,*

J. C. Smuts

[1] Probably C. J. H. Reitz, an attorney.

[2] On 8 March Hertzog introduced a motion in the house of assembly to approve
the report on Dominion status of the imperial conference of 1926. He said, *inter alia,*
that the Union had the right to be neutral but that the matter was largely academic.
Smuts said that the question was a difficult one; that it should not have been brought
up since it was not mentioned in the report; that the house should not commit itself
on the matter because, whatever abstract right of neutrality there might be, in the last
resort hard facts would govern the situation and public opinion would be decisive.
(*See House of Assembly Debates*, vol. 10, cols. 1839–60, 2154–8.)

240   Notes (1928)   Box N, no. 107

NOTES OF CONVERSATION WITH GENERAL HERTZOG
ON NATIVE POLICY, 13 FEBRUARY 1928

Hertzog began by telling me that he had read a recent book called *Africa Thinking* in which the claims of Africans are set out and amount to equality with whites all along the line. He said this was the position they took up in South Africa also, and unless a stand was made now it would in future years become impossible to deal with developments. He said another matter bearing on the question which he had not mentioned in public yet referred to the possible attitude of the Communists who might join hands with the Natives for political purposes, divide the whites very seriously and make a solution of the Native question in future impossible. He therefore thought that the time had come and that no further postponement in dealing with the question was possible. He then proceeded to sketch to me the form his ideas were now taking.

There should be five white representatives in the senate elected by the Natives of the three northern provinces, based on a new franchise system for the Natives all over the Union. At the Cape the Native voters, both those on the existing registers and those to come on the new register, would elect two representatives to the house of assembly, but, not to disturb present political arrangements, the change would be postponed for some time, say until two general elections have passed. During this period the Natives at present on the roll will continue to vote with the whites in white constituencies as heretofore. But there would be no new additions of Natives to the present rolls, all future Native voters at the Cape will have to go on the new register based on the common franchise for the Natives in South Africa.

I pointed out to him that this proposal met only a very small part of our whole question of electoral reform. We were faced with numerous other questions in regard to electoral reform. The franchise laws of the Union still remained on the old provincial basis, and differed all over the Union. Besides, the women were clamouring for the franchise.[1] Moreover, after his settlement with the Indians in Natal,[2] it was only a question of time for the Indians

[1] *See supra*, p. 60, note 2.

[2] A conference between representatives of the governments of India and of the Union of South Africa was held in January 1927. It resulted in the Cape Town Agreement of which the main provisions were: that the Areas Reservation and Registration Bill was dropped, that a scheme of voluntary assisted repatriation to India was devised, that the Union government recognized its duty to 'uplift' Indians domiciled in the country, and that South Africa had the right to maintain western standards of life.

to raise the franchise question, and he must expect them to urge their claims strongly as soon as the franchise had been given to the Natives and the Coloured people all over the Union. There would be no argument against the Indian franchise, once the concession had been made to the Coloured people and Natives. The result would be that if he dealt only with the Native and Coloured question now, we would be up against these questions of franchise and political rights for years to come. And it was a question which he should consider seriously, whether a more comprehensive solution should not be adopted. That is to say, a general franchise reform, constituting a common franchise all over South Africa, based on occupation and income or salary was to apply to all, black and white alike, and while not so high as to exclude the whites, yet to be high enough to exclude the bulk of the Native population. In addition to this common qualification, there might then also be an education and civilization test, applied to all non-Europeans in future, the presumption being that the European was civilized, and that the non-European had to prove his adoption of European civilization. Such a comprehensive scheme would be quite simple, would draw no colour distinctions at all in regard to qualifications, and would only apply a differential civilization and education test which was reasonably justified.

I pointed out that I was not advocating the Indian franchise, but that he should consider the whole question. And certainly so far as women were concerned, there was a great deal to be said for dealing with the question now, instead of waiting for agitation hereafter. I also made it clear that my suggestion for a comprehensive solution was not a definite proposal, but should be considered, as it might prove a better solution of the whole question with which we were faced. Once we departed from a comprehensive solution applying to everybody, we were bound to come up against grave difficulties of colour and race bars, and in view of the state of mind among the Native and Coloured people, it might be wise to explore every means of avoiding these bars and distinctions.

Further discussion took place on the above proposal and difficulties which were involved without adding materially to the above points.

241   Notes (1928)   Box N, no. 108

NOTES OF CONVERSATION WITH GENERAL HERTZOG,
15 FEBRUARY 1928

General Hertzog told me he had thought over our discussion and he felt convinced that the north was not ripe for a solution of the general franchise question. There had been manhood suffrage from the beginning, and he did not think that the time was ripe for carrying a general franchise reform such as I had mentioned. He added that it might still be possible to get large numbers of Indians out of Natal, and he thought it would be a mistake to give them franchise rights at an early date.

I explained to him that I had simply mentioned the matter for his consideration, and that it was, of course, one which he had to consider but which I certainly was not pressing. I said that if the larger scheme was ruled out and we had to fall back on a discussion of his modified proposals, the matter struck me in this way. His proposal from the Native point of view was entirely inadequate. He had said in public that the Natives were the determining factor in at least twelve Cape constituencies,[1] and yet he now wanted to restrict them to two constituencies. After a little interval of time he proposed to abolish substantially the existing Native rights, and the grant of Native rights to the three northern provinces was not considered of a substantial character. He had even gone back on his original proposal to give the Natives in the north five seats in the house of assembly.[2] I pointed out that it was necessary first of all to frame a just and fair proposal which would commend itself to all reasonable men, and that in my opinion, his proposal even in its modified form was quite unfair and therefore unacceptable. It would create a very bad state of mind among the Natives, and in years to come, the Natives might be completely alienated from the whites.

In reply he pointed out that the majority of Native interests were common with the whites, and would be properly represented through the white representatives in parliament, and that it was wrong to minimize the importance of the senate. He was afraid that if too large a representation was given to the Natives in the assembly there would be a danger of a Native block, which might hold the balance between the other parties.

He asked me what I thought would be a fair proposal on this point. I said that he should be prepared to put all his cards on the table, and make a proposal on which the Native leaders could be consulted afresh, and might perhaps take a different view from the

[1] *See* **204**, section III(d).   [2] *See* **204**, section III.

unanimous condemnation of his bills which they had expressed before the select committee.[1] To my mind the least he could do would be to offer the Cape Natives representation according to their present voting strength. I would not boggle over one or two additional seats, provided he could carry Native approval with him, because in a settlement of a large matter like this, we must be prepared to go a good distance. I had for instance offered Rhodesia twelve seats in the case of union[2] although numerically she was not entitled to more than nine. It was essential to satisfy the Natives if possible, and they should get whatever representation they were entitled to on a numerical basis at least. It would probably mean five or six seats in the assembly for the Cape, in addition to the five seats in the senate for the northern provinces.

I also pointed out that it would be necessary to leave entirely untouched the Native voter at present on the Cape register. His rights were apparently completely protected by the second subsection of article 35 of the constitution,[3] and it would be regrettable to make a change where apparently the constitution did not intend it. To my mind the only course left was to leave the Native voters already on the register to vote as at present with the whites in white constituencies for the rest of their lives. The new register would then be built up consisting of new voters, and as the quota of voters was reached for one or more separate Native members, separate Native constituencies would be created at the Cape, until the maximum number was reached. This to my mind would agree with the constitution and would bridge the necessary transition period.

I said I did not put this forward as my own suggestion, and I reserved my opinion on the matter until I had thought it over further and consulted my friends, but to my mind this was the least that he could put forward as a basis, if he wanted to carry the reasonable men and perhaps also the Natives with him.

I suggested that if he put forward some such suggestion, we could then consult afresh with Native leaders and try to carry them with us. And in my opinion it would be very advisable also to consult the leaders of the church, whose opinion he had unnecessarily flouted.

[1] The select committee appointed in October 1927 which reported in May 1928.
[2] In 1922 Smuts had offered Southern Rhodesia ten seats in the house of assembly and five in the senate.
[3] This reads: 'No person who...is registered as a voter in any province shall be removed from the register by reason only of any disqualification based on race or colour.' Article 35 may be repealed only by a two-thirds majority at a joint session of both houses.

He thanked me for my suggestion and thought it might be helpful. I then went on to tell him I was not enamoured of his general council.[1] I feared that he would collect all the Kadalies[2] and Communist agitators in South Africa into a body which might have a very unsettling effect on the Native mind. To my mind it was a far better policy to let the general council stand over, to establish councils under the act of 1920[3] in the various territories, and when these were in full and efficient working, then to consider the question of a general council based on them as a superstructure. In the meantime the present annual Native conference,[4] if made proper use of and given more importance to, will satisfy Native needs and requirements of the case, and be a far safer body than the general council, which seemed to me to be a dangerous leap in the dark. I added that many of my friends felt grave misgivings about the general council project.

He said that there was a similar feeling among many of his friends, and it was a question which might be reconsidered. He had thought that as the Natives were not getting full political rights, the council would be an additional *quid pro quo*.

On the Coloured bills, I said that it seemed to me to be one of the weakest parts of his proposals, and that I doubted whether the system was workable, and feared that a rapidly growing Coloured population might in another generation constitute a new problem and create fresh political troubles. To my mind miscegenation will go on, and the Coloured population of South Africa, which was already about half a million, would continue to grow in numbers.[5] Although large numbers of the Coloured people were of a very high class, and fully deserved equal political status with the whites, there were also large numbers who certainly were not superior in any respect to the Natives. To my mind a distinction was necessary between these two sections, and it was not a wise proposal to give them all equal rights with the whites. I thought the wiser course would be to apply a new franchise and civilization test to all non-Europeans alike, and, if they passed these tests, the Natives would then go on the Native register, and vote in their own constituencies for their representatives, while the Coloured voters would vote with the whites in white constituencies for the future, just as in the past.

He replied that there was a good deal to be said for such a scheme, that he had dealt with the Coloured people in the Coloured Persons'

[1] *See* **204**, section v.   [2] A reference to Clements Kadalie (q.v.).
[3] *See supra*, p. 42, note 3.
[4] The Native Affairs Act of 1920 made provision for holding conferences in order to consult Native opinion and several of these had taken place.
[5] The Coloured population at the 1960 census was 758, 256.

Rights Bill[1] partly from political considerations, and because it was alleged that their protection under section 35 of the constitution was being removed. I said that it seemed to me that we should preserve section 35 for the future and not repeal it, but keep it intact for the protection of Native and Coloured rights in future. He said there was some doubt about the legal aspects of the question. He added that the suggestion made by me would considerably simplify the matter, and he would go into it.

Coming finally to the Land Bill,[2] I said that I thought his scheme much too complicated, and that it would take a long time to get it through parliament. The new areas had been delimited twelve years ago[3] and could no longer be maintained, and it would be wrong to give them a sort of statutory basis. Botha's original idea was to make the new areas purely Native areas, and his provisions for mixed holdings for white and black were subject to very grave criticism. To my mind all that was necessary to lay down by act was that the Natives would be given additional Native areas to the extent of the new areas, without binding ourselves actually to the new areas, and then for parliament to give the government powers of expropriation and the necessary funds to buy out land for necessary Native areas in the neighbourhood of the existing areas until the maximum limit was reached. A bill based on these lines would be quite simple and would go through without much trouble, and a large measure of discretion would naturally be left to the government to act according to circumstances, while no stigma would be placed by law on any present area held by whites. I said that many of my farmer friends held these views, and he would find a simple bill on these lines a better solution than his complicated measure.

He said that in effect this was the very policy which his bill was trying to carry out, but the detailed method of carrying out his idea seemed to him a matter of comparative indifference, and that my suggestion for simplifying the bill might be gone into. I objected to the licensing provisions[4] which he said were to be greatly modified.

In conclusion he said that he thought this frank discussion had much clarified the position, and that he would go into the points mentioned by me and that we could meet again later.

Throughout I made it clear that I was not making any definite proposal to him, but simply trying to induce him to put forward

[1] *See* **204**, section IV.   [2] *See* **204**, section II.
[3] By the Native land commission, under the chairmanship of Sir William Beaumont, which reported in 1916 (U.G. 19 of 1916).
[4] *See* **204**, section II(b).

proposals which might be fair and reasonable and might be suggested as possible to carry the assent not only of reasonable men but also of the Native leaders who were very hostile to his published bills.

242   Notes (1928)   **Box N, no. 109**

NOTES OF CONVERSATION WITH GENERAL HERTZOG ON NATIVE BILLS, 27 FEBRUARY 1928

General Hertzog said he was very glad of our exchange of ideas as they helped him to get along, and he thought that real progress had been made in our talks. He thought that it might be possible to have five Native representatives for the Cape eventually, but that he thought a limit should be put to the time during which the present voters would continue to vote in the white constituencies. He had not made up his mind yet, but he was simply putting to me the feeling among his friends.

I replied that article 35, sub-section 2 of the constitution[1] would prove an insuperable bar to that, as it made no provision for changing the rights of Coloured people already on the roll, and a change could only be brought about therefore by a constitutional amendment. Clearly within the purview of the constitution, Natives and Coloured people on the roll should remain there so long as they are entitled, without any infringement of their existing rights.

He then said that he thought there was a good deal in my view that there should be a uniform franchise all over South Africa, but instead of levelling the North up to something like the Cape franchise,[2] he thought the better course would be to level down the Cape to the manhood suffrage basis of the North. The result then would be that the whites would have manhood suffrage all over South Africa, but for the Natives there would be a franchise based on qualifications plus an education and civilization test.

I said that the point was a very serious one, and might wreck his whole scheme. This differential franchise in my opinion would not prove acceptable either to the Natives or large sections of the whites. To my mind, the qualifications should be the same for everybody, but the civilization test was justified in the case of non-Europeans. This would be additional to the qualifications common to all. I said that to my mind, 5s. a day was the minimum for the unskilled white, and a man who could not even earn that was not entitled to a vote. On this basis, the wages qualifications of the Cape would have to be raised from £50 to £75 a year, and similarly

---

[1] *See supra*, p. 371, note 3.   [2] *See* vol. I, p. 94, note I; vol. II, p. 239, note I.

the occupation qualification would have to be raised from £75 to £100. This qualification I said would, in my opinion, not keep a single decent white man off the roll, nor would it be a bar to a decent Coloured man, or even Native who had reached a certain standard. But it would keep off the register the vast mass of the Native population and also large sections of Coloured people whose standard was no better than that of the raw Native. I said that the whites ought to be prepared for a great reform of the Native question to make some sacrifice of their own. The Labour party might not like it perhaps, some of his own party might not like it. Perhaps some of my own party might not like it, but to my mind differential qualifications were out of the question, and manhood suffrage for the whites together with a high qualification basis for the rest would prove unacceptable and jeopardize the solution of the Native question. I warned him to look at the matter in the most serious light and not make up his mind prematurely as in the end everything might hinge on this.

In regard to the general council, he said he thought that the matter might stand over, and the conference system might be developed in the meantime. He had put forward the general council as a sort of *quid pro quo* for rights which the Natives might seem to lose through the proposed changes in their position.

With regard to the Land Bill, he thought that it could be simplified, and suggested that it might be unnecessary to declare the neutral areas as statutory areas, to use them merely as an indication of the areas within which the Natives might in future be free to buy, and the government to expropriate for the Natives.

I said that in my opinion rights of expropriation were very necessary, as the Natives were not able to buy much land.

With regard to the Coloured people whose position was fully discussed, it was agreed that once they had obtained their position on the register, they should be treated like whites and vote with the whites and no distinction should be made. But it would be necessary for them to submit in future to education and qualification tests together with the other non-Europeans. The position of Coloured people already registered would of course not be affected in any way.

243   Notes (1928)   Box N, no. 110

NOTES OF CONVERSATION WITH GENERAL HERTZOG
ON THE NATIVE BILLS, 12 MARCH 1928

General Hertzog said that he thought the time had come for us to discuss the question of policy in our select committee on the Native bills,[1] but before doing so, he wanted to state his views for my consideration after the talks we had had previously. His views were taking the following shape:

1. *Franchise.* He is in favour of a uniform franchise for non-Europeans all over South Africa which would include an education test, civilization test, and wages or salary or occupation test, some-what on the lines of the Cape system, although the new tests may be higher than those laid down in the Cape system or in his bills. I pointed out that there was a strong feeling among my friends, which I shared, that the wages or salary or occupation test, as well as the education test, should be common to both the European and non-European all over the Union. And that only the civilization test if deemed necessary should be confined to non-Europeans. I said I held a very strong opinion that there should be a general franchise reform for whites and non-whites alike, and that only in the matter of civilization should there be a separate test if necessary. He agreed that this was a matter still outstanding in our discussions.

2. *Registration lists.* He proposed that all non-Europeans at present on the registration lists should remain thereon for the future. And these voters should exercise the vote with the whites in the same way as they had done heretofore at the Cape. With regard to the future, there would be new lists based on the new franchise; the Natives on the new lists would vote for their own representatives in proportion as their numbers reached quotas which could be settled. Future Coloured voters would vote with the whites.

3. *Representation.* There would be a maximum of five members in the house representing the Natives in the Cape province in future, and these five members would be reached gradually according as the full quotas of voters were raised. He suggested that a better way might be that the new members would be voted for not as quotas of new voters were reached, but as quotas of old voters disappeared from the existing voters rolls, so that if, for instance, three thousand Natives dropped off the present rolls at the Cape, a separate constituency would be given for Native representation

[1] *See supra*, p. 371, note 1.

at the Cape. I expressed no opinion on this suggestion. The five
representatives in the senate would be chosen in the three northern
provinces. Here too the process would be gradual, and new senators
would be chosen as quotas of Native voters were reached. These
five senators would eventually take the place of the present four
Native senators,[1] a nominated senator disappearing as an elected
senator was chosen. His idea was that the three northern provinces
would have one common list of voters, irrespective of the provincial
limits, so that the five elected senators would represent the northern
provinces as a whole.

4. *General Native council.* He thought this might be looked upon
as premature and might stand over, whilst the annual conference
was being made effective use of.

5. *Land.* A formula should be found in regard to additional
Native areas, which would render the existing practice of buying
Native lands legal and make it unnecessary to create statutory
released areas.

Hertzog said that he proposed to put forward these suggestions
to the select committee and they might form a basis for our further
discussions.

I said that in my conversations with him hitherto, I had simply
put forward my personal views, but if he was going to raise the
points now in select committee I should like to have an opportunity
to call my friends who are members of the select committee together
and to discuss with them first of all the views which he had laid
before me. It was agreed that I should do this, and that he should
do the same with regard to his members in the select committee.

244   To A. Wyatt-Tilby   Vol. 40, no. 165A

27 April 1928

Dear Mr Wyatt-Tilby, I thank you for sending me your *Quest of
Reality*,[2] which I hope to read with care and interest as soon as our
parliamentary holiday arrives. I have read your letter and the article
in the *Outlook*[3] for both of which I thank you. I have also seen your

---

[1] By article 24, sub-section ii of the South Africa Act (1909) half of the eight
senators to be nominated by the governor-general 'shall be selected on the ground
mainly of their thorough acquaintance...with the reasonable wants and wishes of the
coloured races in South Africa'.   [2] Published in 1927.

[3] Not in the Smuts Collection. The *Outlook* was a weekly review published in
London. The article, written about 9 March, was on a lecture by Jeans which 'seemed
to make rather a hole in one of the underlying assumptions of your philosophy'. *See*
Smuts Collection, vol. 40, no. 249.

review of *Holism* in *The Nineteenth Century*.[1] The points of view
which you develop in that article are interesting and deserve careful
consideration. But I am not sure that the initiative and freedom
associated with the phenomena of life do not mean much more
than merely your surplus energy. However I am looking forward
to reading your book, and seeing how you develop your main idea.

With regard to your criticism of *Holism*, I doubt whether you
have quite apprehended what I am driving at. Certainly your
inference in reference to atheism seems to be wide of the mark. All
that I am concerned with in my book *Holism* is to deny the world-
whole or world-soul, or the world as an entity with a spiritual
persona of its own, whether conscious or unconscious. Dealing with
wholes, it was necessary for me to refer to this subject in the most
general way, as it has often been touched upon by philosophers. But
I do not understand that that is really the problem of theism, nor
do I, directly at any rate, touch on the question of theism at all in
my book. Some people, making just the opposite inferences from
yours, have told me that holism is God. You will therefore see that
different views are taken of my theory which is, however, not intended to be a contribution to theology, but primarily to science,
and secondarily to philosophy.

I read [Sir James] Jeans's article in *Nature*[2] with great interest,
but here too I doubt whether you are right in thinking that his cosmic
speculations make a hole in holism. On my view Jeans is still concerned all the way with wholes, of course lesser wholes, the primitive physical wholes which are the beginnings of the universe, and
not the spiritual wholes of Bosanquet [B.] which you are looking
for. It seems to me the very nature of reality to be synthetic at all
stages, and never to show itself in diffuse primitive stuff which cannot be construed as a whole or wholes of some sort.

Of course you must not be misled by the size of Jeans's universe,
which is so vast and on such a scale as almost completely to dwarf
the importance of the human. The human appears on this view as
a microscopic mouse produced by the great labouring mountain of
the universe. But to my mind questions of size and scale have very
greatly lost their importance in consequence of Einstein's [A.]
General Relativity. What is microscopic from one point of view is
cosmic from another, and vice versa. It all depends on observers,
their frames of reference and their relations of movement or otherwise. Besides, the aspect of waste and mere surplusage seems

[1] *The Nineteenth Century*, February 1927, p. 242.
[2] 'The genesis of the great nebulae' in *Nature*, 26 February 1927, vol. 119, no. 2991,
p. 315.

characteristic of the universe. The tree produces scores of millions of spores on the off-chance of a single reproduction which seldom comes off. Astronomical numbers apply to reproduction in life just as much as to the cosmic universe of Jeans. Man may appear to be a casual by-product, and yet he may in reality express in maturest form the inner essence of the whole movement.

Human personality is to my mind the ripe outcome up to date of tendencies and structures which we find already in the primeval fire-mist. That is all that I am at, and the fact that human personality is a rare thing in the whole universe does not trouble me. Naturally I do not hold that personality is the last word. On other planets of other suns, and under other physical conditions, creative wholes of a much higher order may arise or have arisen. Even on this globe human personality may be a mere stage in the evolution of wholes. Who knows?

Here we are in the region of speculation. All that my book intended to emphasize was the holistic nature of the whole vast plan, which seems to embrace existence at all its stages. And perhaps holism is simply a provisional construction which may on better scrutiny make way for a better hypothesis. We are clearly getting out of the era of mere analysis and atomicity, and have definitely to turn our attention to what to my mind is the most characteristic feature of the universe, both physical and spiritual, and that is the element of synthesis, of structure, and of plan. The law of chance seems to be swallowed up in some bigger law which we may still have to formulate. Holism is merely a suggestion, and it may prove untenable.

I am sorry to have taken up so much of your time, but I felt honoured by your attention and the gift of your book. Yours sincerely,

s. J. C. Smuts

245   To L. S. Amery   Vol. 40, no. 175

House of Assembly
Cape Town
22 May 1928

My dear Amery, I was pleased to receive your letter of 1 May, and thank you for all the nice things you say. I am sure this is not diplomacy, but from the heart. And your writing about Palestine made me think once more of the happy days we spent there together, walking and riding over those downs and up the hills and down the great gorges where the sun stood still.[1]

Let me dispose at once of this question of Palestine that you raise. Colonel [F. H.] Kisch of the Palestine organization which is conducting a very successful propagandist and begging tour in South Africa, put the question to me about the high commissionership. I really did not give the subject any serious attention and probably made an evasive reply to him, which has made him take the action that you refer to.[2] I agree with you that there is other work for me to do, and that Palestine might well be left to many of the staunch men and true who will handle the situation there as well as I could. As for myself, my work at present is here, and it has been uncommonly hard work. The years in opposition have proved to me to be not a bit less harassing than the heavy years in office. Our government has thought fit to tackle a number of the most fundamental issues which are fraught with grave dangers from every point of view. I have done my best all through to defend the old constructive policies which have built up the new South Africa, and which alone can guarantee progress in the future.

Next year we are having our elections, and although the prospect for us appears favourable, the issue is uncertain. I have been so tied down to this country that I have not been able to get away for fresh contacts in the old world. If we win the elections, I shall be at it for some years more. If I am defeated, I may possibly take the hint, and extricate myself from the local situation and take a greater interest in those movements in the larger world in which I have always been profoundly interested. Nothing would give me greater pleasure than to enjoy some freedom to take part once more in the bigger fight for human culture and civilization which lies beyond the African confines.

The larger Africa also attracts me profoundly. I believe that there are the makings on this continent of something very big indeed. Africa from the equator downwards ought within so many generations to take a high place with Canada and Australia, as one of the greatest Dominions in the Empire. For this careful planning is necessary now, and the reservation of sufficient elbow-room for our great white civilization, leaving sufficient land for the Native population for present and future needs. All this sort of work attracts me greatly, but my South African preoccupations have

[1] L. S. Amery had accompanied Smuts when he visited Egypt and Palestine in February 1918 (*see* **816**).

[2] Colonel Kisch (q.v.) had informed the Zionist organization in England that Smuts would seriously consider an invitation to become high commissioner for Palestine (*see* Smuts Collection, Vol. 40, no. 2).

been such that I have not had the time to devote sufficient attention to these larger problems.

I am very sorry that I missed [E.] Hilton Young. His commission[1] was in Cape Town when I was attending some functions up in the Transvaal, and so we just missed each other. Otherwise I would certainly have expounded my grandiose dreams to him. Of course I am aware that his commission has a much more limited scope, but I believe we should keep before ourselves the larger point of view which some day is certain to be attained.

You left us in the flag muddle[2] and at this moment we are almost back in it again. The settlement which was reached last November is once more in danger because of the niggardly and ungenerous spirit in which the government has provided for the flying of the Union Jack in the Union.[3] However, there is a great deal of negotiation going on, and continual goings to and fro, and the government must itself be sensible of the extent to which feeling is boiling up, so that I still hope we shall get round this corner and that the peace will be maintained. I shall certainly do my best to prevent any cleavage developing among our South African people on this delicate sentimental issue.

Your visit here did untold good, as I wrote you at the time. Your constant emphasis on the larger view-point, on Empire comradeship, and on the co-operation which means so much more than a narrowly conceived independence—all that had its effect and helped materially to bring about ultimate success in the settlement of this flag controversy. I followed your tour and your speeches carefully over the rest of the Empire, and I feel convinced that few can appreciate the full scope of the work you have done. It must have been a Herculean labour, but coming at a critical point in Dominion development, the effect must have been very considerable indeed. Your tour must also have had a good effect in Great Britain where people are inclined to be immersed in the post-war struggle and in the reconstruction which it is so difficult to carry through.

You will have noticed that I made a statement on the American peace proposals which was cabled to the London *Times*.[4] I thought

[1] The East and Central African commission to investigate the question of federation or closer co-ordination between the governments in those territories.

[2] L. S. Amery arrived in South Africa on 22 July and left on 22 September 1927.

[3] The Flag Act of 1927 laid down that the Union Jack should fly beside the South African national flag at the houses of parliament, the main government buildings in the capitals of the provinces, the harbours of the Union and such other places as the government might determine.

[4] *The Times*, 19 May 1928, pp. 15–16. F. B. Kellogg, the American secretary of state, after consultation with Briand, foreign minister of France, had declared that the powers should agree to condemn war and renounce it as an instrument of national

it a very opportune moment for us to get away from the difficult atmosphere which had been created between us and America through the breakdown of the Geneva disarmament conference. There is no doubt that the American proposals give a great opening to us not only to put ourselves right with American sentiment but also to link up America more closely with the great peace effort in Europe. By itself the idea of the outlawry of war as a mere affirmation appears futile enough, but it may well be the means of carrying America once more into closer co-operation with the League, and for that reason I would not scan the American idea too hypercritically. I was very pleased to see that the British and Dominion answer has on the whole been favourable, and I hope that in the future development of this question, we shall leave no stone unturned to put ourselves right with America, and to get her more closely associated with the work of the League even if she does not actually join it. But I have already taken up too much of your time, and can only wish you all that is good, and remain, Yours very sincerely,

s. J. C. Smuts

246   To J. H. Hofmeyr

Vol. 40, no. 181

Irene
17 Juni

Liewe Jantjie, Vanoggend kreeg ek een brief van Reitz waarin hy sê dat die Barbertonse kiesafdeling aandring op een nominasie en dat indien sulks nie gebeur nie, een lokale man mag opgeset word. Ek stem saam dat ons een seker mate van gevaar loop en gaan dus aan die kiesafdeling aan die hand gee dat er maar moet genomineer word—met een aanduiding van jou naam. Jy kan natuurlik nie nou al aanneem nie, en aanname kan oorstaan tot sulks doenlik is later. Maar intussen bly die posisie in order en behouden teen lokale indringers. Dit is vir jou private informasie. *t.t.*

J. C. Smuts

policy. Smuts said that such an agreement was consistent with the covenant of the League but would only function successfully in conjunction with the covenant.

TRANSLATION

> Irene
> [Transvaal]
> 17 June [1928]

Dear Jantjie, This morning I had a letter from Reitz in which he says that the Barberton[1] constituency is insisting on a nomination and that, if this does not happen, a local man may be put up. I agree that we are in some danger and am therefore going to suggest to the constituency that a nomination had better be made—with an indication of your name. You can, of course, not accept now,[2] and acceptance can stand over until this is possible later. But in the meantime the matter is in order and the position held against local intruders. This is for your private information. *Totus tuus*,

> J. C. Smuts

247 To L. S. Amery   **Vol. 40, no. 192**

> Irene
> [Transvaal]
> 16 October 1928

My dear Amery, I was very much gratified by the receipt of your last letter and thank you for it.

At this distance the impression created on my mind is that you run a good deal of risk of a Socialist reaction in Great Britain. The figures in the last news of bye-elections are far from reassuring. And under the circumstances it would seem to me wise to deal very circumspectly with the tariff question. I am not sure that on this question Baldwin's more cautious line is not the wise one. I am all for fostering inter-Empire trade; but you have to deal with a more complex situation than that.

When Hertzog's German treaty[3] comes before the house for approval next session, we shall do our best so to amend it as to leave the door open for more Empire preference in future. I think there is not enough now, after the changes made by the Union parliament in 1925. Hertzog has unfortunately in all his speeches on Empire status continually harped on the right of secession, as if it were the essence of our status, instead of a mere questionable

[1] In the eastern Transvaal.

[2] Hofmeyr was at this time administrator of the Transvaal.

[3] This treaty, signed at Pretoria on 16 November 1928, was the first to be concluded between the Union of South Africa and a foreign country and between Germany and a British Dominion. It provided for mutual freedom of trade and shipping and embodied the principle of most-favoured-nation treatment.

accident. The note of co-operation and comradeship he never or very seldom, and then grudgingly, touches.

It is difficult to say how our elections next year will turn out. If the Labour split continues I shall win, but otherwise the issue is doubtful. All good luck to you, Ever yours sincerely,

s. J. C. Smuts

248   From J. H. Hofmeyr   Vol. 40, no. 95

Kantoor van die Administrateur van Transvaal
Pretoria
20 November 1928

Geagte Generaal, Hiermee stuur ek u afskrifte van briewe aan Barry en Andrews wat my posiesie in sake Barberton uiteensit.

Ek wil net dit byvoeg—dit was onvanpas om dit aan hul te sê—ek is op die oomblik onwillig om my definitief aan die S.A.P. te verbind, omdat ek dink dat daar miskien 'n kans is om die gewenste doel beter langs 'n ander weg te bereik. Maar sodra—wat heel waarskynlik is in die loop van tyd—dit my duidelik word dat daar *nie* so'n kans bestaan nie, dan sal ek my tot uw beskikking stel.

Ek hoop dat wat ek nou besluit het u nie sal teleurstel nie—maar vireers altans voel ek dat dit die regte ding is. Met baie hartelike groete, Geheel die uwe,

Jan H. Hofmeyr

TRANSLATION

Office of the Administrator of the Transvaal
Pretoria
20 November 1928

Dear General, Herewith I send you copies of letters[1] to Barry [R. A.] and Andrews [C. T. E.] which explain my position in the matter of Barberton.

I want to add only this—it was inappropriate to say it to them— I am at the moment unwilling to bind myself definitely to the South African party, because I think that there may be a chance to reach the desired goal by better and other means.[2] But—which is very probable in the course of time—as soon as it becomes clear to me that there is no such chance, I shall put myself at your disposal.

[1] Omitted by the editor.
[2] Hofmeyr saw a chance of getting enough Nationalist support to 'break down the present unnatural lines of division' between the two main parties (*see* Smuts Collection, vol. 40, no. 95, enclosure).

I hope that what I have now decided will not disappoint you but, to begin with at any rate, I feel that it is the right thing. With very best wishes, Yours sincerely,

Jan H. Hofmeyr

249   From J. S. Haldane   Vol. 40, no. 83

Cherwell
Oxford
13 December 1928

Dear General Smuts, Though the immediate reason for this letter is a different one, I must first apologize for never having written to thank you for sending me a copy of your book, which I of course read with the greatest interest. I have been giving the Gifford philosophical lectures at Glasgow University for last year and this year, and referred last year pretty fully to the book, though I also ventured to criticize your treatment of conscious behaviour. Before his last illness my brother[1] told me, however, that he had been in correspondence with you on this very point, and that you were considering it further. This being so, and knowing how busy you are, I did not write to you.

The matter I wish to bring before you is this. The British Association is meeting at the end of July and beginning of August at Cape Town and Johannesburg. I have arranged to go myself, and take part in discussions relating to mining troubles (in which I have been much interested for the last thirty years). But I am also very anxious to organize a discussion on 'The Nature of Life', and get you to open it. The president (Sir Thomas Holland) and the secretaries are most anxious that you should consent to do so. The proposal is that the meeting should be a joint one of the physiological and other biological sections. The organizing committees of the various sections meet in London on 4 January to arrange programmes; but I undertook to write to you meanwhile, so as to give you as long notice as possible. I think that a discussion of this sort would be of very great public interest and scientific value.

Perhaps you are not as well aware as I am that among physiologists and other biologists the orthodox conception of life is still, consciously or unconsciously, essentially mechanistic. Anything else is put down as 'vitalism', though, in England at least, some physiologists are now beginning to think more deeply. One of the most significant signs of this was the presidential address of Pro-

---

[1] Viscount Haldane.

fessor Lovatt Evans in the physiological section at the Glasgow meeting of the British Association three months ago. He has come right over.

Our idea is to get the strongest upholders of mechanistic ideas we can, to speak after you. Sir Edward Schäfer, who gave an ultra-mechanistic presidential address to the British Association a few years ago, is hoping to come, and if so I hope he will stand to his guns. But, failing him, there are several other men coming who have committed themselves in a similar direction.[1] They will have your book to bite on, as well as my Gifford Lectures, which will be published about two months from now, the title being *The Sciences and Philosophy*.

I think the discussion should be confined to life as it appears to, say, a physiologist in connection with what appear to be the unconscious activities of the body, or to a botanist; otherwise we shall get rather deeply into philosophy.

As regards a title, it might be something like 'The Nature of Life', or 'The Mechanistic Theory of Life', or 'The Holism of Life', but perhaps you would choose a title if, as I very much hope, you are willing to open the discussion.

Also would you rather have the discussion at Cape Town or at Johannesburg? There will be several days available at both.[2] But if it suited you, there would, I think, be more time available in at least the physiological section at Cape Town.

A formal invitation will be sent to you after the meeting to make general arrangements for the sectional programmes. Yours faithfully,

J. S. Haldane

250   To J. S. Haldane

Vol. 43, no. 39

6 February 1929

Dear Professor Haldane, Thank you very much for your letter of 4 January which I received by the last mail. You will have received my letter in which I agree to your kind proposal to open the discussion on 'The Nature of Life', and I am most pleased that your proposal has met with the approval of the various sections of the Association. I shall be quite willing to come down to Cape Town for the purpose.

[1] The chief speech on the mechanistic view was made by Professor Lancelot Hogben.

[2] The discussion took place at Cape Town on 25 July 1929.

Your proposal that Professor Schäfer[1] or Professor D'Arcy Thompson should open the reply is I think a good one, and it certainly will be most interesting to have [Sir A. S.] Eddington and Wildon Carr to join the discussion. I think it would be desirable to have one or two South African scientists also to join in the discussion, and it would not be difficult to make arrangements accordingly later on. With kind regards, Yours sincerely,

s. J. C. Smuts

251 To C. P. Crewe   Vol. 102, no. 239

House of Assembly
Cape Town
15 February 1929

My dear Crewe, Things are going quite well. We shall beat them on the Native bill and that will then become the great issue for the elections. I don't really fear it, as the north will not show much enthusiasm for Hertzog's proposals to give representation to Natives and Coloured people in parliament. We shall not worry over details of the bills and confine ourselves to fighting at the second and third readings.

They will have a very big surplus and then proceed to buy the railway and civil service votes. Potchefstroom was simply bought. Ever yours sincerely,

J. C. Smuts

252 To H. Mentz   Vol. 43, no. 44

6 March 1929

My dear Mentz, Thank you for your letter about Parrack [W. J.]. I have seen him and talked over Sons of England and politics generally with him. He is a good fellow and means well by us. He does not want to stand this time and in fact thinks that both Benoni and Brakpan are hopeless seats for us.[2] I do not know whether I told you that young Hofmeyr was thinking of standing for Benoni against Madeley if he stood at all. I have cabled him to Jerusalem where he is at present to find out what his intentions are. His sympathies are strongly with us, but he is also a sort of 'hereniging's man', very much as Gys was a year ago;[3] I think that is a point

---

[1] Sir Edward Albert Sharpey-Schäfer (q.v.).
[2] Mining constituencies on the Witwatersrand.   [3] See 212.

on which he is really troubled. As you know, the Hofmeyr mind naturally turns to *hereniging*.[1] I am for it also if we can call the tune, instead of playing second fiddle. If we win this election, as I think we shall, it may be possible to do something in that direction.

Esselen arrived yesterday and I have been going into a number of constituencies with him. I understand from him that Rustenburg[2] has been remitted to the executive committee because I believe Teichmann [W. R. F.] has a majority which is not an absolute majority. All three candidates seem to be too weak to make any impression on Piet Grobler,[3] and if we can find another good man, we may yet have to push him in. If Hofmeyr wants to fight a country seat, this will be the place for him and he may beat Grobler. For the moment, however, the decision is to be between the three candidates, and I do not see how we can pass over Teichmann who obtained a majority. Re-nomination is so troublesome that I doubt whether it is in the interests of the party. Dolf de la Rey is in my opinion the weaker of the two candidates. I am somewhat troubled over the seat as I was very anxious to give Grobler a knock, but unless we can get a man like Hofmeyr to stand ultimately and Teichmann to retire for him, I do not see how this change can be effected.

The Nats feel very sick over the bungle into which they have got over the Native question. They never anticipated that we would vote against the bills clause by clause and make them vote for them clause by clause. They now think that we have laid a trap for them and that Hertzog has bungled the affair.[4] We are certainly on a good wicket and I doubt whether they will be able to make any capital out of this most dangerous issue.

I understand the elections will be on 12 June. This comes to me from many quarters, but of course there is not yet any absolute certainty. However I think we can reckon on this date. Prospects seem good, the government has bungled badly over the German treaty, although I had some difficulty in getting my friends out of, at any rate the appearance, of being anti-German. All good wishes, Yours ever sincerely,

s. J. C. Smuts

[1] A reference to the policy of J. H. Hofmeyr (Onze Jan).

[2] In the western Transvaal.

[3] P. G. W. Grobler was at this time minister of lands.

[4] In February 1929 when Hertzog submitted the revised Natives' Parliamentary Representation Bill and Coloured Persons' Rights Bill to a joint sitting of both houses they failed to get the two-thirds majority required by the constitution although Hertzog had adopted some of the suggestions made by Smuts in their private talks (*see* **240–2**, and C. M. Tatz, *Shadow and Substance in South Africa*, pp. 60–1).

253   To M. C. Gillett   Vol. 43, no. 104

Cape Town
4 April 1929

I have spent a glorious week of quiet at Tsalta after the session. On
Sunday I leave for the eastern province and shall be at it all the
time till 12 June when our election comes...I wrote a paper on
'The Nature of Life' for the British Association which goes on
holistic lines without striking out new ground. All very pleasant
and peaceful and away from the anxieties and strife of politics.

The unexpected news of the death of Lady Courtney came as
a great shock. I had just received a very nice note from her about
the secret Irish negotiations and the king's redrafted speech.[1] She
wanted to know more about it all; and then, darkness and silence.
She was a fine and great soul, and of all the politicals in London
I loved her best.

Thank you very much for your last dear letter (from Madeira),
so full of news and pleasant things...Yes, Tsalta has been good to
us. Like Paradise[2] and similar good places which have passed into
the eternal. And Tsalta will pass too. But there still is East Africa
to beckon us and look forward to. I think four to six months there
will be a great thing indeed—even more so than the last Zoutpansberg trip which even Hutchinson [J.] calls the experience of his life.
It is curious how one turns away from this strenuous life of preoccupation with human affairs and human beings and longs at the
last to be alone with your nearest and dearest and with the
nature that never fails you. The old animal is said to be driven out
of the herd, but is he not half willing to go and be alone and by
himself away from the jostling and the frolicsomeness of the younger
ones? And so he browses quietly on the hillside and surveys the
world with a detached eye. I have not at all the feeling of age but
I do love to get away from politics to that wild nature which is so
sweet and interesting...

Yes, I think the scotching of Hertzog's Native policy was a good
thing; but grave difficulties remain. One can only pray that people
will more and more appreciate that this is not a road for short-cuts
and that patience and far-sightedness are essential to any solution
of the problems that face us. A Fabian policy is on the whole the
wisest in so dangerous a situation. But I sometimes despair of the
Native question. It seems to me that it is demanding almost too
much of human nature to ask black and white to be just and fair
and generous to each other. Still we must do our best and act up

[1] Smuts Collection, vol. 41, no. 94.   [2] *See* vol. III, p. 659, note 3.

to our lights, and God will fulfil himself in ways now dark to us.[1]

Well, dear, I am writing too much, and my poor hand is numb with cold. Ever yours lovingly,

Jan

254   From J. H. Hofmeyr   Vol. 42, no. 29

The Mandeville Hotel
Mandeville Place, W.1
11 April 1929

Geagte Generaal, Van Cairo het ek u geskryf dat ek die vraag van my moontlike kandidatuur by die toekomstige verkiesing nog verder oor sou nadink, en eers tot 'n finale besluit sou kom na ons aankoms in Londen. Dit het ek nou gedoen, en tot die besluit gekom om my *nie* as kandidaat te stel nie. Ek is jammer om u teleur te stel—ook dat ek u nie behulpsaam kan wees nie, maar met die oog op die toekoms meen ek dat dit die regte besluit is. Dit is vir my duidelik dat wat ook nou met hierdie eleksie mag plaasvind, die tyd wel sal aanbreek wanneer daar nouere samewerking sal moet kom tussen ons en die Nasionaliste, en met die oog daarop sal dit miskien van belang wees dat daar iemand op ons kant is wat nie in die stryd deel geneem het nie. Of ek reg is, sal die tyd moet leer, maar dit is in elk geval nie my eie belang wat ek op die voorgrond stel nie. Want die tekens lyk goed vir 'n S.A.P. meerderheid— hoewel 'n klein meerderheid—na die verkiesing, en met die oog daarop sou dit seker meer in my belang wees om in die stryd deel te neem.

Ons plan is dus om ons vertrek so te reël dat ons net kort voor die verkiesing terug keer. Miskien land ons die 10de Junie in die Kaap aan, miskien die 3de. In die laaste geval sou ek miskien nog 'n ietsie kan doen om u te help, deur 'n paar vergaderings op die Rand toe te spreek met die hoop dat ek die onbesliste stem teen die Arbeiders kan beweeg—maar dit is iets wat ek eers later oor sal besluit, en in elk geval sal dit die meeste effek hê as my voorneme om dit te doen nie publiek bekend is nie.

Ek sal u later weer skryf om te sê wanneer ek daar sal wees. Intussen die beste wense—en alle moontlike sukses. Geheel die uwe,

Jan H. Hofmeyr

---

[1] And God fulfils himself in many ways,
  Lest one good custom should corrupt the world.
Tennyson, *The Idylls of the King, The Passing of Arthur*, l. 407.

TRANSLATION

The Mandeville Hotel
Mandeville Place, W.1
11 April 1929

Dear General, I wrote to you from Cairo that I would further consider the question of my possible candidature in the coming election
and reach a final decision after our arrival in London. This I have
now done and have decided *not* to offer myself as a candidate. I am
sorry to disappoint you—and also that I cannot be of help to you
but, with a view to the future, I think this is the right decision. It is
clear to me that, whatever may happen in this election, the time will
come when there will have to be closer co-operation between us
and the Nationalists, and, in view of that, it may be important that
there should be someone on our side who had had no part in the
struggle. Time will show whether I am right but at any rate I am
not putting my own interests in the foreground. For the signs look
right for a South African party majority, although a small
majority, after the election and, in view of that, it would no doubt
be more in my interest to take part in the struggle.

Our plan is therefore to arrange our departure so that we return
just before the election. Perhaps we shall land in Cape Town on
10 June, perhaps on the 3rd. In the latter case I may yet be able to
do a little to help you by addressing a few meetings on the Rand in
the hope of influencing the floating vote against Labour—but this
is something I shall decide later and, in any case, it will have the
greater effect if my intention of doing it is not publicly known.

I shall write to you again later to say when I shall be there. In
the meantime, best wishes and all possible success. Yours sincerely,

Jan H. Hofmeyr

255   To M. C. Gillett   Vol. 43, no. 106

Irene
[Transvaal]
22 April 1929

We are having the most lovely days—medium nights when three
blankets are necessary outside, and glorious sunshiny days when
one finds it impossible to remain indoors. I am spending a week or
so at home to deal with correspondence and all the worries of
politics before I start for the next political tour. It is letter writing,
telephone answering and interviewing almost all the time. Still

'time and the hour run through the roughest day'[1] and I have seen worse times than these. It is now Monday morning. I had to remain here over the week-end for visitors and interviewers, but in an hour's time Andries [Weyers] and I leave for Rooikop to see how things are getting on there. We shall stay only for the night and be back tomorrow at noon. On Friday I am at Bloemfontein for a heart to heart talk with our Free State candidates and next week I shall hold a big meeting at Pretoria to reply to Hertzog's last speech at Smithfield.[2] His election campaign seems based on two charges against us. We are old Unionists in disguise, and we are negrophilists dragging South Africa to ruin. Both dangerous racial stunts which show how we still play with fire in the year 1929. I agree with you that the way I defeated his policy in the last session, quietly and without fuss, was one of my best jobs. But there is a vast difference of opinion on these matters in South Africa and he is appealing to deep-seated prejudices which may be stirred into dangerous activity. It is horrible to fight elections between whites over anti-Native prejudices. My hope is that he will fail to bamboozle the public and stampede them into a Native crisis. If we win now I believe the Nats will break up just as Labour has already broken up. We shall see. Meantime I notice that mechanized electioneering is going on at a great pace in Great Britain. I do not see anything in Lloyd George's programme to cure unemployment.[3] If the unemployed are taken on the roads for a year or two, what is to happen after the roads are finished? To the dole will then be added another trouble, the state labour army on the roads, which could not be demobilized, and so the snowball will increase.

I am deeply interested in the reparation negotiations in Paris which are reported to be at breaking point.[4] I hope a solution will be found. Unless this problem is eliminated and the Rhine evacuated, we shall see vast troubles in the next five years when the occupation period *must* end,[5] and the French will want to hang on

[1] ...Come what may,
Time and the hour runs through the roughest day.
                                    Shakespeare, *Macbeth*, i. iii. 146.

[2] *See* 256.

[3] The Liberal party had issued an elaborate programme set out in five books. One of these was *We Can Conquer Unemployment* (March 1929) which advocated a large public works project including a system of national roads.

[4] In January 1929 a committee had been appointed, under the chairmanship of Owen D. Young, to work out a final settlement of the reparation problem and to deal with the question of the evacuation of the Rhineland.

[5] Under the treaty of Versailles the coal mines of the Saar were ceded to France for fifteen years during which period it was administered by the League of Nations. At the end of the period (1934) a plebiscite of the inhabitants would decide its future government.

to the Rhine. Unless the reparation question is out of the way, the French will make that the excuse for sticking to the Rhine in spite of the peace treaty. If trouble then occurs, as in the Ruhr invasion of 1923, we shall be bound to come in under the Locarno agreement, and matters may easily drift into chaos. But so many troubles have been overcome these last ten years that one hopes and prays that this crisis over the Rhine will also be averted. I was much interested in Snowden's indiscretion over the debts.[1] I suppose this was a calculated move, and that we shall hear more of it in the future. The United States has let off very lightly her other debtors after driving a furious bargain with us, and we have let off our continental debtors even more lightly. The whole position does require looking into, if England is not to be bled white and permanently crippled.

But I am writing too much. Love from yours ever,

Jan

256 Speech (1929) Box H, no. 47A

This election speech was made by Smuts on 30 April 1929 at Pretoria. The document in the Smuts Collection is a typescript corrected by Smuts.

Let me begin by referring to the recent speech of the prime minister at Smithfield.[2] To the Pact it will not prove a very helpful speech, and I don't think we shall hear much of it in this election campaign. It is more full of vainglory and boasting than of real constructive statesmanship. It repeats the platitudes which the prime minister has been saying *ad nauseam* on the platform these last few years. The Pact will require different ammunition if they are to get with some credit through this campaign.

I deplore the prime minister's personal references to his opponents. No wise man expresses public contempt and insult for his opponents in that style. But the prime minister is worried and weary, and allowance must be made for this as well as for his unfortunate methods of public controversy. I fear his followers will go one better, and we shall see the floodgates of personality and

[1] In the course of the debate on Churchill's fifth budget on 16 April 1929 Snowden made a slashing attack on the principle expressed in the Balfour note of 2 August 1922, namely, that Great Britain should take no more from her European debtors than she would be required to pay the United States. Snowden regarded this as 'a policy of quixotic generosity at the expense of the oppressed British taxpayers'. His speech fluttered many dove-cots but did not, in the end, lead to an international issue on war debts.

[2] On 18 April 1929.

abuse opened wide during this election campaign. Already the chief organ of the Nationalists in the Transvaal[1] has called me the successor of Dingaan,[2] and a much more dangerous enemy to white civilization than that Kaffir potentate. And this sort of abuse is called politics. I shall not follow the methods of the prime minister. However deeply I differ from him, I respect him, both personally and in his official position. The time surely is past when such methods of vituperation and abuse should be resorted to in our political campaigning. If I cannot win this fight cleanly I would not care to win at all. Let us not lower public standards further. It is one of my grave charges against the present government that the standard, the tone of public life has been lowered. As a result parliament has gone down in public estimation, and its authority is being gravely undermined. Public life is beginning to be looked upon as not a clean thing and something to be avoided by honest men. Nowhere is this deterioration more noticeable than in relation to the civil service. The civil service is becoming degraded into a mere party machine. Ministers have openly declared their preference for Nationalists in appointments to the service. A political inquisition is held into a candidate's opinions. Favouritism and nepotism are rife. Party politics is creeping in everywhere, and polluting all the channels of public life and public service. The spoils system[3] which has been the curse of other countries is being adopted in South Africa. Jobs for pals is publicly preached by the Pact as a desirable policy. We condemn this as a pernicious policy which will cost this country very dear. Our public service has in the past been above this sort of thing; we have had a high tradition of a clean and impartial public service which has been the pride of this country. The latest instance of this debauching of the service is the railway circular on civilized labour[4] for which the general manager of railways[5] is not responsible, but which he has been forced to issue as a departmental report. It is a political partisan document from beginning to end; and one hears that other similar reports will be published during these elections to provide the Pact party with ammunition. The public and railway services are full of party politics, and if an official resists this policy he runs grave risks and is looked upon with disfavour. No wonder many of our best

[1] *Ons Vaderland*, established in Pretoria 1914–16; title changed to *Die Vaderland* March 1932; moved to Johannesburg June 1936.

[2] *See* vol. IV, pp. 317–18.

[3] The practice in the United States of appointing to public office the supporters of the winning party in an election. Derived from the phrase 'to the victors belong the spoils'.

[4] This remains unpublished.   [5] J. R. More.

men are leaving the service, and that the service is being impoverished and its morale lowered. No greater service can be rendered this country than a clean sweep of these practices and a return to the high tradition of an impartial public service. The self-respect and the independence of a loyal, disinterested civil service is a priceless asset of immeasurable value to the country in every respect. If we are returned to power we shall look upon it as a mandate to make the necessary reforms and to see that in future the service does not remain liable to this sort of party abuse. The service should as far as possible be placed in a position which will protect its independence and its self-respect and prevent its being abused for party purposes—whatever party it may be.

The prime minister makes two great charges against the South African party, and both charges convict him of dangerous racialism. The first is that the South African party is in reality an old-Unionist party, in which the influence of the old Unionists predominates. The second is in effect that the South African party is a pro-Native or negrophilist party and is working for a black South Africa.[1] These charges are not only wild and baseless, devoid of all truth; but they are most dangerous. They are an insult to that section of our white people who formerly belonged to the Unionist party. Natives and Unionists are held up as a menace to South Africa. Judging from the prime minister's charges one can only conclude that the old Unionists and Natives are the enemies of South Africa. Could anything be more puerile and more dangerous? The old Unionists represent a large section of our English fellow-citizens. That seems to be their sin. They are still foreign adventurers.[2] Mr Jagger we are told is not yet a South African, in spite of a lifetime of devoted love and service to this country. Can anything make him a South African except knuckling down to the Pact? Surely these racial insults and taunts are unworthy of the prime minister of this country. They are very wounding and are felt very deeply by people who are as good South Africans as the prime minister himself. We have lost in Sir Thomas Smartt one of the noblest and best South Africans we ever had.[3] The prime minister's conception of South African patriotism is such that there is no place for the Smartts, the Jaggers and the Duncans, for the more recent South

[1] In January 1929 Smuts, speaking at Ermelo (Transvaal), had said the Union should co-operate with the British authorities in developing their territories to the north and had envisaged a future federation of British states south of the equator. Hertzog had replied by issuing his 'Black Manifesto' in which he said that Smuts looked forward to the establishment of 'a black kaffir state' of which South Africa would be only a subordinate part.

[2] *See* vol. III, p. 112, note 2.   [3] He had died on 17 April 1929.

Africans who have thrown in their lot with us. 'Come out of the house of the stranger' is still the appeal which is continually being addressed to the Dutch-speaking Saps. And that is the real appeal of his Smithfield address. Our English-speaking fellow citizens justly pride themselves as much as we do on their South African patriotism, their love of South Africa and its people, their complete identification with the country and its deepest interests. These taunts simply convict the prime minister of deeply rooted racialism. They prove that he has learnt nothing and forgotten nothing since the De Wildt speech of 1912.[1] My unforgivable sin is that in 1920 I invited our English fellow citizens into the South African party on a footing of equal comradeship. Hence this repeated charge of harbouring old Unionists in the South African party. We glory in the step which was then taken. That was the real death-blow to racialism in our politics. Our South Africanism is wide enough to embrace both races on an equal footing. For eight years we have worked together in office and out of office: we have co-operated in perfect loyalty to each other, and it is the pride of our party that no racial issues exist for us in any shape or form. The prime minister charges us with impotence in office. Impotence! The party that has seen South Africa through all its greatest phases of development since Union is charged with impotence. If we had really been impotent in face of all the dangers which threatened this country from within and without General Hertzog would not today be standing on our shoulders and crowing over the sovereign independence of South Africa. In those days the so-called do-and-dare party showed their daring mostly in thwarting our efforts to keep this country safe and its honour untarnished. Their doing consisted mostly in undoing the work of union and in missions and campaigns for the break up of the Union. Now that, owing to our action, their war policy and their secession policy have finally failed and been abandoned they are reaping the fruits of our labours and they show a spirit of boastfulness which ill becomes them under the circumstances. In the years of depression which overcame this country, as they overcame every other country after the war, our efforts were crippled, and we had to strain every nerve to keep things going. And we succeeded, in spite of all the efforts of our opponents to promote lawlessness and to foment strife and unrest. The prime minister says that we left the finances of the country in a deplorable state in 1924. The fact is that our successors found sufficient in the coffers of state to repay our deficits, and from the balance left by us to devote £500,000 to road improvements,

[1] *See* vol. III, p. 123, note 2.

£200,000 to land settlement, and to pay £1,700,000 into the sinking fund for debt redemption. That was the nest egg we left them instead of the bankruptcy they keep harping on. A government that could manage to nurse the finances of the country through the fiercest depression of its history and leave such balances behind for its successors to play with cannot have been so impotent as the prime minister tries to make out. And what, in comparison, is the record of the so-called do-and-dare government? They came into power in the middle of 1924, when the tide of trade was turning in a world-wide movement. They had surpluses during the next four years which totalled over £5 million, but like the spendthrift they lived up to their income, and their expenditure today is £5 million per annum more than it was in 1924. They take £5 million per annum more out of the pockets of the people through taxation than we did. When the day of reckoning comes and the tide of trade turns in its recurrent cycles we may have to face a financial crisis which will inflict the greatest suffering on our people. Through economy in public expenditure we reduced the annual cost of our services between 1921 and 1923 by £2½ million. But all this painful work has been undone and our expenditure in recent years has gone up by leaps and bounds until now, apart from the railways, it costs £30 million per annum to run a country with a white population of less than 1¾ million. In the railways the rate of increased expenditure has been even more rapid and the position is much more alarming, so that instead of an asset the railways are fast becoming a financial liability to the country. The Pact régime in the railways has been one of deficits, and it is only this year that by hook and by crook a small surplus has been scraped together for election purposes. This enormous inflation of our public expenditure means inflation in other directions and an eventual rise in the cost of living which will hit the poorer classes and the development of the country very hard. The value of the pound has already sensibly gone down. The greatest blessing a good government can confer on a country is cheap and economical administration, and judged by that standard the performance of the Pact government is lamentable. The prime minister boasts that all their election promises of 1924 have been fulfilled. What about their promise of economy in the light of these figures? They made the welkin ring with their thunder against our spendthrift policy at a time when we were actually economizing and lowering expenditure in every direction. Instead of carrying out their promise of economy they ran amok when their chance came and they will go down in the history of the country as the most wasteful administration the country has

397

ever seen. Their boast that their big budget surpluses reflected the industrial and manufacturing progress of the country will not stand a moment's examination. Revenue from customs exceeded Mr Havenga's estimates in the three years 1926–9 by the very high figures of £847,000, £991,000 and £1,225,000. The boasted surpluses were largely due to importations into the country and not to internal industrial development. During these three years there were also the phenomenal diamond discoveries in Lichtenburg and Namaqualand, which accounted for another large addition to the revenue, as well as for the swollen importations and customs figures. But for these elements of pure accident and luck the budget of Mr Havenga might have told the same sorry tale that Mr [C. W.] Malan's railway budget has been actually telling the last five years.

The progress of the country in other respects has been quite normal. Industries have developed but not more so than they did under the South African party régime.[1] During the last four years the manufacturing production of the country has increased from roughly £80 million to £100 million in round figures, that is, at the rate of about £5 million per annum, which is very much the same as the average rate during the preceding eight years of the South African party government. And the white employment figures show a similar normal rise. Members of the government have boosted themselves and their financial and industrial policy *ad nauseam* until some people have actually been taken in by their constant iteration. But when the figures are analysed and the facts examined, their record appears to be nothing but the normal expansion of the country in good times, plus the heavy top weight of expenditure which they have imposed on the country and its future development. General Kemp[2] goes about the country with his fairy tale that taxation has been decreased by £6 million under the Pact. It is on a par with the wild and woolly story which he also spins to the backveld that the Native policy of the South African party is to give equal franchise rights to white and black alike, and to male and female alike. The minister of finance does not claim to have decreased taxes by more than about £2 million, and even that figure is disputable, while in spite of that reduction the actual taxation screwed out of the tax-payer has admittedly increased by over £5 million per annum since 1924. These brilliant surpluses cover hardships. The customs duties have been raised, the prices on many of the necessaries of life have increased, and the

[1] Here is inserted in Smuts's handwriting: 'The old Sap. industries going forward. Motors.'   [2] Then minister of agriculture.

cost of living figures have gone up. During 1928 customs collections on blankets amounted to £534,000; on clothing £794,000; and on foodstuffs and other necessaries of life £2,100,000. And these taxes hit the poor far more than the rich. They claim to be a poor man's government, just as they claim to be a poor digger's government. But the poor man has heavier burdens thrown on him than he carried ever before, and the poor digger lies stunned and flattened out under the new Diamond Law[1] and the state diggings, while the Diamond Syndicate has never been more flourishing than under Mr Beyers.[2] During the last five years the public debt has gone up by over £35 million—from £208,000,000 in 1924 to £243,500,000 in 1929. The prime minister boasts, however, that the unproductive debt has gone down by £20 million under the Pact and apparently wishes the inference to be drawn that that debt has been paid off by that enormous amount. Of course nothing could be more misleading. The figure of £20 million is based on a treasury calculation which does not mean actual payment of debt. According to the auditor-general's reports the public debt actually paid off from 1923 to 1928 amounts to no more than £6,128,019. The figures for the last year have not yet been audited. The prime minister is prone to accuse others of inaccuracy. I leave it to the public to judge the accuracy of his statements on this important matter.

I now come to the main issue on which the Pact is fighting this election—I refer to the Native question. The prime minister knows perfectly well that this general election or any other general election will not avail to solve the Native question. What he is really aiming at is not to solve the Native question but to use it as a party stunt to win the general election. It is a purely party manoeuvre and a particularly lamentable and reprehensible one. If he had any serious intention of solving the Native question he would have kept it out of the party arena and out of this election. Along party lines a solution is impossible under the South Africa Act. That Act requires a two-thirds vote of all the members of both houses of parliament at a joint sitting for any alterations of the Native franchise at the Cape. No party is ever likely to get such a majority and it was the clear intention of the framers of the South Africa Act, including General Hertzog, under that unchangeable provision to take the Cape Native franchise out of party politics. Whatever views we may take of the Native question, we must accept it as bedrock fact that under the South Africa Act no solution on party lines or by

[1] The Diamond Trade Regulations Act, No. 1 of 1928.
[2] Then minister of mines and industries.

way of general elections is possible. No one knows that better than the prime minister. His object is to win the election by scaring the people, by playing on their fears and passions, by stampeding them on a matter which, above all others, requires cool and sane statesmanship. His manoeuvre in making the Native question his chief party cry on this occasion is therefore particularly discreditable and deserves the punishment which I trust it will receive in these elections. I hope these elections will teach politicians that it is dangerous to play with fire, and that the game is not only dangerous but will not pay. That they were going to take this fatal step had been clear for some time. Last October Mr Roos declared at Ermelo that the Native question was the best battleground which the Pact could choose for these elections, and he expressed the wish that the South African party would vote for the Cape Native franchise so that they could go to the country on this question. The prime minister has followed his sinister advice. Mr Roos in 1919 sent the prime minister and his colleagues on a wild goose chase to America and Europe for the disruption of the Union, while he himself kept out of the silly farce.[1] In the same way he has launched the prime minister on this fatal expedition. We all sincerely hope he will soon be restored to complete health and public activity.

The prime minister in his Pretoria West speech at the beginning of the year showed clearly that he was determined to make the Native question the football of our party politics. His intention was still more clearly shown shortly after by his black Africa manifesto which will ever remain a black blot on his own fair fame. It was the most disgraceful exhibition to which a party politician has ever lent himself in this country. Mr Ben Jenkins, an ex-chairman of the Labour party, and no friend of mine, but an honest opponent, used language about this manifesto on which I could not improve. 'I have no hesitation in saying', he declared, 'that it is the choicest piece of political blackguardism the world has ever seen.' I leave it at that. But you will know by this time that this misleading false propaganda is the main plank of the Pact in these elections. From every platform in rural South Africa you hear it thundered forth that I am for a black South Africa, that I want to dissolve the Union in a flood of barbarism, that I am a menace to white civilization. And all this because I have advocated, and still strongly advocate, a policy of

---

[1] Tielman Roos had been the chief spokesman for the Transvaal National party at the Bloemfontein congress on 16 January 1919 which met to discuss the question of sending an independence deputation to the peace conference (*see supra*, p. 102, note 1). The deputation did not travel direct to Europe because the crew of an English ship threatened to strike if they came aboard. They took a Dutch ship to New York and there boarded another Dutch ship for London.

friendship and political rapprochement with the young British states to our north which are our real industrial and political hinterland. I look forward to the time when our politics and our resources in African civilization will be linked up, and the name of South Africa will bear a far wider meaning than it does today. I believe there is not a single fair-minded and patriotic South African who does not agree with me in this hope, this outlook, this aspiration for the future. It has been the traditional northward policy of South Africa, and it will influence our future as it has our past. This faith is my sin. The prime minister calls the British states to the north kaffir states, whom to touch would be certain leprosy for South Africa. He must have been made aware by now of the deep resentment he has caused in the north, and the great injury which is being done to our interests by these wild statements. So he is now back-pedalling. The two Rhodesias, although they follow the same Native policy as the Cape, and although they, too, have a vast preponderance of Native over white population, are not included in this ban from any future federation or alliance with us. Well, let me tell him that I myself do not look upon our extension north-wards beyond the Rhodesias as practical politics for our day and generation. I shall be more than satisfied if I could see a fair linking up with the two Rhodesias in my time. The rest I leave to the future. But my policy of friendship and collaboration with the rest of British Africa remains unaffected, and I shall always look upon them as junior members of the family, whom to befriend and support in our common task of civilization would be both a duty and a privilege for the Union.

Besides this mare's nest there is the other, that the policy of the South African party is to give equal franchise rights to black and white alike throughout the Union. This charge is just as baseless as the previous one of a black Africa policy. The equal franchise has never been the policy of the South African party. No such declaration has ever been made with any authority on behalf of the party. Our party programme from 1911 onwards never gave the least indication of such a policy. And only last December our Bloemfontein programme laid down as the broad principles of our Native policy that we respected existing rights, that we aimed at the improvement and better economic use of the existing reserves and locations, and at the extension of Native local self-government in Native areas. Not a word about equal franchise rights. The Natives do not claim and the whites certainly will not concede any such claim. The charge seems to be based on a declaration issued some weeks ago by the Archbishop of Cape Town, Sir James Rose Innes,

Professor Fremantle, Mr Morris Alexander and others.[1] They do not speak for the South African party. A week after Mr Alexander had signed that declaration the prime minister was supporting him in his candidature for Gardens at the Zionist Hall in Cape Town. It is the policy of Mr Alexander, whom the prime minister so fervently backs, but it is not our policy. Anyone who anywhere in these election days says that the equal white and Native franchise is our policy is stating what is false and what he knows to be false. To this I wish to add quite clearly that the prime minister's scheme of parliamentary rights to the Natives of the northern provinces will not receive the support of our party.

This statement of our Native policy does not cover the Coloured people. So far as the Coloured people are concerned I adhere to the policy repeatedly laid down on behalf of our party that the existing Cape basis ought not to be tampered with. As regards our Native policy, it is contained in our Bloemfontein programme as just indicated. We believe in giving our Native fellow citizens justice and fairplay and reasonable scope for self-development; we do not believe in a policy of repression which is certain to recoil on the whites. And as regards political rights we believe that in terms of the South Africa Act no policy is feasible or possible which is not carried by general consent of parties, and in which the Natives are not fairly consulted. The only way to make any progress is therefore to call a national convention to deal with the matter by way of negotiation, understanding and agreement between parties and others interested. This course I advised in 1925 already. To me it is as clear as daylight that no other method will prove of any use in this connection. I hope when we are returned to power that we shall have the co-operation of the other parties in exploring this question by means of such a convention, and I am more than hopeful that in that non-party atmosphere a workable solution will be found—for our time at any rate, even if no permanent solution is possible on so grave and difficult an issue. The Natives themselves welcome and will respond to such a method of dealing with their status and their rights.

In saying this I wish to add that in my opinion the position will never be quite safe for European civilization unless the balance of population is seriously redressed. Six million Natives against one-and-three-quarter million whites is a brute fact which no laws or

[1] This manifesto led to the formation of the Non-Racial Franchise Association in May 1929. Its objects were to defend the Cape franchise against differentiation on the ground of race or colour and to advocate a franchise with a civilization test for the whole Union. It was a strictly non-party organization.

repressive administration can get away from. The only sane and safe policy is a well-regulated system for increasing the European population and altering the ratio of our white and Native population. Immigration has been the policy of our party since its foundation at Bloemfontein in 1911. I believe that a proper immigration policy spread over some generations will work wonders in this respect. But here again we are up against stubborn opposition from the other side. The figures can be redressed by a continuous policy of immigration.

The scare started by a former director of census[1] that the Natives were increasing at such a rate as to doom South Africa to being a black country in future has no substantial foundation. Senator [A. W.] Roberts has reviewed the census figures most carefully and minutely and shown that the Native birthrate is rapidly slowing down and that the position is by no means alarming. If the white birthrate were reinforced by a sound immigration system the position would not only be eased but might cease to inspire fear for our future. To my mind a sound immigration policy is the real and permanent solution of the Native question, in that it will remove the fear which now lies heavily on our future. It is far preferable to the prime minister's hopeless policy. Money judiciously and wisely spent here would be the best investment this country could make to insure its future, to develop its resources, and to increase its inland markets.

I shall now proceed to summarize briefly the main items in the programme of action on which we are fighting these elections. The programme itself was formulated by our party at the Bloemfontein congress last December to which I would refer you for further details. I mention only the main points.

1. *Our status in the Empire.* As regards our national status within the British Commonwealth of nations, we stand by it as it has been declared at the imperial conference, and won for us by the loyal service and sacrifice of our brave sons. We rejoice that this status is now generally accepted and that the policy of secession from the Empire has been definitely abandoned.

2. *Preference within the Empire.* We condemn the German treaty as a breach with the settled policy of preference within the Empire, and as an unnecessary menace to our best foreign market. Unless the treaty is amended in this respect we shall denounce it at the earliest opportunity. Any vote for the Pact will be a vote for the indefinite continuance of this treaty with all its dangers for our producers.

[1] Dr J. E. Holloway.

3. *Our northern policy.* We stand by the northern policy as above indicated, which will, we hope, eventually lead to federation with the two Rhodesias and to co-operation and some loose form of linking up in the future with the other British states to the north.

4. *Women's enfranchisement.* We stand for enfranchisement of women. In view of the difficulties about Native women at the Cape I would favour leaving their rights over for settlement at the convention along with the rights of Native men. But this should not delay the grant of the franchise to our women as one of our first acts if we come into power. I note that the prime minister at Benoni receded from his promise in parliament to introduce such a measure in 1930. He now makes it dependent on the settlement first of the Native questions at some future date. This is a pretty hopeless prospect for our women, and they had better expect nothing from either the prime minister or Colonel Creswell or their parties who have repeatedly betrayed this great cause.

5. *The Native question.* Our policy has been stated above—a national convention.

6. *Asiatics.* Our policy remains unaltered and may be summarized as 'no Asiatic immigration and repatriation as fast as possible and with no chance of return'.

7. *The public and railway services.* We stand for clean services, divorced from politics or tests of a political nature, and for a reformed public service commission. We guarantee existing pay and conditions and fair inquiry into grievances. We oppose appointments from outside except where professional or technical qualifications are required. The civilized labourers on the railways need have no fear of dismissal, and every effort will be made to improve their position on grounds of efficiency.

8. *Social, wage and housing policies.* We stand by the Conciliation Act as the real bulwark of industrial peace, which it has proved to be since it was passed by the South African party government in 1924.[1] The Wage Act[2] will be maintained but will be restricted to unorganized or sweated industries for which it was passed, and will be fairly administered so as not merely to protect the highly skilled but also the semi-skilled worker. The difficulties which have arisen from the wage determinations for shop workers and hotel workers,

[1] The Industrial Conciliation Act, No. 11 of 1924, provides for the setting up of industrial councils or conciliation boards to determine disputes between employers' organizations and trade unions all of which must be registered.
[2] The Wage Act, No. 27 of 1925, laid down minimum wages to be recommended by a Wage Board and distinguished between 'civilized' and 'uncivilized' labour.

as well as in other recent cases show the necessity for a change in its administration. The same wage policy pursued in Australia under the arbitration acts has been severely condemned by the recent British commission of inquiry as a potent source of industrial unrest and upheaval. The Wage Act has scarcely begun to function as many of the determinations have been upset by the law courts, but it may lead to the same trouble as in Australia, unless its application is definitely restricted so as not to affect the organized trades.

We also favour a vigorous prosecution of the national housing policy which was first begun by us and has proved a priceless boon to the workers and to people with small incomes. The beneficial effects of decent housing for all classes cannot be overestimated.

9 and 10. *Land and immigration policies.* We advocate a policy of adequate advances for purchase and improvement of land for approved South African and immigrant farmers alike. Water boring on farms will be cheapened and speeded up on a large scale, and the deplorable state of the cattle and tobacco industries will be vigorously dealt with.

11. *Mining policy.* We condemn the provisions in the Mozambique agreement[1] which curtails the labour supply from Mozambique by 25,000 men in five years, shortens the period of service, compels the repatriation of all Portuguese boys working on farms, and severely curtails trading by Mozambique boys on the Rand. It is our intention to move for the alteration of these provisions at the earliest opportunity. Inquiry should be made how best to prolong the life of the low-grade mines on which the prosperity of the Rand is largely dependent, and every step should be taken to secure a continuance of that life. Prospecting and mining by the small man will be encouraged and made easier in every possible way. The Diamond Law should be amended so as to remove the undue restrictions on diggers' rights and owners' rights which were passed last year. The position of the state diggings in Namaqualand calls for thorough inquiry with a view to putting a stop to the grave abuses to which it has led. The government has behaved with great meanness. What action should be taken with regard to these diggings will depend on such an inquiry. The coal and oil fuel industry will receive, as it will deserve, our strongest support in view of its immense importance for this country.

[1] Since December 1901 a series of agreements had been made with the Portuguese government for the recruitment of Natives from Portuguese East Africa as labourers in the gold-mines (*see* vol. II, p. 399, note 1; p. 564, note 1). The agreement had lapsed in 1923. The chief provisions were renewed in 1925 until a new agreement, which was less favourable to the Union, could be arrived at in 1928.

12 and 13. *Protection and cost of living.* We stand for protection for local industries which legitimately call for support. But we are against state management and undue state interference, and prefer to encourage private initiative and enterprise. We also think that the cost of living should not be raised by such protection, but that the duties on articles not calling for protection should be lowered *pari passu* with the imposition of protective duties. This is mainly a farming and mining country, and to keep the cost of living low should be a matter of cardinal public policy. We condemn the policy of unnecessarily high customs duties which may swell the revenue and create surpluses, but make life harder for the poor and the wage earners and cripple the development.

We stand by the iron and steel industry which has been the policy of the Suth African party since Union. We mean to see the industry through, even if it should eventually involve certain alterations to the existing scheme.

14. *Railway policy.* The South African party considers the present position of our railway system unsatisfactory and favours a reconsideration of railway policy and railway rates in order better to promote general development and give effect to the provisions of the South Africa Act in regard to management on business principles and the development of the interior, and concurrently to make full economic use of motor transport.

15. *Provincial councils.* The South African party considers that the present elaborate and largely political provincial council system should be reviewed and careful inquiry made towards devising a more satisfactory form of local government for the Union, provided that in no province shall the provincial council be abolished unless on a referendum vote of that province in favour of such abolition.

16. *Road policy.* We favour a national road policy with a proper fund, which will co-ordinate the provincial activities in regard to our national and main roads. We do not think the best results will be obtained by the present government policy of occasional subventions to the provinces. There should be a co-ordinated policy for the Union as a whole, and the funds available for motor and petrol taxes ought to be amply sufficient for the purpose.

17 and 18. *Science and natural resources.* The practical application of science will make enormous difference to our resources and more than double the value of many districts. Farming is dependent on science. The botanical and veterinary divisions have done magnificent work which has received world-wide praise. A great forward

movement has become possible, and it is the intention of our party to make a start as soon as we get the opportunity. At the same time a determined effort will be made to prevent veld deterioration, to protect the sources of our river and our water supplies, and to make better economic use of our natural resources. To that policy our party stands pledged. The drift towards waste and senseless destruction must be definitely arrested. South Africa and her natural resources should be treated not as mere alien ground but as our mother, as something dear to us, which we mean to foster and protect and cherish. Young South Africa pouring from the universities has a new national consciousness; science has kindled in them a deeper reverence for all our natural things. And they are going to make use of their new knowledge for the conservation of our unique nature and for making her more fruitful and beautiful. And we mean to back this new attitude, this deeper scientific and aesthetic patriotism in every way. Politics should not absorb all our attention, and our real devotion should be for the things that will improve and enrich and render beautiful our great natural heritage. We want to wed science to life and from that union to create the new South Africa which we are seeking. No party can give a greater lead on this new road than the South African party.

I have explained to you the broad general standpoint which the South African party takes up in the politics of our country. I have necessarily had to omit many details and minor points for which there is no time tonight. As against the narrowness and race or class sectionalism of our opponents we stand for the greater South Africa, and for the wider nationalism which knows no distinctions. We seek to build this great Union on the foundations which General Botha laid, and which have stood the test of time; on comradeship and trust between the races; on loyalty and honour; and on fair and just dealing with rich and poor alike, with black and white alike. That is our tradition from the past, that is our vision for the future. That is the faith which inspires the South African party and which we shall carry into practice to the best of our ability.

May these ideas win in the coming elections. The greater South Africa, the wider nationalism—let that be our slogan in the fight which we shall do our best to win.

257   To J. H. Hofmeyr   Vol. 43, no. 57

Civil Service Club
Cape Town
5 Junie 1929

Waarde Jantjie, Net een regeltjie om jou en Borrie baie hartelik te
verwelkom by jul aankoms aanstaande Maandag. Ek was bly jou
briefies te ontvang en ook die telegram van gelukwens op 24 Mei.

Jy sal self jou idee kan vorm oor die politieke situasie by jou
aankoms. Sover ek kan sien bly die posisie vir ons gunstig; maar die
Pak het verbasend hard gewerk, en niemand kan met sekerheid
profeteer nie.

As ons slaag dan is my plan met jou nog wat dit was te vore. Jy
sal seker sonder versuim af kom na die Transvaal sodat ons sake
kan bespreek as dit nodig word, wat ek verwag.

Die uitslag van die Engelse eleksies is baie interessant. Met die
Arbeiders aan die hoof van sake, is die posisie vir die toekoms taamlik
onseker, en selfs gevaarlik in India en Afrika. Baie grond kan verlore
word indien daar nie met alle waaksaamheid gehandel word nie.
Ek was baie geïnteresseerd in jou beskouinge oor Afrika, die grooter
Suid-Afrika en die kwesties van ons toekoms in hierdie mysterieuse
vaderland.

Welkom met alle goeie wense op wat voor jou lê.

t.t. J. C. Smuts

TRANSLATION

Civil Service Club
Cape Town
5 June 1929

Dear Jantjie, Just a line to welcome you and Borrie very heartily on
your return next Monday. I was very glad to receive your notes and
also the telegram of good wishes on 24 May.

You will be able to form your own view of the political situation
when you arrive. As far as I can see the position remains favourable
for us; but the Pact has worked astonishingly hard, and no one can
prophesy with certainty.

If we succeed, my plan for you is still what it was before. You
will probably come down to the Transvaal without delay so that
we can discuss matters if it becomes necessary, as I expect.

The result of the English elections is very interesting.[1] With

---

[1] The Labour party, having won 287 seats, was the largest party in the house of
commons. But it had no overall majority for the Conservatives had 261 seats and the
Liberals 59. Nevertheless a Labour government took office.

Labour at the head of affairs the future position is very uncertain and even dangerous unless the greatest vigilance is shown. I was very much interested in your views on Africa, the greater South Africa and the questions of our future in this mysterious fatherland.[1]

Welcome with all good wishes for what lies before you, *totus tuus*,

J. C. Smuts

258   To M. C. Gillett   Vol. 43, no. 115

Irene
[Transvaal]
11 June 1929

I am just writing a line to show that 102 is not forgotten. But in view of tomorrow and all the work going on I shall be very brief. I spent last week at the Cape in a series of meetings, and incidentally visited 'Tsalta' in order to get a book which I wanted to consult for my article on 'Life'. I found that my little reading room was very damp and some water must have leaked in there and somewhat spoiled the walls. I cannot imagine how and where the water comes in.

I am very glad the elections are over and only tomorrow remains to record the result. Isie and I will leave in the morning for Standerton to hearten our supporters, but I am sorry that I have to go away at this stage. What the result over the whole country will be I do not worry about, having done my duty.

It has been most annoying that Sir James Rose Innes, Burton, and some others have formed a Franchise Association in support of the Cape Native franchise and for its extension to the north. Their manifestos have been a godsend to Hertzog and he has continually pointed out that the Saps want this extension. Finally, the Association has proceeded to belabour me for my national convention proposal. And then they pose as friends of the Cape franchise! If I had followed their tactics, Hertzog would have won handsomely and the Cape franchise would have been finished for good and all. Can you understand how such clever men can reallly do such a stupid thing? But you will see what difficulties I have between the upper and the nether millstone.

We are having a glorious winter. It has just rained over an inch here and the real cold has not come yet, although it is almost mid-June. I only wish I could go for a week or two to the Bushveld and

[1] Shortly before he returned to South Africa from a holiday abroad Hofmeyr's pre-election statement supporting the South African party was published. It emphasized the need for a realignment of parties after the election. (*See* the *Cape Times*, 6 June 1929, p. 13.)

rest after my labours. But it depends on the result. In any case I hope to have some days of good solid reading at the books you have recently sent me.

I suppose Japie will have gone when this reaches you. If not, give him my love and blessing for his East African expedition. My love also to you and Arthur and the other members of 102. I am thinking much of you. Ever yours,

Jan

259   To M. C. Gillett   Vol. 43, no. 116

Irene
[Transvaal]
19 June 1929

I have just read your last dear letter and, in the press of many visitors, I hurry to answer before the mail leaves. We are so glad that Japie has done well in his exam.[1] He has been a good steady boy and your kindness and the home at 102 must have helped him very much indeed. He will enjoy this return voyage and especially the Kenya visit on a motor bike.[2] Were it not that parliament meets on 19 July and the British Association on 22 July, I would go north with Jannie and share with him in the trip to that glorious country. But probably next year we shall all go to it and make a first-class holiday of it and a good botanical venture. Our elections are over and lost.[3] I do not feel heart-broken over the result. I have worked very hard and expected better things. But Hertzog's black bogey worked wonders in the backveld, and the people were stampeded. Even so we are a clear majority of the electorate over all other parties, and it is our electoral system which has beaten us. But there may be compensations; and I may yet secure my freedom at a favourable opportunity. So I am waiting and thinking. I am endowed with the happy temperament which always looks for good to come out of apparent evil. The last few days I have been working at a new draft of my paper on 'The Nature of Life' for the British Association. I wrote a paper before the elections which was sent to those interested in the British Association. But I was dissatisfied with it and have now made a new draft, with a fuller dose of holism. I do not see why I should not break a lance for holism on this occasion. It seems to be making headway. I have

[1] He had got a double first in the engineering tripos.
[2] On this occasion Japie Smuts climbed to the summit of Kilimanjaro.
[3] The results were: National party 78; South African party 61; Labour party 8; Independent 1.

recently seen a number of biologists (Wheeler [G. C.] in the United States, Donnan [F. G.] and Boycott [A. E.] in England) using at least the language of holism. This meeting is a great occasion for a little propaganda, which I must make use of. I shall send you the article when it is typed out, with a type[script] also of the earlier draft on somewhat different lines.

I suppose I ought to congratulate you on the Labour victory. What use will they make of it? It is a great opportunity after the stupidities of the Austen Chamberlain régime. I hope for the best. The world is ripe for a new lead, and perhaps a Babe (in the shape of the Labour party) will lead them, where the wise and the great have failed.[1] The position of Great Britain and the Empire generally is most unsound and unsatisfactory, and we shall permanently lose the lead in all liberal movements unless we now buck up. The world has been waiting—and only found manoeuvres instead of real wisdom and statesmanship...Thanks for the Swarthmore lecture[2] —a really fine piece of work. I did not know that Eddington was a Quaker. He is now our foremost scientific thinker in England, as Whitehead is in America.

My love to 102. God bless you,

Jan

260   To C. P. Crewe   Vol. 102, no. 247

Irene
[Transvaal]
19 June 1929

My dear Crewe, Many thanks for your kind letter and cheering words. Not that I am depressed, but it is good to feel the sympathy of your comrades.

We have lost the fight but have saved our soul, aye the soul of South Africa. Hertzog has stampeded the people into racialism with his black bogey, and has an awful responsibility before history.

I am glad you are going into the figures. The majority of the people is with us, and the intelligent patriotic majority too. The elections were partly lost two years ago when the delimitation com-

---

[1] Smuts appears to have confused two quotations:

    (a) 'The wolf shall also dwell with the lamb, and the leopard lie down with the kid...and a little child shall lead them.'   *Isaiah* xi. 7.

    (b) '...Thou hast hid these things from the wise and prudent, and hast revealed them unto babes...'   *St. Luke* x. 21.

[2] *Science and the Unseen World*, by A. S. Eddington. This was an annual lectureship, founded by the Society of Friends.

mittee[1] was packed, and later when the black Africa cry was raised.

I am meditating over the future and am in no hurry to decide.

I wish to thank you very sincerely for magnificent assistance in the fight. Yours ever sincerely,

J. C. Smuts

261 To F. S. Malan   Vol. 43, no. 58

Irene
21 Junie 1929

Waarde Frans, Baie dank vir u welkomme brief. Ons sal sake baie ernstig moet bespreek en bedenk. Miskien is sake nie so sleg as hul lyk nie. Maar hul lyk sleg.

Die rasseverdeling is weer daar. Die toestand onder ons Afrikaner volk is onrusbarend.

Maar jy weet hoe wonderlik die keering in hierdie land kom. Miskien sal dit weer gebeur.

Hartelike groete en baie dankie vir al jou uitstekende werk vir die goeie saak. Dit is nie verlore nie. Jou vrind,

J. C. Smuts

TRANSLATION

Irene
[Transvaal]
21 June 1929

Dear Frans, Thank you very much for your welcome letter. We shall have to discuss and consider matters very seriously. Perhaps things are not as bad as they look. But they look bad.

Racial division is again at work. The position among our Afrikander people is disquieting.

But you know how remarkably the swing-over comes in this country. Perhaps it will happen again.

Best wishes and many thanks for all your outstanding work in the good cause. It is not lost. Your friend,

J. C. Smuts

[1] By section 41 of the South Africa Act a delimitation commission of three judges appointed by the governor-general are to carry out in accordance with the provisions of the act a re-division of constituencies after every quinquennial census. Such a commission sat in 1926.

262   To E. F. C. Lane   Vol. 43, no. 58A

Irene
[Transvaal]
28 June 1929

My dear Lane, It was a great comfort to receive your letter, many thanks for it.

Everything would have gone well but for the Native scare which Hertzog raised. Our organization was good, and we carried the great centres where this scare had no effect. But the rural constituencies took fright and I am afraid that even many weak-kneed Saps must have voted Nat in the supposed interests of their children. It was said that we were for social equality etc. etc. And you know what effect that must have had in the backveld. If ever party won on lies and misrepresentations this is the Nationalist party, who are perfectly unscrupulous. It is a sad thing that we are now very much back in the old racial divisions. I am really very sick of the whole business, but under the circumstances we shall hold on and await the future. I feel the Nats are bound to come a cropper. They have had very good luck with prosperous times etc. But I doubt whether this will continue. And the extreme elements among them will probably drive them to extreme courses which will be certain to alienate the man in the street.

Our organization was good and I am satisfied that but for the Native scare we would have been in. As it is we have the majority of voters with us.

I have stuck to my post these last five years without any respite and feel that it would be a good thing to get away in September to England and to see what is happening in the great world. I am getting quite into a backwater. The pity is that so much of the burden and the grind falls on me. But Duncan and Joel Krige would have to bear their share in future. I had hoped that young Hofmeyr would be useful, but his stock has gone down recently and he will not be much use in the near future.

I am sorry to hear about Spilhaus [K.] and only hope that the harm done will not go too far. Dawie[1] is getting old and is by no means the man he was a few years ago. If his wife[2] tackled the job she would probably do much better.[3]

My love to you and Mrs Lane, Yours ever sincerely,

J. C. Smuts

[1] Sir David Graaff.

[2] Eileen, Lady Graaff; daughter of the Reverend J. P. van Heerden; died in 1950.

[3] Lane had written about the affairs of the Imperial Cold Storage Company. Sir David Graaff, one of its founders, wished to dispose of his interests in it. *See* Smuts Collection, vol. 42, no. 68.

PART XV

ALLIANCE WITH HERTZOG

9 AUGUST 1929–12 NOVEMBER 1934

ALLIANCE WITH HERTZOG

The documents in this section again fall into two main groups reflecting Smuts's activities in South Africa and abroad.

In the Union of South Africa there took place during this period a consummation of many earlier attempts at reuniting the two chief political parties. The stages of this process, the pressures that induced it, the new oppositions it engendered, the reservations it implied—on all this there is enlightening material in the Smuts papers. Hertzog damps down republicanism (**293**); Smuts moves nearer acceptance of Hertzog's separate Native franchise (**275, 276, 281, 282, 291, 295**); Tielman Roos appears as catalyst (**302, 324–6**); Smuts curbs the separatists in Natal (**314, 315, 317, 321, 322**); a cautious coalition is effected with Smuts as minister of justice (**327–30**); a year later the National and South African parties fuse (**342, 344, 345**). But there are provisos (**352, 353**); and there are irreconcilables who form new parties (**346–8, 365**); and there are suspicions, notably about Dominion status (**350, 357, 358**). Nevertheless a programme of principles for the amalgamated party is drafted and submitted to the existing party congresses (**363, 367**).

Between 1929 and 1934 Smuts made four visits abroad. He continued to be closely concerned with the, to him, inseparable questions of world peace and security, the fostering of the League of Nations, the strengthening of the Commonwealth. In 1929 he went to England, the United States and Canada to give lectures and visited the problem country—Germany. He spoke at Oxford on African settlement, Native policy and world peace (**263, 264, 272**). In the United States he expounded the misunderstood and still boycotted League. In Canada he urged Commonwealth solidarity. His address to the committee of the Empire Parliamentary Association sums up the gospel he preached (**274**).

He also at this time took a hand in two difficult problems of British policy which were to concern him for the rest of his life—the clash of Arabs and Jews in Palestine and the demands of Indian nationalism. As a party to the Balfour declaration on Palestine Smuts thought it his duty to plead the Zionist cause with the British government (**264, 268, 284–90**). Of British policy in India he was sharply critical (**293–5, 297, 318, 320**) and when he was in London in 1931 both Gandhi and the British authorities sought his 'friendly intervention' (**304, 305, 308**).

Smuts's letters in 1933 and 1934 reflect a growing disquietude not only at the deterioration of economic and political order but at a 'barbarism of the spirit stealing on us' (**359**). He notes the failure of the monetary and economic conference to which he was a delegate, the cruelties of Hitlerism, the departure of Germany from the League and her threat to Austria, the advance of Japan in Manchuria, the inadequacy of British and American statesmanship. In November 1934, in a speech to the Royal Institute of International Affairs, he made a diagnosis of the condition of Europe and some curative suggestions (370).

Smuts continued in these years the philosophical and scientific studies for which he had since 1924 found the necessary leisure. His work received recognition. He became a Fellow of the Royal Society (283) and president of the British Association for the Advancement of Science in its centenary year (1931). His presidential address appears below (298). His new interest in palaeontology produced a notable paper on 'Climate and Man in Africa' read at the meeting of the South African Association in 1932.

263   To M. C. Gillett   Vol. 43, no. 123

Cape Town
9 August 1929

I am afraid I misled you in my last letter as to the date of my departure. I had booked for 30 August but have found since that I have to remain here for the elections to the new senate. The government are going to dissolve the present senate with its Sap majority and get one in which they will have the majority.[1] I am an elector, and it appears that on my vote will depend whether we get an additional Sap senator in the Transvaal.[2] We do not yet know when the government will hold this senatorial election and I have to wait until we know. I may therefore not be able to leave here before the middle of September. This is a serious delay and a great nuisance, as it means that I shall have to go into residence at Oxford pretty well on my arrival,[3] and the prospect of Porthcothan is knocked on the head. I know you will be disappointed but the delay is unavoidable as far as I am concerned. The party may not suffer to give me a holiday. So please go on with your own separate arrangements irrespective of me.

I received a wire from you this afternoon asking me to deliver the Sidgwick Memorial Lecture at Newnham. I have accepted, but simply to please you and Cato [Clark],[4] and to discharge some

[1] Under the Senate Act, No. 54 of 1926, the government might dissolve the senate within 120 days after a general election.
[2] Under the South Africa Act of 1909 the elected senators were, after 1919, to be chosen by the provincial councillors and the members of the house of assembly for each province sitting together.
[3] Smuts was to deliver the Rhodes Memorial Lectures at the University of Oxford.
[4] They were both past students of Newnham College.

obligation to which I am under to Newnham; also some return for dear old Sidgwick's teaching which I never properly appreciated.[1] But upon my soul I do not know what to speak on. The only two subjects on which I am very good and strong are barred—I mean party politics and dogmatic theology! Please tell the principal that under these circumstances I labour under a most serious handicap. I cannot look upon a fee of £10 as proper remuneration and I shall therefore have to return it to the college.

I have already accepted to deliver the anniversary address before the Scotch Geographical Society[2] at Edinburgh; also to address the Royal Colonial Institute[3] at a similar function. So you can see how my troubles are thickening upon me, and I have not had time to prepare a single note yet. It is not going to be much of a holiday— that much is quite clear...Much love to you all,

Jan

264   To M. C. Gillett   Vol. 43, no. 127

Irene
[Transvaal]
28 August 1929

The mail has just arrived, with your letter written on the eve of your continental trip. I hope you have enjoyed this very much and will come back freshened and full of life.

I am in the difficult and unpleasant stage of having to make notes for the Rhodes lectures. You know how I loathe this sort of thing. It makes me positively sick to have to write anything serious. My idea at present is to lecture on some of Rhodes's policies—mostly African settlement, Native policy and the like. My lecture to the Scottish Geographical Society at Edinburgh will be on 21 November and it will also deal with recent developments in Africa. You will there-fore see that I am at present preoccupied with this continent. It is most pleasant to rummage through all sorts of books and to feel the air of Africa blow through my soul, so to say. But I hate writing about it. I am also doubtful whether people are interested in this sort of thing. The really big living issues I am afraid to tackle in my present ignorance. I have been so long away from Europe and feel so out of touch and (let me admit) out of sympathy with much that

[1] The Sidgwick Memorial Lecture commemorated, not Henry Sidgwick, but his wife (*see supra*, p. 245, note 5).
[2] The Royal Scottish Geographical Society, founded in 1884.
[3] Now the Royal Commonwealth Society of London, founded in 1868.

is happening that I feel scarcely justified in public speaking on what is happening. Still I shall have to say something on the League and similar issues.

I note that the Hague reparation conference is on the point of breaking down.[1] Snowden's ruthless attitude[2] will be an eye-opener to the Continent after the suppleness and sloppiness of British ministers the last ten years. But a cold douche is often the real preliminary for good business. And I hope some way out will yet be found. Something more is necessary than a fanatical insistence on our own rights—good as that may be. The building up of the new Europe is a great and urgent task, and Great Britain will remain, I hope, a great active force in this enormous reconstruction of the old world—and not retire to her tents. I cannot understand how they allowed old Josiah Stamp to go so far without warning or pulling up from Downing Street.[3] I am afraid that the U.S.A. will also blame us for this *gaucherie*. However, perhaps a settlement has been reached even before you read this.

Just now our Jews are up in arms over the Palestine pogroms.[4] It is really very disheartening and shows what race feeling continues in spite of appearances of peace and understanding. I had thought our way of dealing with the Arabs so much wiser than the French way in Syria. And then comes this disillusionment!

You will see that I arrive on 7 October and there will not be an opportunity to do more than go to Oxford. Street will have to wait a bit for some vacant week-end. I hope we shall make good use of our week-ends to see our friends and relatives.

I have rambled too long. With much dear love, Yours,

Jan

[1] The Hague conference of August 1929 had been called to deal with objections by some of the states concerned, notably Great Britain, to the report of the Young Committee on reparations.

[2] Snowden was able to induce the conference to concede most of the British claims.

[3] Stamp had been the chief British representative on the Young Committee.

[4] The national rivalry of the Jews and Arabs in Palestine had taken on an increasingly religious character. The dispute centred upon access to the remains of an ancient wall in Jerusalem which was sacred to both the Jewish and Islamic faith. A number of incidents at the 'wailing wall' culminated in August 1929 in a major riot in which 133 Jews and 116 Arabs were killed and many more injured.

265   To S. M. Smuts   Vol. 43, no. 77

102 Banbury Road
Oxford
24 Oktober 1929

Liefste Mamma, Ek is so jammer dat ek laaste week te laat gewag het om te skryf en miskien die boot gemis het. Ek dag dit was nog Donderdag toe dit al Vrydag ogtend was. Maar ek leef in soo 'n gedoente dat ek nie altyd die dag kan onthou nie. Nog nooit het ek dit so woelig gehad op my Londen besoek as nou; daar is een eeuwige correspondensie en toeloop en ek sit letterlik die halwe dag briewe dikteer. Sally is in Londen maar die Sec. van Margaret, Miss Livesey, is baie knap en is byna die heele dag besig met typing en korthand skryf vir my.

My lectures is nou in orde om gegee te word en is al na die drukker daar ek graag die boekie gedruk wil hê en ontslae wil wees van die las van revisie. Dit sal 5 wees als volg:

1. African Settlement ⎫
2. World Peace   ⎬ Rhodes Lectures
3. Native Policy in Africa ⎭
4. Livingstone and After, te Edinburgh and Glasgow
5. Democracy, te Newnham.

Ek het dus geen lecture oor filosofie, maar ek sal seker een of twee meer gee, hoewel ek nie tyd sal vind om hul uit te skryf. Die boonste 5 is gelukkig nou klaar.

Die koning het my al herhaalde maal uitgenooi en ek gaan 23–25 Nov. daarheen op my terugreis van Skotland. Ek waardeer dit dat hy en die koningin beide so begerig is om my te sien. Ongelukkig is Sandringham ver weg op die Norfolk kus, meen ek, en nie maklik om te bereik. Aanstaande week-end gaan ek na Strakosch, wie een aantal finansieele experts by mekaar maak om my te ontmoet. Dit sal interessant wees om te hoor wat hul opinie is oor vooruitsigte vir die toekoms. Die banke dink dat swaar tye aan kom is oor die heele wereld.

Ek was so bly van ogtend te sien dat Jantje so mooi gewen het, en het hom een telegram van gelukwens gestuur. Hy sal ons baie tot nut wees in die parlement en daarbuite.

Ek kry nou baie uitnoodiginge om na Amerika te gaan vir die 10 jaar feesviering van die Volkebond. Die voornaamste manne en assosiasies het my uitgenooi en ek voel half lus om te gaan maar het nog nie geantwoord nie. As ek gaan sal ek nie voor middel Februari of selfs beetje later terug kan wees te Kaapstad, maar miskien is dit die moeite werd. My vriende hier denk dat ek nie sulke uitnoodiginge kan weier nie.

Ek voel baie vris en fluks; Cato en Bancroft was Sondag weer hier en sien daar baie goed uit. Ek hoop dit gaan jul almal baie goed. Ons het pragtige weer gehad, maar Sondag het dit gereent en vandag ook weer. Hutchinson stuur baie groete en wil maar te graag weer uitkom en ons vergesel naar die Victoria Falls. Soentjes van

Pappa

TRANSLATION

102 Banbury Road
Oxford
24 October 1929

Dearest Mamma, I am so sorry that I waited too long to write last week and perhaps missed the boat. I thought it was still Thursday when it was already Friday morning. But I live in such a whirl that I cannot always remember the day. I have never yet been so busy on a London visit as now; there is eternally correspondence and people calling and I literally sit half the day dictating letters. Sally [Richardson] is in London but Margaret's secretary, Miss Livesey, is very capable and is busy almost all day typing and shorthand-writing for me.

My lectures are now ready to be given and have already gone to the printers as I should like the little book to be printed so as to be done with the burden of revision. There will be five, as follows:

1. African Settlement
2. World Peace   } Rhodes lectures
3. Native Policy in Africa
4. Livingstone and After (at Edinburgh and Glasgow)
5. Democracy (at Newnham)

So I have no lecture on philosophy, but I shall no doubt have to give one or two more, although I shall not have time to write them out. The above five are now fortunately finished.

The King has already invited me repeatedly and I shall go there from 23 to 25 November on my return journey from Scotland. I appreciate it that he and the Queen are both so desirous of seeing me. Unfortunately Sandringham is far away—on the Norfolk coast, I think, and not easy to reach. Next week-end I go to Strakosch who is collecting a number of financial experts to meet me. It will be interesting to hear what their opinion is about future prospects. The banks think hard times are coming all over the world.

I was so glad to see this morning that Jantjie had won so well and have sent him a telegram of congratulation. He will be of much use to us in parliament and outside.[1]

I am now receiving many invitations to go to America for the ten year celebration of the League of Nations. The prominent men and societies have invited me and I have half a mind to go but have not yet answered. If I go, I cannot be back in Cape Town until the middle of February or even a bit later, but perhaps it is worth while. My friends here think that I cannot refuse such invitations.

I feel very well and fit. Cato and Bancroft were here again on Sunday and are looking very well.[2] I hope you are all well. We have had lovely weather but it rained on Sunday and again today. Hutchinson sends good wishes and is only too eager to come out again and go with us to the Victoria Falls. Kisses from

Pappa

266   To S. M. Smuts   Vol. 43, no. 83

102 Banbury Road
Oxford
18 November 1929

Liefste Mamma, Maandag namiddag. Ek maak my mail klaar, daar ek die meeste van die week in die noorde sal wees vir my Livingstone lecture. Die laaste Rhodes lecture is gelewer en was een groot sukses. Ek werd gecap en het toe die adres gelewer in cap en red gown as een doctor van die universiteit; die groot Sheldonian was weer meer dan vol en daar was die grootste enthusiasme. Ek stuur die Latynse speech vir Jannie om te ontsyfer. Jy sal daaruit sien dat ek famous is, nie vir hierdie of daardie ding nie, maar as een groot melkboer! Ek kry van Rhodes Trustees die ingeplakte cuttings oor die Speeches en sal die aan jou stuur en dit sal jou seker baie moeite spaar. Daar was ook een League of N. meeting in die Guild Hall in Londen en my korte speech daar het ook baie byval gevind. Nou is ek druk besig om een toer vir Amerika in order te bring. Daar is een gedurige gekabel. Ek vrees die Amerikaners gaan baie lastig wees en ek gaan baie swaar kry. Maar miskien kan ek daar goed doen. In opposiesie in die Kaapse parlement kan ek tog niks doen nie behalwe praatjies verkoop. Dus sal

---

[1] At a bye-election in Johannesburg North J. H. Hofmeyr had stood as the South African party candidate against J. Duthie, the Labour candidate, and had won the seat with a considerably increased majority.

[2] Cato Smuts and Bancroft Clark had married in 1928.

ek maar doen hier wat daar te doen is om een groot saak te bevorder. Gister (Sondag) was ek by Ramsay MacDonald te Chequers en Bancroft en Cato het my daarheen geneem en ons het toe daar gelunch en ek het met Ramsay oor sy en my Amerikaanse toer gepraat. Hy het my goeie tips gegee. Die visiete was een groot sukses en Cato en Ishbel het maats gemaak. Ek het die plek goed leer ken in die ou dae van Lloyd George en Baldwin, en hoewel die winter reeds hier is, was dit nog alles baie mooi en lief daar.

Ek sien daar is moeilikheid met die naturelle, en dat tearbombs en maxims teen hul gebruik word. Wat sou die Nattes gesê het as ek dit gedoen het. Maar wat Hertzog doen is goed. Die *Manchester Guardian* correspondent in Suid-Afrika sê dat dit alles bedoeld is om mense verder bang te maak en Hertzog se wette deur te kry. En die naturelle gaan meer en meer op hol, op hul eie pad.

Ek is nog so vas hier dat ek nie weet wanneer ek kan weg kom na Holland. Tatta. Liefde,

Pappa

TRANSLATION

102 Banbury Road
Oxford
18 November 1929

Dearest Mamma, Monday afternoon. I am finishing my mail as I shall be in the north for most of the week for my 'Livingstone' lecture. The last Rhodes lecture has been delivered and was a great success. I was capped and then gave the address in cap and red gown as a doctor of the university.[1] The big Sheldonian was again more than full and there was great enthusiasm. I send the Latin speech for Jannie to decipher. You will see from that that I am famous, not for this thing or that, but as a big dairy-farmer! I am getting the pasted-in cuttings about the speeches from the Rhodes Trustees and shall send them to you—which will save you a lot of trouble. There was also a League of Nations meeting in the Guildhall in London and my short speech there also met with much approval. I am now very busy arranging a tour in America. There is continued cabling. I am afraid the Americans are going to be very troublesome and I shall have a hard time. But perhaps I can do good there. In opposition in parliament in Cape Town I can in any case do nothing but bandy words. So I shall do what can be done here to advance a great cause. Yesterday (Sunday) I spent

---

[1] The degree of Doctor of Civil Law was conferred on him.

with Ramsay MacDonald at Chequers.[1] Bancroft and Cato [Clark] took me there and we lunched there and I talked to Ramsay about his and my American tour. He gave me some good tips. The visit was a great success and Cato and Ishbel[2] made friends. I got to know the place well in the old days of Lloyd George and Baldwin and, although winter has already come, it was still very lovely and delightful there.

I see that there is trouble with the Natives and that tear-bombs and maxims are being used against them.[3] What would the Nats have said if I had done that? But what Hertzog does is good. The *Manchester Guardian* correspondent in South Africa says that it is intended to frighten people further and to get Hertzog's bills through. And the Natives increasingly run riot and go their own way.

I am still so tied here that I do not know when I can get away to Holland. Good-bye and love,

Pappa

267 From T. W. Lamont   Vol. 42, no. 65

23 Wall Street
[New York]
25 November 1929

My dear General Smuts, I was very glad to receive your letter of October twenty-sixth, stating that you will be with us. We are all looking forward to your visit. I am sorry to note from the crowded itinerary which the people over here are arranging for you that we shan't have you at the house as much as I could wish. Nevertheless, we shall be able to get a little rest for you there. I am planning to give a private dinner for you on January ninth to which I shall invite a few of our elder statesmen.

Looking forward to your arrival and assuring you of the interest and satisfaction which your visit here will arouse among all our people, I am, Sincerely yours,

Thomas W. Lamont

[1] Chequers Court, an estate in Buckinghamshire and the official country residence of prime ministers of Great Britain.

[2] Daughter of Ramsay MacDonald.

[3] On 14 November, after a number of clashes between whites and blacks in Durban, the newly appointed minister of justice, Oswald Pirow, directed an armed police force in a search for Native tax-defaulters in the city. A crowd gathered and was dispersed by the police with the aid of tear-gas bombs. They did not use or carry machine-guns.

268   From C. Weizmann   Vol. 43, no. 168

The Zionist Organization Central Office
77 Great Russell Street
London W.C.1
Personal and confidential   28 November 1929

Dear General Smuts, I should like to sum up a few of the points which I tried to make in our conversation the other day.

In view of the recent events in Palestine, the British government will have to reach a clear decision concerning its future policy with regard to the mandate, and to consider the ways and means of enforcing its decision. Great Britain can do one of three things:

1. Give up the mandate,
2. Continue a policy of 'drift',
3. Carry out the mandate in letter and spirit.

1. It is for the British government to determine how far they think themselves bound by their previous declarations actively to continue the task they have undertaken in Palestine; what value should be set by the friendship and gratitude which the carrying out of the promise embodied in the mandate would earn them from the Jews all the world over; what importance attached to Palestine as a link in the imperial chain and a sentinel on the Suez canal; and what repercussions a surrender before savage terrorism would be likely to have in Asia and Africa. It is not for me to express, still less to urge, any views on these matters. But I wish to point out

(*a*) that while Great Britain can give up the mandate, she cannot cancel it. It embodies a promise to the Jewish people endorsed by all the members of the League of Nations and by the U.S.A.; and even should Great Britain cease to be the mandatory power, she would remain under an obligation to uphold the principles of the mandate, and to see them observed by whatever power was entrusted with it.

(*b*) that, in our view, the only honourable alternative to giving up the mandate is for Great Britain to carry it out in letter and in spirit.

2. The policy of 'drift' requires no decisions, indeed no thinking. During the first years a good case could be made out for restraint so long as this did not degenerate, as unfortunately it often did, into downright obstruction. That policy has anyhow affected our work most unfavourably, and has differed painfully from what had been promised to us in the mandate. Still, I myself repeatedly defended

the actions, or inaction, of the Palestine administration before my own people, incurring unpopularity and bitter reproaches.

As the years went by, I came, however, to see with regret and disappointment that what I had defended on grounds of temporary expediency was becoming the established policy of the Palestine administration, who boasted of 'holding the ring' between Jew and Arab—in reality with a strong bias in favour of the easy *status quo* and against the arduous constructive work of establishing a Jewish national home in Palestine. And when at last they found themselves holding the ring for a murderer and his victim, they still tried to make it appear that these two were combatants. I do not mean to enter into the story of the late pogrom: I trust that the evidence now given before the commission of inquiry will be published in full, and then everyone will be able to form his own conclusions.

We had to press for the fullest and most searching inquiry into the circumstances which have caused the disaster. We have suffered, we have dared to complain and to argue our case, and now, perhaps naturally, we are made to feel the consequences of inconveniencing those against whom there is no appeal. We feel an atmosphere of hostility.

At present it seems to be the practice to explain away our rights, and to whittle down, sometimes without a hearing, the claims we make—whether these concern immigration, security, or compensation for losses. Meanwhile the Palestine administration fails to deal effectively with the Arab murder gangs. It is a matter of comparative indifference to us whether this is because they lack the means or the courage for dealing with those who incite to murder and violence; in either case, we look to his majesty's government to supply what is lacking in Palestine.

Sometimes the ghost of pan-Islamism is conjured by those opposed to the idea of the Jewish national home. We do not presume to argue how much importance should be attached to the pan-Islamic problem and threats, but our rights cannot be made to depend on fears, real or imaginary, or they will be placed at the mercy of agitators whom every success will encourage to attempt further encroachments at our expense. The incident of the wailing wall, in itself the consequence of official dallying, has enabled the Moslem supreme council at Jerusalem to raise the semblance of a religious question, though even this they had to bolster up by lies, assiduously propagated by the Grand Mufti[1] and his entourage (with perfect impunity), that the Jews had thrown a bomb into the

---

[1] Amin el Husseini, appointed Grand Mufti of Jerusalem in 1921.

mosque of Omar.[1] The question of the wailing wall is distinct from that of the national home and must be solved on its own merits; and it is not in our power to contend against fanciful and malicious lies, if the Palestine administration fails to visit them on their propagators. So much, however, is clear—as is shown by the resolutions passed on 26 November by the Egyptian Wafd[2]—that the problem of the Jewish national home as such is of practically no interest to other Moslem countries. But we suspect that pan-Islamism is only too often a convenient bogey for those who are anyhow opposed to the policy of the mandate; and those who have proved unequal to their task, or unwilling to carry it out, no doubt have a personal interest in proving that the task is impossible.

I repeat once more: it would be a terrible blow to us if Great Britain gave up the mandate, but both as a British subject[3] and a Zionist, I would prefer Great Britain to give it up than that she should continue the methods of the last ten years, in circumstances aggravated by Arab terrorism, before which the Palestine administration seems to bow.

3. I pass to constructive proposals—what do we mean by the carrying out of the mandate?

As things stand now we must begin with the question of security, which is the first condition for our work. The Palestine administration has failed, and still fails to secure the lives and property of the Jews who have settled in Palestine on the strength of the international agreement embodied in the mandate. This being so, it is inhuman to refuse us the means for self-defence, nay, to disarm us when faced by massacre. We demand immediate consideration of our requests in this matter, and welcome as a first step the appointment of a committee by the high commissioner[4] to examine the question of the re-establishment of sealed armouries.

Our next demand is for men. Our security depends largely on numbers. Had there been 300,000 or even 250,000 Jews in Palestine, instead of 160,000, the pogrom would probably never have occurred. We have an unlimited supply of men willing to go to Palestine, to face every hardship, and to brave every danger; the recent events have not stopped our pioneers from volunteering for work in Palestine. Their arrival will raise the spirits of those who for more than three months have borne the brunt of attacks. They shall know that come what may the Jewish nation will not abandon or betray them.

[1] The wailing wall is part of the retaining wall of an enclosure containing the Dome of the Rock or the mosque of Omar and the El Aqsa mosque.

[2] The Egyptian nationalist party.

[3] Weizmann was born in Russia in 1874 but became a British citizen in 1910.

[4] Sir Gilbert Clayton, who assumed office in March 1929.

428

Our immigration into Palestine has been hampered all along. It has been considered from a wrong angle. For centuries we have been driven from land to land, and even at present most of the world is divided for us into countries which ask us to go, and countries which forbid us to enter; and now, at the gates of what has been acknowledged as our national home, we are treated by British officials as 'immigrants' entering on sufferance, almost as intruders. Quite recently the alleged existence of some unemployment among Arabs was made into a reason for refusing permission of entering Palestine to a number of Jewish workmen for whom we have asked and whom we require. But indeed, were the settlement of Jews in their national home to be made conditional on there being no Arab unemployed left in Palestine, the promises of the mandate would be turned into derision. We are denizens of our national home, and the two million Jewish unemployed in eastern Europe, who out there seem condemned to moral and physical decay, have to be placed in the scales against the alleged two thousand Arab unemployed in Palestine.

In short, we demand a liberal immigration policy such as is implied in the recognition of the Jewish national home in Palestine.

But the number of Jews who can settle in Palestine depends largely on the economic and fiscal policy of the government. So far our work has received none of the encouragement promised in the mandate. No state lands have been assigned to us, while the most fertile lands in Palestine, round Beisan in the Jordan valley, have been given away to Arab squatters, in excess of their requirements; these are now selling their surplus land to speculators. Agricultural improvements, which in every other country are encouraged, in Palestine are penalized by a system of taxation which is based not on the capacity of the land, but on the actual produce; and not even temporary exemption is allowed to new settlers. Further, the taxation of land and houses is based on the latest purchase price, which means that the Jewish newcomer has to pay very much more than the Arab. On public works undertaken with money, of which a large share is contributed by us, wages are paid on which Jews cannot possibly subsist. We do not ask for any differentiation between Jews and Arabs, but demand a decent rate of wages for Jews and Arabs alike. A human standard of living for the fellaheen may be inconvenient to the Arab effendis, but we mean to work for friendship between Jews and Arabs by raising the standard of living among the Arab working classes, and not by bribing the effendis.

There are many economic and fiscal reforms which we have repeatedly urged on the Palestine administration and the colonial office, but with which it would be useless to trouble you. Everything at bottom turns on one question—how to secure a different attitude on the part of the Palestinian officials, an attitude more in consonance with the spirit of the mandate. If the men 'on the spot' are against us, they will always be able to explain away any general declarations made in London, and any instructions received from the colonial office, especially if they see, as they have seen in the past, that insults inflicted on us are not visited on those who choose to inflict them. And if British officials are suffered to treat us with contempt and dislike (see e.g. the language used by an official even before the commission of inquiry about the Polish, Russian, and 'that kind of Jew'), one cannot wonder if the Arabs conclude that we are outcasts towards whom anything is permitted.

We have not, and do not, put the blame for what has happened in Palestine at the door of the responsible British statesmen on either side of Downing Street. Even in the days of the Hebron and Safed massacres,[1] when, in spite of inadequate protection, arms were refused to our people, we wired to the Zionist organizations all over the world that, while criticizing the Palestine administration, they must refrain from attacking the British government. We did so as a matter of justice, not of policy. We have had sincere friends in Lord Balfour and Mr Lloyd George, in Mr Amery and Mr Ormsby-Gore, and even if they failed to make themselves obeyed by their own officials in Palestine, nothing will ever make us doubt their real friendship and good will towards us. As for the present government, in August of this year it had been in office much too short a time to be saddled with any responsibility either for the persons or actions of the Palestine officials. We therefore honestly dissociated Downing Street from the Palestine administration; and it will depend on his majesty's government, and on them alone, whether after the commission of inquiry has reported, they will be associated in the eyes of the world with what had been done, or left undone, in Palestine.

But whatever the result of the present inquiry may be, we think that we have a right to demand from the British government that they should immediately put an end to the anarchy which now prevails in Palestine, both for our sake and their own, and for the sake of the country itself; and also in order to enable us, after the commission has reported, to enter into negotiations for an honourable understanding with the Arabs. There can be no basis for such negotiations unless it has been proved to the Arabs that

---

[1] Between 24 and 29 August 1929 Arabs attacked the Jewish ghettos in Hebron and Safed. Some 75 Jews were killed and about 80 wounded.

violence does not pay; that neither the British government nor the Jews will give way to it; that they have to accept us as partners with equal rights in the land which has been acknowledged as our national home; that they will not succeed in tricking or jockeying either the British government or ourselves into any so-called constitutional settlement which is to be the means for excluding us in future from our national home; that, in fact, constitutional progress in Palestine depends on a previous free and amicable agreement between Jews and Arabs. Only if the Arabs are taught to look upon us as equal partners and to respect us, and are fully convinced that the British government stands by both aspects of the mandate —that which benefits us no less than that which protects the Arabs —then only will it be possible for us to meet them in a round table conference, and then only will the comity between Jews and Arabs be placed on safe and sound foundations.

Please forgive the length of this letter, and perhaps at some places the sharpness of its tone. I am sure you will bear with me if you understand the amount of suffering and the agony through which we have passed in the last few months. With kind regards and many thanks, Yours very sincerely,

Ch. Weizmann

269 To S. M. Smuts

Vol. 43, no. 86

102 Banbury Road
Oxford
4 Desember 1929

Liefste Mamma, Baie dankie vir jou laaste brief wat ek net gelees het. Ek is net een dag in die week hier en dan kry ek die mail en al die ander briewe en moet maar aanja met die antwoorde. Al my mail briewe is egter klaar en ek eindig nou met een brief aan jou. Ek gaan morre na Londen om die Prince of Wales te sien oor sy reis na Afrika en dan bly ek die aand by die Jellicos vir sy 70ste verjaardag. Die Prins sal een maand in Suid-Afrika wees as ek weg is, en dan 3 maande jag verder noord. My werk is nou klaar en is verbasend suksesvol gewees en word ook baie waardeer. Ooral het ek die mooiste ontvangs geniet. Die beste van al was die Oos Afrika dinner waar von Lettow en sy vrou teenwoordig was. Die geesdrif van die 1,000 ou vuurvreters was groot en die uitwerking van die dinner gaan uitstekend wees. Al die ou bekende kamerade was daar en ons het baie lekker kon gesels. Gister aand was ek in die House of Commons op een dinner waar ek een speech gemaak het oor Empire trade en markets wat die grootste byval gevind het; maar dit was privaat en is nie gerapporteer nie. Een van die ministers het my gesê dis die beste speech oor die onderwerp wat hy nog gehoor het. Die werk was hard maar ooral groot waardering, en dit het dit die moeite werd gemaak. Ek voel na die twee maande hier vris en vluks en hoop dat ek die Amerikaanse toer net so goed sal staan. Maar dit sal daar baie straf gaan na ek vermeen. Dit lyk of ek een groot reputasie in die State het as die werklike auteur van die Covenant, en dit sal vir my baie moeilik wees om my reputasie op te hou. Maar die visiete sal een goeie begin wees. Die League of Nations Assocn. betaal al my koste; dus hoef ek my nie daaroor te bekommer. Ek sal ook drie dae in Canada deurbring. Skryf beetje vir Bibas dat ek na alle waarskynlikheid op 17 Feb. te Kaapstad sal aankom...Ek hoop dat jul reeds begin van Feb. daar sal wees om my af te wag. Die ontmoeting sal hartlik wees na die lange afwesigheid. Hutchinson kom in Juni weer uit om ons na die Falls te vergesel; hy praat nog altyd oor die heerlike tyd by ons. Pole-Evans skryf baie ongelukkig oor sy werk en posiesie. Ek hoop jy sal hom beetje moed in praat. Nyssie se boek word ooral gelees. Ek prys dit ook ooral aan.

...Baie groete en liefde van die Gilletts wat my beter behandel as ek kan beskrywe. Liefde van

Pappa

TRANSLATION

102 Banbury Road
Oxford
4 December 1929

Dearest Mamma, Thank you very much for your last letter which I have just read. I am here for only one day in the week and then I get the mail and all the other letters and must hurry on with the answers. But all my mail letters are done and I now finish with a letter to you. I am going to London tomorrow to see the Prince of Wales about his journey to Africa and I shall stay the night with the Jellicoes for his seventieth birthday. The Prince will be in South Africa for a month when I am away, and will then be hunting further north for three months. My work is now done and it has been remarkably successful and is also much valued. I have had the nicest reception everywhere. Best of all was the East Africa dinner at which von Lettow and his wife were present. Great was the enthusiasm of the thousand old fire-eaters and the effect of the dinner is going to be excellent. All the old well-known comrades

were there and we could have fine talks. Last night I was at a dinner
in the house of commons where I made a speech on Empire trade
and markets;[1] but it was private and not reported. One of the
ministers told me it was the best speech on the subject that he had
heard. The work was hard but everywhere there was much appreciation, and that made it worth the trouble. After the two months
here I feel well and energetic and hope that I shall stand the
American tour just as well. But I hear that it will be very hard
going there. It seems I have a big reputation in the States as the
real author of the covenant, and it will be very difficult for me to
live up to it. But this visit will be a good beginning. The League of
Nations Association is paying all my expenses, so I need not worry
about that. I shall also spend three days in Canada. Please write to
Bibas [Smuts] that I shall in all probability arrive in Cape Town on
17 February...I hope you will be there at the beginning of
February to await me. It will be a joyful meeting after the long
absence. Hutchinson is coming out again in June to accompany
us to the Falls; he still talks about his lovely time with us. Pole-
Evans writes very unhappily about his work and his position. I hope
you will cheer him up a bit. Nyssie's book[2] is being read everywhere.
I also sing its praises everywhere...

Much love and good wishes from the Gilletts, who look after me
better than I can say. Love from

Pappa

270   To S. M. Smuts   Vol. 43, no. 96

Berengaria
29 Desember 1929
Sondag

Liefste Mamma, Ek skryf aan jou vandag omdat ek nie weet wanneer daar weer tyd sal wees om te skrywe. Ons land oormorre, en
morre sal daar baie te doen wees; en in Amerika sal ek soos een slaaf
gedryf word dag en nag. Maar ek vrees dat dit tyd sal neem voor jy
my brief kry, want ek kan die volgende mail van Londen nie meer
vang nie. Dit is darem aangenaam om te gesels, al hoor jy eers baie
later.

Dinsdag het die Gilletts saam met Bancroft en Cato my van
Street na Southampton gemotor en daar op skip gelunch. Kort
daarop het ons vertrek na Cherbourg, waar meer passasiers opge-

---

[1] Not in the Smuts Collection.
[2] D. Reitz, *Commando*, first published in October 1929.

kom het. Woensdag het ek nog opgestaan maar kon maar slegs in my sitkamer bly lê. Ek het pragtige state apartments—slaapkamer, sitkamer, badkamer ens. Donderdag en Vrydag het ek in bed gebly. Die see was vreeslik en self die skip van 53,000 ton het gespring en gewaggel soos 'n klein boot. Gister (Saterdag) kon ek weer vir een tydjie opstaan en rondwandel. Vandag is dit stiller en kouer. Ons is in die Arktiese stroom suid van N. Foundland. Ek hoop dit sal stil bly want ek het baie te doen, notes te maak vir speeches, briewe te skrywe ens. Sally, Philip Kerr en Sir Herbert Baker is met my. Ek is die slegste sailor onder hul maar nie die slegste op skip. In bed kan ek maar net lees. So het ek die paar dae gelees: Graham Kerr: *Evolution*; Lewe van Lloyd George in 2 dele; Siegfried; *America comes of age.* Ons het ook een daaglikse courant wat die wireless news bevat, maar noodeloos to sê is daar niks van Suid-Afrika in. Ek het ook die *Cape Times Annual* en Weinthal se *Annual* gelees as ligte stof. En dan het ek beetje notes vir Canada gemaak. Ek gaan een swaar tyd tegemoet, maar hoop net dat ek dit sal staan en dat ek nie een fool van my sal maak nie.

Ek kan nie verstaan waarom die *Cape Times* die aanvalle op my in my afwesigheid maak en wat daaragter sit. Dit lyk so na Dr Leipoldt maar kan ook iemand anders wees. Ek weet hy skryf vir die *Times*. Hier in Engeland het my werk baie byval gevind by hoog en laag; net in my eie land vind die verkleinering plaas, en wat die rede of motief is is my duister. Dis een snaakse wereld— genoeg om mens fies te maak.

My lectures in Engeland is reeds in boekvorm gedruk en ek het een copie by my, maar die uitgawe vind eers middel Jan. plaas, volgens gebruik in die trade wat stilstaan vir die vakansie. Ek hoop jy sal dit lyk en daar is goeie stof in. Nou is daar een offer om die-selfde te doen vir my Amerikaanse adresse; maar die is nog nie geskrywe nie, en alles hang af van goeie snelskrif rapporte, of dit die moeite werd sal wees om dit te publiseer. Ek weet die stof sal goed wees, maar ek het geen tyd om dit alles weer af te skrywe nie. Sally is nuttig met haar type; maar sy sal nie snel genoeg op die vergaderinge kan skrywe om alles akkuraat af te neem nie.

Ek het 'n allerheerlikste rus te Street geniet. Elke dag 'n paar uur gewandel en verder stil en rustig gehou. Die opening van die Elmhurst Hall ter gedagtenis van die liewe ou Clarks was uiters interessant en die familie was my baie dankbaar vir wat ek oor hul ouers by die geleentheid gesê het. Maar dit was my ook een begeerte van die hart, daar hul my altyd so goed en vriendelik was. Om nie van Leo te praat nie, met sy glas bier! En nou is ons met die liewe familie vertroude. Hoe meer ek van Bancroft sien hoe meer ek van hom hou. Sy moeder is eerste klas; baie bekwaam en goed deur en deur. Ek wil hul graag vir een kuier na Suid-Afrika kry daar Roger ver van sterk is, maar hul praat van eers na Amerika gaan, waar hy groot belange in een skoenfabriek het.

Dit is nou vas dat ek New York op 17 Jan. verlaat en dus van Londen 31 Jan. sal vertrek en 16 Feb. te Kaapstad aankom. Daar sal ek my liefies ontmoet en omarm. Die vooruitsig is soet in al die gewoel en swaar werk wat op my rus. Dit was my swaar om na Amerika te gaan, en dit was baie teen my sin. Maar ek het gevoel dat ek geen keuse had en dat dit miskien goed kon doen. Maar die uitstel sal die ontmoeting des te liefer maak. Soentjies.

Pappa

TRANSLATION

Berengaria
29 December 1929, Sunday

Dearest Mamma, I write to you today because I do not know when there will again be time to write. We land the day after tomorrow and tomorrow there will be much to do, and in America I shall be driven day and night like a slave. But I fear it will be some time before you get my letter because I can no longer catch the next mail from London. Still, it is pleasant to talk, even though you will only hear much later.

On Tuesday the Gilletts, with Bancroft and Cato [Clark], motored me from Street to Southampton and lunched on board. Shortly after we left for Cherbourg, where more passengers came aboard. On Wednesday I got up but could only remain lying down in my sitting-room. I have beautiful state apartments—bedroom, sitting-room, bathroom, etc. On Thursday and Friday I stayed in bed. The sea was terrible and even this ship of 53,000 tons bucked and rolled like a small boat. Yesterday (Saturday) I could again get up for a bit and walk about. Today it is calmer and colder. We are in the Arctic stream south of Newfoundland. I hope it will stay calm for I have much to do—notes to make for speeches, letters to write, etc. Sally [Richardson], Philip Kerr and Sir Herbert Baker are with me. Of them I am the worst sailor—but not the worst on the ship. In bed I can only read and have in these few days read: Graham Kerr, *Evolution*;[1] a life of Lloyd George in two volumes;[2] Siegfried, *America Comes of Age*.[3] We also have one daily newspaper

[1] J. G. Kerr, *Evolution* (1926).
[2] J. H. Edwards, *The Life of Lloyd George*, 2 vols. (1913).
[3] A. Siegfried, *America Comes of Age* (1927).

which contains the wireless news but, needless to say, there is nothing about South Africa in it. I also read, as light stuff, the *Cape Times Annual* and [L.] Weinthal's *Annual*.[1] And I made a few notes for Canada. I am facing a hard time, and only hope that I shall stand it and not make a fool of myself.

I cannot understand why the *Cape Times* makes these attacks on me in my absence and what is behind it.[2] It looks very much like Dr Leipoldt but may be someone else. I know he writes for the *Times*. Here in England my work has been much approved by high and low; only in my own country this belittling occurs and what the cause or motive is I fail to see. It is a funny world—enough to disgust one.

My lectures in England have already been printed as a book[3] and I have a copy with me but it will only be published in mid-January, according to the practice in the trade, which has stopped for the vacation. I hope you will like it; there is good stuff in it. Now there is an offer to do the same for my American speeches;[4] but these have not yet been written, and it all depends on good short-hand reports whether it will be worth-while to publish them. I know the matter will be good but I have no time to write it all down again. Sally is useful with typing but she will not be able to write fast enough at the meetings to take down everything accurately.

I had a most delightful rest in Street. I had a few hours' walk every day but otherwise stayed peaceful and quiet. The opening of the Elmhurst Hall in memory of the dear old Clarks was most interesting and the family were very grateful to me for what I said about their parents on this occasion.[5] But for me also it came from the heart, for they were always so good and friendly to me. Not to speak of Leo,[6] with his glass of beer! And now we are linked by marriage to this dear family. The more I see of Bancroft, the more I like him. His mother[7] is first-class; very capable and good through and through. I should like to get them to South Africa for a visit

[1] *The African Annual*, begun in 1903.

[2] On 18 November 1929 the *Cape Times* published an article by Dr J. S. Marais, then senior lecturer in history at the University of Cape Town, in which Smuts's first Rhodes lecture was criticized. On 25 November a leading article in the same newspaper commented adversely on all his lectures in England.

[3] These lectures were published in 1930 under the title *Africa and some World Problems*.

[4] Smuts's speeches in America were not collected and published as a book, but some were printed as pamphlets.

[5] The Elmhurst County School in Street had been founded by William S. Clark. His children built a school hall as a tribute to him and his wife. On 18 December 1929 Smuts unveiled a memorial plaque in the hall. *See* the *Central Somerset Gazette*, 20 December 1929.

[6] Leopold J. Krige.   [7] *See* vol. IV, p. 230, note I.

as Roger [Clark] is far from strong, but they talk of going to America first where he has big interests in a shoe factory.

It is now fixed that I leave New York on 17 January and so depart from London on 31 January and arrive in Cape Town on 16 February. There I shall meet my darlings and embrace them. The prospect is sweet amid all the bustle and hard work that oppress me. It was hard for me to go to America and much against my inclination. But I felt that I had no choice and that it might do good. But postponement will make the meeting all the dearer. Kisses.

Pappa.

271   To T. W. Lamont   Vol. 46, no. 4

Ile de France
22 January 1930

My dear Lamont, My stay with you is one of the happy memories of a life crowded with happy memories. I could not thank you and your wife sufficiently for your most kind hospitality during my visit to the States. I can only thank my stars for directing my steps to that most hospitable home, where so much kindness was lavished on me, and where I met so many distinguished people. You will have to come to South Africa to see that hospitality is not confined to North America!

The U.S.A. has made a great impression on me. I cannot understand how I could so have neglected my opportunities in not visiting it sooner. I should have gone there ten years ago at least. Life is so short that one grudges the missing of these great opportunities.

We have had a rotten voyage, and the thought of 107 East 70[1] has therefore been all the sweeter. With all good wishes, Ever yours sincerely,

J. C. Smuts

272   To S. M. Smuts   Vol. 46, no. 6

Ile de France
23 Januarie 1930

Liefste Mamma, Ek skryf dit na Tsalta in die hoop dat jy reeds daar is; so nie dan hoop ek dat jy daar aanstaande week sal wees met my aankoms op 16 Februarie. Ek verwag jou stellig daar.

Ek het vir al die drie weke in Amerika nie geskrywe nie, en ook

---

[1] The house of the Lamonts in Manhattan, New York City.

nie kon skrywe nie, daar ek nooit in my lewe so besig gewees het nie. Ek was daar 18 dae en in die tyd het ek meer as 26 lange toesprake moet hou, behalwe oneindige funksies wat my dag en nag besig gehou het. Dit was maar gedurig funksies en praat en dan 'snags per trein van een plek na die ander reis wat my maar min slaap gegee het. Maar nou, na 6 dae op see, is ek weer uitgeslaap en vind ek dit moeilik om weer aan slaap te raak. Die laaste paar nagte het ek wakker gelê lees tot 3 of 4 uur elke ogtend. Ek sal seker spoedig weer normaal wees. Ek land namiddag te Plymouth en sal vanaand by Cato wees en dan na Oxford om te pak; 3 speeches wag vir my in Londen (House of Commons, Institute of International Affairs, S. A. Luncheon Club) en baie kleiner bestellings. Maar 31 Januarie is ek weer op see na huis—dankie. Dit was sedert 7 October een verbasende ondervinding, maar die kroon was in Amerika waar ek een koninklike onthaal had. Ons sal oor dit alles praat: dus genoeg. Soentjes en liefde,

Pappa

TRANSLATION

Ile de France
23 January 1930

Dearest Mamma, I write this to 'Tsalta' in the hope that you are already there; if not, then I hope you will be there next week when I arrive on 15 February. I shall definitely expect you there.

I did not write during the whole three weeks in America and nor could I write, for I have never been so busy in my life. I was there for eighteen days and in that time I had to give twenty-six long addresses, apart from endless functions which kept me busy day and night. There were eternal functions and talking and then travelling at night by train from one place to another—which allowed me very little sleep. But now, after six days at sea, I am again quite rested and find it difficult to fall asleep. For the last few nights I have lain awake reading until three or four each morning. But I shall soon be normal again. I land at Plymouth this afternoon and shall be at Cato's tonight and then at Oxford to pack. Three speeches await me in London (house of commons,[1] Institute of International Affairs,[2] South African Luncheon Club[3]) and many lesser appointments. But I shall be at sea on the way home on

[1] 274.
[2] Entitled 'The British Empire and World Peace', Smuts Collection, Box I, no. 73.
[3] Delivered on 29 January 1930; reported in *The Times*, 30 January.

30 January—thank Heaven. It has been an amazing experience since
7 October, but the crowning-point was America where I had a royal
reception. We shall talk about all that, so enough. Kisses and love,

Pappa

273   From Lord Lugard
Vol. 45, no. 59

Little Parkhurst
Abinger Common
nr. Dorking
Surrey
24 January 1930

Dear General Smuts, In the course of the very pleasant evening
I spent with you at Oxford, at Mr Gillett's house, the conversation
turned for a moment on the Kenya question, when you expressed
the view, with which I am cordially in agreement, that the only
permanent solution of the question of the relation of white and
blacks there is segregation, in so far as it is possible to apply it;
namely, that there should be a separate white colony with its own
legislative council operative only in the settlement, and that the
whole of the rest of the country should be placed directly under
the crown. The laws applicable to the Native areas would be enacted
by the governor as high commissioner for Native territories.

You quoted Basutoland as an illustration of the successful working of this system. These are the lines on which I have consistently
urged that the Kenya question should be dealt with, and I write to
ask you whether you have any objection to my quoting you as being
in support of this policy?

May I venture to offer my congratulations on your very successful
tour in the United States and Canada. It seems to me that this is the
psychological moment to waken interest in the League of Nations
in the States. Very sincerely yours,

Lugard

274   Speech (1930)
Box I, no. 72

Smuts made this speech on 28 January 1930 at a meeting of the committee
of the Empire Parliamentary Association. It was published as a pamphlet.

Mr Chairman and gentlemen, I feel very much honoured by your
presence here this afternoon, and I wish to thank you, Mr Snowden,
very much for the very kind remarks you have made about me.

Sir Howard d'Egville has been pressing me for some time to meet the Empire Parliamentary Association here and address them briefly, but owing to very heavy preoccupations I found it impossible to appear here earlier, and finally I was drawn to America on a mission which I undertook there. It was only after my return from America that I found it possible to come and address you, and so I am here this afternoon after a very arduous time which has left me little opportunity for preparation. I therefore propose this afternoon just to speak in a somewhat casual way in regard to my mission to Canada and the United States. I think it might be useful to refer to what I said there, and to give you a few impressions of my visit both to Canada and the United States.

I spoke principally on two subjects both in Canada and in the United States, and those subjects were the unity of the British Empire, and the League of Nations and the peace movement generally. The line that I took in Canada was this—and I am sure you will all appreciate the point that I was trying to make there; I think it was appreciated in Canada too—that we had finished one phase of our constitutional development in the Empire. We had begun as a unified government and a unified country. We had expanded to a world Empire, but still it remained an Empire in the real sense with a unified sovereignty and unified control; and from that we had developed to the next phase, namely, a group of states with full national status, full freedom accorded to the various parts, and this second phase had also been concluded. This is the post-war phase of the Empire; and I pointed out to our friends in Canada that to my mind, although a great deal had been done during this phase—the phase of Dominion status and its full attainment— that was only a phase of the constitutional development which lies before us, that our task is by no means complete.

We had now the unity of Empire to work out on the new basis, I explained. That unity of Empire had rested in the past on a clearly defined constitutional basis. There was the one king, the one crown throughout the Empire, and there was the parliamentary sovereignty of the British parliament. On that double basis of the one crown and the one sovereign parliament the unity of the Empire had existed in the past. I went on to explain that that unity in the post-war period of Dominion development, the development of Dominion status, had been very largely transformed. According to the present situation, as it was defined in 1926 at the last imperial conference, the parliamentary sovereignty of Great Britain is gone; the Dominions now enjoy an equal parliamentary and legislative status, and they are all equals, equal in authority in every respect before the law. The other basis of unity, the crown, remained, and that is a basis which formerly was not thought much of. Those of you who have studied constitutional history and development know that a generation or two ago, when Bagehot, for instance, wrote his book on the constitution,[1] it was felt that the crown was quite a minor feature of the unity that existed in the Empire, that parliamentary sovereignty was the real sovereignty, and that the crown was quite a minor aspect of authority and of unity. Well, what then was thought the main prop of unity has gone, and it is now the crown alone that remains; and I pointed out to our friends in Canada that we had to be very careful in the next phase of our development. There was the danger, if we were not careful, that the decentralization of the Empire would proceed to such lengths that in the end the unity itself would go, and the Empire might be disrupted, not because people wanted it to be disrupted, not because it was the set policy of any particular part of the Empire, but simply through absent-mindedness, through not clearly appreciating what was happening, through not clearly understanding the trend and the development that was taking place. And I pointed out that to my mind the great task that was now before us, now that Dominion status had been fully realized and the Empire was recognized as a group of equal states, was to see in what way we could develop the unity of the Empire; and that if we did not do that, in the course of time—it might be a process of years, or of generations, but in course of time—we might be left with a situation where something so valuable to the world, something so great and so remarkable in history as the Empire, might have disappeared.

Well, I pointed out that a great deal would have to be made in future of the common crown, the kingship. That is what remains of the past, and in the future constitutional development we shall somehow have to make a much more real and living factor of the crown, of the kingship, in the British Empire, than we did before, because that is what remains now as the only constitutional basis. I also pointed out what is not always fully recognized in all parts of the Empire, that we have only one king, that there is only one common crown, that it is not a case of personal union of five or six independent states, and that it is not a mere casual personal union which binds them together, but that according to the legal theory and the express terms of the Dominion constitutions, it is the British crown which is the crown in the Dominions too, and, therefore, you have not a personal union, but you have one crown, one common

[1] Walter Bagehot, *The English Constitution*, first published in 1867.

king, right throughout the Empire, I think that that will have to be stressed more and more, because there is a tendency in several parts of the Empire to look upon the independence of the Dominions as so complete that there is not a sufficient basis of unity really left. As a matter of history, there is no doubt that the original basis of authority and unity in Great Britain was the king. The legal theory was that all sovereignty was vested in the king, and that parliamentary authority was a sort of derivative agency. After all, according to the theory of the law, it is the king, with the advice of parliament, who makes the law. The king was the real sovereign authority in this island even before there was a parliament and before it was the British Empire, and, in theory, therefore, the unity of the kingship throughout the British Empire remains a tremendous bond which we must try and maintain in every way possible. It was the original bond, and it will remain the final bond. Our task is to give reality and strength to this bond.

It becomes much more important than it was before, when parliamentary sovereignty still existed. If we want to keep the Empire together we shall have to make more of the kingship than we have done before, certainly than we have done for the last few generations. If one reads some of the Victorian books on constitutional law with their minimizing of the importance of the crown, it is quite clear that we shall have to be very careful on this point, otherwise we may one day awake and find that, simply through unconscious processes, without any intention or deliberate policy, we have broken down the biggest political structure that time has ever built up.

I attach also a great deal of importance to the imperial conference. If we are to have a common Empire, there is no doubt that on many points there will have to be common policies, and there must be some organ of discussion, some system of discussion and debate, for hammering out such common policies, and I sincerely hope that in future we shall look upon the imperial conference as a most important practical link and organ in the Empire. If we do not keep up that system of debate and threshing out of common interests through the imperial conference, then there will be the tendency to drift apart in our policies, and in the end differences will develop which may prevent co-operation on vital occasions.

I also look forward to other forms of co-operation in the Empire to keep it together. Exchange of visits and information between members of parliament as arranged through branches of the Empire Parliamentary Association are of first rate value. Organizations like the Empire Marketing Board, and the development of scientific organizations which is quietly taking place now in the Empire, are,

I think, of the utmost importance. There is no doubt that science is becoming of profound importance both from the point of view of production and marketing and from many other points of view, and without trying to create new legal ties in the Empire (which it would be unwise to attempt) you can create a common scientific atmosphere, you can create the atmosphere which leads to common scientific methods, to co-operation in marketing, and so on, which I think will have a far-reaching effect in the long run. I hope that we shall develop the various scientific agencies under the Empire Marketing Board, and other agencies too, as much as possible.

The point that I am at, gentlemen, is this, that unless we are prepared to run a very grave risk in future in the development of the Empire, we shall have to give much more attention to the ties that bind us together, to the natural and historic links that exist, to the sentiments, traditions and practices which make us one group, than we have ever done before. The whole tendency, so far, has been towards emancipation and decentralization, and one can understand that with an Empire spread over the whole world, comprising such virile nations as we have in it, it is inevitable that there should be this process of the extension of freedom and of independence. But that process is now complete, and I hope that in all parts of the Empire we shall in future give our very close attention as responsible leaders to this new phase which is before us. If we do not do that, then we shall be running a very grave risk, and in the end very grave dangers may ensue for the unity of the Empire.

I look upon the Empire as the greatest actual political achievement of time. The League of Nations is a great experiment, which is gradually becoming more than an experiment: it is stabilizing itself and it is becoming a reality; but the British Commonwealth of nations, comprising one-fourth of the human race and of the globe, is an actual fact and is something far greater than has ever existed before in history. It guarantees peace and liberty and freedom to one-fourth of the human race, and when through the process of constitutional evolution you have achieved a result like that, it is your simple human duty to defend it to the uttermost, to stand by it, and to see that it does not crumble to pieces simply through negligence and through oversight.

Now, as I say, I believe that one phase of our development is complete, but the next phase lies before us, and the appeal I made to Canada was this. I said to the Canadians: 'You have been the leaders in this last phase of our evolution in the attainment of Dominion status. There you have taken the lead.' There is no doubt that Canadian statesmen, backed up by statesmen from other Dominions, have taken the lead in that great constitutional development. 'Now,' I said, 'you should become the leaders too of the next phase, namely the phase which will mean a better realization of our unity.' You do not want to create new shackles. I think that is the way to disrupt the Empire. To create new legal bonds is entirely out of the question, but what you can do is to strengthen the sentimental ties, strengthen the sense of loyalty, which, after all, is the biggest force in the world, strengthen the sense of common ideals, the sense of common interests, and thus give new force to those human ties which are, in the end, of much greater strength and power and efficacy than any mere legal nexus. I think the phase that is now before us is to prosecute this task and to prevent the Empire from quietly and insensibly, and perhaps unconsciously, drifting apart, until afterwards we shall have lost what, as I say, is a unique human and historic achievement, and should be conserved by us to the utmost of our power. That is the line I took in Canada, and I think it met with a good deal of response in all quarters.

Passing on to the United States, I dealt more with the question of the peace movement generally and the League of Nations. I was, of course, on very delicate ground, because of the party divisions that existed over the League of Nations ten years ago and since; I had to be very careful not to get involved in any partisan movement in the United States. I did my best to keep out of the party controversy, and to make the people of the United States realize what the League of Nations really is, and what it stands for, and what it has been doing.

I found to my great astonishment, that the gravest misconception prevailed in the United States about the nature and the aims of the League of Nations. You will remember that the first associations that were formed during the Great War for the establishment of the League of Nations originated in the United States, and the most powerful of these groups, the most powerful association, was one called the League to Enforce Peace. That was the word, 'enforce' —the League to Enforce Peace. To that League belonged many of the foremost Republican leaders in the United States, who are to-day still foremost in their party. But the basic idea in those days— that is, twelve or thirteen years ago, was that a League had to be established which would *enforce* peace, which would use force in order to maintain world peace. That was the mentality with which they started, and that is the mentality which prevails to-day still in the United States about the League. The United States is under the impression, the public there is under the impression generally that the League of Nations is such an organization of force. They have themselves completely abandoned the idea now. They have revolted from the idea that there should be a League to enforce peace. Force, sanctions—if you mention the word now it is anathema in the United States; but it was the point where they actually started, and they are under the impression that no movement forward has been made in the Old World at all, that the Old World has simply adopted this baby of theirs, and that the Old World has established an organization to enforce peace, and that the League of Nations is nothing but a banding together of the nations in order, by force if necessary, to maintain the peace of the world.

Well, I had to combat that idea, because to my mind it is not only wrong, but it is ruinous. Once you have that idea of the League of Nations you are not only labouring under a misconception, but you are labouring under a false misconception. I explained to them what took place in the peace conference at Paris, in the League of Nations commission, and the battle that took place there as to the future basis of the League of Nations. One point of view was that the League of Nations should be a system of conference, a round-table system, where any disputes that might arise between any parties would be debated between them in the presence of other impartial powers, and I said that that was the one view which ultimately prevailed in the League of Nations commission and in the covenant. The other view was frankly the original American view, which happened to be strongly backed by certain continental powers. You can well understand that France was inclined that way, and the smaller nations, the younger nations, were all only too anxious to have abundant security, and they saw security only in armies and navies; so naturally there was a strong body of opinion backing this view of the League of Nations. The battle was fought out, and finally, I told them, the view which prevailed in the League of Nations commission, and which is embodied in the covenant, was not the force view, the sanctions view, but it was the round-table view. I said: 'If you look at the essential clauses of the covenant you will see that it is the view of the League as a round-table conference, a method of peaceful argument and agreement, of legal settlement away from force, which has prevailed', and I took them over the clauses, particularly article 12, article 15 and article 16 of the covenant, to show them that that was so.

I showed them that what the nations belonging to the League undertook was this: they undertook, first of all, not to go to war before there had been a discussion of their differences. Either there

445

must be a reference to arbitration, and they undertake to refer their disputes to arbitration or to some legal settlement, or there must be a discussion before the council of the League; and it is only after such a discussion has taken place or such legal means have been exhausted for the settlement of a dispute that they get a free hand to deal with their dispute as they see fit. I said that these were the two undertakings that any member of the League makes. Firstly, he undertakes not to go to war before his case has been submitted under article 12 to arbitration, or under article 15 to conciliation by the council. That is the first undertaking; and the second undertaking is that if there is a unanimous decision against a state, either through arbitration or through the council, that state will then obey it. If a state flouts these two undertakings or either of them, if it goes to war without submitting its case first to arbitration or to conciliation, or if it flouts a unanimous decision against it, if it does either of these two things and breaks these two engagements then it puts itself outside the pale. It ostracizes itself, so to speak, and the penalty of article 16 follows—that is to say, the economic boycott, the severance of commercial and financial relations by other members of the League with the offending state. I said that that was the real scheme of the covenant.

I told them there were certain semblances, certain remnants of the idea of force still left in the covenant. That is found in article 10, which guarantees the boundaries and independence of the members of the League. That guarantee, undoubtedly, may be construed as meaning the application of force in the end. I said: 'I frankly admit that article 10 is against me. But article 10 is a survival of the old order of ideas, that force is necessary to maintain peace.' Similarly there is a clause in article 16 which says that when economic sanctions are applied it is competent for the council of the League to recommend what military or naval or air sanctions should also be applied. That also seems to indicate the application of force in certain eventualities, if the council so recommend. But the point I made was this, that these were two isolated survivals of the older order of ideas, the idea of the application of force, and that it was not an essential part of the scheme at all; that the essential part of the scheme was the round-table, including arbitration and conciliation, but that there remained certain survivals of the other order of ideas in article 10 and in article 16. But more and more, I said, we have learned our lesson; during the last ten years that the League has been in operation we have never acted either under article 10 or under that section of article 16 referring to war sanctions. In no case has there been the slightest attempt to apply that sort of sanction under the League, and the reason for it is this, that opinion has ripened, there has been a development of opinion during the last ten years in the direction that conciliation is the proper method for the League to follow. And I said that today in the Old World, although there is a difference of opinion, there is no doubt that a consensus of opinion is growing up in favour of the conference, the round-table system of the League as the real basis of the League, and if fairly carried out, in the long run that system will probably be sufficient.

Well, I discussed this aspect of the League at many of my public meetings, and at many private meetings too. Of course, the more important meetings which I held were private meetings with leaders and with the responsible people, and they all said to me that the case had been entirely differently represented to them. They said they had all been led to believe that the League was a very different body, and that they were very glad to hear that the League was of this nature, which is more in harmony with their own present trend of ideas. They have themselves abandoned the idea of force. They themselves revolt against the idea of sanctions, and they were very glad to hear that the whole development of ideas and of practice in Europe has been in the direction of peaceful methods of arbitration, legal decision under the world court, conciliation through the council and otherwise, as probably in the long run sufficient to prevent a conflict. My view, I explained to them, was this, that the main revolution created by the covenant and by the League was that a settled regular method of conference would be established, that in 1914 the crisis took place largely because it was impossible to bring the leaders of the European states together, and that if a settled system such as we are now working out in the League, and which is becoming the settled practice and the settled international method, could be stabilized and regularize itself and root itself deeply enough, then in the end probably we should succeed in preventing war. Whenever there is danger of a conflict the nations will gather round the conference table, and there they will thresh out their difficulties, and, in my opinion, probably that will prove sufficient. I do not believe that once the disputants are got round the table, with other disinterested powers to help them to solve their difficulties, there is very grave danger of war left.

I then went a step further and dealt with the peace pact,[1] of

[1] The general pact for the renunciation of war, signed by nine powers on 27 August 1928. Initiated by the United States secretary of state, Frank B. Kellogg, it condemned war as an instrument for settling international disputes but included no provision to enforce the peaceful settling of disputes.

which they are excessively proud in America, but the consequences of which I think they do not realize. The peace pact is, of course, a tremendous gesture; even as a gesture it is one of the great things in history. But I pointed out that it was more than a gesture: it is now international law. I pointed out to them that it had been signed by practically every civilized nation in the world, and whether it had been signed honestly or not it was now international law, and in some way or other it will have to be carried out. Whatever may have been at the back of people's heads, there it is, it is law, and we shall never go back on it again. It is one of those steps in history which if once taken there is no going back upon any more, however much people may in certain eventualities intend to go back upon it. It is a break with the past which creates essentially a revolution, and there is no going back on it. I said we can only go forward, and the question is how are we to go forward and carry out the peace pact? What are you going to do? What machinery are you going to establish to carry out the peace pact?

I did not want to argue with them about the League at this stage, and say, 'The League will be the machinery to carry out the peace pact', because that was not the proper way of approach in America to a problem like this. To my mind the conference system which we have found to be the really efficacious departure in Europe, the new diplomatic instrument, the new diplomatic weapon which was all powerful, or will in time come to be all powerful, is the weapon also through which to apply the peace pact—that is to say, that nations not only in the League, not only within the covenant, but nations and governments generally, in order to carry out the peace pact, will at last have to come back to that method, and will have to confer together when danger threatens. America has already pledged herself to do so in the case of the Pacific. At the Washington conference in 1921, there was not only the limitation of naval armaments agreed upon, but there was the Pacific pact. At that conference the four-power Pacific pact was signed in which America, as a Pacific power, pledged herself, in the case of any danger threatening in the Pacific, to confer with the other Pacific powers and to consult about measures of conciliation and mediation. In regard to the Pacific, the United States is thus already bound to a conference system.

Well, I said, there is a precedent to follow, and to my mind, and apart from the League, even if you decline to join the League, and think that will entangle you in European affairs, you have now signed an instrument with the world which is law, and which you are bound to carry out. You have yourselves set the precedent how to carry it out through the four-power Pacific pact; and to my mind that is the next step to take. We must make the conference system universal, and we must undertake, either by way of supplementary convention or whatever may be the best procedure (with a view to the constitutional difficulties in America), that whether trouble arises in the Pacific or anywhere else the powers concerned in that area will come together and confer. I said that that was the method which is now working under the League; it is really all that survives effectively of the machinery of the League as originally devised in the covenant, and that system, which has been tested now in the last ten years, ought to be applied in the United States, too, under the peace pact.

I thought that that might prove helpful to them. I discussed it, not only in public, but, as I say, at private meetings, and I discussed it with the political leaders. In the United States I urged this very strongly. I said I agreed with their objection against entanglements, and all those arrangements which mean balances of power, and all that. But, to my mind, the conference system, the round-table system is something quite different; it is based on the unity of the human family, it is a large human idea, and it ought to be the basis of a large human institution and of that new, open diplomacy for which America contended in the war, and it should be adopted by America in common with the other states, whether she becomes a member of the League or not. I pressed that as strongly as I could.

Of course, I take an even stronger view. I think it is possible, under the peace pact, to go a good deal further, and to devise specific ways of carrying out the peace pact which will go much further than that; but the best course is to take one step at a time, and if we can get the United States to confer not only in regard to the Pacific, but in other cases where world trouble arises, to my mind, in that way we shall overcome most of the technical difficulties which we feel today in the League and outside of the League, and we shall make a great step forward towards world peace.

I do not want to detain you any longer, but I thought it advisable, briefly, to explain the line that I took on these two matters. I also tentatively pointed out—of course, you have to proceed very tentatively in the United States—that it would be possible in future, with the transformed British Empire—which was no longer the British Empire, but which was now the British Commonwealth of nations —for the United States to co-operate much more whole-heartedly with us than she had done in the past. I said that the British Commonwealth of nations is today not very different from the United States. I said that you have in the British Commonwealth of nations, not only the Old World, you have not only Great Britain, but you have the Newer World. It is newer than you. You call yourselves the New World; well, we of the Dominions are the Newer World. The Dominions have the same outlook, they do not want entanglements with the Old World; they want peace, they want development. They have an entirely different mentality from those war-driven peoples of Europe, who labour under the incubus of the past. They have entirely your mentality; these young nations, which now form a very important part of the transformed British Empire or British Commonwealth of nations, and carry a good deal of weight in the common counsels, have very much the same view as yourselves, and you will find, therefore, that in collaborating with the British Empire you are collaborating with your own friends, who are entirely of your own view of things. I said, Canada thinks very much like you; so does South Africa; so do Australia and New Zealand. We are all very much of the same general outlook in international affairs, and I said you can collaborate much better in future with us than you have done in the past, and you will find it very fruitful, and to my mind, although I am entirely against groupings and balances and that sort of thing, a practical collaboration of the British Commonwealth of nations with the United States will be the most powerful support of peace and progress, and of liberty, that the world has ever seen.

There was one thing that helped a great deal in the plea that I was making, and that is the elimination of the Irish question. I made a good deal of inquiry in the United States as to the position of the Irish factor at present in United States politics, and I was told on the best authority, by those who really know, that although you have still a network of Irish associations in the United States the attitude has changed very largely from the old anti-British attitude of half a generation ago, that these associations are kept going very largely by the older generation; that you find very few of the younger generation joining these Irish associations. The real sting has gone out of the problem. The settlement of the Irish question, I think, quite apart from its effect on the British Empire itself, its internal effect, has had the most extraordinary effect on this larger world question which I am talking about. I feel strongly on it, because to my mind collaboration of the British Empire with the United States should be pivotal in our future foreign policy.

To my mind there is no doubt that the world will remain a dangerous world. We are on the move; forces have been set going by the Great War and since which are incalculable and almost uncontrollable. We see developments in the last ten or fifteen years in Russia, in China, in India, and practically all over the world, forces that are almost beyond human wisdom to measure or control; and therefore, whatever machinery of peace we are building up, the world will remain, in my opinion, for a generation or more to come, a dangerous world. For an empire like ours it is essential to follow lines of safety, and to my mind collaboration with the United States is probably the safest and the best, the soundest and most statesmanlike policy that we can pursue. There is no doubt that the Irish question was a grave stumbling-block in the way of this co-operation. It is gone now. It is quite clear to me from the inquiries that I made, and from the information I obtained in the very best-informed quarters in the United States, that that question has been entirely transformed in the United States itself, and that it will be much better for us, and much easier for us, in future to collaborate than ever before.

So I come to this conclusion. I have been talking about the transformed Empire, the United States, the support that the League of Nations and the whole world peace movement can get from the collaboration of these two great groups; and to my mind, if they can manage to keep together—and I think there is a really good spirit on the other side to keep together with us—we shall achieve something by our collaboration for the future peace of the world which will be of incalculable importance.

Let me just say this in conclusion, that I found a very good spirit in the United States. I have read about the country a good deal. By extensive reading of books I know what others say, but I had never realized what a profound sympathy there is in the United States towards the British Empire. I had never realized it. I had been led to think differently, but it was quite clear to me, and I could speak to them not as an Englishman, but as a man having my own outlook, from my own angle, at things; and I was looked upon there, in the United States, as a person of that standing, somewhat impartial, of an aloof standing, and it was quite clear from the information that was given to me by men of standing, men who really count in all directions, that there is far more sympathy with this country and with the fight it is making in the world today, and with the policies it stands for, the ideals which it is pursuing in the great life of the world, than people in this country realize; and no greater mistake can be made by the British people than to think that America is indifferent to them or to their troubles or viewpoints. I had been told that America was really a different people, a different nation, with an entirely different mentality from the British. Superficially that is so; superficially there is a great deal to support that point of view; but below the surface I found a kindliness of feeling and sympathy, a real drawing towards this country, that no reading of mine, no account I had read of the United States, had led me to infer. All that is very encouraging. I have come back from the United States with the feeling that the things we stand for—peace, progress, liberty, the ideals of human progress and good government that we are standing for, the human good that we are fighting for—are things that are appreciated in America; and in the fight that we are making we shall probably find that they will be allies, not formal allies, but that they will be found collaborating with us whenever any critical occasion may arise in our development.

275   To M. C. Gillett   **Vol. 46, no. 191**

House of Assembly
Cape Town
28 February 1930

I have just finished dictating letters to Sylma[1] and now shall have a chat with you. Miss Richardson has gone to her people to recuperate for a few weeks and in the meantime Sylma is acting as secretary with great efficiency. I am sorry that she will get married next year and then deprive me of the opportunity to serve me. She never talks unnecessarily to me and does her work with great speed and efficiency.

I wrote to Arthur about our visit last week to Blaauwklip[2] and shall not repeat here. I am very satisfied with all I saw there.

On Sunday we spent a glorious day on Table mountain, Isie and Santa [Weyers] climbing with me right up to Maclear Beacon for the memorial service. The governor-general and Princess Alice[3] were with us and must also have enjoyed the day very much. It was hot, but we bathed at a suitable point where you also have bathed before. And there were many plants in flower, and beautiful distant views, and a great mist creeping up from False bay, and banks of white cloud in the south pouring over the Hottentots Holland mountains. Isie feels very proud of her performance, but says never again! A photo appeared in the papers, and all Cape Town has been talking of her feat!

We are once more in select committee over Hertzog's Native

[1] *See* vol. II, p. 451, note 1.
[2] A farm in the western Cape owned by the Gilletts.
[3] The Earl of Athlone and his wife.

bills.[1] The way out is as dark as ever. My own thought is beginning
to come to acceptance of Hertzog's scheme for the Cape only, *plus*
the removal of the colour bar of the South Africa Act[2] (so that
Natives can sit in parliament and represent their own people) and
plus a provision which will enable Natives with a certain education
qualification to remain voting with the whites instead of in separate
Native constituencies. I have consulted some of our more influential Native magistrates and they think the Natives may accept such
a scheme, but I fear the Nats will not look at it. The exclusion of
Natives from parliament is very deeply felt by them and they will
sacrifice much to reverse that provision of the South Africa Act.
The danger is that unless something is done to compensate the
Natives for the change, it may pass (I mean Hertzog's bill may pass)
without any *quid pro quo*, owing to a number of our supporters
having been frightened by recent events in Natal and elsewhere.[3]
I am getting Jabavu [D. D. T.] to Cape Town for a talk over the
whole position. There is a reactionary spirit about, and it even
affects my personal position and influence. Such is the world. Much
love to you dear ones,

Jan

276   To M. C. Gillett   Vol. 46, no. 192

House of Assembly
Cape Town
7 March 1930

...Hertzog introduced the Women's Enfranchisement Bill yesterday, and although the majority of Nats. are against, we have a good
majority for the bill which has a very good chance of becoming law
now.[4] It gives the franchise to European women only throughout
the Union without any qualifications. Most of my men would
have preferred the absence of another colour bar, but in that form
the Nats. and Labourites would have formed a majority against the
bill.

We are still considering Native schemes in our select committee
on Hertzog's Native bills. No headway yet. There is a reactionary

[1] In February 1930 Hertzog again introduced the Natives' Parliamentary Representation Bill in a joint sitting and asked that it be referred to a joint select
committee.

[2] Under articles 26 and 44 members of either house of parliament must be 'of
European descent'.

[3] *See supra*, p. 425, note 3.

[4] The bill duly became the Women's Enfranchisement Act, No. 18 of 1930.

air about. The Natal riots and other difficulties have been skilfully engineered to scare people, with the result that a rotten Riotous Assemblies Bill[1] is before the house for which even some Saps. will vote. It is sad and discouraging and I sometimes feel as if I have outlived my political usefulness in this country. But in the end I decide to drift, wait and see, rather than clear out at a bad time. Depression coming and everybody grousing. My dear love,

Jan

277   To Sir Thomas Holland Vol. 46, no. 25

12 March 1930

My dear Holland, I was very highly gratified to receive your cable some days back telling me that the British Association committee had unanimously elected me as their president for next year. I cabled back immediately my acceptance and thanks. I wish to convey to you and through you to the council of the Association my gratitude for the great honour they have done me. My personal claims are but slender, but I recognize that this is an effort to do honour to the younger parts of our great Commonwealth. I am sure it will be viewed in that light, and that all over the Empire abroad, this generous action on the part of the British Association will be gratefully appreciated.

An idea has occurred to me in this connection to which I wish you to give some consideration. This will be the centenary meeting of the Association, and it will have, I believe, for the first time a Dominion president. I would go a step further, and invite a strong representation from each of the Science Associations in the Dominions so that your centenary meeting may be in the fullest sense representative of Empire science, and form in effect a reunion of all the Science Associations of the Empire. No extra expense should be involved for you, and Dominion scientists may welcome an opportunity of being in London in large numbers on so great an occasion, and may even be prepared to abandon for next year their own local annual meetings. The occasion has great potentialities, if it is properly exploited, and it has occurred to me that a great reunion of British scientists next year in London will be a symbol

---

[1] Carried as the Riotous Assemblies (Amendment) Act, No. 19 of 1930. It empowered the minister of justice to expel from any magisterial district, or, in the case of persons not born in the Union, to deport anyone whose presence, in the opinion of the minister, might lead to the creation of hostility between whites and non-whites.

and expression of Empire unity of a most striking character. There may be difficulties with the British Association, or with the local Science Associations of the Dominions which I am not aware of, and which may prevent the idea from being practicable, but it is at any rate worth exploring.

I hope that you will not mind my troubling you with this suggestion, and if you think it the better course, you can pass it on to Howarth [O. J. R.] for consideration through the usual channels. With sincere regards, Yours very truly,

s. J. C. Smuts

278   To M. P. A. Hankey   Vol. 46, no. 51

21 March 1930

My dear Hankey, I have had a talk with an engineer of very high standing from Northern Rhodesia, Charles Kingston, whom I have asked to have a talk with you when he is in London. I shall be very glad if you will go into the point which he has raised with me which I consider one of very great importance.

The position is this. In Northern Rhodesia one of the great copper fields has been discovered within the British Empire. Kingston, who is very well informed from the inside, is convinced that the Americans are making every effort to collar this field and secure the copper for the American refineries, from where it would once more be exported to England for English consumption. To my mind this would be a very serious matter if Kingston's fears are justified. We have already to pay the Americans a vast annual war tribute, and in addition enormous sums for cotton, petrol and copper. If we could secure the copper for refineries in the Empire, we would materially reduce this heavy annual bill. The question is what can be done to secure the refinement of Rhodesian copper either locally or in Great Britain, and prevent the danger which Kingston fears and which may be quite real.

I hope you will go into the matter with the colonial office as it seems one of great imperial importance. Unless we use the undeveloped resources of the Empire to secure our financial and industrial position in the world, I foresee very grave difficulties from the burdens which our peoples are called upon to bear. I am not sufficiently acquainted with the terms of the Congo treaty or the colonial legislation in Northern Rhodesia to decide which is the better course to take, and the point is very well worth going into.

Please excuse me for troubling you in this matter. My letter is principally intended to tell you about Kingston and his ideas. With all good wishes, Yours very sincerely,

s. J. C. Smuts

279   From M. C. Gillett   Vol. 44, no. 155

102 Banbury Road
Oxford
26 March 1930

My dear Jannie, We see the Women's Enfranchisement Bill is through the second reading but I have not much hope from the senate. I think it is right to put it through for white women; seeing that the whole question of the blacks' status is before you, it seems reasonable to deal with each on its merits and not take them interwoven.

We feel very sorry for the situation about the Natives. It seems as though reaction becomes more powerful just as a liberal spirit was becoming more diffused (as I feel sure it is in the twenty-five years I have known South Africa) and one can understand the psychology of this. What I do feel uneasy about is your own position. I can't think it right that through drifting you should seem to acquiesce in what is reactionary and against all your instincts and faith. You can't go on to shape South African policy the way you would like with your own hands; this is too long a business for the space of your life, especially seeing what the disposition of parties now is. But it must not be supposed that what you envisage and what you would support is contrary to your whole nature and history, because that would be a dead weight in the wrong direction for your successor.

When you are dead, perhaps before then, perhaps while you are still active and influential in League work, you will come to be seen in a truer proportion in South Africa and what you have said and done about blacks will count for much. I think that you can put a thing out into the world there that will live. It will be a shock; it won't be accepted at once; but it will move and have its being and help your successor to carry something through. I think if you could get it out, so that it can't be blinked, (and you have all the authority with which this could be done, so that it can't be ignored) you could then leave it, and South Africa would have to digest it, to struggle over it; but once said it can't be unsaid—South Africa would be changed. And I think it will be more fruitful, more permeating, more like leaven, if you can then leave it and trust the future to the great powers. You say you feel you may have outlived political usefulness; it only means that here is a stage at which you yourself can't water and prune and train. But it's you that will go on in the sayings you will say and you yourself will come over to the League or whatever civilization [sic] asks you to, and not complicate the development of the seed in South Africa. I am so afraid you will hinder your own work by never taking a chance to float your creation off. The reviews[1] show how little your creation has got out of your brain yet. It is a delusion which seems to obsess political leaders that they must be leaders to the end of the chapter. We none of us like to think our affairs can get on without us! But I, nevertheless, persist in believing my affairs here can go on while I absent myself from 13 June till half through September!

Is 13 June time enough for us to sail? It all depends on Arthur not collapsing. He is working harder than I have ever known him, and the course is much obstructed, and just now very difficult...

280   To E. Oppenheimer   Vol. 46, no. 66

29 March 1930

My dear Oppenheimer, I was most pleased to get kind birthday wishes from Lady Oppenheimer and yourself. It is nice to be remembered by one's friends. Please give my thanks to Lady Oppenheimer and also to Imroth [G.] who joined in your telegram.

We are on the point of closing our session, and are very glad to get away from these scenes of talk. On the whole, I think we have done quite well this session as a party, and the nakedness of the government has been thoroughly exposed. I hear that their position is rapidly weakening up north, and that the Nationalists are joining a new organization in large numbers. This so-called 'United party' will have to be carefully watched although at present I am not inclined to take it very seriously. There is no doubt that the government is proving quite impotent in face of the present depression. In the unemployment debate, they could not make any suggestion, and Creswell seemed to rely entirely on road-making as the way out.

In July I shall be in Northern Rhodesia having a good look round not only for plants but also for prospects of future development. Bad times generally contain the seeds of future progress, and

[1] Probably the reviews of his speeches in Great Britain, Canada and the United States.

I think this is the time to have a good look round up north. With kind regards and best wishes. Yours very sincerely,

s. J. C. Smuts

281   To M. C. Gillett

Vol. 46, no. 201

House of Assembly
Cape Town
8 April 1930

...I have carefully noted what you say about the Native question and the *quids* and *pros*. Jabavu has just written a most able letter to the press to say that he stands pat and will not compromise the present franchise position away until the Natives get the right to sit in parliament. The curious thing is that this is one of the points we are discussing in the committee. I doubt whether we shall agree, but a hard fight is being put up to remove this original colour bar from the South Africa Act. If the government agrees to this, I think it a fair compromise to agree to a differential franchise for white and black, seeing that the Natives so outnumber the whites. The idea is to allow the Natives to put their own Native representatives into the senate, but no proposal goes the length of putting them into the assembly. I do not know what will come of all this, but it serves a good purpose to discuss these and similar matters with the Nats. who seldom hear these views.

Sunday I spent on the mountain by myself—a glorious autumn day, full of the dreaminess of the season. On Saturday we went to Moorreesburg to see the brothers;[1] coming back I almost killed a pedestrian who crossed in front of the car in Claremont and was violently knocked over. It was a mercy he escaped with pains and bruises and was not killed outright. He smelt of liquor, poor devil. As usual, I was not to blame!

There is a change in the air, a feel of winter coming without having arrived yet. It is always the most glorious part of our year. You can take big exercise without feeling the strain too much. I think we shall find it a great deal colder in the Transvaal, where heavy rains have fallen. Recently, I have been reading Spinoza again, and find him full of good things as I wrote you last week. He was a deep spirit—of the lines of the great prophets and seers. My dear love to you all,

Jan

[1] J. A. and B. de V. Smuts, both of whom farmed near Moorreesburg in the south-western Cape.

282   To M. C. Gillett   **Vol. 46, no. 203**

Library of Parliament
Cape Town
30 April 1930

When I arrived back at Cape Town a day or two ago I found your last welcome letter, the previous mail having been missed owing to an oversight. It so happens that I also missed last week owing to my being on a long travel, so that as regards that we are quits! I had to go to Bloemfontein to attend a congress; from there to Johannesburg for a Jewish function; from there to the Bushveld to see cotton and cattle; and so I found no time for the weekly note to you.

Rooikop we found again a dreamland; Andries [Weyers], Isie and I went and spent the night. Du Plessis[1] has a very nice wife who will I hope be a real success. The weather was a joy, as it has been all this glorious April. We found the grass good, the cattle fat and happy, the cotton splendid, and in fact I felt happy over everything I saw. I even saw a Koodoo bull for the first time on the farm, although there are fair numbers of Koodoo. Impala in plenty; and those funny warthogs of which you and I once saw several specimens on Droogegrond. Unfortunately, there was a fly in the ointment—in the form of minute pinhead ticks which burrow into your flesh and disappear, causing an itch for some days. I am still spotted on my legs with these inconvenient things. But what matter, when all else is so good?

I came back here two days ago and have been hard at it in parliament. We resume our Native committee also this week. I see little prospect of an agreement over the Native franchise. In fact, we are pretty well split over the question, Natal going even further than Hertzog in his dangerous proposals, while we favour a differential franchise which will retain a white majority in the electorate but keep the advancing Native with the white voters. This I fear Hertzog will not accept, and so Hertzog and Natal between them may put through something reactionary. The Natives in the meantime are becoming more sullen and suspicious and have lost faith in the white rulers, and nurse their suspicions and resentments. I fear the Cape Native franchise is doomed in any case, and what we propose (a differential franchise for them) is the best under the circumstances and finds acceptance among many of their best friends. I note what you say about unholy compromise on vital principles, and that is why I trouble you with the above. The matter will

---

[1] Dreyer du Plessis, manager at Rooikop until 1930.

not again come before parliament till next year, as our committee will take still months of wrangling over the divergent viewpoints.

I am glad you and Jan will sail on 6 June with Hutch.[1] But do try and persuade Arthur to join us. Nothern Rhodesia ought to have a visit from him—personally or officially. It is going to be the great copper field of the world I am told by American engineers, and he should see things in their beginnings, so that ten or twenty years hence he may regale his friends on what he saw before the great change had come. With decent luck, we ought to have a wonderful trip, although winter is not the best time to botanize. With love to you all, ever,

Jan

283 To E. Rutherford   Vol. 46, no. 176

30 May 1930

My dear Rutherford, To my surprise and I must admit intense pleasure, I received your cable this morning announcing that I had been recommended by the council of the Royal Society for election as a Fellow.

I have cabled you my thanks and I wish once more to say how grateful I am for this honour. With all good wishes, Yours very sincerely,

s. J. C. Smuts

284 To J. R. MacDonald   Vol. 46, no. 180

Telegram

From: Smuts

To: MacDonald

Dated 22 October 1930

As one of those responsible for Balfour declaration[2] I feel deeply perturbed over present Palestine policy which marks retreat from declaration.[3] Declaration was definite promise to Jewish world that

---

[1] John Hutchinson.

[2] Smuts had been a member of the British cabinet when the declaration was made on 2 November 1917. *See supra*, p. 19.

[3] Following the disturbances of August 1929, Sir John Hope Simpson was sent to Palestine to report on Jewish immigration and land settlement. His report was published in October 1930, accompanied by a White Paper (Cmd. 3692) defining the policy of the British government. Both documents were regarded by Zionists as a departure from the pledges of the Balfour declaration.

policy of national home would be actively prosecuted and was intended to rally powerful Jewish influence for allied cause at darkest hour of war. As such it was approved by governments of the United States and other allies and accepted in good faith by Jews. It cannot now be varied unilaterally by British government. It represents debt of honour which must be discharged in full at all costs. Circumstances of original declaration were far too solemn to permit of any wavering now. I would most strongly urge government statement to be issued that terms of Balfour declaration will be fully carried out in good faith and government's Palestine policy be recast accordingly.

285   To D. Lloyd George   Vol. 46, no. 181

Telegram

From: Smuts
To: Lloyd George
Dated 22 October 1930

Weizmann will show you cable I have sent MacDonald. Shall appreciate very much if you would make similar representations. Your authority would clinch the matter.

286   From D. Lloyd George   Vol. 45, no. 50

Telegram

From: Lloyd George
To: Smuts
Dated 23 October 1930

Am entirely in accord with your views on Palestine. Incredible breach of faith. Am supporting your protest.

287   From J. R. MacDonald   Vol. 45, no. 63

Telegram

From: Ramsay MacDonald
To: General Smuts
Dated 23 October 1930

I feel sure that the views which you have expressed in your telegram of 22 October must be based upon an incomplete telegraphic summary of the contents of the statement of policy by his majesty's government in the United Kingdom and of the important report by Sir John Hope Simpson. When you have read text of these two documents (see full summary in *Times* of 21 October) you will, I think, admit that, in the light of the facts recently brought to our notice, the statement of policy cannot fairly be described as a retreat from the Balfour declaration. The Balfour declaration explicitly provided that nothing should be done which might prejudice the civil and religious rights of existing non-Jewish communities in Palestine. Since the acceptance of the Palestine mandate the trend of events and in particular some of the methods adopted in the establishment of the Jewish national home have tended to endanger the position of the non-Jewish communities to a degree which, in the light of the Hope Simpson Report, has given us grave concern and convinced us of the necessity for special measures to ensure that the double obligation contained in the mandate is fulfilled. His majesty's government in the United Kingdom have affirmed the view, endorsed by the permanent mandates commission and the council of the League, that the obligations laid down by the mandate in regard to the two sections of the population are of equal weight. You will also recall that the permanent mandates commission expressed the view that, had the mandatory government concerned itself more closely with the social and economic adaptation of the Arab population to the new conditions due to Jewish immigration, it would have served the interests of both sections of the population. Our present policy is in conformity with that suggestion and envisages a scheme of more methodical agricultural development, which, as is shewn in the Hope Simpson Report, is the only method whereby additional Jewish agricultural settlement will be possible consistently with the conditions laid down in article 6 of the mandate which enjoins that the rights and position of other sections of the population are not to be prejudiced. His majesty's government have made it clear in the statement of policy that measures for development are envisaged, in the benefits of which Jews and Arabs can both share. Neither as regards land policy nor as regards immigration do his majesty's government aim at crystallizing the Jewish national home at its present stage of development. Statement of policy contains no stoppage or even suspension of colonization on the large amount of land yet undeveloped already in Jewish ownership. As regards non-rural immigration, it has been the consistent policy of succeeding governments that Jewish immigration should not exceed the economic capacity of the country to absorb new entrants. The new statement reaffirms this principle in language which recognizes that, owing to various causes, it has been imperfectly applied in the past. His majesty's government in the United Kingdom recognizes that the policy which they have outlined is bound to be a disappointment to the hopes of the more zealous elements of both communities, but they are confident that, on a fuller appreciation of the facts and consideration of the policy based upon them, an increasing body of unbiased opinion will be convinced that, in its main lines, this policy is not only in accordance with our mandatory obligations but is designed in the best interests of the two sections of the Palestine population, whose welfare is a matter of sincere concern to his majesty's government.

288   To J. R. MacDonald   Vol. 46, no. 183
Telegram

From: Smuts
To: MacDonald
Dated 24 October 1930

Much appreciate your prompt and full reply which will remove some misconceptions. I specially welcome your assurance that recent statement does not definitely crystallize government's policy on national home as my impression remains that both as regards land purchase and immigration government's statement does not correspond to active obligation for national home undertaken in Balfour declaration. In view of public importance of your cable I take the liberty of publishing this correspondence for general information.

289   From J. R. MacDonald   Vol. 45, no. 64
Telegram

From: Ramsay MacDonald, London
To: General Smuts, Irene
Dated 24 October 1930

As there was no indication in your first telegram that you wished to publish I had not contemplated that your correspondence would be given to the press.

290   To J. R. MacDonald   Vol. 46, no. 184

Telegram

From: Smuts
To: MacDonald
Dated 25 October 1930
My first cable asked for public statement and I therefore inferred
your answer meant for publication. Very sorry for misunderstanding.

291   To M. C. Gillett   Vol. 46, no. 228

Irene
[Transvaal]
25 November 1930

I am again writing in anticipation of the mail as I leave tomorrow
(mail day) for meetings at Witbank.[1] Last week I was in the western
Transvaal, had most successful crowded meetings, but the weather
was awful, with the result that I returned with a bit of what is
called 'sun'—an addled brain, headache, earache and the like. I am
still far from well, but the engagement tomorrow is one for which
I have no understudy, and so I go hoping for the best.

I notice the *Observer* has suggested that I should go to India.
This somewhat silly suggestion is in line with others and make
things rather awkward for me here. The Nats. say that I have not
my heart in this country and its affairs and that I am responsible
for these hints. The argument is therefore used against me and
suspicion is kept going. For the present I am tied to this show,
perhaps for a long time, although I quite recognize that I could
render better service elsewhere. It is a most difficult question and
for me the dice is always loaded in favour of this dear country.

I agree with you that Hertzog has on the whole behaved quite
sensibly at the conference.[2] Of course you must bear in mind that
if nothing particular came out of the conference the Nat. game,
such as it is, is clearly favoured, as they do not like any gifts from
the Greeks.[3] But I agree that he has been less stupid and provoca-
tive than some of his colleagues. But this does not apply to his statements of Native policy. At Geneva[4] he spoke of the menace of

---

[1] A town in the southern Transvaal which is the main coal-mining centre in that
province.   [2] The imperial conference of 1930.
[3] That is, treacherous gifts. The reference is to Virgil, *Aeneid* II. 49: 'I fear the
Greeks, even when they offer gifts.'
[4] For Hertzog's speech on 12 September 1930 to the assembly of the League of
Nations *see Die Burger*, 13 September, p. 7.

Africa to our civilization, and all through he has been the apostle
of the narrow doctrine of fear and self interest. Of course, the stupid
White Paper on paramountcy has played into his hands,[1] but surely
there is a middle way of wisdom and moderation, which will leave
the door open to the Native in his endeavours to raise himself above
barbarism. Christianity here gives the keyword to politics, but of
course we don't willingly take our religion as seriously as that!
Hertzog will land next Monday and then we shall hear a lot about
these things. Unfortunately, he speaks with one voice on imperial
matters in London and with quite another in South Africa. We
shall be extremely busy with politics till the middle of December,
when the political truce usually begins. Dingaan's Day[2] has its
drawbacks from the Native point of view, but in other respects it
does mark a halt to the year's oratorical spate—for which one is
duly grateful. I hope the Native aspect of the day will be more and
more forgotten and that it will become a sort of 4th of July day[3] for
South Africa, when national policies and viewpoints of a wider
character are brought before the people.

Howarth [O. J. R.], the Secretary of the British Association,
has sent a sketch of the presidential banner to which Joan has
made some changes. The idea is the Tree of Knowledge, Igdrasil,[4]
growing round the world, especially the British world, and I have
worked Table mountain in somewhere so as to hold our end up.
It is not a successful effort—I mean Howarth's—but I am no judge,
nor do I attach importance to these matters. I had a very nice letter
from dear old Haldane [J. S.] who urges me to talk holism in my
presidential address and says it is expected of me! I wonder; and
yet the sketch I have so far made is full of the spirit of holism. This
is a spiritual universe, in the scientific, not perhaps in the religious
or ethical sense. And this is a point which I might bring out. You
cannot implant a soul in a mere mechanism, and a divided universe
is thus an impossibility. It is like Lincoln's saying about the United
States[5] not enduring half slave and half free. Fancy, the last few
days I have read through old Asa Gray's book on Botany which

---

[1] The *Memorandum on Native Policy in East Africa* (the Passfield White Paper—
Cmd. 3573 of 1930) recognized Native development as the first charge on any territory
and stated that Kenya could not receive Dominion status until the Natives could
share self-government.

[2] *See* vol. III, p. 147, note 1.

[3] Patriotic holiday in the United States commemorating the adoption of the
Declaration of Independence.

[4] In Scandinavian mythology a tree that with its roots and branches connects
heaven, earth and hell.

[5] 'I believe this government cannot endure permanently, half slave and half free.'
Abraham Lincoln, *Speeches and Letters* (1907), Speech, 17 June 1859.

I first read in 1886. It is really most interesting still. Good-bye dear, love to you all,

Jan

292   To M. C. Gillett   Vol. 46, no. 230

Irene
[Transvaal]
4 December 1930

How time flies! Near the end of another year. Last year this time I was having a royal life at 102, dictating letters all the morning, long walks in the afternoon and mostly convivialities at night. A fire was kept burning for me, and tender care protected me against too much pressure from my fellowmen. And now I sit in my study in sweltering heat, still surrounded by piles of letters, still protected against the inhuman pressure, and still scheming how to defeat and escape the convivials! Another year gone, when every moment of time is so precious and what remains is so short.

Your last letter was full of good things. You wrote...about Jan [Gillett] changing over from zoology to physiology—very wisely, for biology has now become largely physiological. Physiology is more experimental research but also more difficult work, and it is pleasant to think that he has embraced it voluntarily. And his views of Winston's politics. Of course, the Labour party is not anxious to have Winston, who with all his brilliance has largely lost confidence—I mean people's confidence, for I don't believe he ever could lose his own! He sent me his biography. It is a most delightful book—the best written of the whole lot—simple, humorous, sincere far beyond his other works which are too much of a pose. If he did not have that instability and had a better judgment (the same thing) he would be one of the great ones. Nor has he a mind for the inner things, the things of the spirit. His lights are all external, and always turned on.

I did my political meetings all right last week, although I was still suffering from the sun. But I gradually improved, and now there is only the occasional singing in the left ear left. This week *every* night is occupied with something or other at Pretoria or Johannesburg. It is a great waste of time, but I suppose it is in the course of my duty as a public man. It is a mild form of propaganda, for you really keep more or less in touch with the world, which otherwise so soon forgets you.

This is to wish you a very happy Christmas and New Year. May

1931 be another record year in your life. I rejoice to think that I shall see more of 102 and that we shall have an opportunity to get about a bit more than last year. Last year was really too crowded and too much of a rush. I don't quite know how to manage it next time, but I am sure you will be ready with a plan. The rush for engagements will come, and how to resist them? Picard Cambridge, who is now vice-chancellor at Sheffield (of which I am a doctor), has written to ask me to lecture on some subject connected with the war before that University. I have a mind to accept, as there will be some payment and Sheffield treated me very well years ago. But once I give in, I shall be awfully pestered for other engagements...

It remains very dry and hot; this is one of the most exceptionally dry years I have seen. The farmers are literally in despair. What with low prices and drought, ruin is staring thousands in the face. And the drought becomes part of people's psychology—you see a dull anxious expression, you know *that* is what all are thinking about, you see the soft spots in character go and the mind hardens. The Arab character is desert bred; so, largely, is that of the Jews. The psychology of the desert is creeping over South Africa too. Somebody ought to write a book about it, because I think it is true. Poor whites are nomads of the desert, who have gone under in the drought mostly. Here at Doornkloof it is green and beautiful, but this is quite exceptional, and I have seen most other parts of the country dead as Ezekiel's bones.[1]

Tonight we go to a big farewell dance at Government House. My love, dear, to all the dear ones at 102.

Jan

293   To M. C. Gillett

Vol. 46, no. 232

Irene
[Transvaal]
17 December 1930

Last night I returned from Dingaan's celebration at Standerton and today I cope with a heavy mail....It is a full life and I get little time to think or read. And so the few remaining years are running out. You remember that this time two years ago we were at Louis Trichardt and Schoemansdal for the Dingaan feast. What a time we had at Wylie's Poort, and Funduzi and Witvlag![2] I have just

---

[1] 'The hand of the Lord was upon me...and set me down in the midst of the valley which was full of bones...and, lo, they were very dry' (*Ezekiel* xxxvii. 1–2).
[2] In the northern Transvaal.

had a note from Hutchinson that he had had a bad time with an appendix and gastric trouble, but that he is now convalescing. He also writes that that *Pteronia* found on the Delectable Mountain[1] was a real new find—2,000 miles and more from the last find.[2] And the waters of the Lunzua, are they not more thirst-quenching than those of Alph the sacred river?[3]

We have had some interesting political developments since last week. Hertzog came back with the message that the status question had been finally settled and that the next great task was racial conciliation and national unity. He also made a fierce attack on his republicans and threatened them with excommunication. At our Bloemfontein congress immediately after I gave my blessing to his new policy, pointing out that it was our *old* policy. This has made him very angry and sarcastic. His is a strange mind, without a spark of humour, that savingest of the Christian virtues. I have given him full credit for sincerity, but I have my doubts whether this may not after all be merely a political stunt. I cannot imagine the Nats. calmly embracing the English, the old Unionists, and all the other wild beasts of their imagination. We shall see; meanwhile I hold on till the mists clear up. It is more difficult to get out of politics than to get into it.

The latest news about the India conference is far from favourable.[4] The nettle will have to be firmly grasped but it requires great courage and singleness of mind. A Campbell-Bannerman would be very useful today. MacDonald has not tenacity and phlegm enough, and the others are, I fear, wandering in darkness still. Churchill has just been making an exhibition of himself. But the disarmament fiasco does cut one to the quick. I can't understand Bob Cecil; our attitude at this conference does not even strike me as quite sane.[5]

[1] 'They came to the Delectable Mountains.' John Bunyan, *Pilgrim's Progress*, part 1.

[2] This shrub with a Protea-like flower was found on a mountain top south of Lake Tanganyika separated by over a thousand miles from its congeners—a discovery of great phytogeographical interest. It was named *Pteronia Smutsii*.

[3] *See* vol. 1, p. 603, note 1. Smuts's party camped on the Lunzua river about eight miles south of Lake Tanganyika.

[4] Following the publication of the Simon report on the working of the Government of India Act of 1919, the Labour government called a round-table conference which met in London on 12 November 1930 but the Congress party boycotted it.

[5] Since December 1925 a preparatory commission appointed by the council of the League had been clearing the way for the calling of a final disarmament conference. In 1930 it seemed about to complete its task. But the death of Stresemann and the rise of the Nazi party revived Franco-German antagonisms and, apparently to avoid a breakdown of the preparatory commission, the British representative, Lord Robert Cecil, opposed some of the German resolutions and was criticized for retreating from his earlier attitude and moving towards *rapprochement* with France. By the end of the year a draft disarmament convention was adopted by the commission—but by a majority vote.

Is it Cecil or the foreign office officials once more repeating the *gaucherie* of 1928 over naval disarmament?

This is the end of the letter. It is my dear wish that 1931 may be a good and happy year for you and yours.

Jan

294   To M. C. Gillett   Vol. 48, no. 157

Tsalta
[Cape Town]
11 February 1931

Yesterday was your birthday and we duly remembered and lovingly discussed you in the small Tsalta circle. It is also the day I left for East Africa in 1916 to spend one of the hardest years of my life. I have no other campaign before me, and when nearing 61 there is not much more of active career to look forward to. Your letter is full of various interesting things to which I must refer. First, our little holiday next August or September before the British Association. Here I find it impossible as yet to contemplate any programme. The political situation may detain me here till too late for such a trip. In any case, we had better think of no arrangements, even provisional, for the present. I shall write again later. But it would be more than pleasant to spend a few days at Porthcothan and a few weeks in south Germany, if that should prove to be feasible.

Then about the Indian conference. MacDonald has done far better and far more than had been thought possible. I believe the turning point was the falling into line of the princes;[1] after such a gesture, a new atmosphere was created which made great things possible.

C. F. Andrews is here and had lunch with me today. He thinks it will all come right now, but that the Moslems and Hindus must come to an agreement and that it would be fatal for the British government to impose an arrangement. Let us hope they will agree, but I doubt. He says the young men and women are determined to agree and eliminate the religious divisions but the older school are still too much influenced by the past. But it is all to the good that the conference left such a friendly feeling behind and removed so much suspicion and misunderstanding. It is a peace and a solution of understanding that is above all wanted.

Then the antics of Australian politicians. It would be a dreadful

---

[1] MacDonald presided at the round-table conference. The Indian princes agreed to a future federation of the states.

shock to the world and a first class blow to the Empire, if Australia were to default. For one of our premier Dominions to get off the rails like that would be almost unthinkable. And yet it is going to happen. Australia has for years flouted economic wisdom and experience, and is now up against the results. I take this matter very seriously.[1]

I hear from East Africa that the peak of Kilimanjaro which Japie climbed in 1929 was a new one—and indeed the highest of all—and that it has now been named Reusch-Smuts from the two men who climbed it first. Japie has not yet heard this and is still under the impression that it was the Kaiser Wilhelm Spitze which he and Reusch climbed. Rather exciting, isn't it?

...We are hard at it in parliament, and it is perhaps as well that I have these breaks and intervals to prevent me from growing to despair of human nature. In parliament the usual torrent of invective and misrepresentations. I believe it is the tone as much as anything else that is tending to kill the modern parliament. The wordy struggle loses its higher human quality and becomes a nuisance to those not concerned in it and, I fear, even more to some of those in the struggle. My pen is becoming very dry and calling on me to dry up too.

Yes, you also write of the Persian exhibition. That must be a wonder. With our western prejudices we can scarcely believe that any good can come from the East. And then we read the Psalms and the Prophets, and we think of the Teacher from Galilee, and of all that matchless art which has come from India and Persia and China; and we stand reproved as the barbarians we are. And yet we too have something to show besides capitalism—science and Shakespeare and the British Commonwealth. And in years to come they will add the League as the greatest of them all. My love dear to you all,

Jan

[1] A sharp fall in the world prices of wool and wheat led to an acute economic depression in Australia. In October 1929 a Labour government, with J. H. Scullin as prime minister, took office. In 1931 Scullin, in spite of the reluctance of George V to depart from custom, nominated Sir Isaac A. Isaacs, the chief justice and an Australian, as governor-general. Scullin had, at the imperial conference of 1930, maintained that the king should in this matter be advised by his Australian ministers.

295   To M. C. Gillett   Vol. 48, no. 159

Tsalta
[Cape Town]
19 February 1931

Your last letter contained the sad news about Ed New.[1] I have a vivid memory of him as a dream-person; and I have that beautiful London hanging at Doornkloof.[2] Peace be with him.

The latest Indian news is very favourable—Gandhi and Irwin[3] are talking things over. That means that the Congress[4] is prepared to make a deal, and the sooner they bring it off the better. Their best chance is while MacDonald is still in command, and as shrewd people they know it and also must know that MacDonald's tenure of office is precarious. Am I right in thinking that Lloyd George is moving towards Labour? He is certainly keeping the government in office; this may be because he fears a general election from the Liberal point of view; or it may mean that he sees no chance of co-operation with Baldwin. We all admired very much the courageous warning which Snowden gave the other night on the general financial position, and were much taken aback to see George follow on by attacking the 'money barons' and apparently appealing to the disgruntled left wing of Labour. But it is difficult to follow these manoeuvres at this distance. George remains a puzzle and the devil in him seems to pop up very strongly now and then. His ambition remains irresponsible and the higher patriotism does not appeal to him. (Just what my opponents say of me!)

...In parliament we toil on—with little or with negative results. The Native bills committee is pursuing its mischievous course, and I fear the Natives will be completely excluded from the house of assembly. The anti-Native current in South Africa shows no abatement and forms a most melancholy and mischievous sign of the times. But perhaps the worse now, the better later. Surely a reaction must come, and the very extreme course now pursued by our rulers must hasten Nemesis. But I dislike even thinking of this topic.

All well at Tsalta and Doornkloof. Isie comes down first week in March...With love ever,

Jan

[1] Edmund Hort New, a graphic artist and friend of the Gilletts.
[2] An engraving of London by E. H. New.
[3] Lord Irwin, then viceroy of India, later Viscount Halifax.
[4] The Indian National Congress, the mainspring of Indian nationalism, was founded in 1885 by an Englishman, Allan Octavian Hume. From 1920 its real leader was M. K. Gandhi.

296   To A. Adler   Vol. 48, no. 77

House of Assembly
Cape Town
5 March 1931

Dear Dr Adler, I was very much gratified by your letter of the
31st January in reference to my book *Holism and Evolution*. I am
glad you think it may be useful in the study of psychology and that
you think it worth translating.

I have no objection to your making arrangements either with
Professor [D.] Oppenheim or Professor [O. E.] Kraus for translating the book into German and for its publication; nor do I stipu-
late for any financial benefits in regard to this issue. I shall feel
sufficiently rewarded if the book is read and its fundamental idea
is popularized. The book is now in its second edition in English,
but I wish to make a number of small alterations, mostly of a verbal
character, which might be incorporated into the translation. If you can
make arrangements for the translation I shall send you from time to
time a number of chapters thus corrected for the use of the translator.[1]

I have not yet received your article 'Individual Psychology' or
your book *Science of Living*. I shall however read them with much
interest when they arrive, and in the meantime thank you for your
kind courtesy.

As a practical man immersed in public affairs I have never had
much time for study, and such views as I have may therefore seem
to be somewhat unrelated to much of the recent work in psychology
and philosophy. With friendly greetings, Yours sincerely,

s. J. C. Smuts

297   To M. C. Gillett   Vol. 48, no. 164

Cape Town
11 March 1931

Isie arrived a few days ago so that we had a pleasant week-end
together. We went for lunch to Vergelegen[2] on Sunday and that afternoon on to Blaauwklip and Stellenbosch...we saw the Nicholsons[3]

---

[1] *Holism and Evolution* was translated into German by Dr Erwin Kraus but its
publication could not be financed. *See* Smuts Collection, vol. 52, no. 43 and vol.
VI, p. 126.

[2] An estate with an historic house at Somerset West in the western Cape. It was
bought in 1917 by Florence, Lady Phillips, and restored.

[3] Sir William Nicholson (q.v.) married Edith Minnie Stuart-Wortley, born
Phillips, on 6 October 1919.

also at the Li Phi's[1]—they are on a visit. I mean the son-in-law who painted me—not too well.[2]

It is a great consolation to have Isie here. Soon Santa [Weyers] and her small family will return north and then we shall be a very small circle, and it is good to have Isie with us. I feel dreadfully tired physically from all this parliamentary grind and am inclined to become irritable from sheer exhaustion, and she is like balm to the spirit with her calmness and strength.

Thank you very much for the John Bright book[3] which I shall enjoy looking or rather browsing through quietly. Wolff gave some offence by his reference to J. B. in that far-away mid Victorian setting.[4] But I saw no offence in what he wrote, as that world and its ways and mannerisms is incredibly remote from us. I saw at a meeting of Oxford undergraduates companionate marriage had been advocated by a girl or girls as a pleasant variation in the monotony of undergraduate life. What J. B. would have thought of such an idea! Although we still disapprove (I mean we elders) we are not shocked in the same way. The thing is to know what essentials in our institutions to cling to in these days. So much that was accepted is now once more questioned, and rightly so. I feel really sorry for this generation that has so little guidance from public opinion and accepted rules...

What is up with Stanley Baldwin? The cables yesterday said that he had decided against further Conservative participation in the Indian conference. Winston and his die-hards seem to have won. But it is a dreadful position for a great party to take up at this stage, and especially for Baldwin who has so far stood firm against his extremists on this issue. I still remember his magnificent speech in the commons supporting Irwin in an attack made by Lloyd George last year, when he (Baldwin) spoke in moving terms of the two branches of the Aryans, separated millennia ago, at last coming together as friends and comrades in India.[5] It seemed to me that after the London conference the government was bound to go to

---

[1] Sir Lionel Phillips acquired this nickname when he supported the importation of Chinese labourers for the gold mines in 1905.

[2] *See* vol. III, p. 498, note 4.

[3] R. A. J. Walling (editor), *The Diaries of John Bright* (1930).

[4] The following reference to John Bright occurs in *Rambling Recollections* by Sir Henry Drummond Wolff (1908): 'Mr. Grantley Berkeley, who was never on good terms with Mr. Bright, had some difference with him. Mr Bright quoted some friend of his as observing that if Mr. Berkeley had not been born a gentleman, he would have been a gamekeeper. To this Mr. Berkeley replied that if Mr. Bright had not been born a Quaker, he would have been a prize-fighter.' (vol. I, p. 118.)

[5] Baldwin made this speech on 7 November 1929. *See House of Commons Debates*, vol. 231, col. 1308.

almost any length—short of dishonourable surrender—in meeting
the Congress people and getting them into the further stages of the
conference. A constitution without the Congress would be a dangerous
farce, as they would have to work it. Baldwin is a puzzle to me, now
more than ever. His movement should have been in the opposite
direction to what it seems to be.

I have a letter from Eddington speaking in very high terms of my
address and suggesting a number of minor changes, mostly in expression. The argument he approves of—which I am thankful for; he
seems to be becoming more and more of a holist. By the way, some
Vienna professors want to translate *Holism and Evolution* into
German and I have agreed. Few sales now take place in England.
I am not satisfied with the reception which holism has so far
received, as I am more and more convinced it is the sound view.
Love,

Jan

298   Address   Box C

This presidential address, entitled 'The Scientific World Picture of Today',
was delivered by Smuts on 23 September 1931 at the centenary meeting of
the British Association for the Advancement of Science.

After what I said at the opening this afternoon it is unnecessary for
me to emphasize further the significance of this centenary meeting
of our Association. It is a milestone which enables us to look back
upon a hundred years of scientific progress, such as has no parallel
in history. It brings us to a point in the advance from which we
can confidently look forward to fundamental solutions and discoveries in the near future, which may transform the entire field of
science. In this second and greater renaissance of the human spirit
this Association and its members have borne a foremost part, to
which it would be impossible for me to do justice. I shall therefore
not attempt to review the achievements of this century of science,
but shall content myself with the simpler undertaking of giving
a generalized composite impression of the present situation in
science. The honour of presiding over this historic meeting, which
was not of my seeking, and for which I was chosen on grounds other
than my personal merits, is indeed an almost overwhelming one,
and I confidently appeal for your indulgence in the difficult task
which awaits me tonight.

I am going to ask the question tonight: What sort of world-
picture is science leading to? Is science tending towards a definite

scientific outlook on the universe, and how does it differ from the traditional outlook of commonsense?

The question is not without its interest. For our world-view is closely connected with our sense of ultimate values, our reading of the riddle of the universe, and of the meaning of life and of human destiny. Our scientific world-picture will draw its material from all the sciences. Among these, physical science will—in view of its revolutionary discoveries in recent years—be a most important source. But no less important will be the contribution of the biological sciences with their clear revelation of organic structure and function as well as of organic evolution. And last, not least, the social and mental sciences will not only supply valuable material, but especially methods of interpretation, insights into meanings and values, without which the perspectives of our world-picture would be hopelessly wrong.

Can we from some reunion or symposium of these sciences obtain a world-picture or synoptic view of the universe, based on observation and calculation, which are the instruments of science, but reaching beyond the particular phenomena which are its immediate field to a conception of the universe as a whole?

That was how science began—in the attempt to find some simple substances or elements to which the complex world of phenomena could in the last analysis be reduced. The century over which we now look back, with its wonderful advance in the methods and technique of exact observation, has been a period of specialization or decentralization. Have we now reached a point where science can again become universal in its ultimate outlook? Has a scientific world-picture become possible?

Of course there can be no final picture at any one stage of culture. The canvas is as large as the universe, and the moving finger[1] of humanity itself will fill it in from age to age. All the advances of knowledge, all the new insights gained from those advances will from time to time be blended into that picture. To the deeper insight of every era of our human advance there has been some such world-picture, however vague and faulty. It has been continually changing with the changing knowledge and beliefs of man. Thus, there was the world of magic and animism, which was followed by that of the early nature gods. There was the geocentric world which still survives in the world of commonsense. There is the machine or mechanistic world-view dominant since the time of Galileo and

---

[1] The Moving Finger writes; and, having writ,
    Moves on.

Edward Fitzgerald, *Omar Khayyám*, edition i, li.

Newton, and now, since the coming of Einstein, being replaced by the mathematician's conception of the universe as a symbolic structure of which no mechanical model is possible. All these world-views have in turn obtained currency according as some well-defined aspect of our advancing knowledge has from time to time been dominant. My object tonight is to focus attention on the sort of world-picture which results from the advances of physical, biological and mental science during the period covered roughly by the activities of our Association.

Science arose from our ordinary experience and commonsense outlook. The world of commonsense is a world of matter, of material stuff, of real separate things and their properties which act on each other and cause changes in each other. To the various things observable by the senses were added the imperceptible things—space and time, invisible forces, life and the soul. Even these were not enough, and the supernatural was added to the natural world. The original inventory was continually being enlarged, and thus a complex empirical world-view arose, full of latent contradictions, but with a solid basis of actual experience and facts behind it.

Speaking generally, we may say that this is substantially still the commonsense view of the world and the background of our common practical beliefs. How has science dealt with this commonsense empirical world-view? The fundamental procedure of science has been to rely on sense observation and experiment, and to base theory on fact. Thus the vast body of exact science arose, and all entities were discarded which were either inconsistent with observed facts or unnecessary for their strict interpretation. The atomic view of matter was established. Ether was given a status in the physical order, which is now again being questioned in the light of the conception of space-time. New entities like energy emerged; old entities like forces disappeared; the principle of the uniformity of nature was established; the laws of motion, of conservation, and of electro-magnetism were formulated; and on their basis a closed mechanistic order of nature was constructed, forming a rigid deterministic scheme. Into this scheme it has been difficult, if not impossible, to fit entities like life and mind; and the scientific attitude has on the whole been to put them to a suspense account and to await developments. As to the supernatural, science is or has been agnostic, if not frankly sceptical. Such, in very general terms, was the scientific outlook of the nineteenth century, which has not yet completely passed away. It will be noticed that much of the fundamental outlook of commonsense has thus survived, though clarified and purified by a closer accord with facts. This scientific view retained unimpaired and indeed stressed with a new emphasis the things of commonsense, matter, time and space, as well as all material or physical entities which are capable of observation or experimental verification. Nineteenth-century science is, in fact, a system of purified, glorified commonsense. Its deterministic theory certainly gave a shock to the common man's instinctive belief in free will; in most other respects it conformed to the outlook of commonsense. It is true that its practical inventions have produced the most astounding changes in our material civilization, but neither in its methods nor in its world-outlook was there anything really revolutionary.

But underneath this placid surface, the seeds of the future were germinating. With the coming of the twentieth century, fundamental changes began to set in. The new point of departure was reached when physical science ceased to confine its attention to the things that are observed. It dug down to a deeper level, and below the things that appear to the senses, it found, or invented, at the base of the world, so-called scientific entities, not capable of direct observation, but which are necessary to account for the facts of observation. Thus, below molecules and atoms still more ultimate entities appeared; radiations, electrons and protons emerged as elements which underlie and form our world of matter. Matter itself, the time-honoured mother of all, practically disappeared into electrical energy.

> The cloud-capp'd towers, the gorgeous palaces,
> The solemn temples, the great globe itself:[1]

yea, all the material forms of earth and sky and sea were dissolved and spirited away into the blue of energy. Outstanding among the men who brought about this transformation are two of my predecessors in this Chair: Sir J. J. Thomson and Lord Rutherford. Like Prospero, like Shakespeare himself, they must be reckoned among the magicians.

Great as was this advance, it does not stand alone. Away in the last century, Clerk Maxwell, following up Faraday's theories and experiments, had formulated his celebrated equations of the electro-magnetic field, which applied to light no less than to electromagnetism, and the exploration of this fruitful subject led Minkowski [H.] to the amazing discovery in 1908 that time and space were not separate things, but constituent elements in the deeper synthesis

[1] Shakespeare, *The Tempest*, IV, 1. 148. The passage goes on as follows:

> Yea, all which it inherit, shall dissolve
> And, like this insubstantial pageant faded,
> Leave not a rack behind.

of space-time. Thus time is as much of the essence of things as space; it enters from the first into their existence as an integral element. Time is not something extra and superadded to things in their behaviour, but is integral and basic to their constitution. The stuff of the world is thus envisaged as events instead of material things.

This physical concept or insight of space-time is our first revolutionary innovation, our first complete break with the old world of commonsense. Already it has proved an instrument of amazing power in the newer physics. In the hands of an Einstein it has led beyond Euclid and Newton, to the recasting of the law and the concept of gravitation, and to the new relativity conception of the basic structure of the world. The transformation of the concept of space, owing to the injection into it of time, has destroyed the old passive homogeneous notion of space and has substituted a flexible, variable continuum, the curvatures and unevennesses of which constitute to our senses what we call a material world. The new concept has made it possible to construe matter, mass and energy as but definite measurable conditions of curvature in the structure of space-time. Assuming that electro-magnetism will eventually follow the fate of gravitation, we may say that space-time will then appear as the scientific concept for the only physical reality in the universe, and that matter and energy in all their forms will have disappeared as independent entities, and will have become mere configurations of this space-time. Einstein has recently indicated that for further advance a modification in our space-time concept will become necessary, and that the additional element of direction will have to be incorporated into it. Whatever change may become necessary in our space-time concept, there can be no doubt about the immense possibilities it has opened up.

I pass on to an even more revolutionary advance of physics. The space-time world, however novel, however shattering to commonsense, is not in conflict with reason. Indeed, the space-time world is largely a discovery of the mathematical reason and is an entirely rational world. It is a world where reason, as it were, dissolves the refractoriness of the old material substance and smoothes it out into forms of space-time. Science, which began with empirical brute facts seems to be heading for the reign of pure reason. But wait a bit; another fundamental discovery of our age has apparently taken us beyond the bounds of rationality, and is thus even more revolutionary than that of space-time. I refer to the quantum theory, Max Planck's discovery at the end of the nineteenth century, according to which energy is granular, consisting of discrete grains or quanta.

The world in space-time is a continuum; the quantum action is a negation of continuity. Thus arises the contradiction, not only of commonsense but apparently also of reason itself. The quantum appears to behave like a particle, but a particle out of space or time. As Sir Arthur Eddington graphically puts it: a quantum of light is large enough to fill the lens of a hundred-inch telescope, but it is also small enough to enter an atom. It may spread like a circular wave through the universe, but when it hits its mark, this cosmic wave instantaneously contracts to a point where it strikes with its full and undivided force. Space-time, therefore, does not seem to exist for the quantum, at least not in its lower multiples. Nay, more: the very hitting of its mark presents another strange puzzle, which seems to defy the principles of causation and of the uniformity of nature, and to take us into the realm of chance and probability. The significant thing is that this strange quantum character of the universe is not the result of theory but is an experimental fact well attested from several departments of physics. In spite of the strange Puck-like behaviour of the quantum, we should not lightly conclude, with some prominent physicists, that the universe has a skeleton in its cupboard in the shape of an irrational or chaotic factor. Our macroscopic concepts may not fit this ultra-microscopic world of the quantum. And our best hopes for the future are founded on the working out of a new system of concepts and laws suited to this new world that has swum into the ken[1] of science. The rapid development of wave mechanics in the last four years seems to have brought us within sight of this ideal, and we are beginning to discern a new kind of order in the microscopic elements of the world, very different from any type of law hitherto imagined in science, but none the less a rational order capable of mathematical formulation.

We may summarize these remarks by saying that the vastly improved technique of research has led to physical discoveries in recent years which have at last completely shattered the traditional commonsense view of the material world. A new space-time world has emerged which is essentially immaterial, and in which the old-time matter, and even the scientific mass, gravitation, and energy stand for no independent entities, but can best be construed as configurations of space-time. And the discovery of the quantic properties of this world points to still more radical transformations which loom on the horizon of science. The complete recasting of

---

[1] Then felt I like some watcher of the skies
When a new planet swims into his ken.
                    Keats, *On First Looking into Chapman's Homer*.

many of our categories of experience and thought may ultimately be involved.

From the brilliant discoveries of physical science we pass on to the advances in biological science which, although far less revolutionary, have been scarcely less important for our world-outlook. The most important biological discovery of the last century was the great fact of organic evolution; and for this fact the space-time concept has at last come to provide the necessary physical basis. It is unnecessary for my purpose to canvass the claims and discuss the views represented by the great names of Lamarck, Darwin and Mendel, beyond saying that they represent a progressive advance in biological discovery, the end of which has by no means been reached yet. Whatever doubts and differences of opinion there may be about the methods, the mechanism, or the causes, there is no doubt about the reality of organic evolution, which is one of the most firmly established results in the whole range of science. Palaeontology, embryology, comparative anatomy, taxonomy, and geographical distribution all combine to give the most convincing testimony that throughout the history of this earth life has advanced genetically from at most a few simple primitive forms to ever more numerous and highly specialized forms. Under the double influence of the internal genetic and the external environmental factors, life has subtly adapted itself to the ever-changing situations on this planet. In the process of this evolution not only new structures and organs, but also new functions and powers have successively appeared, culminating in the master-key of mind and in the crowning achievement of human personality. To have hammered the great truth of organic evolution into the consciousness of mankind is the undying achievement of Charles Darwin, by the side of which his discovery of natural selection as the method of evolution is of secondary importance.

The acceptance of the theory of evolution has brought about a far-reaching change in our outlook on the universe and our sense of values. The story of Creation, so intimately associated with the groundwork of most religions, has thus come to be rewritten. The unity and interconnections of life in all its manifold forms have been clearly recognized. And man himself has had to come down from his privileged position among the angels and take his proper place in the universe as part of the order of nature. Thus Darwin completes the revolution begun by Copernicus.

Space-time finds its natural completion in organic evolution. For in organic evolution the time aspect of the world finds its most authentic expression. The world truly becomes process, where nothing ever remains the same or is a duplicate of anything else, but a growing, gathering, creative stream of unique events rolls forever forward.

But while we recognize this intimate connection between the conceptions of space-time and organic evolution, we should be careful not to identify the time of evolution with that of space-time. There is a very real difference between them. Biological time has direction, passes from the past to the future, and is therefore his-torical. It corresponds to the 'before' and 'after' of our conscious experience. Physical time as an aspect of space-time is neutral as regards direction. It is space-like, and may be plus or minus, but does not distinguish between past or future. It may move in either direction, backwards or forwards, while biological time, like the time of experience, knows only a forward flow. Hence cosmic evolution, as we see it in astronomy and physics, is mostly in an opposite direction to that of organic evolution. While biological time on the whole shows a forward movement towards ever higher organization and rising qualities throughout the geological ages, the process of the physical world is mostly in the opposite direction†—towards disorganization, disintegration of more complex struc-tures, and dissipation of energy. The second law of thermodynamics thus marks the direction of physical time. While the smaller world of life seems on the whole to be on the up-grade, the larger physical universe is on the down-grade. One may say that in the universe we witness a majority movement downward, and a minority movement upward. The energy which is being dissipated by the decay of physical structure is being partly taken up and organized into life structures—at any rate on this planet. Life and mind thus appear as products of the cosmic decline, and arise like the phoenix from the ashes of a universe radiating itself away. In them nature seems to have discovered a secret which enables her to irradiate with imperishable glory the decay to which she seems physically doomed.

Another striking point arises here. Organic evolution describes the specific process of what we call life, perhaps the most mysterious phenomenon of this mysterious universe. When we ask what is the nature of life we are curiously reminded of the behaviour of the quantum referred to. I do not for a moment wish to say that the quantum is the physical basis of life, but I do say that in the quantum

† No doubt there are exceptions to this broad generalization. In astronomy stars and solar systems and galaxies are probably still being formed, while in physics syntheses of elements may possibly still be going on. In the same way we find in organic evolution minor phases of regression, degeneration and parasitism.

the physical world offers an analogy to life which is at least suggestive. The quantum follows the all-or-nothing law and behaves as an indivisible whole: so does life. A part of a quantum is not something less than a quantum; it is nothing or sheer nonentity: the same holds true of life. The quantum is perhaps most easily symbolized as a wave or combination of waves, which can only exist as a complete periodicity, and whose very concept negatives its existence as partial or truncated. In other words, it is a specific configuration and can only exist as such: the same holds true of life. The quantum does not fall completely within the deterministic causal scheme: the same seems true of life. Significant, also, is the fact that quantum phenomena underlie secondary qualities such as colour and the like, which the older science in its mechanistic scheme ignored, but which are specially associated with life and consciousness. Apparently the quantum does not fall completely within the causal deterministic scheme: the same is true of life. Life is not an entity, physical or other. It is a type of organization; it is a specific principle of central or self-organization. If that organization is interfered with we are left, not with bits of life, but with death. The nature of living things is determined, not by the nature of their parts, but by the nature or principle of their organization. In short, the quantum and life seem to have this in common, that they both behave as wholes.

I have before now endeavoured to explore the concept of life in the light of the more general concept of the whole. A whole is not a sum of parts, or constituted by its parts. Its nature lies in its constitution more than in its parts. The part in the whole is no longer the same as the part in isolation. The interesting point is that while this concept of the whole applies to life, it is according to the recent physics no less applicable to the ultimate physical units. Thus the electron within an atom is no longer a distinct electron. There may be separate electrons, but when they cease to be separate they also cease to be. The eight electrons which circulate in an oxygen atom are merged in a whole in such a way that they have lost their separate identity; and this loss of individuality has to be taken into account in calculations as to the physical behaviour of the atom. The physicist, in fact, finds himself unable to look upon the entity which is one-eighth of eight electrons as the same thing as a single electron. At the very foundation, therefore, of physics, the principle or category of the whole applies no less than in the advanced structure of life, although not in the same degree. In the ultimate analysis of the world, both at the physical and the biological level, the part or unit element somehow becomes shadowy and incoherent, and the very basis of mechanism is undermined. It would almost seem as if the world in its very essence is holistic, and as if the notion of individual parts is a practical makeshift without final validity in the nature of things.

The general trend of the recent advances in physics has thus been towards the recognition of the fundamental organic character of the material world. Physics and biology are beginning to look not so utterly unlike each other. Hitherto the great gulf in nature has lain between the material and the vital, between inorganic matter and life. This gulf is now in process of being bridged. The new physics, in dissolving the material world of commonsense and discovering the finer structure of physical nature, has at the same time disclosed certain fundamental features which it has in common with the organic world. Stuff-like entities have disappeared and have been replaced by space-time configurations, whose very nature depends on their principle of organization. And this principle which I have ventured to call holism, appears to be at bottom identical with that which pervades the organic structures of the world of life. The quantum and space-time have brought physics closer to biology. As I have pointed out, the quantum anticipates some of the fundamental characters of life, while space-time forms the physical basis for organic evolution. Physics and biology are thus recognized as respectively simpler and more advanced forms of the same fundamental pattern in world-structure.

The older mechanistic conception of nature, the picture of nature as consisting of fixed material particles, mechanically interacting with each other—already rudely shaken by the relativity theory—is now being modified by the quantum physics. The attack on mechanism, thus coming from physical science itself, is therefore all the more deadly. Even in physics, organization is becoming more important than the somewhat nebulous entities which enter into matter. Interaction is more and more recognized to be not so much mechanical as organic or holistic, the whole in some respects dominating not only the functioning but the very existence of the entities forming it. The emergence of this organic view of nature from the domain of physics itself is thus a matter of first-rate importance, and must have very far-reaching repercussions for our eventual world-view.

The nature of the organic whole is, however, much more clearly recognized in its proper sphere of biology, and especially in the rapidly advancing science of physiology. Here, too, the correct view has been much obscured by the invasion of mechanistic ideas from the physics of the nineteenth century. A crude materialism all but swamped biology for more than a generation. At the Belfast session of this Association in 1874 a famous predecessor of mine in this Chair[1] gave unrestrained expression to this materialistic creed. All that is passing, if not already past. It must be admitted that up to a point mechanism has been useful as a first approximation and fruitful as a convention for research purposes. But if even in physics it has lost its savour, *a fortiori* has it become out of place in biology. The partial truth of mechanism is always subtended by the deeper truth of organicity or holism. So far from biology being forced into a physical mould, the position will in future be reversed. Physics will look to biology and even to psychology for hints, clues, and suggestions. In biology and psychology it will see principles at work in their full maturity which can only be faintly and fitfully recognized in physics. In this way the exchanges of physics, biology and psychology will become fruitful for the science of the future, and lay the basis for a new scientific monism.

A living individual is a physiological whole, in which the parts or organs are but differentiations of this whole for purposes of greater efficiency, and remain in organic continuity throughout. They are parts of the individual, and not independent or self-contained units which *compose* the individual. It is only this conception of the individual as a dynamic organic whole which will make intelligible the extraordinary unity which characterizes the multiplicity of functions in an organism, the mobile, ever-changing balance and interdependence of the numerous regulatory processes in it, as well as the operation of all the mechanisms by which organic evolution is brought about. This conception applies not only to individuals, but also to organic societies, such as a beehive or an ants' nest, and even to social organizations on the human level.

As the concept of space-time destroys the purely spatial character of things, so the concept of the organic whole must also be extended beyond the spatial limits of the organism so as to include its interaction with its environment. The stimuli and responses which render them mutually interdependent constitute them one whole which thus transcends purely spatial aspects. It is this overflow of organic wholes beyond their apparent spatial limits which binds all nature together and prevents it from being a mere assemblage of separate interacting units.

It is time, however, that we pass on to the world of mind. From matter, as now transformed by space-time and the quantum, we pass step by step through organic nature to conscious mind. Gone is the time when Descartes could divide the world into only two

[1] John Tyndall, born 1820; professor of natural philosophy, Royal Institute 1853–66 and superintendent 1867–87; died 1893.

substances: extended substance or matter, and thinking substance or mind. There is a whole world of gradations between these two limits. On Descartes' false dichotomy the separate provinces of modern science and philosophy were demarcated. But it is as dead as the epicycles of Ptolemy[1] and ultimately the Cartesian frontiers between physics and philosophy must largely disappear, and philosophy once more become metaphysic in the original sense. In the meantime, under its harmful influence, the paths of matter and mind, of science and philosophy, were made to diverge farther and farther, so that only the revolution now taking place in thought could bring them together again. I believe, however, their reunion is coming fast. We have seen matter and life indefinitely approaching each other in the ultimate constituents of the world. We have seen that matter is fundamentally a configuration or organization of space-time; and we have seen that life is a principle of organization whereby the space-time patterns are arranged into organic unities. The next step is to show that mind is an even more potent embodiment of the organizing, whole-making principle, and that this embodiment has found expression in a rising series, which begins practically on the lowest levels of life, and rises ultimately to the conscious mind which alone Descartes had in view in his classification. I have no time to follow up the matter here beyond making a few remarks.

Mind is admittedly an active, conative, organizing principle. It is for ever busy constructing new patterns of things, thoughts or principles out of the material of its experience. Mind, even more than life, is a principle of whole-making. It differentiates, discriminates and selects from its vague experience, and fashions and correlates the resulting features into more or less stable, enduring wholes. Beginning as mere blind tropisms, reflexes and conditioned reflexes, mind in organic nature has advanced step by step in its creative march until in man it has become nature's supreme organ of understanding, endeavour and control—not merely a subjective human organ, but nature's own power of self-illumination and self-mastery: 'The eye with which the universe beholds itself and knows itself divine.'[2]

[1] Claudius Ptolemaeus, flourished 127 to 141 or 151, Greek astronomer and mathematician. His chief work is the *Almagest* in which a system of astronomy is set forth based upon a stationary spherical earth as the centre of the universe with the sun and other heavenly bodies revolving round it. This view held the field in Europe until it was superseded by Copernican astronomy.

[2] I am the eye with which the Universe
Beholds itself and knows itself divine.

Shelley, *Hymn of Apollo*.

The free creativeness of mind is possible because, as we have seen, the world ultimately consists, not of material stuff, but of patterns, of organization, the evolution of which involves no absolute creation of an alien world of material from nothing. The purely structural character of reality thus helps to render possible and intelligible the free creativeness of life and mind, and accounts for the unlimited wealth of fresh patterns which mind freely creates on the basis of the existing physical patterns.

The highest reach of this creative process is seen in the realm of values, which is the product of the human mind. Great as is the physical universe which confronts us as a given fact, no less great is our reading and evaluation of it in the world of values, as seen in language, literature, culture, civilization, society and the state, law, architecture, art, science, morals and religion. Without this revelation of inner meaning and significance the external physical universe would be but an immense empty shell or crumpled surface. The brute fact here receives its meaning, and a new world arises which gives to nature whatever significance it has. As against the physical configurations of nature we see here the ideal patterns or wholes freely created by the human spirit as a home and an environment for itself.

Among the human values thus created science ranks with art and religion. In its selfless pursuit of truth, in its vision of order and beauty, it partakes of the quality of both. More and more it is beginning to make a profound aesthetic and religious appeal to thinking people. Indeed, it may fairly be said that science is perhaps the clearest revelation of God to our age. Science is at last coming into its own as one of the supreme goods of the human race.

While religion, art and science are still separate values, they may not always remain such. Indeed, one of the greatest tasks before the human race will be to link up science with ethical values, and thus to remove grave dangers threatening our future. A serious lag has already developed between our rapid scientific advance and our stationary ethical development, a lag which has already found expression in the greatest tragedy of history. Science must itself help to close this dangerous gap in our advance which threatens the disruption of our civilization and the decay of our species. Its final and perhaps most difficult task may be found just here. Science may be destined to become the most effective drive towards ethical values, and in that way to render its most priceless human service. In saying this I am going beyond the scope of science as at present understood, but the conception of science itself is bound to be affected by its eventual integration with the other great values.

I have now finished my rapid and necessarily superficial survey of the more prominent recent tendencies in science, and I proceed to summarize the results and draw my conclusions, in so far as they bear on our world-picture.

In the first place we have seen that in the ultimate physical analysis science reaches a microscopic world of scientific entities, very different in character and behaviour from the macroscopic world of matter, space, and time. The world of atoms, electrons, protons, radiations, and quanta, does not seem to be in space-time, or to conform to natural law in the ordinary sense. The behaviour of these entities cannot be understood without the most abstruse mathematics, nor, apparently, without resort to epistemological considerations. We seem to have passed beyond the definitely physical world into a twilight where prophysics and metaphysics meet, where space-time does not exist, and where strictly causal law in the old sense does not apply. From this uncertain nebulous underworld there seems to crystallize out, or literally to materialize, the macroscopic world which is the proper sphere of sensuous observation and of natural laws. The pre-material entities or units condense and cohere into constellations, which increase in size and structure until they reach the macroscopic stage of observation. As the macroscopic entities emerge, their space-time field and appropriate natural laws (mostly of a statistical character) emerge *pari passu*. We seem to pass from one level to another in the evolution of the universe, with different units, different behaviours, and calling for different concepts and laws. Similarly, we rise to new levels as later on we pass from the physical to the biological level, and again from the latter to the level of conscious mind. But—and this is the significant fact—all these levels are genetically related and form an evolutionary series; and underlying the differences of the successive levels, there remains a fundamental unity of plan or organization which binds them together as members of a genetic series, as a growing, evolving, creative universe.

In the second place let us see how commonsense deals with this macroscopic world. On this stage commonsense recognizes three levels of matter, life and mind as together composing the world. But it places them so far apart and makes them so inherently different from each other, that relations between them appear unintelligible, if not impossible. The commonsense notions of matter, life and mind make any relations between them, as well as the world which they form, an insoluble puzzle. The older science therefore attempted to reduce life substantially to terms of matter, and to put a question mark behind mind; and the result was a predominantly materialistic view of the world. The space-time relativity concept of the world has overcome the difficulty by destroying the old concept of matter, and reducing it from a self-subsistent entity to a configuration of space-time—in other words, to a special organization of the basic world-structure. If matter is essentially immaterial structure or organization, it cannot fundamentally be so different from organism or life, which is best envisaged as a principle of organization; nor from mind, which is an active organizer. Matter, life, and mind thus translate roughly into organization, organism, organizer. The all-or-none law of the quantum, which also applies to life and mind, is another indication that matter, life, and mind may be but different stages or levels of the same activity in the world which I have associated with the pervading feature of whole-making. Materialism has thus gone by the board, and the unintelligible trinity of commonsense (matter, life, mind) has been reinterpreted and transformed and put on the way to a new monism.

In the third place, the iron determination of the older science, so contrary to direct human experience, so destructive of the free activity of life and mind, as well as subversive of the moral responsibility of the individual, has also been materially recast. It was due to the Newtonian causal scheme which, as I have indicated, has been profoundly shaken by recent developments. Relativity reduces substance to configuration or patterns, while quantum physics gives definite indications of indeterminism in nature. In any case, life through the ages shows clearly a creative advance to ever more complex organization, and ever higher qualities, while mind is responsible for the creation of a whole realm of values. We are thus justified in stressing, along with natural necessity, an increasing measure of freedom and creativeness in the world, sufficient at least to account for organic evolution and for the appearance of moral law and endeavour. This liberation of life and spirit from the iron rule of necessity is one of the greatest gains from the recent scientific advances. Nature is not a closed physical circle, but has left the door open to the emergence of life and mind and the development of human personality. It has, in its open flexible physical patterns, laid the foundation and established the environment for the coming of life and mind. The view, to which Huxley once gave such eloquent and poignant expression, of a dualism implanted in the heart of nature, of a deadly struggle between cosmic law and moral law, is no longer justified by the subsequent advances of science.

But, in the fourth place, another dualism of a wider reach has appeared, which makes the universe itself appear to be a house divided against itself. For while the stream of physical tendency throughout the universe is on the whole downward, towards disintegration and dissipation, the organic movement, on this planet at least, is upward, and life structures are on the whole becoming more complex throughout the course of organic evolution. From the viewpoint of physics, life and mind are thus singular and exceptional phenomena, not in line with the movement of the universe as a whole. Recent astronomical theory has come to strengthen this view of life as an exceptional feature off the main track of the universe. For the origin of our planetary system is attributed to an unusual accident, and planets such as ours, with a favourable environment for life, are taken to be rare in the universe. Perhaps we may even say that at the present epoch there is no other globe where life is at the level manifested on the earth. Our origin is thus accidental, our position is exceptional, and our fate is sealed, with the inevitable running down of the solar system. Life and mind, instead of being the natural flowering of the universe, are thus reduced to a very casual and inferior status in the cosmic order. A new meaning and a far deeper poignancy are given to Shakespeare's lines:

> We are such stuff
> As dreams are made on; and our little life
> Is rounded with a sleep.[1]

According to astronomy, life is indeed a lonely and pathetic thing in this physical universe—a transient and embarrassed phantom in an alien, if not hostile, universe.

Such are some of the depressing speculations of recent astronomical theory. But in some respects they have already been discounted in the foregoing. For even if life be merely a terrestrial phenomenon, it is by no means in an alien environment if, as we have seen reason to think this is an essentially organic universe. In its organic aspects the universe is on the way to life and mind, even if the goal has been actually reached at only one insignificant point in the universe. The potencies of the universe are fundamentally of the same order as its actualities. The universe might say in the words of Rabbi Ben Ezra:

> All I could never be,
> All, men ignored in me,
> This, I was worth to God.[2]

[1] *The Tempest*, IV, 1. 148.
[2] Robert Browning, *Rabbi Ben Ezra*, xxv.

Then again, the very possibility of perception, of knowledge and science depends on an intimate relation between mind and the physical universe. Only thus can the concepts of mind come to be a measure for the facts of the universe, and the laws of nature come to be revealed and interpreted by nature's own organ of the human mind. Besides science we have other forms of this inner relation between the mind and the universe, such as poetry, music, art and religion. The human spirit is not a pathetic wandering phantom of the universe, but is at home, and meets with spiritual hospitality and response everywhere. Our deepest thoughts and emotions and endeavours are but responses to stimuli which come to us, not from an alien, but from an essentially friendly and kindred universe. So far from the cosmic status of life and mind being degraded by the newer astronomy and physics, I would suggest an alternative interpretation of the facts, more in accord with the trend of evolutionary science. We have seen a macroscopic universe born or revealed to consciousness out of a prior microscopic order of a very different character. Are we not, in the emergence of life and mind, witnessing the birth or revelation of a new world out of the macroscopic physical universe? I suggest that at the present cosmic epoch we are the spectators of what is perhaps the grandest event in the immeasurable history of our universe and that we must interpret the present phase of the universe as a mother and child universe, still joined together by a placenta which science, in its divorce from the other great values, has hitherto failed to unravel.

Piecing together these clues and conclusions we arrive at a world-picture fuller of mystery than ever. In a way it is closer to common-sense and kinder to human nature than was the science of the nineteenth century. Materialism has practically disappeared, and the despotic rule of necessity has been greatly relaxed. In ever varying degree the universe is organic and holistic through and through. Not only organic concepts, but also, and even more so, psychological viewpoints are becoming necessary to elucidate the facts of science. And while the purely human concepts, such as emotion and value, purpose and will, do not apply in the natural sciences, they retain their unimpaired force in the human sciences. The ancient spiritual goods and heirlooms of our race need not be ruthlessly scrapped. The great values and ideals retain their unfading glory and derive new interest and force from a cosmic setting. But in other respects it is a strange new universe, impalpable, immaterial, consisting not of material or stuff, but of organization, of patterns or wholes which are unceasingly being woven to more complex or to simpler designs. In the large it appears to be a decaying, simplifying universe which attained to its perfection of organization in the far-distant past and is now regressing to simpler forms—perhaps for good, perhaps only to restart another cycle of organization. But inside this cosmic process of decline we notice a smaller but far more significant movement—a streaming, protoplasmic tendency; an embryonic infant world emerging, throbbing with passionate life, and striving towards rational and spiritual self-realization. We see the mysterious creative rise of the higher out of the lower, the more from the less, the picture within its framework, the spiritual kernel inside the phenomenal integuments of the universe. Instead of the animistic, or the mechanistic, or the mathematical universe, we see the genetic, organic, holistic universe, in which the decline of the earlier physical patterns provides the opportunity for the emergence of the more advanced vital and rational patterns.

In this holistic universe man is in very truth the offspring of the stars. The world consists not only of electrons and radiations, but also of souls and aspirations. Beauty and holiness are as much aspects of nature as energy and entropy. Thus 'in eternal lines to time it grows'. An adequate world-view would find them all in their proper context in the framework of the whole. And evolution is perhaps the only way of approach to the framing of a consistent world-picture which would do justice to the immensity, the profundity, and the unutterable mystery of the universe.

Such in vague outline is the world-picture to which science seems to me to be pointing. We may not all agree with my rendering of it, which indeed does not claim to be more than a mere sketch. And even if it were generally accepted, we have still to bear in mind that the world-picture of tomorrow will in all probability be very different from any which could be sketched today.

299   To F. Lamont[1]   Vol. 48, no. 136

102 Banbury Road
Oxford
4 October 1931

My dear Florence, When I arrived at the end of August last I found your sad letter full of disasters and disablements. You might have anticipated that your Greek tour in the company of the highbrows would lead to mischief, but of course you could not guess the form it would take. I felt deeply sorry for you, and only trust you are well again by now and able to get about in the usual way. In the course

---

[1] Florence Haskell Corliss married T. W. Lamont (q.v.) on 31 October 1895.

of my slippery life I have had to break both my ankles and I can therefore sympathize with you. I have done so most deeply, and you have often been in my thoughts in these hectic days. And hectic they have been. I have now finished with the Faraday Centenary,[1] the British Association and the Clerk Maxwell Centenary.[2] For two weeks I have moved familiarly with the potentates of science, and I feel very much exhausted at the end. Some of your own great ones were here also—Fairfield Osborn, Millikan [R. A.] and many others. As president of the Association I had to take my full share in whatever was doing, and my unfamiliarity with the world of science and scientists made the process all the more exciting and arduous. I am glad to report that I managed to conceal my errors and shortcomings with some success and that the meeting itself has been all that could be wished. I send you some copies of my presidential address which, as you will see takes up high holistic ground and in which I bear testimony to my faith in the future emergence of a more unified science than we have at present. Science is the only hopeful sign at present on our horizon. Everything else is sad and sombre to a degree. Europe seems to be sinking deeper into a financial morass, and some great social breakdown is not beyond the range of possibility. I proceed to Germany in a fortnight to gather such impressions as I can. England is at last also giving way under the strain, and the ark of the covenant—the pound sterling —has gone. It will never be 20s. again.[3] I hear curious rumours of difficulties in the U.S.A. also. The future is indeed dark, with the agricultural population of the world in a condition of economic enslavement, with industry disorganized, with unemployment rapidly growing, and with the finance in a mess. I wonder what Tom [Lamont] thinks of it all. I have not yet seen Austin [Lamont] or his wife, and hope to do so after the term begins, if they will still be here. It will be great fun to see them. I have seen the Gilbert Murrays, but on the whole I have moved in very scientific circles and feel steeped in world-views. But the more I see of all this the more I cling to the purely human as the only real thing in the world. The smallest things are indeed the dearest and the greatest in life.

My love to you and Tom and the children. Yours ever,

J. C. Smuts

[1] The Faraday Centenary Exhibition was held at the Royal Albert Hall from 23 September to 3 October 1931. On 28 August 1831 Michael Faraday discovered the production of electricity from magnetism.

[2] To commemorate the birth, in 1831, of James Clerk Maxwell, the Scottish physicist, best known for his theory of electro-magnetic waves.

[3] On 21 September 1931 Great Britain went off the gold standard and the pound fell from about $4.86 to $3.80.

102 Banbury Road
Oxford
6 Oktober 1931

Liefste Mamma, Ek het jou laaste brief gelees en daar ek vir die
rest van die week weg sal wees sal ek dadelik antwoord. Ek het jou
laas geskrywe naby die end van die B.A. meeting. Die is met groot
sukses en éclat afgeloop en die opinie oral is dat die Meeting een
uitstekende sukses was. Selfs word die President baie lof toegeswaai
vir die aktiewe deel wat hy in the werksaamhede geneem het. Die
einde was een recepsie wat ek by Down House (die ou woonhuis in
Kent van Chas. Darwin) vir een gedeelte van die B.A. gegee het.
Jy sal seker baie biesonderhede in die cuttings sien; dus sal ek jou
nie oor dit alles skrywe nie. Woensdag was die einde en Donderdag
ogtend is ek toe na Cambridge om die Clerk Maxwell Centenary by
te woon. Die was ook een uitstekend sukses; my deel was in die
processies in skarlaken kleeren, en een speech aan die einde die
laaste aand. Voor die einde moes ek een dinner van A. Bailey in
Londen bywoon, gegee aan die oorblywende leiers van die Groot
oorlog. Daar het ek baie van die ou vrinde ontmoet; o.a. Allenby
wat na jou gevra het en baie groete gestuur het. Die Prins of Wales
was ook daar en ek het langs hom gesit en ons het lekker gesels.
Ons kom goed klaar, hoewel ek meer van sy pa as van hom hou.
Saterdag het ek met die Gilletts terug gemotor na Oxford; hul was
saam op Cambridge en kon my dus oorbreng en op weg het ons een
goeie wandeling geneem. Ek was baie moeg en mat en die wandeling
het my goed gedoen. Sondag ogtend moes ek aan korrespondense
wy—oor die 20 briewe moes geskrywe word. Maar die namiddag
weer na die Downs vir een verder wandeling wat ek biesonder
geniet het. Maandag (gister) het Margaret my uitgemotor na die
oude Rowntrees waar ek $1\frac{1}{2}$ uur vertoef het; toe na die Passfields
wie nie thuis was; en toe vir die nag na Sir Graham Bower een ou
man van 83 jaar wat onthullings aan my oor die Jameson Raid wou
maak. Hy was Imperial Secretary van Sir H. Robinson in 1895 en
volkome op die hoogte van daardie gebeurtenis. Hy het my die
geskiedenis vertel waaruit blyk dat Chamberlain nie alleen alles
geweet het nie, maar alles opgesteek en aangehits het—dus erger
selfs as gewoonlik gedenk word. Terwyl ek daar by hom was kwam
daar een telefoon van die koning die wou weet waar ek was. Ek is
toe van ogtend na Londen en het hom een besoek gebreng. Dit
blyk toe dat daar gister een groot cabinetskrisis was—MacDonald
sou bedank ens. En die koning wou—net so as in die Ierse moeilik-

heid van 1921—my advies inwin oor die heele saak. Gelukkig vir my is die Cabinetskrisis in die nag beslis en was alles oor toe ek van ogtend daar aankwam. Maar dit wys watter vertroue die liewe ou koning in my het en hoe graag hy by my om hulp en advies kyk. Hy siet daar goed uit en lyk nie na een invaliede nie.

Dit is nou besluit dat Bancroft nie met my na die Vasteland sal gaan maar na Ierland; die beide Gilletts gaan met my en ons sal Tona dan in Duitsland optel. Ek is bly sulke liewe maats to hê. Cato was nooit by die B.A. maar al daardie tyd te Porthcothan. Ook maar beter so. Morre is ek weer in Londen vir interviews en in die aand vir een dinner by Sir Lewis Richardson. Dan die volgende morre vertrek ek na Sheffield waar ek die aand die Basil Hicks lecture sal gee. Soentjies vir almal en liefde.

Pappa

TRANSLATION

102 Banbury Road
Oxford
6 October 1931

Dearest Mamma, I have just read your last letter and, as I shall be away for the rest of the week, I shall answer it at once. I wrote to you last towards the end of the British Association meeting. This went off with great success and *éclat* and the general opinion is that it was an outstanding success. Even the president has been much praised for the active part which he took in the proceedings. They ended with a reception which I gave at Down House (Charles Darwin's old house in Kent) for part of the British Association. You will no doubt see many particulars in the newspaper cuttings, so I shall not write about all that. It ended on Wednesday and on Thursday morning I went to Cambridge to attend the Clerk Maxwell centenary. This was also an outstanding success. My part was to walk in procession in scarlet robes and to make a speech at the end on the last evening. Before all was over I had to attend a dinner given by A. Bailey in London to the surviving leaders of the Great War. There I met many of the old friends—among others Allenby, who asked after you and sent greetings. The Prince of Wales was also there; I sat next to him and we had a pleasant chat. We get on well although I like his father better than I do him. On Saturday I motored back to Oxford with the Gilletts; they were at Cambridge and so could bring me back and we had a good walk on the way. I was very tired and limp and the walk did me good. Sunday morning I had to devote to my correspondence—more than twenty letters had to be written. But in the afternoon we could go to the downs again for another walk which I particularly enjoyed. On Monday (yesterday) Margaret motored me out to the old Rowntrees[1] where I stayed for one-and-a-half hours; then to the Passfields, who were not at home; and then for the night to Sir Graham Bower's—an old man of eighty-three who wanted to make disclosures about the Jameson Raid to me. He was imperial secretary to Sir H. Robinson in 1895 and knew all about that occurrence. He told me the story, from which it appears that Chamberlain not only knew everything but instigated and incited it all—even worse than is usually thought. While I was with him there was a telephone call from the King who wished to know where I was. So I went to London this morning to see him. It then appeared that there was a big cabinet crisis yesterday; MacDonald was to resign, etc. And the King, as in the Irish difficulty of 1921, wished to have my advice about the whole matter. Fortunately for me the cabinet crisis was decided during the night and all was over when I arrived there this morning.[2] But it shows what faith the dear old King has in me and how much he likes to look to me for help and advice. He looks well—not like an invalid.[3]

It has now been decided that Bancroft [Clark] will not go with me to the Continent but to Ireland. Both Gilletts are to go with me and we shall pick up Tona [Gillett] in Germany. I am glad to have such dear companions. Cato [Clark] was not at the British Association but at Porthcothan all that time—which was really better. Tomorrow I shall be in London again for interviews and, in the evening, a dinner at Sir Lewis Richardson's. The next morning I leave for Sheffield where I shall that evening deliver the Basil Hicks Lecture.[4] Kisses and love to all.

Pappa

[1] The parents of Joan Boardman.

[2] MacDonald was at this time prime minister of a National government formed on 24 August 1931 to deal with the financial crisis. It consisted of four Conservatives, four Labour men and two Liberals. When a general election had to be held the question arose of how the government should go to the voters and how the party differences within it were to be accommodated. MacDonald talked of resignation. George V dissuaded him. On the night of October 5 it was decided that the government would appeal to the voters for a free hand to cure the country's ills—'a doctor's mandate'. *See* H. Nicolson, *King George V*, p. 493.

[3] From November 1928 to September 1929 the King had had a prolonged and severe illness which left him prematurely aged and delicate.

[4] Smuts's subject was 'The Disarmed Peace' (Smuts Collection, Box I, no. 74A).

301 To S. M. Smuts
Vol. 48, no. 142

Hotel Adlon
Berlin W.
28 Oktober 1931

Liefste Mamma, Ek het jou laas uit Holland geskrywe. Vir die laaste
9 dae is ek met die Gilletts en Sally nou hier in Berlin en het ek een
uiters interessante tyd gehad. Ons het die museums en gallerye
besoek, die universiteit en Prof. Planck, die botaniese tuine te
Dahlen en feitlik alles wat werd is om te sien. Ons was te Potsdam
en Sans Souci—een 45 minute per trein van hier. Ek het die ver-
naamste politici en financiers ontmoet en sake met hul bespreek—
die kanselier Dr. Brüning, Dr. Luther, die vorige kanselier, nou
hoof van die reichsbank, en talle van ander vername mense.
Hindenburg alleen het ek nie gaan sien, omdat mijn besoek by hom
een officieele kleur aan die saak kan gee. Ek het die inwendige
toestande en die internasionale posiesie taamlik volledig met hul
bespreek en voel taamlik op die hoogte van wat mens hier denk en
voel. Dit was waarlik een baie leersame ondervinding vir my. Die
Gilletts het dit ook baie geniet. Arthur betaal die onkoste van die
trip en ek kan hul nie dankbaar genoeg wees vir all die goedheid en
liefde waarvoor vir my gesorg word. Ek vind ook ooral een ope deur
vir my. My naam is goed en gunstig bekend. Môre (Donderdag
29 Oct) vertrek ons terug na Londen waar ons die volgende Vrydag
ogtend om 8.30 aankom; dan na Oxford om opgehoopte briewe af
te werk en gedagtes te versamel. Die volgende week—die eerste
van Nov. sal ek seker in Londen moet besig wees sodat ek vrees dat
ek nie op 6 Nov. sal weg kom soos ek gehoop had. Maar ek wil graag
my bes doen vir hierdie lydende wereld en sou nie met halfgedane
sake wil terugkeer. Dus as dit noodig mag blyk sal ek een week of
selfs twee weke langer in Londen vertoef as ek gemeen had. Dinge
lyk oneindig sleg hier en ek vrees dat sake heelmaal na chaos en
economiese verval kan loop als er nie ernstige stappe geneem word
om die posiesie te red terwyl daar nog tyd is. Ek sien uit die koerante
van ogtend dat die 'national government' in Engeland een volslae
sukses behaal het en die Arbeiders uit die veld geslaan is. Dit is
miskien die beste wat kon gebeur het op hierdie oomblik, maar
breng ook sy gevare vir die toekoms. Hoe dit ook sy, ek wil graag
een paar weke in Londen vertoef om dinge daar goed na te gaan en
met die voormanne te bespreek. Die Duitsers maak een baie goeie
indruk en die reis het op my en my vriende baie gunstige herin-
neringe gelaat. Liefde van

Pappa

TRANSLATION

Hotel Adlon
Berlin W.
28 October 1931

Dearest Mamma, I wrote to you last from Holland. For the last nine days I have been here in Berlin with the Gilletts and Sally [Richardson] and have had a most interesting time. We visited the museums and galleries, the university and Professor [M.] Planck, the botanical gardens at Dahlen and practically everything worth seeing. We were at Potsdam and Sans Souci, forty-five minutes by train from here. I met the most important politicians and financiers and discussed things with them—the chancellor, Dr [H.] Brüning, the former chancellor, Dr [H.] Luther, now head of the Reichsbank, and numbers of other important people. Only Hindenburg[1] I did not go to see as a visit to him might give an official colour to the matter. I discussed internal conditions and the international position rather fully with them and am now fairly *au fait* with what people here think and feel. It was really a very instructive experience for me. The Gilletts also enjoyed it very much. Arthur is paying the expenses of the trip and I cannot be grateful enough to them for all the goodness and love with which they care for me. I also find an open door everywhere. My name is good and favourably known. Tomorrow (Thursday, 29 October) we return to London where we shall arrive next Friday morning at 8.30. During the next week—the first in November—I shall probably have to be busy in London so I fear I shall not be able to get away on 6 November as I had hoped. But I want to do my best for this suffering world and would not like to return with the work half-done. So, if it appears necessary, I shall stay in London for a week, or even two weeks, longer than I had intended. Things look extremely bad here and I fear they may lead to complete chaos and economic ruin if serious steps are not taken to save the situation while there is time. I see in the newspapers this morning that the 'national government' in England has had a complete success and that the Labourites are disconcerted.[2] Perhaps this is the best thing to have happened at this moment but it also has its dangers for the future. However, I want to stay in London for a few weeks to look into things carefully and to have discussions with the leading men. The Germans have made a very good impression

[1] General Paul von Hindenburg was then president of the German Republic.

[2] The National government scored a landslide victory with 556 seats, of which 472 were held by Conservatives. The Labour party suffered a heavy defeat, returning only 46 members as against 287 in 1929.

and the journey has left me and my friends with favourable memories. Love from

Pappa

302 From L. Esselen to T. Roos Vol. 47, no. 55

The document in the Smuts Collection is a typed copy initialled in the handwriting of Louis Esselen and annotated as follows: 'Gold standard issue. Roos goes off the Bench.'

Personal 11 November 1931

My dear Tielman, I am sorry I missed you in Johannesburg on Thursday morning and again in Pretoria the same afternoon. The enclosed (see marked portion)[1] rather perturbed some of our friends in the Union Buildings,[2] but I quite understand and to all intents and purposes it has probably helped. [O.] Pirow has indicated to me that if it can be arranged by Oom Jannie[3] he will meet you two so that matters can be discussed, and I may add that this has the concurrence of General Hertzog. Oom Jannie is quite willing and the only thing remains now as to how you want me to arrange the meeting. I would suggest that you and the chief first have a conversation and he can then send for Pirow.

For the good of South Africa and all of us, I want to make an earnest appeal to you to help us in obtaining what you and I and many others have striven for for a long time. With a little give and take I feel confident that our efforts will be crowned with success. The new party must come and the sooner the better, and I feel sure that in a year or two you will emerge a greater man than you have ever been before. There are many friends anxious to help you and the only thing that has kept them back is the uncertainty of your future movements and on account of some of the people you have round you. I have explained to Oom Jannie and Pirow that you might want something done for Hjalmar [Reitz] and they both agree and can see no difficulty.

As far as Oom Jannie is concerned I may very definitely tell you that you have a very good friend in him and probably much more than you may realize.

It is unfortunate that I have to go to Natal to assist in the Umbilo bye-election and will not be back before the 21st instant as I would much rather have explained matters to you personally instead of

---

[1] Not in the Smuts Collection. [2] The main government offices in Pretoria.
[3] Familiar name of Smuts.

writing. Oom Jannie will be back on the 17th and a meeting can be arranged any time after that.[1]

Will you kindly on receipt of this drop me a line to Box 1694 Durban, which will be my address while I am there, the telegraphic address being 'Safrican'.

Instead of posting this letter, I will ask our mutual friend K.[2] to hand it to you. *Beste wense, Opreg jou vriend*[3]

L. E.

303   From C. F. Andrews   Vol. 47, no. 8

Telegram

From: C. F. Andrews

To: General Smuts

Dated 15 November 1931

Saw Lord Irwin personally this morning and intended coming Oxford today carrying letter from him to you as he and Mr Gandhi wished me to see you as soon as possible. I found out by telephoning you had gone to Sandringham.[4] Could you kindly either telephone me Sloane 4232 or telegraph me 88 Knightsbridge London where I could see you soonest and whether I should post Lord Irwin's letter[5] or bring it with me.

304   From Lord Irwin   Vol. 47, no. 149

Private

88 Eaton Square
S.W.1
14 November 1931

Dear General Smuts, Will you forgive me for presuming on a very slight acquaintance to write to you on a matter which I know, to you as to me, will seem of very great importance?

---

[1] On 13 November 1931 Smuts, then in England, sent the following telegram to Louis Esselen: 'Can attend meetings mentioned. Entirely disapprove suggested tactics. No such co-operation possible unless proposal from other side and agreement first on all outstanding questions. Otherwise merely trap for us. Advise sustained attack on government policy now clearly proving ruinous to country. Advise united party action in this first-class emergency. Show telegram friends.'
                              (Smuts Collection, vol. 48, no. 146.)
[2] Louis Karovsky, a house agent in Brits, Transvaal. He was a leading member of the Labour party and a close friend of Tielman Roos.
[3] Best wishes, sincerely your friend (Afrikaans).
[4] Country seat of the royal family near King's Lynn, Norfolk.
[5] **304.**

The situation, as you know, of the Indian round-table conference is very grave[1] and on it hangs, in my judgment, the future well-being of India—and her relations to the Empire. And a good deal else.

Gandhi came to see me this morning, and I know how great your influence is with him. He told me of the interest you have been taking, and this is only to beg you to continue to exert your good offices in the cause of settlement. I will not bore you with the ins and outs of the difficulties; you probably know them well enough. A good deal will depend on what the government actually does; but a great deal, and perhaps more, upon whether or not Gandhi believes in their sincerity. Now, I believe that from your exceptional position, you can do more than perhaps anyone else to convince him of that (if you are yourself convinced) and to convince the prime minister of the immense risks involved in rupture.

I saw the prime minister today and I think he hopes to get hold of you without delay. For this there is indeed no room. I doubt the prime minister being able to do all that Gandhi wants; but for Gandhi, as you know better than anyone, it is the spirit rather than actual steps taken that very often counts heaviest. But, apart from Gandhi, the knowledge that you were interesting yourself in the matter would, I fancy, exercise a most useful and salutary effect upon the mind of the Conservative party, and of the British public generally. What is needed is to get it into their heads that Great Britain and India simply cannot afford the risks to both of failure to reach an agreement. Yours very truly,

Irwin

305   From M. K. Gandhi   Vol. 47, no. 64

17 November 1931

Dear General, I duly received your affectionate letter. My observations since our last meeting lead me to the conclusion that you may not withdraw from the friendly intervention you began so happily last week. If necessary you should postpone your departure to South Africa for a cause you rightly believe to be the world's cause.

Thank you once more. Yours sincerely,

M. K. Gandhi

[1] The second round-table conference on India met in September 1931. Gandhi attended as the only delegate of the Indian National Congress. He opposed the main decisions and the conference foundered on the question of communal and minority electorates.

306   To M. C. Gillett   Vol. 48, no. 197

R.M.S. Arundel Castle
2 December 1931

Isn't that good news from 'Hindhayes'?[1] A cable reached me on his birthday and gave great joy. And so the great stream of life rolls on through these curious human units. Whence? Whither? And yet, as the holist says, it is not a process of mere rolling but of creation, of creative movement all the time. 'To God who is our home.'[2] Yes, but whence? For if there was perfection at the beginning, why this painful process of realization through time? Why the apparent farce of individual life, when life perfect and universal has been there all the time? 'We ask and ask. Thou smilest and art still.'[3] My answer is that the perfect life has not been there, but it will be there in the final consummation if that were possible. Did I tell you that I have been reading Russell's *Scientific Outlook*[4]—not up to his usual standard, and Professor C. G. Darwin's *Conceptions of Matter*[5]—very good. Darwin makes plain that matter shows diffraction and interference just as does light, and must therefore be of the nature of waves. But its actual place and speed are matters of probability only, so that, as Russell comically puts it, matter is a wave of probability undulating in nothingness. This is pretty far from common sense and ordinary experience. But it helps to show how far we have gone in the interpretation of experience when waves of probability become solid matter to experience.

I have also been much interested in Leakey's book,[6] and I have worked out certain parallelisms for climate and man in South Africa, which I may write up later if I have time.[7] It is a fascinating subject—the oscillations of climate with the appearances of man through the ages. The evidence from South Africa and East Africa supplement the European information in a curious way, and vice versa. Did I tell you that *The Mahdi of Allah* (by Bermann)[3] is such

---

[1] Jacob Daniel, the first child of Bancroft and Cato Clark, had been born. Their house in Street is called 'Hindhayes'.

[2] But trailing clouds of glory do we come
From God, who is our home.
　　　　　　　　　　　Wordsworth, *Ode, Intimations of Immortality*, iv.

[3] Matthew Arnold, *Sonnet, Shakespeare*.

[4] B. Russell, *The Scientific Outlook* (1931).

[5] C. G. Darwin, *The New Conceptions of Matter* (1931).

[6] L. S. B. Leakey, *The Stone Age Culture of Kenya Colony* (1931).

[7] A lecture, entitled 'Climate and Man in Africa', was delivered by Smuts on 6 July 1932 at a meeting of the South African Association for the Advancement of Science at Durban. It was printed in the *South African Journal of Science*, vol. 29, pp. 98–131, October 1932.

[8] Richard A. Bermann, *The Mahdi of Allah* (1931).

an interesting book. It tells the story of the Sudan revolt in the 'eighties from the Mahdi's point of view—a curious psychological study, based on information obtained from the natives on the spot.

I have done my four to eight miles at least every day and am looked up to as the champion 'hiker' on board. I feel very fit and have shaken off the weariness which work and disappointment[1] have brought in England. I blame myself for not having fought harder at Paris (1919), for if I had done so I might today have been in a position which would have enabled me to be a real force in the present situation. Instead I am more like a spectator—which is often very galling. But the work of today can really only be done by the new men, and not by those who, like myself, come from that generation of blood. This I believe is what the prophets said to old David. Still, I would rather be an erring David than a wise Solomon.[2] Ever yours,

Jan

307   To M. C. Gillett

Vol. 48, no. 201

Irene
[Transvaal]
23 December 1931

Your welcome mail letter has just come in, but I have no time to answer, as I am off to a party meeting. It is now all politics over here, and science is as dead as the dodo. I have joined issue with the government over the gold standard and have some hope of beating them over it. The 30% exchange is building up a wall round South Africa which is killing our exports and ruining the country. Besides I don't like our present autocratic and racialistic rulers, as you know. Not that I itch for office, I assure you.

The rains are slowly beginning and the weather is cooler. Isie and the children leave for Tsalta on 26 December but I remain behind for the fray. Good-bye, dear. Luck and happiness for the New Year. Ever yours,

Jan

[1] Smuts had given a statement on the international situation to Reuter's for publication on his departure. It received very little notice in the press. He also thought the British government were 'making a mess of India'. See Smuts Collection, vol. 48, no. 200.

[2] 'And David said to Solomon, My son...it was in my mind to build an house unto the name of the Lord my God. But the word of the Lord came to me saying, Thou hast shed blood abundantly, and hast made great wars: Thou shalt not build an house unto my name.... Behold, a son shall be born to thee, who shall be a man of rest... his name shall be Solomon...he shall build an house for my name...' 1 Chronicles xxii. 7–10.

308   To M. C. Gillett   Vol. 49, no. 212

Irene
[Transvaal]
5 January 1932

And so we have reached a new year—and one which may prove unusually fateful. May Heaven be with us in our troubles. I am spending a most unusually quiet time—alone in the big house, and only down on the farm[1] for meals. I don't remember such a quiet time for many years. I have been mostly reading anthropology and finished my article on our pre-historic 'Climates and Man'. I have used the sequence of the European Pleistocene as a key to unlock our southern mystery—all very interesting to me, and probably an advance in science. Now the time for meetings has arrived and I begin a campaign at Standerton tomorrow which will take the rest of the week in the eastern Transvaal. Then home for the week-end, and next week again in the western Transvaal. Then on to Cape Town for the session. Mostly the gold standard and all the evils in its train—loss of money, loss of markets, and the rest. The government is sitting tight, and with their big parliamentary majority they may defy public opinion and hang on for the present. But the country is suffering deeply. I believe a new coinage is coming to keep the new flag company.

Meanwhile big things are moving in the great world. India is once more in the crucible, Gandhi in gaol,[2] and in Europe the conferences are gathering, as they always do in times of trouble. MacDonald is going to pay dearly for not following my advice and clinching the bargain over the constitution while he still had Gandhi in London and the situation was still well in hand. Now I fear—even if the present policy beats the Congress—an agreed solution is farther off than ever; and it is possible that the policy of repression may fail—in India as in Ireland—with results which will be calamitous. The Congress lot are of course quite impossible and have played straight into the hands of their opponents. But a peace of understanding is receding into the blue. As regards Europe I am anxious to see what will happen at the conference a few weeks hence.[3] With the U.S.A. sitting out and France on her

[1] That is, at the house of the Weyerses on the farm Doornkloof.

[2] On his return from London Gandhi resumed the civil disobedience campaign and was again imprisoned.

[3] A conference was to meet at Lausanne in January 1932 to adjust all inter-governmental debts but was postponed until June. A resolution of congress against reduction or cancellation of foreign debts prevented the participation of the United States in the conference.

high horse I fear no first-class move towards doing away with debts and reparations and setting hope going again will be possible. We shall have some more temporary palliatives and drift on to what may yet be the rocks. I see nothing but revolution in Europe and America the way things are going now. And yet, so many dangers have already been surmounted that one does not quite lose hope or heart. My old friend Professor Lotsij has died. I wrote him a long letter from Berlin, but even then he must have been under sentence of death. I saw Joan and Boarders[1] on New Year day—both well and flourishing. Love to you and Arthur and the household.

Jan

309   To F. Lamont

Vol. 49, no. 176

House of Assembly
Cape Town
22 January 1932

My dear Florence, Here I am again for the session of parliament, and shall be till June. Here too I found your last interesting letter for which I thank you. I was very glad to read all you say, especially that your foot is once more in order. It must have been a bad business. And all the good news about the children who evidently are pressing on in the great race of life. They have got a good start in life, but will find their generation one of the most difficult and puzzling in all history. The fact is that we have no longer accepted norms or rules of the game of life and are in for an era of experiment, with all the pain and failure and disillusion that must bring with it. I do not think the world has been for centuries in such a critical phase as it is passing through today. There is no danger of reversion to barbarism, as some think, but there is grave danger of colossal set-backs unless great wisdom and large-heartedness is given to us. From the British Association I went to Berlin and spent some weeks exploring their situation with the German statesmen and financiers. I got the impression of a drowning world, of a society essentially bankrupt in pocket and in soul, which had been kept going with foreign support since the peace. I fear for the future unless the helping hand continues. Germany is very sick, so is the rest of central Europe. It is only now that we are beginning to realize what the Great War has really meant for the world. It is not only a failure of statesmen and economists, but a great spiritual im-

---

[1] Howard Boardman, born 16 July 1894; emigrated to South Africa 1925; at first a farmer, then partner in a furniture factory in Johannesburg.

poverishment which has overtaken the world. No wonder that in
this confusion young people begin to look to Russia with serious
hopes for the future. I found this attitude to Russia everywhere.
Here at any rate was a plan, and a faith resolutely practised. You
must have tremendous difficulties in the States too, and Tom must
be in the thick of it all. There has never been such a test applied to
our economic civilization, and it is still a question whether we can
pull through without serious damage to our spiritual heritage.

But let me pass to pleasanter subjects. I am so glad that you
enjoyed reading my presidential address. I believe it created a great
impression. It was a plea for a more spiritual approach to the universe, towards which science appears at present to be pointing. My
dear Florence, we must recapture the essence of that spiritual order
in which we were brought up, but which has been largely lost in
our time, and for want of which the world is perishing. I don't mean
the orthodox formulas, which are dead and gone. But behind those
formulas, just as behind the sayings and teachings of all our great
intellectual leaders of the past, there lay a world which was dimly
apprehended and which we are fast losing for good and all. What is
finest in us is really also fundamental in the universe although
embodied in material and physical forms which often hide the
truth.

You raise interesting and indeed vital points in connection with
my address. I pointed out the vast anomaly which arises on the
second law of thermodynamics. But it is today the accepted basis
in the higher physics and I had to take it at that. Millikan's theory
of cosmic creation is not regarded seriously in Europe and must be
placed to the reserve account. But it would be an enormous advance
if the second law could be eliminated somehow. Then about
values; I *do* consider them real and not merely subjective. But you
must remember my view that the human mind *is* a natural force
and part and parcel of the natural order. Its creations are therefore
entitled to high respect in the order of nature. I do not really go
counter to dear old Aristotle. Your third point about *the* Whole is
very cute, and quite right. The world is not an assemblage of little
wholes, but there is something more. Only I still hesitate to call
this *the* Whole, as so many philosophers and theologians are prone
to do. There remains for me a mystery—the *Bond* which unites all
but is different from all. I can't get at it yet in any tangible form,
although my mind is moving towards something. How nice it would
be to talk over all this, but I fear the prospects are not good.

Your African trip still remains my dream on which I fondly
dwell. But I doubt whether you will have the time for it. Remember

the best time is June to August when you can move freely about this continent without risk of catching malaria. If there is any chance, let me know and I shall arrange my plans accordingly. With the Smuts family you will be quite happy, but I want you to see something of this mysterious continent with its unique appeal. This year, next year, any year—let us keep the idea before us, to realize before too late. I spent six of the most interesting weeks of my life in 1930 motoring to central Africa. I like to browse on hopes for the future. They are almost as good as the realization.

Please congratulate Corliss [Lamont] on his Ph.D. Corliss appeals very much to me. But I *don't* believe in behaviourism or other forms of the discarded materialism. The movement is from matter to something different. Perhaps Austin [Lamont] will find the secret in the nerves of the frog. Or perhaps Eleanor [Lamont] will find it in the society of the Beloved. The Toms[1] will *not* find it in finance! Perhaps we shall find it on the African veld!

But I must stop. Will the fellow never dry up, I hear you say. No, I have not read Walter Lippman since he left the [*New York*] *World*. But there is great stuff in him.

Good-bye, dear Friend. My love to all your little family. Ever yours,

J. C. Smuts

310   To C. van Riet Lowe   Vol. 49, no. 179

House of Assembly
Cape Town
3 February 1932

My dear van Riet Lowe, You will remember our conversations on anthropology on board the *Arundel Castle* which to me were in many ways the most interesting part of the voyage. I told you that I was reading through Leakey's book with much interest, and that it seemed possible to me that his work might throw great light on the problem of our past climates.

During the Christmas holidays I brought together such information as I had on the subject and tried to piece it together into a theory on the basis of Leakey's work in East Africa. I send you by this post a copy of the rough draft which I have made, which I hope will interest you. It seems to me that anthropology can be used as a very powerful instrument to throw light on our recent geology

---

[1] Thomas William Lamont and his son, Thomas Stilwell Lamont, were both bankers.

and climate, and I therefore made an attempt to apply it as an instrument of research into our immediate past. The subject has always interested me very much, and I have now another reason for dealing with it. The S_2A_3 have kindly asked me to deliver the evening lecture at their meeting at Durban next July. I have accepted this invitation and am thinking of using the material of this paper for the purpose of such an address. Nothing can be more interesting than climate and man in their sequences and interactions in the past of South Africa, and a lecture on such a subject might appeal to a large public, and at the same time show them what interesting results can be expected through the study of our anthropology.

Please read the paper and tell me frankly how the matter strikes you; which of my facts are wrong, and what other facts can be adduced to strengthen my viewpoint. If you are not interested, and you think I am on a wrong tack, I shall not mind your telling me so. But if you think there is something in my line of argument, I shall be very pleased to have all possible sources of error eliminated from the very start.

I am also sending a copy to my brother-in-law, Krige [L. J.], and Dr [A. W.] Rogers, for their remarks from a purely geological point of view. I know they are both very deeply interested in this question of our past climates from a geological point of view. Of course you are at liberty to talk to them if you so desire.

With very kind regards both to you and Mrs van Riet Lowe, Yours sincerely,

s. J. C. Smuts

311   To A. B. Gillett   Vol. 49, no. 218

House of Assembly
Cape Town
4 February 1932

I am writing [in the] early morning in bed in reply to yours of 7 January. Thank you very much for it. I am sorry to see that electricity has been left in such a state that it will require much further attention from you.[1] You have been so long locked up with that affair that I had hoped for your release. I hope you will let others get a show in now, and not fondle and coddle this ugly baby too much. Bear in mind that you are a farmer in South Africa and

[1] A. B. Gillett was engaged in the reorganization of an electricity supply company in Oxford that had got into financial difficulties.

[have] valuable interests to look after; also friends who are anxious for an early visit. I think it will do you good to come out as soon as possible and perhaps protect your bank also against the policy of our Union government. Frankly I don't know what we are coming to. The government appear determined to keep the country on gold, and the country is without money or credit, business is very bad, and we shall soon be at a standstill. How the public finance is to be done beats me. Further taxes won't help, as the limit of productivity has been reached. They can print Reserve Bank notes without the gold cover, but that is not the gold standard; or they can try to raid or force the banks once more—though I am not clear how this can be done. Anyhow keep your eyes open and yourself free for an African visit soon.

Then India. Nothing can be done at this stage. Willingdon has blundered in refusing even to see or talk to Gandhi. I admit he had great provocation, but big people are patient with smaller ones. Now the new method must go on till it fails and then a change will be made. Indian self-government is itself so difficult an experiment and with such small chance of success that one cannot be very keen about the whole subject. But I do feel sorry that the British government has made this blunder, which must prove both costly and fail in the end.

And now the young Communists. Of course, I dislike the whole matter very much, as the boys are far too ill-informed and crude in their ideas to justify such a sudden change in their outlook. Still there it is; and there is also their sincerity and disinterestedness. They have nothing to gain and they know their parents and friends are grieved. There is no other course but to leave the thing to run its course—which may lead to worse, or may work its own cure. One danger is that their new enthusiasm will interfere with their studies and proper preparation for life. But again this fear may prove groundless. I am sorry that I don't quite know what Communism is—as distinct from socialism. I have always taken it to mean a *violent* bringing about of the change over. Now how does this square with the Quaker faith and its adherence to non-violence? Perhaps the best thing for the boys will prove to be their good Quaker upbringing. I hope they will stick to the creed of their fathers and to the Meeting. Do you see any sign of weakening in this respect? I hope not. As long as they remain good Quakers I think they are safe. But in such a deep convulsion of their natures it is difficult to foresee what will happen. I can understand and most fully sympathize with your anxiety. And yet you must respect their personalities, and you must remain the same friendly comrade you have ever been to them. Where there is so much deep-seated goodness I have faith that all will come right—although perhaps not in the way we old fogies think. I love the boys and don't bother very much over this idiosyncrasy of theirs. I was at Sylma's on Sunday and on Sneeukop[1] with the Coaton boys. I missed you and yours. The mountains are so good. Love ever,

Jan

312   To A. B. Gillett   Vol. 49, no. 229

House of Assembly
Cape Town
24 March 1932

Many thanks for your letter by last mail. It is always specially pleasant to decypher your scrip and to feel that it has been worth while! I suppose protection in a mild form had to come,[2] and as I am not prejudiced either way I am prepared to watch the experiment with interest. The chief danger is in what is called the 'bargaining weapon'. There is nothing so dangerous as the temper which hucksters and bargains. And I can conceive a pretty mess in the Commonwealth as well as in the world, when the spirit of bargain has full play. Still, we must face this also. We shall have to bargain with de Valera, for instance. It will not do to crush him with a sledge-hammer. Perhaps he wants to pick a quarrel and feed the nationalist flame. But we have no use for this sort of thing. And I don't want to settle another Black and Tan terror. We are knowing hard times. The gold standard means a measure of deflation which will be cruel indeed. I prefer the other way. The English people have shown their profound political instinct by abandoning the golden calf as soon as it became a real nuisance. We still worship the poor beast with a religious fervour.

At home all well and happy. The two grandchildren[3] (Santa's) are to me like what a Bach symphony is to you. Oh the blessed release, and the surge of the pure human into our consciousness. We are going to Hermanus and later the Doornkloof party will return home, while I keep hanging on the flanks of the government and the gold standard. But I look forward to the Bushveld in

[1] A peak (5,240 feet) in the Slanghoek mountains near Wellington in the south-western Cape.

[2] The passage of the Import Duties Act, operative from 1 March 1932, marked the final abandonment of the free trade policy of British governments since c. 1860. It imposed a general customs duty of 10% on almost all imports.

[3] Jan and Louis Weyers.

June. And still more to the good time when 102 will be here. My love to you and Margaret and the young Communists.[1]

Jan

313   To M. C. Gillett

Vol. 49, no. 245

Doornkloof
[Irene, Transvaal]
4 June 1932

I never write to you on a Saturday night as there is generally something or other going on. But tonight I shall make an exception as I may not have an opportunity to do so next week. On Monday I have to be in Johannesburg in connection with an address before the university, and on Tuesday I hope to leave for the eastern Transvaal for a week's botany in Schoeman's Kloof—that is to say, it is ostensibly a botanical trip, but really I want to get away to the wilds...So far I have only found the valuable Andrew[2] as a companion...But even alone I shall enjoy the change very much. My next letter will say how I have fared.

I had a beautiful letter from you from Land's End and I have reread it because it so brought that mystic country before my mind. What a wonderful dance that Helston Flurry was and how I long to have seen it.[3] I suppose it originated as a ceremony to purge the houses of evil spirits. Why are these ancient and obsolete things so fascinating to us?

...Yes, I believe in prayer—not in the variety which tries to cajole or circumvent the deity, but in the unutterable longing and waiting for the real behind it all and in reunion with that whole to which we belong. We are but temporary moments in the eternal current of being, and in the thought of that whole there is rest and blessedness and refreshment for us. Surely prayer is this mystic reunion and escape from the bonds of our mere individual being into Being itself. By the way I see in the last *Manchester Guardian* that C. F. Andrews (Gandhi's friend) has written a book *What I Owe to Christ* which is spoken of with the highest praise. Please get it for me and first look through it for yourself. The reviewer says no such book on religion has been written for a long time. I am always deeply interested in this sort of thing. The last and highest phase of holism is religion and the subject is often in my mind. But it is a conception of religion which is very unorthodox—almost

---

[1] *See* **311**.   [2] An African servant at Doornkloof.
[2] The ancient festival at Helston in Cornwall is known as the Flurry.

a religion without God, I fear. The ordinary terms of religion are so vitiated by popular use that one likes to avoid them and state our pure human experience in fresh terminology. But at bottom I do firmly believe that all the great spirits of the world have felt the same thing and passed through the same phases of the inner life. I think holism is a great clue in these matters if one only had the time and the ability to work it out fully. In the end the religious motif remains the deepest in human life. At present it appears to be all economics; finance dominates the world. And yet I feel that in the end we shall have to evolve a deeper and truer religious outlook if man has to save his soul. We live by faith, we feed on ideals, and nothing else in the end will satisfy us. I think the New Testament can be modernized in holistic language and thus rid of all the antiquarianism which now sounds so strange and far off to us, trained as we are in a modern outlook. Of course it will take generations of groping, of trial and error before we once more see a clear light. But I have no doubt that it will come and that it is the one thing necessary.

Meanwhile, we shall have our hands full in saving civilization from shipwreck. I watch developments in Europe and America with the gravest misgivings. We are today drifting as never before and the rocks are not far off. Leadership seems impotent, if not blind. Poor Hoover seems to have lost all grip on reality, Brüning has for the moment gone and Germany has put up the danger signal.[1] You say MacDonald is played out, and there is nobody in France. Meanwhile the position is threatening in the extreme. I don't believe in Communism. The faith in which we were brought up remains the only creed for me—human liberty, personal initiative and the spirit of adventure and not safety first. I do not think the slowest should set the pace, and that the great ones should have their heads chopped off. What is wanted is a new spirit of service—of human service. But the regulation and regimentation should be definitely kept in check. Otherwise we become like the ants and bees—which seems to me to be the Communist ideal, where the individual is enslaved to the whole, and life becomes a deadly routine. 'The soul for ever' as old Walt Whitman sang.[2] Nothing can take its place. This may sound old-fashioned, but it has been the faith and the vision of our best for thousands of years.

---

[1] On 30 May 1932 Brüning was dismissed by President Hindenburg and Franz von Papen was appointed chancellor in his place.

[2] Ever the undiscouraged, resolute, struggling soul of man...
　Ever the soul dissatisfied, envious, unconvinced at last;
　Struggling today the same—battling the same.

Walt Whitman, Life.

Forgive this dull screed, but your letter somehow has made me write like this. And I conclude with love, deep love, to my dear 102's.

Jan

314   From P. Duncan   Vol. 49, no. 31

House of Assembly
Cape Town
13 June 1932

My dear Smuts, Since you spoke to me on Monday last I have had an opportunity of reading the resolutions of the Natal members and [G. Heaton] Nicholls's letter, and before leaving I want to let you know what I think about them.[1]

To me this action seems to be a piece of almost inconceivable weakness and folly. I cannot imagine how the whole party including [C. F.] Clarkson[2] allowed themselves to be stampeded by the leaders.

But however that may be, I feel very strongly that they have created an impossible position as far as the rest of the party is concerned. We cannot have within the party a group with its own separate caucus looking to its own elected leader and acting independently of the party caucus—a group, moreover, which is pledged to a policy of federation which you and the rest of the party definitely reject. Imagine the position if we came into power with the help of this group. I see no prospect of our being able, at any rate for some time, to come to hold office with a majority which would make us independent of them. They would simply have us by the throat and enforce their own terms on us. Our position would be intolerable. I can't imagine our remaining in office on such conditions.

I think you should make it very clear to them that federation is not the party policy and that you are not prepared as leader to

[1] Since 1930 there had been a movement in Natal to oppose centralization and increase the powers of the provincial council. Its aims varied from 'devolution' or 'home rule' for Natal to secession from the Union in order to reconstitute it as a loose federation. On 17 May 1932 a letter from G. Heaton Nicholls was published in the *Natal Mercury* in which he advocated the formation of a 'Natal group' within the South African party 'pledged to further federation'. On 4 June the Natal members of parliament met and agreed to form a 'Natal federal group as a wing of the South African party and to be bound by the caucus of the group'. *See* G. Heaton Nicholls, *South Africa in my Time*, pp. 217–27.

[2] C. F. Clarkson was at this time chairman of the South African party in Natal and a member of the executive committee of the Natal provincial council.

recognize them as members of the party so long as they are bound
by these resolutions. Nothing but a firm attitude will do any good
with them or restore our prestige with the people in Natal who are
still loyal to us.

I am sorry to be going away just at present. It is a difficult time
for you but I am sure that a clear and firm course is going to be the
best and the easiest in the end. Yours sincerely,

Patrick Duncan

315   From J. H. Hofmeyr   Vol. 49, no. 124

778 Schoeman St.
Pretoria
Maandag [Junie 1932]

Geagte Generaal, Ek stuur u hiermee 'n brief van Egeland, (wie u
seker nie onbekend is nie—hy was Rhodes Scholar en later Fellow
van Brasenose). Ek voel baie sterk dat ons rekening moet hou met
die nie onaansienlike aantal Natallers wat voel soos hy voel.

Wat hy sê oor Mackeurtan is deur M. self bevestig (ek het hom
vandag hier op Pretoria gesien). Dit lyk asof M. en sy vriende 'n
bietjie onthuts is deur die ongunstige ontvangs wat hul laaste streek
deur die hele land gekry het. Daar is g'n twyfel dat die gevoel teen
die Natallers baie hoog loop beide op Pretoria en op Johannesburg
veral onder ons Engelse vriende.

Wat my betref kan ek nie anders dan voel dat in die huidige
omstandighede daar niks meer oorbly dan vir ons om te breek met
die Natallers—om hul hul eie party te laat vorm—en dan met hul
'n soort van Pakt te maak vir die volgende eleksie op die basis, dat
ons hul kandidate nie sal opponeer nie, en hul ook deselfde sal doen
met ons mense, soos bv. Friend en Nel.

Ek het Mackeurtan in daardie gees gepols—en sy terugwerking
daarop was gunstig. Met beste wense, Geheel die uwe,

Jan H. Hofmeyr

TRANSLATION

778 Schoeman St
Pretoria
Monday [June 1932]

Dear General, I send you herewith a letter from Egeland [L.] (who
is probably not unknown to you—he was a Rhodes Scholar and later
a Fellow of Brasenose). I feel strongly that we must take account of

the not inconsiderable number of people in Natal who feel as he does.[1]

What he says about Mackeurtan [H. G.] has been confirmed by Mackeurtan himself (I saw him today here at Pretoria). It seems that Mackeurtan and his friends are a bit upset at the unfavourable reception which their latest dodge has had throughout the country. There is no doubt that feeling against the Natal men is running very high both at Pretoria and Johannesburg, especially among our English friends.

As for me, I can only feel that in the present circumstances nothing remains for us but to break with the Natal men—to let them form their own party—and then to make a sort of Pact with them for the next election on the basis that we will not oppose their candidates and they will do the same for our men, such as, for instance, Friend [G. A.] and Nel [O. R.].

I sounded Mackeurtan in that sense and his reaction was favourable. With best wishes, Yours sincerely,

Jan H. Hofmeyr

316 To F. Lamont

Vol. 49, no. 205

Irene
Transvaal
13 July 1932

My dear Florence, Your last, most welcome, letter arrived a mail or two ago. And the notice of Eleanor's wedding[2] arrived the day *after* the event! While letters travel slow, events travel fast, and the world has moved on since you wrote so dolefully. Your presidential candidates have been nominated,[3] the Wet Banner has been raised once more;[4] Lausanne has come and gone, and Geneva is still brooding over disarmament. I cannot be enthusiastic over Lausanne. The agreement was good, but it may never come into force.[5] The time-

---

[1] Egeland had written that Graham Mackeurtan and Kingston Russell, editor of the *Natal Mercury*, had brought about 'a reconciliation between the Devolutionists and the Parliamentarians', that is, the Natal members of parliament and that he could not, in these circumstances, join the South African party (*see* Smuts Collection, vol. 49, no. 124, enclosure).

[2] Eleanor Allen Lamont (1910–61), daughter of T. W. and F. Lamont, married Charles Crehore Cunningham.

[3] They were Herbert Hoover (Republicans) and Franklin D. Roosevelt (Democrats).

[4] Roosevelt favoured repeal of the eighteenth amendment to the constitution which imposed prohibition in the United States.

[5] At the Lausanne conference, which met in June 1932, reparations were abolished subject to conditions which involved a satisfactory settlement of war debts. *See supra*, p. 503, note 3.

table of the world seems all wrong. While America will be thinking till next November or longer what to do with debts, Hitler will be in command in Germany,[1] and chaos everywhere. We may thus see a repetition of the Hoover moratorium fiasco of last year on a much larger scale.[2] And if the Lausanne arrangement fails I don't see how even a good measure of disarmament (even if it were possible) would help. Civilization is like a big army fighting a battle on a broad front, and something for ever goes wrong somewhere and united action is impossible.

Still, I don't think western civilization will go to pieces. I don't see you going hungry yet, even if it might not be such a bad thing in itself! Our economic system is a fairly tough structure and will not topple easily. The crisis will drag on—with ups and downs—until we have adjusted ourselves to a new world order. It will not be the Russian order. I do not believe that an economic system is possible in defiance of ethical principles. Our ethical heritage is our most valuable asset from the past, and if it perishes, nothing else could endure. Religion and high endeavour, freedom and personal initiative will remain and become the basis of a new social system. Economic values will go down, money will be cheaper and more plentiful, leisure will be there in abundance, and will have to be properly organized and not wasted in the form of unemployment as now. New leaders will arise, new political institutions, and the objectives of our human march will change. But I believe it will be a long slow evolution, and the Russian experiment will not be repeated. Russia fell because her religion, her ethical system had decayed and become rotten. The church and the state had fallen, and so all that world toppled. But I don't believe this is the state of affairs elsewhere.

Now about private affairs. I have been back from parliament for about two months and have had a blessed time of meditation and reading. I have got through a great deal of botany (my beloved subject) and even some philosophy. The last week has been devoted to Whitehead's *Process and Reality*.[3] Whitehead seems to me to be living in a world apart, in which evolution has not taken

[1] In September 1930 the Nazis won 107 seats in the reichstag. In April 1932 Hitler gained 13,400,000 votes in the presidential election and from June the Papen government ruled with the support of the Nazi party.

[2] On 20 June 1931 President Hoover, in an attempt to curb the spread of the Austro-German financial crisis, had proposed a moratorium of one year on all inter-governmental debts. But French objections delayed acceptance of the moratorium. Meanwhile financial chaos overtook Germany and a crisis developed in Great Britain. Moreover, both parties in the United States, in view of the imminent presidential election, opposed any cancellation of war debt.

[3] A. N. Whitehead, *Process and Reality* (1929).

place, and in which mathematical forms play an undue role and flit about in a flare of events. I want an answer to the insistent question: how has value become a reality? How have we risen from primordial inorganic beginnings until life and mind have dawned, and personality has emerged, and the spiritual values and ideals have become our new world! How has this *more* come out of the preceding *less*? What has been that Holy Spirit which has held our hand in this pilgrimage? I cannot get a clear idea from White-head. And this problem—the reality of what we call evolution in its broadest sense—is the great problem of our time. I still find no better word than holism, but am willing to learn from anyone. I have not very much time for reading of general literature and so am getting somewhat out of date. But one must limit oneself. I can do no writing at present.

Yes, I think next summer, any time from May or June, will be a very good time for you and Tom to visit South Africa. Barring a general election in this country at that time—which is just pos-sible—I shall be free to see much of you and to direct your move-ments and show you something of this continent. Africa remains the mystery among the continents—serene, aloof, dreaming—and no place like it for getting away from the shocks and anxieties of the great world. Tom must be needing some real change. I wonder whether J. D. Rockefeller Jr. will also come; or is he not much in your line? I am sure you will both enjoy the novel experience, and find out that in African simplicity and barbarism there is a good deal of compensation.

My family is very well. Three daughters married now, with their children, and one still at school. Two boys in the mines, one a very brilliant boy who is wasted there, but one must live. My wife is wrapt in her public work and her grandchildren. And such a husband to look after!

My love to you and Tom and the children. I feel very near to you and to 107 East 70. Ever yours affectionately,

J. C. Smuts

317   To M. C. Gillett   Vol. 49, no. 252

Irene
[Transvaal]
13 July 1932

I am back again from Natal, having spent a very enjoyable week at Durban and Pietermaritzburg. At the latter place I met a party conference to discuss the federal movement and came to a satisfactory conclusion which will leave the party position in that province intact.[1] There was serious danger of a split, and I was prepared for half a dozen Natal M.P.s to hive off from the South African party and establish their own independent group. But in the end they fell into line. But the temper in Natal remains bad. The government have been overdoing bilingualism and racialism, and Natal too has a good dose of original sin; hence this revolt of sentiment, partly against Hertzogism but also partly against the 'Dutch'. At Durban I joined in some of the Science Association work and delivered my address on 'Climate and Man'. A big meeting of about 2,000 people gave me a wonderful hearing, and the slides helped to make the difficult matter go down. It was a great success, and I hope will give a good fillip to anthropology in South Africa. One whole day was spent on a botanical trip to a part hitherto unexplored, although quite close to Durban. It was most enjoyable and we found heaps of plants new to me and some new to everybody in the party. Miss Forbes,[2] our Durban botanist, was with us. I wish we could spend a day or two in some such area, because it is so full of new things. *Wrightia Natalensis* was recognized by me only, though Miss Forbes is very well versed in the flora of Natal. It was a deep gorge where a new pipe-line is being laid, with wooded sides and a stream at the bottom. I shall leave the collection intact, to go through with you when you are next here. Oh when will that be! I have just read your last letter, telling all about that good time at Aston Tirrold,[3] but also saying that Arthur is less likely to come, and you unlikely to come without him. It is these 'less likelies' and unlikelies that take the bloom off things. I still wait for a change of plans and still hope to see you both here this year. I am very pleased with Jan's first, and would not have forgiven him if he had failed to get it. I shall drop him a line. What a good time you must have had at the cottage and how I enjoyed reading of that night walk to Lowbury.[4] But these things are best in the best company!

We have lost the Colesberg election—or rather we did not succeed in capturing the seat from the Nats, who are naturally jubilant.[5]

[1] On 9 July Smuts met the executive of the South African party in Natal and made it clear that a Natal group within the party would not be allowed.

[2] Helena M. L. Forbes, government botanist at the Natal Herbarium, Durban.

[3] A village under the downs west of Moulsford and near the 'Paradise' country. *See* vol. III, p. 659, note 3.

[4] The Gilletts had a cottage, 'Crossways', at Aston Tirrold. Lowbury is an eminence on the downs.

[5] The result of the bye-election at Colesberg, Cape Province, on 6 July 1932 was as follows: Rev. C. W. M. du Toit (National party) 3090; J. J. de Villiers (South African party) 2,889.

It is a blow to us, but I don't feel it overmuch. I always have that inner faith that all things work together for good in the order of the universe. I have been looking through Miss Emmet's book on *Whitehead's Philosophy of Organism*.[1] It is a good piece of work, but Whitehead—in spite of great insight and power—remains difficult to translate into plain sense. I think I begin to understand him, but the more I understand the less inclined I feel to agree. But there is something very valuable in his thought—only difficult to say exactly what.

I fear Lausanne has come too late to save central Europe and too early for America. It is the time-table that is wrong, just as we felt in Berlin. When the United States has seen the light, Germany and the rest will have gone under in Fascism. And Ireland is unspeakably bad.[2] I have done my best to warn Thomas [J. H.]. If Ireland hives off, South Africa is sure to follow sooner or later. Patience and long suffering are divine qualities. Love ever,

Jan

318   To M. C. Gillett   Vol. 49, no. 260

Irene
[Transvaal]
15 August 1932

I am afraid my last letter was very desultory. But sometimes we strike a bad patch, and I find it most difficult to cope with my letters when my hand is stiff with cold. It seems to affect my mentality also. And you must have some trouble to decypher my script, for sometimes when I look over what I have written I find it difficult to make out all the words and have to be guided by the context! Your handwriting on the contrary retains the definiteness and clearness of outline of a Newnham undergraduate. My friends have repeatedly advised me to learn typing, so that I might be saved the trouble of scribbling and at the same time save my friends the trouble of decypherment. I only grudge the time this learning will take and think how many books I could read through in that time. For it is not the writing that is my main trouble but the finding of the time to do the necessary intellectual work in my busy practical life. I suppose we muddle through somehow, like the British Empire

[1] Dorothy M. Emmet, *Whitehead's Philosophy of Organism* (1932).

[2] In 1932 De Valera became prime minister of the Irish Free State. On 21 April he introduced a bill to abolish the oath of allegiance and exclude the treaty of 1922 with Great Britain from the constitution. On 1 July land annuities due to the British government were withheld.

which just now is doing more muddling than I have seen in recent years. We cannot make out what is really happening at Ottawa,[1] and in the end nothing worth speaking of may happen at all. I was foolish enough to look to Ottawa as an occasion on which we might do real good work by hammering out a decent currency policy. It will be impossible for Great Britain to keep drifting very long on the changing tide of exchange, and sooner or later we shall have to devaluate and return to a fixed currency; and all the Dominions are in the same boat. Ottawa could have done the Empire and the cause of world recovery a real good turn by tackling this task. But it has been shelved indefinitely, and instead a bargaining for sops and favours has unfortunately been resorted to. Fixing the £ at something like 12s. will have done more for the Empire than all this hopeless and dangerous haggling. We would have secured the higher prices we talk about, and would have preserved a uniform Empire system. That chance is now gone. I don't see what we can now expect from a world economic conference in the late autumn.[2] This conference will bar reparations and debts and will have no lead from the Empire on the grave currency question. I feel sure a general currency settlement for the Empire at Ottawa will have helped enormously to give a pointer to the coming conference.

I have seen reports in the press recently to the effect that Japan may leave the League of Nations because it is expected that on the advice of the Lytton commission the League will go against Japan's Manchurian policy.[3] Perhaps it will be as well, if thereby the League itself is saved for the world. It seems to me quite hopeless to go on as things have been going on in Manchuria in recent months. Japan is preparing for herself an Alsace-Lorraine[4] of the future, and the League must keep out of that entanglement. Unless it keeps its soul the machinery will become useless and a nuisance. Have you ever discussed the point with Gilbert Murray? This is a first-class issue.

From the point of view of the British Empire India is quite the most important and dangerous issue at present. I frankly cannot grasp the British policy. It seems to me a sheer muddle to put the Congress in gaol, to alienate the moderates, and yet to think of going

[1] An imperial economic conference met at Ottawa in Canada in July 1932 to discuss mutual tariff preferences to members of the British Commonwealth.

[2] The world monetary and economic conference did not meet until June 1933.

[3] The League of Nations commission of inquiry into Japanese action in Manchuria, presided over by Lord Lytton, left for China in February 1932. Its report, published on 2 October was, in general, a condemnation of Japan.

[4] Border territories between France and Germany the possession of which has been in dispute between those countries since 1681.

forward with the grant of a new constitution. Who will work this constitution and who will have any responsibility for its success? I can understand frank reaction or the strong hand. I can also appreciate a more or less liberal policy of trust such as that of Campbell-Bannerman. But what is this monstrosity, which now keeps in gaol the people who must necessarily work the new constitution? Is there anybody who follows what is happening, or is the present policy going to be scrapped a little later? Gandhi is and remains the best friend and should be dealt with as such, and strengthened against his extremists. I am convinced that he has real good will and with reasonable government backing will be able to get India to fall into line in a constitutional way. But with Gandhi in gaol and Sastri [S.] indignant, we might as well scrap this constitution which will deepen the confusion. Then there is Ireland. She is now being hopelessly ruined. After De Valera hopeless bankruptcy, and civil war perhaps. What is the sense of forcing things to such fatal issues? Surely Great Britain must be the strong friend and elder brother. I do believe there is a way out of this entanglement, which smacks too much of old Unionist[1] tactics. Patience and magnanimity is a great game, or rather a sure winner in the great game. How often we have learnt that lesson and how soon we forget it! It is hopeless to identify Ireland with a mad fellow like De Valera. Now we make all the innocent suffer for his idiosyncrasies. I really thought the Empire had turned its back finally on such things. We have moved into a new world; we must work through good will and consent. Dragooning through tariffs may be no less fatal than through Black and Tans.[2] But why do I disburden my mind like this, and to you who can help just as little? I can but put my thoughts to you, and they are dismal. I believe that none of these policies are necessary, and yet I don't see how in my position and at this distance I can publicly condemn them. And so I grouse and growl in the company of my friends. There is nothing else to do. We seem to have lost faith in the great saving principles and are gripped by the spirit of reaction which is abroad in high places. But I am convinced that only the good old Liberal ideals really put to the test can save the world in this crisis. My dear love to you all, dear children.

Jan

[1] *See supra*, p. 96, notes 1–2.
[2] When land annuities were withheld the British government imposed special duties on certain Irish imports whereupon the Irish Free State put equally high duties on certain British imports into Ireland.

319   To S. G. Millin   **Vol. 102, no. 22**

Irene
[Transvaal]
13 September 1932

Dear Mrs Millin, I have spent two days in reading through your *Rhodes* MS[1] from beginning to end, and I may tell you that I have done so with enormous pleasure. I congratulate you on a most notable piece of work. Only you could have written it. What a picture of the great man! I find Rhodes nowhere swamped in the details, but every chapter is dominated by him, and his great bizarre figure stands out ever more clearly as the book proceeds. Vivid, vivacious, enormously interesting I found it from beginning to end. Rhodes's star is in the ascendant, and your book will help very much this process. I am sure it will be a great success. I find it written in the right spirit—he is quoted objectively like a natural phenomenon, where praise or blame is equally difficult.

Let me now note a few points. I have read the book rapidly to get a general impression and hence not had time to pause for detailed consideration. But here are a few points.

1. Your remarks on p. 16–17 about South Africa *before 1870* will be very much resented. Besides, I don't agree with you. We have our background, our spiritual roots, and it is barefaced materialism to date us from diamonds and gold. I think those paragraphs should be deleted or toned down.

2. I find your history somewhat weak. You should read Hofmeyr's *historical* notes.[2] Thus you exaggerate the *slavery* motif of the Greak Trek. Thus p. 59–60 ought to be reviewed. Was Bulwer Lytton ever colonial secretary? p. 62.

3. I also agree with Hofmeyr that the Bond was separatist only in its *pre-Hofmeyr* (du Toit) phase,[3] and it would be a great mistake to create the impression that the great Afrikander Bond in its palmy days was against the British connection. Just the opposite. p. 74.

4. 103–4. A small point. The name was Groot *Adriaan* de la Rey.[4] The Boers always called him simply *Groot Adriaan*, and as such I knew him.

5. You are surely wrong in thinking the Jameson Raid not very significant in its consequences. It was *the* disaster. It inflamed the national psychology of the Boers, made racial trust impossible, and created the very mentality for the Boer War. Some sentences ought to be deleted here.

[1] Published in 1933.   [2] In J. H. Hofmeyr, *South Africa*, published in 1931.
[3] *See* vol. I, p. 32, note 2.   [4] *See* vol. I, p. 356, note 3.

6. I find no undue attention given to Matabeles. In fact the most brilliant chapters deal with the Matabeles, Lobengula,[1] and the Raid.

7. I wish you could sometimes give dates in footnotes. The book will remain the classic on Rhodes, but the historian will rightly blame you for jumping backwards and forwards without giving dates where necessary. This is not a mere biographical pamphlet but a serious historical work. However, I can but note this point.

I am very pleased with the work, which paints a great picture of a great man in a great way. Ever your sincerely,

J. C. Smuts

320 To M. C. Gillett Vol. 49, no. 271

Irene
[Transvaal]
27 September 1932

I am writing this in advance of the mail which only comes tomorrow, as I intend going to the Bushveld tomorrow morning with Andries. News has arrived of fine rains at Rooikop and as we have had a phenomenal drought in the Bushveld, the temptation is great to go and see what has happened...I shall have a more or less quiet week, when I shall be able to do some much needed reading. I find that when reading is so intermittent and for days or weeks I don't look at a book, the benefit is small indeed. You have continually to pick up lost threads and can never sufficiently concentrate on the argument as a whole. But unfortunately that is all I am nowadays able to do. I like to read a book through from end to end, then to glance back through it, and review the argument as a whole. But the opportunities to do so are very limited. As for writing, that is entirely out of the question. I can scarcely make notes for speeches.

I see that Knollys [E. G. W. T.] has left for good to take up residence in England. I wonder whether Barclay's will have another resident director. What about A. B. G.?[2]

Gandhi has made a great achievement. He is really one of the wariest calculators I have ever seen, and his threat of starvation has brought the Hindus to heel and sent his stock soaring up.[3] I hope the government will let him out of gaol and get his co-operation for

---

[1] *See* vol. I, p. 554, note I.   [2] Arthur B. Gillett.
[3] Gandhi undertook his fast in protest against separate electorates for untouchables. On the seventh day Hindu leaders proposed a compromise on the matter and Gandhi broke his fast.

other aspects of their constitutional scheme as well. What a waste to see such a power and influence for good in gaol at such a time! And without Gandhi's co-operation the new institutions will never even begin to function properly.

Germany, again, may have made a very astute move in abstaining from the disarmament conference until the question of status is settled.[1] I say this because I think, rather than see her rearm, the others will agree to drastic curtailment of their own armaments. We shall see. Great Britain does not come well out of this business, and [Sir John] Simon is on the way to become as egregious a failure as poor Austen [Chamberlain]. And now the papers report a secession of the Liberal ministers. They have swallowed so much that I am really surprised by this action.[2] But I suppose a public reaction against the government has already set in, and the Liberal ministers think it wise to rat now. There is nothing further to report from here. We are all beginning to look forward keenly to the end of November. Love to you and Arthur and 102.

Jan

321   To G. Heaton Nicholls   Vol. 49, no. 207

Irene
[Transvaal]
14 November 1932

Dear Nicholls, Your letter of 5 November[3] has only just reached me on my return from the Cape Province.

I was bound to dissociate myself publicly from the views which you had expressed in your Empangeni speech.[4] Those views as reported in the press were contrary to the principles of our party and damaging to its interests, and I had to make it clear in my first public utterance thereafter that you were voicing personal opinions from which the party completely dissociated itself.

Your contemptuous reference to racial co-operation which is

[1] On 16 September 1932 Germany gave notice of withdrawal from the disarmament conference because her claim to equality of armaments with the other powers was rejected. On 12 December the German claim had, however, to be recognized.

[2] Although the supporters of free trade in the National government had remained in the cabinet when a general tariff was imposed (*see supra*, p. 509, note 2), Sir Herbert Samuel, Sir Archibald Sinclair (Liberals) and Philip Snowden (Labour) resigned when the Ottawa agreements on imperial preference were signed.

[3] Smuts Collection, vol. 49, no. 158.

[4] On 29 October 1932 Nicholls had made a prepared speech at this village in his constituency in Natal. On 4 November in a speech at Turffontein, near Johannesburg, Smuts repudiated it.

our declared policy, your reference to the English attitude to the language clause in the South Africa Act,[1] as well as other statements not only deeply offended loyal members of our party all over the country, but gave our opponents much needed ammunition of which they have since made ample use. Your suggestion that Natal and the Free State should become unilingual provinces was not only in conflict with our principles but was calculated, unless promptly repudiated, to drive every Afrikaans-speaking member in Natal out of the party. How could we be party to such a betrayal of our loyal members (English-speaking in the Free State, Afrikaans-speaking in Natal) without covering ourselves with dishonour? And you can understand with what deep resentment such views were heard, coming as they did from a Sap member of parliament sitting on the front bench of the party.

Nothing said or done at the recent Pietermaritzburg conference justified such a declaration on your part, and if the Natal members of our party were committed to your views by the terms or the implications of the resolutions there taken, they would never have agreed to it and would immediately have repudiated it. Nor did the resolution mark a completely new situation as you appear to think. In substance it but repeated the principles already affirmed in the Natal provincial council resolution of last May, to which our Natal M.P.s also agreed. The [F. C.] Hollander memorandum was accepted, not *in toto* or in detail, but as a basis, and as such it will usefully serve in the further discussion and working out of this important subject.[2]

In view of your critical reference to myself I may say that my remarks on your speech were only made after I had convinced myself that I was dealing not with mere random extempore statements, but with a carefully prepared declaration. And such your speech has since been admitted to be. It is a pity, in view of this admission, that neither in your letter under reply nor in any statement to the public you have seen fit to put yourself right with our party whom your statements have so deeply offended. Yours sincerely,

s. J. C. Smuts

[1] Nicholls had said that it was impossible to build up a 'South African' national sense and that the English at Union had really aimed at anglicization (*see* G. Heaton Nicholls, *South Africa in my Time*, pp. 252–4).

[2] For an account of the decisions on these matters taken at the South African party conference at Pietermaritzburg on 14 October 1932 *see* Nicholls, *ibid*. pp. 247–50.

322   To G. B. van Zyl   Vol. 49, no. 208

Irene
[Transvaal]
15 November 1932

My dear van Zyl, I rejoice to hear that you will be in force at the congress.[1] We shall have to deal with the provincial question. The resolution should embrace

(1) retention of all existing provincial rights and privileges;
(2) extension within the framework of the South Africa Act;
(3) future curtailments to be subject to petition from the provincial councils.

I had a talk with Stuart Helps and Mackenzie [T. W.], and they are much concerned over (3)—arbitrary withdrawal of power by the Dr Malans[2] of the future. With wisdom and tact I think we shall carry Natal with us. But Nicholls and Marwick [S.] are queer fellows, and I don't know what they will do. I have had some sharp correspondence with Nicholls.

Your telegram is quite in order and strengthened my hands. The midlands is O.K.

Very kind remembrances to you and Mrs van Zyl.[3] Ever yours sincerely,

J. C. Smuts

323   From M. R. Drennan   Vol. 49, no. 30

University of Cape Town
2 December 1932

Dear General Smuts, Many thanks for sending me a copy of your excellent paper on *Climate and Man in Africa*. It is a real landmark in the science of anthropology and I feel certain that it is going to be much sought after as a classic on the subject.

Valuable as it is to us who have become gradually familiar with the new African terms, it must be priceless to students in other countries for whom you have done an immense service in explaining how the various climatic phases and cultures might be correlated in the light of existing knowledge.

[1] A congress of the South African party was to meet at Bloemfontein in the first week of December 1932.
[2] Dr D. F. Malan, then minister of the interior.
[3] Marie Elizabeth van Zyl, daughter of Sir John George Fraser of Bloemfontein.

I hope therefore that you will see your way to send copies to institutions and individuals overseas who, I feel sure, would appreciate this very much. With best wishes, Yours sincerely,

M. R. Drennan

324   To J. Martin   Vol. 50, no. 137

Irene
[Transvaal]
6 January 1933

Dear Martin, Many thanks for your note[1] which I very much appreciate. The idea you suggest has already formed the basis of my plan for the opening of parliament, if nothing happens before then to necessitate a change.

You will have seen from this morning's [Rand Daily] Mail how far I have actually gone with my own party in dealing with the subject of a coalition.[2] In anything I do I have, of course, to make certain that I carry the party with me, and it will be difficult to get them to move too fast or too far. It may be that I may have to ask you to come down to Cape Town at some stage of the session for consultation. The situation is now fluid, and we may just have a chance of achieving some lasting good. Kind regards, Ever yours sincerely,

J. C. Smuts

325   To S. M. Smuts   Vol. 50, no. 138

Tsalta
11 Januarie 1933

Liefste Mamma, Na 'n heerlik warm rit deur die Karoo had ons gister 'n verbasende ontvangs in Kaapstad. Jy sal seker alles in die koerante gelees het maar kan geen idee vorm van die gedrang en gedoente. Baie grooter as die ontvangs aan Roos gegee. By Tsalta was alles in orde, waarvoor ons die liewe Jouberts te dank het...

[1] This letter from John Martin is not in the Smuts Collection.

[2] The question of coalition became acute when Tielman Roos resigned from the appellate bench and re-entered politics on a pledge to force the Pact government to leave the gold standard (21 December 1932). His support in the country was so great that the government was obliged to announce the abandonment of the gold standard on 28 December. Roos had enough followers in both the National and South African parties to enable him to negotiate with Smuts for joint action to overthrow the Pact and form a coalition government.

Dit lyk my of die Roos onderhandelinge nie te goed loop en of dit nog alles in mislukking sal eindig. Roos insisteer op homself of 'n ander Nat as P.M. en dit sal ons party nie staan nie. Nou is daar 'n sterk gerug hier dat die Regering besluit het op 'n sessie van 'n paar weke, en dan dissolusie en een vroege eleksie. Dit lyk waarlik of daar iets in die gerug is. Dus moet jy maar spoedig afkom, anders sal jy glad geen sessie hê nie! Na al die moeite wat ek geneem het om my vir 'n sessie in te rig!

Ek had 'n lang onderhoud met ons Kaapse lede gister en vandag sal daar weer baie interviews met party en publiek wees. Ek sal taamlik besig wees tot die naweek. Ek probeer Jan Dommisse in die hande te kry om vir Jannie met sy mathesis te help. Nou 'n soentje;

Pappa

TRANSLATION

Tsalta
[Cape Town]
11 January 1933

Dearest Mamma, After a lovely warm trip through the Karoo we had an astonishing reception yesterday in Cape Town. You will no doubt have read all about it in the papers, but you can have no idea of the crowds and the doings. Much bigger than the reception given to Roos. At 'Tsalta' everything was in order, for which we have to thank the dear Jouberts...

It looks to me as if the Roos negotiations are not going too well and as if it will all end in failure. Roos insists on himself or another Nationalist as prime minister and that our party will not tolerate. Now there is a strong rumour here that the government has decided on a session of a few weeks and then dissolution and an early election. It really looks as if there is something in the rumour. So you had better come down soon, or you will have no session at all! After all the trouble I took to arrange my affairs for a session!

I had a long interview yesterday with our Cape members and today there will again be many interviews with party and public. I shall be fairly busy until the week-end. I am trying to get hold of Jan Dommisse to help Jannie with his mathematics. Now a kiss;

Pappa

[1] Captain F. A. Joubert and his wife Enid, born Goldman.

326   From J. du Plessis

Theologies Seminarium
Stellenbosch
10 Februarie 1933

Hooggeachte Generaal Smuts, Die berig dat daar 'n waarskynlikheid bestaan dat die Unie binne weinige dae onder bestier van 'n Koaliesie Regering sal staan het ook my verbly, nie slegs omdat ek, netsoos die meeste denkende en onpartydige mense moeg is van die twiste van die party-politiek, maar ook en veral omdat ek die hoop koester dat ons die groot Naturelle Vraagstuk nou eenmaal uit 'n ruim nasionaal standpunt sal besien en behandel.

Daarom waag ek dit om reeds nou aan u te skryf, om u te bid om nie die S.A. Party te bind insake die oorweging en voorgestelde oplossing van ons Naturelle Probleem nie. Dit word gesê dat daar 'a large amount of agreement' bereik is in die Selekt Komité, dog aangesien die bevindings van daardie Komité nog nie gepubliseer is nie, kan die groot publiek geen oordeel vel oor die punte van 'agreement' nie. Ek verkeer al lank onder die oortuiging dat daar geen bevredigende oplossing van ons Naturelle probleme kan verwag word nie, alvorens die hele kwessie bo die peil van die party-politiek verhewe is.

Nou kom daar in die voorsienigheid van God sulk 'n geleentheid opdaag. 'There is a tide in the affairs of men', etc. Ek hoop en vertrou van harte dat u as vertroude leier van die S.A. Party nie net terwille van die ooreenkoms enige beleid in naturellesake sal aanvaar nie, wat gebore is uit die gees van agterdog en vrees. Daardie gees kom maar al te dikwels tot openbaring, veral by sommige Transvalers. Ek is daar diep van oortuig dat dit 'n verkeerde en verleidelike gees is, wat die ware vooruitgang van ons land in die weg staan, en wat uitgewerp moet word voordat ons die ses miljoen Naturelle binne die Unie met simpatie en regvêrdigheid kan bejeën.

Dit is nou nie die tyd vir my om in besonderhede te tree nie. Ek wil alleen herhaal—(a) dat ons nou die kans het om die hele Naturellekwessie met 'n 'clean sheet' te behandel, dat hierdie kans en geleentheid van verbygaande aard is, en seker nie in u en my leeftyd sal terugkeer nie—ons is al albei sestigers!—en miskien nooit weer in die geskiedenis van ons Volk sig sal aanbied nie. En (b) dat daar nou 'n etiese toets sal toegepas word op ons jong Suidafrikaanse nasie, waaruit sal blyk of ons die agterlike rasse in ons midde nou waarlik in 'n gees van edelmoedigheid en selfopoffering gaan behandel. Die Naturelle Vraagstuk is op die keper beskou nie 'n ekonomiese of politieke kwessie nie, maar 'n etiese, en die manier waarop ons dit oplos sal openbaar of ons in wese, en nie slegs in naam nie, 'n Kristelike volk is. U is meermale 'n idealis genoem. Dit is 'n erebenaming, want die idealiste is die enige mense wat verbeelding het, en verbeelding en voorsig regeer tog maar die wereld.

Vergeef my dat ek in hierdie vir u drukke tyd nog my beskouings aan u opdring. Ek begroet die huidige krisis met blydskap en dankbaarheid, dog ook met bewing; en daarom spreek ek. *Dixi et salvavi animam meam.*

U steeds die leiding van die Voorsienigheid toebiddende, Verblyf ek, hoogagtend, U toegeneë vriend,

J. du Plessis

P.S. G'n antwoord is nodig nie. Miskien sou u hierdie brief aan Hennie Hofmeyr wil toon.

TRANSLATION

Theological Seminary
Stellenbosch
10 February 1933

Dear General Smuts, The report that it is probable that the Union will within a few days come under the guidance of a coalition government[1] has gladdened me also, not only because I, like most thinking and impartial people, am tired of party-political quarrels, but also, and especially, because I cherish the hope that we shall now envisage and deal with the Native question from a broad national standpoint.

That is why I dare write to you now—to implore you not to bind the South African party in regard to the consideration and the proposed solution of our Native problem. It is said that 'a large amount of agreement' has been reached in the select committee; but, as the findings of that committee have not yet been published, the great public cannot judge as to the points of 'agreement'. I have long been convinced that no satisfactory solution of our Native problem can be expected before the whole question is raised above the level of party politics.

Now, by God's Providence, such an opportunity has appeared. 'There is a tide in the affairs of men', etc.[2] I hope and fervently

---

[1] The negotiations between Smuts and Roos had by this time failed and been superseded by arrangements for a coalition between Smuts and Hertzog. The two leaders met for their first talk on 16 February.

[2] There is a tide in the affairs of men,
Which, taken at the flood, leads on to fortune.
Shakespeare, *Julius Caesar*, IV. iii. 217.

trust that you, as the trusted leader of the South African party, will not accept, merely for the sake of the agreement, any policy in Native affairs which is born of a spirit of suspicion and fear. That spirit is revealed all too often, especially in some Transvaalers. I am deeply convinced that it is a wrong and deceptive spirit which obstructs the true progress of our country and which must be cast out before we can approach the six million Natives in the Union with sympathy and fairness.

This is not the time for me to go into details. I only wish to repeat (a) that we now have a chance to deal with the whole Native question with a clean sheet; that this chance, this opportunity, is of a transitory nature and will certainly not return in your and my lifetime—we are both in the sixties—and will perhaps never again offer itself in the history of our people; and (b) that there will now be applied to our young South African nation an ethical test, from which it will appear whether we are really going to deal with the backward races in our midst in a spirit of magnanimity and self-sacrifice. In the last resort the Native question is not an economic or political, but an ethical question, and the way in which we solve it will show whether we are in reality, and not only in name, a Christian people. You have, at times, been called an idealist. That is a name of honour, for the idealists are the only people who have imagination and, after all, imagination and foresight rule the world.

Forgive me for intruding my views upon you in this, for you, busy time. I greet the present crisis with joy and thankfulness, but also with trembling; and that is why I speak. *Dixi et salvavi animam meam.*[1]

Ever praying that Providence may guide you, I remain, Your sincere friend,

J. du Plessis

P.S. No answer is necessary. Perhaps you would like to show this letter to Hennie Hofmeyr.[2]

---

[1] I have spoken and saved my soul.   [2] J. H. Hofmeyr.

327   To M. E. van Zyl   Vol. 50, no. 141

House of Assembly
Cape Town
24 February 1933

Dear Mrs van Zyl, Your gift of fruits comes to me as a gift of so
much more from the heart and so welcome and precious to me.

If we have sacrificed much, it is all for South Africa. Let us pray
that the sting of poison will at last be drawn from our politics, and
the hymn of hate cease to be our national anthem.[1] Yours
affectionately, Ever,

J. C. Smuts

328   To J. Martin   Vol. 50, no. 142

House of Assembly
Cape Town
2 March 1933

My dear Martin, Your letter has given me deep pleasure. The small
sacrifice I have made[2] is as nothing compared to the prospect of
agreement which is now opened up before the people of South
Africa. Of course we shall have our difficulties. So many seats we
could have won. So many candidates now to be halted. And in the
Nat. party pinpricks will no doubt be continued from time to time.
But I trust and pray that our people will now rise to the occasion.
With kind regards, Yours ever,

J. C. Smuts

329   From Lord Clarendon   Vol. 50, no. 20

Private and personal

Westbrook
Rondebosch
[Cape Town]
3 March 1933

My dear General, I feel that I must write you a line on the part
you have played in the recent political events. When you and
General Hertzog came to see me a few days ago I think I made it
clear how delighted I was that coalition between you and him was

[1] Smuts and Hertzog reached agreement on a coalition government on 21 February
1932 (*see* O. Pirow, *James Barry Munnik Hertzog*, pp. 156–7).
[2] Smuts had agreed to serve under Hertzog as minister of justice and deputy prime
minister.

a *fait accompli*. But what I particularly want to say to you now is how much I feel South Africa owes you for the great part you have played in, what I cannot help considering is, one of the greatest and most important events in her history. In spite of the general expectation of the success of yourself and your party at the next election, you put aside all personal and party advantages in favour of a step which, in your vew, was in the best interests of the Union. This self-effacing action on your part has, I am confident, earned you the affectionate esteem and unbounded admiration of one and all, not only here in South Africa but outside as well, and I hope you will allow me to say that this very grand thing you have done is a deed which will gloriously enrich the pages of South African political history. Yours very sincerely,

Clarendon

330   Speech (1933)   Box I, no. 79A

This speech on coalition which Smuts made in the City Hall, Cape Town, on 7 March 1933 is taken from a verbatim report in the *Cape Times* of 8 March.

Mr Chairman,[1] ladies and gentlemen: I am very gratified at this very fine meeting tonight. It is a meeting, if I may say so, that is worthy of the occasion. We meet tonight on one of the most out-standing occasions in the history of our country, and we are seeing an occasion such as we have never seen before.

It has all happened very suddenly, and has been very spectacular. How sudden the change that has come over this country is you will realize when you remember that only a couple of months ago our prime minister declared that the coming general election would be the bitterest ever fought in our history.

Well, it does not look like that tonight; the storm has passed. We find South Africa in an entirely different mood, and we do not look forward to a bitter general election. For the first time in our history as a Union the two great political parties have combined to form a national government for this country.

Something which wise men have been looking forward to for many years, and one which many people thought would never take place, has happened suddenly and unexpectedly, and we are face to face with a great moment in our life as a nation.

South Africa is once more true to its reputation of being a land

---

[1] Major G. B. van Zyl.

of surprises. The unpredictable always happens here, and it has once more happened.

I must say that some months ago I was looking forward to the coming struggle in this country with dread and foreboding; I thought it might prove a very serious setback. Now it is all past, and we have come to what, I believe, is a grand political settlement, whose after-effects may be far greater than what we foresee today.

The question is: Is it a good thing that has happened? I think the answer of South Africa to that is overwhelmingly 'Yes'.

Major van Zyl has rightly pointed out that we are only pursuing a course on which we embarked thirteen years ago. Then the old South African party, which was very largely Afrikaans, combined with their English friends to steer a new course in the politics of South Africa, and today we are simply proceeding one step further on the great road which we then entered upon.

If we would wish to understand the truth and significance of what has happened, we have to bear one important fact in mind, and it is this: that this movement for a national government is not a 'plant' by any statesman or politician; it is not a political manoeuvre on the part of two party leaders.

This movement has been born of the people, and unless we understand that fully we shall not understand the events of the last two months. There has been an overwhelming desire on the part of the people of South Africa to draw together, to call a halt, to make a truce and to make a new start in the politics of the country.

It has been the most popular movement in politics that I have ever seen in my lifetime; in fact it has been like a whirlwind, and it has shaken the old parties to their foundations; it has shaken the old system, and now, at the behest of public opinion, as the result of this great popular movement, we are going to try this great experiment of governing South Africa together.

This movement for union, for co-operation, has been the result of our sufferings under the gold standard. There is no doubt that out of that great misfortune in our political history has been born this great good for South Africa.

What did we see during the gold standard régime in South Africa? We saw the government embarked on a course which was exceedingly unpopular, which inflicted great sufferings on the people.

We, as an opposition, had naturally to attack the government on their policy to the best of our ability; but the mere fact that we had to take that line only made them harden their hearts and hold faster to the gold standard.

The people saw that in the game of politics as played in this country there was no material advantage to them, and, although we were doing our duty faithfully and loyally as an opposition, the result was that we only hardened the hearts of our rulers and did not succeed in getting them off the gold standard.

I think that brought home more closely to the people of this country the danger of these political divisions, the danger of excessive party government and party spirit than anything else could have done.

The idea, as I say, was the desire for a national government. I needed no convincing: I have stood on that platform, of unity, for many a year.

I have not been taken by surprise. I have made overtures year after year—in guarded terms, naturally, as was my duty as a party leader—I made overtures from time to time to our opponents to work with us.

It was only after these momentous events—it was only after General Hertzog had realized that here was a movement which was to carry parties and politicians off their feet—that he realized the truth and that he, too, became a convert to this movement.

Today we all believe in it, with the exception of Dr Malan,[1] and perhaps he may be converted yet—who knows?

Mr Tielman Roos, with his sure instinct and fine sense for public opinion, saw at once what the tendency of public opinion was. Mr Roos appeared in the arena and his appearance on the political stage had a great effect. Behind him ranged large numbers of people. It was not the Roos movement, as many people thought; he was simply giving expression to a vague and widely spread public opinion which existed all over the country.

The movement was there. It only needed some centre round which to crystallize, and Mr Roos gave the opportunity, he rendered the service. But as a matter of fact the movement went much deeper and much wider. Large numbers of people, faithful and loyal South African party men and women, supported him in that cause, and up to a certain point the effect of that movement was very great and very good.

But tonight—now that that episode is over, and now that we can look back on events—we can see that the Roos idea would have been a mistake. We would not have achieved anything essential by that.

[1] Dr D. F. Malan and twenty-nine National party members of parliament issued a manifesto in which they set out their objections to coalition but accepted it under protest for the sake of party unity on condition that it should be a temporary measure and that it should not proceed to fusion (see D. F. Malan, *Afrikaner Volkseenheid*, p. 156).

Even if the Roos idea as to coalition had gone through, we would not have had that peace and cessation from political strife which we were longing for. We would have had a solid Nationalist party fighting to a bitter end against that idea, and the fact of Mr Roos's leadership would have made the conflict deeper.

The Nationalists would have looked upon him as a traitor, and the result would have been a deepening of suspicion, and the real longing of the people for peace would not have been satisfied.

However good the motive and the instinct behind this movement, I am sure it would not have been the right thing, and what has happened now is the right thing.

If there was to be peace, it had to be concluded between the two great political parties. The vast bulk of politically-minded people are ranged in these two parties. The South African party and Nationalist party include practically every man and woman who thinks politics in this country, and, if we are to have unity and co-operation then it was impossible to exclude either of these parties. A peace had to be made between them and that is what has happened.

No, it has not been the work of any leader in particular. This work, result and achievement which we see today has been practically forced on leaders by the march of events—by public opinion. And it is very often so in public life. Leaders, politicians, are very often puppets, and it is public opinion that pulls the strings and this is one of the occasions where this has happened.

There has been an overwhelming feeling for union, and it is in obedience to that feeling that men who have fought the movement year after year for a lifetime have at last given this movement their blessing, and have helped to bring out this result—a national government in South Africa. That is the true explanation of what has happened.

I have read General Hertzog's speech at Smithfield, in which he gave his explanation as to why this thing has come about, why, at long last, the Nationalist party has been willing to give the hand of friendship to their old opponents.

General Hertzog has given his explanation at Smithfield, and Dr Malan has given his at Worcester. You have read the speeches, and no doubt you have been enlightened by what they said; but I always think that when parties start making explanations and giving reasons, that they are very often wide of the mark, perhaps unconsciously.

There is no doubt, however, whatever explanation was given by these gentlemen, that the real reason that moved the people and the leaders was this overwhelming force of public opinion.

General Hertzog, for instance, said at Smithfield that, looking at events from his watch-tower, he was afraid that the South African party might fall into the wrong through 'these extremists in Natal, the devolutionists', people who had not a South African orientation; and thus he feared there was a danger that the moderate South African party man might be driven to rely more and more upon these people, that General Smuts might have to rely more upon Natal, and that great damage might be done to the body politic.

Let me say this: I have worked for many years with my Natal friends, and—I give you my sincere and honest opinion—it is that there is no danger in them to South Africa.

I think there is no more conclusive proof of the correctness of what I say than this, that the people of Natal—not only those who belong to the South African party, but those who do not belong to our party—have all accepted, and loyally accepted, so far as I understand, the arrangement in regard to the provinces which has been come to by General Hertzog and myself.

That arrangement is not a dangerous one; it does not mean any disaster to South Africa. They have accepted the arrangement as satisfactory from their point of view. This, I think, is proof positive that, in striving for the extension and improvement of the provincial system, even if they talk about federation and secession, they never mean anything harmful to South Africa.

There was, perhaps, more in the bark than in the bite. There was, perhaps, louder talk than was meant. Speaking for my Natal friends, both inside and outside the South African party, and knowing them after long years and close political association, let me say that you will find them a source of strength in this greater re-union which we are bringing about. There is no reason to point a finger at them, or to blame them. They will be good and loyal; they are good South Africans and they will be another source of strength to this unity in our politics.

Various reasons have been given for the steps which have been taken to bring about coalition. The fact is that there has been this urge of the people; the unconscious instinct of the people of South Africa has moulded this movement, and the politicians have fallen into line. They may even invent reasons, if they like, but the true reason is that the people have been wiser than their leaders; they have wanted the right thing, and in the end they have got it.

Major van Zyl has said that this movement means sacrifices. It means sacrifices for the South African party. I have no doubt that we have had more to sacrifice in the arrangement than the other side. Events may prove me to be wrong, but to my mind we have been called upon to surrender a great deal.

I do not talk of leadership, because you know my attitude all these years has been that personality does not count with me at all. I have stood for a lifetime for certain large principles, which I want to see carried out and triumph in this country, and to me it does not matter whether it is A or B, myself or another, who leads in this movement. That is not the sacrifice I am talking about.

But there is another kind of sacrifice. Our party has been for years in the desert, and there has been very hard fighting against very great odds, and I cannot be sufficiently grateful to the members of the South African party of both races for the fight they have put up and for the sacrifices they have made in order to work up our cause and to bring our party to the state in which it is today.

Our prospects have improved very much. The position today is this: Our prospects are such that if a general election were fought under present circumstances, the South African party has every chance of capturing a large number of seats. Our party has been improved in position owing to the sacrifices of its members, and of the hard work of the men and women in the party. The party has improved its position until it stands at a place where a great vista opens out before it.

That is the sacrifice we have made. We have to call a halt to our ambitions, and we have said, 'We are going to make peace.' It is hard for human nature to call a halt, just when you are in sight of victory and the hour has struck. That is the sacrifice we are making. But, ladies and gentlemen, we are making the sacrifice for South Africa. We are not going to gain by it, from the commander-in-chief to the man in the ranks, but the country is going to gain. We are going to have peace; we are going to call a halt to those differences which were not leading to racial peace and prosperity in this country. That is what we are going to do.

The South African party, by the action it is taking today, is probably making a greater contribution to the future peace and welfare of South Africa than it would have done by the most over-whelming victory that it could have won at the polls.

To my mind the greatest service that we can render to South Africa today is not to win a party victory, however great the prospects of that may be, but to put South Africa on the right track once more.

That we are doing. We are using our strength, we are using our prospects, we are using these great chances that are in front of us, not for ourselves, not to get into power, but to put things right in South Africa.

No, we are making sacrifices; and it was almost with a sore heart that I have had to say to candidates who have worked hard and are now in sight of their goal—it has been hard to say to them: 'Stop! Leave the seat to your opponents whom you have fought so successfully for the last year or two.'

But as I say, it is for the country, and I think it is the greatest victory of all that we are winning when we do it for our country and not for ourselves.

But we are not the only people to make sacrifices. Our opponents are making a sacrifice. They are running very grave risks, as you know.

I think General Hertzog has shown real statesmanship and courage in the steps that he has taken. In a way he is running a greater risk; he is courting greater dangers than we do.

After all, I have a united party behind me. On every side in this great business, when I have consulted my friends in parliament, my colleagues, my caucus, my head committee, I have had unanimous approval for the step taken. The South African Party comes very well out of this business.

You know the taunt that has been flung at us year after year, that this is not a party, it is a collection of fragments, brought together for political purposes. But today you see how at the great moments in the life of this country, when great decisions have to be made when at the turning of the road we have to take new courses, this party, man, woman and child, stands like one—no division.

I am very proud that that is the situation—that in spite of the different shades of opinion which we represent—and we have great latitude of opinion in our party on the great issues which concern the future of this country—we all look in the same direction, and we all, at critical moments move in the same direction.

General Hertzog has not been equally fortunate and that is why I applaud the courage and statesmanship of his action and the sacrifice that he is making.

You have read the papers. You know the rumblings that are going on. You have seen what attitude Dr Malan and his friends are taking.

I do not know whether they are a powerful faction or not, but I know they are serious men, and they are men who in the end may bring about very serious mischief in the Nationalist party.

General Hertzog has faced up to all that, and he is backed by a large section of his party. When we talk about sacrifices I want you to bear in mind that he also has faced a great situation; he is facing great risks and is doing so for the sake of South Africa, just as we are doing.

I notice, both in the Nationalist press—or rather let me say in Dr Malan's press, because I do not think it represents Nationalist opinion—and also in the speeches of Dr Malan, the insinuation that the South African party has been aiming at the disruption of the Nationalist party.

The insinuation was that, in this move that we have made for racial peace and co-operation, our undisclosed object has been to drive a wedge between the two sections of the Nationalist party and so divide them in order that we may rule. Nothing has ever been further from my mind.

I never even dreamt there would be division in the ranks of the Nationalist party when I made these overtures to General Hertzog. If there is one person who is going to divide the Nationalist party it will not be myself, but it will be Dr Malan.

No, this has been a clean business. I have had no party objects, either for myself or as regards my opponents. If I had thought of party I would have stood out of this business, and I would have fought the next general election as hard as I could.

But I did not think of party. I thought of this country, this young country, these people longing for peace and quiet, these people suffering and bent on seeing better days in this country. I was thinking of them and not of party.

It is entirely due to the great forces moving in this country that we have at last reached the goal which our statesmen have often looked to from a distance and never until now achieved. After twenty-one years of intense political warfare between the great parties in this country we have at last, I say, reached the prospect of peace.

What a twenty-one years those have been from 1912—those awful days in Johannesburg, the Great War, the rebellion, the further events that followed it, and all that time the people of this country hopelessly divided into two camps and at each other's throats!

We had these twenty-one years of embittered strife, and not only amongst the Dutch. You had these divisions, all this bitterness which split families and communities, which made social life impossible. There was another very sinister side. More and more this intensity of political struggle took on a racial tinge.

More and more South Africa became divided again into two camps. It was once more the true patriot and the *uitlander*;[1] and that division has been intensified for the last twenty-one years until at last many serious people began to think that it might lead to more serious consequences in the future again.

[1] Foreigner (Afrikaans).

Well, that phase is over. The happy fact has at last come to South Africa, and after the storms we have again the prospect of peace. I cannot call it more than a prospect. We stand at the beginning of things. It is only an experiment which we are going to try, and it is for the people, even more than for the leaders, to make that experiment a success.

My prayer is that the people of this country, who have been primarily responsible for this movement, from whom this movement was born, that they will continue to look upon this work as their own, and that they will not allow party feeling once more to come between the people. The beginning has been your work, and you must see that the experiment becomes a success.

But, whatever happens to this movement for a national government, certain results will in my opinion remain permanent for ever. The first result is this: that here you have the political leaders of the two great parties making peace and shaking hands.

Now you know there has been the popular suggestion that General Hertzog and myself were the real offence in this country; that we were the cause of all this bitterness which was living in this country. Many honest people thought that politics was merely a duel between the two Generals, and they said it would be a good thing for this country to clear both of them out. These two old men, bringing their hates from the past, not giving the people a chance, fighting each other and indulging their private hatreds at the cost of the country—that is the popular picture of us two. And there was an insistent call for us to clear off.

Well, it would have been a poor exit, a pitiable exit, if leaders who had been responsible for this country for many years, should have to leave the stage in that way, like old, wounded bears slinking to their dens, licking their wounds.

There was a better way, and I am very glad—and it is something that nothing can undo in future—that the better thing has happened. And before we leave this stage—and we shall soon have to leave it in the ordinary course of events as *anno Domini* is on our tracks—we two have helped to bring peace to this country.

I think that is a real service. We have set the example, and let the rest of you who have criticized us so severely follow that example. Let us make peace all round. Let peace percolate from the top to the bottom, and let us see right through the country the spirit of the leaders permeating the people of this country.

I am sure that that is what the people want, and what South Africa calls for. I think this is the best way that the matter could have been brought about. The men who still had the influence and commanded the confidence and loyalty of South Africa had to put it to the test, and had themselves to start the movement that was in the hearts of the people. And it has happened.

For myself I only claim this small credit—that for many long years, even in the darkest years when we were fighting hardest and most bitterly, I have foreseen that something like this might happen in the end, and that is why you have never heard a bitter taunt or a bitter word flung at my opponent.

I know that large numbers of good South African party men and women have often asked the question: 'Why does not the General hit out? Why does he lie down under the attacks made upon him?' I was looking ahead. I knew my time to strike would come, and this is my time.

I think that this game has paid in the end, and it has paid, not me, but South Africa. We have been able to make a peace, without any bitterness or *arrière pensée*, which I think will be an enduring peace in the politics of this country.

That I call one of the permanent results of this movement which no one can ever undo. But there is another, greater, permanent result, that in future, after this, no one South African can call another unpatriotic, or names, again.

You will remember how the taunt has been flung at me for years that I had joined hands with the old Unionists. You will not hear that again. That is finished. We shall all be now old South Africans, old Unionists or whatever our past or our origin or language—we shall all be supporting one National government, and it will be impossible hereafter to call a part of our people unpatriotic, *uitlander* or whatever opprobrious terms have been used in the past.

Now, that, I think, is a great result we are going to achieve. There are no longer to be two camps; no longer shall we separate people into two camps, patriotic and unpatriotic people. Whatever our opinions may have been in the past, we shall all now be in the same camp, and one chapter is closed for ever.

That is a great thing to achieve, and, mind you, after this event we shall never be able to return again to those charges, to those taunts and to those insults which from time to time have been flung by one section against the other.

I do not blame anyone in particular for this, but it is a good thing when we have reached a stage when this chapter is closed, and when in future we are going to work together and look upon one another as friends and comrades. These two things stand there, and I am satisfied with them.

I think something more may happen. I think, ladies and

gentlemen, when you do a right thing you can never foretell the consequences, because the right thing is a fruitful thing and contributes to further right.

I think we will find that we are only at the beginning of something which can be very far-reaching in the politics of South Africa. I do not think we can ever return again to the old party lines and spirit which we have seen for the last twenty-one years.

It is true we are keeping our parties, and you will have seen the statement issued by the prime minister and myself that we are safeguarding the identity and the maintenance of the parties in the co-operation that is going to take place. It is right to do that, because this thing may be for a short time or a long time, but no one can foresee the future.

We in the South African party ought to see that we keep up our identity, that we are free to defend the principles for which we stood and that we do not through slackness give up the position which we have tried to achieve in this country. Whilst I say that, I also feel that it will be impossible after this co-operation in one government in South Africa to return again to the old ruts, to the old, bitter feeling, and to the old spirit of the old fight.

Who knows whether we have not builded better than we knew;[1] whether in coming together at this time we have not laid the foundation for something bigger? We have seen great changes in South Africa, and we have read of great changes in the history of the world. It is quite possible that this peace we have concluded in the politics and public life of South Africa may be the beginning of a very great development which will mean far more for peace and unity and ultimately for prosperity than we can foresee today.

One thing that struck me very much during my talks with General Hertzog was this: there was no division, there was no difference of opinion between us, on fundamentals. That to me was one of the most significant things in this whole tremendous business—no differences of opinion on the vital questions.

You will remember that after General Hertzog had published his seven points[2]—he, like President Wilson, believes in points, you know, but whereas President Wilson had fourteen points, General Hertzog, fortunately, had only seven—after those seven points were published, our local press, both the *Cape Times* and the *Cape Argus*, referred to them as platitudes. They said, 'These

---

[1] He builded better than he knew;—
The conscious stone to beauty grew.
Ralph Waldo Emerson, *The Problem.*

[2] For these *see* O. Pirow, *James Barry Munnik Hertzog*, p. 157.

things we can all subscribe to. Why differ about these things?' To me it was very salutary to hear that in our press.

When I talked things over with General Hertzog, I found that was so. We were not divided. We might differ in our phrasing, in our emphasis, but on the real business we were not divided.

Take the question of our status. We all agreed on our dual status, this country an independent sovereign country among the nations of the world, and also a loyal co-operating member of the British Commonwealth of nations. No difference of opinion about that. There were years when we differed bitterly—you remember the days of republicanism and secession—but we agreed about the status of this country.

Take the flag! What a great struggle have we had in this country over the flag. We accept today the position; we recognize our two official flags; we recognize the national flag floating over this country; we recognize the Union Jack, which symbolizes our affiliation to and membership of the greatest empire on earth.

Our dual language—no difference of opinion about that. I know it is spoken of, but in principle—take it from me—from one end of South Africa to the other the people of this country are agreed to accept the two official languages of this country.

And we do it because it is the law, it is the constitution; and we do it also because we know this will never be a happy country, never a united people, until we have learned to respect each other's language, and we show a respect for our neighbour by learning his language.

I believe even my friends the devolutionists of Natal are agreed now to abide by the essential basis of unity laid down in the South Africa Act. Nobody outside a lunatic asylum questions that.

So you may go through the whole list of the seven points. I think it is a great thing for us in South Africa to have reached the point that we are agreed on essentials. I remember in my lifetime how we disagreed on every essential. We fought over it. We fought politically, and we fought with rifles and guns over essentials. Now we accept them all. The basis for national unity and for national co-operation is well and truly laid in this country.

And where you have the people of this country so united on the great essentials you have a basis to build on for the future.

There was one point on which we differed. In the seven points there was one in which we differed. That was the Native question —no doubt the biggest of them all.

There is no doubt that the Native question raises issues which far transcend the elements of South Africa, and there we agreed to differ. General Hertzog in his seven points laid down a certain basis, but he knows that not only are there differences between his party and my party, but there are differences which cut right across parties.

Here is a question which is world-wide and is profoundly ethical. And we came to this measure of agreement: that we shall not unduly use the steam-roller against each other, but that our object is to reach a solution by agreement rather than mere fighting by majority. We shall not force the pace unduly, but we shall honestly try to explore the method of agreement.

That may take years, but what are a few years in the Native question? Our grandchildren two hundred years hence will still be labouring at the Native question. It is our problem. It is the great problem which has been entrusted to South Africa.

We differ, but we agreed to differ, and we also agreed to explore methods of agreement as to the solution of this problem in the future.

Our Coloured people, of course, do not fall under the section dealing with the Native people. Our Coloured people, we are all agreed, should be dealt with as part and parcel of the body politic of South Africa. There are social differences, and there may be other differences, but as far as political rights are concerned we draw no line, not in this province anyhow.

I do not want to detain you too long. I have now dealt mostly with the large political issues, the high politics of the situation, and I have tried to prove to you that every consideration of high politics and nationhood and those things which are dear to us in our aspirations point to national co-operation as highly necessary and desirable.

But the economic situation in this country calls equally imperatively for united action. The economic situation is a most powerful argument for united action. If ever there was a time when we ought to pull together in the government of this country, it is now.

This country is in a parlous condition. I, personally, have never held out greater hopes in our departure from the gold standard than this—that thereby we would secure two enormous advantages. One was that we would be able to export our primary products to the world markets, and get the full world price for them without any deduction. There would not be the handicap which there was under the gold standard. That was number one.

Number two: I conceived that if we went off the gold standard, we would have a return of money to this country on a large scale, and that we would have cheaper money. Both these points have been proved very convincingly by the events of the last couple of months.

At the end of last year we went off the gold standard, and the result has been that our primary producers have got 40 to 50 per cent more for whatever they exported than they got before under the gold standard. We also see that the country is choc-a-bloc with money; I understand the banks do not know what to do with the money. Not much of it has come my way. I do not know whether you are more happily situated. We have the assurance that we have a plethora of money, and the interest rates have to come down very considerably.

So far what I expected to happen through our departure from the gold standard has come about; but it is not enough. The economic situation of this country remains parlous in the extreme. We have to pay our debts; this country is overburdened with debt. Our agricultural community is in a state of poverty. I might almost say ruination, such as they have never been in before in our lifetime.

You can imagine what that means in the immediate future if these debts have to be paid. You can understand how much easier it is for a united government to deal with this situation than it is for a government which has to fight to put their measures through parliament.

In an economic alliance one doctor prescribes what he thinks is a very good remedy, and another doctor appears on the scene and strikes out the prescription, while the patient gets worse all the time.

Now we are going to have one doctor, and we are not going to have the difference between the doctors. There will be no more cancellation of prescriptions, and you are going to give this country what they have learned to call in England 'a doctor's mandate'.[1]

That is what the change will mean. You are going to tell your new government representing the two great parties, to go ahead and to prescribe for the economic illness, and there will be no one to cancel the prescription.

Right or wrong, the work will go on. You will have every reason to expect that a government like that will have a much better chance to deal with the ailments of the country successfully than a government which has to meet bitter opposition, and whose measures are very often difficult to put into practice.

[1] The National government of Great Britain had no common programme to put before the voters in the general election of 27 October 1931. Ramsay MacDonald, in an election speech, asked for 'a doctor's mandate' to diagnose and prescribe for the ills of the country.

No, that is the position. If we want to pull through this economic mess in South Africa today, if we want to weather the storms that are ahead of us, then, as wise people, we shall pool our energies and resources, our brain-power and politics, and we shall constitute a national government such as I have mentioned.

But it is not only the South African situation that calls for this. You cannot open your papers without seeing what the situation is in the great world beyond our borders. But yesterday the United States of America bestrode the world. Where is that country today? What has become of that proud country, the richest and most powerful economically in the world?

You want no more striking proof of the dangers that await us along our future path than what is happening in the United States today.

It is not only in America. Look at Europe; look at Germany; look at the whole of central Europe; look at Asia, and you see a world such as has not been seen, I believe, for the last thousand years—a world in turmoil, rocking on its foundations from one side to the other.

We here in South Africa—we are the fly on that wheel. That wheel is moving round by a fate which certainly we cannot control, but we are linked up in the closest manner with that wheel.

We are linked up in the closest manner with the fate of Europe. Our markets are found there; our money comes from there; all our affiliations in commerce and economics are with that great world which is reeling and rocking on its foundations.

You can see the danger ahead of us. We must realize it. We must realize that in the next few years the great world, and we also in South Africa, may be tested as never before. I think we shall build wisely if we take counsel beforehand, if we take the necessary precautions, and secure a government which will be strong enough and united enough to withstand all the trials and dangers that lie on that path.

I think that, quite apart from high politics and from our aims and ideals, that economic situation of South Africa and of the world is by itself sufficient to justify to the full the step now being taken. I believe I need not say anything further on that point. You are all in agreement with me.

There is one more word I want to say before I conclude. It may appear, from what I have said, and from what has appeared in the press, too, that this is a combination between the two great parties of this country to the exclusion of all others.

You have seen the statement that the future government will

consist of twelve—six from each of the two great parties.[1] There will be no Labour representative in that government according to that statement, and the inference may be drawn that this government will not have that contact with Labour and that sympathy with Labour that it should have.

Let me say I want to dispel that impression at once. In the arrangements that have been made the very fullest safeguards have been provided, not only for the two big parties, but also for the Labour party, which no longer exists.

If there had been a Labour party today, they would have been in this national government also, but there is no Labour party, and that is why it was impossible to put any representative of Labour in that government. Such a representative might only stir the ill will of other sections of Labour.

But we have done this. Although it was not possible to put a representative of Labour in the government, we have done our best to maintain, as far as we can in the circumstances, the representation of Labour in parliament. As you will remember, Labour was, in the last parliament up to recently, represented by eight members. One of those seats has since gone to the South African party in the resounding victory which we won at Germiston.[2]

One of the Labour members has come over to the South African party, and is now a member of our party.[3] That leaves six. Of those six, two are resolutely opposed to the national government,[4] promise us every measure of warfare, and it is very difficult to make provision for them. They have made their bed, however, and they must lie on it. But with regard to the other four,[5] we are making provision to give them seats. Three of these seats are given by the South African party. We are giving three safe South African party seats and are making a present of them to Labour.

I am afraid it is a fact that there will be in these constituencies

---

[1] The National party ministers were: J. B. M. Hertzog, N. C. Havenga, P. G. W. Grobler, O. Pirow, J. C. G. Kemp and A. P. J. Fourie. The South African party ministers were J. C. Smuts, P. Duncan, D. Reitz, J. H. Hofmeyr, C. F. Clarkson, R. Stuttaford.

[2] In the Germiston (Transvaal) bye-election on 1 December 1932 J. G. N. Strauss won the seat for the South African party with 4,257 votes. The National party candidate polled 3,076 votes and the Labour party candidate 132.

[3] This was Morris Kentridge, member for Troyeville, Transvaal.

[4] These were R. T. McArthur, member for Umbilo, Durban and W. Madeley, member for Benoni (Transvaal).

[5] In the general election of 1933 F. H. P. Creswell became coalition member for Bellville (Cape Province); F. Shaw became coalition member for Bloemfontein North; H. W. Sampson was defeated by H. J. Reitz of the Roos group at Jeppe (Transvaal) and J. Christie was defeated by W. Bawden of the South African party.

a considerable grievance felt by the members of the South African Party at the action we have taken. But we have taken it in order to show that this method [*sic*] towards a national government has no feeling, carries no hostility whatever, against the progress of this country or those people who represent it.

We are making them a present of these seats, and we did it as a message of good will to the workers of this country. And the workers may rest assured that, not only are we doing our best to keep their representation in parliament—if we did not do so they would probably not have representation at all—but they may be assured that we shall continue to watch over their welfare, and we shall look after the interest of the workers of this country to the very best of our ability.

It is not for me to announce the policy of the new government; but I do hope that the programme which I sketched for the South African party at the last Bloemfontein congress will become a guide to the new government in their attitude on this question. And the electoral arrangements will apply not only to the Union parliament, but also to the provincial council elections.

In conclusion, I only want to say that this is a great chance which has come to us at a time of sore trial and suffering. I remember a case many years ago when, out of a dire calamity in South Africa, a great hope was born. I am speaking of Union.

Union was preceded by years of very acute and grave depression; 1907 and 1908 were years of great suffering, especially for people of this province and Natal, and I felt persuaded at the time, that but for the depression which was driving these two colonies to link up their fate with the interior, we would not have seen the unification of the colonies in a united South Africa.

It was the calamity under which there was born a united South Africa. Today we see something very similar, and it may be something in the end even bigger for the people of South Africa.

Out of the calamities, and out of the depression which has spread over the world, we have seen this new policy, this movement towards a united government and this desire for a cessation of party strife. My hope is this: that this new spirit which has come to us in this almost providential way will be turned to the best account by the people of South Africa. My hope is that just as Union became a medium of destiny in the history of South Africa, so we will turn our present opportunity into a moment of destiny, and, through this great movement, we shall date an era in the history of South Africa when, more than ever before, the races will draw together; there will be a cessation of the party strife that has divided them;

there will be more national unity growing up, and from this date we shall, perhaps in years to come even more than from Union date the true unity of the people of South Africa.

331 To F. S. Malan

Irene
27 Maart 1933

Waarde Frans, Binne 'n paar dae sal die nuwe regeering gevorm word en ek skryf jou hierdie reëls om my spyt uit te druk dat dit nie moontlik gevind is 'n plaas daarin aan jou to offereer nie. Dit is nie te wyte aan onwil van eenige kant—inteendeel. Maar met die volste en ernstigste konsideratie van die heele kwestie is dit finaal besluit om jou daaruit te laat. Vir my was dit 'n baie pynlike besluit. Ons het sovele jare saamgewerk in die politiek van die land dat ek baie onwillig was jou buite die nuwe regeering te sien. Maar 'n menigte van konsideraties het ten slotte tot daardie resultaat gelei.

Dis onnoodig vir my om te sê met watter volle vertroue en vol-hartige sympathie ek jou bejeën. En ek vertrou dat hierdie ge-dwonge stap geen verandering wedersyds teweeg sal breng nie. Nooit het ons grooter moeilikhede ondervind met die vorming van 'n Kabinet, en ek persoonlik is ver van tevrede met die uitslag. Maar in die politiek is dit nie die beste wat gekies word nie, maar die beste onder al die omstandighede. Hertzog was jou geheel welgesind, en dit is alleen die omstandighede wat ten slotte die deurslag gegee het.

In liefde en met volle versekering van my vertroue, Steeds getrou die uwe,

get. J. C. Smuts

TRANSLATION

Irene
[Transvaal]
27 March 1933

Dear Frans, The new government will be formed within a few days and I write you these lines to express my regret that it has not been found possible to offer you a place in it. This is not because of unwillingness on any side—on the contrary. But, after the fullest and most serious consideration of the whole question, it was de-cided to leave you out. For me it was a very painful decision. We have worked together in the politics of the country for so many years that I was very unwilling to see you out of the new government. But numerous considerations led, in the end, to that result.

It is unnecessary for me to say with what complete trust and deeply felt sympathy I regard you. And I hope that this forced step will not bring about any change between us. We have never had greater difficulty in forming a cabinet and I, personally, am far from satisfied with the result. But in politics it is not the best who are chosen, but the best under all the circumstances. Hertzog was altogether well-disposed towards you and only the circumstances decided matters in the end.

In love and with the full assurance of my confidence, Ever faithfully yours,

J. C. Smuts

332   To G. B. van Zyl   Vol. 50, no. 144

Irene
[Transvaal]
27 March 1933

My dear Van Zyl, In a couple of days the new government will be formed, and it is a matter of bitter regret to me that it has not been possible to include you in it. Your political services, your unwearied devotion to the party would have been a complete justification of the step. But the prime minister and I have not been able to overcome the difficulties in the way. We found it essential to give representation to commerce and the widespread commercial interests of the country, and after prolonged consideration it was regretfully decided to waive your strong claims and to give the appointment to Stuttaford [R.]—without portfolio.

I only wish to say to you how strong and complete my confidence is in you, and what a disappointment it was on this occasion not to be able to offer the seat to you. But I feel sure that you will understand my difficulties and accept my assurance that only dire necessity has made me take the course I have taken. The formation of this cabinet has been more difficult than any other with which I have been associated, and the difficulties have arisen out of the nature of the case and not of ill will on the part of anybody.

With kind regards and in all true loyalty to you, Ever yours sincerely,

s. J. C. Smuts

333   From G. G. A. Murray   Vol. 50, no. 107

Yatscombe
Boar's Hill
Oxford
28 March 1933

My dear Smuts, I have been watching affairs in South Africa with
the keenest interest, and need not say how glad I am to see that you
are again in the saddle, though I could wish, for the sake of the horse,
that others were not sharing it with you. Do you remember how we
wished you to stay here and lead the Liberal party after the war?
I constantly think of that time and wonder how much of the
present evils you could have saved us from. I have been looking
back lately over our history, as given in the *Survey of International
Affairs*,[1] and have been made to reflect again and again *quam parva
sapientia mundus regitur*.[2] I do think however that the poor governments have had an unusual amount of bad luck as well.

I am asking the press to send you a copy of my new book on
Aristophanes.[3] If you have time to read it I hope some of the
parallels with modern times may amuse you. He fought a splendid
fight against the jingo mob of his own day. Yours ever,

Gilbert Murray

334   To M. C. Gillett   Vol. 50, no. 177

Doornkloof
[Irene, Transvaal]
29 March 1933

Another week has passed—with many a look back at the golden
days spent together.[4] But the march of events is terrific. Meetings,
cabinet making, endless correspondence and interviews. But the
sweetness of the flowering time remains. I have written on an average
thirteen to thirty letters every day and have had to keep flying
between this dear home and the office and government buildings at
Pretoria. And now the real difficulties will begin. On Friday the
new government will be sworn in, and after that most of my days
and day time will be spent in office once more. What an unpleasant

---

[1] An annual series published by the Royal Institute of International Affairs,
founded in 1920.
[2] 'With how little wisdom is the world governed?' (Count Axel Oxenstierna (1583–
1654), chancellor of Sweden).
[3] G. G. A. Murray, *Aristophanes: a Study* (1933).
[4] The Gilletts had been on holiday in South Africa in January and February 1933.

prospect! I have really enjoyed this life of semi-privacy of the last nine years very much, and would pray that it might remain my lot to the end. But it may not be. And so to the collar and the harness once more. I shall be minister of justice—one of the very few portfolios I have never held since the old days when I was state attorney to the Republic. I may end where I began—with many ups and downs between. Duncan, Hofmeyr, and Reitz will be my principal Sap colleagues. A good band of faithful and true comrades. The Nat team will interest you less, just as it does me. The Nats have reserved all the big patronage portfolios for themselves; but they are also the most critical and dangerous jobs—railways, agriculture, Natives included. If there is going to be breaking of necks it will be in these jobs. We take justice, mines, lands, interior, which is an *omnium gatherum*[1] affair given to the brilliant Hofmeyr. Tomorrow I go to Standerton to preach the new gospel of racial co-operation and national unity. If successful, this will be my last and best service to South Africa. If unsuccessful, well, then I have at least made a gallant attempt. And time must follow it up and bring it to fruition. All that matters in this world is a great and stout heart; and the rest is time's work, done or undone.

I notice that MacDonald has had some success both at Geneva and Rome—that some semblance of disarmament may yet come, and that the great word *treaty-revision* has at last been spoken in high quarters.[2] Why not when Stresemann and Brüning were sacrificing themselves for European civilization? But the good is always too late in this world. Hitler may succeed where the good men failed—in making people realize the dangers ahead. But Japan has walked out of the League,[3] and India is worse than ever so far as a settlement is concerned. And where is the economic conference which is to save us from the coming Communism? And our leaders stand like Hamlets and curse their fate.[4] I have done little botany and no philosophy since my last letter. And the Gillett family is enjoying the high seas. Good-bye,

Jan

---

[1] Mock Latin, meaning a miscellaneous collection.

[2] From 16 March 1933 MacDonald attended the disarmament conference to which he submitted a new draft convention. It contained proposals which were to be substituted for the disarmament clauses of the treaty of Versailles. On 18 March MacDonald and Simon were in Rome for discussions with Mussolini on a four-power pact.

[3] When the League assembly adopted the Lytton report condemning her occupation of Manchuria, Japan at once gave notice of her intention to resign from the League.

[4] The time is out of joint; O cursed spite,
  that ever I was born to set it right!
  Shakespeare, *Hamlet*, i. v. 118.

335   From R. I. Steyn   **Vol. 50, no. 132**

Vreugde
Oliver Weg
See Punt
2 April 1933

Liewe Generaal Smuts, Veel mag ek nie skrywe, maar dit is 'n behoefte van my hart om u te sê, nou dat die nuwe kabinet tot stand gebring is, dat ek hoop die samewerking tussen u en Generaal Hertzog van die beste sal wees.

Toe ek van die koalisie gehoor het, het die teks my dadelik te binne geskiet 'God kan groote dingen doen, die men niet doorzoeken kan; wonderen die men niet tellen kan'.

As 'n Engel uit die hemel my einde Januarie vertel het dat dit gaan gebeur, sou ek dit nie geglo het.

Nooit het ek gedink dat u gewillig sou wees om onder Generaal Hertzog te dien. U groot moedigheid en opoffering eer en bewonder ek.

Ek herinner my nog so goed toe ons in London in 1909 was, toe u en G. Hertzog die Hotel saam binne gestap het dat President na my om gedraai het en gesê het, met twee sulke knappe jong Afrikaners is ons Land veilig. U het hy altyd besonder brilliant beskou.

Die blyde dag is weer vir Suid-Afrika aangebreek dat u beide in tyd van groot nood saam span om ons Volk te red.

My bede is dat veel sukses op u werk sal rus, en sê ek met Ds. Kestell 'Ons hou ons hart vas, en gee Land, Volk en Voormanne aan God oor.'

Met innige liefde groete aan Mev. Smuts en u, en met die harte wens dat ons Volk nou die eenheid mag bereik waarna ons almal so vurig na verlang, Bly ek, liewe Generaal, U liewe vrindin,

R. I. Steyn

TRANSLATION

Vreugde
Oliver Road
Sea Point
[Cape Town]
2 April 1933

Dear General Smuts, I may not write much but it is in my heart to say, now that the new cabinet has been formed, that I hope for the best co-operation between you and General Hertzog.

When I heard of the coalition I at once remembered the text, 'Which doeth great things past finding out; yea, and wonders without number.'[1]

If an angel from Heaven had told me at the end of January that this would happen I would not have believed it.

Never did I think that you would be willing to serve under General Hertzog. I honour and admire your great courage and sacrifice.

I remember so well, when we were in London in 1909[2] and you and General Hertzog walked together into the hotel that the President turned to me and said, 'With two such able young Afrikanders our country is safe.' You he always regarded as particularly brilliant. The happy day has again dawned for South Africa when you both, in a time of great need, stand together to save our people.

My prayer is that much success will rest upon your work and I say, with the Reverend Mr [J. D.] Kestell, 'We hold fast in our hearts and leave our country, our people and our leaders to God.'

With loving greetings to Mrs Smuts and to you and with the fervent wish that our people may now achieve the unity for which we all so ardently long, I remain, dear General, Your dear friend,

R. I. Steyn

336   To C. P. Crewe   Vol. 102, no. 258

Irene
[Transvaal]
4 April 1933

My dear Crewe, Old comrades like us do not part with angry words, and although you appear not to want an answer to your last letter I think it due to our longstanding friendship that I should send a few words in reply. Your judgment is unfair to poor [Brigadier-General J. J.] Byron, especially to Duncan, to the whole case of coalition; and finally you pull me also into your angry condemnation. My dear old friend, surely we know each other too well after long years of the severest testing! I have not undergone a sudden change. The things we stand by remain the same, and I hope to prove true to ideals for which I have in the past sacrificed a lot. So let us remain friends and comrades even if there is a difference of opinion.

[1] *Job* ix. 10.
[2] The occasion of this visit was the passage of the South Africa Act through the parliament of Great Britain.

Remember the country craves for rest and peace from all this racial and political strife. The English section even more than the Dutch. They went head over heels in favour of coalition. You say we would have won next year. Would we—with Roos creating havoc in the ranks of the South African party? The Rand members, the [Cape] Peninsula members confessed in caucus that with Roos in the field a large number of our seats were in danger and would be lost. We would have had three parties next year, and it was doubtful whether we could win. Racialism would have remained rampant and the old pre-Boer War atmosphere would have been steadily created. Half the country is bankrupt; Bolshevism is invading the *platteland*[1] where all the talk is of moratorium, repudiation and like dangerous stuff. It is because I am conscious of all this and a good deal more that I have attempted to create once more a new spirit, to invoke the benign genius of South Africa which has so often come to our assistance in the past. Of course I may fail; but also I may succeed. And be sure that I don't mean to surrender. If I see my faith and confidence is abused, I shall once more appeal to the people of South Africa and that time as one who had gone all out for saving her.

So do not simply condemn coalition. It is undertaken in a great faith which may yet prevail. May I just add how sorry I am to hear how unwell you are. May you soon be better. It would grieve me to think I have added to your worries and your illness. Ever yours sincerely and comradely,   J. C. Smuts

I hope you can read this scrawl which is written late at night.

337   To M. C. Gillett   **Vol. 50, no. 178**

Irene
[Transvaal]
4 April 1933

This is the third letter I write you since your departure, so I suppose you have already landed and reached 102. Well, I hope you have found it all O.K. Since my last letter I have been to Standerton to explain coalition and make others understand the vision of a new South Africa. I have also been sworn in and have started at my office where I have been busy for three or four days. It is really funny that I should be back at the very job I had thirty-five years ago when I started as attorney-general of the Republic at the

---

[1] The rural districts.

mature age of twenty-eight! The same job now and at less pay![1]
And they call this a department of *Justice*! However, I shall not nurse
a grievance against fate but go right forward, following the lead of
a great faith, wherever it may take me. The egregious Roos who
was to have retired to his farm on the accomplishment of our coalition has already changed his mind and is putting up candidates
against us right and left. 'This is not the coalition *he* intended.'
Such is personal politics, which has been the curse of this country
of people on the make.

But why write about us when the poor old world is reeling on
her foundations! The Russian business is once more getting bad.[2]
And Hitler is frightening or squeezing the life out of the Jews.
There he is making a first-class blunder though. The Jews have
their hands on every lever in every civilized country, and Hitler
will find that he has undertaken the impossible. But you can imagine
how perturbed my friends out here are. We seem to be getting
back to mediaeval barbarism. But I suppose all this is to happen
before there is a real turn for the better. The bitterness must come
to the surface and show its own futility everywhere before sanity
will once more return. I have not lost faith. I feel sure we are
groping to the new light. Even the failures of the League of Nations
may prove an incentive to more sincere relations, because many
statesmen must get frightened to see how this prop is also going.
Our idealism requires a stronger dash of realism and downright
sincerity; and all the recent blows will but tend that way. At least,
so I hope and pray. The desertion of Japan may make America
realize how dangerous her own attitude to the League and the
world is, and she may yet come to see that in the end she may have
to face Japan alone and single-handed in the Pacific. I don't think
the Lord has forgotten us.

Most nights I go to bed with some botany book. My work is now
too much to permit of philosophy at that late hour. But botany is
like a sweet opiate, expelling the day's interests and preoccupations.
Love to you all,

Jan

P.S. Webster: *The League of Nations [in Theory and Practice*
(Allen and Unwin) please.

[1] The salary of a cabinet minister was at this time £2,500 a year. Smuts's salary
when he was appointed state attorney of the South African Republic in 1897 was
£2,250 a year.
[2] In 1933 a large number of political arrests and trials took place in Russia, including
that of several engineers employed by the Metropolitan-Vickers Company in Moscow.
They were accused of sabotage and spying. Six of them were British subjects.

Office of the Department of Justice
Union Buildings, Pretoria
20 April 1933

My dear Murray, Thank you very much for your kind letter and good wishes which I very much appreciate. You must have been surprised at recent political developments in South Africa as most people here have been surprised. Things happen so suddenly here and often when least expected. This latest move for a joint government is, however, not the result of a sudden impulse, but has deep underlying causes which have at last come to the surface. My expectation is that we shall now see a cessation of the orgy of racial politics which has been the stock-in-trade of our public life. With luck we may see this country launched on a new path which may carry it far from the bitternesses of the past.

A contemplation of the European scene is much less pleasing. I deeply regret the action of the British government in placing an embargo on Russian trade, especially as it was clear from the mild sentences on the English accused that the Soviet were retreating as fast and as gracefully as they could after the Moscow trial.[1] Unless there is something undisclosed, this British action may prove a very serious blunder. But we know very little here, and there may have been more than mere newspaper propaganda to influence the British government.

There are not many rays of hope in this darkness. Japan has almost torpedoed the League, and the League has shown little strength to react against this almost fatal attack. Then also Continental policies are taking a turn which seems to me to be entirely away from the League spirit, and the original intentions of its founders. I cannot persuade myself that Mussolini's new concert of great powers[2] is any real improvement, and not rather a set-back in our ideas of world peace. I shall not be surprised to see it a source of fresh world troubles. And on top of it all comes Hitler with his ruthless barbarism reminiscent of something worse than the old Prussia, and especially with his baiting of the Jews which carries us back to the Middle Ages. It is difficult to see any point from which

[1] The foreign accused were either deported or acquitted. The British government suspended negotiations for a new trade treaty with Russia and put an embargo on about 80% of Russian imports.

[2] Mussolini's proposal of a pact between Great Britain, France, Germany and Italy was apparently aimed at separating France from those powers which opposed the revision of the treaty of Versailles in favour of Germany. The four-power pact was accepted on 8 June but in a form which hardly affected existing international relations.

one might try to turn the flank of this tide of reaction. I suppose at the root of it all today is the economic and financial situation which even more than political wrongs seem to be driving the peoples to madness. The only ray of hope is that the very extremity of the crisis may drive the governments together in more earnest attempts at solution. The fact that America is in it right up to the neck may also be helpful and may probably lead to the abandonment of the somewhat selfish and cowardly policy which she has followed since the great days of Wilson. I do not think that the occasion is one for despair, but what is so aggravating is that one feels so helpless. I do not blame anybody, but I only feel that there has been great weakness and slackness at a time when the utmost vigilance was demanded from those to whom we are looking for leadership. Perhaps the economic conference may succeed amid all this failure and may give us a new start for which we are looking.

I am sorry to write such a depressing letter, but I must frankly confess that at this distance the whole stiuation is to me intensely disquieting. I had not looked forward to spectacular advances on the path of peace, and recovery, but I had looked forward to a generation of slow and painful movement forward, during which the new world would have grown up, and a new atmosphere arisen among the nations. Now it seems as if even in our own brief day we may once more be precipitated into the gulf.

It is possible that I may be coming to the economic conference whenever that may be, and in that case I shall look forward to a real exchange of ideas with you on these matters which it is so difficult to write about.

With very kind regards and all good wishes both to you and Lady Mary, Yours ever sincerely,

J. C. Smuts

339   To F. Lamont

Vol. 50, no. 151

Irene
Transvaal
25 April 1933

My dear Florence, This is not a letter in answer to your last, but my notice that I shall be in London at the economic conference to represent South Africa.[1] I am most anxious that Tom and you

---

[1] The world monetary and economic conference met in London on 12 June 1933. The Union of South Africa was represented by Smuts, N. C. Havenga, then minister of finance, and O. Pirow, minister of railways and harbours and of defence.

should be there too, and I appeal to you two to be there, whether officially or in a private capacity does not matter so much. I am longing to see you two once more, and I also feel that Tom should be on the spot. Some of the most momentous decisions will have to be taken. Perhaps the real economic peace will be written or begun to be written at this conference. I do not know whether Tom is *persona grata* with the powers that be in the U.S.A. But I look upon him as the American financier who, more than anyone else, has a right to be there and to take part or to watch developments. So please make your plans accordingly. It will be a joy to see you once more and to hear all you have to say about that interesting world of which I had only the briefest and most illusive glimpse.

I believe things are coming to a head in the Old World—and it will not be the same after this conference. It will move one way or the other. And may we all help to safeguard what is precious in its heritage. With love to you both and to the children within reach, Ever yours,

J. C. Smuts

340   From J. B. M. Hertzog   Vol. 50, no. 77

Kantoor van die Eerste Minister
Pretoria
29 Juni 1933

Waarde Jan, Dank vir jou brief uit Salisbury. Mitchell is 'n paar dae gelede hier gewees, en nadat hy my meegedeel het die sake wat hy graag sou opgelos wil hê, het ik hom die gelegentheid gegee om dit met Kemp en sy departement te bespreek. Kemp is besig om sy best te doen om Rhodesia tegemoet te kom, en Mitchell skyn dan ook tevrede met wat voorlopig aan hom toegesê is geword. Natuurlik behoor ons hul tegemoet te kom waar dit mogelik kan sonder die Unie te seer te benadeel, of aan gevaar bloot te stel. Kemp is dan ook besig om die sake uit daardie oogpunt te oorweeg.

Die Rand spekulateurs het alles in hul vermoë geprobeer om ons op hol te set in verband met die goud-premie en naar ik nou verneem is die Rand Club alles behalwe 'n veiligheids oord vir lede van die Regering! Die agitasie metodes deur hul aangewend, is presies weer gewees die van voor die boer-oorlog. Hul bluf is misluk en weer eens heers daar stilte by die *Mail* en *Star*—alsof daar nooit enig kwessie was van ontevrendenheid. In die harte van hul wat hul laat byt het deur te onversigtig te spekuleer, sal dit wel minder rustig wees.

Ik hoop dat die Konferensie meer vrugte sal dra dan wat dit tot
nou toe nog beloof het! Met beste wense aan jullie almal,

J. B. M. Hertzog

TRANSLATION

Prime Minister's Office
Pretoria
29 June 1933

Dear Jan, Thanks for your letter from Salisbury. Mitchell [G.]
was here a few days ago, and after he had informed me what
matters he would like to have settled, I gave him an opportunity to
discuss these with Kemp and his department.[1] Kemp is doing his
best to meet Rhodesia and Mitchell seems to be satisfied with what
has provisionally been promised him. Of course we ought to meet
them wherever possible without doing the Union too much harm
or exposing it to danger. Kemp is considering matters from that
point of view.

The Rand speculators tried everything in their power to stampede us in connection with the gold premium[2] and I understand that
the Rand Club is anything but a safe place for members of the
government! The methods of agitation which they used were again
exactly those used before the Anglo-Boer War. Their bluff has failed
and once more calm reigns at the *Rand Daily Mail* and the *Star*—
as if there had never been any question of dissatisfaction. In the
hearts of those who allowed themselves to be bitten by rash speculation it will doubtless be less peaceful.

I hope that the conference will be more fruitful than it has so far
promised to be! With best wishes to you all,

J. B. M. Hertzog

¹ The department of agriculture.
² In the budget of 30 May 1933, the government had proposed a special tax of
£6 million on gold premium profits. Patrick Duncan, as acting minister of finance,
had to face heavy attacks from the Chamber of Mines, the Rand newspapers, the
Johannesburg stock exchange and members of parliament, notably Sir Robert Kotze.
See **342.**

341   From J. Hutchinson   **Vol. 50, no. 82**

The Herbarium
Royal Botanic Gardens
Kew, Surrey
30 June 1933

My dear General, I have finished revising the names of your Schoemanskloof etc. collection, and have prepared a complete list to accompany your notes on the vegetation. I have added a few interesting notes on the distribution of some of the species.

You know, when you go on these trips you set an example to the botanical department at Pretoria, and the publication of results will perhaps stimulate some of them to leave their office stools a little oftener.

You collected a new *Crassula*, a new *Erythrina* (hitherto referred to *Caffra* but now found to be quite different), a new *Dimorphotheca*, and a new *Anisopappus* (Compositae),

As you expressed a wish to see the paper before it was printed, should I ask the director to send it to you? Or could you come a little earlier on Tuesday and glance at it in my room?

I am going to Wimbledon today. Kindest regards, Yours ever,

J. Hutchinson

342   From P. Duncan   **Vol. 50, no. 29**

Department of Mines
Pretoria
11 July 1933

My dear Smuts, I was very glad to get your letter by last mail. I hope this will reach you before you leave England. From the news of the conference which we get in the papers here it seems to be living from day to day on the brink of dissolution but I imagine it will try to do something before it goes out or at any rate to arrive at some common understanding as to what can be done.

The session of parliament was not satisfactory. It met in an atmosphere of haste—quite unnecessarily—and by the end of the second week members were all on edge to get away. Morning sittings were put on after the first week and you know what that means when measures are before the house raising all sorts of intricate questions, with deputations urging this or that amendment. There was simply no time to give proper attention to them. I had to see through most of the things and to endure a real bombardment of letters and telegrams in all the keys of wrath and indignation.

The mines taxation raised a veritable storm. I remember nothing like it on the Rand since the agitation for Chinese labour. I do not believe the taxation itself is likely to stop the expansion of the industry. As far as I know all the main new developments which were on the *tapis* before the budget are still going on. But it certainly gave a bad shock to the market and to the investing public and the Chamber set up an intensive propaganda which increased the alarm.

To some extent we have ourselves to thank for this. The scheme as originally introduced was much too complicated and the White Paper issued by the treasury was a case of *obscurum per obscurius*.[1] No one could tell without elaborate calculation what the effect would be on particular mines and the market got into a panic. The scheme was launched without enough time for full consideration and elucidation. It was faulty in certain respects in its incidence and to meet the criticisms of the Chamber representatives— Anderson [P. M.] and Lawrence [W. H. A.]—I had to drop it and produce a substitute which is both simpler and more equitable towards low grade mining. It was produced at high pressure and is not perfect. Anderson and Lawrence and their advisers were at Cape Town and were most helpful. Their contention was that we were taking £2 million too much and that we should have taken a straight percentage. I would not agree about departing from our figure of £6 million but agreed to limit the special tax to that amount for this year, for next year to take not more of the excess profits than we budget for this year from the new tax and the income tax on the excess profits, i.e. £7.4 million, and for the next three years not more than 50% of the excess profits. I do not like binding future years but I thought we must do something to reassure intending investors as to our future policy and I think 50% of the excess profits is as much in any case as we ought to take. 'Excess profits' of course will lose its meaning with currency stabilization and we should then recast our taxation system. We are also allowing mines not yet at the producing stage to set off expenditure on shaft sinking and underground development against the tax on excess profits when they come to the taxable stage—a very important concession—and the new gold law amending bill[2] which has been published is a revolution in the method of dealing with new mineral areas. So altogether, with all these things and gold at 124s. 6d. an ounce (as against 120s. on which our calculations were made), the industry should make a good recovery and the indications are all that it is doing so.

---

[1] (Explaining) an obscurity by something more obscure.
[2] Gold Mines Excess Profits Duty (Amendment) Act, No. 43 of 1934.

The Farmers Mortgage Bill is a rather crude affair.[1] I am not very proud of it. It will have some effect in bringing interest down but I fear it will throw a large number of farmers' bonds on to the Land Bank and discourage private investment in farm bonds.

Inside the government everything goes smoothly. In the country the Nat and Sap branches want to amalgamate—at least in the Transvaal. I feel that we must go a bit slow over that so as to take our town people with us. Cape Town is suspicious and on the Rand Stallard has been carrying on a campaign against the mines tax which (though he professes loyalty to the coalition) has alienated from us a number of our people who say they were let down by the South African party. Stallard, of course, is a political comet but we shall have to give people on the Rand a little time to cool down. Best wishes from us all, Yours sincerely,

Patrick Duncan

343   To M. C. Gillett   Vol. 50, no. 192

Khartoum
28 August 1933

We arrived here today at 5.15 after having flown about 1,200 miles today from Cairo. This is the longest single day flight of the trip[2] and in spite of the heat it has passed off well. We started at 3 a.m., having got up at 1.30 this morning. It was most noisy at the Continental Hotel where we were staying, so you can understand that I had little sleep last night. (In fact the same should be said about the night before at Athens, where the noise prevented sleep, and at 4 a.m. we had to get up.) So you can see I am entirely dependent for sleep on what I can get in the machine. The heat was great and at Atbara where we came down for lunch at 2.30 the thermometer showed 107 in the shade, although our party felt sure it was a mistaken reading for 127! I felt a bit squeamish at one point where the machine wobbled terribly, but that soon passed. The trip so far has been pleasant and enjoyable, with good company bound for most of the countries we pass through or to. It was a sight after a day of the African desert to come down at Khartoum and find the country green. Copious rains have been falling here recently and even now a great storm is raging nearby. The lions are roaring

[1] Farm Mortgage Interest Act, No. 63 of 1933. The Act relieved farmers by providing government assistance in paying the interest on farm mortgages and limiting the interest chargeable on such mortgages.

[2] This was Smuts's first air journey. He was the first South African cabinet minister to fly from the Union to Europe.

loudly, and the jackals join in a grand chorus—just as at Groote Schuur—only louder. There must be a zoo near the hotel.[1] Evidently the storm reminds these children of the wilds of their native land, where the approach of the storm means green grass and plenty of game to feed on! The hotel is on the Blue or Abyssinian Nile which is in flood, having risen 26 feet from the condition it was in when last I stayed here, and even then it was no mean river—the size of the Rhine at Bonn I should say. (The chorus continues crescendo, poor things.) No, here it *is* Africa; at Alexandria, and somewhat less at Cairo, you still feel the transition *to* Africa. I smell Africa here, especially after the storm. A donkey is braying near, to heighten the impression. Darkness has come on since I started writing this letter, so different from the long English dusk. A beautiful breeze is now starting after the storms, and I feel quite refreshed. There is a growing hush, unlike that awful jabber which continues all day in Athens and Cairo, and seems to grow worse at night. This is Africa, and I feel at rest.

I have been much struck by the continuous graduations from the white type in northern Europe to the African negro as this trip progresses—English—French—Italians—Greeks—Egyptians—Soudanese, and so on to the Bantu and the negro. The change of shading and of type is most marked. And the characteristics vary even more. I suppose all this variety is really an enrichment, whatever one may think of the comparative values of these types. I must say that after the Nordic I like the real African best; but that may be my continental 'provinciality' as Whitehead would call it. In any case the fascination of Africa—both human and geographic—is undeniable...

Jan

344   To G. B. van Zyl   Vol. 50, no. 172

Palace of Justice
Pretoria
4 September 1933

My dear van Zyl, Just a line of friendly greeting on my return to this dear land in which I am glad to be back. The trip in the air was to me a most pleasant and interesting experience, and the conference—though not a success—was also a great experience in many ways. I believe it has done good, and at the right time

[1] There is a zoo near Groote Schuur, the Cape Town house of the prime minister of South Africa.

solutions will yet be reached. But today the times are out of joint, and the future is more uncertain in the old world than ever before.[1]

Duncan showed me your letter, and Hofmeyr has also reported. I think the Transvaal executive acted with undue haste, and I shall have to tone down somewhat the roseate picture they have attempted. But the fact is that in the rural Transvaal the urge towards fusion is very great and the executive probably had its hand forced. I shall see that there is proper consultation and co-operation between all sections of the party. But of course I agree and believe fully that in the end there is likely to be fusion. Dr Malan and his stalwarts may soon split off, and that too may ease the position for many troubled Saps. If there is anything special please let me know. I send you and Mrs van Zyl my kind regards and good wishes. Every yours sincerely,

J. C. Smuts

345   To M. C. Gillett   Vol. 50, no. 194

Doornkloof
[Irene, Transvaal]
5 September 1933

My last letter was a rapidly scribbled one from Broken Hill. My hand was so shaky from the vibration of the machine that the letter must have been barely legible. For all that it was a most enjoyable flight from Mbeya that morning. We once more crossed the Zambesi—Kafue Junction—and with a favouring wind arrived quite early at Salisbury. We had to fly high, so I could not see whether a big herd of big game south of the Zambesi was elephant or buffalo. But I have seen more big game (I mean biggest game) on this return trip than ever before—especially on the White and the Victoria Niles. Did I tell you what a glorious sight Lake Kioga was? Perhaps the finest of the whole trip. After leaving the Victoria Nyanza at Jinja the Nile spreads out into a series of lakes, some very large; from Mazindi Port where we crossed this Victoria Nile we had a beautiful view of this series of lakes—for fifty or a hundred miles eastward. And in the morning sun they presented a sight such as one but seldom sees. But to go on. With a wind behind us we moved at 136 miles an hour from Broken Hill to Pietersburg and

---

[1] The world monetary and economic conference adjourned on 27 July having failed in its main purpose—currency stabilization. The vacillating attitude of the United States really killed the conference.

from there to Johannesburg. We were everywhere much in advance of time. Once more we flew right over Rooikop and by Doornkloof. At the airport Isie was with the rest of the Doornkloof family. Jan and Louis [Weyers] were in great form and seemed to attract more attention than Oupa. It is a fact that small children are always a centre of interest and joy to elders. I think there is something deeply psychological in this. Louis knew me at once and rushed like lightning at me. After that his preoccupation was with the many aeroplanes at the aerodrome, and his interest in me sensibly abated. It was a great homecoming, with family and heaps of friends about. Saturday I went through piles of correspondence and papers, and Sunday I gave the usual reception to the uninvited public of Pretoria. And so I am once more plunged in the routine of office and of politics. Heavy programmes of meetings and tours are growing. And it is all such an intolerable bore to me. Still, there are compensations. And I have the pleasant memories of unrivalled holidays on the downs with the dearest of friends. I certainly have no reason to complain of life, and I do not complain but return thanks with a full heart all the time.

Our political situation here is somewhat troubled and complicated because a strong section among the Dutch in both great parties are pressing hard for a complete fusion instead of a coalition, and Hertzog has espoused this cause for tactical reasons of his own. Dr Malan in his party and to a lesser extent the English following in my party are resisting this—Malan because he is a racialist and loathes co-operation with the English, my English friends again because they do not trust the Nats, and do not feel safe in that camp. I shall have my work cut out to meet these difficulties and prevent a rupture between the two wings of the coalition. The English naturally do not feel quite at home with the Nats; and Hertzog keeps harping on *nasionaal* and *Afrikaners*, which words are not liked by the English, as you can understand. I tell you this simply to give you the hang of things here...

Jan

346   To M. C. Gillett   Vol. 50, no. 202

Doornkloof
[Irene, Transvaal]
7 October 1933

Your nice, long, newsy letter has just come (Saturday morning) and I have enjoyed reading it. As I leave tonight for the Cape and shall be away for some nine or ten days with little opportunity to write letters, I reply now at once...

At Cape Town I shall be busy with my Cape congress over the matter of joining hands with the Nats. I fear it will be a ticklish and unpleasant job. The Saps there don't love the Nats, and have not yet forgiven me for surrendering the prospects of power when it was within my grasp. It is a difference between the near and the far view of things. I was right, but I admit all appearances were against me. The question remains whether victory at the cost of deepening animosities would have been worth while.

Hertzog has just had his Cape congress at Port Elizabeth and has been soundly beaten by Dr Malan.[1] The Cape Nats will not look at the 'old Unionists'—the English section of our party. Their outlook remains narrowly racial, and the vision of the larger nationalism has not visited them yet. The whole position is clarified by this breakaway of the die-hard Nats; but on the other hand it is going to make things frightfully difficult for Hertzog. It may be a case of Sap predominance, with a Nat prime minister with a small following of his own. You have that situation in England and it does not work well.[2] In South Africa it will work even less smoothly. The Cape Saps may also take the bit between their teeth and say (like Dr Malan) 'we prefer to go our own way rather than join the Nats whom we don't really like'. Then I too shall be beaten. My next letter will enlighten you. I hope with caution and patience to carry the day[3] but nobody knows in this count. Hertzog felt certain of victory at his congress and got badly beaten. Meanwhile my thoughts are very much at Geneva. We felt happy over South Africa as president of the assembly.[4] But I shall not feel at ease till something substantial is done in disarmament. Some big new move is essential, but I don't see clearly what and how. The only bright point is that all nations are *at present* horribly afraid of war, and we shall still have another chance in the near future. Love,

Jan

[1] The vote against fusion was 142 to 30.

[2] In Great Britain J. R. MacDonald was Labour prime minister in a National government dominated by Conservatives.

[3] Both the Cape and the Natal congress of the South African party gave Smuts a decisive vote for fusion. Those who opposed him formed the Dominion party under the leadership of Colonel C. F. Stallard.

[4] C. T. Te Water, chief delegate of the Union of South Africa in the League assembly from 1929 to 1939, was president of the assembly in 1933.

347   From T. Roos to L. Esselen   Vol. 50, no. 119

45 National Mutual Buildings
Johannesburg
11 November 1933

Dear Louis, I will meet General Smuts and Mr Pirow at any time that suits them—from next week Tuesday morning I will be in Pretoria with a trial case.

May I suggest 4 o'clock on Tuesday at General Smuts's office in the Palace of Justice?

Before receiving your letter I gave a message re congress to the *Star*, which will publish it this afternoon.[1]

Kindly assure General Smuts that I am making no claim on behalf of anyone, and believe that I will bring my crowd into the fused party, if, as a result of the meeting, they and I are officially invited to help to make fusion a success. Sincerely yours,

Tielman Roos

348   To T. Roos   Vol. 50, no. 175

Pretoria
1 Desember 1933

Waarde Roos, Na aanleiding van die gesprek wat Pirow en ek gister met u gehad het wens ons te herhaal die versekering wat ons u toe gegee het, dat u medewerking met die nuwe party ons aangenaam sal wees en dat ons die stap hartelik sal verwelkom.

Pirow wens nadruk daarop te lê dat sy versekering ook weergee die houding van sy Transvaalse kollegas.

Weens die ingewikkelde machinerie van die bestaande partye en die noodige konsultasies daarmee neem die stigting van die nuwe party 'n beetje tyd, maar ons twyfel nie aan volkome sukses. Ons beskou u eventueele toetreding as die natuurlike ding, en voel versekerd dat dit sal bydra tot die bereiking van daardie breë basis van nasionale samewerking wat ons almal beoog het met die koalisie beweging en wat ons verwag spoedig sal lei tot die totstandkoming van die nuwe party. Geheel die uwe, *t.t.*

J. C. Smuts

---

[1] In his press message Roos said that a congress of his group would meet on 31 January 1934. Its purpose was to advance fusion; it was not aimed at the government. He hoped that steps to relieve the burden on farmers would be taken and declared that the problem of unemployment must be solved.

TRANSLATION

Pretoria

1 December 1933

Dear Roos, In connection with the conversation which Pirow and I had with you yesterday, we wish to repeat the assurance that we gave you then that your co-operation with the new party will be a pleasure to us and that we shall heartily welcome such a step.

Pirow wishes to emphasize that his assurance also reflects the attitude of his Transvaal colleagues.

Because of the complicated machinery of the existing parties and the consultations with it that are necessary, the founding of the new party is taking a little time, but we have no doubt of complete success. We regard your eventual accession as the natural thing and feel sure that it will contribute to the achievement of that broad basis of national co-operation which we all envisaged in the coalition movement and which we expect will soon lead to the establishment of the new party. Yours sincerely, *totus tuus*,

J. C. Smuts

349   To J. L. Landau   Vol. 52, no. 97

21 January 1934

Dear Dr Landau, I feel deeply honoured by the suggestion of the South African Zionist Organization that a tract of land in Palestine should be called after my name. To be thus associated with the Zionist cause and to have my name placed on the map of the Holy Land is indeed a rare distinction, and I am deeply moved by the generous feeling which has inspired the suggestion.[1]

My work for Zionism has from the first been a labour of love and gratitude. The services of the small Jewish people to humanity have been incomparably great and our western civilization today still lives largely on the visions of Hebrew prophets and seers. That such a people should continue exiles from their ancient homeland throughout the ages was an historic anomaly and injustice which called for reparation. Hence my original connection with the shaping of the policy of the national home and my deep interest in its execution ever since.

I believe that that policy was one of the noblest and truest inspirations of the Great War and will outlast most of the other

---

[1] The settlement, about 600 acres in extent, in Palestine named after Smuts was called Kfar Jochanan Smuts and is in the region Emek Zebulun, near Haifa.

results of that period. Up to date the success has been most striking. Jewish immigrants and generosity have already made of Palestine the most prosperous little country of the Old World. With the persistence for which the Jewish people are famous this process will continue until ancient prophecy is fulfilled and the glorious return is finally consummated.

There is much in the Jewish situation today that is disquieting and even menacing. But the people who taught the world the supreme value of faith is not likely to be daunted by temporary setbacks. They will follow their star to the end. Now that they have recovered their base in the ancient homeland they can look forward with ever increasing confidence to the future.

The national home will be built anew, as the Temple was rebuilt after the captivity. The waste places will be restored. In the desert the deep spiritual springs will be set flowing, to fertilize once more the thought and the spiritual life of mankind. The Isaiahs, the Spinozas, the Einsteins will once more be guiding lights on our human path.

I gratefully and humbly accept the honour of having my name placed on the map of the Holy Land. Yours ever sincerely,

s. J. C. Smuts

350   To A. B. Gillett   Vol. 52, no. 145

Tsalta
[Cape Town]
31 January 1934

Thank you for your last letter and your reflections on the times. I note your perplexities and doubts. But who today is not full of them? And why should we always look for a clear and straight road before us? The later nineteenth century had that smooth and smiling appearance. And you know how we were all horribly taken in and deceived by those appearances. When the storm burst on us in 1914 we thought it incredible that there could be such folly and madness in high places. No, it is much better to see and to know that it is a dangerous world and that our way is risky and difficult. I think it is good for all this to have come into the open. It is not really a worse world. I believe there is today as much genuine good feeling and religious aspiration as there has ever been in the past. But evil and wrong are more open and therefore better provided against. It is the decay of the old liberal principles and practices which I feel most as a distinct deterioration. Democracy, having reached all the masses, has taken on more than it can handle. The dark instinctive forces in society are coming to the surface and find expression in autocracy, denial of liberty and free thought. Bolshevism, Fascism and Nazism are upon us. But it only means that the fight for freedom has to take place in new forms and on a new stage. The old freedom has fallen into decay and inefficiency, as all good things do in time. The new freedom will arise and our children will be all the better for having had to fight for it again.

Jan

351   To L. S. Amery   Vol. 52, no. 99

Office of the Minister of Justice
Cape Town
1 February 1934

My dear Amery, Thank you very much for your welcome and interesting letter which arrived by last mail. It is always a great pleasure to hear from you.

In spite of the international situation, the economic position does seem to be improving in most countries. Here in South Africa, we are probably on the eve of remarkable developments. The depreciation of the pound has meant a rise in the price of gold such as was never thought possible, with the result that the mining industry is now expanding on a scale beyond all our fondest dreams. New properties are opening in all directions, and old low-grade ore which was never thought capable of being worked is now being worked all over the Rand.

Besides this, we have had, and are having, a great rainy season, such as I have never seen in this country. Wool and other agricultural prices are up, and we may therefore look to a rapid agricultural recovery. Mining and agriculture will therefore lead to an era of prosperity in this country which will make a very great difference after the bad years we have behind us.

I think Roosevelt's policy of working down the dollar has been undoubtedly right. The most unfavourable part of his policy is the huge debt he is running up in times of peace. However, I suppose the United States can carry a big increase of debt, hoping by it to have a recovery as early as possible, whatever the ultimate consequences may be. It would be a fatal thing for your export trade if the pound does not keep step with the dollar, and I sincerely hope Chamberlain [N.] will depreciate the pound so that the dollar does not steal a march on us.

It is difficult to form any opinion on the international situation. To all appearances, it has been getting worse and worse in recent months. And yet one has a feeling that behind appearances there may really be the makings of a revival and improvement. It depends largely on what is really at the back of the German mind. If Hitler[1] really means to make peace with France as he keeps saying, then I have no doubt that we may see a change for the better in the political atmosphere of the Continent. The League has suffered grievously in recent months,[2] and yet it is not impossible that there may be a recovery there too. The United States government is evidently becoming more friendly and helpful. It is quite possible that the defection of Germany may make Russia look more favourably on the League.[3] Things are in a state of flux, and developments may be very different from what one would imagine from the circumstances of today. It is quite possible that both Germany and Japan may well find that they have made a mistake in leaving the League. I do not therefore look upon the situation as one for complete pessimism.

You may be right also that new groupings of a permanent character are in the making on the Continent. There was undoubtedly too much cutting up and starting of new shows after the Great War, but the movement towards new groupings may be full of life and helpful towards the future peace of Europe.

I note what you say on the question of honours. It is doubtful whether the general question of honours will ever be reopened in South Africa.[4] But the case is different with the privy council, and it may be possible to revise the situation there. By the way, it is a thousand pities that in a recent privy council case, the policy which was followed since Union in 1910 was apparently reversed. I refer to the Pearl Insurance case where leave of appeal was granted by the privy council. It was laid down shortly after Union by Lord Haldane as lord chancellor that no appeals from South Africa would be allowed except when great constitutional principles or great principles of law were raised, and this decision has been followed every since, with the result that the privy council always declined

[1] Hitler had become chancellor of Germany on 30 January 1933.

[2] Modifications of the disarmament convention (*see* p. 552, note 2) were proposed on 14 October 1933 whereupon Germany withdrew from the conference. On 23 October she left the League of Nations. On 8 December Italy announced that her continued collaboration with the League would be conditional on its radical reform.

[3] The Soviet Union joined the League of Nations on 19 September 1934.

[4] On 24 February 1925 A. Barlow, a Labour member, moved in the Union house of assembly that an address be presented to the king praying that no honours be in future conferred on his South African subjects. The motion was adopted two days later by a majority of 71 to 47.

leave to appeal in the ordinary sort of case. Now the privy council has reversed this judgment and expressed the opinion that Lord Haldane's judgment was a mere *obiter dictum*,[1] with the result that a very difficult situation has arisen in South Africa. We may be compelled very much against our will to introduce legislation to abolish privy councils altogether. These dear old gentlemen in the house of lords do not know what repercussions their views may have in far distant portions of the Empire. Here in South Africa they have raised a hornets' nest which may have very untoward results. Perhaps you may interest yourself in the matter. We do not want to raise it officially, and the only action we can take is to bring in legislation for doing away with the appeal altogether.[2] Under the South Africa Act our courts cannot give leave to appeal, and the object of this provision was to limit appeals to the privy council as much as possible. You can imagine the hardship to the ordinary South African litigant if his wealthy opponent takes him to an expensive appeal court in London.

In other respects our political situation is developing quite favourably here. The new national government works well together, and I have no doubt that in the near future you will have the Nationalists and the South African party fused into a big central party, which will be a real contribution to political and racial peace in the future. With kind regards and all good wishes, Yours ever sincerely,

s. J. C. Smuts

352   To J. B. M. Hertzog   Vol. 52, no. 101

352 and 353 were published in both the English and the Afrikaans daily newspapers.

18 February 1934

My dear Hertzog, Since the publication of the correspondence which has passed between you and the head committee of the Cape National party you and I have talked over matters in order to avoid any difficulties and misunderstandings which may arise in consequence of that correspondence. In view of the widespread public interest in the correspondence, and the interpretation which has in certain quarters been placed upon it, I consider it advisable for the objects we both have in view that I should put to you in

---

[1] An incidental remark.

[2] Appeal to the privy council was abolished in the Union of South Africa by statute in April 1950 (Act No. 16 of 1950).

writing some of the points which seemed to me likely to give rise to difficulties.[1]

In the first place there is the question of procedure for the further negotiations for the purpose of formulating a draft programme for the new party. The impression is that a change has been made in the procedure which has hitherto been followed in our discussions, and that in future a draft programme will be drawn up by you in consultation with the federal council of the National parties, and presented to me. If this impression is correct, it would become necessary for me similarly to call in the assistance of the head committee of the South African party, and in that case we should have the two parties, instead of their two leaders, discussing at arm's length points of difficulty which might arise, perhaps with little chance of agreement. I am sure that you can publicly remove such an impression and give the assurance that the procedure hitherto followed will be continued, and that the discussions of the draft programme between you and me will proceed unhampered, subject of course to the ultimate decision of our respective congresses.

We have also discussed certain matters raised in the correspondence which appeared to me to go beyond the seven points upon which coalition was based. I mention these points here in order that they may be cleared up in such a way as to avoid public misunderstanding:

(a) *Definition of status*

While you have refused to agree to specific issues arising from our status being raised in the programme of principles, you have expressed yourself personally on such matters as the divisibility of the crown, the right of neutrality, and the right of secession. As you know, while I wholeheartedly accept our sovereign status, as confirmed by the Statute of Westminster,[2] I do not subscribe to these conceptions as being inherent in that status. I assume there-

---

[1] When negotiations for fusion of the South African party and the National party began, the Cape National party, under the leadership of D. F. Malan, opposed full amalgamation. They sought and obtained assurances on a number of points from Hertzog and correspondence between them was published on 16 February 1934. Smuts then told Hertzog that this public agreement with the Cape Nationalists had made his own position impossible and proposed to end further negotiations for fusion. On 17 February he sent Hertzog, for publication, a letter which Hertzog considered to be 'aggressive'. After discussion between them Smuts wrote the revised letter of 18 February. (*See* O. Pirow, *James Barry Munnik Hertzog*, pp. 164–79.)

[2] This statute, enacted on 11 December 1931, gave effect to the resolutions on status passed by the imperial conferences of 1926 and 1930.

fore that these are matters of interpretation on which we differ and have differed, and that they are not matters on which we are called upon to come to an agreement in drawing up a programme of principles.

(b) *Nationality*

In view of the general and somewhat indefinite reference to this matter in the correspondence, I thought it necessary to raise the subject with you, as I was not prepared to agree to the inclusion in the programme of principles or otherwise of anything which would mean a substantial modification being made in respect of our common status within the British Commonwealth alongside of our Union citizenship. I was reassured by what you said to me and feel certain that a similar statement by you will reassure public opinion.

(c) *Republican propaganda*

This matter arising out of the correspondence was also discussed between us. While not desiring to impose restrictions on the expression by members of the party of their individual opinions as to the form of our constitution, I consider it necessary that any references to this in the statement of principles should be governed by a clear declaration that the party as such stands for the maintenance of the constitutional position as laid down in the South Africa Act and the Statute of Westminster. I have hitherto understood that we are agreed on this matter and trust that you will be able to remove any public misconception thereon.

With any possible misunderstanding as to our position removed by our conversations and this correspondence, I hope it will be possible for us to resume at once the discussions which we had at Pretoria on the draft programme of principles, and that the achievement of the great object of national unity which we both have in view will before long be an accomplished fact. Yours sincerely,

s. J. C. Smuts

353   From J. B. M. Hertzog   Vol. 51, no. 145

Prime Minister's Office
Groote Schuur
18 February 1934

My dear Smuts, I have just received yours of even date saying that 'in view of the widespread public interest in the correspondence between me and the head committee of the Cape National party', you consider it 'advisable for the objects we both have in view' that you should put to me 'in writing some of the points which seemed to you likely to give rise to difficulties'.

The first point you raise is that of *procedure*. I wish at once to assure you that there is no idea with me of changing the method of procedure which from the first I intended to follow in respect of our discussions, and with which already in Pretoria an informal commencement had been made before our coming down to Cape Town for the session. As far as the published correspondence with the head committee of the Cape National party is concerned, it was never contemplated thereby to do anything more than to determine the procedure within the National party. I have, therefore, no hesitation in giving you the assurance you ask for.

As to the following points mentioned by you, I desire to make the following answers:

(a) *Definition of status*: Re the questions of divisibility of the crown, the right of neutrality and the right of secession, I agree that these are matters of interpretation on which we differ and that they are not matters on which we are called upon to come to an agreement in drawing up a programme of principles.

(b) *Nationality*: The question of our common status within the Commonwealth, as also that of our Union citizenship are matters which were dealt with at the last imperial conference and decided upon, so that there is no necessity for including in the programme of principles anything which would mean a substantial modification in respect of either of these matters.

(c) *Republican propaganda*: On this point too I think we are in complete agreement, viz. that while the programme of principles of the new party should clearly state that the party as such stands for the maintenance of the constitutional position as laid down in the South Africa Act and the Statute of Westminister no member of the new party will be prohibited from expressing his personal opinion as to the form of our constitution or from advocating any change therein.

In conclusion I wish to assure you that I shall be only too glad to resume discussions with you the moment parliamentary and other public business will allow us to do so. I feel confident that the people of the Union will rejoice most heartily if we could accomplish our great task on a basis of true national unity. Yours sincerely,

J. B. M. Hertzog

354 To M. E. van Zyl   Vol. 52, no. 102

Cape Town
21 February 1934

Dear Mrs van Zyl, Ever so many thanks, first for the beautiful figs, and now for your sympathetic note on recent developments. One is often reduced to something like despair. Yet, knowing how pure our own intentions and how deep the longing of the people for racial and political peace, we can but go on in faith and hope, but open-eyed and knowing it is dangerous going. Ever yours lovingly,

J. C. Smuts

355 To M. C. Gillett   Vol. 52, no. 149

Tsalta
[Cape Town]
21 February 1934

Louis [McIldowie] and I have just returned from our evening after-dinner walk. We are in the habit of going as often as we can to Kirstenbosch after supper and enjoy the experience very much. Of course it is not comparable to the after supper walks which we had from 'Crossways'[1] to Lowbury. But could anything be as good as that? Even to think of it is to fill me with a mild ecstasy. But this is also quite good in its way and helps to keep me fit and her weight down...

No, last air mail brought nothing from you, and so there is nothing to answer. But even so I never have difficulty in filling a letter to you with nonsense talk. And firstly, you will be amused to hear that I have had this week a most hectic time politically. General Hertzog took it upon himself to make peace with Dr Malan and to conclude the peace in an exchange of letters which left the poor South African party in the air. My little plan seemed all gone and I was beginning to make other plans for the future. But then I tackled the General with the result that he left the Doctor in the air, and again returned to unity with the South African party.[2] A right-about-face in one week! That is how we carry on in South Africa. What Dr Malan is now thinking of it all Lord only knows. But I am not yet rejoicing as there may be another somersault soon. The Malanites are determined to wreck the fusion of parties and the coming together of the races. But Hertzog cannot now drop the South African party without coming a nasty cropper, and I think

---

[1] The Gilletts' cottage at Aston Tirrold.   [2] *See* **352, 353.**

he genuinely desires racial peace. To me it is a funny thing that Nel [Petronella] van Heerden is now violently anti-Hertzog and anti-fusion. What harm she sees in us poor Sappies I cannot make out. The Steyn family is hopelessly split—Gladys and Colin are with Roos, Mrs Steyn with Hertzog (and me), Emmie[1] and the van der Merwes[2] are violently pro-Dr Malan. But these antics of the ants don't perhaps amuse you, I fear.

So poor Dollfuss [E.] has suppressed his Socialists and handed himself over to the tender mercies of the Nazis.[3] His only chance seemed to me to carry the Socialists with him against Hitler. But now he must take his medicine. I am very sorry, for he was a gallant soul. Meanwhile a first-class situation must be developing over Austria. Disarmament is more and more receding into the background and rearmaments (and the devil) coming into the picture. And yet, and yet, I don't lose heart quite. Somehow I cannot believe the world is going quite mad. However powerful a force passion is, reason backed by self-interest (as in this case of Europe) *must* in the end prevail. And the soul sickness of Europe cannot continue for ever.

I am leaving this week for Kimberley to unveil a monument to our Coloured troops who fell in the war. It is a great bother to me, but I like to honour the memory of these brave men—Coloured men too. I shall be back on Tuesday and in time to write you again, I hope. Isie and the rest very well and happy. Dear love to you and your and my dear ones. Ever,

Jan

356   To R. J. K. Russell   Vol. 52, no. 108

Library of Parliament
Cape Town
24 March 1934

Dear Russell, I return your letter of 18 March to you as I cannot accept such a letter from you. Not only does it give a garbled and inaccurate account of our conversation last September, but it levels a veiled charge of betrayal of trust at me which I cannot accept

---

[1] Third daughter of President Steyn; married J. S. du Toit.

[2] N. J. van der Merwe and his wife, Isabella Gordon, youngest daughter of President Steyn. *See* vol. IV, p. 394.

[3] Dr E. Dolfuss, chancellor of Austria, opposed by both the Nazis and the Socialists, had assumed a virtual dictatorship. In February 1934 the Socialists, having been goaded into armed action, were suppressed by the Heimwehr using artillery and killing hundreds.

from anyone. This letter does you no justice, and nothing in our past relations justified such a communication from you to me. I am sure you will on reflection agree with me. A communication like this ought really to end relations between us. But I have always tried to be patient with you, and do so again. But this note I cannot possibly accept. Yours sincerely,

s. J. C. Smuts

ENCLOSURE

The Natal Mercury
Durban
18 March 1934

General Smuts,
Minister of Justice.

Dear General, A point seems to have been reached at which a definite issue of personal honour is raised, and I propose to state it to you with the frankness which our relations have always encouraged.

I wish to recall to you the circumstances under which I made my visit to Pretoria to see you and the prime minister last September. It was made very clear to you, I think, that the main reason for my interview with you was the acute concern felt in Natal at the demands of the Malanites, as an essential condition of their co-operation in fusion, for the abolition of British nationality and citizenship in the Union, the interpretation of the new constitutional status so that this country would be able at any time to declare its neutrality (that is by the device of dividing the crown), and for the right to continue active propaganda within the new fusion party, for the establishment of a republic. This concern was heightened by the fact that in his speeches in the Free State immediately prior to my visit the prime minister had publicly accepted the Malan claims and had even committed yourself to the promise that you would agree.

I represented to you what our views were on these matters, and that I had been requested to obtain from you assurances which would allay the unrest in Natal, so that the *Natal Mercury* might continue to work wholeheartedly for a re-alignment of parties on the non-racial basis of the seven coalition points.

You will also recall that I expressed to you the doubts left in my mind after my long talk with the prime minister, when I found him harping constantly on the fact that, in the light of the imperial conference declaration of 1926 and the Statute of Westminster, British citizenship in the Union was now an anachronism which had to be replaced by a vague and entirely undefined thing called the 'common status'. Your reply to me (which, in the discharge of my duty, I reported to those to whom I am responsible) was very definite and unequivocal on these points. You indicated that you greatly resented the prime minister's action in seeking to commit you to acceptance of the things he told the Free State he 'was sure' you would gladly concede in the new party. You remarked to me, with an emphasis which I have never forgotten, 'You may rest assured I shall never betray my English-speaking followers, who have been so loyal to me.' And to give special point to that remark you drew my attention to the fact that in the act of Union the qualification for membership of the senate and the house of assembly was that one *must* be 'a British subject of European descent'. This foundation of British South African rights in South Africa you assured me could never be removed with your consent, and, as far as my memory serves me, I think you went on to state a point I have heard you make in public on several occasions—that in your opinion any amendment of the act of Union touching fundamental rights, either as regards the division of the crown or changes in the basis of citizenship qualification, would require also an amending act by the parliament of Westminster. In concluding the assurance, you roughly outlined to me what you proposed to say in your speech at Johannesburg on the following evening, and you told me that, if I bore in mind the special difficulty you had in too bluntly stating an attitude which might at that stage tend to drive Hertzog back into the arms of Dr Malan, I would be perfectly satisfied with your assurances at that meeting: you were not going to budge an inch beyond the coalition points, and you were going to reject all those apples of discord as regards nationality, division of the crown, etc.

From first to last, until the last week, I have never once doubted your assurances on these points. You will therefore understand with what acute personal concern I regard the knowledge that you appear to have acquiesced in an amendment of the act of Union deleting the qualification of 'British subject'. If this change takes place it is quite futile for us to rely on the fact that under the Union nationality laws, as they exist at present, a Union national is defined as one who possesses British citizenship, for the prime minister has himself declared the intention to change that British citizenship into a 'common status', and you yourself, in your letter to Hertzog after the publication of the Malan–Hertzog correspondence, threw in a carefully prepared phrase which, by implication, accepted the change to a 'common status' as not a 'substantial modification' of our nationality.

There are few things about which I am concerned, but one of them most definitely is my personal honour, and I cannot square the assurances I gave to my directors and others here in Natal after my interview with you in Pretoria with the plain fact of the proposed deletion of 'British subject' from the act of Union. If there is to be a betrayal of our trust on this point I cannot possibly remain a silent party to it, and I hope that if my conscience ever urges me to speak on the subject you will absolve me from any implication of confidence as regards what I have here related concerning our talk in Pretoria. Yours sincerely,

R. J. Kingston Russell

357   To M. P. A. Hankey   Vol. 52, no. 108A

Library of Parliament
Cape Town
7 April 1934

My dear Hankey, Your letter of 11 March was very welcome and read with much interest. I am glad you are having this holiday to Australia this year and hope you and Lady Hankey[1] will thoroughly enjoy the change. I also had an invitation from Australia to attend the centenary functions, but as I have to be in Scotland in October as rector of St Andrews[2] I cannot go and I fear I may even be on my way to England by air when you arrive here at the beginning of September. It would, however, be a great pity if you don't see Johannesburg and Pretoria and I would strongly advise you to go north between the 3 and 17 September and either join the *Ceramic* at Cape Town or at Durban. The north is the hub of the Union. The government will be up there in September.

We are having some trouble over Hertzog's Status Bill[3] which has been represented to our English friends as preparing the way for secession and neutrality. This is, of course, nonsense. But many people here have never accepted the new status of the Dominions, and I am afraid that we are in for a good deal of political unpleasant-

[1] Born Adeline de Smidt, daughter of Abraham de Smidt, formerly surveyor-general, Cape Colony; married M. P. A. Hankey in 1903.

[2] Smuts had been elected rector of St Andrews University in 1931.

[3] Enacted as the Status of the Union Act, No. 48 of 1934. It asserted the sovereignty of the Union parliament by providing that no legislation of the British parliament would apply in the Union unless specifically enacted by the parliament of the Union. *See also* **358**.

ness. As this is a recurrent trouble it is better to get through it now. The status question has largely divided the English and Dutch population into two racial camps in the past, and from all points of view it should now be cleared out of the way. It is a great step to accept our sovereign status *within* the Empire as the settled policy of this country. The alternative is a sort of Irish mentality on Empire matters.

I am deeply interested in all you write about disarmament and other European troubles. I am afraid that we are not halfway through those troubles yet. While Hitler has done much for Germany morally and politically, the economic position (which is basic) is getting steadily worse. I fear a collapse of Germany and of Hitler, and then the real trouble will start; Communism has only been driven underground. In France, too, the position looks very unstable. The nations founded and run on freedom may find themselves opposed to a chaotic world, and unless America co-operates with us, the situation may become very serious. I do not fear war so much as this decay in the structure of our civilization, the disappearance of liberalism and liberty, and the return to chaos and tyranny. Happily, for the moment, most countries within our Commonwealth are on the upgrade, and in England the signs of revival appear fairly sound. I pity the statesmen who have to lead the world under the troubles of today. It may all be very interesting, but it is very difficult for those who have to act and not merely watch the scene.

I am glad you are getting away from the strain for a few months. There is a good deal of hard work ahead. With kind regards and all good wishes, Ever yours sincerely,

J. C. Smuts

358   Speech (1934)

Smuts made this speech on 11 April 1934 in the house of assembly during the second reading of the Status of the Union Bill. (*See House of Assembly Debates*, vol. 23, cols. 2071–83.)

The minister of justice: I am sure that we have all listened with the greatest interest to the suggestive and thoughtful speech of the honourable member for Cathcart (Mr [C. M.] van Coller). He has put a number of categorical questions to my friend, the minister of railways,[1] and perhaps I can relieve the honourable member's anxiety by dealing with them very briefly. At the outset I should

[1] O. Pirow.

explain that I have been prevented by circumstances from taking part in the debate at an earlier stage, but there are things which will best come from me, and I would like to state to the house and the country the view I take of this bill and its provisions and their bearings. In the first place, I wish also to pay a tribute to the high level of this debate and the good spirit in which it has been carried on. The debate has been a credit to this house. I also wish to say how much I have appreciated the reception given to these bills[1] by the country generally. There is no doubt that these bills have brought large sections of our people in South Africa up against a very difficult situation, and the way that our people all over the country, with a few exceptions, have viewed these bills and accepted them is to my mind very creditable indeed to their intelligence and patriotism. There are certain exceptions, small areas of this country, in which there has been a tendency to work up an agitation, but that has been more due to newspaper action than to the independent action of the people themselves. I think on the whole the country has taken these bills calmly, and I am sure that the debate which is taking place in this house, both by friends and by opponents of these bills, will help to pacify and calm feeling, and to make people understand really what these bills mean, what their import is. A somewhat unfortunate impression has been created partly by the press. When I refer to the press I must say this in fairness to the press, that on the whole I think the press has behaved magnificently in connection with this contentious matter, and when I refer to the press I do not do so in a spirit of fault-finding. But a section of the press has stated that there is something sinister in connection with the introduction of these bills. It has even been suggested that there is some secret agreement between the prime minister and myself, and that we are on dangerous ground and have to tread very warily. I would remind the house that in the governor-general's speech these bills were announced. We said there, right at the beginning, that bills were going to be introduced. And for what purpose? The language was important because it was carefully considered at the time—'Bills would be introduced to bring the Union's legislation in harmony with the present constitutional position.' That was the intention announced in the governor-general's speech, and that is the intention which we are trying to carry out in these bills. No, sir, there is nothing to hide; there is nothing to shirk as far as I am concerned in these bills. I am

---

[1] The Royal Executive Functions and Seals Bill complemented the Status of the Union Bill. The subsequent act secured the complete independence of the Union executive.

confident that we have an absolutely good case for these bills, a one hundred per cent case, and I am prepared to argue out the whole matter from beginning to end. I have from the very first moment taken my party into my confidence over these bills. Before they were introduced into this house, I read them with my friends in caucus and we discussed them carefully, in an earlier form and in their subsequent form, and on the whole my party, with a few exceptions, were quite agreed to accept these bills. There were exceptions; my party has not been entirely agreed. It has been an old charge against us that we are not always in agreement, a very honourable charge, and at times I have had a very difficult job with some of my friends. And I had it here. But I know that they are honest and sincere. I know that some of them are severely troubled in their minds, and I for one am prepared to bear with them. I only ask them to bear with me too. We discussed these bills most fully in caucus before they were introduced, and I gave my party all the information at my disposal. The suggestion has been made that these bills come before this house in order to carry out certain promises which the prime minister made to the head committee of his party according to recent correspondence. I have already quoted the object of these bills, and explained how they were introduced and announced on the very first day of the session, long before this correspondence took place, and I have stated, for the information of the country, how these bills were dealt with by the government. The bills were originally drafted in the prime minister's office by the special legal adviser to the prime minister's department, and they were entrusted to the minister of railways, as he seemed a more neutral person than the prime minister or myself.

Mr Madeley: An umpire.

The minister of justice: We discussed these bills, especially the Status Bill which is now before us, clause by clause, not once, but repeatedly, over and over again, until finally this bill emerged in a form which was entirely new, and honourable members may take it from me that this bill which we are now discussing in its present form is the bill absolutely and truly of the whole cabinet. You may say that if ever a bill was drafted in cabinet by the whole cabinet, this is the bill. I may let the house into a further secret, and it is this, that some of the most contentious clauses, some of the clauses over which controversy has raged hottest, emanated from the members of the South African party in the cabinet. I say that in answer to my honourable friend when he says that this bill represents an effort of the honourable member for Calvinia (Dr D. F.

Malan), and the members of the head committee of the Nationalist
party in the Cape Province. So far from that, these bills are the
work of the whole cabinet. This bill which we are discussing is
the work of the whole cabinet, and I assume the fullest responsibility for these bills. This matter has been going on for a long
time, and these bills have been for months under my personal consideration. I have searched my conscience, I have searched my
legal knowledge, I have searched my experience of a lifetime in
the working of constitutions, and I am satisfied that nothing is done
here, and nothing is asked from the people of the country here,
which ought not to be asked of them. We must bear in mind that
there are some lawyers in the cabinet, too, and men with a good
deal of knowledge not only of the law but of the actual working of
constitutions, which is an even more difficult matter; men of very
good practical experience in these matters; and where we have
come to an agreement, not as a matter of compromise but as a
matter of trying to do the right thing, I think some weight ought
to be attached to the immense experience and training in these
matters which lie behind this bill. Let me say this, and this is more
important still—that the whole cabinet was absolutely unanimous
in their intention that nothing should be done but to express the
existing constitutional position—that formula I read for the king's
speech absolutely governed the whole situation as far as we were
concerned. We had nothing to do with the controversies which
have been raised on the floor of the house and in the country. Our
object was simply to put into legal language, as far as human
knowledge could do, the actual constitutional position as we
understood it. No, there was no intention whatever to deal with
contentious issues or to go a step beyond the existing position.
I have in writing the prime minister's promise that the points on
which we had differed in the past would not be touched; that we
would continue to differ on them.[1] My honourable friend did not
refer to that part of the correspondence. I do not think it was right
for him to refer to the correspondence with the head committee
without referring to the correspondence, which was far more important, which dealt with these matters. I had his promise, and we
were perfectly agreed on that—that we never intended to raise
those issues on this bill. This bill is a measure of common agreement
on the vital issues of our constitution. I mention this because it is
most important. The country should know it, the house should
know it, and the future should know it—that there was no intention
on the part of the cabinet to go a step further than to express in

---

[1] *See* **352, 353.**

legal language the existing constitutional position. And what is more, here we come to the house and we state that to the house and we state that fact to the country. My honourable friend the minister of railways and harbours has done so; my honourable friend the minister of mines[1] has done so, and my honourable friend the minister of education[2] has done so. I am doing so, and whatever minister here speaks in the debate will tell you that within our purview and intention as we view the matter, this Status Bill does not go one inch beyond the existing legal constitutional position in this country. Well, that is very important for the working of this bill in future. The light by which it should be interpreted is this governing declaration which is made here, which has been made by my colleagues and by myself, and on which we are unanimous. It is human to err; I do not say we have erred; but this is what underlies this bill. It does not travel one inch beyond the existing position but states the position as we understand it, and as it is. If, in future, there are questions of interpretation, that is the governing principle. We understand this bill to be merely declaratory of the present position, and it ought to be interpreted in future, and we ought to be guided in future, in that spirit. Now I think, in the light of this statement, the importance of which ought to be appreciated, there ought to be no difficulty. It is an idea which seems to be in some minds, and to which I am afraid expression has been given by the honourable member for Cape Town (Gardens) (Mr [C. W. A.] Coulter), that there is some other object to be achieved by these bills; that is entirely wrong. We simply wanted to express, as far as we were able, the existing position. Now I come to this bill itself. I am going to test the clauses of this bill in the light of this declaration I have just made. What does this bill say? It begins with a preamble which deals quite clearly and frankly with, and sets out quite fully, the whole position as it has developed since 1926. It starts with that basic declaration of 1926—the Balfour declaration of 1926,[3] sets forth what happened subsequently, the Statute of Westminister,[4] and in that way the preamble sets forth the whole position under our common law, that we have a system of states equal, autonomous, free, none subject to the other; that we are a free association in the British Commonwealth of nations, and that we owe common allegiance to the crown. The matter is followed up by a schedule, which sets out the Statute of Westminster—not only the operative clauses, but even the preamble of the Statute of Westminster so far as it applies to South Africa. This

[1] P. Duncan.   [2] J. H. Hofmeyr.
[3] *See supra*, p. 335, note 3.   [4] *See supra*, p. 574, note 2.

bill then goes on to make certain provisions and I am going to mention under these provisions those which seem to be important and
ought to be discussed in this house. In the first place, we have the
provision which says who our king is in the constitution.

Mr [F. C.] Erasmus: And his heirs and successors.

The minister of justice: The present king is known and settled, and
we extend the provision to his heirs and successors too, to provide
for the future. There is no change in that and it has been the practice hitherto, and has been laid down in the South Africa Act of
1910. No change is made there. And surely it is a matter of great
importance that we should have this solemn reaffirmation, in what
will largely be our constitution in future, of the position of the crown
as existing hitherto, and as was laid down in the South Africa Act.
Surely in the light of all the controversies which have raged in this
country, it is a matter of profound importance that it should be
done. No change is made. We are expressing once more for the
present and for the future the existing constitutional position of
the crown. I look upon that as most important. This is the first
important provision. The second provision that is important deals
with what is called here 'the sovereignty of parliament'. I submit,
and honourable members will agree with me, that in this clause we
do not travel beyond what is and has been the existing position both
in practice and as laid down in the Statute of Westminster. I am not
going to cover the position which my honourable friend, the member for Roodepoort (Colonel Stallard), and also the honourable
member for Cape Town (Gardens) (Mr Coulter) raised here
whether there is still a residuary legislative power of the British
parliament. All that we say here in this provision of the bill is this,
that no British act shall apply to this country unless it is covered
by an act of our own parliament. There may be some residuary
power left in the British parliament. I do not know. It is not a
matter that we need argue upon now, but we make the position
perfectly plain as far as we are concerned, that is, that only an act
of our parliament will bind South Africa in future. If there is a British act and it has to have any relation to us, we must make it our
act. That is what is laid down here. Surely we are not travelling
in the least beyond either the existing practice or the Statute of
Westminster. The Statute of Westminster uses the words 'agreement and consent', but honourable members will understand that
that is a vague expression. The question is: how is parliament going
to give its 'agreement and consent'? We do it by act and we lay
down here that it is only by act of our own parliament that any
law passed elsewhere shall apply to us. That is the Statute of West-

minster and that has been the practice. I do not remember a single case since we had our constitution given us in 1910 where a British act has been applied except by our own act. Take a very important case which has special reference to us here, that is, the British naturalization act. The imperial conference agreed that there should be a uniform naturalization act throughout the Commonwealth. A model act was passed in the United Kingdom and it was applied here to us by our own act, just as we are doing in the bill today. The practice of the law as laid down in the Statute of Westminster is carried out here and we do not in intention or in language go an inch beyond that. Now we come to the executive government, and that is the provision which the honourable member for Roodepoort (Colonel Stallard) has made the most of. It is provided that in executive government, both in internal and in external affairs, the king acts on the advice of his South African ministers. I ask whether that has not been the practice. There is only one answer to that. It has been the uniform and invariable practice in this country ever since we received a constitution in 1910. There has never been any other way of acting. The king or the governor-general as his deputy has always and invariably acted in the executive government of the country on the advice of his ministers. It has been our practice, it is the British practice. As long as there is a government the king acts on its advice, and no innovation whatever is made here on the practice that has existed hitherto. It is the very nature of responsible government. Responsible government means that the king acts on the advice of his ministers and if he did not, there would not be responsible government, there would be autocracy. I am trying to prove my case that we have not travelled an inch beyond the existing practice and the existing law. These are the provisions, the really important and governing provisions, in this bill—who is our king in South Africa, what is the authority of our parliament and who is our executive government? And I say that in the provisions laid down here, which were very carefully considered in the cabinet and drafted and re-drafted, over and over again, we have tried to express what is the existing position in practice and what has been agreed to at imperial conferences and laid down in the Statute of Westminster. The honourable member for Roodepoort (Colonel Stallard) says we have travelled in two or three respects beyond the existing position. I am going to deal with the exceptions which he says we have made to the existing position. He says that where we use the words 'sovereign independence' in the preamble, that is new, and travels beyond the existing position. There may be some difference of

opinion as to the wisdom and expediency of using those words, but
if you ask me the question whether we have the right and are we
right to call our present status by that name, then I have no doubt
whatever, and I think there can be no doubt. The whole position
rests on that fundamental and governing declaration of the conference in 1926. It is set out here, in the preamble, and to my mind
the most important part of that declaration, which is often overlooked and which I am afraid my honourable friend has overlooked,
is what I may call the equation between Great Britain and the
Dominions. That is the governing thing. That was the most daring
part of the declaration of 1926, to equate Great Britain with the
Dominions. She is mentioned with them, she is lumped together
with them, in this declaration. That I call the great equation of
Commonwealth, upon which our Commonwealth rests. If that
equation is fundamental, if that is really what this great declaration
of 1926 meant, then how can you conceivably argue that the Dominions are not sovereign international independent states, without
denying that Great Britain, which is equated with them, has that
status in the world? It seems to me an utter absurdity, and it is only
the unwillingness of some of my friends to face that situation that
makes them boggle over this language. The British statesmen did
not boggle over it. This formula was agreed to by the most powerful
Conservative government that Great Britain has ever had. This
formula was drafted by two of the most able and experienced ministers that England has ever had. Lord Balfour is especially associated
with this declaration. Surely he was not the man to be caught nap-
ping, or to use words in absent-mindedness. He wrote down this
formula, and the other man who was responsible more than any
other was the lord chancellor of that day, probably the most brilliant lord chancellor England has had in our generation, Lord
Birkenhead. These were two of the brilliant men on the British
side. Lord Birkenhead stood out amongst the lord chancellors of
our day and was probably one of the ablest men to have held that
position. Then we had Lord Balfour. His experience, wisdom and
knowledge of the Empire was such as no one could question. These
men were not afraid. These men wrote down the grand equation
of the Commonwealth which equates Great Britain whith the
Dominions. Do not let us boggle over the words. If Great Britain
is a sovereign international state, then by the laws of Euclid, by
the laws of thought, the same thing can be applied to any of the
Dominions. This was not only great statesmanship but it was great
faith in the future of the Empire, of the Commonwealth. These
men knew the traditions of their race. They knew the essence of

the British constitution, they knew and they had faith in the other members of the Empire and they did not boggle over the formula of equality. Do not let us do it. Although some of us may not like the word, some of us may hark back to the past and to what my honourable friend has somewhat ungenerously called the 'crown colony mentality'; do not let us here in this country do that. Let us have equal faith and equal pride in British institutions and in the nature of the great group to which we belong. Freedom, equality are the essence of it. I do not think we have made a departure there, except in the mere form of words. Nothing is implied in the words 'sovereign independence' which is not implied by the whole full Balfour formula as written down. It has been pointed out in this debate that sovereign independence in the preamble is defined by those resolutions and declarations of the past. That is so. But I am not labouring that point. I think we are on safe ground by pinning our faith to that grand equation that was laid down in 1926 and which is the very foundation and will continue to be the foundation of the Empire. If there is to be any question of that equation, then it will be a bad day for our whole group. Now I come to the second point which my honourable friend says is new. He says that in providing that the king in his government in South Africa acts on the advice of his ministers, we have divided the crown; he says that we have intended doing it and we have done it. He says that under the Statute of Westminster, the possibility arises of divided counsels, and therefore if the Empire has to be kept together on great critical and crucial occasions, there must be some authority to keep the Commonwealth together, and he says that we have taken that power away. He says we are binding the king, or his deputy in South Africa to act on the advice of ministers here. He says the king can no longer exercise that prerogative of personal decision on critical occasions which will allow him to save the Empire. Now my answer to that is this. There is no such prerogative. I tried to push my friend for precedents on other occasions where the king had exercised that prerogative of personal action in case of difference. *Mr Nicholls*: Surely, although they have not arisen, they may arise. *The minister of justice*: There is no such prerogative, and if there were such a prerogative left in England, then the British constitution would be an entirely different thing from what it is. The king would be an autocrat. *Col. Stallard*: The necessity may arise as a result of the Statute of Westminister. *The minister of justice*: The honourable member has a quarrel to pick with the Statute of Westminster. I do not agree with him.

Col. Stallard: I have no quarrel with it.

The minister of justice: The argument of the honourable member is this. The Statute of Westminster leaves the opening or creates the opening for divided counsels, and therefore the king must have this prerogative which will make united action possible. He must in the last resort take personal action and make a personal decision. I know my British constitution. I know it from the books, I know it because I have seen it work, and I have actually taken part in its working, and I can assure my friend that there is no such action possible for the king, there is no such prerogative. That prerogative stopped hundreds of years ago, it is a feudal prerogative, which goes back to the Stuart times or earlier. The king has no prerogative of acting on his own without the advice and counter signature of his ministers. What is the prerogative of the king today? He has one undoubted prerogative, and that is to appoint his prime minister. We have all agreed that that is the king's prerogative.

Mr Coulter: He can dissolve parliament and appeal to the country.

The minister of justice: I am inclined to think so myself but I just want to tell my honourable friend that there is no agreement about that. There is no agreement that the king can dissolve parliament and dismiss his ministry without their being first defeated in parliament.

Mr Coulter: It was done in 1842.[1]

The minister of justice: I qualify my statement on this point. I am quite sure that constitutional lawyers are unanimous in thinking that the king has the prerogative of appointing his own prime minister without consulting anyone. Sometimes he does consult, but he need not. There is the celebrated case where Mr Gladstone resigned in 1893, and Lord Rosebery was appointed by the Queen as his successor without Mr Gladstone being consulted. That appears from the correspondence which was published since. There is no question about that. It is customary for the king to consult his trained advisers, but he has undoubtedly the prerogative of deciding who the prime minister is to be, and the governor-general here acts in the same way. But it is perhaps questionable whether he has the other prerogative. That is the prerogative of the king. What else is there? You may say that he has the prerogative to veto a bill passed by both houses, but it is more than questionable whether that veto is still part of his prerogative. It has not been exercised, I believe,

---

[1] 'No Government has been dismissed by the Sovereign since 1783. The general impression in 1834 was that Lord Melbourne's Government was..."turned out neck and crop". The facts now available do not substantiate this conclusion...There was no example after 1834 and it is inconceivable today.' Sir Ivor Jennings, *Cabinet Government* (1937), pp. 299–301.

for more than two hundred years, and if it is part of his prerogative, it is a dead prerogative. There is no prerogative on the part of the king to act on great occasions on his own. He cannot declare war on his own, he must act on the advice of his ministers, and whatever proclamation is issued must be countersigned by his ministers. He cannot make peace on his own. It is done on the advice of his ministers. The king has no prerogative such as my friend there has suggested.

Mr Nicholls: There is no law against it, only practice.

The minister of justice: There is no such prerogative. My honourable friend says that a state of chaos would arise in a crisis. That has been the position and it may be the position again, but it does not arise. The British constitution rests on common sense, it rests on wisdom, it rests on insight, it rests on great experience and on human nature and on none of these technicalities of law to which my honourable friend alludes. If the king did otherwise, he might lose his head as has happened before, or he would initiate a revolution.

Mr Coulter: Why should we have a bill at all?

The minister of justice: With the evolution of the Dominions the British government has agreed to that. They thought it wise to make this necessary far-reaching declaration in 1926 and after that they departed in the Statute of Westminster from the old practice of an unwritten constitution. There is no such prerogative, and if such a crisis were to arise we have only to rely on the innate sense of statesmanship, prudence and deep-seated sentiments that bind together our great group of nations, for there is no prerogative in law but only common sense and human wisdom. These are the points of new departure which my honourable friend has mentioned. There is no such prerogative as he says we take away. I would like to say a few words as to the points made by the honourable member for Cape Town (Gardens) (Mr Coulter); he took a different line. He was also very strongly opposed to the use of the term 'sovereign independence', and he also thought that there should be a central authority for the day of emergency. The king has no such functions in the British Empire and never will have; he is in quite a different position. The honourable member added another argument, that the South African party has always stood for a clear position. We have fought secession, neutrality and a republic and all these things he thinks are wrapped up in this constitution. He says we are making a surrender of what we have stood for. I would say to him that I stand absolutely where I stood before. I have said so to the prime minister and he has agreed. We

want in this document to lay down that broad basis of a constitution on which 95 per cent of the people are agreed. To my mind
these things, secession, neutrality and the like are impracticable and
academic. I do not believe that anything we can say in a constitution
will settle our attitude or influence it when we come to the day of
secession or to the day to declare our neutrality. These events, if
ever they come to pass, would shake the whole British Empire and
perhaps the whole world to its foundations. It is futile. You may
talk about these things in a debating way if you are a debating
society, but men who have been through the ordeals we have been
through attach no importance to formulae of words. Consider, for
example, the position of the United States of America during the
war. The United States did her utmost to keep out of the Great
War. She fought a presidential election during the war to keep out
of it, and everybody was pledged to the full to keep out of the war,
but in spite of all in a couple of months she was in the war. She
could not maintain her neutrality. Whether it is neutrality or secession or any of these things, they will be decided, not by legal documents or the phraseology of a bill like this, but by the ordeal of
facts, of great events which might shake not only this country, but
even the world, to its foundations. But sufficient unto the day is the
evil thereof.[1] Wise men leave these things alone. There is nothing
in this bill which we are offering the people of this country to which
I think any legitimate exception can be taken. I know the fears,
I know the misgivings of some of my friends, but I give them my
solemn assurance that, having studied these documents to the full,
having given them as much attention as I can give them after
a lifetime of experience in these matters, I find nothing in them
that I cannot ask my people to ratify and to agree to. I go further,
and I would say this here today, that this is the sort of settlement
which, in the light of my experience, I would recommend my party
and my people in South Africa to accept, because this is the sort of
settlement that seems to me, and that always seemed to me, to make
for the abiding peace of South Africa. Full sovereign status, freedom
to the utmost without limit, but always in the group of comrades
and friends with which we have marched hitherto in our history.
Here you have it. This bill gives us a full sovereign status and is
intended to give that; but it also, at the same time, equally empha-
sizes the other aspect of our position, and that is that we belong to
a group of friends, a free world-wide association of states. We may
leave it in the ripeness of time, but that is the group to which we
belong. The king is the symbol of this free association, and common

----

[1] *St Matthew* vi. 34.

allegiance to him, right through this great group, keeps it together. It seems to me that this is the sort of settlement which I would, if I were a dictator, dictate to South Africa. So far from betraying the position I have stood for, and the confidence of my friends, so far from doing anything that ought to shake their confidence, this is the sort of solution that, if it were in my power, if I were a dictator, I would prescribe to South Africa.

Mr Coulter: Does our British nationality remain unimpaired?

The minister of justice: Absolutely. My honourable friend can accept the assurance which was given here the other day by the minister of railways, not only on the authority of his colleagues of his government, but on the authority of the resolution that was passed by the last imperial conference, that our status as British subjects will not be touched, except by common agreement.

Mr Coulter: I spoke of nationality.

The minister of justice: I ask my honourable friend not to quibble with me. I do not say he is quibbling, but I know there are turns and twists of phrases, and I do not want to be caught. I am simply pinning my fath to the language which is adopted in this document: 'common allegiance to the king'.

Mr Coulter: I only want to make it clear that 'common status' means 'British nationality'.

The minister of justice: My honourable friend has the assurance of the minister and of the government that nothing will be done to touch that common status without common agreement, and there we may leave it. We may raise a fight over it, and he may then be alongside of me—one never knows. One never knows in this country what the next phase will be. But I have profound faith in this country, and I would ask my friends who do not quite agree with me to have faith in South Africa. I have quoted to them the case of the British statesmen who had faith in what they call the 'British Empire'—not only in their little island people, but faith in the whole group spread over the world; and I ask my fellow citizens here in South Africa: 'Have faith in South Africa.' After all, we have come grandly out of the struggles of the past—through all that South Africa has gone [through], and it has been tested as no other young nation has been tested in history. In our generation she has been tested to the utmost, and she has always come out with flying colours, and she is still moving forward. There has been no wreckage; there has been no fatal mistake by her people, but they have always been guided by sound sense—a nose, so to say, for the right; and I have the fullest faith that South Africa will continue like that. Do not fear. Do not look to phrases and to words, but look to the character of the people. They have struggled in the past and have had controversies which seemed to shake the country. But again they have come together and have co-operated. They have done their duty on great occasions and have not let their country down. And I say, when we deal with a document like this, and launch forward into the dark future—a future which is darker for the whole world than for South Africa—let us have some faith in the people of South Africa—in their innate sense of what is fair and right, and in their wisdom and their practical statesmanship. The past has taught us that in that faith we do not go wrong. I appeal to my friends to accept the bill in that spirit, and I appeal to the country also to do so. I was profoundly moved the other night by what my honourable friend, the honourable member for Graaff-Reinet (Dr [K.] Bremer) said about *nasie trots* (national pride). I know it goes very deep. To a large section of our people their pride is not only a national pride, but a personal pride. We shall never have peace in South Africa until we satisfy that. We must settle it once for all. We have had two roots of division in the past; one root was racial and the other was constitutional. The racial root is withering. More and more you see people fraternizing, and doing away with the dead racial issues of the past. We shall continue to have difficulties and racial questions—all is not yet lovely in the garden. But the root is withering, as I say. Let us now cut the other root. I hope that this bill will cut the root of the constitutional controversies which, for a generation, have divided South Africa and convulsed it to its foundations. In cutting it we are rendering South Africa the greatest service possible and laying a sure foundation for the future. Unless we remove these fundamental causes of difference, we shall have no peace in this country. Do not think you will be able to discuss your economic questions in a fair and proper spirit. Do not talk about that, because over it all will be the poison of this controversy, this feeling that justice has not been done to the people of this country, that their status has not been recognized. Remove that, satisfy that feeling. It is a good and proper feeling, it is a human feeling of national self-respect, which nobody should resent. What we are doing here, and we are asking our friends who have that feeling, also to agree, is to confirm our friendship and our association with our group. I know that my English friends especially are profoundly attached to what is called the British connection. Whatever can be said in human language to affirm the British connection, is said in this bill. That being so, and both sections of our population being satisfied and their aspirations being fairly met, let us accept this bill. Let us not start a controversy among our people. Do not let us divide them, because we honestly mean to do the right thing by them, and to keep them together. Let us accept this bill, and give it to South Africa as one of the foundation stones of her future unity and strength.

Mr Speaker:[1] I allowed the right honourable minister to proceed beyond his time limit. I feel sure that I interpreted the feeling of the house in allowing him to do so.

359 To M. C. Gillett

Vol. 52, no. 159

Tsalta
[Cape Town]
15 April 1934

Again Sunday morning, and as air mail now leaves Tuesday morning and Monday is usually too busy for private correspondence, my letters to you will now have to be done on Sundays—which is a very good thing. I generally feel cheerful and easy on Sundays before the worries of the week have grown thick around me. Besides, Sunday is really the day for one's friends and nearest.

We have a very interesting week behind us. We finished the second reading of the Status Bill which has raised quite a storm among the English. Fortunately, owing to a timely and, I am told, persuasive speech by me in the house,[2] the situation suddenly and almost miraculously cleared up and only seven voted against, including only three Saps. This was a very happy ending to a sad mess. I have had great congratulations, even from such ardent opponents as Nico van der Merwe. The speech itself was nothing particular, and was delivered half way through an attack of malaria. But I suppose its spirit and deeper appeal did the trick. All are pleased—friend and opponent alike.

Then we have had a wonderful budget such as the country has never seen before. All due to the shackles of the gold standard being broken from the growing limbs of this young country. We have remitted about £2¼ million taxation and are back in penny postage and many other good things. It would almost seem as if abounding times of prosperity are ahead of us if we could only overcome the deadly diseases which the Old and the New Worlds are suffering from. I do not see how we could have permanent prosperity here if things don't come right in the great world which forms our markets.

[1] Dr E. G. Jansen.   [2] *See* **358**.

I see from the papers that four hundred Evangelical German parsons have applied to the *Pope* (!) to intervene against the new paganism of their country. Think of it! Luther and Calvin now applying to the Pope to save them from their own (Nazi) government. I may be old-fashioned in my ideas, but I look upon the destruction of liberty in all its spiritual forms as in many ways a greater menace to civilization than even war itself. A barbarism of the spirit is to me worse than anything I can conceive. But it is steadily stealing on us and making our fair world hideous with its repressions and suppressions and tyrannies. When will the day break again?...

360   From S. G. Millin   Vol. 52, no. 48

> 34 Pallinghurst Road
> Westcliff
> Johannesburg
> 23 April 1934

Dear General Smuts, Perhaps I have not made myself clear. I don't want to write exactly a *Life* of you.[1] Didn't I say 'a book *about* you'? I didn't mean a personal, private, prying affair. I mean a study of you as you affect the business of the world: the things you have done and experienced and thought and believed; your work in South Africa, the Empire and the World War; your association with people whose actions had consequence; your philosophical ideas. I am not competing with Mr Levi! You don't want Mr Levi's book[2] to stand as the final expression of yourself! I shall hope, of course, that you will give me some necessary material: opinions, information, perhaps some letters of consequence. But I am a quick worker. I shall try not to make myself tedious. A day now and then on your part would do it.

Don't you think, really, such a book ought to happen? And while the flavour of my *Rhodes* success still hangs over me?[3] Who knows what may happen later? Here I am, able to write. Here you are, only thirty miles away, who ought to be written about. One day somebody else will do it who can't do it. There is a biography being written at the moment about Bernard Shaw which will make future generations wonder what people ever saw in him—I have

---

[1] S. G. Millin's biography of Smuts entitled *General Smuts* was published in two volumes in 1936.

[2] *See* vol. III, p. 367, note 1.

[3] S. G. Millin, *Rhodes*, first published in 1933, had appeared in a third impression by 1934.

read the first volume.[1] If I find I can't make a big affair of this thing I'll certainly give it up. Say yes, General! Please.

I am still in bed with this cartilage. My doctor thinks I may need an operation. But I disagree with him. I shall get better without.

Three more days and the new version of *The South Africans* is done. It is right up to date, and I think it improves on the original book.[2] There is some more Smuts in it. Also Dr Malan now appears. I have been reading up a lot about Dr Malan. Awfully fascinating. Yours,

Sarah Gertrude

I want this book about you to have *meaning*. I want to write *around* my subject. I can't just write novels any more. The real world troubles me too much.

361   To F. Lamont   Vol. 52, no. 110

House of Assembly
Cape Town
29 April 1934

My dear Florence, It is eight months since we last saw each other, and no word has passed between us since then. Is this not wrong? Perhaps I am to blame. But in all this time, when the U.S.A. has bulked so large in the news you and Tom have never been far from my thoughts. He specially must have had a very anxious time in all this National Recovery policy[3] of the government and I only hope that he is maintaining his high courage and good health. General [Hugh S.] Johnson must be enough to try the strongest nerves. You, I hope, are quite recovered from your innumerable operations and as alive and vivid as ever. What a world to live in today! But it requires good health and sound nerves to do justice to it.

I shall be in England again next September and October as I am rector of St Andrews University and have to go there to discharge my one and only duty as rector—deliver a rectorial address. My election by the student body was of course a very high honour, and I must not disappoint them because of my heavy duties in South Africa. I wonder whether you and Tom will be in England again at

[1] Apparently the biography by Frank Harris, first published in 1931.
[2] This was first published in 1926.
[3] The National Industrial Recovery Act of 16 June 1933 provided for the organization of industry in the United States according to a series of 'codes' approved by the federal government and also for a public works programme of over three billion dollars. General Hugh S. Johnson was head of the federal body set up to implement the act.

that time, and whether (if so) it will not be possible for us to see more of each other than we did last year in the stresses of that futile economic conference. There is so much to talk about, so many notes to compare, and life is so short, and so little of it remains in any case. Ah me, what gnats we are to buzz around problems which we never solve. And we neglect the great perennial problems of the personal life which at bottom are the most important of all. Economics pass by; the human soul remains for ever, the centre of our human universe. Is it not the very essence of the Christian message that the soul is the great thing. 'What profits it a man if he gains the whole world and loses his own soul?'[1] But of course by soul we no longer mean personal salvation, but rather the great spiritual ideals which have been the very life-blood of our civilization. And there our failure today is even more poignant than our economic chaos. What remains of our great spiritual heritage today? Looking round at the doings of the brigands and dictators, and their worship by half Europe, I ask where is that freedom—of life and thought and self-expression—which was the proudest achievement of our civilization? Who cares today a rap about it? I fear this spiritual failure is symptomatic of a vast setback, and is far more serious than our economic troubles and disarmament fiascos. Tyranny is a worse evil than war or the danger of war. People nowadays talk of the passing of a civilization, and think of the disorganization in our trade and economics and affairs. But what is passing away is a much sadder business, and touches our fate far more deeply. Economic troubles seem to be submerging all the great values which represent the heritage from the past. And I always ask myself what really is happening in the world. Is what is happening in Asia—in Japan and China—not far more important than what is happening in Europe and America at the moment? If Japan is allowed to dominate and organize China, will that not lead to one of the greatest and most fateful movements in the history of the world?

What are you thinking of, and how is America reacting to the amazing developments in Europe and Asia? Or is she so preoccupied with internal affairs that she cares for none of these things? Above all, write to me and break this long silence. Kindest regards to you both and the family. Ever yours affectionately,

J. C. Smuts

[1] 'For what shall it profit a man, if he shall gain the whole world, and lose his own soul?' *St Mark* viii. 36.

362   To S. G. Millin   Vol. 102, no. 33

House of Assembly
Cape Town
29 April 1934

My dear Sarah Gertrude, I am afraid you have persuaded me and
I shall have to give in. I was very much opposed to a *Life* at this
stage. But a book about South Africa is a different proposition, and
under the circumstances and on your insistence I can but agree
and wish you luck. I fear it will be a difficult job. I am a more difficult subject than Rhodes, as I have touched life at so many points.
And Rhodes sailed home on the big imperial wave, while I have been
largely associated with less popular causes, and do not make the
appeal he made. I am also more of a puzzle to people. Winston
Churchill once said to me that I was the ablest man he had met who
was devoid of ambition! He was puzzled. The outside world simply
does not understand and is not interested. No, it is a difficult subject, and you may here break your record of unbroken success.
So I would advise that you count the cost before you start. My wife
can give you much information. I shall only have time for personal
explanations and communications as I cannot wade through vast
accumulations of stuff. Besides, you may not want to be bothered.

You will find the philsophical and scientific aspects very puzzling
and strange. Still, if you feel tempted to jump in, I shall not
dissuade you. You will be objective and not spare me or my fail-
ings—that I am glad to know. And now good-bye and good luck.
Ever yours,

J. C. Smuts

363   To A. B. Gillett   Vol. 52, no. 166

Cape Town
26 May 1934

I have just finished my weekly letter to Margaret in which all the
news is told. So I shall confine myself here to other items. Your
dear letter arrived last mail, in which you write of your bank doings.
I was much interested. Of course you suffer from the inferiority
complex and always under-rate your powers and your performance.
But in my honest opinion you compare more than favourably with
the financial and banking big wigs whom I meet from time to time.
I know this will not, unduly, influence you so I don't mind writing
as I do. If you could practise an air of authority and decisiveness

and finality, you will at once be accepted as a great banker. But you are doubtful and hesitating and uncertain (as all wise men are) just where a little air of appearance will do the trick. In politics too we have to appear far more confident and assured than we in reality are. The world does not accept those who doubt or appear to doubt themselves and who hesitate when they should simply close the argument with an air of assurance and finality. I myself have never practised this art successfully because I also suffer from this inferiority complex! So there you have it!

We have weathered the storm over the status bills. Many expected confidently that my party (mostly English) would not follow me here and would go to pieces. But so far the indications are the other way. On the contrary Hertzog, who thought he would strengthen his party position by these measures, has suffered, and I doubt whether he will keep his party together when we come to amalgamation of the two parties.

We have drafted a basis of principles for the new party,[1] and are now preparing for the congresses which will deal with the matter. I shall be busy with this work in July and August so that I may be free for my Scottish visit in September. It is really most awkward that I shall have to be away from South Africa during this critical year. But St Andrews is, as you know, an old-standing engagement out of which I cannot decently get. I should so wish to see something more of Europe in these fateful times, but South Africa is a most exacting mistress, and I am in her service and cannot get out of it.

We are all very well. Isie has been very happy here with her two daughters and two grand-daughters, but we shall be happy to go home at the end of the session which will be the end of this week or some time next week. Love to you ever,

Jan

364   From F. C. Kolbe   Vol. 52, no. 19

The Monastery
Sea Point
[Cape Town]
6 June 1934

My dear General Smuts, I understood of course how busy you must have been during the whole session, and am very glad to have seen

---

[1] The programme of principles of the United South African National party was issued on 5 June 1934. It is printed in D. W. Krüger, *South African Parties and Policies 1910–1960*, pp. 85–8.

so much of you as I did. The improvement of health goes on, and I can walk twice as far as a month ago.

I am writing myself because I am going to say some things that my secretary must not know. Do you tell your secretary everything?

But first let me tell you I have been having a little success. There is a hymn in our liturgy called *Ubi caritas*. From internal evidence I have identified it with the hymn which Pliny mentions in his letter to the emperor,—a hymn sung *alternatim* and *Christo tanquem Deo*.[1] Why nobody else has so identified it I don't know. But my theory was checked by Abbot Cabrol (English, though the name doesn't sound like it), who wrote in the *Tablet*[2] that *Ubi caritas* has been found to be part of a medieval hymn. I tried to get a copy of that hymn, but failed. At last I could wait no longer, and boldly declared that the medieval hymn would prove to be a descant based on the ancient *Ubi caritas*. Now I have found the medieval one, and my surmise has proved quite correct. I am wickedly triumphant! Done an abbot in the eye! By the way, Protestants ought to be interested in this. Why do they leave everything to us? A hymn of the second century, the first metric hymn in Christendom, ought to belong to them by their own principles. I suppose it is because it is Latin. Once, when a boy, I left my Cicero on the waiting-room table. A farmer came in, took it up and glanced at it, then flung it down in disgust saying, *Rooms!*[3]

But the chief matter for my letter is Hamlet's ailment. Purposely I submitted my MS[4] to two doctors. Leipoldt knows the sickness well, and testifies that I have described it aright. He says it is common among missionaries.[5] 'Otherwise', he adds naively, 'they wouldn't become missionaries.' In history, I fancy Martin Luther and Shelley are conspicuous examples. (By the way, did you know that all Luther's direct descendants are now in America, and are all Catholics? I fear I am in an impish mood tonight.) But my own study of it is from life. The family I spoke of (about two hundred

---

[1] Pliny the Younger, born A.D. 61–2, Roman statesman, became the representative of the emperor Trajan in the province of Bithynia and Pontus in A.D. 111. His *Letters* reflect the life of his times. Writing to Trajan from his province on the problem of the Christians he says that one group when examined declared that 'they had met regularly before dawn on a fixed day to chant verses alternately among themselves in honour of Christ as if to a god'. (*The Letters of the Younger Pliny*, translated by Betty Radice, p. 294.) Pliny died A.D. 113.

[2] A Catholic weekly paper established in 1840 and published in London.

[3] Roman Catholic (Afrikaans).

[4] Not in the Smuts Collection.

[5] Kolbe's father, Rev. Frederick William Kolbe, came to the Cape Colony in 1853 as a member of the Rhenish Missionary Society and later joined the London Missionary Society.

persons) is my own, chiefly the Elliott branch.[1] Did you not see something of it in Sir Charles Elliott? I could see it in his eyes. While three at least of his sons are above the average, two of them are in a mental asylum. I could have added many more details, but I was afraid of betraying family secrets. I have a good deal of it myself, and have often had great ado to conceal it. Since coming here I have had several spells of hysterical delirium. I got into a jaundiced way of looking at things and thought I was being unjustly dealt with. Thus I fell into a quarrel with a colleague. Finally (without thinking of Laertes) I decided to jump off it on the right side, and wrote, 'Don't remember what a sick mind says when racked with fear and anxiety.' The letter put things right, but I should be very sorry to be cross-examined on the whole matter. When I speak of *dual personality* I qualify it by the words 'a sort of'. Hamlet remains the same person, and *knows it*, throughout. Jekyll and Hyde is merely clever tomfoolery. You will have a lot to discuss when you come to 'personality' in your next volume. Leipoldt is quite a man to discuss it with—not without caution.

About publication, there is a hitch. Why in the world won't they let a man express himself freely and be natural? Professor [W. S.] Mackie is the obstacle. I think he must be a newcomer, and he is Scotch. He seems quite surprised that I can write good English.[2] We ought to have a university press—not confined to physical science.

I hope you will be having a kindly rest. My love to Mrs Smuts. The children have been asking after the Duchess.[3] Yours affectionately,

F. C. Kolbe

365   To M. C. Gillett   Vol. 52, no. 171

Pretoria

25 June 1934

...I have a very busy week behind me. All about fusion of parties. I met our Sap head committee, the Transvaal head committee, and

[1] Kolbe's mother was Isabella, daughter of William Elliot who was sent to South Africa by the London Missionary Society.

[2] Professor W. S. Mackie recalls that he considered Kolbe's explanation of a passage in *Hamlet* to be wrong.

[3] Kolbe wrote a column called 'Children's Corner' in the *Southern Cross* under the name 'Uncle Joe'. His name for Isie Smuts was 'The Duchess of Biltong'. In a memoir of Kolbe in the *Southern Cross* of 29 January 1936 Smuts wrote that his wife used to send Kolbe 'finely powdered *biltong* which was most grateful to him in his toothless condition'.

the general council of the party at Johannesburg—all agreed to fuse with the Nats. Dr Malan and his friends have definitely split off. The Cape Province will largely follow Malan, and in the Free State a small party under Dr van der Merwe.[1] These people have definitely a racial complex and think the Dutch should keep together and apart. To me that attitude is utterly hopeless, and we see in Ireland what in the long run it leads to. Here in South Africa the position is complicated by the fact that among the English there is also a fairly strong party who favour English isolation, and they will probably form an English party under Colonel Stallard.[2] Our work is just now also made difficult by the turmoil among our mealie farmers who are hit by low prices following on depression and severe drought in past years. Tielman Roos is exploiting this dissatisfaction, and as he is a past master in political agitation we have to be up and doing. Much of this work falls on me and I am kept on the move all the time. Hertzog is singularly silent and taking things comparatively easy. I think he is ageing and his mind is not retaining the necessary suppleness and adaptability for politics.

You know how little this sort of work appeals to me. And yet one has to do the job, or clear out. I chuckle when I read your reflections on Q. M. and Y. M.[3] and all the conferencing, and small activities you have to take your part in. Life seems to consist mostly of these minor matters, the sort of roughing which must be added to the real nutritious food. But how much rather one would give all one's strength to the real work. Here I have been sitting for more than two hours in my office dealing with petitions and grievances and useless things. And when one is through with them, the time is past, and one has very little strength left for the things that matter. I shall stop now as I must write again this week. On Saturday I leave for Port Elizabeth to open the Science Association and new law courts, and hold a public meeting. I shall be away for almost a whole week. And when I return my office will be chockful with delayed papers and correspondence. Such is life. And it could be so different and so good. Good-bye dears. Ever yours,

Jan

[1] Popularly known as the 'purified' National party, it was represented in the house of assembly by nineteen members of whom one was a Transvaaler, four were Orange Free Staters and the rest from the Cape Province.

[2] This became known as the Dominion party deriving its support chiefly from Natal. It had seven members in the house of assembly.

[3] The quarterly and yearly meetings of the Society of Friends.

Doornkloof
[Irene, Transvaal]
9 July 1934

This is Monday evening. I am sitting by the fire in the sitting-room after supper. It has been exceptionally cold the last week and more. Last night eleven degrees of frost, the night before thirteen degrees and so on. Tonight is again very cold, and I keep close to the fire. At the same time we read in the cables of your heat wave, of forest fires and the like. It is a topsy-turvy world, in more senses than one. At last the bust up has come in Germany which I had been expecting all along, and it may only be the beginning. Hitler is moving to the Right and extinguishing his Left supporters.[1] But I fear his stock must be very low, and the economic position most desperate. It must therefore follow that the agony of the masses *must* lead to further trouble—probably this winter. But what a brutal way of dealing with your opponents! The Nazis are almost worse than the Bolshevists. It is almost inconceivable that such summary executions could be tolerated in any civilized country. But then our civilization appears to be at a very low moral ebb just now...

If I have the time we might visit the new archaeological station at Mapungubwe next door to Burnett's on the Limpopo, where Neville Jones and Schofield [J. F.] are doing the work I had intended Miss [G.] Caton-Thompson to do, but the Pretoria University in their wisdom and prejudices decided otherwise. I should like to know whether any of the Zimbabwe[2] puzzles have been resolved at this station, and should also like the change. I have been very hard at it all the time since I came from Cape Town. Most of my colleagues have been on holiday or 'tours of inspection' which come to the same thing. Hertzog has been now for more than two weeks away on his farm,[3] excogitating new fulminations against his enemies. Of course I shall get my change next October and November but it is very hard to be at work when it is so cold and dismal.

Your last letter had the enclosure about Neubauer.[4] It is indeed

---

[1] On 30 June 1934 the Nazi leaders carried out an extensive purge by summary execution of the more radical wing of their party and of other suspected enemies. Among the victims were General von Schleicher, Ernst Roehm and Gregor Strasser. Seventy-seven executions were officially admitted but there were, in fact, many more.

[2] Extensive stone ruins in Southern Rhodesia discovered in 1868. Both their age and their origin remain in dispute.

[3] Waterval, on the Wilge river east of Pretoria.

[4] Dr Jeodor Neubauer, a member of the reichstag and a schoolmaster, suffered repeated periods of imprisonment in Nazi concentration camps. The Society of

a pitiable case and one would gladly do all in one's power to help these people. I am afraid the recent happenings will only make their position worse, as Hitler seems to fear Communists more than ever—and now with added reason. My difficulty is the danger of making Dr Neubauer's position actually worse by making representations. The German government of course know that his wife is in England and will at once realize that she is behind this move, which they would resent as dangerous propaganda against the Nazis. Poor Neubauer may therefore find himself treated with additional harshness and brutality. From here I could not do anything. Most Germans in South Africa are either extreme Nazis or Jews without any influence on the German government. It may be that the extremely influential petition you mention may do good, but I fear that it may be a dangerous weapon to use with terrorists such as are now in power in Germany. Dreadful as it may be to say so to Mrs Neubauer I fear anything attempted from the outside can only harm her husband, and whatever can be done must be done *inside* Germany. In her case this would be nothing at all. But what can one do? I see no light on the matter at all at present, though the situation may be different when I come in October— if poor Neubauer is then still in the land of the living. I have thought over the case from many points of view, but can only advise her to approach Nazi friends (if she has any) *in* Germany to enlist their sympathy and support. This is longwinded, but you see my mind is in a state of real perplexity in view of the danger of any move from the outside. Poor dear people! What a hell this world has been made! How much better off he would have been if he had been fatally gassed in the war. So many thousands and millions have been saved—for only worse to come. How faltering, cruel and blood-stained is our human advance through the ages! And yet we must not lose faith in Good. Far, far off the light shines, while we are toiling through the night, in which so many of us are destined to perish miserably on the march. To me this faith in Something Good beyond is the greatest thing in the world. There is some harmony at the heart of the universe, and the hope of reaching it is the real motive power which keeps us going in spite of every indication of sure defeat. The vision of God is the lure of the universe, the Eros of which Plato and Whitehead speak. 'Though He slay me, yet shall I cling to Him.'[1] Have ever deeper words been wrung out of the human soul by sorrow and anguish? Through sorrow and

Friends tried to obtain his permanent release but he either died or was executed in a camp. (Note by M. C. Gillett.)

[1] 'Though he slay me, yet will I trust in him.' *Job* xiii. 15.

suffering and defeat mankind is finding its soul, and laying hold ever more firmly on the ideals which lure us on to the better life and the fairer world. Though our hopes for the present are dashed, we should never be defeatists in the warfare of the soul. But what can one say to Mrs Neubauer? Perhaps I may see her in England, if that is not too late...Love from,

Jan

367   To F. C. Kolbe   Vol. 52, no. 119

Irene
Transvaal
20 August 1934

Dear Dr Kolbe, Last night I saw an article in the London *Times* on S. T. Coleridge[1] which I thought may interest you and so I enclose it for you. It reminds me very much of your 'Hamlet ailment'. There is the same inner frustration and incapacity to act. Something in the inner machinery is out of gear and there is a pulling in different ways at the same time. I don't know whether you consider Coleridge's case an illustration of the Hamlet malady, but at any rate it seems to be something not quite dissimilar.

I have been fearfully occupied and rushed since I left Cape Town and have scarcely had a free day. I should so much like to see our political house put in order before I leave for Scotland at the end of September. Next week I have to attend three party congresses and thereafter the real work of reorganization will begin. I doubt whether I shall come down to the Cape before I leave and fear I shall not see you before my return and indeed before the reopening of parliament. I shall fly both ways. I trust that your health is maintained and that you are pleasantly occupied with your own thoughts and doings. Your life has been a very rich one and has been abundantly blessed. And it is pleasant to think of peace and quiet at the end. Ever yours lovingly,

J. C. Smuts

My wife sends her dear love to you.

[1] 'S. T. Coleridge. A dweller in two worlds. The lost poet'. *The Times*, 25 July 1934, pp. 13–14.

368 From students, St Andrews Vol. 52, no. 196

Telegram

To: General Smuts, Railway Station, St Andrews

From: Students, St Andrews (Thomson, president)

Dated 19 October 1934

Students' heartiest good wishes to rector and Mrs Bancroft Clark on leaving Scotland. Delighted with visit, eager to meet again. Three cheers for rector. Best wishes for his country.

369 To M. C. Gillett Vol. 52, no. 185

Savoy Hotel
[London]
20 October 1934

Just back and seen your letter, among so many others. You will be most welcome *any* time next week. And I too shall be glad when your Millfield labours are over.

St Andrews proved a great success, as Cato [Clark] will tell you. But I feel the strain of the last four days. This afternoon I go on to Cambridge, to speak in chapel tomorrow[1] and attend the royal functions on Monday, and speak in the evening at the King's College dinner.

The Irvines[2] have been more than kind to me, and I give them a return dinner here on Thursday night with some of their friends. She was Mabel Williams.

Cato was a brick right through. From Isie comes nothing but good and most interesting news. And my thoughts have often been at Crossways and 102. Ever yours,

Jan

370 Speech (1934) Box I, no. 91

This speech was made by Smuts as the guest of the Royal Institute of International Affairs at a dinner at the Savoy Hotel, London, on 12 November 1934. The institute originated at the Paris peace conference in 1919.

[1] Smuts spoke on 21 October 1934 in the chapel at Christ's College on 'Human values'. *See* Smuts Collection, Box I, no. 89.

[2] Sir James and Lady Irvine. He was principal of St Andrews University at this time.

I should like at the outset to pay my tribute to the work of the Royal Institute of International Affairs. The Institute is discharging a most useful and necessary function as a forum for discussion and study of international questions. This work is all the more necessary in view of the growing importance of international relations in the modern world, the preoccupation of public men with the daily affairs of their own peoples, and the necessity of arriving at clarity on fundamental principles which should guide foreign policies. The Institute is, so to say, doing the work of a general staff for foreign affairs.

I am here tonight to speak to you on the present international outlook. I do so in no dogmatic spirit, but only in order to join in this process of study and discussion, and in that way make my contribution to the work of the Institute. It is my intention to discuss the present situation quite frankly, and with the seriousness which its grave character calls for. If I drop any bricks, the blame and responsibility will be all my own.

Looking at the European situation today, as distinct from the wider world situation (to which I shall refer later), I am deeply impressed by the fact that two underlying forces are today creating and shaping policies—the fear complex and the inferiority complex. Both are dangerous complexes, the symptoms of disease and not of healthy growth, and unless they are treated on wise lines they may in the long run produce very serious consequences for the public mind and life of the world. It may seem a humiliating confession to make, but it appears to be a fact that fear is today the real driving force in our European relations. Fear, the meanest of human motives, is today the master of us all. The victors of the Great War, so far from feeling secure in their victory, are, in fact, obsessed with this almost neurotic fear. And the vanquished are reacting in the obvious and inevitable way by refusing to accept their enforced inferiority and their position as second-class nations in the comity of civilization. The victors are actuated not by confidence, but by fear of the defeated; the defeated are determined to reconquer their lost equality with the victors. The mental reactions seem, in fact, to be reversing the roles created by the Great War.

It is all a very absurd and topsy-turvy state of affairs. But it is this mental topsy-turvydom which is today driving Europe forward on the road to chaos. In these obsessions reason is in abeyance, the finer human instincts are paralysed, and a wrong twist is being given to our future development as a well-ordered continent. Every urgent question becomes insoluble in this atmosphere of distortion. Disarmament has almost suffered shipwreck when every solid reason points to its necessity; and international co-operation is endangered where every common European interest calls imperatively for it.

If Europe is to get back to the right road again, it seems to me necessary that the nations, both victors and vanquished, should be cured of their Freudian obsessions, should recover their common-sense and sanity, and should once more see things in their right and normal relations. There is no super-psychoanalyst to do this trick, but it is at least necessary to diagnose the disease, to recognize that it is a disease, and not a healthy normal condition. Once Europeans admit to themselves that they are perhaps a little mad, the cure would come of itself. A sense of humour, of good humour, and a little laughter at themselves will do the rest. 'Know thyself' was the wise oracle;[1] 'Know thyself' is the word to be spoken to Europe today in its temporary obsessions and aberrations. There is no doubt that the present spell will pass, but what irreparable mischief is not being done while it is on! Let statesmen become the courageous doctors to their sick peoples, and the spell will soon pass.

One of the symptoms of this fear complex is the war talk which is now so common. It is represented that we are on the brink of another war, that war is waiting just round the corner. This war talk is creating a war atmosphere, and is more likely to lead to war than anything else. To me it seems all a vicious and dangerous mistake. And the curious thing is that pacifists are most responsible for the scaremongering. In their well-meant efforts to frighten people into disarming and to a sense of dangers to come they are actually fomenting the mentality that leads to war. To me it seems that the only shrewd, wideawake people who indulge in war talk are the manufacturers and vendors of munitions. With all the emphasis at my command, I would call a halt to this war talk as mischievous and dangerous war propaganda.

The expectation of war tomorrow or in the near future is sheer nonsense, and all those who are conversant with affairs know it. Conditions today are very different from those of 1914. Then war in the near future was a set policy for which the old empires were feverishly preparing. They all had their 'day' to which the general staffs looked eagerly forward. Today nobody wants war; every statesman knows it will be the ruin of his country and the end of himself. With perhaps one exception, not a single nation is today prepared for war, and war will simply mean internal revolution.

[1] This piece of advice of the oracle of Apollo at Delphi has also been attributed to Thales, Solon, Socrates, Pythagoras and others.

And even in the case of the exception I refer to, the people itself is today profoundly pacific.

Today it is not the military but the economic front which dominates the thoughts of statesmen. We are continually being told of what is happening beyond the Rhine, of the secret arming and drilling and preparing. That may be all true, and a great deal of it must be true; but it is probably no more than the workings of the inferiority complex. It is not real militarism, but only military dope applied to the masses. Those wild doings create a blessed sense of satisfaction and relief in those who consider themselves inferior or humiliated by their neighbours on the other side of the Rhine. The real war spirit is another and very different thing. It may possibly revive again if we are unwise enough to let things drift, but for the present it lies buried under the ruins of 11 November 1918. To tell me that the German people really desire war and are deliberately preparing for it is asking me to believe that they are madder than any people could be today. Let us stop this senseless war talk, the mischievous tendency of which is to translate itself into fact sooner or later. I do not mean to deny that the times are full of dangers and anxieties, but they do not justify this loose and dangerous war talk and war propaganda.

The remedy for this fear complex is the Freudian way of dragging it out from its hidden depths, bringing it into the open, and exposing it to the light of day. And this is exactly the method of the League of Nations. The League may not be a satisfactory source of security; it may be wanting in that element of sanctions which many consider so necessary. But, at any rate, it is an open forum for discussion among the nations; it is a round-table for the statesmen, around which they can ventilate and debate their grievances and viewpoints. The 'open diplomacy' for which Woodrow Wilson so ardently pleaded is enshrined in the covenant, and is today the settled and accepted method of international intercourse in the League. The League was designed to be first and foremost the round-table of the nations, and at that table and in open discussion the secret fear complex can be treated along truly human and scientific lines.

There are those who say that this is not enough—that as long as the League remains merely a talking shop or debating society, and is not furnished with 'teeth' or proper sanctions, the sense of insecurity will remain, and the fear complex will continue to dominate international relations. It is also felt that the inability of the League to guarantee the collective system by means of force, if necessary, is discrediting it and leading to its rapid decay. It is said that the crucial case of Manchukuo[1] has exposed its real weakness and shown that, unless armed with force to carry out its policies, it is doomed. My answer to this is twofold.

In the first place, I cannot visualize the League as a military machine. It was not conceived or built for that purpose, it is not equipped for such functions. And if the attempt were now made to transform it into a military machine, into a system to carry on war for the purpose of preventing or ending war, I think its fate is sealed. I cannot conceive the Dominions remaining in such a League and pledging themselves to fight the wars of the Old World, and if the Dominions leave it, Great Britain is bound to follow.

I cannot conceive anything more calculated to keep the United States for ever out of the League than its transformation into a fighting machine, pledged to carry out its decisions by force of arms if necessary. And remember, the United States has still to join the League before it will ever be its real self. Membership of the United States was the assumption on which the League was founded; defection of the United States has largely defeated its main objects. And the joining up of the United States must continue to be the ultimate goal of all true friends of the League and of the cause of peace. A conference room of the nations the United States can, and eventually will, join; it can never join an international war office.

Remembering the debates on this point in the League of Nations commission which drafted the covenant, I say quite definitely that the very idea of a League of force was negatived there; and the League would be false to its great mission as the board of conciliation and settlement for the nations if it ever allowed itself to be turned into something quite different, something just the opposite of its original idea—into a League of force. The solution of the difficulty does not lie in that direction.

But, in the second place, experience since the inception of the League has in fact taught us the way out. Locarno[2] has been incorporated into the League or the collective peace system. And Locarno establishes the principle of limited sanctions, of a smaller group within the League entering into mutual defensive arrangements under the aegis, and subject to the control, of the League. This does not throw the obligation to use force willy-nilly on all members, but binds only those who on grounds of their special situation and interests choose to enter into such arrangements.

[1] In 1932 the province of Manchukuo in Manchuria was turned into a puppet state controlled by Japan. The League failed to take effective counter-action.
[2] *See supra*, p. 258, notes 2 and 3, p. 259, notes 1 and 3.

The Eastern Pact or Locarno, which the late M. Barthou proposed for eastern Europe, as modified by the British government, would, if it does not miscarry, be another such system of limited sanctions to buttress peace within the League.[1] Its present prospects are somewhat uncertain, but it may be that eventually some such pact or pacts may yet be found feasible in eastern Europe and in other parts of the world.

If the fear obsession in Europe can be removed only by sanctions, then let it be on some such limited basis, and within the circumscribed area of those interested, and not by a departure from the principles of universality and conciliation enshrined for ever in the covenant. To endeavour to cast out the Satan of fear by calling on the Beelzebub of militarism,[2] and militarizing the League itself, would be a senseless, and indeed fatal, proceeding. Whatever forces are used to support peace must be national, and not League, forces and must be assembled and employed by mutual defence arrangements of those concerned, made under the general supervision and sanction of the League.

I have so far referred only to the fear complex and the way to deal with it. But the other or inferiority complex is very closely associated with it—in the same way that the mentalities of victor and vanquished are closely associated. If we desire peace, it is little use dealing with the one without courageously tackling also the other. It is no use piling up sanctions to remove fear if at the same time we do not strike at the root of the inferiority complex. The fear increases as the inferiority complex becomes more inflamed and threatening. The inferiority complex again becomes more inflamed as the fear complex arms itself with defensive weapons. They reinforce and augment each other, and both together lead to a policy of fresh defensive armaments. Unless both are therefore dealt with we shall continue to keep moving in a vicious circle of the two complexes and of increasing armaments. Unless both the complexes are healed, I fear the policy of disarmament will continue to suffer the reverse which it has so far encountered. It is simply a case of cause and effect. The removal of the inferiority complex from Germany is just as essential to future peace as the removal of fear from the mind of France; and both are essential to an effective disarmament policy.

How can the inferiority complex which is obsessing and, I fear, poisoning the mind, and indeed the very soul of Germany be

---

[1] The parties to the Eastern Pact were to be the Soviet Union, the Baltic states, Poland, Czechoslovakia and Germany. The project came to nothing because of the opposition of Poland and Germany.

[2] 'ye say that I cast out devils by Beelzebub'. St Luke xi. 18.

removed? There is only one way, and that is to recognize her complete equality of status with her fellows, and to do so frankly, freely, and unreservedly. That is the only medicine for her disease. And when we have summoned up sufficient courage to treat her in that human way, as our equal in the comity of nations, then, and not till then, will the old wound cease to fester and poison the life of Europe and the world. As long as recognition of her equal position is denied her, the sense of grievance and injury will continue to rankle. This is perfectly human, and it is this human situation which we should face with wisdom and courage.

While one understands and sympathizes with French fears, one cannot but feel for Germany in the position of inferiority in which she still remains sixteen years after the conclusion of the war. The continuance of her Versailles status is becoming an offence to the conscience of Europe and a danger to future peace. Surely there is sufficient human fellow-feeling left in Europe to see that the position has become intolerable and a public danger. There is no place in international law for second-rate nations, and least of all should Germany be kept in that position half a generation after the end of the Great War. Fair play, sportsmanship—indeed every standard of private and public life—calls for frank revision of the position. Indeed, ordinary prudence makes it imperative. Let us break those bonds and set the captive, obsessed soul free in a decent human way; and Europe will reap a rich reward in tranquillity, security, and returning prosperity.

Some people consider magnanimity out of place in international affairs. I have seen it in my own country recreate a position of dangerous potentialities into one of everlasting friendship between victor and vanquished. That is the way we humans are built. But if there is no place for magnanimity and generosity in European politics, at any rate here is a case where necessity and prudence point in the same direction and call for the same action. Let us take that action before it is too late. Only such action can bring healing to the sick souls in Europe and lay the ghost of that inferiority complex which is rapidly becoming a flaming portent of danger to the future of our European system. The time is come to call halt to these devastating passions and to make peace—to complete that true peace which we admittedly failed to make at Versailles.

Germany's equality of status has already been conceded in principle. This was done in December 1932 when the great powers at the disarmament conference agreed to accord Germany 'equality of rights in a regime of security'. If this declaration had been followed up and acted on in the conference itself Germany would today still be a member of the League,[1] and not a disturbing factor outside it, and we should probably have had an agreement on a far-reaching measure of disarmament. Now she is out of the League, her armament position is wrapped in obscurity and danger, and the opportunity for a general measure of disarmament seems further off than ever. It is the story of the Sibylline books.[2] The circle of the two complexes and of growing armaments is tightening round Europe. Let us hurry to untie the knot and set the good genius of European civilization once more free from the bonds which may strangle her in future.

The call to Europe is becoming ever more insistent to set her house in order, and not to allow present tendencies and complexes to become chronic. We dare not bequeath to the coming generation a legacy of chronic disorder which may prove more than they can bear. The suffering, fear-driven peoples of Europe, filled with anxieties and forebodings for the future, appeal with outstretched hands to their political leaders for wise guidance and courageous leadership. Is it too much to hope that, with a great lead from the leaders now, a new atmosphere may even yet be created, and a new situation arise in which we could return to the more hopeful outlook which obtained more than a year ago, and in that friendly atmosphere resume the threads which were then so rudely broken off? A really great gesture even now may avail to dispel the fear and inferiority complexes and to render possible a new start in European relations and a propitious resumption even of the disarmament conversations. Europe may yet be steered into calmer waters and into an era of friendly collaboration. My point is that time is passing, and that what has to be done should be done quickly.

Germany declared at the end of last year that, if she was in principle accorded equality of rights, she was in practice willing to limit her defensive armaments so as to be no danger to her neighbours. The specific proposals in respect of her rearmament which she made were admitted by authoritative opinion, at least in this country, to be a not unreasonable basis of discussion. Why should a great opportunity to secure European peace, and so make a new start in European co-operation, be wantonly jettisoned? Repugnant as the principles of Nazism may be to many other western peoples, that is no reason why Germany's equal international position should not be recognized and the obsessions which lie at the root of Nazism thereby removed. Russia, in spite of her

---

[1] Germany's withdrawal from the disarmament conference in October 1933 was followed by her resignation from the League.

[2] *See* vol. I, p. 308, note 1.

Communism, has at last been welcomed into the circle of the League.[1] Surely the necessity for recognizing Germany's equal international status is no less imperative, whatever her internal political system may be.

Unfortunately there is a spirit of fatalism and defeatism abroad. People shrug their shoulders and despair of anything being done. This is a spirit which ill becomes those who have learnt the lesson of the Great War. A resolute and determined effort even now may avail to save the situation, to bring Germany back to the disarmament conference and the League, and probably to lead to a substantial step forward in agreed disarmament. But European statesmanship must clear its mind of obsessions, and screw up its courage and boldly take the necessary steps in declaring Germany's equal status. If this is not done by agreement, it may soon come of itself. But with this difference, that whereas the future armament of Germany could have been a matter of agreement with her neighbours, her self-asserted unilateral equality may lead to complete freedom in the matter of her rearmament. It will be with disarmament as it already is with reparations: in default of reasonable action and agreement while there is yet time both may founder and become obsolete issues in the march of events. Statesmanship will have abdicated and events will then decide.

So far I have confined my remarks to the European situation. Europe, like the poor, is always with us. But in the Far East a cloud is appearing which, although it is at present no greater than a man's hand,[2] may come to overshadow the whole international sky in time. Already on its mere appearance it has severely shaken the League and led to menacing reactions in several directions. People instinctively realize that here is a phenomenon of first-class order, which may have the most far-reaching effects on the fortunes of peace, and indeed of our civilization. Manchukuo is perhaps not yet the parting of the ways, but it is the warning that we are coming to the parting of the ways and may soon have to make a very solemn choice in national policy.

I have always looked upon the Washington treaties of 1922[3] as probably the greatest step forward yet taken since the peace on the road to a stable future world order. In 1921, at the imperial conference of that date, I stated my view that a great change was coming over world politics, and that the scene was shifting from the Atlantic

---

[1] The Soviet Union became a member of the League with a permanent seat on the council in September 1934.

[2] 'Behold, there ariseth a little cloud out of the sea, like a man's hand.'

1 Kings xviii. 44.

[3] *See supra*, p. 110, note 2.

to the Pacific. It was felt, and not by me only, that the future of the world would probably be decided, not in the Atlantic, but the Pacific ocean and countries. The pot might continue to boil in Europe for perhaps another generation, but in the end it would simmer down. Europe would settle her essentially family quarrels in the end, and a state of more or less peaceful equilibrium would be reached. That feeling I have still. But for these tiresome and obstinate neuroses to which I have referred, Europe would probably already be settling down. The storm centre will pass away from the countries of Christian civilization and shift to the Far East. There the hand of destiny is still writing in its unknown script—in a language and in ideas which are scarcely intelligible to the western mind.

The achievement of the Washington conference was just this— that in this new danger zone of the future a concert or collective system of the powers concerned had been built up, a loose conference system, founded on certain vital issues, which might do for the Far East what the Geneva League was attempting to do in the West. Comparative naval power, the integrity of China, the open door in that immense potential market, were agreed in principle, and in case of any differences or danger arising the conference would meet for discussion. Here was the most promising thing for world peace which had yet taken place since the covenant. The question which is now being raised is whether the promise of Washington will be fulfilled and not prove to be a mere mirage. Manchukuo, as I said, pointed the danger signal. Now the treaty on naval ratios seems to be in danger; and if that goes the other issues settled at Washington may also be reopened and the whole Pacific concert may collapse. Here is something far more dangerous for the future than these present temporary and passing differences in Europe.

At present we are very much in the dark as to what is actually going on. Conversations are taking place here between the parties to the four-power treaty, the outcome of which is still uncertain. Under these circumstances it would be futile, and may even be harmful, to enter upon a discussion of the merits of the naval questions involved, and I do not propose to do so now, even supposing I had the competence to do so. There is, however, an air of pessimism about the outcome of these conversations which gives food for thought. In view of this, and in view also of the far-reaching issues involved, it may perhaps be permissible to refer to certain broad aspects of the whole question and the fundamental considerations of policy which, I submit, should be steadily borne in mind, without going into the particular naval points which are at present the subject of secret exchanges. I therefore address myself to a few general observations on the underlying policies which strike me as pertinent.

In the first place, this threat to the continuance of the Washington arrangements and the Pacific concert, with all it may ultimately involve, must be another serious call to Europe to put her house in order without undue delay. It must be plain to everybody that the rift in the lute now beginning in the East may have very disturbing effects on the European concert as well. Whereas Europe left to herself may in the end come to some working equilibrium, the new trouble in the East may easily destroy that prospect. Adversity makes strange bedfellows, and those who have in the past talked loudest of the Yellow Peril may in future be tempted to look for friends in that unlikely quarter. The day when Europe calls in the Far East to redress the balance of the West[1] will be an evil day for western civilization and the peace of the world. In view of the situation now developing in the Far East, European statesmen should redouble their efforts to compose European differences before it is too late. The dangers I allude to are so evident that I need not dilate further on this point.

In the second place I would appeal most earnestly and in the friendliest spirit to Japan, as our old friend and war-time ally, to pause before she puts in motion machinery which will in the end imperil the concert in the Pacific. She has already given notice of withdrawal from the League.[2] If, in addition, she withdraws from the Washington treaties, the whole collective system goes, so far as she is concerned. For herself this might mean a position of isolation which experience in the Great War has shown to be most dangerous, even for the greatest of military powers. And for all, the disappearance of the Pacific concert would be a matter of the gravest concern. The collective system is probably the most beneficent of all post-war changes in international affairs, and its weakening or destruction might involve dangers the magnitude of which none can foresee today. I therefore pray for the most serious reflection before the final plunge is taken.

In the third place everything possible in the power of diplomacy should be done to avoid even the appearance of antagonism between the East and West. The potentialities of the situation are inherently serious enough, and should not be rendered worse by one-sided diplomacy. Asia is at a curious phase of her awakening. Complexes

[1] 'I called the New World into existence to redress the balance of the Old.' George Canning in a speech of 12 December 1826.

[2] On 27 May 1933 Japan announced her intention to withdraw from the League. The withdrawal was to take effect in two years.

there, too, are forming. The old exploitation or ascendancy policies are out of place in such a situation, and should be carefully avoided for the future. The past record of the West in the East is not one to be proud of or to be further copied. While mindful of our duty and responsibility as trustees for the greatest civilization that this earth has ever known, we should avoid the assumption of superiority. Not the mailed fist, but the friendly helping hand, should be in future the symbol of our association with Asia.

We are facing the greatest, most intriguing, most testing human situation which has probably ever arisen in history. It may well be that western civilization will stand or fall in this matter of its contacts with the immense human masses of the East. Here let it put its best foot forward and show that it is a universal system, based on the broadest and highest human principles, and not merely a local system for the European peninsula. In this spirit I would say, even if the present negotiations for naval ratios fail, do not let us depart from an attitude of friendliness and large human good will towards Japan. Good will, good temper, friendship, will solve the hardest problems of statesmanship yet. And they are specially called for as the ultimate instruments of diplomacy in our dealings with Asia. If we cannot and should not be allies, we can at least be friends, and proceed to the unknown dangers of the future in a spirit of understanding and friendliness. The old Japanese alliance may have been, and in my opinion was, a mistake.[1] A policy of friendliness and understanding can never be a mistake, and will keep or make friends without thereby making enemies.

Fourthly, and subject to what I have just said, I wish to make another point which I consider no less important and vital. This is a difficult world, in which we have to walk warily, in which even good will may not be enough, and in which we are called upon to exercise a wise discretion as an insurance for the future. In this spirit I would say that to me the future policy and association of our great British Commonwealth lie more with the United States than with any other group in the world. If ever there comes a parting of the ways, if ever in the crises of the future we are called upon to make a choice, *that*, it seems to me, should be the company we should prefer to walk with and march with to the unknown future. On that path lie our past affiliations, our common moral outlook, our hopes and fears for the future of our common civilization. Nobody can forecast the outcome of the stormy era of history on

---

[1] The Anglo-Japanese alliance of 1902 which recognized Japan's interests in Korea and provided for common action should either party become involved in war with more than one power.

which we are now probably entering. Our best insurance in this unknown territory is to be with those with whom we have an instinctive and historic sympathy.

The British Commonwealth has its feet in both worlds. Through Great Britain its one foot is firmly planted on this old continent. Through the Dominions it has its other foot as firmly planted in the outer newer world, where the United States already plays so great a part. The Dominions have even stronger affiliations towards the United States than Great Britain has. There is a community of outlook, of interests, and perhaps of ultimate destiny between the Dominions and the United States which in essence is only the first and most important of them. Through the Dominions British policy is ultimately tied up with the United States in a very profound sense, which goes much deeper than the occasional jars which, perhaps, are more acutely felt at any particular moment. That fundamental affinity, coming from the past, stretching to the future, is, or must be, the real foundation of all British foreign policy. Any policy which ignores it, or runs counter to it, is calculated to have a disruptive effect on the Commonwealth as a whole. We are here on bedrock, which we ignore at our peril.

While therefore our Far Eastern policy should, I submit, be based on friendship with all, and exclusive alliances or understandings with none, the ultimate objectives of that policy should continue to conform to that general American orientation which has distinguished it since our association with the United States in the Great War. In this way our policy will correspond to the actual general situation of our Commonwealth in the world of today— a situation which goes much deeper than, and underlies, all public policies, and on which alone it is possible to base stable and enduring policies for the future. Any other course would mean building our Commonwealth policy on quicksands, and placing the future of this group at the mercy of incalculable accidents.

In saying this I do not wish to import any note of exclusiveness in our policies or our world outlook. The day is surely gone for the old exclusive outlooks of the past, and for the alliances and balances of power which were based on that outlook. In spite of all appearances to the contrary, we have in this respect made progress in the post-war period. The principle of universality on which the covenant and the new world order are based is slowly making headway. More and more the recognition is winning through that there really is a society, and not merely a collection, of nations. The League of Nations in itself implies a society of nations. Not in our separateness and exclusiveness, not in mere nationalism, either political or economic, lies the way out of our present troubles, but in our steadily increasing sociality, in the interweaving of interests, viewpoints and ideas, in the open door and the removal of barriers and restrictions, in the dominance of large human principles transcending national boundaries, and in the recognition that in mankind we are members one of another. More and more we are recognizing that, in spite of racial and political barriers, humanity is really a whole.

It is in this steadily growing mutuality of our relations, in this every-increasing wholeness of our human relationships that I see the only possible ultimate solution of our present discords. Here lies the true line of progress for the future. And the more we recognize this wholeness of mankind, this integral character of all our relationships, the surer our success will be in the great adventure of human government, and the brighter the prospects will be for that world of ordered liberty and peace which we are out to build. The driving force in this human world of ours should be, not morbid fears or other sickly obsessions, but this inner urge towards wholesome integration and co-operation. The drive towards holism, which I have elsewhere pointed to as at the basis of nature and the creative process in this universe, is equally operative in our human society. Unless it is artificially interfered with and thwarted, it will lead us forward to sanity, wholeness and wholesomeness, and rid us of the pathological obsessions which are today producing so much friction and dislocation at every step of our advance.

I thank you for the patience with which you have listened to me, even when you may not have agreed with some of my views. What I have said in all sincerity is simply meant as a plea for understanding by one who has no axe to grind and whose sphere of work lies far from the political battlefront of Europe. Ever since Versailles, where I entered my first protest,[1] I have felt very deeply that the real peace was still to come, and that it would be a peace, not merely of mechanical arrangements of the territorial or economic kind, but something psychological, something in the nature of European reconciliation, something reaching down to and resting on our common human and Christian foundations. In that spirit I have once more pleaded for peace tonight. I hope that our statesmen will yet lead us to that peace before it is too late—that is to say, before new, sinister forces have advanced and taken possession of the field and imperilled what centuries of European effort have accomplished for our human advance. I feel the hour for action has come, or is rapidly coming, and we all pray that our leadership, for which we feel the profoundest sympathy, will not fail us in this crisis of our fate.

[1] *See* **1043**.